Exploring China's Past

NEW DISCOVERIES AND STUDIES IN ARCHAEOLOGY AND ART

International Series in Chinese Art and Archaeology • No 1

Exploring China's Past

New Discoveries and Studies in Archaeology and Art

Translated and edited by
Roderick Whitfield and Wang Tao

Saffron

Exploring China's Past: New Discoveries and Studies in Archaeology and Art
Tanslated and edited by Roderick Whitfield and Wang Tao

ISBN 1 872843 20 4 [paper]
ISBN 1 872843 25 5 [cloth]

Saffron Books International Series in Chinese Art and Archaeology • No 1

Cover *Bronze sculptures from Sanxingdui, Sichuan, Shang/Zhou period*

Published by Saffron Books, an imprint of Eastern Art Publishing

Managing Editor Sajid Rizvi

Eastern Art Publishing
 P O Box 13666
London SW14 8WF
United Kingdom

Telephone   +44-[020]-8392 1122   {+44-[0]-181-392 1122}
Facsimile   +44-[020]-8392 1422   {+44-[0]-181-392 1422}
E-mail   saffron@eapgroup.com
Web   www.eapgroup.com
              www.eapgroup.co.uk

Typeset and designed by Prizmatone Design Consultancy
Printed and bound in Scotland

British Library Cataloguing in Publication Data
A catalogue record of this book is available from the British Library

We dedicate this volume to Su Bingqi (1909-1997) and Wang Xu (1930-1997), both of whom passed away during the preparation of this book. Their contribution to the studies of Chinese archaeology and their warm friendship will be forever remembered.

Contributors • 8

Introduction • 11-14

Chinese Archaeology and the Origins of Chinese Civilisation • 15

Su Bingqi A New Age of Chinese Archaeology • 17-25

Yu Weichao New Trends in Archaeological Thought • 27-32

Xu Pingfang Archaeological Research on the Origins of Chinese
Civilisation • 33-40

Mou Yongkang and **Wu Ruzuo** A Discussion on the 'Jade Age' • 41-44

Guo Dashun An Archaeological Investigation of the Wudi • 45-48

Chinese Archaeology in the West • 49

Robert Thorp Studies of Chinese Archaeology/Art History in the
West: a Historic Review • 51-62

Sarah Allan Chinese Bronzes through Western Eyes • 63-76

Agriculture and Early Cities • 77

Ren Shinan Prehistoric Agriculture in China • 79-85

Zhang Chi and **Okamura Hidenori** Excavations of Cities: Shijiahe and
Yingxiangcheng • 87-94

Duan Yu The Origin, Structure and Network of Early Shu Cities • 95-103

Zou Heng The Early Jin Capital Discovered: a Personal Account • 105-109

Wang Tao A City with Many Faces: Urban Development in pre-Modern China • 111-121

The Cultural Frontiers • 123

Chen Fangmei Bronze Weapons from the South: the Xin'gan Case • 125-136

Tu Cheng-sheng The 'Animal Style' Revisited • 137-149

Li Kunsheng The 'Bronze Age' of Yunnan • 151-162

Contents

Sacrifice, Rituals and the Afterlife • 163

Chen Xiandan The Sacrificial Pits at Sanxingdui: Their Nature and Date • 165-171

Tang Jigen The Burial Ritual of the Shang Dynasty: a Reconstruction • 173-181

Li Boqian Jades from Tomb M63 at the Jin Cemetery at Tianma-Qucun • 182-188

Alain Thote Continuities and Discontinuities: Chu Burials during the Eastern Zhou Period • 189-204

Art and Technology • 205

Wang Xu The Eight-Pointed Star Pattern and the Prehistoric Loom • 206-211

Filippo Salviati Decorated Pottery and Jade Carving of the Liangzhu Culture • 212-226

New Discoveries • 227

Wang Tao with the assistance of **Li Xinwei** The Important Archaeological Discoveries: 1991-95 • 228-245

Chinese Historical Chronology • 246
Glossary • 247-254
Bibliography • 255-275
Index • 277-286

Contributors

Sarah Allan, Burlington North Professor of Asian Studies, Dartmouth College, Hanover, New Hampshire, USA

Chen Fang-mei 陈芳妹, Curator of Ancient Bronzes, National Palace Museum, Taipei, Taiwan

Chen Xiandan 陈显丹, Deputy Director, Sichuan Provincial Museum, Chengdu, China

Duan Yu 段渝, Deputy-Director, Institute of History, Sichuan Academy of Social Sciences, Chengdu, China

Guo Dashun 郭大顺, Honorary Director, Liaoning Provincial Institute of Archaeology, Shenyang, China

Li Boqian 李伯谦, Professor, Head of Department of Archaeology, Peking University, Beijing, China

Li Kunsheng 李昆生, Director, Yunnan Provincial Museum, Kunming, China

Li Xinwei 李新伟, Assistant Research Fellow, Institute of Archaeology, Chinese Academy of Social Sciences, Beijing, China

Mou Yongkang 牟永抗, Research Fellow, Zhejiang Provincial Institute of Archaeology, Hangzhou, China

Okamura Hidenori 冈村秀典, Associate Professor, Institute for Research in Humanities, Kyoto University, Kyoto, Japan

Ren Shinan 任式楠, Research Fellow, former Director, Institute of Archaeology, Chinese Academy of Social Sciences, Beijing, China

Filippo Salviati, Lecturer in Art and Archaeology, Department of Oriental Studies, University of Rome 'La Sapienza,' Rome, Italy

Su Bingqi 苏秉琦, formerly Research Fellow, Institute of Archaeology, Chinese Academy of Social Sciences, Beijing, China

Tang Jigen 唐际根, Associate Research Fellow, Institute of Archaeology, Chinese Academy of Social Sciences, Beijing, China

Robert Thorp, Professor, Department of Art History and Archaeology, Washington University, St Louis, USA

Alain Thote, Head of Research Unit, Centre National de la Recherche Scientifique, Paris, France

Tu Cheng-sheng 杜正胜, Director, Institute of History and Philology, Academia Sinica, Taipei, Taiwan

Wang Tao 汪涛, Lecturer in Chinese Archaeology, School of Oriental and African Studies, University of London, UK

Wang Xu 王㐨, formerly Research Fellow, Institute of History, Chinese Academy of Social Sciences, Beijing, China

Roderick Whitfield, Percival David Professor of Chinese and East Asian Art, School of Oriental and African Studies, University of London, UK

Wu Ruzuo 吴汝祚, Research Fellow, Institute of Archaeology, Chinese Academy of Social Sciences, Beijing, China

Xu Pingfang 徐苹芳, Research Fellow, former Director, Institute of Archaeology, Chinese Academy of Social Sciences, Beijing, China

Zhang Chi 张驰, Associate Professor, Department of Archaeology, Peking University, Beijing, China

Zou Heng 邹衡, Professor, Department of Archaeology, Peking University, Beijing, China

Acknowledgments

The editors gratefully acknowledge the support of the Chiang Ching-Kuo Foundation for International Scholarly Exchange which has provided part of the publication cost for this volume. The foundation has made a great contribution for the international studies of Chinese culture. We have a pleasant memory of Professor Li Yih-yuan, the President of the Foundation, and Madame Yu Shufen, the secretary, when they paid a visit to London and SOAS in 1994. We are also indebted to our contributors, for their selfless help and in particular their enduring patience.

The project started in November 1992 when a one-day symposium on Chinese archaeology was held at SOAS. Several of the original speakers are among the authors in this volume. When we began to expand our coverage, many other leading Chinese archaeologists kindly sent texts. Several authors actually worked on their contributions when they visited London: Duan Yu and Tang Jigen were supported by the KC Wong Fellowship of the British Academy; Chen Xiandan, Li Boqian and Ren Shinan were in London with the Mysteries of Ancient China Exhibition (1997) at the British Museum. We would also like to thank these institutions. The Chinese characters in the glossary were typed by Miss Cai Wei, a former student at SOAS. We thank her for her labour and enthusiasm.

Finally, we would like to express our appreciation and gratitude to our publisher Sajid Rizvi who has taken on this difficult project with considerable success. We certainly hope this is only the beginning of our cooperation.

WT and RW

Introduction

Students of Chinese art and archaeology in the West face two major hurdles: the lack of a general overview of current developments in Chinese archaeology, and the daunting amount of material published in Chinese and seldom translated. This book aims to tackle these problems.

Part One includes five articles written by China's leading archaeologists. One of the most important people in Chinese archaeology is the late Su Bingqi, who sadly passed away during the preparation of this book. During his long and very distinguished career, Su had a profound influence on Chinese archaeology, and this volume is dedicated to him. As we approach the new millennium, there is no better person than Su to present his reflection of the past and his thoughts on the future of Chinese archaeology.

Scientific archaeology from the west was introduced to China at the beginning of the 20th century. In 1928, Chinese archaeologists made their first independent excavations at the Shang dynasty site at Anyang, marking the birth of modern Chinese archaeology. Although, the study of prehistory in China did not begin to take shape until the 1960s, by the 1970s an increasing number of archaeological sites were being unearthed. Su analysed the regional pattern of neolithic cultures and arranged them into several distinctive types and branches, known as the *quyu puxi* theory. His theory differed from the traditional view that Chinese civilisation originated and diffused from the middle valleys of the Yellow River. It is in this new framework that the majority of Chinese archaeologists today begin to interpret their findings and make sense of their data. And it is on this basis that Su argues for the 'Chinese school of archaeology' and predicts that a new age in Chinese archaeology is already on its way.

Chinese archaeology has always been thought to be lacking in theoretical approach, or to be based solely on paradoxical Marxist theory. Yu Weichao's article *New Trends in Archaeological Thought* may change this presumption. In this article, Yu deals with such questions as periodisation and theory in archaeology, both in China and the West. His comments on the introduction of western theories to China are important and he strongly encourages a more open approach to new ideas and methods.

One of the main tasks in Chinese archaeology over the last 20 years has been to investigate the origins of Chinese civilisation. Three very interesting articles consider this subject. Xu Pingfang reviews the background to this important question and summarises the most representative studies. He also

Bronze container (detail), unearthed at Jiangchuan Lijiashan. See page 152

points out key areas demanding further research.

In the discussion of the origins of Chinese civilisation, one crucial question is whether Chinese civilisation developed along a different path to that of western civilisation. The assertion by Mou Yongkang and Wu Ruzuo that there may have been a Jade Age in China has caused controversy, especially among supporters of the traditional 'Three Ages.' It is significant that their joint study is based on both recent archaeological research on jade artefacts and the evidence offered in ancient texts. Archaeologists have to decide whether to employ literary evidence in archaeological interpretation, and if so, how it should be used. This is a particular dilemma in Chinese archaeology, which has a very strong tradition of using textual references, because the literary records are abundant and have often been proved correct. Guo Dashun's article on the legend of the Five Lords shows that early legends can be traced in the archaeological remains. It is important to point out, as Guo argues, that the function of archaeology is not merely to testify to the accuracy of the records, and to realise that in this case both the legend and material evidence of the Five Lords are essential elements in the cultural identity of 'the Chinese.'

Part Two includes two articles by distinguished western scholars on the study of Chinese art and archaeology in Europe and North America. Robert Thorp's article is a substantial contribution to our understanding of how Chinese art and archaeology was perceived in the West between 1900-1950. His analysis of the historical and intellectual framework in Europe and the USA before the arrival of 'Chinese archaeology,' and of the underlying eurocentric and sinocentric stances clearly demonstrates that the two different traditions did not develop in comparable ways and that they are likely to remain in contrast for some time. From Sarah Allan's analysis of western scholarship on Chinese archaic bronzes it emerges that there exists a conceptual gap between Chinese and western scholars, which has affected their respective interpretations of ancient ritual bronzes. Allan considers the recent progress in Chinese archaeology and puts forward her own hypothesis on the meaning of the Shang ritual bronzes.

Progress in a subject is usually stimulated by the discovery of new material or a new theoretical interpretation. There is a vast wealth of new archaeological material in China, and we are fortunate to have a number of exciting and up-to-date articles in Part Three. Ren Shinan gives a descriptive account of the most recent discoveries of the ancient cultivation of rice, cereal crops and the domestication of various animals, including pigs, cattle, dogs, sheep, horses and silkworms. Ren also argues that there was a division between north and south China from a very early time. The evidence amply supports his conclusion that China was one of the earliest centres for the origin of agriculture. We now have evidence of rice cultivation going back 10,000 years, which qualifies Jiangxi Wannian rice as the earliest cultivated rice in the world. The importance of this is not to prove that China was always the earliest in everything, but to put China in the perspective of a world archaeology.

The difference between north and south is reflected not only in agriculture, but also in the development of urban settlements. Zhang Chi and Okamura Hidenori explore early urbanisation in the south. By the time of the Qujialing and Shijiahe cultures (c2800-2300 BC), large walled settlements were appearing in the middle reaches of the Yangzi River. Many early walled enclosures have been discovered in both north and south China, as well as in the central plains. The construction of the walls of the Shijiahe and Yingxiangcheng sites in the south are very different from the rammed-earth structures usually found in the north. The new evidence will undoubtedly reinforce the theory of independent cultural development in the south. The excavation of the cities of the Shijiahe culture reported by Zhang Chi and Okamura provides first-hand material for further exploration of the emergence of cities in early China.

However, two important questions remain: How much do we know about the settlement plans of these sites and the life of the ancient people who lived in them? And what are the criteria for qualifying a site as a 'city,' rather than a 'village'? Duan Yu's article offers a theoretical discussion. Taking a comparative study of early cities in Sichuan as a base, Duan argues that there were two different types of early cities and that they originated for different reasons and developed in different ways: one was driven by economic forces; the other by political and military power. This theory throws new light on the subject and needs to be tested fully in different cases. Zou Heng's article also looks at the archaeology of cities in early China, but is presented from a very different angle. Zou is credited with numerous important archaeological studies, of which the discovery of the Jin state capital in Houma, Shanxi province, is supremely important. In his article, Zou recalls the excitement of the discovery and excavation of the site. His personal experience shows once again just how important it is for an archaeologist to have mastery of the textual sources, in addition to skills in archaeological surveying and excavation.

The three articles in Part Four all deal with the bronze culture in China, but do so from different regions, or more precisely from those different cultural traditions which fall outside the mainstream of the central plains. Chen Fang-mei's study of the weapons unearthed at Xin'gan Dayangzhou, Jiangxi province, demonstrates that an independent tradition existed in the south. This tradition cannot be defined as belonging to the Shang tradition at Anyang, although it was certainly influenced by the latter. It is more closely linked to an indigenous southern tradition reaching back to the neolithic period.

Tu Cheng-sheng's article deals with another distinctive bronze culture, that of the 'northern zone,' or Ordos bronzes. The question of the 'animal style' has attracted attention for a long time. Here, Tu reviews the earlier studies and puts forward a new hypothesis. It seems true that the 'animal style' developed through different stages and that it represents a nomadic culture different from the more settled Huaxia culture of the central plains. Tu's study will certainly stimulate further interest in the study of nomadic culture of the north. Focusing on a very different geographical area, Li Kunsheng presents another indigenous tradition, namely the 'Dian bronzes' of Yunnan. Here, bronzes also differ from the central plains in both technology and subject matter. They depict everyday life and ritual scenes more directly, in an explicit and realistic manner. The article begs some interesting questions: Were these people very different from the 'Chinese'? And would ethnographic studies of the minority peoples living in Yunnan today help us to understand the Dian culture of the past?

The archaeology of ritual and sacrifice has always been a fascinating topic. We have four articles on the subject in Part Five: the famous Sanxingdui sacrificial pits, the Shang dynasty burial ritual, the Jin royal cemetery at Tianma-Qucun, and the Chu burials of the Eastern Zhou period. Since their discovery in the mid-1980s, the pits at the Sanxingdui site have attracted enormous interest. They have also posed many questions. The scale and sophistication of the site suggests that the people who constructed the site had already formed a complex society. Recent archaeological work has also confirmed that in the Erlitou period, about 2000 BC, there already existed a developed civilisation in the Sichuan basin. But because this area is beyond the central plains and is less well known in the literary records, its significance in the development of Chinese civilisation has not been fully realised. As one of the original directors of the excavation, Chen Xiandan discusses the date and function of the pits, which are essential for any advance in interpreting the significance of this important archaeological discovery.

Tang Jigen focuses on some well-known material, the Shang dynasty tombs at Anyang, but offers a new and different approach. With the new theory of 'processual archaeology' in mind, he tries to reconstruct the behaviour pattern of the burial practice of the Shang people, and furthermore, to explain the social structure and belief system of Shang society.

Li Boqian's article presents the recent excavation of the Western Zhou Jin royal cemetery at Tianma-Qucun. He identifies the owners of the tombs with the Jin rulers recorded in historical texts, and in particular focuses on the jade objects found in Tomb M63, which is believed to be that of one of the consorts of Marquis Muhou. The context of the discovery reveals an interesting fact: the jades placed in a specially packed box found in the tomb are not of Western Zhou date, but of the earlier Shang dynasty. Most probably they were the personal collection of the tomb owner and were used very differently from the original context in which they were made. This find reflects the change of peoples' perception of artefacts in different times.

Alain Thote's article also deals with the question of continuities and discontinuities, this time as reflected in Chu burials. In recent years, the study of the Chu culture has been one of the most fruitful areas in Chinese archaeology. As one of the best-informed western scholars in the field, Thote gives a systematic analysis of various aspects of Chu burial, such as tomb construction, artefact typology and assemblages. He arrives at the conclusion that the changes in burial custom paralleled formation of the ideology of the afterlife. This study will definitely be of benefit to any study of material culture of the Eastern Zhou period and early Chinese religion.

The two articles in Part Six look at weaving technology in prehistoric times and jade carving of the Liangzhu culture. The late Wang Xu, who has been greatly missed since his death in 1997, focuses on the eight-pointed star pattern frequently found on prehistoric materials such as pottery and bronzes. With his exceptional knowledge of visual and textual sources, he has convincingly reconstructed the earliest loom on the basis of archaeological evidence.

Filippo Salviati makes the iconography of Liangzhu jade carving the focus of his discussion, but explores the wider contexts of technology and the natural environment. By comparing the motifs found on both jade and pottery and the context in which they were unearthed, he tries to interpret the meaning to Liangzhu society of items bearing those motifs.

Part Seven is a brief summary of the most important archaeological discoveries made between 1991 and 1995. Fifty sites from the palaeolithic to the Yuan dynasty (50,000 bp-14th century AD) have been selected by the Chinese authorities as representing the most important advances in archaeology. These sites are significant in themselves, either for the new knowledge they convey or the important artefacts they yield. At the same time, they also reflect the way Chinese archaeologists regard their work and how the Chinese government relates archaeology to its policies and to society. It is as important to recognise the association between Chinese archaeology and politics today as it is to understand the history of Chinese archaeology.

This volume assembles a large number of papers of vastly different nature and content, and it would be pretentious even to attempt a detailed assessment of them in such a short introduction. We have striven to integrate all the papers into a coherent body, in the hope that it will help students and scholars in the West to understand current developments in the field of Chinese archaeology. Our personal observation is that Chinese archaeology in the 1990s has been as exciting as it is challenging. The old picture presented the study of Chinese archaeology as little more than a few dynasties and tombs. Now a much greater diversity has been recognised. New material appears all the time, and if we can approach it with an open mind we may be able to pool ideas and come closer to establishing a firmer understanding of China's past. The contributors of this first volume are scholars from China, Taiwan, Japan, Europe and the United States. It is our genuine hope that this series will be truly 'international,' and serve to integrate Chinese archaeology into the broader global context of world archaeology.

Wang Tao and Roderick Whitfield

Chinese Archaeology and the Origins of Chinese Civilisation

SU BINGQI

A New Age of Chinese Archaeology

C HINESE archaeology has three major tasks: *a)* writing national history; *b)* extending this to periods which have no written records; *c)* establishing our own archaeological school. First of all, we have to overcome the limitations of traditional literary records. Archaeology is not simply a matter of authenticating the classics and supplementing historical records: its main aim is to discover material evidence from the ground, as important evidence for the writing of national history. Archaeology is a branch of historical science, but needs to establish its own discipline distinct from that of history.

The second task, of extending into areas which have no written records, refers to what Guo Moruo wrote in the preface to his book, *Zhongguo gudai shehui yanjiu* (The Study of Ancient Chinese Society*)*, proposing that one should write a supplement to Friedrich Engels' *The Origin of the Family, Private Property, and the State*, which has proved extremely influential and has been reprinted many times since it was first published in 1929. Guo Moruo was emphasizing that the object of research into ancient Chinese society was "to give a clear account of Chinese society" and "to throw light on its development."[1]

The third task, of "establishing our own archaeological school" was a suggestion first made by Professor Yin Da, then Director of the Institute of History, Chinese Academy of Social Sciences (CASS), whom I had invited in 1958 to speak in the Department of History of Peking University. Yin saw it as an important duty to establish Chinese archaeology within a Marxist framework.

Since the establishment of the People's Republic in 1949, or rather from the setting up of the Institute of Archaeology in 1950, one can roughly distinguish three main periods. The first period, in the 1950s and 1960s, is a period of many doubts and gradual understanding; the second period, covering the 1970s and 1980s, is a historical turning-point, marked by the appearance of a Chinese school, when the theory of regional developments was put forward and validated; in the third and most recent period, the 1990s, the new task is to reconstruct ancient history, and to welcome the new age of Chinese archaeology from a global perspective. The present paper represents the reflections of an old hand on the threshold of the 21st century.

[1] Guo Moruo 1954: *Zhongguo gudai shehui yanjiu*. Beijing: Renmin chubanshe, 'Preface.'

This article is based on 'Yingjie Zhongguo kaoguxue de xin shiji,' first published in *Dongnan wenhua*, 1993(1).

All the above are basic tasks in Chinese archaeology. During the 1950s, we invited Russian scholars to teach us the differences between old Russian archaeology and the new Soviet archaeology, in the hope of solving these problems. Good intentions, however, were not enough: in practice we were fully occupied in excavating, classifying objects and writing reports. If we look at the textbooks then used in Peking University for teaching archaeology, and at the displays in the National Historical Museum, we cannot be satisfied. It is too simplistic to think that the sole purpose behind the study of Chinese history was simply to add some new artefacts in a general history of social development. By the end of the 1950s, we had no clue as to the solution of these problems, and this led to confusion. The problem was that we had not found the right balance between theory and practice.

In 1958 and 1959, during the excavation of Huaxian Quanhucun, I began to try a new direction of thought, starting with the classification of material from the site. Comparing the material from Quanhucun with material from the so-called Yangshao culture, there was a breakthrough to a more detailed understanding of the latter, and a redefinition of traditional types. The old definition of the Yangshao culture was too broad: from the Gobi desert in the north to Hubei and Hunan in the southwest, and as far east as the western part of Shandong, all painted pottery was classified as belonging to the Yangshao culture; this was obviously not correct. Because of the complexity of the artefacts, we then designated three groups of artefacts, each of two types, as representative criteria of the Yangshao culture. Group I consists of amphorae or jars with a narrow mouth and pointed base, which occur in two different types, with a gourd-mouth, or with a double lip. The pottery of Group II has painted animal motifs, including fish and birds. That of Group III has painted floral motifs, either rose or chrysanthemum. All of these six types developed within the area from Baoji in Shaanxi province to the Yihe and Luohe rivers, a distance of about 800 *li*, which we have defined as the core area of the Yangshao culture. The two amphora types at first coexisted in the lower level of the Beishouling site at Baoji; later they split into two trends. After painted pottery became popular, both fish and bird motifs show a parallel development from concrete images into abstract patterns. At the Quanhucun site, plant and bird motifs coexisted, and both rose and chrysanthemum motifs appeared with their own sequences of development; but at Miaodigou there is only an incomplete sequence of the rose motif, and even fewer examples of the chrysanthemum motif. We named these last two motifs as the Banpo type and the Miaodigou type, respectively. They were redefined as having the same origin and a parallel development in terms of stratification. Although at some sites the Miaodigou type was found above the Banpo type, this did not contradict our conclusion that they derived from the same source and had developed in parallel. Beyond the core area, we could still see these representative types of the Yangshao culture, but not in a systematic manner. The most prominent motif is the rose motif, which spread into many different areas. We can treat them as being under the influence of the Yangshao culture.[2]

Having defined the geographical extent of the Yangshao culture, we also investigated its vertical development. The Yangshao culture of the central plains (the core area) covered two millennia from c5500-c3500 BC, and can be divided into early and later phases, each lasting about 1,000 years. Its origins lay in a culture which we termed the pre-Yangshao type or Laoguantai culture. This was first recognised in the lower level of the Beishouling site, dated earlier than 5500 BC. There was also a post-Yangshao period, known by some scholars as a regional type of the Longshan culture. This also lasted for 1,000 years. We can therefore divide the development of agriculture in the core Yangshao area into four phases, the last two of which date from c4500-c3500 BC and from c3500-c2500 BC. We need to emphasise 4500 BC as the time when society in this area developed from a tribal society into a state. This is not to say that the state had already appeared in a mature form; this was simply a turning-point when tribal society had reached its climax and had begun to decline, while elements of civilised society had begun to appear. In the same period there were many

[2] Su Bingqi 1984: 'Guanyu Yangshao wenhua de ruogan wenti,' *Su Bingqi kaoguxue lunshu xuanji*. Beijing: Wenwu chubanshe, 157-189.

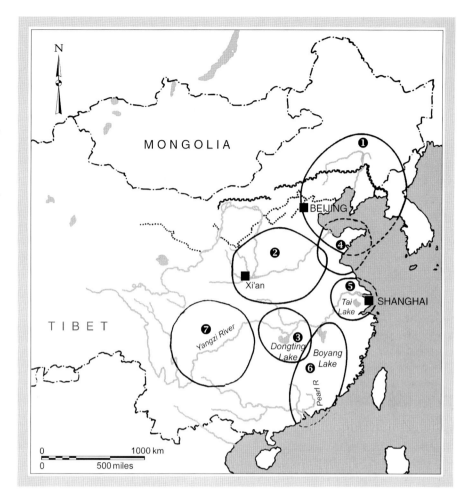

technological breakthroughs. With the division of labour, society also was stratified into classes. The painted pottery did not consist of everyday utensils, but was specially intended for religious use, probably by priests. The settlement of the Jiangzai site, dated to 4500 BC, reflects the kin relationships and social organisation of the tribal system; while the settlement at Daheishan dao Beizhuang on the Bohai Gulf, dated later than 4500 BC, shows the decline of the tribal system and the appearance of social divisions. By comparing these two examples, we can see the changes that had taken place at the basic level of society, which amount to an historical transformation. Of course, this generalisation cannot replace our study of historical facts from different regions.

To sum up, through the analysis of the Yangshao culture we realised that we had to follow this direction in order to complete the three tasks. Engels did not say that there was only one path for human society to enter civilisation. Based on the evidence then available, he suggested that there were three main types of state development, those of Athens, Rome and Germany. These three models each had their own characteristics; human society developed from barbarism into civilisation along different paths. Our study of the Yangshao culture clarified the history of the development from tribe to state in this particular region, and cannot serve as an overall model for the development of civilisation throughout China. However, it is the most important building block in the history of Chinese civilisation and the development of the Chinese as a nation.

The Regional Diversity of Chinese Archaeology

Chinese archaeology attained its maturity in the 1970s and 1980s. After the explorations of the 1960s, we finally found the right path for Chinese archaeology, that is to develop a basic practical theory, based on cultural divisions and interactions.[3] In August 1975, in my lecture to the students and teachers of Jilin

[3] Su Bingqi 1984: 'Guanyu kaoguxue wenhua de quxi leixing wenti,' *ibid*, 225-234.

University, I proposed this theory for the first time, laying the foundations for studying the origins of Chinese culture and civilisation, the development from tribe to state, from state to empire, the formation of "the Chinese" as a unified body with its individual parts drawn from different sources. In researching all these important historical questions we must first pay attention to the subdivisions within divisions, namely seriations and types. We can divide the intensively populated region into six divisions, three of which face the Eurasian landmass, and three of which face the Pacific (figure 1).

These six divisions are not simply geographic, but show their own origins, cultural characteristics and development. More importantly, different types within each division had their own paths of progression, which were not always parallel to each other. In archaeology, only certain core areas can reveal all their characteristics and the whole of their unique path of development. Each division has its own core areas. There are links and interactions between the different regions, but we have to admit that there are imbalances between them. In the following, I will review the archaeological work that has been carried out in the 1970s and 1980s. During this period, the major advances have been made in the peripheral areas; in particular, Sichuan archaeology has become significant only in recent years.

Archaeology of the Northern Region

In terms of its cultural geography, the north of China can be divided into three: the northwest, north, and northeast. The dividing line between the north and northwest lies between Baotou and Hohhot, and that between the north and northeast is Mt Yiwulü and the Liaohe River. The study of the cultural divisions of the north is an enormous cultural project, covering the following aspects:

First, the influence on the points where the northern cultural region adjoins the central plains: between 1979 and 1982 we selectively excavated the Xiheyin site along the Huliuhe River, Zhangjiakou in Hebei province, and the Taigu Baiyan site in Jinzhong, central Shanxi. The results were outstanding, proving that the Shanxi Taiyuan basin is the southern frontier of the northern cultural region and that northern Hebei around 4500 BC was the meeting-point between the Yangshao culture, represented by the painted pottery with the rose motif, and the Hongshan culture to the south and north of Mt Yanshan. A thousand years later, the same place became the dividing-point for the post-Yangshao culture, the post-Hongshan culture, and the ancient Ordos regional culture, which is represented by ovoid vessels. The meeting and integration of several different cultures fostered the Hongshan culture in the areas of the Laohahe and Xilamulunhe rivers leading it towards cultural maturity and social changes.

Secondly, there has been great progress in the Yanshan and Liaohe regions, stimulated by the discovery in 1983 of the ritual altars of Dongshanzui and the jade dragons of the Hongshan culture. We conducted investigations in the adjoining areas of Jianping, Kazuo and Lingyuan, and successfully brought to light sacrificial altars, temples and tombs with ritual jades in sets or groups of the later Hongshan cultural period, dating to 3500 BC. These discoveries show that society had already formed some sort of hierarchical structure above the level of communes, or more precisely, that there was some sort of early state. Some important remains, dating to before 5500 BC, were also found at Fuxing Chahai, Xinglongwa and Zhaobaogou at Aohanqi. We can therefore define a new cultural type, traditionally known as microlithic culture, with comb-patterned and zigzag decorated pottery. This provided a primary solution to the question of the origins of the Hongshan culture.

Considerable progress has also been made in research on the Lower Xiajiadian culture. The discovery of a large cemetery of this culture in Dadianzi, Aohanqi, and of a number of military fortifications parallel to the later Great Wall in the region of the Yan, Zhao and Qin states led us to realise that no later than about 2500 BC society in the Yanshan region had already developed beyond the stage of primitive states. The *fangguo* regional state, an organisation of several chiefdoms linked by chains of fortifications for defensive purposes, had already appeared.

We have also found six ritual pits oriented northeast and southwest and containing bronze ritual vessels in the areas adjoining Jianping, Kazuo and Lingyuan. They date to the late Shang and early Zhou periods. These finds indicate that here was an important historical stage 3,000 years ago. Between 1985 and 1986, we discovered the foundations of the Jieshi Palace of the Qin empire on the western coast of the Bohai Gulf. Taken together, these three finds, the ritual complex of the later Hongshan culture, the Xiajiadian fortifications, and the palace and Great Wall of the Qin empire, formed a complete series of development from primitive state, regional state, and empire. These archaeological discoveries in the Yanshan region corroborated our theory of the development of cultural divisions, announced at the 1985 Xincheng symposium, which proposed a progression from ancient culture to ancient city and finally to ancient state (these stages were later elaborated as 'primitive state,' 'regional state' and 'empire'). To draw a general conclusion from the above discussion, this progression from tribe to state took place in each of the cultural divisions.

The conference on Inner Mongolian archaeology held in 1984 in Hohhot discussed the cultural divisions within the central and southern parts of Inner Mongolia. The excavation of the Zhukaigou site helped us to understand the basic development of this region and its relationship with the cultures of the central plain. Between 1500 and 500 BC this region was the centre of the northern bronze cultures, related to the Shang and Zhou cultures in the central plains, but with its own characteristics. This was the source of the Ordos bronze culture.

The question of the Great Wall regional archaeology was discussed in the Lanzhou conference in 1986. West of Lanzhou city and Baotou was the so-called Great Northwest region. The Dadiwan culture was specifically discussed at this conference: this culture in fact was located farther to the east but basically belonged to the Yangshao cultural system and not to that of Majiayao. Although the Majiayao culture had a very developed painted pottery, the mentality of its people was quite different from the people of the Yangshao culture. The topography of the Dadiwan site at Qin'an, Gansu is significant. It is about one square kilometre, facing a river and backed by mountains, surrounded by natural defences. In the late phase of the Yangshao culture, about 3500 BC, there appeared the architectural foundations of some kind of a palace.

Archaeology of the Jin Culture

The study of Jin culture is one of the most important themes in the archaeology of the central plains as well as of the north. Just as central Shanxi is the southern frontier of the northern cultural region, southern Shanxi is the northern edge of the central plains cultural zone. As pointed out earlier, between 4500 and 3500 BC, social development in the late Hongshan culture of the northern region was more advanced than that of the central plains and other regions, being the first to witness the formation of a state with royal power: we can call it the dawn of Chinese civilisation. However, after 3500 BC, the Hongshan culture declined and was replaced by the early Hetao regional culture. By the middle of the second millennium BC the cultural centre had moved towards the southern part of Shanxi in fusion of different elements from the central plains, the Hetao region, the north, east and southeast, resulting in the appearance of the Taosi culture. The Taosi culture reached a higher social level than the late Hongshan culture, as the centre among a number of regional states. It is the *zhongguo* (central kingdom) which appears in pre-Qin texts, just as the sages of Yao and Shun laid the foundations for the Huaxia. In the Western Zhou dynasty, Tang Shu was assigned this land and established the Jin state; although it was a vassal of the Zhou dynasty, its foundations were largely based on a local tradition, a combination of Huaxia (Chinese) and Rongdi (nomadic) elements.

Archaeology of the Hua'nan Region

Hua'nan refers to the area whose axis is the Poyanghu Lake, the Ganjiang River and the Pearl River delta. Typical finds are shouldered stone tools, while the core area shows a complete sequence of stamped pottery, with flat-based *ding*, *dou* and *pan* vessels decorated with geometrical stamped patterns. The origins of this culture can be traced to the Cave of the Spirits in Wannian, Jiangxi province, dating back 10,000 years. It spread to neighbouring regions, eastward to the south of Lake Taihu and Fujian, the eastern part of Guangdong and Taiwan, westward to the south of Lake Dongting and the region of the Xiangjiang and Xijiang Rivers, and northward to the border area of Hunan, Hubei, Anhui and Henan. The distribution of shouldered stone tools spread to the south towards the Indian ocean; segmented implements spread to the east towards the Pacific; flat-based *ding*, *dou* and *pan* became prototypes of early ritual vessels.

The Shixia culture at Qujiang and the remains of its upper layers are important evidence for exploring the development from tribe to state in the Lingnan region. It is also important to see its relationship with other cultural divisions: the tombs at this site had the ground prepared with sand, and were interred with stone *yue* and *cong*, as well as pottery ritual vessels such as polished black pottery and sets of tools. Such tombs obviously belonged to military leaders, priests and craftsmen. In a developed tribal system, these three professions enjoyed a higher social status, but there was little difference in the ownership of private property between them and ordinary members of society; however, at Shixia, the tombs of such people can be distinguished, indicating that labour divisions had already led to social divisions. The traditional tribal system had been breached and society had entered a new phase of development.

The discovery of a Shang dynasty city in Wucheng, Jiangxi, was an important breakthrough. Civilisation here was related to the Shang civilisation in the central plains, but with strong local characteristics. It was probably a *fangguo*, or regional state, which coexisted with the Shang dynasty and which was in the same phase of social development. The discovery at Xin'gan Dayangzhou was another significant example of the regional development in the late Shang and early Zhou period. In the western part of Guangdong, along the Xijiang River, a number of tombs dated from the Western Zhou to the Spring and Autumn Period have been excavated. From the tomb structure and the bronze objects found within the tombs, they show individual characteristics: stone and bronze *ge*, and large-mouthed *zun* from Shantou and Meixian also display local and period characteristics. To sum up, the development of ancient society in the Hua'nan region proceeded in parallel to that of the central plains, starting from 6500 BC in the early neolithic, and turning from a tribal society into a primitive state around 4500 BC, and finally from a primitive state into a *fangguo* regional state about 2500 BC. Two thousand years ago, this region was integrated into the Qin and Han empires, but its cultural divisions and development are far more complicated than those of the central plains: this area still has many ethnic groups, and the question of the cultural divisions of ancient Hua'nan has begun to be explored, but needs further research.

Archaeology of the Lower Reaches of the Yangzi River

In October 1977, at the Nanjing conference on the neolithic cultures of the Lower Yangzi River, agreement was reached on the following:

- The large area along the southeast coast shared some cultural characteristics and parallel social development with the central plains and the northwest. This area played an important part in the integration of the Chinese people and the formation of the state.

- There are different cultural divisions within this area. What is known as the Qinglian'gang culture had different divisions: *a*) the Dawenkou-Longshan culture in Shandong and that part of Jiangsu north of the Huaihe river, *i e* the area traditionally known as the ancient Xuyi and Huaiyi cultures; *b*) the area bordering on Jiangsu,

Shandong, Henan and Anhui; *c*) the Ningzhen area, centred on Nanjing and the northeastern part of Ganjiang, which is the ancient Wu and Yue cultures; *d*) the region around Taihu and the Qiantangjiang , belonging to the Majiabang-Songze-Liangzhu culture; finally *e*) the area between the Yangzi and the Huaihe, which basically belonged to the Songze-Liangzhu culture.

In the 1980s, we further subdivided the region around Taihu into the three areas of the Ningshao plains, Hangjiahu and Susong. Field archaeology has made great progress in this region and the discovery of the Liangzhu tombs with jade ritual objects, artificial platforms and large-scale cemeteries has made a significant contribution to the study of the origins of Chinese civilisation. Current debate on the Liangzhu culture focuses on the question of whether it had entered the period of *fangguo* or regional state.

Archaeology of Shandong and the Bohai Area

At the same conference, we also proposed that the Jiaodong and Liaodong peninsula followed an independent cultural progression. Even the prehistoric culture of Changdao should become a separate research topic. In 1987, the first archaeological conference for the Bohai area was held in Yantai. It discussed principally the material from the Heishandao Beizhuang site. A second conference was held in 1988 at Lingzi, and focused on the ancient cultures of the southwestern part of Bohai. A concept was formed of 'Qingzhou archaeology'. We began to consider the cultural foundation of the later Qi state. Two further conferences were held in Dalian and Shijiazhuang in 1990 and 1992, both of which used the point of view of divisions and types, first to examine the cultural development and characteristics of the Bohai region, and then to set these in relation to the Pacific and northeastern Asian background. At these conferences a number of overseas scholars participated and agreed with the proposed scheme of cultural divisions.

Archaeology of the Lake Dongting Region

At the first congress of Zhongguo kaogu xuehui (The Association of Chinese Archaeology) in 1979, it was proposed that the study of the Chu culture should be emphasised in the broadest sense. Before the unification of Qin in 221 BC, and afterwards, the Chu culture was a strong cultural system that influenced southern China, although it was not static nor so large in prehistoric times. The purpose of research into the Chu culture is to solve puzzles concerning its origin and development. In order to study this topic we could either begin with the prehistoric materials from their origin to the later development, or else trace back from the later materials to their origins. Because most of the available materials are from tombs of the Eastern Zhou period, we selected some of the most important cultural elements, such as the *li* vessel in Chu style, from the Jianghan region, roughly contemporary with Shang and Zhou dynasties. The Chu-style *li* is different from the *li* of the Shang and Zhou: it was created by the ancestors of the Chu people and developed independently in parallel with the latter. The early type can be found among pottery vessels of the Shijiahe type of Hubei Longshan culture and in the upper layer of the Qinglongquan site. This Chu-style *li* is similar to the *li* of the early Shang period, that is to say, its first appearance dates back 4,000-5,000 years. Beyond this, the origin for the Shijiahe culture might be found in the Qujialing culture, and several other primitive cultures which existed in northwestern Jiangxi and along the Yichang region of the Yangzi at Sanxia. The cultural contents may not be exactly the same at all these sites, but the appearance and development of the Chu-style *li* and its distribution in different cultural regions in the Jianghan area reflects its relationship with the Xia, Shang and Zhou cultures in the central plains, which were also undergoing similar social and cultural changes. In Pengtoushan, Hunan, we have found neolithic cultures dating to 6000 BC and archaeological work in

Hunan and the bordering areas of Hubei, Anhui and Jiangxi indicate that this region might be an independent cultural division.

Archaeology of the Sichuan Basin

The Sichuan basin and the area north and south of Dongting Lake belong to the same cultural division, but the Sichuan basin is comparatively independent. In 1984, during the meeting of the National Fieldwork held in Chengdu, we examined pottery sherds from Chengdu and Guanghan Yueliangwan which showed that both places had early cultures dating back to 3500 BC. Later, the discovery of two sacrificial pits at Sanxingdui and of architectural remains at the Chengdu Shierqiao site made us realise that the Sichuan basin had its own development of ancient culture. Three or four thousand years ago it had developed a very distinctive bronze culture which was associated with the Xia and Shang cultures of the central plains. It was undoubtedly a regional state. More significantly, in the Chengdu plain, there seemed to have continuously coexisted the two states of ancient Shu and ancient Guanghan. By the Qin and Han periods, Shu and Guanghan were two prefectures about 50 kilometres apart.

The Chinese Archaeology School

In 1987, I wrote a short article "Aspiring to the establishment of a Chinese School" on the occasion of the tenth anniversary of the Chinese Academy of Social Sciences (CASS). In this article, I cited a speech by Professor Hu Shun, then Director of CASS, in 1975. He had emphasised that we should establish our own schools in all disciplines, including archaeology, with Chinese national characteristics, and to establish a methodology. In the last two decades, archaeology has followed his directive. We have been exploring two aspects of the same question: the first, to divide China into six great divisions according to archaeological features, characteristics and development, three of these divisions facing Asia, and three the Pacific. This multifaceted unity is the historical and structural foundation on which 10 million Chinese people came together; secondly, on the question of the origins of Chinese civilisation, Chinese archaeology has provided a key to open the door of the long formation of the Chinese cultural tradition.

The positive cultural elements in the Chinese cultural tradition gave the Chinese people a national spirit which can be summed up under the following main topics:

- Good at techniques, good at thinking. From the lithic tradition of palaeolithic times to the pottery making of the neolithic period, China has developed a craftsmanship which has been associated with thoughtful design and the hard-working characteristics of the Chinese people. It has created a rich material culture, with spiritual aspects as well.

- The ability to absorb elements from different sources. The formation of the Chinese as a nation is the result of the interaction, mutual influence and integration of many different cultural divisions, which as the result of a process of endless rejoining became culturally identified and economically integrated. It has a solid historical foundation.

- The Chinese writing system played an important role in linking different cultural elements. Chinese characters reflected the special mode of thinking of the Chinese, using images and suggesting meanings.

- The social function of jade was to reflect the moral ideals and value judgements of Chinese culture. Jade embodies feelings and thoughts that are characteristic of Chinese culture. We have found evidence for the use of jade at the Chahai and Xinglongwa sites as early as 7,000-8,000 years ago. Five thousand years ago, in the Hongshan, Dawenkou and Liangzhu cultures, jade had become the symbol of prestige and a vessel for communication between the spiritual world and the people, justifying the relationship between man and nature. Later still, jade was associated with various social virtues: this association actually derived from prehistoric times.

Chinese archaeology now appears poised for takeoff. In order best to enjoy the fruits of this golden age, we need to adopt several strategies. Foremost among these is to reconsider the integration of the discipline. For example, at the moment, archaeology of the palaeolithic and of the neolithic periods is divided into different institutions, but these should not be kept separate any longer. Secondly, we should keep a balance between inland archaeology and that of the frontier regions, and between world archaeology and Chinese archaeology. Thirdly, we need to increase international academic exchange, with clear guidelines and well-organised programmes, sending students out, inviting people in, as a long-term plan for the systematic investigation of Chinese culture. We have found our own path and built our own theoretical foundation and framework for reconstructing ancient Chinese history; we have also found our own position in the world, in both past and present reality. We are standing on the new runway, ready to embark on a scientific phase after one based only on experience. Facing the world and facing the future, let us welcome the arrival of the new age of Chinese archaeology!

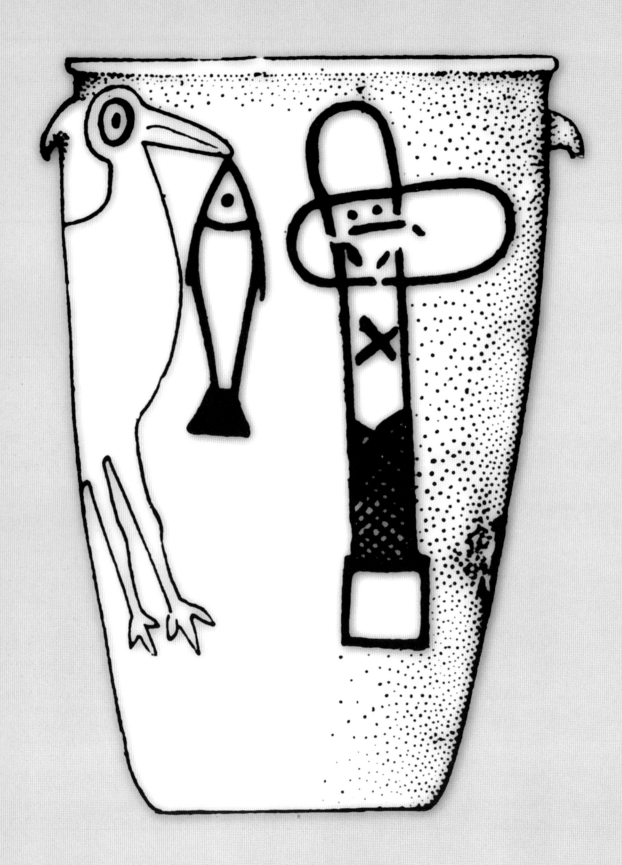

YU WEICHAO

New Trends in Archaeological Thought

*S*INCE the end of the 1970s, after the disruption of the Cultural Revolution, Chinese archaeologists have been gradually learning the new developments in international archaeological circles, in particular the theory and methodology of the New Archaeology that appeared in the 1960s in the United States and Europe. Their opinions and reactions vary greatly. In fact, the New Archaeology itself later developed several different branches and there is no unity of agreement among them. Generally speaking, however, it represents a new trend in archaeological research. The understanding of its position in current archaeology should be, as I see it, based on the history of the development of archaeology as a discipline.

Periodisation

In the last 10 years, many European and American scholars have tried to divide the history of western archaeology into different phases. Willey and Sabloff divided the development of American archaeology into four periods:[1] the speculative period (1492-1840); the classificatory-descriptive period (1840-1914); the classificatory-historical period; and the explanatory period (1960 onwards). American archaeology was transplanted from Europe, and this periodisation is in fact closely related to the development of European, in particular British, archaeology.

The so-called speculative period is similar to Antiquarian studies in Europe and to *jinshixue* (study of bronzes and stone stelae) in China. In the second phase, the classificatory-descriptive period, a scientific classification was applied to artefacts; stratigraphy and typology were established in archaeology and were used to record and explore the function and evolution of artefacts. In the research of human remains, anthropology was also taken into consideration. The third phase, the classificatory-historical period, refers to the effort of using material remains to reconstruct the past; the main aim here was to provide a fuller picture of history. In the final phase, the explanatory period, the aim is to establish a model of cultural development; in other words, to search for the dynamics of cultural progression. To achieve that goal, various methods have to be used, including scientific means, to obtain the maximum of information from

[1] Willey, G R and Sabloff, J A 1980: *A History of American Archaeology,* 2nd edition San Francisco: Freeman.

Facing page • Pottery urn, c3900 BC Linru Yancun, Henan

This was originally written as the preface for *Dandai waiguo kaoguxue de lilun yu fangfa* (ed Zhongguo lishi bowuguan kaogubu), Xi'an: San Qin chubanshe, 1991.

limited archaeological remains. In this phase, scholars are fully aware of the interaction between the natural environment and human society.

In 1981, K Kristiansen divided archaeology in Denmark also into four periods:[2] in the first, from 1805-1850, archaeology had become a discipline, which used materials to explain national or historical events; the next, 1850-1900, saw the birth of modern archaeology and a period of expansion: archaeology combined with various disciplines to study prehistory and changed the traditional view of human history; in the third period, 1900-1960, the foundations of archaeology were further strengthened by the use of systematic excavation and artefact typology, which would allow us to establish a reliable prehistory of different areas and of different peoples: archaeology had also become a common area of interest and knowledge for the general public; finally, from 1960 to the present, there is a new phase of changes and development in which archaeological research is becoming more and more professional. As the social and natural sciences have developed, many new technologies and theories have been introduced into archaeology; the definition of archaeology itself has been altered and the result is unknown. The general trend is that archaeologists are trying to relate their research within a much broader social and scientific context.

In Britain, Colin Renfrew briefly reviewed the history and problems of explanation in archaeology.[3] He divided the history of archaeological interpretation in the West into three periods:

a) **The early ferment**: before the later half of the 19th century, there were some theoretical advances in archaeology. In 1859, Charles Darwin published *The Origin of Species* and his work was reflected in the writings of Pitt-Rivers. In anthropology, several pioneers were also trying to explain the fundamental problem of human origins in a fresh way; ethnographic methods were applied to archaeology.

b) **The long sleep**, between the 1880s and the 1950s: in this period, there was hardly any theoretical discussion on the basic questions of principles of archaeology, but Oscar Montelius's (1843-1921) typological study of artefacts is a great advance in methodology; Gordon Childe's (1892-1957) book *Man makes himself*, published in 1932, raised some questions that later became important in the new "processual archaeology". In the United States, in 1948, W Taylor published his doctoral dissertation *A Study of Archaeology*, challenging the existing paradigm, but his work was not taken up by other archaeologists.

c) **The great awakening**: in 1960, R B Braithwaite's *Scientific Explanation* inspired archaeologists to seek a clear and explicit reasoning in their study of material cultures. Many archaeologists, such as Lewis Binford, David Clarke, and Renfrew himself, all tried to answer some of the key questions in theoretical archaeology. The New Archaeology was influenced by Carl Hempel's philosophy of science, and led to a debate on theoretical issues in archaeology. However, in order to understand the phenomenon of "cultural regularity", the New Archaeologists such as Binford tried to establish a universal interpretative scheme which was based on deductive method, and this has led to the present confusion in archaeology.

Renfrew, Kristiansen and Willey and Sabloff's periodisations of Western archaeology share many things in common. The main difference is that Renfrew's approach focuses on the development of archaeological interpretation, and therefore he did not pay much attention to the early "speculative" period.

In March 1989, at the National Round Table meeting of Cultural Relics held in Nanning, Guangxi province, I gave a speech in which I briefly reviewed the development of archaeology in Europe, North America, the Soviet Union and China and divided archaeology on a global scale into three main periods:

a) **The birth of archaeology**: This includes the early collecting and study of antiquities: its real beginning is in the Renaissance when people suddenly realised that there had been a golden age before the medieval dark ages. They wished to find a new world and to establish a new order. Ancient works of art, Greek and Roman sculptures in particular, attracted peoples' attention; in ancient

[2] Kristiansen, K 1981: 'A social history of Danish archaeology (1805-1975),' Glyn Daniel, ed, *Towards a History of Archaeology*, London: Thames and Hudson, 20-44.

[3] Renfrew, Colin 1982: 'Explanation revisited,' A C Renfrew, M J Rowlands and B A Segraves, eds. *Theory and explanation in archaeology*, New York: Academic Press, 5-23.

art they discovered a perfect world. Art history therefore developed. Consequently, many sites and ancient remains were discovered and people became interested in collecting ancient weapons, tools and ornaments. Classification was developed for the purpose of sorting out these objects. By the beginning of the 19th century, several Scandinavian scholars began to use stone, bronze and iron as the main criteria of their classification, representing the three main stages of the development of human technology. Studies in art history and antiquities laid the foundations of modern archaeology.

b) **The Modern Phase:** Compared to the more recent trends, archaeology remained traditional. Stratigraphy and typology are the two main keystones of its methodology. Stratigraphy was introduced into archaeology from geology. The publication of Sir Charles Lyell's *The Principles of Geology* in the early 1830s marked the real beginning of the doctrines of stratigraphic geology, which were then borrowed by archaeologists. Between 1825 and 1841, J MacEnery excavated Kent's Cavern at Torquay and found some flint implements. As a Catholic priest, MacEnery attributed these implements to "a very remote period", but he did not publish his finds. In France, Jacques Boucher de Perthes (1788-1868) also discovered many palaeolithic remains in Abbeville and the Somme Valley. In 1859, a group of English geologists and archaeologists visited Abbeville and confirmed de Perthes's discovery. For the first time, the orthodox Christian doctrines and the myth that God made man was challenged and the true value of archaeology was recognised. However, the use of stratigraphy in archaeology was not common until fifty years later, when Heinrich Schliemann (1822-90) and Augustus Pitt-Rivers (1827-1900) adopted stratigraphic principles in their excavations.

Typology developed from the classification of antiquities, but was influenced in the first place by the method of classification used in biology. In the early 19th century, several northern European antiquarians had already started to use this method; and by the early 20th century, archaeological typology became a mature methodology, marked by Montelius's systematic study. Willey, Sabloff and Kristiansen all considered the time between the middle of 19th and the beginning of the 20th century as a separate period, for the reason that the typology and stratigraphy were still in a stage of development and the archaeological chronology of different regions was not yet in place.

From then onwards, until the 1950s, archaeologists in many countries took these two methods to be the main methodology in archaeological research. The cultural chronology of Mesopotamia, Egypt, Europe, South Asia and East Asia was established by the use of such methodology. As the British archaeologist W Flinders Petrie (1852-1943) said, the ultimate aim of archaeology is to reconstruct the life of the past. Traditionally, archaeologists' understanding of a culture is based on archaeological evidence, such as pottery, architectural remains, orientation of tombs, and ornaments; based on such evidence, the archaeologist could speculate on whether there was a migration or diffusion of the culture. The general pattern of cultural development is, however, not the goal of archaeological exploration.

However, after the facts have been established, one starts to think about more abstract questions. As early as 1932, G Childe argued that after the use of fire, the invention of agriculture and the domestication of animals are the most important revolutions in food production in human history, which naturally led to the concept of a 'neolithic revolution' later proposed by him after World War II. In the 1950s, Childe proposed another new concept: the 'urban revolution' which occurred after the neolithic revolution.[4] Childe proclaimed that he himself was a Marxist. His archaeological research was obviously influenced by Marx's theory of historical materialism which emphasises the law of social development.

In Russia, after the October Revolution, Soviet archaeologists adopted Marxism and tried to explain the pattern of social development, but detailed and concrete case studies were often sacrificed for the sake of a rigid interpretation of theoretical principles. For example, Marr's linguistic theory and Pokelofski's historical theory dominated Soviet studies in the fields of archaeology and

[4] Childe, Gordon 1950: 'The Urban Revolution,' *Town Planning Review* 21: 3-17.

history. From 1919 to the 1950s, the Institute of Archaeology at the Russian Academy was renamed the Institute for the Study of Material Cultures. The aim of archaeology, which should include the total study of material production, spiritual life and social relations, etc, was narrowed down to the study of the force of material production alone. Even if the initial aim was plausible, the way in which it had been carried out was wrong.

c) **The New Archaeology**: This arrived at the end of the 1960s, and has since been the dominant force in the West. W Taylor is really the pioneer of New Archaeology. As mentioned earlier, in 1948, Taylor challenged traditional archaeology.[5] He argued that the aim of archaeologists was not only to conduct excavations and publish reports, and that typology and stratification should not be the final goals of archaeological research. He claimed that American archaeology in the 1940s was too much obsessed with objects, and that not enough attention was being paid to non-material aspects. Taylor thought that archaeology should integrate more with other disciplines and should investigate human behaviour as reflected in the artefacts made by them; to him, archaeology is a science of human behaviour and culture is a synthetic concept; to study prehistory, we need a multi-disciplinary methodology.

[5] Taylor, W 1948: *A Study of Archaeology,* American Anthropologist Memoir 69, Washington DC.

Theory in Archaeology

In the 1950s the new evolutionism, represented by J Steward (1902-72), influenced American and western anthropology. The philosophy of science led by C G Hempel and Oppenheim also made a great impact on both anthropology and archaeology. L A White used the system theory and energy cost to measure the degree of human progress. American history is comparatively short, which gave an advantage to anthropological study. In the American tradition of archaeology, anthropology is always dominant. It was against this cultural background and with the movement of neo-evolutionary thought, that the new movement called New Archaeology appeared first in the United States, then in Britain and other European countries.

This new beginning was marked by the publication in 1962 of Lewis Binford's article entitled 'Archaeology as Anthropology.'[6] Binford argued that archaeology shared the same aims as anthropology, that is to "explain the total range of physical and cultural similarities and differences characteristic of the entire spatial-temporal span of man's existence." According to him, "the formal structure of artefact assemblages together with the between element contextual relationships do present a systematic and understandable picture of the *total extinct* cultural system."

[6] Binford, Lewis 1962: 'Archaeology as Anthropology,' *American Antiquity* 28-2: 217-25.

The New Archaeology proposed that we should use a systems theory to interpret this cultural system, which can be divided into three classes of artefacts: technomic, socio-technic and ideo-technic. To study the initial function of an artefact is to relate it to its natural environment, and to explain technical and economic changes. We should take into consideration both the technical content and the changing social circumstances to reconstruct a picture of an environment which is no longer extant. Apart from technomic and socio-technic artefacts, archaeologists also study a third category of artefacts, that is the ideo-technic artefacts, such as figures of deities, clan symbols and symbols of natural agencies. Binford's theory expanded archaeological research into new fields, including material and spiritual culture, and social relations, all of which are aspects of human activity, and emphasised the ecological condition of human existence. The philosophical foundation of this new movement is cultural materialism: its aim is to understand the process of human behaviour and the dynamics of human history. Therefore, it is known as processual archaeology.

To achieve its goals, the New Archaeology introduced social theories and methods from the natural sciences and social sciences, such as demographic analysis, settlement patterns, ecological analysis, and evolutionary theory. There are many new branches, including environmental archaeology, experimental archaeology, social archaeology, economic archaeology, and ethno-archaeology. In 1982, Renfrew summarised the new approaches in current western archaeology and divided them into five different schools:[7]

[7] Renfrew, *ibid.*

a) **Historiographic**: Archaeologists of this school emphasise the study of particular events. They take the approach that one can put himself into the shoes of the actor, to have a fuller understanding of the historical background, and to provide a detailed analysis and description of a particular culture.

b) **Hypothetical-Deductive**: Archaeologists of this school believe there to be a general law which can be applied in archaeology, and that by using deductive methodology, one can determine the outcome based on a knowledge of given circumstances.

c) **Systems Behaviour**: This school draws its vocabulary and concepts from systems theory, in order to interpret the changes and development of human behaviour, but in practice they rarely discuss the context or background of this behaviour.

d) **New Marxist**: They reject vulgar materialism, which was practised by Soviet archaeologists in the 1920s and 1930s; however, they use the concepts and theories of Marxism, such as production mode and the relations between production and the labour force, in order to interpret archaeological events.

e) **Structuralist**: This school appeared in the 1960s and had a huge impact on all branches of the social sciences and the humanities. The structuralist approach mainly relies on the study of ideology and semiotics. For archaeologists, it is difficult to observe the spiritual world and therefore this approach has not been widely used.

Among these schools, some have been more popular than the rest, such as the historiographic approach, which derives from traditional archaeology but which improved upon it greatly, in particular through the use of scientific method. In the 1980s, after the debate between traditional archaeology and New Archaeology, the two in fact drew closer together. The hypothetical-deductive method was derived from New Archaeology, and criticised traditional archaeology as a low-level study, based only on reductive method; they themselves emphasised the deductive method, using a general rule to explain events occurring in different areas. However, we know that it is extremely difficult just to use limited generalisations to interpret the cultures of different regions, and that this often leads to pitfalls.

At present, the controversy between traditional archaeology and New Archaeology has not yet been settled, and in the meantime some new movements have emerged, such as post-processual archaeology in Britain, of which the representative figure in the 1980s was Iain Hodder. Hodder argues that behavioural archaeology treated the human factor as the passive result of the outside environment, ignoring the subjective activity of the protagonists. Processual archaeology emphasised that social change is not an isolated process, but derives from the historical limitations and should be treated independently. To understand social change one has to understand the ideology of those who enact the changes. In other words, archaeologists have to study ideology and its role in human behaviour and social change.[8]

[8] Hodder, Iain 1986: *Reading the Past: Current Approaches to Interpretation in Archaeology*, Cambridge: Cambridge University Press.

In the New Archaeology, since individual cases are used only to demonstrate the general pattern, no successful case studies have been produced. This has been criticised by many other archaeologists. Traditional archaeology has also taken human behaviour and processes to be its subjects; there is an integration of old and new, in both research design and methodology. By looking at this phenomenon, we can understand that archaeology has entered a new phase. In Russia, the Marr school was abandoned by Soviet archaeologists; consequently, some American and European archaeologists also influenced Soviet archaeology, and detailed case studies once again were at the centre of archaeological research. By the 1970s, Soviet archaeology had gone into a new expansionary diversity: there are schools of historical archaeology, ethno-archaeology, social archaeology, descriptive archaeology, technical archaeology, ecological archaeology, systems-theory archaeology. Some of them are obviously influenced by the New Archaeology in Europe and America: however, they all share the same goal, which is to reconstruct the past and to explain the patterns of social development. They only differ in certain aspects and in the means or methodology used in research. In the last 10 years, Russian archaeology has integrated with European and American archaeology.

In China, modern archaeology was introduced from the West in the 1920s. Before the establishment of the People's Republic in 1949, archaeology was disrupted by the Sino-Japanese war and by civil war, so that in fact it had a history of only about a dozen years. In that period, some archaeological advances were made, such as the discovery of Peking Man, Hetao Man, the Upper Cave Man, and microlithic cultures in the north. The Yangshao and Longshan neolithic cultures had been discovered, as had the Shang-Yin bronze culture and the impressed pottery culture in the south. Despite all these discoveries, we knew very little of the prehistory of China. In the 1950s, Chinese archaeology closely followed Soviet archaeology. We emphasised that the task of archaeology is to reconstruct ancient society and to explain its development. In the last 40 years, many Chinese archaeologists have treated archaeology as the study of human behaviour. In the latter part of the 1950s, Chinese archaeologists started to explore the social relationships of ancient society and people's spiritual life, rather than the mere study of technology and production. However, on the whole, the foundation of Chinese archaeology was still weak, and the priority was to establish the framework of different cultural developments and their mutual relationships. For the last thirty or forty years, with some interruption during the Cultural Revolution, Chinese archaeologists have been working hard to establish a cultural chronology for different regions. Thus, Chinese archaeology although having the aim of a higher level, similar to the third period of western archaeology, has actually remained in the second level, of establishing a cultural chronology. There have been some important studies in terms of archaeological thinking and practice: subjects such as the social pattern of the Yangshao culture, the relationship between topographical change and cultural settlements in Shandong, experimental archaeology of Longshan eggshell black pottery, the social ranking systems of the Shang, Zhou, Qin and Han periods, and cosmology. These studies have reached a high level of interpretation and particularly during the last decade, the trend away from a descriptive to a more interpretative archaeology has accelerated. We can estimate or predict that Chinese archaeology will soon enter a new phase.

Conclusion

Finally, a remark should be made on the question of why China has not produced many different archaeological theories as has been the case in Europe and America. I have been exchanging views with Chinese archaeological colleagues and I think that there are probably three reasons for this. Firstly, archaeology as a discipline has not been highly developed in China; secondly, in most European countries and in America there is no single dominant social theory: everyone can pursue his own social or historical theory to explain cultural progress and dynamics; thirdly, in the West many archaeological theories are actually middle-range theories, that is, theory between concrete historical details and the highest generalisation of historical process. This is necessary for theoretical exploration, but in China we have become used to using Marxist historical materialism to explain archaeological events, without recourse to middle-range theory. Without middle-range theory, many historical events cannot be fully understood and integrated into a generalisation. For this particular reason, I trust that the younger generation of Chinese archaeologists will continue their efforts in the field of theoretical exploration in archaeology.

XU PINGFANG

Archaeological Research on the Origins of Chinese Civilisation

*T*HE study of Chinese civilisation is to study the historical progress through which China became a civilised society, as marked by the formation of classes and a national state. Due to the different understandings of the word civilisation, most discussions equate civilisation with culture, which has led to some confusion; therefore we first have to discuss whether Chinese civilisation is an indigenous culture or one imported from outside China. This question has long been the subject of discussion.

Since the latter half of the 18th century and until the 1940s, the theory of the western origins of Chinese civilisation was dominant in the West.[1] The time was one of the expansion of western capitalism and colonisation, so it is not surprising that this view was influential. The Swedish scholar Andersson's initial discovery in 1921 of the painted pottery in Yangshao village, Shunchi, Henan province seemed to support this view. However, recent archaeology gives no support to the diffusionist theory according to which Chinese civilisation was imported from the West. In his later years, Andersson modified his view on this question, but the problem has not gone away completely. The Russian scholar L S Vasilev still insists, in his book *The Problem of Chinese Civilisation* (in Russian) published in 1976, that the formation of Chinese civilisation was largely influenced by civilisations of the Near East and Central Asia.[2]

After the establishment of the People's Republic, Chinese archaeology has proved that the old theory of the western origins of Chinese civilisation was from the beginning completely false. All the major elements of Chinese civilisation, such as agriculture (the northern millet culture and southern rice culture); domestication of animals (mainly pigs and dogs); the invention of sericulture; architecture based on stamped-earth foundations, with a wooden frame structure and enclosed courtyard layout; cities as centres of politicised religious activities; the use of ritual jades and bronze vessels; a script based on ideographic principles; clan-based ancestral worship: all these distinctive features suggest the indigenous origin of Chinese culture. These facts are readily recognizable, if one has no eurocentric prejudice.

However, when China became a civilised society is an important issue in

[1] The French scholar Joseph de Guignes first promoted the theory that the Chinese were migrants from Egypt (de Guignes, *Mémoire dans lequel on prouve que les Chinois sont une colonie égyptienne*, Paris, 1758). James Legge also recklessly claimed that the Chinese were the descendants of Noah (Legge, *The Chinese Classics*, HK/London 1861/72). Later, Terrien de Lacouperie argued that Chinese civilisation was linked to that of Mesopotamia (de Lacouperie, *Western Origins of the Early Chinese Civilisation from 2300 BC to 200 AD*, London: 1894).

[2] Vasilev, L S 1976: *The questions of the origins of Chinese civilisation* (in Russian, Chinese translation, *Zhongguo wenming qiyuan wenti*, Beijing: Wenwu chubanshe, 1989).

This paper was first presented at the International Conference on Sinology (January 1995, Haikou, China) organised by the Chinese Academy of Social Sciences.

Chinese history. In the 1930s the question was the subject of heated debate, in association with other topics of Marxist theory concerning the Asiatic production mode and social history of China. Guo Moruo wrote in the preface to his book *Zhongguo gudai shehui yanjiu* (The Study of Ancient Chinese Society) as follows: "China is still a blank page in the history of world culture. Engels' *The Origin of the Family, Private Property and the State* mentions nothing of Chinese society. We Chinese should write on this page."[3] Again, he wrote: "My book is a supplement to Engels' work." Guo acutely sensed the significance of the question of the origins of Chinese civilisation and treated it in the framework of world cultural history. Unfortunately, the conditions for studying this question did not exist at the time. In the 1950s, Chinese historians once again debated the periodisation of ancient Chinese history: the question of the origin of Chinese civilisation was touched upon but the main focus of that debate was the periodisation of Chinese slave and feudal societies. We can therefore see that from the 1930s to the 1960s the discussion on the origins of Chinese civilisation could not make any progress due to a lack of evidence. The birth and origin of Chinese civilisation took place in the neolithic period, in which there were no written records. The study of prehistory has to rely mainly on archaeology, and archaeological research is the key to the exploration of this question. The archaeology of prehistory in China has accumulated materials in the last few decades: in particular the theory of regional divisions and types by Su Bingqi has provided a framework for the archaeology of prehistory in China and paved the way for an investigation of the origins of Chinese civilisation.[4]

[3] Guo Moruo 1954: *Zhongguo gudai shehui yanjiu*. Beijing: Renmin chubanshe, 4-5.

[4] For Su's theories see his paper in this volume. Also, Wang Tao 1997: 'Establishing the Chinese Archaeological School: Su Bingqi and contemporary Chinese archaeology' and Su's 'Hua people – Descendants of the dragon-Chinese: an archaeological seeking after roots.' *Antiquity* 71- 271, 31-39.

The Views of Xia Nai and Su Bingqi

In 1983 Xia Nai, the director of the Institute of Archaeology, formally proposed to conduct archaeological research on the problem of the origins of Chinese civilisation. He said: "In my view, the origins of Chinese civilisation, like those of other civilisations, should be resolved through archaeological research, because this was a period when writing had not yet evolved to maturity. Even were there some written records, they may not have survived: we have to rely largely on artefacts as our evidence. Since 1928, the beginning of archaeological excavations at Xiaotun, Anyang, after the first few years of fieldwork, a considerable harvest of materials was produced. By the 1930s, we were able to confirm that Shang culture was already a splendid civilisation, but at the time most scholars still regarded the Yinxu culture at Xiaotun as the earliest Chinese civilisation. Some people even thought that the birth of Chinese civilisation took place there, but we know that the Shang culture at Yinxu was already a highly developed civilisation: this would be like the legend of Laozi who was born as an old man with a long white beard." Xia Nai considered that the cities, writing, bronze-casting technology and other elements found in the Shang culture at Yinxu could be traced back to the Erligang culture at Zhengzhou and the Erlitou culture at Yanshi, Henan province, and even might be closely associated with some neolithic cultures such as the late Henan Longshan culture, the late Shandong Longshan culture, the Liangzhu culture in Zhejiang, and the late Yangshao culture in Gansu. He continues that "China is not completely isolated from the rest of the world: Chinese civilisation likewise cannot have developed in isolation. But Chinese civilisation has been growing in this land, having its own characteristics, style and traits. There are already some cultural elements with Chinese characteristics in the major neolithic cultures in China. The formation of Chinese civilisation was based on these foundations."[5]

[5] Xia Nai 1985: *Zhongguo wenming de qiyuan*. Beijing: Wenwu chubanshe, 79-106.

In 1986, in order to explore the origins of Chinese civilisation, Su Bingqi also proposed a number of new concepts — 'ancient culture,' 'ancient city' and 'ancient state.' He explains: "What is the definition of Chinese civilisation? 'Ancient culture' refers to the primitive cultures. 'Ancient city' refers to the towns and cities in the early urbanisation, which were not yet the capitals that developed in the later periods. 'Ancient state' refers to the stable and independent political institution above clans and chiefdoms…The links and evidence for these three concepts are major settlements and tombs which are distinct from ordinary village sites and graves, and which coincide with the division of labour and the social stratification of relationships. The time when these changes took place was the period of the late phase of primitive society, between 5000 and 4000 bp."[6]

Su cited the archaeological site of the Goddess Temple and piled-stone tombs at Niuheliang, western Liaoning province, of the late Hongshan culture (c3500 BC), as evidence that, as early as 5,000 years ago, there was a form of social organisation which transcended that of ordinary tribes or chiefdoms. Su Bingqi's new concept made an impact on the study of the origins of Chinese civilisation. In 1989, Su, as President of the Association for Chinese Archaeology, declared that the most important research to be conducted in the following decade should be on the origins and formation of Chinese civilisation, thus marking a new era in this research.[7]

Debates in the 1980s and 1990s

In September 1989 and November 1991, the Institute of Archaeology, Chinese Academy of Social Sciences, and the editorial board of *Kaogu*, twice held seminars to discuss the topic of the origins of Chinese civilisation. They summarised previous research and discussed the direction and content of future endeavours. They reached a consensus on some basic concepts, and agreed on several points, as follows:[8]

• We need to clarify the definitions of 'culture' and 'civilisation'. Civilisation refers to an advanced cultural level in the development of human history, marked by the transitions from a classless society to one in which classes are distinguished; from chiefdom to state; from primitive society to slave society. As defined by Engels, "the state is the crystallisation of a civilised society." The word 'culture' is defined in the study of sociology or anthropology as including material, moral, spiritual and religious traditions of people.[9] Culture in archaeology refers to the cultural remains in a certain area at a certain time which share common characteristics of human behaviour, such as their artefacts. It reflects the distinctions and relationships between different groups or types of human activities and represents in general the historical development of human society. By clarifying these two concepts, we have gained some agreement on the object and scale of our research.[10]

• It is important to define the elements in the origins of Chinese civilisation. The primary question for the study of the origins of Chinese civilisation is to ask with what qualities and elements China eventually entered the ranks of civilised societies. Gordon Childe has summarised the elements for the birth of a civilised society as city, writing, metal technology, irrigation, etc.[11] In the Chinese context, Xia Nai identified the invention and development of the writing system, bronze-casting, the city and state.[12] Other scholars argue that elements such as the invention of writing, bronze-casting technology and cities are naturally important but that account must be taken of the stratification of social classes as reflected in the archaeology of the middle and later neolithic periods, and particularly in the ritual jades which reflected social ranks and social values, and in the palace and temple sites invested with political and religious significance. All of these factors, they say, should be taken into consideration in the formation of a civilised society, because the cultural contents differ according to circumstances, and the elements to identify each cultural type would also be different. In general, the elements of a civilisation must reflect the changes in the essential nature of a society.

• We also have to clarify the differences between two separate questions: one is the birth of a civilised society, and the other is the elements constituting a civilisation. The origins of Chinese civilisation and the birth of a civilised society occurred during the period in which the nature of Chinese society went through a great transformation, a process leading from changes in number of elements, to arrive eventually at a new society. The birth of a civilised society represents

[6] Su Bingqi 1986: 'Liao Xi gu wenhua gucheng guguo,' *Wenwu* 1986(8), 41-44.

[7] *Zhongguo kaoguxue nianjian* 1990. Beijing, Wenwu chubanshe, 1991, 8.

[8] *Kaogu* 1989: 'Zhongguo wenming qiyuan zuotan jiyao: September 9, 1989,' *Kaogu* 1989 (12); *Kaogu* 1992: 'Zhongguo wenming qiyuan zuotan jiyao: November 27-30,' *Kaogu* 1992(6).

[9] Tong Enzheng 1989: 'Youguan wenming qiyuan de jige wenti,' *Kaogu* 1989(1): 51-59.

[10] Zhang Zhongpei 1994: 'Yanjiu kaoguxue wenhua xuyao tansuo de jige wenti,' in his *Zhongguo kaoguxue lilun shijian fangfa*, Zhengzhou: Zhengzhou guji chubanshe, 97-110.

[11] Childe, Gordon 1950: 'The Urban Revolution,' *Town Planning Review* 21: 3-17.

[12] Xia Nai 1985: *op cit*.

a big leap forward in terms of the development of the society. Divisions between agriculture and craftsmen, changes of the production force and the relationship of productions, the emergence of surplus and private property, the birth of classes and the state: these were lengthy processes. Accordingly, individual elements of civilisation may have emerged earlier, but their common development led to the transformation of society and the birth of a civilised society. This was something that happened much later. There is a clear distinction between these two concepts.

• We must emphasise that research on the origins of civilisation and its development should be based on the theory of regional divisions and types of prehistoric cultures. Scholars have also presented arguments concerning the Longshan, Liangzhu, Hongshan, Erlitou, Taosi and Xindian cultures.

Among those who have discussed the origins of Chinese civilisation, Shi Xingbang, Zhang Zhongpei, Yan Wenming, Zou Heng, Gao Wei, Shao Wangping, K C Chang are the most representative. In the following, I will comment on their respective views. Shi Xingbang discussed the historical progress of the origins of Chinese civilisation as early as 1983; he argues that it was during the late Yangshao culture, between Majiayao culture and the Dawenkou culture that the system of private ownership emerged; bronze technology and male domination appeared. In architecture this period saw a much more complex structure and layout with many rooms and a differentiation of main room and side rooms. Wild and domesticated animals were used in burials. Men and women were buried in areas designated for the purpose, reflecting the decline of matriarchal society. A new society with patriarchal elements developed, and there were changes in the positions of male and female, both socially and, later, economically. During the period from the late Dawenkou culture and the Banshan-Machang culture, there was an increase of elements representing male power and private ownership. Changes in technology and production led to further changes in means of production and material life. There was a gap between rich and poor. Males and females were buried together, with wives, concubines and slaves indicating the existence of the patriarchal society and the use of slaves. The clan or chiefdom society disintegrated and was replaced with divisions and classes. The emergence of states and the formation of a class structure finally took place in the Longshan and Qijia cultures period. Technology and agriculture were further developed, while the accumulation of private property caused a number of social changes. Division between agriculture and craftsmanship speeded up the process of exchange and widened the gap between rich and poor. The emergence of cities and the use of oracle bones indicated the existence of an élite class; ideographic writing was invented; heads of clans became heads of a patriarchal society. Power was inherited in the male line. A primitive form of the state had been born.[13]

In 1994, Shi further pursued his argument on the characteristics of the origins of Chinese civilisation:

• The development of Chinese culture continued to be based on an agricultural economy, unlike the commercial trade developed in the West. The cultural development of this society was inward and relatively stable: regional cultural units were integrated into a common body.

• The blood ties within Chinese clan society remained very strong. In the West, territorial affinity replaced traditional social relationships based on the blood-ties of the clan: in China, even with the appearance of a civilised society, this system of blood ties did not disappear, but developed into a social system (*zongfa*) based on ancestral worship, adopting a restricted social hierarchy. This is one of the main traits of ancient Chinese society.

• During the formation of Chinese civilisation, the ideology of the superstructure played an important role. It was under the guidance of ideology, together with a combined development of technology and social organisation, that Chinese civilisation grew. Early religious leaders, together with heads of

[13] Shi Xingbang 1983: 'Cong kaoguxue wenhua tantao woguo siyouzhi he guojia de qiyuan wenti,' *Shiqian yanjiu* 1983(1): 27-45.

[14] Shi Xingbang 1997: 'Zhongguo wenhua yu wenming fazhan he xingcheng de kaoguxue tantao,' Tsang Cheng-hwa ed. *Zhongguo kaoguxue yu lishixue zhi zhenghe yanjiu*, Taipei: Zhongyang yanjiuyuan, 85-130.

[15] Zhang Zhongpei *forthcoming*: 'Yangshao shidai - shiqian shehui de fanrong yu zhuanbian,' K C Chang and Xu Pingfang eds. *Zhongguo wenming de xingcheng*, New Haven/Beijing: Yale University Press and China New World Press.

[16] Yan Wenming 1992 'Luelun Zhongguo wenming de qiyuan,' *Wenwu* 1992(1): 40-49.

[17] Yan Wenming 1997: 'Longshan shidai chengshi de cubu yanjiu,' Tsang Cheng-hwa, ed. *Zhongguo kaoguxue yu lishixue zhi zhenghe yanjiu*, Taipei: 235-256.

[18] Zou Heng 1987: 'Zhongguo wenming de dansheng,' *Wenwu* 1987(12): 69-74.

chiefdoms, became the joint holders of political, religious and spiritual power in society. This is another characteristic of Chinese civilisation.

• The diversity of regional divisions and types in prehistoric times led to the later existence of many different cities and regional states. There were many centres in the development of Chinese civilisation, but in this process the mainstream is the central plains (the Yangshao and Longshan cultures). They formed the earliest civilised states.[14]

Differing from Shi, Zhang Zhongpei argued that the transformation of matriarchal to patriarchal society took place as early as in the Yangshao culture, which can be regarded as on the threshold of a civilised society. This point of view is presented in a forthcoming book entitled *The Formation of Chinese civilisation*.[15]

Yan Wenming, in his article 'A brief discussion on the origins of Chinese civilisation,'[16] presented his view that "during the Longshan period, almost every culture had already entered the door of civilisation, some of them having already developed into early civilised societies. In this respect, Chinese civilisation is not a single unit, but has a multiple origin. However, these cultures were not isolated from each other, but were mutually influenced and stimulated. They formed a cultural zone. Accordingly, the origin of Chinese civilisation should be treated as a singular process, which eventually developed into the Xia, Shang and Zhou civilisations." He also argues that the transitional period from a prehistorical to a civilised society probably happened in China during the period in which both stone and metal were being used, and which underwent two important phases. The first phase roughly corresponds to the later Yangshao culture, 3500-2600 BC. During this period, the gap between rich and poor widened, and there was an early division into classes. Some centres were superior to other settlements; stone axes buried in tombs indicate that warfare was prominent in this time. The second phase is about 2600-2000 BC: cities and fortifications appeared, some of which might have been early capitals. Some mound burials may be associated with the nobility. Other types of craftsmanship and material culture also developed. Some form of early state organisation seems to have appeared to cope with the problems of conflict between classes. This situation coincides with the accounts in the historical tradition. Yan Wenming also discussed the question of the origin of Chinese civilisation in connection with city sites of the Longshan period.[17]

From a very different angle, Zou Heng argues that the origin of Chinese civilisation is the Erlitou culture. He points out that: "the birth of civilisation and the emergence of states can be regarded as occurring simultaneously. So the formation of states is an indication of the beginning of the civilised age. The Erlitou culture, particularly that of western Shanxi, was derived from a local tradition. We have seen a number of elements of the Erlitou culture latent in the Longshan culture. Another significant fact is the transition that took place from the Longshan culture to the Erlitou culture in regard to palace architecture, namely the appearance of an early capital, with bronzes used for casting ritual vessels and weapons, and the invention of writing. All of those are elements that were shared by the Shang and Zhou civilisations, but which had not appeared during the Longshan period. This indicates that the Erlitou culture is the threshold of Chinese civilisation, from which the Shang and Zhou civilisations developed directly. We are therefore able to identify the origin of Chinese civilisation from archaeological evidence, and this Erlitou culture is the Xia civilisation. Starting from this base, the so-called Three Dynasties began a new phase of civilisation."[18]

Gao Wei, investigating the question of the ritual system of the Longshan culture period, found that along the middle and lower reaches of the Yellow and Yangzi rivers, in the later Dawenkou culture, the Shandong Longshan culture, the Longshan culture in the Central Plains, the Xiejiagang culture, the Liangzhu culture, and the somewhat earlier Hongshan culture in the Yanshan region of western Liaoning, there have in every case been unearthed lacquers, jades and pottery made in unusual shapes. Judging from their form and decoration, these objects were quite distinct from those intended for daily use, and were probably ritual objects similar in intention to the bronze vessels of the Shang. They were owned by a minority in society, indicating privilege and carrying a specific meaning; in other words, they are *liqi*, ceremonial objects. This social phenomenon was quite common, and follows a certain pattern. The combinations of *liqi* in the Longshan culture period varied according to regions and cultures. The ritual and ceremonial systems represented by the *liqi* are, together with other marks of civilisation such as cities, writing, metalwork and monumental buildings, the most important indication that Chinese civilisation had begun.[19]

Shao Wangping agrees that the formation of early Chinese civilisation took place during the Longshan culture period, c3000 BC, along the Yellow River and the middle and lower reaches of the Yangzi. This Longshan cultural sphere is the basis of early Chinese civilisation. She divides the Longshan culture into four subdivisions: the middle reaches of the Yellow River, the east coast region, the Jianghan region (between the Yangzi and the Han Rivers), and the Taihu region (around Lake Taihu). The transition from a primitive culture to the civilised culture of the Longshan culture period first took place separately within these four areas, and the interaction between them led to the simultaneous emergence of early Chinese civilisation. Such interaction also led to the appearance of a "central kingdom". During this formative period, there were some changes in settlement patterns. In the early Longshan culture period, the *yi* (urban settlement) appeared, corresponding to a simple social stratification.

By the later Longshan period, accompanying the multilayered social structure, there appeared *cheng*, cities, walled cities or terraced cities, which became centres of political power. Apart from *yi* and *cheng* there were *du* capitals. The three types of settlement, *du*, *yi*, and *cheng*, formed the early city states which multiplied within the Longshan cultural sphere. One of the significant foundations of the new social order of the early states of the Longshan period was the ritual system. It was also one of the most important characteristics of early civilisation in the Yellow River region. In the course of the progress of early civilisation, religion filled the role of serving the needs of political authority, and became another important support for the new social order. In this new social structure of the Longshan period, the clan system was not completely abandoned, and blood ties were still effective, later being transformed into the *zongfa*, a social system based on ancestral worship.

In the course of the formation of the ritual system during the Longshan period, the best craftsmanship was reserved for the production of *liqi*, ceremonial objects which, being designated by the rulers as marks of social status, thus themselves became symbols of political power. The production of *liqi* became a prerogative of the ruling house, and they were not a trading commodity. In other words, they could not promote the economic development of society. Bronzes of the Longshan culture period had not yet acquired the ritual function of later *liqi*, therefore they were not a necessary element of early Chinese civilisation. If we consider writing as a means of social communication, we can treat some symbols found in the Longshan culture as precursors of a writing system: for example inscriptions found on pottery from the Dinggong site and from the Liangzhu culture appear as signs with regulated form to express a certain meaning, so that they can be considered to be the ancestors of Chinese characters.[20]

K C Chang's theory is most systematic. He has proposed that the key stage for the appearance of Chinese civilisation and states was the transitional period between the late Longshan culture and the beginning of the Bronze age with the Three Dynasties.[21] In this period, he argues, "all regional cultures in time became more extensively distributed and interaction between them was intensified, resulting, during the fourth millennium BC, in the sphere of interaction that set the geographical stage for the first historical Chinese civilisations."[22] He has further argued that "by the beginning of the Longshan period, around 3000 BC, there were ten thousand small villages and settlements

[19] Gao Wei 1989: 'Longshan shidai de lizhi,' *Qinzhu Su Bingqi kaogu wushiwu nian lunwen ji*, Beijing, Wenwu chubanshe, 235-44.

[20] Shao Wangping *forthcoming*: 'Wenming de xingcheng - Longshan shidai yu Longshan jiaofu zuoyong quan,' K C Chang and Xu Pingfang, eds. *Zhongguo wenming de xingcheng*.

[21] For the detailed discussion of his ideas, see Chang, K C 1986: *The Archaeology of Ancient China* (4th edition), New Haven: Yale University Press, chapters 5, 6.

[22] Chang, K C 1989: 'Zhongguo xiangfu zuoyong quan yu wenming de xingcheng,' in *Qinzhu Su Bingqi kaogu wushiwu nian lunwen ji*. Beijing, Wenwu chubanshe; see also Chang, K C 1986: *The Archaeology of Ancient China* (4th edition), 234.

along the Yangzi River and the east coast. Several cities and settlements would make up a 'state'. Within and outside such a state, individuals would belong to kinship groups in the form of *zongfa*. The social structure of these groups is stratified. On the upper level the ruling class accumulated great wealth by political means, firstly through warfare, conquering neighbouring cities and taking over their wealth and, secondly, by increasing the labour force, either through increased productivity or by adding to its numbers. No matter what, the ruler had constantly to increase his political power. One important way to increase such political power was to monopolise religion and religious practices."[23]

[23] Chang, K C *forthcoming*: 'Wang de xingqi yu chengbang de xingcheng,' K C Chang and Xu Pingfang, eds. *Zhongguo wenming de xingcheng*.

Chang made an interesting observation on the "*wu*-shamanistic" elements in Chinese religion: "One of the significant characteristics of Chinese civilisation has been the communication between Heaven, Earth and Man through shamanistic practices. The monopoly of such techniques is a major phenomenon in early Chinese society. Such a monopoly, in a class society, is achieved through politics, or the relationships between people. The major changes in the course of transformation from the primitive stage into a civilised society are changes of the relationship between people and between Man and Nature. The latter is a technological change, and is secondary in character. In this transition from prehistory to civilisation, Chinese society exhibits important and manifold elements of continuity."[24]

[24] Chang, K C 1986: *Kaogu xue zhuanti liu jiang*, Beijing, Wenwu chubanshe, 1-24.

Chang also compared the formation of Chinese civilisation with the origins of western civilisation from the angle of cultural history, pointing out that "in western social sciences, there is a general recognition that the emergence of civilisation has been marked by writing, cities, industrial metalwork, religious buildings, and art. The emergence of civilisation is accompanied by the appearance of a stratified society; this amounts to a revolutionary transformation of society. The difference between barbarism and civilisation lies in the fact that civilised man distances himself from the natural or primitive environment. An important implication of this is that civilisation is formed in a new technological and economic environment...however, the basic characteristics of early Chinese society differ from this general pattern of the origins of civilisation as proposed by western social scientists."[25]

[25] Chang, *ibid.*

K C Chang thinks that Chinese civilisation is similar to the Maya civilisation in Meso-America, which belongs to a type that is different from that represented by the Sumerian civilisation of the Near East. He goes on to argue that "by comparing Chinese civilisation with the Maya and Sumerian civilisations, we consider that on a world scale the Chinese example represents the main form of transformation into a state of civilisation, while the western example is an ancillary form. In consequence the general pattern deduced from western experience of the social sciences cannot be universally applied. I would call the Chinese example one of 'continuity' and the western example 'revolutionary.'

"From the standpoint of world prehistory, we can propose two main types of transformation: one I shall call the non-western type, of which China is the principal example; the second is the western type. One of the important characteristics of the first type is a continuous development from primitive society to a civilised society, during which many social and cultural elements continued, mainly concerning the relationship between Man and Nature, and between the individual and society. In contrast, the western style is revolutionary, and the relationship between man and the natural environment consists in a breakthrough of the limitations of the ecological system through technology, trade, and other new elements."[26] Chang emphasised the importance of the Chinese experience in studying world ancient history. He claims that, "based on Chinese ancient history, we can perceive a new pattern in the development of human history, which probably represents a worldwide process of continuous transformation, seen in most regions. Therefore, to establish a general theory, we cannot rely solely on western experience, but need to consider the Chinese historical experience as well."[27]

[26] Chang, K C 1993: *Meishu, shenhua yu jisi*, Taipei: Daoxiang chubanshe, 147-57.

[27] Chang, K C 1986: *Kaogu xue zhuanti liu jiang*, 24.

Conclusion

At present, archaeological research and discussions on the origins of Chinese civilisation have reached some commonly accepted ground. The majority of scholars agree that the birth of Chinese civilised society was during the late Longshan culture period and that the stage of formal civilisation was reached in the Erlitou culture. Some elements of this civilisation were conceived in the middle phase of the Yangshao culture. The process took in all about two millennia (c3500-1500 BC). There are several topics that have attracted much attention, such as the formation of early cities, the appearance and formation of the *liqi* and the ritual system, the relationship between political power and early religion, and between remnants of clan kinship and the *zongfa* system, while the question of the model of Chinese civilisation and its position in world history is also worthy of further exploration.

In the last decade, the exploration of Chinese civilisation has greatly promoted the archaeological discipline in China, in particular that of prehistoric archaeology. One of the basic tasks for archaeology is to use archaeological results to interpret history. However archaeology and history are two different disciplines, differing in terms of their subject matter and methodology. For archaeologists to interpret history, we need a combination of different disciplines and methods, which is to some degree extremely positive for the development of our discipline. We may say that the topic of studying the origins of Chinese civilisation is, quite apart from its own academic significance, very important for the future development of archaeology in China.

Finally, in regard to the aims of current research, I would like to offer some thoughts on several areas that need our special attention:

• To select several different types of early city sites from the Longshan period, planning and conducting a comprehensive excavation of each to obtain detailed archaeological data. This would be of the utmost significance for the further research into the characteristics of early cities.

• To investigate further and excavate sites relating to settlements, cities and capitals, comparing their different types and relationships. This would furnish extremely important material for our understanding of the formation of states, regional states, city-states and the actual layout of cities in the early history of Chinese civilisation.

• In order to study the whole process of a cultural type in the evolution of civilisation and society, we must see that different cultural types have had their own specific path to enter civilised society. Only after the study of the paths followed by such different cultural types will we be able to understand the general pattern of the emergence of Chinese civilisation.

• In order to attain these research goals and to enhance their quality, it is necessary for Chinese prehistoric archaeology to pay attention to all manner of evidence in field archaeology, collecting information that would otherwise disappear immediately after excavation and removal from the site. To achieve this we should use all the most modern available scientific means.

Looking back, and forward to the future, we can envisage that our task is difficult, and the road long, but that the results will be glorious!

MOU YONGKANG AND WU RUZUO
A Discussion on the 'Jade Age'

The view proposed by us that there was a Jade Age in the prehistory of China, characterised by jade ritual objects, has caused considerable interest as well as controversy among archaeological circles. Since we first raised the question in 1990,[1] several scholars have argued against our theory. They insist that jade was not used for production tools, and that there was no consistency in its geographical distribution; therefore we should not propose that jade should be considered like stone, bronze or iron as a principal criterion of prehistoric development.[2] In this article, we would like to refine the concept of the Jade Age, and examine its significance for the study of Chinese archaeology.

The Definition of the 'Jade Age'

We should first look at the concepts of 'labour force', 'production tools' and 'production technology'. These are interrelated but not synonymous concepts. Production tools and technology can only result in production in combination with the labour force. The appearance of agriculture and pastoralism represent different production modes from earlier hunting and gathering: agriculture is a crucial step forward in terms of social production, marking what is known to historians as the agricultural revolution or the neolithic revolution. The Stone Age is divided into palaeolithic and neolithic according to the differing technology of the manufacture of stone tools. The Bronze Age represents another revolution in social production, during which alloys of copper and tin were used to make better production tools. By the Iron Age iron came to be used as the principal material for making tools. On each occasion, the use of tools made with the new materials would increase social production. However, production tools on their own would not lead to revolutions in technology, without the participation of the labour force. The combination of these elements forms a 'production mode', which is what we should concentrate on when discussing the concept of the Jade Age in the Chinese context.

The appearance of jade implements represents a breakthrough in the history of human technology. Jade is a hard material: although the working of jade is a part of lithic technology, it is a stage which could only take place following the development of advanced methods. In order to shape jade, sand must be used as an abrasive material, with cords to make cuts, and a final polish. This process involves a much more complex technology than the making of ordinary stone tools. The majority of jade objects that have been found are not

[1] Our article (Mou Yongkang, Wu Ruzuo 1997: 'Shi lun yuqi shidai-Zhongguo wenming shidai chansheng de yige zhongyao biaozhi,' Su Bingqi, ed. *Kaoguxue wenhua lunji* 4: 164-87, Beijing: Wenwu chubanshe) was written in the spring of 1990. On July 5, 1990, *Guangming ribao* published a short abstract of our arguments. We published an outline version, 'Shi tan yuqi shidai-Zhonghua wenming qiyuan de tansuo,' in *Zhongguo Wenwubao*, November 1, 1990.

[2] For instance, in February 1994, at the international conference held in the Chinese University of Hong Kong, Professor An Zhimin questioned the theoretical basis of a Jade Age. The topic has also been discussed by Gu Fei 1993: 'Ping Zhongguo yuqi shidai,' *Kaogu* 1993(6) and by Xie Zhongli 1994: 'Yuqi shidai — yige xin kainian de fenxi,' *Kaogu* 1994(9): 832-836.

production tools, but a few pieces are indeed associated with weaving technology. The latter include jade spindle whorls and loom parts, found in tombs M23 at Fanshan and M11 at Yaoshan: both are Liangzhu culture sites (c3100-2200 BC). We shall discuss the social functions and meaning of these objects elsewhere, and concentrate first on the technology of jade-working: whether it is derived from stone technology or whether it has its own origin.

The earliest jades have been found at the Fuxin Chahai and Xinlongwa sites in northeast China, dating to c5500 BC, when cord-cutting methods were employed. Similar evidence has also come to light on the jade earrings of the Majiabang culture in the south. This technology was not used for the making of stone tools. Comparing the methods for making jade and stone, we find that jade technology is much more difficult and complex and much more labour-intensive. Another significant element is that jade craftsmen were much more concerned with economy in the use of the raw material, reflecting the precious nature of jade. On occasions, however, similar methods were used for making jade and stone tools, for instance several jade axes and stone implements found in the lower Guojiacun, Lishun, Liaoning province, on which there remained the evidence of chipping. In the Liangzhu and Longshan cultural period, cord-cutting techniques were also applied to the making of stone tools, which were also given a final high polish. These techniques were usually applied to both jade and stone. Thus the two materials to some degree shared the same technology.

More significantly, in northwest China, where jade carving technology was not very advanced, some jade production tools have been found. At the Longgangsi site in the southern part of Shaanxi, 19 tombs of the Banpo type of the Yangshao culture, circa 4500 BC, proved to contain 24 jade axes, spades, chisels and arrowheads.[3] Sixteen of the tombs had male occupants. According to the archaeological report, these jade objects retained evidence of chipping and cutting; at the same time, these jade tools had not been used. M345, much larger than any of the other single-occupant tombs, had five or six times the quantity of burial objects compared to the other tombs. Among the objects buried in it, two large stone spades bore no traces of having been used. Probably they symbolised the power or social status of the occupant.

In Minghe, Qinghai province, where more than 200 tombs belonging to the Banshan and Machang types have been excavated, some large-size stone axes have been found which also show no traces of having been used. One axe made of quartz has traces of sawing, cutting and polishing. These are all techniques commonly seen in jade carving. Five arm bangles of marble from the same group of tombs had also been polished and drilled. The archaeologists who excavated the site believe that these stone axes were some sort of ritual implements. The arm ornaments also indicated the status of the tomb occupants: "they might have been shamans, or have combined the roles of shaman and community leaders."[4] These characteristics and the social function of these objects differentiate them from ordinary stone tools. The technology for jade carving therefore developed independently from stone technology. In later times the two different traditions may have borrowed from each other.[5] As Ren Shinan has pointed out, in the jade-using areas, jade production became a specialised profession, and its advanced craftsmanship ensured that carved jade became the representative of the highest material culture of its time.[6]

The use of jade in early China is closely associated with ritual practices, as well as being part of a ritual system. Jades have also been called sacred objects. Ritual itself appeared much earlier than ritual systems in their social sense; the former reflects the relationship between man and god, while the latter concern human relationships in society. Before jade was used in ritual, painted pottery was probably the most common material used for funerary vessels and objects; however, it did not reflect the social hierarchical system. Musical instruments such as drums may have been used in the worship of gods, and so may be called ritual objects, but they are not necessarily indicative of the existence of a ritual system. The Shang and Zhou bronze ritual vessels were transformed from purely

[3] Shaanxi 1990 (Shaanxi sheng kaogu yanjiusuo): *Longgangsi*, Beijing: Wenwu chubanshe, 96-98, 182.

[4] Qinghai 1990 (Qinghai sheng wenwu kaogu yanjiu suo): *Minhe Yangshan*, Beijing: Wenwu chubanshe, 59, 64, 110, 143.

[5] Professor Ke Jun, in his paper presented at the conference on the Dingcun and Jin cultures at Taiyuan, Shanxi, in September 1994, argued that the technology of gem production was an important stage in the development of technology before the advent of metallurgy.

[6] Ren Shinan 1993: 'Zhongguo shiqian yuqi leixing chuxi,' Zhongguo shehui kexueyuan kaogu yanjiusuo ed. *Zhongguo kaoguxue luncong*: Beijing: Kexue chubanshe, 106-130.

ritual objects into objects that denote social status. However, the appearance of jade, in particular the appearance of jade axes, in relation to other jade objects, marked the beginning of such a transformation.

The characteristics of jade *yue* axes include not only their non-utilitarian character and highly-polished physical appearance, but more importantly, their symbolism. The elaborate decoration on stone axes used for burial was first seen in the Xiejiagang and the Daxi cultures. In the Liangzhu culture, the jade *yue* axe acquired additional accessories. The handle was also inlaid with pieces of jade (such as the *lun* and *dun*, adorning the top and bottom of the wooden handle). The *lun* is usually shaped in the form of a folded cap, which is an important part of the human-beast image found on Liangzhu jades, which is incised on the *lun* and *dun* from tomb M7 at Yaoshan, while the blade of the jade *yue* from tomb M12 at Fanshan bears the same image, together with flying birds. This type of shafted *yue* axe is different from those used as tools or weapons: it has become a purely ritual object, symbolic of power. Such *yue* axes are usually highly polished and were bound with cords to the shaft.

In addition to the imposing jade *yue* axe, other jade ritual objects, such as *ge, zhang,* and *gui*, also appeared, probably in association with handles and decoration, to mark important changes in the ritual system. *Cong* tube, *huang* circular plaque and three-pronged jades as well as loom parts and spindle-whorls occurred in groups with the same significance. Their positions in the tombs also suggest some essential changes in the ritual system.

'Jade Age' and the Traditional Periodisation

Periodisation is an important method in archaeological research: its aim is to establish a chronology of cultural and social development. It is crucial to determine the boundaries between different phases; however, different re-searchers may apply different criteria, from different angles, which thereby result in differences of periodisation.

Periodisation, to a certain degree, is also classification. Different disciplines have different classifications, and even within the same discipline there may be varied classifications, which often reflect the development and progress of the subject. The Three Age periodisation of Stone, Bronze and Iron originally put forward in 1816-19 by the Danish scholar C J Thomsen (1788-1865) is the theory currently still dominant. However, many scholars have challenged this theory: Glyn Daniel, in his book *150 Years of Archaeology*, doubted whether the Three Age system would continue to remain useful in the study of European prehistory, and he further remarked on the difficulties encountered in trying to apply the Three Age system outside the framework of European prehistory.[7]

In archaeology, apart from the Three Age system, we also encounter various terms such as palaeolithic, neolithic, microlithic, and chalcolithic, some of which overlap, reflecting the diversity of the development and interpretation of archaeology. This is part of the study of archaeological methodology. Before the advent of metallurgy, jade represented the acme of technological achieve-ment; yet after the advent of metallurgy, jade continued to occupy an important position in the development of material culture, and there were further developments in jade-working techniques.

The core issue in proposing a Jade Age is whether the development of Chinese civilisation followed its own path, with its own characteristics. Huang Shenzhang has pointed out that in order to define Chinese civilisation, we have to look at three aspects: first, the special characteristics unique to the Chinese; second, those shared with other countries, but having special Chinese features; and third, those features which in China were especially important or developed earlier than anywhere else.[8] Zhang Xuqiu also argues that in China, between the neolithic and the Bronze Ages, there was a Jade Age.[9] Although this theory has not been widely accepted, we believe that the appearance of jade in the form of ritual objects marked the dawn of civilisation in China. K C Chang has said that western archaeology talks about the Three Ages system

[7] Daniel, Glyn 1975:*150 Years of Archaeology*, 2nd edition, London: Duckworth, 249.

[8] Huang Shenzhang 1992, ed: *Yazhou wenming*, volume II, preface. Hefei: Anhui jiaoyu chubanshe.

[9] Zhang Xuqiu 1992: *Changjiang zhongyou xinshiqi shidai wenhua gailun*, Wuhan: Hubei kexuejishu chubanshe, 306.

of Stone, Bronze and Iron, but is not concerned with the Jade Age, because in the West, jade is less important, while in China, the Jade Age represents the transition from the Stone Age to the Bronze Age, from primitive society to state and city. This transition has its own characteristics in the development of Chinese social history.[10] The views of all these scholars have reflected a new trend in the study of Chinese archaeology.

To conclude, recent archaeology has provided a basis for the theory of the Jade Age. The discoveries of the Hongshan and Liangzhu jades have been most significant. We still have some unanswered questions concerning the use of jade in the early period: for example, in the northwest, new materials have been emerging and will need further study. However, to answer these questions, we have first to overcome our traditional prejudices and preconceptions. This short paper has only provided some preliminary ideas of the Jade Age; we need further fieldwork and more careful observation of the evidence, as well as robust scholarly discussion of the issues.

[10] Chang, K C 1986: "Tan 'cong' jiqi zai Zhongguo gushishang de yiyi," Wenwu chubanshe biejibu ed. *Wenwu yu kaogu lunji,* Beijing: Wenwu chubanshe, 252-260.

GUO DASHUN

An Archaeological Investigation of the Wudi

*I*n Sima Qian's *Shiji* (Records of the Historian) the first chapter (*Wudi benji,* Biographies of the Five Lords) consists of the biographies of Wudi, the Five Emperors or Five Lords.[1] It is customary to talk about the Wudi when discussing the 5,000 years of Chinese civilisation. Although Huangdi or the Yellow Emperor has always been regarded as the ancestor of the Chinese, the period of the Wudi is treated as legendary by modern historiography, because there is no material evidence to prove their existence. Thus, the beginning of Chinese civilisation can only be traced back 4,000 years to the Xia dynasty (traditional date 2205-1766 BC). Compared to the other centres of ancient civilisations, China is almost 1,000 years later than the Indus civilisation, and 1,500 years later than the civilisations of Mesopotamia and Egypt.

Searching for traces of the Wudi now becomes an important task for Chinese archaeologists, and an important issue also for all those of Chinese descent. Since the 1980s, under the guidance of a scientific methodology, Chinese archaeology has made enormous progress. In the study of many important archaeological discoveries such as the Hongshan culture (c3500 BC), the Liangzhu culture (c3100-2200 BC) and the Taosi culture (c2500-1900 BC), there is a trend to combine archaeological evidence with historical records and legends. Scholars have suggested that the Taosi culture relates to the Taotang clan in legend,[2] and that the Liangzhu culture is proto-Xia.[3] The discussions on the Hongshan culture are even more heated. Was the dragon-shaped jade related to Chiyou, a mythic figure who was enemy of Huangdi? Was the goddess-worship related to Nüwa, the creator of mankind? Could advanced religion and ritual be associated with Zhuanxu, one of the Five Lords and the reformer of early religion? Several scholars have even associated the Hongshan culture with Yandi (the Flaming Lord) and with Huangdi.[4] In the introduction to the second volume of the newly published multi-volume *Zhongguo tongshi* (A General History of China), Su Bingqi has argued that Chinese archaeology should combine with historical research.[5] He has also suggested that the period of the Wudi should be considered in archaeological terms.

Can we identify the period of the Wudi with any archaeological evidence? Numerous archaeological discoveries in different regions show that from the middle and later Yangshao period (c4000-3000 BC), many early cultures began a transformation in terms of their cultural and social development and of the relationships between them. Within the Yangshao tradition, there are the

[1] *Shiji* (by Sima Qian, b 145 BC) Beijing: Zhonghua shuju, 1969, juan 1.

[2] Tian Cangwu 1986: 'Xian Xia wenhua tansuo,' *Wenwu yu kaogu lunji*, Beijing: Wenwu chubanshe, 93-109; Yu Weichao 1991: 'Kaogusuo sishinian chengguo zhan bitan,' *Kaogu* 1991(1): 75-76.

[3] Chen Shenyong 1995: 'Xia wenhua dongnan shuo,' *Xungeng*, 1995(1): 10-13.

[4] Gan Zhigeng and Sun Shoudao 1992: 'Guanyu Niuheliang zhi xing de tongxin,' *Beifang wenwu* 1992(3); Fu Langyun 1993: 'Niuheliang, Nüshenmiao, zushu kao,' *Beifang wenwu* 1993(1); Qi Yuchen 1993: 'Zhonghua diyi cun lanshen,' *Beifang wenwu* 1993(1); Lu Sixian 1993: 'Hongshan luoti nüshen wei Nüwa kao,' *Beifang wenwu* 1993(3).

[5] Su Bingqi 1994, ed, *Zhongguo tongshi*, vol 2. Shanghai: Renmin chubanshe.

Banpo type and the Miaodigou type; they may have their own origins, and the latter spread across a much broader area: many neighbouring cultures under Yangshao influence in fact related directly to the Miaodigou type. At the same time, the typical painted pottery amphorae of the Yangshao culture diminished in importance.

During that period, we have found an early 'palace', as large as 400 square metres, divided into front hall, rear hall and left and right wings, at the Qin'an Dadiwan site in Gansu province. We have also found a tomb at the Hua xian Qianhucun site, Henan province, with a polished black owl-shaped wine vessel, which obviously belonged to a person of a special status. Recently, in the western part of Henan, a stamped-earth city wall and platform have been found, also belonging to the late Yangshao period.[6]

[6] *Guangming ribao*, May 14, 1995.

Outside the Yangshao cultural zone, we can see other cases which are indicative of similar transformations. For example, in the second phase of the Shandong Dawenkou culture (c3500-2500 BC), there are marked differences in the burial goods of different tombs. Some important ritual objects arranged in groups, including carved ivory tubes and ornaments, and stone *yue* axes, indicate the social status of the tomb occupant. Beyond the Great Wall, in the western part of Liaoning, large-scale ritual centres appeared, with huge altars, stone cist tombs with many ritual jades, and a temple for goddess-worship. During this period, there was an intensified interaction and integration of different cultures, the most important being the contacts between Yangshao and Hongshan, Yangshao and Dawenkou. These cultures in different parts of China began to meet and to interact.

The beginning of the Wudi period can thus be identified with the late Yangshao period, about 3000 BC. The next question is, when did it end? In the historical tradition, the period of the Wudi was succeeded by the Xia dynasty. There has been a controversy about the Xia in Chinese historiography as well as in archaeology. Some recent progress has been made, particularly the discovery and investigation of many proto-Shang cultures. At the international conference on Shang culture, held at Yanshi, Henan province in May 1995, it was debated whether the Erlitou culture belonged to a different cultural system, although it shared some characteristics with the late Longshan culture which preceded it and with the early Shang culture which followed it, on account of the individuality reflected in its artefacts. So it can be argued quite convincingly that the Erlitou culture belonged to the Xia. The end of Longshan period, preceding the Erlitou culture, should also represent the end of the Wudi period. Thus we are able to define the Wudi period in terms of archaeology, as corresponding to the period from Late Yangshao to the end of the Longshan period, between 3000-2000 BC, lasting about 1,000 years.

We can further divide the Wudi period into early and later phases; the former is represented by the rule of Huangdi, who is credited with many inventions, such as agriculture and transport. The war between Huangdi and Yandi and Chiyou is very famous, ending with the unification of many tribes. During this early period, another important figure is Zhuanxu, who was a religious leader who ordered his minister Chongli to rearrange the cosmic order. His achievement in religious reform made him as important as Huangdi. In early societies, religion occupies an important position in the transformation of society; religious figures who had the ability to communicate with spirits were highly respected and powerful.

The later phase of the Wudi period is represented by Yao and Shun. According to the historic tradition, at the beginning of Yao's reign, the flood which occurred in the Yellow River region reached to the sky. At Handan, Luoyang, and Wugong, archaeologists have actually found traces of floods, dating back to 2000 -2500 BC, which may not be just a coincidence.[7] Controlling the floods became the major task of the government, reinforcing the administrative structures of the state. According to the *Yaodian*, the four Yue and twelve Mu consisted of an aristocratic committee; there was a proper governmental organisation including Si Kong, Si Tu, Hou Ji, Shi, Gu and the

[7] Su Bingqi, 1994: Preface, *Zhongguo kaogu wenwu zhi mei*, 10 vols, Beijing/Taipei: Wenwu chubanshe and Guangfu shuju, 17-20.

departments for military operation, law and punishment, music and listening to grievances. In other words, the state machine was very developed.

In archaeology, the division between these two phases is clear: the transition took place between the Yangshao and the Longshan culture about 2500 BC. On a large scale, many early cultures underwent changes almost at the same time, and many new cultural elements appeared. For instance, black pottery gradually replaced the painted pottery and geometrical patterns came to dominate pottery decoration; the amphora with pointed base was gradually replaced by the *jia* and *li* with three hollow legs; the appearance and spread of the *li* is an important landmark; many large settlements with stamped earth city walls were constructed; and bronze-casting appeared. The new period, represented by the Longshan culture (2500-1900 BC), arrived. Each distinctive culture of different regions moved towards the formation of a common body. Warfare also played an important part. It is said in the *Shiji* that after the Shen Nong clan declined, different lords began to attack each other. The characteristics of this time might reflect the beginning of a new historical period.

At this time there were two major cultural centres, *a*) the Liangzhu culture in the region of Lake Tai, marked by earth-constructed altars, burials with jades to indicate religious and royal power; and *b*) the Taosi culture in the southern part of Shanxi, whose characteristic features were painted lacquer or pottery dishes, stone *qing* chimes and crocodile-skin drums which were probably used for temple rituals.

If we can accept this archaeological definition and periodisation of the Wudi period, then the next important task is to investigate the relationship between historical figures and their activities with the archaeological divisions. Su Bingqi recently emphasised two important achievements of archaeological fieldwork in the 1980s, which might provide some important clues. The first is the study of cultural remains in Shanxi province, where the cultures of the central plains meet those of the northern regions. The second is the discovery of the altar and the goddess-temple of the Hongshan culture in the western part of Liaoning.[8] Su Bingqi has argued in many of his articles that the ritual complex of the Hongshan culture was sparked by the meeting of two different cultures, represented by the flower (Yangshao) and the dragon (Hongshan) motifs. It had already a social organisation more advanced than the chiefdom, that is to say, it corresponds to the historical transition from chiefdom to state, and was more advanced than anywhere else in China at that time. In the Taosi culture of southern Shanxi, we can again see elements from different cultures: the pottery basin painted with a red dragon came from the Hongshan culture, the flask from the Dawenkou culture, the L-shaped stone implement from the Liangzhu culture, while the *jia* with three hollow legs is a result of the combination of the amphorae of the Yangshao culture and the ovoid vessels of the Hetao region of Mongolia. The typology of the *li* tripod is most complete in the Taosi culture, indicating that the characteristics of this culture were not the result of radiation from the centre but rather were gathered from various sources to be concentrated in the Central Plains. This pattern of development corresponds to the literary record that during the Yao and Shun period all the different states came to pay tribute to the central kingdom. As later commentators have remarked, *Zhongguo* (Central Kingdom) means "the king resides in the centre." The most recent archaeological discoveries and researches have revealed that in the early phase of the Wudi period the centre was in the north, around Mt Yanshan, and represented by the Hongshan culture. The ritual complex found in Niuheliang was its highest cultural point. The key issue for this period is the cultural relationship between the Hongshan and Yangshao cultures.

In the later phase of the Wudi period, the centre moved towards the south, to the southern part of Shanxi, represented by the Taosi culture. The Taosi site is the highest cultural centre of this period, and its relationship with other cultures was that of a gathering point of influences from different sources. The study of the Hongshan culture in the north also proves the reliability of the literary records: it is said that the Huangdi clan was migratory with no permanent

[8] Su Bingqi 1994: 'Liushinian yuanyi meng,' *Huaren - longde chuanren - Zhongguoren - kaogu xungenji*, Shenyang: Liaoning University Press, 1-2.

settlements, similar to the way of life of the northern nomads in more recent history. The war between Huangdi and Chiyou took place in the suburbs of Zhuolu, which lies in the San'gang River region of Zhangjiakou, northern Hebei. It is recorded that King Wu of Zhou enfeoffed the descendants of Huangdi at Ji, which is at the southern foot of Mt Yanshan, near the Great Wall. It is also recorded that the Five Lords were most active in Jizhou, one of the nine prefectures, situated in the western part of Liaoning. The *Yugong* (Tribute of Yu) says that "the soil of Jizhou is white," obviously referring to the white sandy soil of the Yanshan region, not the loess or yellow earth in the central plains. Archaeologists have found many leaf-shaped stone implements in the Hongshan culture and the Zhaobaogou culture (c5200-4200 BC), found in Inner Mongolia. These were obviously used for ploughing the soft sandy soil. An abundance of both literary records and archaeological evidence thus supports the argument that the Yanshan region was the centre in the Wudi period.

To conclude, we will gain new insight if we revise the old framework that China is an unchanging unity, a concept which is rooted so deeply in people's psychology. We should look at the different cultural divisions within "Chinese civilisation" which were just as sophisticated as the mainstream and which were interacting continuously with the central plains. Chinese civilisation is the centre of East Asia and an important part of world history. The study of ancient Chinese culture and history will further our understanding of the history of mankind. The Wudi or Five Lords period is most important for the formation of our national identity and cultural tradition; it is the dawn of Chinese civilisation. This period is most important for the formation of our national cultural tradition; it is the result of the integration and reorganisation of many different cultural elements. We should write this first chapter of the history of Chinese civilisation in great detail, not just a few lines.

Chinese Archaeology in the West

ROBERT L THORP

Studies of Chinese Archaeology/Art History in the West: a Critical Review

S cholars who study the material legacy of ancient China are usually called either archaeologists or art historians. Both professions flourish today in China, North America and Europe, but the number of practitioners in each region differs significantly. The profession of Chinese archaeology is far more populous in China than elsewhere, while on the other hand Chinese art history may actually be more common in North America than in Europe or China. Some practitioners, like myself, see themselves as having one foot in each camp, and have become acutely aware in recent years of the important differences in goals and methods that distinguish each group. Anthropological archaeologists and humanist art historians who study ancient China may share a common research target in the most general terms, but in 1993 they approach their tasks in very different ways. Chinese and non-Chinese archaeologists likewise have important differences in outlook determined by the history, institutions and theories of their respective scholarly traditions. Not least, practitioners of art history in North America and Europe and of its analogue, *meishu kaogu* in China, also deploy different critical vocabularies and methodologies.

This paper discusses the goals and methods of western scholarship on ancient China as it was written by scholars active in the prewar decades and the immediate postwar period (c1900-1960). My comments are an effort to reflect on the nature of early western archaeological and art-historical practice and its consequences for the present-day study of ancient China. These reflections ought to be of some value in facilitating future research efforts, especially those that build on earlier scholarship or which attempt to integrate archaeological and art-historical methods. At the same time, these ruminations are also an implicit critique of many existing protocols of art-historical scholarship, and a call for approaches that might yield new scholarship.

Archaeology or Art History

From the Renaissance period onwards, investigations of the past in Europe privileged the legacy of classical antiquity, the civilisations of ancient Greece and Rome, both their literary traditions and their material relics, most especially

---

This paper was first presented at the opening of the Arthur M Sackler Museum of Art and Archaeology, Peking University, May, 1993.

ancient architecture and sculpture.[1] From the outset, it was assumed that literary, epigraphic and material evidence (sometimes on the same object) could be juxtaposed in a meaningful and complementary fashion so that each would shed light on the other. It was considered possible and highly desirable to recover material objects that had been described by writers in antiquity as well as objects that had been used by actors within the historical dramas of that era. A burgeoning antiquarian love of ancient things led to the widespread looting of ancient sites such as Pompeii and, gradually, to a regimen of field practice for excavating and recording those sites.[2] Systematic collecting and connoisseurship grew from this passion, and with them critical vocabularies for the evaluation of ancient things, especially in qualitative or aesthetic terms. These practices and this vocabulary still underlie or inform many approaches within both Eurocentric classical archaeology and art history. Many comparisons could be made here with the activities of Chinese antiquarians and their specialised writings, especially from the Song period (10th century AD) onwards.[3] Most significant is the belief that history and archaeology were seamlessly connected and the view that the latter was a handmaiden to the former.[4]

A canon of the Fine Arts as Architecture, Painting and Sculpture was defined during the enlightenment period,[5] and interest developed in the study of 'modern,' (that is, contemporary as opposed to antique) arts. Only in the 19th century, however, did these studies take on the character of a recognised scholarly discipline with its own institutional identity, particular goals and specific methods. This new discipline became known in Germanic languages as *Kunstgeschichte* and in English, in a literal translation, as 'art history.' *Kunstgeschichte* addressed topics both ancient and modern. Its methodologies were tailored to the canon of the fine arts. The particular European experience of these arts in the Renaissance and post-Renaissance periods conditioned many of its most basic concepts and goals.[6] Investigations were framed within an historical paradigm in which individual makers (artists) and their products (their oeuvre) were taken as basic units for analysis. Biography was often the explicit armature on which art-historical studies such as catalogues were built. The actors in these biographies were akin to the great men of history-writing;[7] their actions and personalities determined the history of art. The traits of an individual 'artistic personality' could be read from (or more properly into) the physical and stylistic properties of objects. A history of artistic productions was written in which the fundamental concepts of genius and style were dominant. In pre-modern China, the best analogy to some of these practices and concepts can be found in the literature of painting.[8]

Studies of non-canonical objects and of non-European things more generally were often propelled by the idea that racial and cultural identity rather than an individual's traces were inherent in the objects being studied. Often the grand narratives that connected these objects were conceived in terms that today are felt to be transparently Eurocentric, imperialist and racist.[9] In some contexts it was normal to study such topics with little regard to other factors or related subjects. Critical and aesthetic judgements woven into the narratives of art-historical writings carried these texts into a special realm of discourse, one detached from the specifics of actual history and infused instead with assumed universal impulses and abstract patterns. Germanic philosophy offered a conceptual frame and vocabulary by which such matters could be theorised and described.[10] Such writings are comprehensible only within their own frame of reference, and often now seem antiquated. The late 19th and early 20th-century vogue for such discourse has passed, but its legacy is everywhere in conventional art-historical formulations and writings, and is no less felt in writings that attempt to set themselves apart from traditional practice.

In general the most enduring art-historical scholarship has been well aware of wider realms of inquiry. For example, specialised studies of the subject-matter of classical and Christian art became codified as 'iconography' and the pursuit of the same cannot be circumscribed within narrow disciplinary

[1] Haskell, Francis and Nicholas Penny 1981: *Taste and the Antique: The Lure of Classical Sculpture. 1500-1900.* New Haven: Yale University Press.

[2] Daniel, Glyn 1968: *The Origins and Growth of Archaeology.* New York: Crowell.

[3] Rudolph, Richard C 1963: 'Notes on Sung Archaeology.' *Journal of Asian Studies* 22, 169-177; Wu Hung 1989: *Chinese Pictorial Art.* Stanford: Stanford University Press, 38-45.

[4] Snodgrass, Anthony M 1987: *An Archaeology of Greece: The Present State and Future Scope of a Discipline.* Berkeley: University of California Press, 37.

[5] Kristeller, Paul O 1965: 'The Modern System of the Arts'. *Renaissance Thought II: Papers on Humanities and the Arts*, New York: Harper, 163-227.

[6] Gombrich, E H 1966: 'Norm and Form: the Stylistic Categories of Art History and their Origins in Renaissance Ideals.' *Norm and Form*, London: Phaidon, 81-98; and 'The Renaissance Conception of Artistic Progress.' *ibid*, 1-10; Preziosi, Donald 1992: 'The Question of Art History.' *Critical Inquiry* 18: 363-386.

[7] Burke, Peter 1992: *New Perspectives on Historical Writing.* University Park, Philadelphia: Pennsylvania State University Press.

[8] Soper, Alexander C 1976: 'The Relationship of Early Chinese Painting to Its Own Past' in *Chinese Culture*, 21-47 Princeton.

[9] Mitter, Partha 1977: *Much Maligned Monsters: History of European Reactions to Indian Art.* Oxford: Clarendon Press; Kubler, George 1991: *Esthetic Recognition of Ancient Amerindian Art.* New Haven: Yale University Press.

[10] See Podro 1982.

[11] Panofsky, Erwin 1955: 'The History of Art as a Humanistic Discipline', *Meaning in the Visual Arts: Papers in and on Art History,* New York: Doubleday, 1-25.

[12] Antal, F 1949: 'Remarks on the Method of Art History.' *Burlington Magazine* 91: 49-52 and 73-75.

[13] Carpenter, Rhys and James Ackerman 1963: *Art History and Archaeology.* Englewood Cliffs: Prentice Hall.

[14] Ridgway, Brunhilde Sismondo 1986: 'The State of Research on Ancient Art.' *The Art Bulletin* 68.1: 7-23; Snodgrass, Anthony M 1987: *An Archaeology of Greece: The Present State and Future Scope of a Discipline.*

[15] Trigger 1989: *A History of Archaeological Thought.* Cambridge: Cambridge University Press; Willey and Sabloff 1974: *A History of American Archaeology.* San Francisco: Freeman.

boundaries.[11] It has never been possible strictly to delimit the boundaries separating art history and cultural history once subject-matter became the target of investigation. Perhaps the most significant development in eurocentric art history prior to the second world war was the explosion of content-based studies under the general rubric of iconography and iconology. This in turn led to contextualised approaches, a social history of art in which knowledge about society became accessible through the study of art.[12]

In tandem with European political imperialism of the 18th and 19th centuries, specialised archaeologies developed to investigate the ancient cultures of Egypt (Egyptology), the Holy Land (Biblical Archaeology), and Mesopotamia (Assyriology). Like classical archaeology, as created by their European practitioners these outfields assumed an historical paradigm, and they also exploited ancient languages whose epigraphic and textual resources transmitted valuable data that was then juxtaposed with material remains. The rationale for the study of these subjects was generated from the self-definitions of European scholars. Many scholars saw the ancient cultures of Egypt and Mesopotamia in particular through the lens of Biblical accounts or as sources for the classical tradition from which European high culture had grown. The material records left by these ancient cultures did not in all cases supply evidence for the (canonical European) Fine arts, and some highly specialised fields developed in response to specific categories of objects such as numismatics and seals. The artistic legacy was sufficiently rich, however, to allow a range of studies that paralleled the art-historical investigations of Renaissance and post-Renaissance Europe (for example with reliefs taking the place of painting). Thus new methods were generally not called for, and the achievements of these early cultures could readily be used to preface conventional histories of Mediterranean and European art and culture.

During the 20th century, the study of classical antiquity has gradually been disengaged from art history, although the break has never been consistent or logical.[13] Today in North America, for example, classical archaeologists may work in college and university departments of Classics, of Art and Archaeology or of Art History, while some programs exist independently. Separate professional associations and journals serve the two groups (the Archaeological Institute of America and its journals, the College Art Association and its journals). Some classical archaeologists continue to emphasise fieldwork, while others pursue art-historical analyses not dependent on excavations.[14] In the field, classical archaeologists now deploy most of the same techniques that other archaeologists exploit, from geophysical prospecting to flotation. In general, classical archaeologists have at least a rudimentary command of classical languages, history, and even of art history. As a result they tend to view the modern landscape in which they work through the eyes of an informed and historically-conscious viewer even if the modern language, population, and culture are radically different from those of antiquity.

Since the 19th century, however, another stream of archaeology has developed in northern Europe and in the Americas to investigate ancient peoples and cultures outside the classical world.[15] Just as the prehistoric eras in continental Europe and the British Isles differ from those in North and South America, so do too the histories' trajectories. The study of prehistory in North America became a recognised division within anthropology early in this century. Since mid-century, anthropological archaeologists have become more numerous on college and university campuses than classical archaeologists, and their graduate programs, professional associations and journals now dominate the larger realm of archaeology. Thus today in North America both humanistic, classical archaeologists and anthropological archaeologists work in Europe and the Mediterranean on sites from classical antiquity. Anthropological archaeologists also study other culture areas on every inhabited continent. Moreover, the methods of modern archaeology are now applied to historic sites such as those of the Roman and mediaeval periods in Great Britain and on the continent, and the post-contact period in the Americas. In this respect, archaeology is neither confined to a distant past nor limited by Eurocentric cultural definitions, which contrasts with the views of archaeologists in China.[16]

Within this eurocentric historical narrative and conceptual framework, the archaeology of ancient China has had no obvious or necessary home. In order to understand that situation we must look at early studies of Chinese art and archaeology by non-Chinese scholars.

Eurocentric and Sinocentric Paradigms

Even though China was never colonised by the European powers, the pursuit of China's antiquities began in the 19th century within an imperialist paradigm in which Europe was regarded as the centre of the world, and European concepts and values were assumed to constitute a norm against which all else should be judged. In recent years, the term orientalism has been adopted to designate the relationship of Europeans with the Islamic world,[17] and indeed some of the same mechanisms were at work in the ways in which European scholars addressed China in the late 19th and early 20th centuries. Classical humanism and Christian morality strongly affected the ways in which Europeans perceived China and its cultural heritage.[18] Any wholesale appropriation of the concept of orientalism, however, is in my view inappropriate to the Chinese case. Like India,[19] there were distinctive factors that made the European relationship to China different from the experience with Islam, not least the considerable strength of the Chinese empire through the 18th century, the initial fascination of European intellectuals with Confucian culture,[20] and the European appreciation for Chinese decorative arts and crafts.[21]

European and American amateur archaeologists of the late 19th and early 20th centuries, some of them self-styled sinologists, established many of the goals and methods sustained in this field to the present day. Some of these amateurs adopted the outlook of their Chinese scholar contemporaries. They began to collect certain objects in a spirit much akin to the antiquarians of the Song and Qing periods. Édouard Chavannes' (1865-1918) photographic albums employed a modern technology to record stone images and inscriptions that Chinese scholars had traditionally recorded by making ink rubbings.[22] John C Ferguson (1866-1945), having embraced Chinese scholars' taste, produced a handbook to antiquities organised by the media-based categories they themselves used.[23] Berthold Laufer (1874-1934) collected all manner of things under the general rubric of ethnology during his trips to China, from baskets to Daoist images to Han pottery to jades, relying on the same Chinese agents who also supplied local Chinese collectors. Laufer then catalogued his materials using Chinese encyclopaedias and other reference works.[24] Bernhard Karlgren (1889-1978), after extensive philological studies of the Chinese classics, studied bronze vessels on the basis of the judgements of his Qing and Republican-era peers, using their catalogues as his database.[25]

Such studies appeared in a European and American world in which bona-fide experts were few and far between, and in which common intellectual goals and cultural values could be assumed among Europeans and Americans. The works of Chavannes and Karlgren explicitly validated the goals and methods of Qing dynasty scholarship and by extension proclaimed China's respectability as a great ancient culture. China in the early 20th century might be politically, militarily and economically weak, but her cultural traditions had ancient roots and her best scholars were worthy of emulation. Within a European context, the categories of objects given attention by these writers were exotic: ceremonial jades, ritual bronzes, engraved pictorial stones and calligraphic inscriptions; and stood apart from the trade goods and collectibles then in vogue. Most scholars unselfconsciously adopted a vocabulary taken wholesale from the lexicon of European antiquarians: stelae, bas-reliefs, tumuli, etc. The enfolding historical matrix that Chinese scholars employed was likewise taken for granted. Karlgren's investigations of bronzes were after all an attempt to improve on the rather vague datings to the Three Dynasties then in use by his Chinese contempo-

[16] On the limits of archaeology in China; see Xia Nai and Wang Zhongshu 1986.

[17] Said, Edward 1978: *Orientalism*. New York: Knopf.

[18] Zhang Longxi 1988: 'The Myth of the Other China in the Eyes of the West.' *Critical Inquiry* 15 (Autumn): 108-131.

[19] Mitter 1977.

[20] Mungello, David 1985: *Curious Land: Jesuit Accommodation and the Origins of Sinology*. Stuttgart: Steiner.

[21] Lach, Donald F 1965-77: *Asia in the Making of Europe*. 2 vols. Chicago: University of Chicago Press.

[22] Chavannes, Édouard 1913: *Mission archéologique dans la Chine septentrionale*. Paris: E Leroux.

[23] Ferguson, John C 1919: *Outlines of Chinese Art*. Chicago: University of Chicago Press.

[24] For example, Laufer, Berthold 1912: *Jade: a Study in Chinese Archaeology and Precision*. Chicago: Field Museum of Natural History. (Reprint edition. New York: Dover, 1974).

[25] Elkins, James 1987: 'Remarks on the Western Art Historical Study of Chinese Bronzes, 1930-1980.' *Oriental Art* 33.3: 250-260.

[26] Laufer 1912: 29, 120-68, for discussions of *cong* and *bi*.

[27] Mirsky, Jeannette 1977: *Sir Aurel Stein: Archaeological Explorer.* Chicago: University of Chicago Press.

[28] Hopkirk, Peter 1980: *Foreign Devils on the Silk Road.* London: John Murray; see also Table A.

[29] Ségalen, Victor *et al* 1923-24: *Mission archéologique en Chine. 1914 et 1917.* Paris: P Geuthner. *The Great Statuary of China.* E Levieux, trans. Chicago: University of Chicago Press 1977.

[30] Abe, Stanley K 1993: 'Wonder House: Buddhist Art and the West.' Unpublished MS.

[31] Beasley, W G and E G Pulleyblank 1961: *Historians of China and Japan.* London: Oxford University Press.

raries. Laufer, as a critical modern scholar of his time, doubted the existence of a neolithic stage in Chinese prehistory, even as his study of jades illustrated what we now know to be such objects.[26] These non-Chinese scholars were both serious and credulous. As experts in an arcane field their role was to introduce exotica to the larger world in terms that would be credible to their non-Chinese audiences. Their project was an informed translation, based on advanced scholarship in China, that normalised Chinese things within a conventional Chinese frame of reference.

Other European amateurs pursued an agenda more akin to that of their peers active in Egypt or in Mesopotamia. Sir Marc Aurel Stein (1862-1943) is perhaps the most famous of these archaeological explorers, who "conducted reconnaissances in Chinese territory, selectively to carry back to his sponsors in the British Empire."[27] Many other European explorers, driven by a mixture of scholarly and nationalist zeal, crossed the ancient trade routes of present-day Tibet, Xinjiang and the steppes, and their collections came to decorate the museums of many European capitals.[28] Sven Hedin's (1865-1952) expeditions were exceptional in their Sino-Swedish sponsorship, and the provisions made to work with Chinese scholars on the one han, and to leave collections in Chinese hands on the other. French and German explorers shared much of the glory for their remarkable discoveries; their exploits parallel those of British and Dutch colonial archaeologists in India and Indonesia. Unlike colonial archaeologists, who had putative authority to investigate and collect, the Europeans in Central Asia were taking advantage of a political vacuum. There was no one to stop them most of the time, and their removal of objects could be rationalised by recourse to a racist orientalism, in which native peoples could not be trusted to preserve their own cultural heritage. By contrast, Victor Ségalen's (1878-1919) harvest was photographic and literary. His experiences became the basis for one of the earliest synthetic accounts of Chinese sculpture.[29]

If Chavannes, Ferguson and Karlgren operated within the conceptual categories of their Chinese intellectual peers, albeit with a transposed European vocabulary, writers like Stein and Ségalen were fixated on a vision of World History and World Art in which the classical civilisations of the Mediterranean were the point of reference, and in which, therefore, eurocentric criteria determined the value and interest of Chinese things. Rather than operating within a coherent (albeit sinocentric) view of China's antiquity, Stein and Ségalen saw China instead as a distant civilisation beyond the eastern borders of *their* classical world. Stein's fascination with China was fuelled by his desire to connect events in this classical world to the lands beyond. He was ecstatic to find the traces of an artisan-painter named Tita (Titus) at Miran on the southern Silk Road in Xinjiang, and like others of his day saw the Buddhist art of China as Greco-Buddhist, firmly ensconced within the legacy of Hellenistic culture.[30]

In spite of their different frames of reference, however, Chavannes and Stein shared a common intellectual goal: to understand the past through a conflation of its literary and material traces. For both scholars, archaeology was an historical project, ancillary to the primary tasks of reading and interpreting received historical texts. It is a coincidence that in both the Chinese and European historiographical traditions, archaeology served the role of supplementing and correcting received records.[31]

For both Chinese and non-Chinese scholars, therefore, great prestige was attached to the recovery of textual or epigraphic sources (Shang oracle-bone inscriptions, Zhou bronze inscriptions, Han slips, Dunhuang manuscripts). For both groups of scholars, history was the arbiter of the significance of a find or site. If a sand-buried city could be correctly identified with historical people and events, it was unquestionably important; prehistoric and ahistoric finds were another matter. In their earliest phase, therefore, archaeological investigations of ancient China were carried forward by non-native scholars who accepted the same goals and deployed the same methods that drove the practice of classical archaeology and art history in European and Mediterranean lands.

Table A | Archaeological Works 1900-1937

Author	Publication

1 • EXPEDITIONS AND EXCAVATIONS

Author	Publication
Andersson, J G	*Preliminary Report on Archaeological Research in Kansu* (1925)
	Children of the Yellow Earth (1934)
Arne, T J	*Painted Stone Age Pottery* (1925)
Black, D *et al*	*Fossil Man in China* (1933)
Chavannes, E	*Les Documents Chinois* (1933)
	Mission Archéologique (1913, 1915)
Conrady, A	*Die Chinesischen Handschriften* (1920)
Grünwedel, A	*Bericht über Archäologishe Arbeiten* (1906)
	Altbuddistische Kultstätten (1912)
Palmgren, N	*Kansu Mortuary Urns* (1934)
Pelliot, P	*Les Grottes de Touen-Houang* (1920-24)
Ségalen, V	*Mission Archéologique* (1923-24)
Stein, M	*Ancient Khotan* (1907)
	Serindia (1921)
	Innermost Asia (1928)
von le Coq, A	*Chotscho* (1913)
	Die Buddhistische Spätantike (1922-23)
	Bilderatlas zur Kunst (1925)
Warner, L	*Buddhist Wall-paintings* (1938)
White, W	*Tombs of Old Lo-Yang* (1934)

2 • GENERAL WORKS

Author	Publication
Hentze, C	*Chinese tomb figures* (1928)
Laufer, B	*Jade: A Study in Chinese Archaeology and Religion* (1912)
	Chinese Pottery of the Han Dynasty (1909)
	Chinese Clay Figures (1914)

Table B | Art-Historical Works 1915-1937

Author	Publication

1 • CATALOGUES

Author	Publication
Anonymous	*The Chinese Exhibition* (1936)
Janse, O	*Briques et Objets céramiques* (1936)
Kummel, O	*Chinesische Kunst* (1930)
Laufer, B	*Archaic Chinese Jades* (1927)
Nott, S	*Chinese Jade* (1936)
Pelliot, P	*Jades Archaïques de Chine* (1925)
Rostovtzeff, M	*Inlaid Bronzes of the Han* (1927)
Salmony, A	*Sino-Siberian Art* (1933)
Yetts, P	*The George Eumorfopoulos Collection* (1929-32)

2 • GENERAL WORKS

Author	Publication
Fischer, O	*Die chinesische Malerei der Han-Dynastie* (1931)
Hobson, R	*Chinese Pottery and Porcelain* (1935)
	The Art of the Chinese Potter (1923)
Rostovtzeff, M	*The Animal Style* (1929)
Sirén, O	*A History of Early Chinese Art* (1929-30)
	Chinese Sculpture (1925)

Early Collections: Chinese Antiquities and the Canon

The collecting of antiquities that raged in China in the decades leading up to the second world war yielded a critical mass of objects in non-Chinese museums and private collections.[32] At much the same time the earliest modern public museums in China were being established. Both inside and outside China, museums became repositories for a great range of material, most of which was not, however, central within any eurocentric canon of the Fine Arts. Chinese collections were always polyglot, speaking the languages of ethnography, history, archaeology, and art. Various carved and inscribed stones belonged to the one category common in Chinese collections that most resembled eurocentric notions of a fine art: sculpture. Although there were almost no famous names in ancient Chinese sources who could be plausibly associated with such stones (excepting calligraphers, who in any case did not themselves carve the stelae bearing their texts), Han reliefs, Buddhist images and calligraphic inscriptions could be studied and criticised using much of the critical vocabulary of classical archaeology and art history. Stones were of course also durable, and could be studied in many cases through the convenient medium of rubbings. Moreover, many stones had long attracted the interest of Chinese antiquarians due to their inscriptions, which in turn illuminated their content as well as their provenance.

The other canonical European fine arts, architecture and painting, however, posed more serious problems, both conceptually and pragmatically. Buildings in themselves and their designers or makers had no status within the pre-modern native Chinese context that might have allowed them to be evaluated as an art. Noble ruins akin to those of Greece and Egypt were in short supply; almost no ancient examples seemed to survive above ground with the exception of a few gate towers and offering shrines noted early on by Chavannes and Ségalen, and ruined brick and stone Buddhist pagodas. Sites where famous buildings had once stood were almost without exception the home of much later structures or, like the Afang or Weiyang palaces, were now desolate. And except for eaves tiles, there was no pre-modern tradition of collecting architectural artefacts. When Liang Sicheng and Liu Dunzhen began their systematic investigations of the oldest extant structures, they were creating a new discipline in China, one modelled explicitly on a non-native conceptual framework.[33] That discipline has continued to flourish in China, but not as an art-historical pursuit; instead such studies are rationalised and promoted as a branch of the history of Chinese science and technology.

In the early 20th century ancient Chinese painting seemed to be almost totally lost. Chinese histories of painting and critical texts began in earnest in the Six Dynasties period and flourished from the Tang onwards. The earliest accessible pictorial art was confined to various Han engraved stones[34] and, after Stein and Pelliot's expeditions, Dunhuang paintings. Anyone assessing the early history of Chinese painting prior to Tang in the 1920s or 1930s was forced to rely primarily on literary testimony.[35] As a practical matter, aside from Han stones and their rubbings, there was little material that might be collected. Collectors did augment true painting with other related materials in a way reminiscent of the study of Greek vases: lacquer wares, pictorial bronzes and stamped bricks were defined as analogues of painting. These materials offered a wider range of examples of both subject-matter and styles, and in turn permitted scholars to adduce literary sources that describe or discuss painting in the early periods. The materials that came to dominate collections were objects reflecting traditional Chinese antiquarian taste, on the one hand, and the accidental archaeology of railway construction and tomb looting, on the other.[36] Jade carvings and archaic bronzes, traditional targets of Chinese collecting, bulked large in both private hands and museum holdings. Ceramics, from painted urns of the Gansu neolithic cultures to the mortuary figurines and wares of Han, Six Dynasties and Tang, were also assembled in large numbers.[37] These ceramics were collected largely in response to the market created by non-Chinese enthusiasts. Thus western museum holdings came to resemble in some ways the collections of Egyptian, Mesopotamian, and Classical antiquities: durable objects, many of them from

[32] Clunas, Craig 1993: 'East Asian Art and Oriental Antiquities: British and American Views,' unpublished MS; Cohen, Warren I 1992: *East Asian Art and American Culture*. New York: Columbia University Press.

[33] Fairbank, Wilma C 1984: 'Liang Ssu-ch'eng: A Profile.' *A Pictorial History of Chinese Architecture* by Liang Ssu-ch'eng. Cambridge: MIT Press.

[34] Wu Hung 1989: *Chinese Pictorial Art*. Stanford: Stanford University Press.

[35] Waley, Arthur 1923: *An Introduction to the Study of Chinese Painting*. London.

[36] Fontein, Jan and Wu Tung 1973: *Unearthing China's Past*. Boston: Museum of Fine Arts; Goodrich, L Carrington 1957: 'Archaeology in China: The First Decades.' *Journal of Asian Studies* 17: 5-15.

[37] March, Benjamin 1929: *China and Japan in Our Museums*. New York: Institute of Pacific Relations.

burial contexts, some connected to history, epigraphy and antiquarian taste, some redefined as analogues to the true fine arts.

Unlike those fields, however, there was little contemporaneous archaeology taking place in that allowed the objects to be contextualised. An early 20th century curator of Chinese antiquities had few archaeological publications to draw on compared to his counterparts in departments of Egyptian or classical antiquities. Chinese collections became the focus of a combination of sinological exegesis and hybrid connoisseurship. Relatively few catalogues of these collections were compiled in the prewar years.[38] Those that did appear, most notably catalogues of archaic bronzes, generally aped their Chinese predecessors in format and range as well as in judgements about authenticity and historical significance.[39] It was often enough to assign an object to a block of time several centuries in duration and to affirm its importance because of its supposed rarity or sheer antiquity. These first stages of western scholarship (c1900-1930) on ancient China were a hybrid of antiquarian and archaeological approaches in which traditional Chinese attitudes and imported European ones were merged. A survey of scholarly publications on China held by American libraries illustrates how disconnected were the accounts that non-Chinese scholarly writers had produced at the time.[40] (See Tables A and B). I take the literature catalogued in Gardner's survey as a reasonably accurate snapshot of the kinds of activities most non-Chinese scholars interested in early China had pursued during the first four decades of the century. Publications derived from the various central Asian expeditions and catalogues of collections comprise most of the 'serious' literature. In spite of the evident respect some Sinologists showed their Chinese peers, few Chinese scholars themselves participated in these publications.

New Agenda: Writing about the History of Chinese Art

Professional art historians first came to the study of ancient China in the 1920s and 1930s. I refer to such important figures as Ludwig Bachhofer, Otto Kümmel, Max Loehr, George Rowley, Alfred Salmony, Osvald Sirén and Laurence Sickman as professional art historians, because they earned degrees and/or pursued careers within the institutional matrix of academic art history and art museums. Some of these scholars had only a modest acquaintance with the Chinese language or even with China itself. Perhaps only two could claim to be true Sinologues: Max Loehr (1903-1988) and Osvald Sirén (1879-1966), both of whom lived and travelled for extended periods in China. Several of these scholars—Bachhofer (1896-1976), Rowley (l895-l962), and Sirén—came to Chinese art through a side-door (such as Indian art) or as a second field (after medieval or Renaissance European art). Indeed, one detects traces of their previous specialities in their approaches to Chinese topics, such as Sirén's annotated lists of Chinese painters which mimic Berenson's compilations of Italian Renaissance painters.

Writings by these scholars cover a considerable array of topics and are not easily lumped together or summed up. Only the amazingly prolific Osvald Sirén engaged the whole range of canonical topics —architecture, sculpture, and painting—as manifested in China in his writings. Sirén's works are notable because they relied on extensive photographic documentation of sites in China and objects in lieu as well as on his first-hand familiarity with objects in Chinese collections. His *History of Early Chinese Art* (1929-30) attempted to address a wide range of subjects, but most of his books focused instead more closely on a single topic, such as sculpture, the walls and gates of Peking, gardens or painting.

Several scholars—notably Olov Janse, Michael Rostovtzeff, Alfred Salmony, and Walter Perceval Yetts—published catalogues of Chinese objects in collections, in particular the holdings of the prominent dealer C T Loo. Several of these figures do not fit my arbitrary definition of professional art historians, and indeed their works are a medley of several kinds of description and analysis.

[38] See Table B

[39] Wenley, A G 1946: *Descriptive and Illustrative Catalogue of Chinese Bronzes Acquired during the Administration of John Ellerton Lodge.* Washington: Smithsonian Institution; Thorp, Robert L 1991: 'Bronze Catalogues as Cultural Artifacts.' *Archives of Asian Art* 44: 84-94.

[40] Gardner, Charles S 1938: *A Union List of Selected Western Books on China in American Libraries.* 2nd edition. American Council of Learned Societies.

[41] Wiseman, James 1984: 'Scholarship and Provenience in the Study of Artifacts.' *Journal of Field Archaeology* 11: 67-77.

[42] Alsop, Joseph 1982: *The Rare Art Traditions*. New York: Harper and Row; Cohen 1992: *East Asian Art and American Culture*. New York: Columbia University Press.

[43] Bachhofer, Ludwig 1946: *A Short History of Chinese Art*. New York: Pantheon; see also Vanderstappen, Harrie 1977-78: 'Ludwig Bachhofer (1894-1976).' *Archives of Asian Art* 31: 110-112.

[44] Bachhofer 1946.

In compiling these catalogues, these scholars began the tradition of serving the interests of dealers, collectors and museums. Such owners, of course, have several interests. In addition to the genuine desire to know more about their objects, there were the needs to establish authenticity and justify value or significance. Simply to be catalogued and published brings new status to any object. To be authenticated, dated, and assessed in qualitative terms makes an ordinary or undistinguished object into an important one.[41] The symbiosis of collectors and scholars was by no means confined to the new field of Chinese antiquities; it is endemic to art history in European and American society.[42]

As a professional art historian, Ludwig Bachhofer produced the first serious one-volume survey of Chinese art in English.[43] Bachhofer concerned himself explicitly with the fundamental question of all formalist studies: why do things look the way they do?

> No explanation should be necessary for the great emphasis laid upon problems of *form*. Form is the only means of expression an artist has at his disposal, whatever considerations may have determined his subject matter. It is form alone that makes a vessel, a statue, or a painting a work of art. But form never remains the same. It changes continually, and I saw my main task in describing these changes. They revealed themselves as so many phases of a logical, orderly, and organic evolution.[44]

These few sentences are pregnant with important methodological assumptions. Form makes things works of art; artists express themselves through form; changes in form are logical and evolutionary. This is as succinct a statement of the professional art historian's credo as I have found in English writings. A new discourse was thus brought to bear on Chinese objects, and the traditional terms used by Chinese antiquarians hereafter would be less in evidence.

As a group, the common goal of professional art historians was to deploy eurocentric art-historical concepts and methods on Chinese materials. First, certain kinds of objects were defined for operational purposes as art (whatever their status may have been or be within pre-modern or modern Chinese culture). As such they were assumed to express the maker's (artist's) intentions and to manifest specific stages in a logical evolution. Thus the scholar's goal was to unlock the pattern of that evolution through the closest and most perceptive visual scrutiny of his objects. Certain patterns were to be expected, most notably a development from simple to complex, and a reaction against that complexity that has been described as a cycle of archaic, classic, and baroque.[45] The description and interpretation that art historians produced I call 'style narratives.'[46] The critical first step in such a narrative was careful visual description leading to the formal and qualitative categories developed within eurocentric art history. Whenever possible, stylistic sequences were correlated with datable monuments. Since the persuasive power of a sequence depended in many cases on establishing such correlations, serious arguments might arise over the authenticity and/or dating of certain key monuments.

[45] Fong, Wen C 1980: 'The Study of Chinese Bronze Age Arts: Methods and Approaches' *The Great Bronze Age of China*, 20-34. New York: Metropolitan Museum of Art.

[46] To compare: Davis, Whitney 1990: 'Style and History in Art History' *The Uses of Style in Archaeology*, ed. M Conkey and C Hastorf. New Directions in Archaeology. Cambridge: Cambridge University Press.

[47] Bachhofer 1946: 63-85.

[48] Loehr, Max 1953: 'The Bronze Styles of the Anyang Period (1300-1028 BC).' *Archives of the Chinese Art Society of America* 7: 42-53.

[49] Soper, Alexander C 1966: 'Early, Middle and Late Shang: A Note.' *Artibus Asiae* 28: 5-38; Spiro, Audrey 1981: 'Max Loehr's Periodisation of Bronze Vessels.' *Journal of Asian Culture* 5: 107-133; Thorp, Robert L 1985: 'The Growth of Early Shang Civilisation: New Data from Ritual Vessels.' *Harvard Journal of Asiatic Studies* 45: 5-75.

Perhaps the most long-lived of these master sequences and style narratives were Bachhofer's interpretation of Chinese Buddhist sculpture from the Six Dynasties through the Song,[47] and Max Loehr's interpretation of Shang bronze styles.[48] In each case particular observations and a rigorous logic generated a sequence in which each step seems convincingly to be the necessary outcome of what came before and the essential way station to what must come next. In Bachhofer's sculptural studies, a good supply of dated objects, few of problematic authenticity, made his overall framework that much more secure. In Loehr's case with Shang bronzes, the sequence was eminently logical but not well supported by more than logic until excavations of the 1950s and 1960s were published.[49]

The ordering that each scholar achieved was considered, in art-historical terms, a notable contribution in itself, just as many striations dependent on careful formal analysis of pottery have been accepted as significant in archaeological terms. Like archaeological series, Bachhofer and Loehr imposed a shape onto the processes of time, and deduced a mechanism—progress toward a goal that the later scholar could discover—that 'explained' the mechanisms of those changes. What had been inchoate or incoherent prior to their studies became an obvious pattern that could be easily grasped and readily applied to new materials. From such sequences it was then possible to ascend to a higher level of more abstract analysis, and to offer opinions about larger historical trends. The patterns were expressed in conventional terms and relations taken wholesale from eurocentric art history. It is hardly surprising, therefore, that non-Chinese scholars were inclined then to make universal claims about art and its history, to assert that fundamental processes were common to all humans.

This art historical approach was not universally accepted in Europe and America, much less adopted by scholars in China. John Pope's (1906-1982) caustic review of Bachhofer's *Short History* was a forceful critique of the application of art-historical terms and methods of analysis without, or in preference to, sinological grounding.[50] He wrote:

> "Lacking the essential tool of language and relying on stylistic formulae which had been tried and proven in the European field, the art historian ventured into the vast and complex field of Chinese art. The results of his efforts provide ample evidence that his equipment has been unsuited to the task…"

> "What I regard as the shortcomings of this volume are, I believe, the inevitable shortcomings of the art-historical method when applied to this field of endeavour…" [51]

Pope wrote in the context of an underdeveloped field which he believed could only advance "once [we] begin to realise how little we really know … Future progress will depend in great measure on how much we can *find out about* the circumstances under which objects were made…"[52] From this point of view, art historians like Bachhofer were guilty of a sin of commission: not working to understand the culture of which the art objects were a part and product. While their colleagues studying European objects might adequately appreciate the larger patterns and meaning of European civilisation, Pope maintained that Chinese culture was insufficiently understood to allow such self-confident analyses.

When the great majority of specific objects discussed resided in collections and had no ascertainable archaeological provenience, as was the case with Bachhofer, the pitfalls of an art-historical approach were multiplied. The interpretation may have been suited to its objects, but what was the relation of those objects to the larger (unstudied) whole? To give the accumulation of objects in collections a systematic and rational structure, the art historian had to assume or infer the aesthetic choices and traditions of the makers. To the extent that such assumptions or inferences were derived from European experience (even if they were assumed to be universal), the structure was merely hypothetical or logical and not necessarily true to the Chinese case.

The net result of early art-historical studies was very like the time-space systematics of much 20th-century archaeology. In this situation, field archaeology was useful primarily as a ready source of new materials, and especially for better clues to dates and to points of origin.[53] Ultimately in such art-historical projects, however, all objects, with or without provenience, were treated as equal and discriminated on the basis of quality and rarity within the context of the style narrative. A large array of objects (or of photographs of objects) was actually more important than a large fund of data about each object, since it was the inferred connections deduced from the visual properties of the objects that held the system together.

[50] Pope, John A 1947: 'Sinology or Art History: Notes on Method in the Study of Chinese Art.' *Harvard Journal of Asiatic Studies* 10: 388-417.

[51] Pope, John 1947: 389, 393.

[52] Fontein and Wu 1973: 417.

[53] *Ibid*: 417.

Post-War Syntheses *in Absentia*

From the 1940s through the 1960s, these art historical methods dominated the literature in Europe and North America. Access to China itself was hard to come by, especially for American scholars, and anthropological archaeologists, with few exceptions, turned away from Chinese studies because of the lack of field opportunities. Art historians themselves devoted their energies primarily to objects that were accessible at first hand in non-Chinese museums and private collections (and the collections on Taiwan). Their research targets were therefore a curious mixture of a relatively small number of objects of perceived high quality and a rather larger fund of less interesting and valuable material. All had come to light as a by-product of construction, looting and collecting in the first decades of the century and had passed through the various stages of the prewar antiquities trade prior to their acquisition by their current owners. The requirement for first-hand access is understandable and even commendable as a methodological bias. When the self-imposed limitations of this evidence are not acknowledged, however, the way is open for misleading scholarship.

While the range of accessible objects was reasonably diverse, it was also in many respects highly stereotyped: neolithic pottery from the Gansu corridor, Late Shang bronzes (many with an unconfirmed Anyang provenience), Eastern Zhou materials from such mysterious sites as Liyu, Luoyang, Shouzhou and Changsha, Tang grave furnishings from Henan and Shaanxi, and so on. If these holdings were plotted on a time line and a map, they would be a highly impressionistic assortment drawn only from certain episodes and a few places. Certain museum collections indeed had a pronounced regional character. The Museum of Far Eastern Antiquities in Stockholm was known for its Gansu pottery; the Royal Ontario Museum was strong in all manner of things from Henan; the Field Museum (Chicago) was full of Laufer's Xi'an acquisitions; the John Hadley Cox collection (now Yale Gallery of Art) was largely comprised of material from Changsha. These regional specialisations reflected the collecting habits of donors rather than systematic acquisitions programs. In many collections objects from pairs and sets were represented by single specimens, their mates consigned to other hands through the vagaries of the antiquities market.

Much of the writing of the 1950s was produced by scholars with an acquaintance with China from the prewar or wartime years (for example: Richard Edwards, Wilma Fairbank, Richard Rudolph, Laurence Sickman and Michael Sullivan, all of whom had interests in early China). In their works, sites and monuments in China were frequently juxtaposed with objects in non-Chinese collections. For such scholars, a site like Longmen or the Forbidden City was real if then inaccessible, and objects in non-Chinese collections were the tip of an iceberg of related materials to be found in China. Notions of rarity or of importance were therefore informed and tempered by a sense of the larger whole, and there was an understood, if not always well articulated, sense of a larger framework into which these discrete objects fit.

In the 1950s, it became the task of academic art historians and museum curators to synthesise a picture of the material and aesthetic culture of an ancient civilisation from these randomly collected but durable traces. Some scholars and curators, like Laurence Sickman,[54] collected and displayed all manner of things for their own beauty, but accorded serious art-historical status only to those things that might stand within a narrative of the history of the Chinese canon. To carry this program forward a serious accommodation was necessary: objects were given expected canonical roles. Thus grave goods could function as early evidence in a history of sculpture, and Han reliefs and lacquer wares might stand as evidence for the pictorial art of the period. If the earliest examples adduced therefore were crude or *archaic,* that was to be expected as part of a universal pattern, rather than understood as a property of their original identity. If the subjects and styles represented in the available evidence were skewed in one direction or another, such as the Wu Liang

[54] Sutton, Denys 1973: 'The Lure of Ancient China.' *Apollo* 97 (March 1973): 2-11 and Wilson, Marc F 1989: 'Laurence Chalfant Stevens Sickman (1906-1988),' *Archives of Asian Art* 42: 82-84.

shrines, that characterisation might then be transferred to the larger subject being addressed, the history of Han painting as a whole.[55] Thus the selection of objects and their redefinition had a strong determinative effect on the generalisations of even the most sensitive and well-informed scholars.

Conclusion

There are comparable overviews to be written for recent scholarship outside China, for the early history of archaeology in China, and for archaeology in China since 1949. In all of these assessments, the 1940s are a kind of watershed defined by the war and by the founding of the People's Republic in 1949. The practical circumstances under which archaeology has been practised have differed significantly before and after that decade both inside and outside China.

Before that decade and inside China, field archaeology was little practised by non-Chinese scholars with the notable exception of the Zhoukoudian excavations (and the activities of Japanese scholars in Manchuria). While expeditions were possible in the waning years of the Qing, little was attempted and less realised in the decades between the wars, under the Republic and its rivals. But it was precisely during this interval that eurocentric art history accommodated Chinese subjects and found a home for them within its own vocabulary and methodologies. More important than access to China or ongoing archaeological investigations were the collections that dealers, individuals and institutions were forming, making use of a very advantageous economic situation that channelled valuables out of China and into European and American hands. Scholarship followed this process and would not have developed as it did without it. This prewar situation determined the character of much scholarship on early China well into the postwar decades. It defined the rules of the game that still dictate how much scholarly work is conceived and executed. Since this kind of situation never developed in China, it is hardly surprising that a comparable scholarship did not develop, or that art history as it is defined in Europe and America has been slow to grow within Chinese academic institutions.

[55] See Powers, Martin J 1991: *Art and Political Expression in Early China*. New Haven: Yale University Press, for a critique.

SARAH ALLAN

Chinese Bronzes Through Western Eyes

estern scholars who study China and Chinese scholars who study their own tradition often find themselves confronting one another in mutual incomprehension, each locked in their own traditions with a sense that they have some critical knowledge or methodology which the other side is missing. This is nowhere more apparent than in the study of ancient Chinese bronzes, where Chinese and western scholars have approached the vessels from radically different perspectives. Nevertheless, a particular value of the intercourse between two cultures, such as that of China and Europe or America, is that in attempting to explain ourselves to others, we become more aware of the particularity of our presuppositions.

My aim is to make the concerns and methodologies of western scholarship in this field more understandable to a Chinese audience by tracing their history. I also wish to make the context and rationale behind my own hypotheses concerning meaning in Chinese bronzes more explicit.[1] Although I have made a number of revisions in the following account, it remains a history of western, as opposed to Chinese, scholarship on Chinese bronzes.

[1] Allan, Sarah 1993: 'Art and Meaning' and 'Epilogue,' in Whitfield, Roderick 1993, ed: *The Problem of Meaning in Early Chinese Ritual Bronzes, Colloquies on Art and Archaeology in Asia*, 15, London: Percival David Foundation of Chinese Art, School of Oriental and African Studies (SOAS): 9-33, 161-76.

Western Studies of Chinese Bronzes in the 20th Century

Chinese bronzes carry a different meaning in the context of western museums and collections from that which they carry in China. Chinese have always valued bronzes as historical objects and studied them for the light which they shed on their ancient history. Thus, Chinese scholars have been most interested in inscriptions and their interpretation. Furthermore, although a great many bronzes were collected and often handed down through generations before the advent of modern archaeology, a much greater number of bronzes have been excavated archaeologically during the last 40 years. Since 1949, these bronzes, which may be studied within a known context, compared with other objects and dated accordingly, have become the focus of scholarly attention.

In the West, however, Chinese bronzes have been seen primarily as art objects to be displayed in museums alongside other non-western objects, to be admired for their intrinsic beauty, often by people with little knowledge of or interest in ancient Chinese civilisation. Since the bronzes were robbed from tombs or hoards rather than excavated scientifically, their provenance can only be surmised or deduced. Each bronze stands in isolation, its original context left to the imagination, and so the studies have often been highly theoretical and highly contentious. In the following, I will recount briefly some of the contributions of western scholars to the study of Chinese bronzes. Many of the flaws are now, with the hindsight of modern archaeological evidence, obvious, but the methodologies are nevertheless of interest, as are the critiques which have been made of them. I will also discuss some of my own attempts to resolve some of the issues which others have raised before me. I will confine myself here to the studies of Shang (c1700-1100 BC) and early Western Zhou dynasty (c1100-771 BC) bronzes which have, in any case, been the focus of western scholarship.

The first comprehensive studies of Chinese bronzes by a western scholar were made by Bernhard Karlgren in the 1930s and published in the *Bulletin of the Museum of Far Eastern Antiquities*, Stockholm. Most important were his 'Yin and Chou in Chinese bronzes,' published in 1936,[2] and 'New Studies on Chinese Bronzes,' published in 1937.[3] These articles followed an exhibition of early Chinese bronzes held in Stockholm in 1933 on the occasion of the 13th International Congress of the History of Art which had excited considerable interest and for which Karlgren had written the catalogue. In 1935, the Chinese government lent pieces to an exhibition held in London and it too aroused interest among western art historians.

[2] Karlgren, B 1936: 'Yin and Chou in Chinese bronzes,' *Bulletin of the Museum of Far Eastern Antiquities*. 8: 9-156.

[3] Karlgren, B 1937: 'New Studies on Chinese Bronzes,' *Bulletin of the Museum of Far Eastern Antiquities*. 9: 1-117.

Karlgren was a sinologist and had already done extensive work translating and annotating classical Chinese texts. He was well acquainted with Chinese scholarship and, of course, knew about the excavations at Yinxu of the last Shang dynasty capital, but the results of these excavations were not yet published and his researches were entirely based upon the bronzes themselves. Karlgren made no reference to any archaeological material in these studies. Instead, he attempted to create an internally consistent 'scientific' system by means of which they could be dated and classified. Because they were primarily interested in the bronzes as art objects, many of the bronzes that western collectors valued most highly were uninscribed. Nowadays, comparison with archaeologically excavated pieces is the primary means of dating such objects; but in the thirties, Chinese archaeology was just beginning and there was no archaeological context which could be used for dating. Karlgren's problem, then, was to derive a means of dating uninscribed bronzes entirely on the basis of their appearance.

Karlgren's method was very ingenious. His aim was to use the inscribed bronzes to provide a scientific means of dating uninscribed bronzes on the basis of their style. Thus, in order to distinguish Yin (*i e* Shang) from Zhou vessels, he first examined a large number of inscribed bronzes which included 'real texts' — texts with content other than formulaic expressions — in order to determine whether they were made by the Zhou. By this method, he determined that certain formulaic expressions such as *ju* (as he transcribed the character), *xi zi sun* and the *ya*-shaped cartouche, never occurred in inscriptions which were clearly identifiable as Zhou. Having dated the bronzes by this means, he then classified the motifs typologically and determined that certain motifs only occurred on vessels which he had classified as Yin, and others only on those which were Zhou. Thus, the motifs (and certain other stylistic elements such as vessel shape and type) could be used as criteria to date other uninscribed bronzes to the Yin or Zhou Dynasties. He then went on to establish similar criteria for use in distinguishing early Zhou bronzes from those cast after the reign of King Mu (c956-918 BC). He called Zhou bronzes cast before the reign of King Mu 'Yin-Zhou' since he regarded their style as a continuation of Shang bronze styles.

Figure 1 • A bronze gu, *Middle Shang period, height 23.2 cm, Linden Museum, Staatliches Museum für Volkerkunde, Stuttgart (OA 20.340L). Photo courtesy of the museum*

In 'New Studies,' Karlgren made a typological classification of the motifs on bronzes which he had previously determined were in the Yin style. His purpose was to discover which motifs could occur together with one another on the main body of the vessels. Thus, he divided the motifs into three groups, A, B, and C. The A elements were more pictorial and included such motifs as

Figure 2 • A bronze li-ding, Western Zhou period, Museum of Far Eastern Antiquities, Stockholm (110.04:170). Photo courtesy of the museum

the mask *taotie*, the bodied *taotie*, bovine *taotie*, the cicada, and the vertical dragon. B elements were more abstract and included such motifs as the dissolved *taotie*, the animal triple band, the de-tailed bird, the eyed spiral band, the eyed band with diagonals, the circle band, the square with crescents, compound lozenges, spikes, interlocked Ts and vertical ribs. C elements, usually found in a subordinate position, included the deformed and the dragonised *taotie*, trunked, beaked, jawed, turning, feathered, winged, S and deformed dragons, birds, snakes, whorl circles, blades and spiral bands. A and B elements, he argued, were mutually exclusive, whereas C elements could occur with either A or B elements. Therefore, he concluded, there were two distinctive, though closely related styles and workshops in the late Shang period.

Although Karlgren's analysis was criticised early on, it has nevertheless exerted considerable influence. The names which he gave to the various motifs are still in common usage and his argument for the coexistence of two styles has, for example, been used by K C Chang as evidence to support his theories concerning the dualistic nature of the Shang royal house. Karlgren considered his A style which included the more animalistic types of *taotie* and the cicada to be primary, whereas the B style which included a number of geometric motifs, the so-called dissolved *taotie* and the animal triple band was secondary. The B style derived from the A style, but the A style continued and coexisted with it. Karlgren's assumption that A was prior to B was primarily for theoretical reasons. He assumed that the earliest *taotie* must be relatively realistic; thus the plastic representations with realistic animal features would come before such motifs as the animal triple band which he interpreted as an abstraction of the more realistic forms of the *taotie*. He was also influenced by the predominance of geometric motifs on Zhou bronzes after the reign of King Mu. He saw this 'middle Zhou' style as a natural development of his B style, thus confirming his hypothesis of a progression from realism to a dissolved geometric style.

Karlgren continued to write about bronzes until his death in 1968 without substantially revising his original hypothesis, even though it was strongly criticised by many other scholars. For example, H G Creel, who had been present during some of the excavations at Yinxu and was better acquainted with the excavated materials, criticised Karlgren's analysis of the inscriptions, pointing out that even short inscriptions were relatively late in the Yin sequence.[4] Moreover, the art historian J Leroy Davidson recognised a distinction between two types of abstraction which Karlgren had grouped together, the 'dissolved *taotie*' (actually an Erligang-style *taotie*) and the 'animal triple band,' and that the former was earlier than the latter (see, for example, figures 1 and 2). Thus Davidson became the first western scholar to successfully place Erligang-style vessels at the beginning of the Shang sequence.[5]

Anyone acquainted with bronze inscriptions today will know that the type of bronze inscriptions which Karlgren used to establish his Yin and Zhou styles—inscriptions which were long and complicated enough to be considered 'real texts'—were all Zhou or at least very late Yin Dynasty. Another problem with Karlgren's analysis which has not been generally recognised is that he did not distinguish between cast and inscribed inscriptions and that he included many fake inscriptions in his analysis. Thus, for example, a *yan*-steamer from the Museum of Far Eastern Antiquities at Stockholm is included by Karlgren in his 'Yin and Chou in Chinese bronzes' as an example of Yin bronze because it has the single character *ju* which is one of his Yin criteria

[4] Creel, Herlee G 1936: 'Notes on Professor Karlgren's System for Dating Chinese Bronzes,' *Journal of the Royal Asiatic Society,* 1936, 3: 463-473.

[5] Davidson, J Leroy 1937: 'Toward a Grouping of Early Chinese Bronzes,' *Parnassus* 9.4 (April 1937): 29-34, 51.

(figure 3). However, an examination of the vessel (which was also available to Karlgren) shows clearly that the inscription was engraved, not cast. Furthermore, the bronze is demonstrably Western Zhou by comparison with excavated pieces.

Although we now know by comparison with archaeologically excavated bronzes that this *yan* is Zhou not Yin, the bovine *taotie* which decorate its legs are the type of realistic, animal-like *taotie* that Karlgren placed at the beginning of the Yin period and assumed were its most primitive form. In his scheme, *taotie* of this type are an A element, though the detailed birds in the top band are a B element; and Karlgren acknowledged that this type of vessel, as well as a similar *yan* with an animal triple band motif on the upper part of the steamer, were exceptions to his rule. Indeed, he used the latter vessel to support his claim that the animal triple band was a dissolved form of the realistic *taotie*, taking it as the equivalent of the de-tailed bird which logically could only derive from a bird to which the tail was still attached. (Interestingly, Karlgren made a similar assumption of the priority of realism in his studies of early myth and legend— *i e*, that myth, being unrealistic, must derive from real historical prototypes; however, in both cases he worked from a theoretical premise and offered no concrete evidence).

In contrast to Karlgren's theories, which were based upon a statistical analysis of individual motifs and upon the premise that realism precedes abstraction, were the theories of the art historians Bachhofer and Loehr. Bachhofer was a student of the great German historian of European art, Wölfflin, who believed that the art of a given period and place represented the spirit of the people (their 'Zeitgeist'). This school was concerned with overall style and their theories were both evolutionary and deterministic. Thus, Bachhofer rejected Karlgren's theory of two rival workshop traditions because of his premise that in any one era "one style must reign supreme." [6] His analysis of Chinese bronzes was also strongly influenced by European art-historical categories, such as classical, baroque, and neoclassical. In terms of Chinese bronzes, this meant that he saw a 'restrained' Anyang style as preceding an 'ornate' style with raised relief and projections in the early Western Zhou which in turn gave way to a 'severe' style during the reign of King Cheng (c1042-1006 BC). Bachhofer's analysis of particular bronzes was not particularly successful, however, and he was immediately challenged by, for example, Otto Maenchen-Helfen, who pointed to contradictory styles among contemporaneous inscribed bronzes, such as the so-called Nie Ling and Chen Chen sets.[7]

More influential than Bachhofer himself has been his student Max Loehr. Loehr criticised Karlgren's typological studies, stating:

> "The order arrived at is an historically incomprehensible grouping of Shang vessels into three categories based, not on styles, but on motifs … It is a system that rests on the *a priori* concept of the absolute earliness of 'the true, realistic' *taotie*. It does not offer a logical explanation of the supposed subsequent changes, a history of styles. Consequently, the system is strangely static; the earliest stage is 'already highly developed, magnificent bronze art' … Likewise, the style supposed to be at the end does not tally with what we do know of the Early Western Chou." [8]

Loehr's first article on Chinese bronzes appeared in 1936, but that for which he is most famous was published in 1953.[9] In it, he successfully established a sequence of five styles based entirely upon art-historical criteria without reference to archaeology or inscriptions. The priority of his first three styles was confirmed by the publication of the excavations at Zhengzhou and Huixian.

Figure 3 • *A bronze* yan, *Western Zhou period, Museum of Far Eastern Antiquities, Stockholm (K.14.756). Photo courtesy of the museum*

[6] Bachhofer, Ludwig 1944: 'The Evolution of Shang and Early Chou Bronzes,' *The Art Bulletin* 26: 107/16.

[7] Maenchen-Helfen, Otto 1945: 'Some Remarks on Ancient Chinese Bronzes,' *The Art Bulletin* 27: 238-243; see also Bachhofer, Ludwig 1945: 'Reply to Maenchen-Helfen,' *The Art Bulletin* 27: 243-246.

[8] Loehr, Max 1953: 'The Bronzes of the Anyang Period,' *Archives of the Chinese Art Society of America* 7:44.

[9] Loehr 1953: 42-53; and Loehr 1936: 'Beiträge zu Chronologie der ältern Chinesischen Bronzen,' *Ostasiatische Zeitgeist* 22 (N F12): 3-41.

Figure 4 • A bronze li-ding, *Middle Shang period, from Christian Deydier Oriental Bronzes, London (formerly Neiraku Bijutsukan collection, Nara). Photo by Prudence Cuming Associates*

Loehr further elaborated upon his sequence in a book, *Ritual Vessels of Bronze Age China*.[10] Loehr emigrated from Germany to the United States after the end of World War II and he has had great influence through his students such as Alexander Soper, James Cahill, Virginia Kane and Robert Bagley, as well as by his own writings.[11] Since many art historians still use his stylistic sequence as a means of describing Shang bronzes, I will summarise it briefly below.

Loehr's Styles I and II are the characteristic styles of bronzes of what we now know to be the Erligang period. Style I is "executed in thin relief lines on a smooth surface. [The motifs] are arranged in horizontal friezes, which are usually bordered by rows of small circles. The motif consists of meanders: bands with oval eyes connected by diagonal lines or tangential curves." Style II (figure 1) "differs from the first style in that the ornaments appear to be incised." Loehr placed Style I before Style II because the raised relief of Style I could be made by incisions on a mould whereas Style II requires a more complex casting process with incisions on a model. Style III (figure 4) differs from Style II in that the decoration is no longer contained in narrow bands but has expanded to fill the surface of the vessel. A peculiar feature of this style is that hooked lines, often called quills, rise from the bodies of the *taotie*. In Karlgren's terminology this motif is a B style 'dissolved *taotie*,' but Loehr has placed it correctly in sequence before the fully developed *taotie* motif.

In Loehr's Style IV (figure 5), the *taotie* is clearly delineated and the image is distinguished from the ground. There is now a *leiwen* (squared spiral) background, but the motifs are still flush with the surface. Style V (figures 6, 7) differs from Style IV in that "the ornaments now rise above the meandered ground in sharply outlined, somewhat simplified and thus clarified forms, which are arranged in a rigid order." Loehr further distinguished three subtypes of his Style V: *a*) with all-over *leiwen* ornament on a *leiwen* ground; *b*) ornament without *leiwen* on a *leiwen* ground; and *c*) without *leiwen* on the ornament or on the ground.[12]

Loehr first analysed the bronzes stylistically, by comparing them with one another, and then, having established his sequence, he turned to other evidence, such as inscriptions and comparable vessels which had been excavated archaeologically, to date the changes which he had already discerned. He originally assumed that his sequence all took place during the Yinxu period. The discovery that the first three styles were already present in the Erligang Period was nevertheless regarded as a validation of the sequence. More recently, of course, the discovery of the Fu Hao tomb has indicated that the entire sequence had already taken place by the reign of Wu Ding. Furthermore, as Robert Thorp has observed, there is still no archaeological evidence for the priority of Style I over Style II (both Erligang period) or of Style IV over Style V. Thus, these styles can also be regarded as artistically complementary, rather than as sequential developments.[13]

Figure 8, a square *yi* with a rather crude, incised *taotie* as its main decor, set off by the raised relief of Loehr Style Vb in the bands above and below, is an interesting anomaly. Loehr did accept that there might be an overlap in style periods, but his assumption of a single line of development, as William Watson observed, tends to reduce all stylistic variation to a problem of sequence.[14] Although Loehr's hypothesis concerning the direction of development has been confirmed by the archaeological evidence, many style elements, such as plastic modelling, cannot be explained by a unilinear scheme of development on the

[10] Loehr 1968: *Ritual Vessels of Bronze Age China*, New York.

[11] See, for example, Soper, Alexander C 1966: 'Early, Middle, and Late Shang: A Note,' *Artibus Asiae* 28: 5-38; Kane, Virginia 1973: 'The Chronological Significance of the Inscribed Ancestor Dedication in the Periodisation of Shang Dynasty Bronze Vessels,' *Artibus Asiae* 35: 335-370, Kane 1975: 'A Re-examination of Anyang Archaeology,' *Ars Orientalis* 10: 93-110; Bagley, Robert W 1987: *Shang Ritual Bronzes in the Arthur Sackler Collection*, Cambridge, Mass: Arthur M Sackler Foundation.

[12] Loehr, Max 1953: 48.

[13] Thorp, Robert L 1988: 'Archaeology of Style at Anyang: Tomb 5 in Context,' *Archives of Asian Art* 41: 47-69—1985: 'The Growth of Early Shang Civilisation: New Data from Ritual Vessels.' *Harvard Journal of Asiatic Studies* 45: 5-75.

[14] Watson, William 1968: 'The Five Stages of Shang,' (Review of Max Loehr, *Ritual Vessels of Bronze Age China*), *Art News* 67.7 (November 1968): 42-47, 62-64.

Figure 5 • A bronze gu, Late Shang period, Staatliches Museum für Volkerkunde (52-14-2), Munich. Photo courtesy of the museum

Figure 6 • A bronze square gu, late Shang period, Museum für Ostasiatische Kunst (C76.4), Köln. Photo courtesy of the museum and Rheinsches Bildarchiv

central plains. More recent archaeological evidence suggests that regional innovations and influence played an important role.

Loehr had criticised Karlgren's analysis on the grounds that the realistic animal forms which he assumed were the earliest forms of the *taotie* represented a fully developed bronze art. Loehr, on the other hand, assumed that neolithic painted pottery with geometric motifs would eventually prove to be the origin of Shang bronze art. Just as Karlgren assumed that realism must precede abstraction on theoretical grounds, Loehr was committed to a theoretical view that geometric design precedes abstraction. Thus, in *Ritual Vessels of Bronze Age China*, Loehr quoted Susanne K Langer's *Feeling and Form*:

> "The fundamental forms which occur in the decorative arts of all ages and races—for instance, the circle, the triangle, the spiral, the parallel—are known as motifs of design. They are not art 'works,' not even ornaments, themselves, but they lend themselves to composition, and are therefore incentives to artistic creations … A comparative study of decorative art and primitive representational art suggests forcibly that form is first, and the representational function accrues to it." [15]

[15] Langer, Susanne K 1953: *Feeling and Form*, New York, 69-70.

Langer had not, however, made a comparative study: her position here was simply a theoretical, philosophical one.

An important concomitant of Loehr's thesis that Shang art derived from geometric design was that it could not have any symbolic or iconographic meaning. This question of the meaning of Shang bronze art is also one which has excited much interest and argument among western scholars. According to Loehr:

> "If the ornaments on Shang bronzes came into being as sheer design, form based on form alone, configurations without reference to reality or, at best, with dubious allusions to reality, then, we are almost forced to conclude, they cannot have had any ascertainable meaning—religious, cosmological, or mythological—meaning, at any rate of an established literary kind."[16]

[16] Loehr 1968: *Ritual Vessels of Bronze Age China*, New York.

This denial of meaning has been passed down to Loehr's students, most prominently Robert Bagley, who has declared, "The history of the motif suggests that Shang decoration is an art of pure design, without any specific symbolism attaching to particular motifs. The later versions of both dragon and *taotie*, with their protean shapes and incessant permutations, would seem to bear out this suggestion which was first made by Max Loehr."[17]

[17] Robert W Bagley in Fong, Wen C 1980: 'The Study of Chinese Bronze Age Arts: Methods and Approaches' in *The Great Bronze Age of China*, 20-34. New York: Metropolitan Museum of Art: 101. See also Bagley 1987: 49 -50.

In contrast to the Loehr school, a number of early attempts were made by western scholars to interpret the meaning of Shang bronze art, none of which are followed by modern scholarship. Karlgren himself wrote an early article on fecundity symbols in which he identified the cult of the earth god, *she*, as a phallic cult and identified the so-called 'bottle-horn' of the *kui*-dragon as a phallic representation.[18] Similarly, Phyllis Ackerman's *Ritual Bronzes of Ancient China*,[19] based on her studies of Near Eastern art, gave a prominent role to phallic symbols. Not only did Ackerman assume a common mode of thought between the Near East and China and interpret Chinese motifs accordingly, she believed in the diffusion of Near Eastern forms to China, as did many western writers of this period.

[18] Karlgren, Bernhard 1930: 'Some Fecundity Symbols in Ancient China,' *Bulletin of the Museum of Far Eastern Antiquities* 2.

[19] Ackerman, P 1945: *Ritual Bronzes of Ancient China*, New York.

The most prolific early advocate of an iconographic interpretation of Shang bronze motifs was Carl Hentze. Hentze theorised that lunar myth and symbolism was fundamental to early Chinese religion. On bronzes, buffalo horns represented the moon because of their crescent shape. The *taotie* was also a lunar divinity, representing not death and darkness but the liberator of light and life. In later studies, he included the sun and star cults in his interpretations and he brought the Chinese materials together with those of American Indians in an attempt to find circum-Pacific cultural links.[20] Florance Waterbury, on the other hand, argued that the *taotie* was a tiger and a solar rather than a lunar deity.[21]

[20] Hentze, Karl 1932: *Mythes et symboles lunaires*, Anvers. Hentze 1937: *Frühchinesische Bronzen und Kultdarstellungen*, Antwerp; Hentze 1941: *Die Sakralbronzen und ihre Bedeutung in den Frühchinesischen Kulturen*, 2 volumes, Antwerp.

[21] Waterbury, Florance 1942: *Early Chinese Symbols and Literature: Vestiges and Speculations*, New York.

These interpretations have had very little influence on later scholars. One reason is that Loehr's argument that the *taotie* originated in abstraction and that zoomorphic representations are relatively late and unimportant in Shang art has been very influential. It is impossible to understand the *taotie* motif with its continual permutations as having any representational model and so it cannot be understood as the depiction of any particular animal or deity. Another reason is that neither the psychological and the diffusionist hypotheses were formulated upon an analysis of early Chinese culture. They are entirely theoretical, built up upon suppositions about early China without any evidence from contemporaneous inscriptions or archaeological evidence and, as evidence has accumulated subsequently, they have not found any support.

A more recent response to the problem of understanding the meaning of the *taotie* and other bronze motifs has been the use of anthropological analogy. This analogy is made with Native American art which, as Hentze observed early on, often looks very much like Shang art although it is much later in time. Both Jordan Paper and Elizabeth Childs-Johnson have argued that the *taotie* represents a shaman's mask. According to Paper, the *taotie* is a "horned, jawless mask with body or remnant of body symmetrically attached to each side." He also noted that such split animal designs are circum-Pacific in occurrence and that in America a special headdress with horns or feathers was characteristic of shamanistic garb, the horns—a male characteristic in animals—symbolizing

Figure 7 • *A bronze* ding, *Late Shang period, Staatliches Museum für Volkerkunde (56-6-1), Munich (formerly von Lochow collection). Photo courtesy of the museum*

Figure 8 • A bronze yi, *Late Shang period, Museum Rietberg. Photo courtesy of the museum.*

superior power.[22] Childs-Johnson has also identified the *taotie* as a shaman's mask, stressing the mask's connotation of transformation of the spirit. In her analysis, she has also sought confirmation in the oracle bone inscriptions, citing, for example, the characters *gui* and *zhu* as evidence of the use of such masks in Shang times.[23]

K C Chang's interpretations of Shang bronze motifs are well-known through publications in Chinese as well as English. Chang has also relied on anthropological analogy with Native American cultures, as well as citing later Chinese texts, such as the *Shanhaijing*, which may have their origins in earlier oral traditions. Chang's interpretation places particular emphasis on a group of bronzes in which a man is held in the mouth of a tiger, such as the famous *you* jar in the collection of the Cernuschi Museum, Paris, said to have come from Hunan province (figure 9) and the almost identical vessel in the Sumitomo Collection, Kyoto. The same theme also occurs at Anyang—on a *yue* axe from the tomb of Fu Hao and the handles of the Simu Wu *ding*, but the other excavated examples are southern.

Parallel motifs are found in America and are associated with the idea of an alter ego — *i e* a child is given an animal at birth by a shaman who then acts as his protector, helper, companion and alter ego. The jaguar was associated with the highest ruling class in South America and had a mythological particular significance. Thus, Chang suggests, the tiger may also refer to the king in China and the man-beast motif to the king in his role of supreme shaman performing the act of crossing to the other world. Chang has further argued that the bronzes are decorated with mythological animals which served as agents of the shamans (*wu*) in communicating with the other world.[24]

Western scholars have criticised Chang's analysis on a number of different grounds. One objection is that the bronzes upon which his analysis is based are characteristically southern and not representative of the Shang. Another is that there is no evidence for shamanism in Shang religion as known from the oracle bone inscriptions. Shamanism is usually understood as involving spirit travel or possession from which divine knowledge is obtained, but the cracks on the oracle bones were a physical manifestation of the spirits' will which performed the same function as a shaman's flight. With the discovery of the Liangzhu jades, this criticism is less powerful than it appeared earlier. They cannot prove the existence of shamanism in the Shang, but they do include a motif in which man and animal are combined and the human figure wears a feathered headdress, the characteristic garb of a shaman; and this motif may well be the origin of the *taotie*.[25] A further objection is an art-historical one: Chang's thesis that the bronzes are decorated with mythological animals implies that they are representations and he assumes a realistic prototype. In this regard, he has made use of the sequence of development determined by Li Chi that is similar to Karlgren's in assuming the priority of realism and rejected by most modern art historians.[26]

In *The Shape of the Turtle: Myth, Art and Cosmos in Early China*, I attempted to resolve the problem of the meaning of the *taotie* and other motifs on Shang bronzes and proposed a new hypothesis concerning the meaning of the *taotie* and other Shang bronze motifs.[27] In order to meet the objections raised against previous theories, any hypothesis should be able to: *1)* account for the many permutations and transformations of the *taotie* in the Yinxu period; *2)* make sense of the historical development of the *taotie* from the Erligang to the Yinxu period, and also from the earlier Liangzhu jade motifs which influenced the bronze motif; *3)* relate the bronzes to Shang religion as known from oracle bone inscriptions and other archaeological remains.

A difficulty in attaching any particular meaning to the *taotie* as it appears

[22] Paper, Jordan 1978: 'The Meaning of the T'ao-t'ieh,' *Journal of the History of Religions* 18.1: 18-41.

[23] Childs-Johnson, Elizabeth 1987: 'The Ancestor Spirit and Animal Mask in Shang Ritual Art,' paper prepared for the International Symposium on the Yin-Shang Culture of China, 10-16 September, 1987, Anyang.

[24] K C Chang's works on this topic in English include Chang 1981: 'The Animal in Shang and Chou Bronze Art,' *Harvard Journal of Asiatic Studies* 41: 527-54; Chang 1983: Art, Myth and Ritual: The Path to Political Authority, Cambridge, Massachusetts: Yale University Press; Chang 1990: 'The Meaning of Shang Bronze Art,' *Asian Art* 3.2 (Spring 1990): 9-17.

[25] Li Xueqin 1993: 'Liangzhu Culture and the Shang Dynasty *taotie* motif,' in Roderick Whitfield 1993: 56-66.

[26] A summary and evaluation of the critiques of K C Chang's theories is given in Kesner, Ladislav 1991: 'Taotie Reconsidered: Meanings and Functions of Shang Theriomorphic Imagery,' *Artibus Asiae*, 41, 1/2: 29-53.

[27] Allan, Sarah 1991: The *Shape of the Turtle: Myth, Art and Cosmos in Early China*, Albany, New York.

on Yinxu bronzes is that it is continually changing. Its only constant feature is a pair of eyes, either round animal eyes or human eyes with pupils. It normally has a nose, at least an upper jaw, often with two fang-like canine teeth, ears and/or horns. The horns are those of various animals, most commonly sheep, oxen and deer. Ears may replace horns above the eyes (which often have human eyebrows), either the round ears associated with a tiger, or pointed ears which are difficult to identify. Human ears may also be placed at the side of the head. The animal face may have two bodies attached on the sides, often making a visual pun of a split animal which is also two animals facing one another. These bodies are most often one-legged, suggesting a water creature, and may detach themselves to become separate dragons. Even the horns themselves may be transformed into dragons.

The *taotie* has many different permutations and there is no clear line which divides one type of *taotie* motif from another. Since further potential permutations are always implied, a comprehensive classification of the different types of the motif is not possible. Yet anyone acquainted with Shang bronze art, however superficially, can readily identify the motif. Furthermore, although the constant permutations suggest that no real or imaginary creature could have served as a model, it is clearly animalistic with an admixture of human features. Western scholars who have offered iconographic interpretations have suggested that it is an ox, a tiger, a lion-griffin (a mythological creature in ancient Iran) and a mythological deity; but since it has no definite form, all of these suggestions must be rejected as Loehr and his students have argued. How then are we to interpret it, or should we accept their argument that it is simply meaningless design? We should, I believe, look for a different kind of meaning.

Shang art has many features in common with other so-called primitive arts. Thus I have formulated an hypothesis concerning the nature of primitive art more generally in order to provide an interpretative framework. This involves a broader theory which encompasses the nature of myth and mythic thought. The characteristic feature of myth, as I have defined it, is that it breaches the boundaries of natural reality. It does so not because early men were unaware of the limitations of the natural world, but deliberately, in order to force a suspension of ordinary logic. The breach serves as a sign that the tale is sacred rather than mundane, with a meaning which transcends that of ordinary reality. Similarly, so-called primitive art breaches the boundaries of physical reality, combining parts of different creatures, stretching this and shrinking that, making flat what should be round or round what should be flat. Such art is not abstract or geometric, but neither is it representational.

Many scholars have noted that writing is essential for the development of historical as opposed to mythological thinking.[28] Clearly, the Shang had a fully developed writing system with a long history before the Yinxu Period from which we have extant oracle bone inscriptions. My argument is that it is not writing itself, but the development of a corpus of literature which changes the way men think. In Shang times, the uses of writing appear to have been limited primarily, at least, to divination and prayer. Although there may have been some other documents, literature only became extensive during the Zhou. Historical records allow man to recognise historical change by giving the past a definite form which cannot be reshaped as memory becomes weaker and events more distant. Literature also has another important aspect: it allows us to externalise our thoughts. Once written down, our ideas have a life of their own and we can think about them, criticise them and contemplate their reality. Thus, at a certain point, a mode of artistic representation develops in which art is secondary to concepts, illustrating ideas that are essentially verbal. Such art may be interpreted iconographically because the symbols refer to literal concepts, but in mythic art, the motifs derive directly from the structure of religious beliefs rather than secondarily from articulated ideas. They allude to themes which are also present in myth but do not depict them.

In Shang bronze art, the many permutations of the *taotie*, *kui*-dragon, and other motifs are characteristic of primitive art as I have understood it. The

[28] See, for example, Goody, Jack 1968 ed. *Literacy in Traditional Societies*, Cambridge: Cambridge University Press, especially the paper by Jack Goody and Ian Watt, 'The Consequences of Literacy.'

Figure 9 • *A bronze* you, Late Shang period, Musée
Cernuschi, Paris (MC6155)

techniques by which reality is violated include disjunctions in which parts of different animals are combined in a single image, double images in which two animals can be seen simultaneously as one, transformations in which one creature or one of its parts becomes another. With a few very rare exceptions, even on the most representational bronzes, realism is contradicted by incongruous features, such as the wings of owls becoming snakes or horns added to a human face. Since the motifs are continually changing, the artist is clearly not seeking to portray real or even imaginary creatures, but he does make use of the natural world in forming his images. If we look to the oracle bone inscriptions and other archaeological remains for the religious context in which these images should be interpreted, we can begin to understand something of their meaning.

Shang bronzes include vessels and weapons. The vessels are analogous to those used by the living, but they were used to feed the dead or, in the case of water vessels, for ritual purification before offerings were made. Weapons are decorated with the same motifs as the vessels and were used for killing, either symbolically if they were ritual weapons, or actually. They include such types as *yue* axes used specifically for the killing of sacrificial victims and *ge*, also used for beheading (as in the character *fa*), either in ritual sacrifice or in warfare (which was in any case a means of garnering sacrificial victims). This cult of sacrifice was the focus of Shang religion, and I have argued that the entire system of oracle bone divination was intended to determine the appropriate sacrifices to the spirits so that they would not wreak random violence on the Shang people because of any unfulfilled needs.[29] We should look then to this context of ritual sacrifice and food offerings to the spirits for our understanding of the motifs which decorate the bronzes.

[29] Allan 1991: 112-23.

Many scholars have noted that the horns and ears of the *taotie* are those of animals used in sacrifice, such as sheep, oxen, deer, and tigers and, as I mentioned above, the motif often includes human as well as animal elements, such as eyebrows and human ears or nose. Thus they have argued the *taotie* represents sacrifices. My argument is, however, that it alludes to these animals and the theme of sacrifice, but it does not represent them. The *taotie* is also in part a dragon. Dragons, which also stand as an independent motif, are associated with the Yellow Springs, the watery underworld of the dead. Commonly, the *taotie* has an open mouth or the upper jaw alone may be depicted. Since these are, after all, implements in a cult of food offerings to the spirits, this suggests a theme of eating.

K C Chang has noted that an open animal mouth signifies passage to the other world in many cultures and argued that the man-in-tiger mouth motif on the Cernuschi *you* represents the crossing of the shaman or shaman-king to the other world. Since the animal is a tiger (at least primarily, for even on this vessel the motif is an admixture of animals) and the tiger was the prototype of a man-eating animal in Chinese culture, we may more reasonably suppose that the passage implied is that of death. As mentioned above, Chang's theories have been criticised on the grounds that they rely heavily on a small group of bronzes, mostly from the south. If, however, we look at the motifs on *yue* axes, we find that the theme may be implied even where it is not depicted. One of Chang's examples is a *yue* from the tomb of Fu Hao in which a human head is held between two tigers (figure 10b). This appears to be a split version of the same motif and the bottom border of the motif is also the upper jaw of a tiger. Thus the blade descends from the tiger mouth, as it does in another example from the Fu Hao tomb in which the motif is a simple *taotie* (see figure 10c). *Yue* with only a human face or simply eyes, such as figures 10e and 10f,

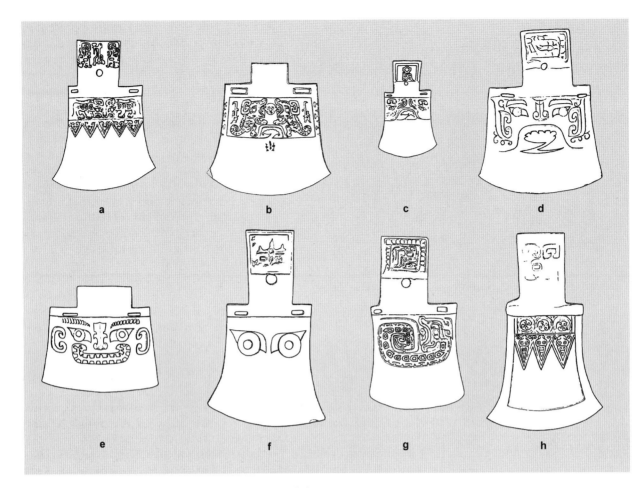

Figure 10 • Examples of bronze yue *axes of the Shang period*

may also be an abbreviation of this same theme, in which eating, killing and sacrifice are all associated.

Shang bronze motifs include allusions to a certain number of animals which were not used in sacrifice, such as snakes, cicadas, owls and elephants. Significantly, these animals are ones with unusual natural features that are used in many cultures throughout the world for their metaphoric value. Snakes are poisonous, slough their skins as they revive after hibernation and cause a physiological reaction of fear in all higher primates. The cicada burrows in the roots of trees, the number of years varying according to the species, and sheds its skin several times before emerging as a pupa and transforming itself into a flying insect. A more dramatic metaphor for transformation after death is difficult to imagine. Owls, associated in later Chinese folklore with death and therefore a bad omen, are birds of prey who come out at night. Animals such as these also suggest the themes of death and passage to the other world. The elephant, on the other hand, is the largest of all land animals and with his strange trunk appears almost supernatural, to breach the bounds of normal reality. In sum, although the motifs on the bronzes cannot be interpreted in the 'traditional literary sense' as iconography or understood in detail, they do make sense as allusions to the passage of death, eating and sacrifice, which was the central focus of Shang religion in which they functioned as vessels and weapons. The motifs are not representations, but their strange language allows the boundary between living and dead to be transcended.

Clearly, this complex imagery is not present in the Erligang period motif in which the *taotie* consists of two staring eyes, the suggestion of an animal face, and undefined bodies on each side. However, this interpretation allows us to make sense of the manner in which the *taotie* develops. All of the allusions

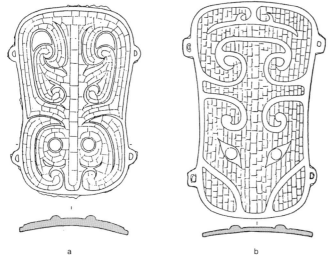

Figure 11 • *Bronze plaques inlaid with turquoise, the Erlitou culture, c1900 BC*

a

b

present in the later forms are not present in the Erligang period, but the early motif contains the seeds of the later complex imagery. The two staring eyes in the face of an animal —which is suggested but not clearly defined in the early motif—simply allude to the other world, that which sees, but cannot be seen or known precisely. As time passes, the motif is elaborated with familiar themes in Shang religion to become a more complex imagery alluding to the passage to the other world, as I have described briefly above. Such techniques as disjunction and continual permutation and a more precise form of double imagery replace the lack of clear definition in the earlier form. We can no longer, furthermore, see the *taotie* as beginning in the Erligang period and imagine, as Loehr did, that its origin was geometric design. Indeed, its ultimate origin appears to be the man and animal motif of Liangzhu jades. Bronzes were extremely crude in the Erlitou period and so largely undecorated (technological limitations may also account in part for the simplicity of the Erligang motif). However, even at Erlitou, a prototype of the *taotie* motif occurs on bronze plaques inlaid with turquoise (figure 11).

The theoretical nature of any interpretative framework for bronze motifs means that no analysis can be more than a plausible hypothesis, and my interpretations have proved no less contentious than earlier theories. My analysis began with the hypothesis that the bronzes do have meaning and attempted to discover what that meaning might be in the context of what we know about Shang religion and the ritual function of the bronzes. Robert Bagley, in a colloquy held in London in June 1990, argued that this involves an *a priori* assumption of meaning and that the *taotie* and other motifs on Shang bronzes may be ornament without any particular religious meaning. In a similar vein, Jessica Rawson argued that the *taotie* is a status marker. I accept that my argument is based on a premise of meaning, but I believe that such an assumption is more logical than the contrary premise that they are formal design without meaning. The motifs are not geometric abstractions even in their earliest stages. They clearly incorporate allusions to animals and people in a manner makes sense in terms of the ritual function of the bronzes in the Shang sacrificial cult and Shang religious beliefs more generally as known from contemporaneous inscriptions. Moreover, although participation in sacrifices which use bronze ritual artifacts was an elite activity, the suggestion that the *taotie* motif *per se* is associated with social or political status is purely theoretical. It is not supported by the pattern of occurrence of the motif itself.[30]

[30] Allan, Sarah 1993.

Just as Shang bronzes have been more highly regarded by western collectors than those of the Zhou, western scholars have, in general, been less interested in Zhou bronzes than those of the Shang. In *Yin and Chou in Chinese Bronzes*, Karlgren stressed the continuity of the early Western Zhou with the Shang and used his inscriptional analysis to define the reign of King Mu as the critical period in which Yin-Zhou style ceded to the Zhou. In her study of the Western Zhou bronzes in the Sackler collection, Jessica Rawson has taken up this theme, deeming the change of decorative motifs and the loss of certain vessel types, such as the *jue* and *gu*, in King Mu's reign as a 'ritual revolution.'[31]

[31] Rawson, Jessica 1990: *Western Zhou Ritual Bronzes from the Arthur M. Sackler Collections*, Cambridge, Mass: Arthur M Sackler Foundation.

A more sophisticated account of the changes which took place at the beginning of the Western Zhou has recently been offered by Wu Hung in his *Monumentality in Early Chinese Art and Architecture*. By carefully analysing the evolution of inscription formulae, Wu Hung demonstrates a gradual change of the ritual and social function of bronze vessels at the beginning of the Zhou. Thus, he sees the increasing patternisation of Zhou bronze styles as reflecting a change of emphasis from ancestor to living devotee and from temple to palace, reflected in both bronze inscriptions and ritual practice.[32]

[32] Wu Hung 1995: *Monumentality in Early Chinese Art and Architecture*, Stanford: Stanford University Press, 53-63, 77-78.

Conclusion

In the last 20 years, Chinese archaeology has spread across the country and Shang bronzes have been found in almost every province, many of them from the early period of the dynasty. These finds have outstripped the materials in western collections and the study of Chinese bronzes is now at a critical juncture. Entirely new theoretical models are required to account for this archaeological evidence. These are some examples of current problems:

• Shang and Zhou bronze art can no longer be seen as a self-generating stylistic evolution which took place on the central plains and spread from there outward. A new, non-linear model which can explain the stylistic interplay between the central plains and other contemporaneous cultures is required.

• The only model for stylistic development of bronze motifs in the Shang period remains that of Max Loehr. However, we now know that all of his five styles were fully developed at the beginning of the Yinxu period, so that there is no longer any stylistic model for the development of bronze decoration at Yinxu.

• Most scholars now accept that there was a connection between the man and animal motif on Liangzhu jades and the *taotie*, but how this transformation took place stylistically remains unclear and its implications for the interpretation of the *taotie* have not been fully explored.

Agriculture and Early Cities

REN SHINAN

Prehistoric Agriculture in China

Neolithic culture in ancient China was principally based on farming activities. The discovery of abundant remains of both cultivated plants and domesticated animals, together with those of related wild species, indicates that China was one of the centres where agriculture originated. It is possible that agriculture may have developed simultaneously with pottery making and signalled the beginning of the Neolithic Age. As early as the initial stage of the Chinese Neolithic Age, pottery has usually been found in association with the remains of cultivated plants.

This paper discusses mainly the remains of cultivated plants and domesticated animals in the prehistoric context, leaving aside other problems such as the environment, farming implements, methods and stages of cultivation, and their social implications.

Recent Discoveries of Rice Cultivation, c10,000 BC

In southern China, two cave sites have recently been excavated, containing the earliest remains of rice so far discovered. This constitutes an important advance in the study of the origin of rice cultivation, although the actual remains were scanty. At Daoxian Yuchanyan, Hunan province, chipped stone tools and polished bone artefacts were excavated in association with coarse black-brown pottery sherds containing charcoal fragments. Examination of the remains of seeds, peel, husks, shells, leaves and stems, including a very few rice husks, revealed more than 40 species of plants.[1] Both wild rice and rice with the characteristics of cultivated rice (*Oryza sativa* L) were identified. The two types of cultivated rice were *xian*, the long-grained, non-glutinous type (*O. sativa* L subsp *Hsien Ting*); and *jing*, round-grained (*O. sativa* L subsp *Keng Ting*). Such a mixture indicates an early stage in the development of rice cultivation. In addition, fossilised remains of rice have been detected. The same strata contained a large assortment of 30 or 40 types of animal bones including mammals, birds, domestic fowls and aquatic creatures. Thus, although hunting, fishing and gathering served as the principal means of subsistence, an early form of rice cultivation had appeared. A radiocarbon

[1] Yuan Jiarong 1996: 'Yuzhanyan huo shuidao qiyuan xin wuzheng,' *Zhongguo wenwubao*, March 3, 1996.

This paper was first presented at a conference at the British Museum in December 1996 in conjunction with the exhibition, *Mysteries of China*.

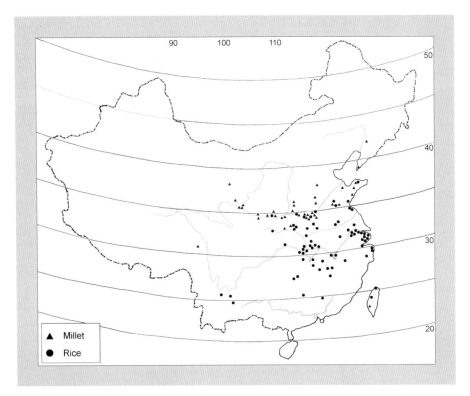

Figure 1 • Millet and rice cultivation sites

date of 10,110 ± 120 BC (uncalibrated) is available from a similar site, the Sanjiaoyan cave site.

At Wannian Diaotonghuan, Jiangxi province, the lower strata of a rock shelter site yielded chipped stone tools but no pottery sherds, while the upper strata included partly polished stone tools, bone artefacts, perforated shell objects and coarse pottery sherds, with numerous animals bones and plentiful remains of pollen and fossilised remains similar to rice.[2] This site appears to have been a temporary camp and slaughterhouse, while the nearby Xianrendong (Spirit Cave), which had previously been excavated and which has similar cultural features, was a dwelling. According to the C14 dates for the two sites, the upper strata of Diaotonghuan can be dated to c12,000-7000 BC, that is to the early neolithic, while the lower strata may be from the end of the palaeolithic or from the mesolithic.

[2] Liu Shizhong 1996: 'Jiangxi Xianrendong he Diaotonghuan fajue huo zhongyao jinzhang,' *Zhongguo wenwubao*, January 1, 1996.

Rice Cultivation in Central, South China and the Yellow River Valley

More than 140 prehistoric sites have yielded remains of rice cultivation. The majority, about 80 per cent, are found in the middle and lower reaches of the Yangzi River valley, between latitude 33° and 28° North (figure 1). At present there is a gap between the earliest evidence of rice cultivation and its distributions in the middle neolithic period. In the middle Yangzi River valley, evidence of rice cultivation occurs in a series of neolithic cultures from the Pengtoushan culture (c6900-6300 BC) onwards. At the Li xian Pengtoushan site in Hunan province, impressions of rice husks were discovered in lumps of burnt clay, and carbonised rice husks and small rice-straw fragments occur in the tempering in the clay body of pottery sherds.[3]

In the Daxi culture (c4400-3300 BC), analysis of carbonised specimens from the Chengtoushan site showed 79 per cent of long-grained *xian* rice (mainly small-grained subspecies of average 4.27mm length), 18 per cent round-grained *jing* rice, and three per cent of intermediate species. In the Qujialing culture in Hubei province, impressions of rice-husks from the Jingshan Qujialing site (c3000-2600 BC) measured on average 6.97 mm long and 3.47 mm wide; they belong to the *jing* type, with larger-sized grains.[4]

[3] Gu Haibing 1996: 'Hunan Lixian Chengtoushan yizhi chutu de xinshiqi shidai shuidao jiqi leixing,' *Kaogu* 1996 (8), 81-89, Pei Anping 1989: 'Pengtoushan wenhua de daozuo yicun yu zhongguo shiqian daozuo nongye,' *Nongye kaogu* 1989(2): 102-8.

[4] Ding Ying 1959: 'Jiang Han pingyuan xinshiqi shidai hongshaotu de daoguke kaocha,' *Kaogu xuebao* 1959(4): 31-34.

In the lower Yangzi valley, large quantities of rice remains were found in the Hemudu culture (c5000-3300 BC) and the Majiabang culture (c5000-4000 BC). At the Yuyao Hemudu site and Tongxiang Luojiajiao sites, both in Zhejiang province, most of the rice found was of the long-grained *xian* type, with 23-24 per cent of *jing* rice, and four per cent of intermediate types. The rice grains from these sites are estimated to have weighed 22g per thousand grains.[5]

The southernmost site of rice cultivation yet discovered in China is at the Qujiang Shixia site (c3000-2000 BC) in Guangdong province (latitude 24°41' North). Rice and husks were found in storage pits, tombs and in lumps of burnt clay on building sites. Both *xian* and *jing* types were found, the former in the majority. The length and width of the grains vary, suggesting that various species were mixed together.[6]

In the prehistoric cultural system of the Yellow River valley, where foxtail millet was extensively grown, remains of rice have been recorded at more than 10 localities, providing evidence of the simultaneous cultivation of different cereal crops in prehistoric northern China.[7] The earliest remains are from c6000 BC, represented by the Dadiwan culture sites of Xixiang Hejiawan and Lijiacun, Shaanxi province, and the Peiligang culture site of Wuyang Jiahu in Henan province. At the Jiahu site, impressions of rice husks and stems and fragments of rice phytolith were found in lumps of burnt clay: most of them were *xian* rice, with a smaller proportion of *jing* rice.[8] Later evidence of rice cultivation recurs in sites of the Yangshao culture and Central Plains Longshan cultures in the middle reaches of the Yellow River valley, and in the Dawenkou and Longshan cultures in the lower reaches of the Yellow River valley. The chronology of these sites shows the advance of rice cultivation from south to north. The northernmost site of rice cultivation in prehistoric China occurs in the Shandong Longshan culture at the Qixia Yangjiaquan site (c2300 BC; latitude 37°18' N), where *jing* rice and fox-tailed millet were discovered together in a storage pit.

Rice culture in Asia resulted from the domestication of ordinary perennial wild species (*O. sativa* var. *spontanica*), with the long-grained *xian* rice appearing first, and the round-grained *jing* rice occurring as a variant type. The main conditions for such a transformation are changes of climate and selective cultivation. Another opinion holds that the two types of *xian* and *jing* evolved independently from two wild species. Further research is needed on this question.[9]

In general, *xian* rice is not as resistant to cold as *jing* rice. Such differences in adaptability led to differences in their respective regional distribution. However, within certain climatic limits, by taking into consideration the nature and characteristics of the rice types, and adopting the appropriate preparation of the ground for cultivation, both *xian* and *jing* may be cultivated in the same place. From the morphological aspect the ratio of length to width varies, from 2.3:1 upwards for *xian* rice, and from 1.6:1 to 2.3:1 for *jing* rice.

The differentiation of the two species occurred at an early date in prehistoric China. The general pattern is that the earlier the date, the greater the proportion of *xian* rice, and the later the date, the greater the proportion of *jing* rice. However, there was not such a clear differentiation between the two species as there is today between different types of modern rice. With Hemudu rice as example, the size and morphological characteristics of the grains vary to some extent, and a small number of intermediate types are still present: these all came from the same site, which provides evidence for the multifarious nature of early rice cultivation.

Dry Land Cereal Crops: Foxtail Millet and Broomcorn Millet

Prehistoric farming in the northern, northeastern regions of China and on the Tibetan plateau was mainly a dry land millet agriculture. Remains of millet have been discovered at some 60 sites (figure 1), the earliest of which, represented by the Cishan and Peiligang cultures, can be dated to c6000 BC. At the Wu'an Cishan site, Hebei province, 88 pits with foxtail millet were excavated.[10] The cereal remains in them had been piled up to a thickness of 0.3 to 2.2 m. This is the richest

[5] Zhejiang 1978 (Zhejiang sheng bowuguan ziranzu): 'Hemudu yizhi dongzhiwu yicun de jianding yanjiu,' *Kaogu xuebao* 1978(1): 95-107; You Xiuling and Zheng Yunfei 1995: 'Hemudu daogu yanjiu jinzhan ji zhanwan,' *Nongye kaogu* 1995(1): 66-70.

[6] Guangdong 1978 (Guangdong sheng bowuguan): 'Guangdong Qujiang Shixia muzang fajiu jianbao,' *Wenwu* 1978(7): 1-15; Yang Shiting 1978: 'Qiantan Shixia faxian de Zaipeidao yiji,' *Wenwu* 1978(7): 23-28.

[7] Wu Yaoli 1994.

[8] Zhang Juzhong *et al* 1994.

[9] Tang Shengxiang, Wen Shaokai and Y I Sato 1994: 'Zhongguo jingdao qiyuan de tantao,' *Nongye kaogu* 1994(1): 59-67.

[10] Hebei 1981 (Hebei sheng wenguanchu and Handanshi wenguansuo): 'Hebei Cishan yizhi,' *Kaogu xuebao* 1981(3): 303-338.

find of this type of millet in the prehistoric period in China. The other early site is the Xuchang Dingzhuang site of the Peiligang culture in Henan province, where carbonised millet was found, with grains of length 1.73 mm, width 1.68 mm and thickness 1.36 mm. Their size and weight per thousand grains show that the quality of this millet reached the level of present-day spring-sown millet, and was even superior to summer-sown millet as grown today in North China, indicating the advanced level of millet cultivation in prehistoric China.[11]

Broomcorn millet (*Panicum miliaceum*) has been found in fewer sites, about 10 in all, than foxtail millet. At the Qin'an Dadiwan Phase I site in Gansu province, Xinzheng Peiligang in Henan province, and the lower stratum of Shenyang Xinle site, Liaoning province, all dating from c6000-5000 BC, broomcorn millet was found. After c5000 BC, there is evidence for this cereal found at sites extending from Gansu and Qinghai provinces to the Shandong coastal area.

One should note that some important evidence for the cultivation of wheat and barley (*Hordeum vulgare* L) has been discovered in recent years. At Yanzhou Xiwu site of the Shandong Longshan culture, the cultural deposits yielded plentiful quantities of pollen of certain grasses (Gramineae) of a type close to wheat (*Triticum* cf *aestivum* L).[12] At the Wugong Zhaojialai site in Shaanxi province, straw embedded in wall plaster has been identified as wheat straw by two independent institutions.[13] The Zhaojialai site also yielded carbonised foxtail millet. These two sites can be dated to c2500-2200 BC.

In the Bronze Age, at Minle Donghuishan site in Gansu province, carbonised grains were found in quantity, including three different types of wheat, two types of barley, foxtail millet, broomcorn millet, and sorghum (*Sorghum vulgare*).[14]

Cultivation of Vegetables and Other Plants

At Qin'an Dadiwan I site (c5600-5400 BC) in Gansu province, some rape seeds were excavated from a storage pit,[15] together with the broomcorn millet mentioned above. At Xi'an Banpo site (c5000-4500 BC) in Shaanxi province, a small pottery jar was found to contain Chinese cabbage seeds (*Brassica chinensis*), probably stored for sowing.

In the lower reaches of the Yangzi River, after 5000 BC, a series of sites such as Yuyao Hemudu, Tongxiang Luojiajiao in Zhejiang province, Qingpu Songze near Shanghai, Hangzhou Shuitianfan in Zhejiang province, and Wujian Longnan in Jiangsu province, all yielded gourd seeds and peel. The young fruits and tender leaves of gourds can be used as food, but they have to be picked from cultivated species, as wild gourds are very bitter and astringent. It is generally accepted that the gourd was brought into cultivation in prehistoric times. Apart from their use as food, gourds can be used to make containers, floats, and musical instruments.

From the fourth stratum at the Hemudu site, seeds and pollen of legumes were unearthed: these have been identified by some scholars as the remains of soya bean (*Glycine max*), and by others as black soya bean. Seeds of legumes were also discovered at Nanzhen Longgangsi, Shaanxi province. The above two sites can be dated c5000 BC or slightly later. In the Miaodigou II culture, calcified beans were found in a pottery jar at Fufeng Anban site, Shaanxi province;[16] legume seeds were also present in Lixian Chengtoushan, Hunan province, a site of the Daxi-Qujialing culture. Both are dated to c3000-2600 BC.

In the Dongxiang Linjia site, Gansu province, belonging to the Majiayao culture (c3100-2700 BC), two pottery jars from a dwelling foundation contained hemp seeds, identified as carl-hemp (*Cannabis sativa*).[17] They may have been used for sowing, but hemp seeds can also be used as food after steaming, or pressed to make edible oil. Hemp fibre is also a traditional textile material.

Domesticated Animals and Their Uses

Domesticated animals in prehistoric China included pig, sheep, dog, horse and fowls. In addition, the silkworm was reared for the production of silk. The earliest evidence for the domestication of dogs (*Canis familiaris* L) is found at Xushui

[11] Zhang Fupeng 1986: 'Guzi de qiyaun yu fenleishi yanjiu,' *Zhongguo nongshi* 1986(1): 110-115.

[12] Guojia 1990 (Guojia wenwuju kaogu lingdui peixunban): *Baozhou Xiwusi*, Beijing: Wenwu chubanshe, appendix 3.

[13] Zhongguo 1988 (Zhongguo shehui kexue yanjiuyuan kaogu yanjiusuo): *Wugong fajue baogao - Huxizhuan yu Zhaojialai yizhi*, Beijing: Wenwu chubanshe, 156.

[14] Li Fan *et al* 1989: 'Gansu Minle xian Huishan xin shiqi yizhi nongye yicun xin faxian,' *Nongye kaogu*, 1989(1): 56-69, 73.

[15] Gansu 1982 (Gansu sheng bowuguan, Qinan xian wenhuaguan): 'Yijiu baling nian qinan Dadiwan yiqi wenhua yicun,' *Kaogu yu wenwu* 1982(2): 1-4.

[16] Xie Wei 1988: 'Anban yizhi huitu zhong suojian dao de nongzuowu,' *Kaogu yu wenwu*, 1988(5/6): 209-213.

[17] Gansu 1984 (Gansu sheng wenwudui *et al*): 'Gansu Dongxiang Linjia yizhi fajue baogao,' *Kaoguxue jikan* 4: 111-161, Xibei 1984 (Xibei shiyuan zhiwu yanjiusuo and Gansu shen bowuguan): 'Gansu Dongxiang Linjia Majiayao wenhua yizhi chutu de ji yu dama,' *Kaogu* 1984(7): 654-655.

[18] Baoding 1992 (Baoding diqu wenguansuo, Beida kaoguxi, Hebei daxue lishixi): 'Hebei Xushui xian Nanzhuangtou yizhi shi jue jianbao,' *Kaogu* 1992(11): 961-970.

[19] Nanjing 1981 (Nanjing bowuyuan): 'Jiangsu Pi xian Dadunzi yizhi dierci fajue,' *Kaoguxue jikan* 1: 27-81.

[20] The character *jia* ('family') may provide further evidence of the domestication of the pig. The meaning of the character is to settle down in a house, and it consists of two elements: the roof of the house and a pig. It can be inferred that raising pigs may have become a basic activity of domestication and that pigs under the roof had come to represent property as an important indicator of wealth.

[21] Li Youheng, Han Defeng 1978: 'Guangxi Guilin Zengpiyan yizhi dongwuqun,' *Gujizui dongwu yu gu renlei* 16-4: 244-254.

[22] Shaanxi 1990 (Shaanxi sheng kaogu yanjiusuo): *Longgangsixinshiqi shidai yizhi fajue baogao*, Beijing: Wenwu chubanshe.

Nanzhuangtou, Hebei province (c10000-8700 BC).[18] After 6000 BC, dog bones are frequently found in sites of different regions. They are usually broken: even the skulls are often badly broken, suggesting that dogs were consumed as food. In Pi xian Dadunzi site of the Dawenkou culture, Jiangsu province, a clay model of a house was incised with a dog on the wall, implying the use of dogs as watchdogs.[19] Sometimes dogs were intentionally buried in pits as sacrificial victims and, in a few cases, dogs were buried in tombs beside the dead, perhaps in order to guard the spirit.

Like dogs, the remains of domesticated pigs have been found in considerable numbers. Being easy to feed and reproducing at a considerable rate, the pig has always been a principal source of meat supply.[20] Pig bones have also been unearthed from the Nanzhuangtou site. A considerable amount of evidence is found at the Cishan site, dated to c6000 BC, where the pig remains belong mainly to piglets, slaughtered when still young. At the Dawenkou site, after 4000 BC, the pig bones that have been found are usually larger in size and belonged to adult pigs, reflecting an advance in animal husbandry. In southern China, pig bones occurred at Daoxian Yuchanyan, Hunan province, dating earlier than 8000 BC, although these cannot be confirmed as belonging to a domesticated species. At the Guilin Zengpiyan site (c7000-5500 BC) in Guangxi province, pig remains were discovered in quantity: they had been raised for one or two years before slaughtering. At one period, pig mandibles were commonly buried in tombs as funerary offerings, presumably to indicate the wealth of the occupant.[21] This custom prevailed especially in the prehistoric cultures of the Yellow River valley.

Cattle raising appeared very early in the Hua'nan region in the south. Its beginning can be traced to c6900 BC, as buffalo bones (*Bubalus bubalus*) were unearthed from Lixian Pengtoushan and Shimen Zaoshi, both in Hunan province, and from Zhijiang Chengbeixi, Hubei province. Remains of swamp buffaloes with short horns were found at Hemudu. It is very likely that in southern China the buffalo was used for field treading, an important part of soil preparation before sowing. In northern China the earliest finds of cattle bones come from the Cishan and Peiligang cultures, dated from c6000 BC. Later, oxen (*bos exiguus*) became the main species in prehistoric cattle-raising, although in some areas buffaloes were bred along with oxen (at Wangyin and Keshengzhuang) or alone (at Jian'gou).

Sheep made their first appearance in the Dadiwan and Lower Zaoshi cultures, dating from c6000 BC. The early evidence is scattered, but they occur more frequently and in increasing quantity in sites of the Yangshao culture; an outstanding example is the Nanzhen Longgangsi site in Shaanxi province, where 61 sheep bones were unearthed and have been identified as the remains of domesticated sheep (*Capra* sp).[22] Among the various domestic animals found in this locality, sheep were found in the highest numbers. By the time of the Longshan culture, sheep breeding had become very common in both north and south China: both the sheep (*Ovis aries*) and the goat (*Capra hircus* L) were raised.

Bones of the horse (*Equus* sp) have been discovered in small numbers. It would seem that horses had begun to be bred by the Longshan period.

The history of domesticated fowls also began extremely early in prehistoric China. Chicken bones were discovered at Xuzhuangtou. Other finds came from the Cishan site in Hebei province: they represent a species that was larger than the present-day wild chicken (*Gallus gallus* L), but smaller than the present-day domesticated chicken (*Gallus gallus domesticus* L). The remains are largely bones of male birds, probably reflecting the use of cockerels for food and sacrifice, while hens were kept to lay eggs. Evidence of chicken breeding was recorded at the Jiahu site of the Peiligang culture in Henan and the Beixin site of the Beixin culture in Shandong. Chicken remains have frequently been discovered in the sites of later periods, showing that the chicken had become one of the major types of domestic fowl in the prehistoric economy.

In addition, statistic analysis of deer-bones (*Cervus* sp.) from the Lintong Jiangzhai site of Yangshao culture, Shaanxi province, shows that remains of the sika deer (*Cervus nippon*) are the most numerous, second only in number of individuals to those of the domestic pig from this site.[23] Their age, like that of the pigs, was rather young. The sika deer is relatively easy to domesticate, due to its habits and character. Archaeologists and scientists believe that the deer may have already been bred and controlled by man at this time.

Discoveries of the silkworm have been made in the Yangshao culture: one half of a silkworm cocoon was excavated at Xiaxian Xiyincun, Shaanxi province,[24] while silk and hemp textiles survived in a child's burial at Xingyang Qingtaicun, Henan province. Two clay silkworm models found at Zhending Nanyangzhuang, Hebei province, are much like the larva of the domestic silkworm.[25] Their appearance and proportions of length and width, especially the horizontal segments between thorax and abdomen, are like those of the domestic silkworm, suggesting that the maker of these models knew their features very well. Another pottery model of a silkworm was found at Ruicheng Xiwangcun, Shaanxi province, while other evidence includes four jade silkworms from Naisitai, in Barin youqi, Inner Mongolia and a silkworm-shaped marble ornament from Jingxi Shaguotun, Liaoning province. All of these finds show that from c4000 BC onwards, people had begun to engage in the rearing of silkworms and in silk weaving.[26]

The most striking discovery was made at Hangzhou Qianshanyang, Zhejiang province, where ribbons made of silk and fragments of plain weave silk were unearthed from a site of the Liangzhu culture.[27] At the same time, the silkworm was depicted on a black pottery vessel from Wujian Meinian, Jiangsu province. Prehistoric silkworm rearing must have originated and developed independently in north and south China.

Conclusion

In agricultural economy and production man works directly on the land to grow crops and obtain food. The emergence of agriculture is not an isolated event, but is the culmination of a long process leading from the gathering of food to the cultivation of plants and the domestication of animals, in which process people gained a high level of skills and knowledge of techniques for the production of food and other commodities. At the end, from simply gathering materials from nature, this led to the increase and improvement of food supplies. In particular, grain cereals were especially easy to gather and to store for seasons when the harvest failed.

In the vast territory of prehistoric China, animal husbandry served to supplement farming, and became in a wide sense an integral part of agriculture. Both omnivorous and herbivorous domestic animals existed, but pigs and dogs were dominant. In certain areas in the Bronze Age, herbivorous animals such as sheep, horses and oxen were bred, together forming the basis for an independent pastoral economy

New evidence from Daoxian Yuchongyan and Wannian Diaotonghuan suggests that in the initial stages of agriculture, with the restrictions of a limited productive workforce, people tended to live in the foothills of mountains, so that they could alternate between cave-dwelling and living in the open, according to changes in the weather; there were no permanent architectural settlements. Hunting, fishing and gathering were still the principal means of survival, but at the same time small-scale horticultural farming came into being and people began to grow vegetables, melons and root-crops alongside a small proportion of cereals. Animals began to be domesticated at the same time. We may call this a mixed economy. Simple plain pottery was also made at this time. Evidence for this type of production goes back to 10000 BC. Around 7000 to 6000 BC the proportion of agricultural activities increased, to become predominant in economic production, and more permanent settlements appeared, forming an agricultural society in the full sense of the term.

[23] Xi'an 1988 (Xi'an Banpo bowuguan): *Jianzhai - xinshiqi shidai yizhi fajue baogao*, Beijing: Wenwu chubanshe, appendix 3.

[24] Li Chi 1927: *Xiyingcun shiqian de yicun*. Peking, Qinghua xuexiao yanjiuyuan congshu, No 3.

[25] Guo Ru 1987: 'Cong Hebeisheng Zhengding Nanyangzhuang chutu de taochangyong shilun woguo jiachang de qiyuan wenti,' *Nongye kaogu* 1987(1): 302-309.

[26] Gao Hanyu 1981: 'Cong chutu wenwu zhuishuo cansiye de qiyuan,' *Cansang tongbao* 12 (1): 17-24, Tang Yunming 1985: 'Woguo yuchang zhichou qiyuan shidai cutan,' *Nongye kaogu* 1985(2): 320-323.

[27] Xu Hui, Ou Qiuming 1981: 'Dui Qiansanyang chutu sizhipin de yanzheng,' *Sichou* 1981(2): 43-45.

To put this subject in a global perspective, China is one of the earliest centres in which agriculture originated. Due to its vast territory, comprising both hinterland and coastal areas, there is a large difference of environment between different regions. However, in terms of both domestication and cultivation, there were two types of agriculture, southern and northern, with the Qinling and Huaihe as the dividing line. This division holds good for rice and millet, as well as for pigs of southern and northern type, buffaloes and cattle, all of which might have originated independently in the different regions where early agriculture was first developed. We should pay special attention to such new evidence. There is an important link between prehistoric types of wheat and the wild species to which they are related within China: just as there are many regional variant types of modern wheat in China, so it is reasonable to assume that Chinese wheat also has an indigenous origin.

Artefacts from the Shijiahe site (detail)

ZHANG CHI AND OKAMURA HIDENORI

Excavation of Cities: Shijiahe and Yinxiangcheng

T he discovery of large walled sites from the middle Yangzi River valley during the 1990s has provided the impetus for examining the development of complex societies. Our discussions about the origins of Chinese civilisation have focused on the walled sites during the third millennium BC.

Shijiahe

The Shijiahe site is located within Tianmen county, Hubei province, in the middle reaches of the Yangzi and Han Rivers. Its discovery, excavation and research are important for the study of the prehistory of the middle reaches of the Yangzi. In 1954, rescue excavations were conducted at the Shijiahe area (figure 1), including Guanpingyuan (Yangjiawan), at Sanfangwan, Shibanchong and Luojiaboling; at Luojiaboling, excavation covered an area of over 1,400 square metres and revealed large-scale architectural remains and a group of distinctive red pottery with regional characteristics.[1] In the 1960s and 1970s, remains of the same type were found in the middle reaches of the Yangzi River, and were variously named as Qinglongquan culture III, Guihuashu culture III, Jijiahu culture, or Hubei Longshan culture. In the mid-1980s, a general agreement was reached to rename these cultures as the Shijiahe culture, after the Shijiahe site where the culture was first identified, dated to c2500-2000 BC.

Apart from a number of small-scale surveys conducted during the early 1980s, no further archaeological work was undertaken at the Shijiahe site during this period. In the later 1980s, the department of Archaeology of Peking University, the Hunan Provincial Institute of Archaeology and Cultural Relics, and the Jingzhou Regional Museum, collectively conducted major excavations of Shijiahe sites, including the Xiaojiawuji,

[1] Shilong 1956 (Shilong guojiang shuiku zhihuibu wenwu gongzuodui): 'Hubei Jingshan Tianmen kaogu fajue baogao,' *Kaogu tongxun* 1956(3): 11-21.

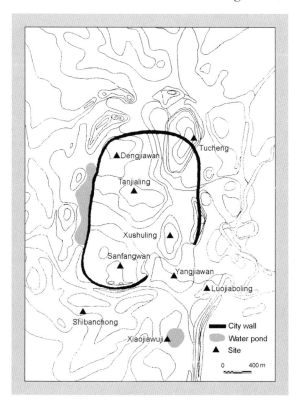

Figure 1 • Map of the Shijiahe site

Tanjialing, Dengjiawan and Tucheng sites.[2] Archaeologists realised that the Shijiahe site constituted a large-scale settlement of 20 to 30 smaller sites. In 1990 and 1991, a comprehensive survey and further excavation revealed that the Shijiahe neolithic site can be divided into three different phases. The earliest settlements, which belonged to the middle to late period of the Daxi culture (c4000-2800 BC),[3] were located near the centre of the site, but the actual scale of these settlements is not clear. The second phase is that of the Qujialing culture and the early to middle Shijiahe culture phase (c2800-2300 BC). During this period, the site was at its most developed, with settlements covering about eight square kilometres, 2.4 kilometres from east to west and 3.6 kilometres from south to north. By the later period of the Qujialing culture, a large walled city had already been constructed in the centre of the site, and this city was used continuously throughout the early and middle period of the Shijiahe culture, and abandoned thereafter. During the later Shijiahe phase (c2300-2000 BC), the archaeological remains, extending over a million square metres, lay mainly in the southeastern section of the site. The following report will discuss the newly discovered walled settlement of the Qujialing culture and the early-middle Shijiahe culture.

The Shijiahe site is in fact a group of settlements, the main part of which consists of the walled city in the centre, with simple small settlements around it, dating to the Qujialing culture and the early-middle Shijiahe culture. Because these settlements are interrelated, we can treat them as a single site. This is located in the northern part of the Jiang-Han plain, in the middle reaches of the Yangzi River, now Tianmen county, Hubei province. The topographical features of the area present a combination of hills which are the eroded lower slopes of Mt Dahong to the north, and the Jiang-Han plain to the south, formed by the floodplain of the Tianmen River, a branch of the Han River. The major part of the Shijiahe site is located at the junction of these two types of terrain, between two rivers whose confluence is located in the southern part of the site. The west river has a deep-cut waterway that shows no evidence of having changed course, while the east river is rather shallow, and may have changed course in the past. Over the past 40 years, the southern part of the site has been affected by man-made construction. In the western part of the site, the settlements reach only as far as the west river, but to the east there are many settlements beyond the east river. The walled city was constructed during the Qujialing culture period, in the triangle formed by the confluence of the two rivers. It slopes down from the northwest to the southeast. The city was an oblong rectangle with rounded corners, 1,300 metres from south to north, and 1,200 metres from east to west. The city wall, built in lightly stamped layers of about 10 centimetres each layer, is 50 metres wide at the base, and 15 metres wide at the top. From the bottom of the outer ditch to the top of the wall is about six metres. The southern and western sections of the city wall remain in good condition; the northeastern corner was infringed by a smaller city wall and ditch dating to the Western Zhou period. The eastern wall survives for a length of 400 metres, and there is a missing section of about 450 metres in the southeastern corner, the lowest area of the city, perhaps to allow for flooding; there may originally have been a wooden fence. The ditch around the outside of the walls is about 4,800 metres long, and is between 80 and 100 metres wide at its widest, and 40 to 60 at its narrowest point. The bottom of the ditch still has an accumulation of thick black-brown silt, indicating that it was once filled with water: some sections of the ditch still contain water, as in the eastern section at Luojiabo. Beyond the ditch in the southwest and northwest there is a platform; this probably resulted from the digging of the ditch and was left after the wall had been constructed. It is difficult to calculate the actual amount of soil moved, but at a rough guess, it must have been at least 500,000 cubic metres.

The scale of the city is over 1,200,000 square metres, with the northern, west and southern areas higher than the remainder. At the highest point is the Tanjialing site, and the lowest point is in the southeast. The cultural remains

[2] Shihe 1990 (Shihe kaogudui): 'Hubei sheng Shihe yizhiqun 1987 nian fajue jianbao,' *Wenwu* 1990(8): 1-16; the same author, 1994 (Shihe kaogudui): 'Hubei Tianmen Dengjiawan yizhi 1992 nian fajue jianbao,' *Wenwu* 1994(4): 32-41; Zhang Chi 1990: 'Shijiahe yizhi diwuci fajue huo xin chengguo,' *Zhongguo wenwu bao* May 4, 1990.

[3] Beijing 1992 (Beijing daxue kaoguxi): 'Shijiahe yizhi diaocha baogao,' *Nanfang minzu kaogu* 5: 213-294.

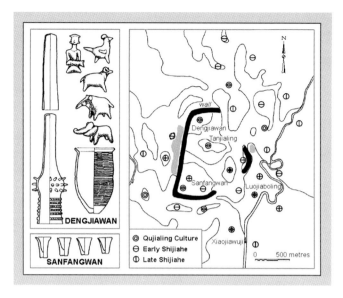

Figure 2 • The Shijiahe site and artefacts discovered

within the city were mostly deposited within the period of the Qujialing culture and the early-middle phases of the Shijiahe culture. A ground survey revealed large-scale architectural remains of burnt clay in the southeastern section, in the centre and in the northern section. Since the mid-1980s, there have been excavations at three points in Tanjialing, where the remains of architecture as thick as two to three metres have been found. Their stratification is complicated, indicating a long period of occupation. Houses were divided into rooms with walls about one metre thick. Holes for pillars have a diameter of about 30 centimetres, set about 50 centimetres apart. The excavation was conducted on a small scale, and no complete multi-roomed house could be excavated. In 1987, archaeologists exhibited six house foundations of the Qujialing culture, among which there was a single-room building, of rectangular shape, 4.76 metres long and 3.34 metres wide. The wall is 40 centimetres thick. There are two entrances, in the north and east. In the southern part of the room a carbonised bamboo mat was found. In the centre, towards the south, was a circular hearth. There are pottery vessels such as adouble-based bowl and double-based stem bowl, water jar with tall neck, lids for vessels, and spindle-whorls, besides stone implements. In the lower section, between Xushuling and Tanjialing in the centre and Sanfangwan in the south, there was a thick layer of disturbed soil in which were found a large number of pottery sherds and other artefacts.

Excavations have also been conducted at the Dengjiawan site in the northwest corner of the city. A cemetery was found and more than 100 tombs have been excavated. They are mostly vertical pit-tombs, some with a second platform. The corpse is generally placed face up. Burial goods were usually a set of 10 pieces, comprising small cups, small *ding* tripods and small jars. There are about a dozen urn-burials, using a pair of pottery vessels as a coffin. Near the cemetery there are two circular pits, within which over 1,000 small clay sculptures were found, including tiger, elephant, pig, turtle, sheep, dog, bird and chicken, and a man holding a fish (figure 2). Sculptures of this type are commonly found in other cultural deposits. Several remains nearby also revealed pottery tubes of strange shapes, and pottery urns joined together, which could be as long as several metres, arranged in two rows. Some of the pottery jars bore incised symbols, such as *yue*-axe, horn-shaped trumpets, cup-shapes, semi-lunar knife shape, and tall-stemmed cups: such jars were probably used in ritual activities.

Within the enclosure, in the southern section, there is an unusual cultural deposit at Sanfangwan. A trial trench indicated that there were several layers of stratification comprising a yellowish clay, burnt red clay, and yellow clay tempered with charcoal and stones. There was a great number of red pottery cups. We estimate that this deposit, which is 1 metre to 1.75 m deep, extends over an area of 90 by 75 metres. Accordingly the number of red pottery cups might be between several thousand and several hundred thousand.

From the analysis of the evidence, the enclosure represents a comparatively complete settlement, consisting of dwelling area, burial area, and areas devoted to religious activities.

Outside the enclosure there are about 20 high platforms adjacent to the ditch, except at the northwest corner. These platforms were originally dwelling areas, and were related in groups. The areas which have been excavated include Xiaojiafangji and Luojiaboling. The excavations of Xiaojiawu have been conducted over several seasons; based on the information from material published before the 1990s, we can date the architectural remains, storage pits, drainage, burials and stoves to the Qujialing cultural period and to the early and middle stages of the Shijiahe culture. The architectural remains are of two types: one is a triangular single construction; the second is a long row of buildings divided into different rooms. The foundations are heavily damaged, in most cases only traces are left, but the stamped earth contains some pottery bowls and jars. Some of the long houses have burnt red earth with fragments of pottery jars. Sometimes pottery jars were buried in rows, with obvious purposeful arrangement. The burials found here are scattered, usually found in groups next to dwellings. Most of the tombs had few burial goods: occasionally there are some specially made goods for burial, such as a small *ding*, and some lids for vessels. However, there is a small number of tombs with more lavish burial goods, such as M7. This tomb is 3.22 metres long, 2.35 metres wide, and about one metre deep. The tomb occupant is male, lying face up. The tomb has a second platform on which burial goods were placed. They consist of 62 pottery jars with tall necks, two deep-bellied jars, and three bowls. In the pit, below the feet of the occupant, there are 32 red pottery cups, finely made with thin walls, arranged in five rows. Placed on the body of the occupant are four small *ding* with lids, and a small axe. To the left side of the head there is a jug and a cup. This tomb obviously belonged to a powerful individual: it has a large tomb pit, more burial goods, and the stone axe is an indication of social status. The contrast between it and other small tombs is obvious. If we put this evidence together with the architectural remains, which also show different forms of construction, we can assume that there were significant social divisions within that society. From the distribution of the burials, the cemeteries near the houses probably belonged to family groups, and there is no larger clan cemetery.

At Luojiaboling, archaeologists have excavated architectural remains in a courtyard style.[4] The remaining section is U-shape in plan. There were two long triangular houses joined by a wall, 39.5 metres long and 10 centimetres thick, surviving to a height of between 20 centimetres and 1.2 metres. This wall was supported by 42 wooden poles; its foundation is about 40-80 centimetres wide and 30-50 centimetres deep. The building on the southeast side is poorly preserved, but the one on the northwest has two triangular rooms, 40 metres long and 4.2 to 5.5 metres wide. The southern room is smaller and is further sub-divided into three small rooms. All the walls have wooden posts placed in the foundation, 90 centimetres apart. The function of the building is difficult to determine at present. There is a further architectural remnant of uncertain form and relationship, on the west side of this courtyard. This is so far the largest group of architectural remains that have been excavated at the Shijiahe site. Because it is located outside the enclosure, it is unlikely to have been the most important building: we can assume that there would have been even larger or more important buildings within the enclosure.

We have dated this Shijiahe site and enclosure to the Qujialing culture and the early and middle stages of the Shijiahe culture. In fact, there is no clear division between these two periods of development. The evidence suggests that they are more or less contemporary and that the appearance of this large-sized walled enclosure is very good proof of the cultural development which began in the Qujialing cultural period.[5]

The interaction of neolithic cultures in the middle reaches of the Yangzi River increased and cultural remains of this date spread to the whole region of the middle Yangzi, far beyond the cultural zone of the Daxi culture. The most noticeable expansion was to the north, where the Qujialing culture entered the middle reaches of the Han river and the Nanyang basin, previously dominated by the Yangshao culture. Some time after that, the remains of the early and middle Shijiahe culture are found further northeast, in the upper reaches of the Huai River, and the southeast region of Henan province. Sites with this type of remains numbered over a thousand and they often overlap. There are more Shijiahe cultural sites than Qujialing ones. According to size, they can be divided into four categories: the largest

[4] Hubei 1994 (Hubei sheng wenwu kaogu yanjiusuo, Zhongguo shehui kexueyuan kaogu yanjiusuo): 'Hubei Shijiahe Luojiaboling xin shiqi shidai yizhi,' *Kaogu xuebao* 1994(2): 191-229.

[5] Zhang Xuqiu 1992: *Changjiang zhongyou xin shiqi shidai wenhua kailun*, Wuhan: Hubei kexue jishu chubanshe; the same author, 1994: 'Qujialing wenhua gucheng de faxian he chubu yanjiu,' *Kaogu* 1994(7): 629-34.

is the Shijiahe site itself (1,200,000 square metres), which is the only one of its kind; sites of the second category, such as Jingshan Qujialing, are usually around 500,000 to 1,000,000 square metres; sites of the third category are usually between 100,000 and 200,000 square metres; the fourth category are smaller sites, around 10,000 or more square metres. Apart from Shijiahe enclosure settlements, there are several other enclosures which date to the same period and which have a similar structure, but which are much smaller in size. Sites of the third category, about 20 of which have been investigated, include Shishou Zhoumaling, Jiangling Yinxiangcheng, Fengxian Chentoushan and Jijiaochen, and Jingmen Majiayuan. In these sites there are no dwellings outside the enclosure. The majority of the remaining sites have no enclosure at all.

The walls of these settlements have uniform characteristics of form and construction technique. They were often constructed near a river or lake, and the soil from the ditch was used for building the wall. The ditch itself is usually very wide. Within the enclosures, the topography is sloping, with dwellings usually occupying the higher ground and drainage the lower areas. Some of the walls on the lower side have special watergates through them, so that there is no problem of flooding. The walls were probably not intended for defence, however, as they were usually very wide but not very high; they could only have served a defensive purpose in combination with the wide ditch. Comparing the scale and structure of the Shijiahe site with the other smaller enclosures, the former has some special features. Firstly, the area of the Shijiahe settlement is eight square kilometres, nearly 10 times as great as the other settlements. The central area alone, enclosed by the wall, is 1 million square metres. The division of the dwelling areas is also complicated. Outside the enclosure, there are several surrounding groups of settlements. They relate both to the main settlement and to each other. They were probably clan groups, constructed at the same time as the walled enclosure, and their defence was also served by the latter. It is like a large community or tribe. The population of this large settlement was probably over 10,000, qualifying as a prehistoric city. This is the only example of such a size in Chinese prehistory. Though smaller than the later cities of Zhengzhou, Yanshi and Sanxingdui, it was bigger than Erlitou in Henan and Wucheng in Jiangxi. If we regard the Shijiahe enclosure as being an early city, its structure is similar to those of Yinxu and Zhouyuan: we can call it a clan settlement, different from the later cities of the Eastern Zhou.

After the middle stage of the Shijiahe culture, the Shijiahe enclosed settlement was abandoned. Remains of the later Shijiahe period are mostly in the southeast section of the site, but were on a much smaller scale. Within the settlement, there are large-scale cemeteries in which the major burial form was that of the large ceramic jar. At Xiaojiawuji over a 100 such burials were excavated and many jade objects were found in them. The later settlement sites of the Shijiahe culture are still the largest ones in the middle reaches of the Yangzi river in that period, but compared to the early periods, they are much smaller. These later sites are mostly in the northwest of the middle reaches of the Yangzi river, they are fewer in number and many of the earlier settlements had been abandoned. Some late Longshan cultural elements from the northern central plains appeared in the late Shijiahe culture. In particular, pottery types appeared which are basically similar to those of the central plains in style and technique. Several scholars have argued that there is no direct link between the later period and the early and middle periods of the Shijiahe culture. The decline of the Shijiahe culture is probably the result of the expansion of Xia culture from the north. The exploration of this question should of course follow the identification of the Xia culture, but archaeological evidence indicates a direct relationship between the Longshan culture from the central plains and the Shijiahe culture. It is the result of the social and cultural transformation, rather than of other reasons such as the natural environment.

Yinxiangcheng

The Yinxiangcheng site is located on a plain drained by the Juzhang River, a tributary of the Yangzi Changjiang River, some 25 kilometres northwest of Jingzhou, Hubei province.[6] This site faces flatlands to the south and Mt Jingshan to the north across the Zhangjiaban River flowing down to join the Yujia Lake. Portions of the walls and moats are visible on the surface. Because the settlement was built on an elevated mound, the height of the walls appears even greater from the outside, some 3-5 metres above the surrounding plain. The entire plan of the walled enclosure is an irregular oval with the long axis oriented east-west, about 580 metres, but we estimate that flooding from the Zhangjiaban River has destroyed the northern third of the enclosure. The area of the original enclosed settlement is estimated at about 17 hectares (figure 3).

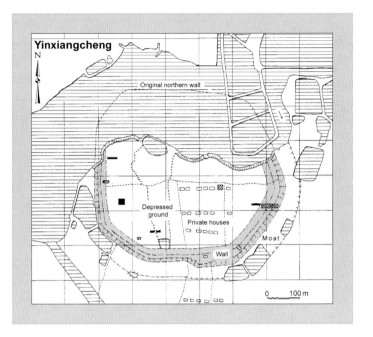

Figure 3 • Map of the Yinxiangcheng site

Although only a small part of the site has been uncovered, we have been able to throw light on the dates of wall construction, the size of the enclosure, structural features of walls, internal settlement organisation, the evidence for the wet cultivation of rice and for craft production. The cultural debris of this site was almost two metres thick and is divisible into four cultural layers: Daxi (c4000-2800 BC), Qujialing (c3000-2500 BC), Shijiahe (c2500-2000 BC) and Western Zhou (c1100-771 BC).

According to the evidence of the test trenches excavated into the eastern and western walls, we have recognised three phases of wall construction: Phase I was in the period of the Qujialing Culture, Phases II and III were in the Western Zhou Period. The eastern wall of Phase I is about 40 metres wide at the base and five metres wide at the top. After that enclosure had been abandoned, the area was reused and the wall extended in Phase II. Phase III was built on top of Phase II, and the section of the eastern wall that remains expands to about 65 metres in width at the base, 16 metres in width at the top and five metres in height. The layers of earth that were formed were slanting and irregular in thickness. The construction was not of rammed earth, but was created by alternately layering two kinds of earth. The remaining sections of the moats are more than 45 metres wide.

Beneath the inner side of the wall, ditches of the Daxi culture village were found. The section of ditch under the western wall was about 10 metres wide and three metres deep. The village consisted of two ditched enclosures, each in the form of an irregular oval with the long axis oriented north-south. It is evident that the Qujialing culture walled enclosure was constructed above the Daxi culture ditched village. During the Western Zhou period the walls were extensively repaired and continued to be used.

The houses of the Qujialing culture were built at ground level, their wall foundations being dug into the earlier house floors which had been baked to brick-like hardness. House No 10 was about 10 metres by seven metres in size, partitioned into three rooms, and oriented according to the four cardinal directions. The door was in the south wall. Several burial urns were found in these houses.

Three pottery kilns of the Shijiahe culture were located close to each other on the inner side of the western wall. The Qujialing-Shijiahe pottery, in contrast to the Daxi pottery, was predominantly grey and black, wheel-made and high-fired. This intensive manufacture of finely made pottery vessels represents a specialised profession.

Many thousands of carbonised rice grains were found in some storage pits in the dwelling area; these have been identified as cultivated rice (*Oryza sativa*

[6] The Archaeology Team of the Jingzhou Museum, Hubei, the Fukuoka Municipal Board of Education and The Institute for Research in Humanities, Kyoto University, jointly excavated a medium-sized walled site at Yinxiangcheng in 1995-96 and simultaneously undertook archaeological surveys of other walled sites. A fuller report is published in Okamura Hidenori and Zhang Xuqiu 1997: 'Kohoku Inshojo ishi kenkyu (I),' *Toho Gakuho*, Vol 69: 459-510.

japonica). Improvements in agricultural technology such as paddy fields and irrigation facilities for the cultivation of wet rice could have caused the population to increase throughout the region. Research at the Caoxieshan site, Jiangsu province, has revealed the early systems of paddy fields and irrigation facilities of the Majiabang culture (c4000 BC). Small sections of similar field systems of the Daxi culture have been uncovered at the Yinxiangcheng site.

Conclusions

We have investigated altogether five large sites with walls in the middle Yangzi valley. Based on the excavations at Shijiahe and Yinxiangcheng, we can summarise the common characteristics of the cities of the neolithic period in the middle reaches of the Yangzi River.

1 **Form of the Cities:** The Yinxiangcheng enclosure is an irregular oval while the Shijiahe site is triangular; the Chengtoushan site is roughly circular. These various forms are determined by the natural topography, such as the rivers and hills. At several enclosures, such as Majiayuan, Chengtoushan, Zoumaling and Yinxiangcheng, a river was used as part of the defensive moat, or its course was altered to lead it into an artificial ditch (figure 4).

Cities of the Shijiahe Culture

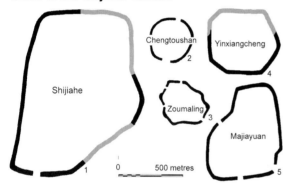

Figure 4 • Form of the Shijiahe culture cities

2 **Construction of the Walls:** The eastern wall of the Yinxiangcheng site was constructed with soil excavated from the ditch. Soils of different colours were piled up in layers and compressed slightly. As the various soils had different strengths, they could make the wall stronger. Such methods can also be seen at the Shijiahe and Zoumaling sites. The western wall of Yinxiangcheng is constructed not of the soil from the outer ditch, which was a river, but of soil from the dwelling area within the enclosure.

3 **Morphology of the Ditch and the Wall:** Outside the wall there is a ditch, forming a double ring surrounding the settlement. The ditch at the Yinxiangcheng site is 45 metres wide, and presently one metre deep. The foundations of the eastern wall are over 46 metres wide, with a remaining height of 5.1 metres, and an outer slope of 15 degrees. The slope of the wall at the Shijiahe site, according to the report, is of 25 degrees. The slope of the walls at Majiayuan and Zoumaling is slightly steeper; however, all of these city walls have comparatively shallow slopes and wide ditches.

4 **Date:** The wall at the Yinxiangcheng site was constructed between the early and late periods of the Qujialing culture. The enclosures at Shijiahe, Zoumaling, and Chengtoushan were constructed in the later period of the Qujialing culture. For a while, all these city walls coexisted. The wall at Yinxiangcheng was later repaired, probably in the Western Zhou period, but at the other sites the walls fell into disrepair in the later Shijiahe period.

5 **Scale of the site:** These enclosures can be divided into large and small types. The Shijiahe site is the only large one. The next largest are the Majiayuan and Yinxiangcheng sites on the northern bank of the Yangzi River. If we take the settlement changes of the Daxi culture, the Chengtoushan walled enclosure was derived from a Daxi culture settlement surrounded by a ditch, without enlargement. However, the Yinxiangcheng site was developed from two neighbouring Daxi culture settlements. It is significant that they were formed in the process of agricultural settlement based on the cultivation of rice; their scale relates to the population.

6 **Use of land within the enclosure:** During the excavation of the Yinxiangcheng site, we noticed areas of low ground within the enclosures. The same feature can be seen in other sites. At Shijiahe and Yinxiangcheng sites, we can even see an alteration of the river course to surround the walled enclosures. This feature continued into later periods in the middle reaches of the Yangzi River. These areas of low ground were not used for dwellings: at the Yinxiangcheng site, workshops were found in such areas. When calculating the size of the population, we have to realise that the city was not completely inhabited. A future task will be to determine the size of the population and the social organisation within the enclosures, in order to understand the progression from the ditch settlement of the Daxi culture to the walled settlements of the Qujialing culture.

In general, it appears that these walled sites were constructed during the period of the Qujialing culture. There is an intriguing variation in the size of the walled enclosures. More than 40 settlements existed inside and outside the enclosed area at the Shijiahe site, making it the largest walled site complex now known. Except for some houses, storage pits and burials, the major find at the site is a ritual structure. Among the ritual objects the big-mouth *zun* beaker with incised symbols, typical of the Dawenkou culture, is of the utmost significance. There can be no question that the Qujialing-Shijiahe culture and the Dawenkou culture were in direct contact with each other, and that the Shijiahe site served as the ceremonial centre and the centre for long-distance exchanges within the regional political unit.

DUAN YU

The Origin, Structure and Networks of Early Shu Cities

C ities are the most important landmarks for civilisation. They mark the end of prehistory and the emergence of new ways of production, social organisation and urban life. In his most influential article 'The urban revolution,' Gordon Childe has defined the 'urban revolution' as the most important step after the 'eolithic revolution' in human history, marking an important "change in the economic structure and social organisation of communities that caused , or was accompanied by, a dramatic increase in the population..."[1] Childe has listed a number of features that separate prehistoric villages from cities, including large-scale habitation areas not based on blood relationships, concentration of surpluses, increase in population, division of labour, writing, the calendar, professional artists and commercial exchange.

In 1956, R M Adams further argued that the crucial transformations in the process of urbanisation are changes in social organisation and an increase in scale and complexity of the community; accompanied by the emergence of new structures in politics and religion.[2] Thus, if we look for the physical evidence of the existence of early cities, they are: *1)* palaces for the rulers; *2)* temples and other religious structures (these royal and religious structures are separate from the houses occupied by ordinary people); *3)* lavish royal tombs; and *4)* large works of art and writing (inscriptions on stone). Moreover, trade is also an essential part of cities, where the exchange and redistribution of goods can take place. The question here is whether the general theory can be applied to the non-western model of urbanisation. In view of these theoretical definitions of early cities and studies of the process of urbanisation, I shall discuss the archaeological and historic evidence relating to early cities of the Shu kingdom in what is today the Chengdu plain, Sichuan province.

Two Early Cities in the Chengdu Plains

Recent archaeology has revealed two early cities, in Guanghan Sanxingdui and in Chengdu. At Guanghan Sanxingdui, archaeologists have discovered enor-

[1] Childe, Gordon 1950: 'The urban revolution,' *Town Planning Review* 21: 3-17.

[2] Adams, R M 1956: 'Some hypotheses on the development of early civilisation,' *American Antiquity* 21: 227-232.

An early version of this paper was presented at the international conference on Ba Shu culture, held in Guanghan, Sichuan province, 1-6 April 1992, and was published in Li Shaoming, Lin Xiang and Zhao Dianzeng, eds. *Sanxingdui yu Ba Shu wenhua* (Chengdu: Ba Shu shushe, 1993) under the title 'Ba Shu zaoqi chengshi de qiyuan.'

mous city walls of the Shu culture, at a site which they believe was the ancient capital of the Shu kingdom, contemporary with the Shang period (c15th-11th century BC)[3] (figure 1).

In archaeology, the city wall which has been found is over 40 metres wide at the base narrowing to 20 metres at the top. Archaeological surveys have revealed ancient walls in the east, west and south of the site, which is about 1,600 to 2,100 metres east to west, and 1,400 metres north to south. The city, with a total area of 2.6 square kilometres, was surrounded by a moat. From this enormous walled area and the scale of the palace buildings, which lie on the axis of the city, we can estimate that the city had a comparatively large population, which both would create wealth as well as consume a large amount of natural resources.

The habitation area of Sanxingdui city has been excavated and has yielded a large number of pottery wine vessels and food containers, but few agricultural tools. The production tools mostly come from the workshop area, showing that some kind of division of space according to function had probably already been made. The architectural remains include small houses with a wooden structure and clay walls, only about 10 square metres in size, as well as larger houses with a hall and a central beam, over 60 square metres in size. The drainage system of the city has also been discovered, as well as many clay animal sculptures, ritual jades, carved wooden objects and musical instruments. One stone sculpture represents a slave with his hands tied behind his back.

Within the city, the life of the people must have been very different from that of people in the prehistoric village, being much more complex in social organisation and political structure. There was probably a division between ordinary workmen and professionals such as artists, traders and priests. All the evidence from the early Sanxingdui city indicates that it was a centre of urbanisation with multiple products and activities, and a complex social structure. At the summit of society, there was the power of the king and his priests, while slaves were at the bottom of society. As monuments, the enormous city wall and wide and deep moat are the result of the productivity of the labour force as well as a symbol of the huge gap and intensified conflict between classes. In 1986, the famous pits Nos 1 and 2 were discovered, in which a large number of bronzes, jades and gold objects were found, in contrast to the poorly furnished tombs of ordinary people found in the city.[4] A central government must already have been in place and the existence of priests and of the king had strengthened the operation of the state machine. The early Shu kingdom probably also had a writing system,[5] which is the result of the emergence of an élite class. Society was strictly controlled.

The second city, which was contemporary with the Sanxingdui city, is known as the early Chengdu.[6] At Shierqiao, which is located in the western part of modern Chengdu city, archaeologists have discovered large quantities of archaeological remains over an area of 15,000 square metres, including wooden architectural remains with a corridor attached, and a number of small timber houses arranged in rows nearby.[7] Judging from the scale and spatial arrangement, the wooden architecture is obviously an official building, probably the royal palace. At the site, artefacts such as bronzes, jades, pottery, bronze and stone implements have also been found and most are dated to the Shang period (c15-11th centuries BC). But there are some objects which belong to later dates, such as the Warring States period (480-221 BC), indicating the site was also used in later periods.

The strata of the Shierqiao site can be divided into early, middle and late phases. The early phase corresponds to the early Shang period (c15th century BC), the middle one is contemporary with the first period of Yinxu (c13th-12th century BC), and the late phase corresponds to the late Shang and early Western Zhou (c11th-10th century BC). Each of these phases lasted over a hundred years. The development is continuous and comparatively stable. In the

[3] Chen De'an, Luo Yaping 1989: 'Zaoqi Shuguo ducheng cu lu duanni,' Zhongguo wenwu bao, September 15, 1989; Wang Yi 1988: 'Chengdu shi Shu wenhua yizhi de faxian ji yiyi,' Chengdu wenwu 1988(1): 10-16.

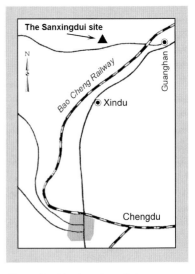

Figure 1 • The location of the Sanxingdui site. After Kaoguxuebao 1987(2): 227

[4] See Chen Xiandan's article in this volume.

[5] Duan Yu 1991: 'Ba Shu guwenzi de lianxi jiqi qiyuan,' Chengdu wenwu 1991(3): 20-33.

[6] Luo Kaiyu 1989: 'Chengdu cheng de xingcheng he Qin de gaijian,' Chengdu wenwu 1989(1): 56-61.

[7] Sichuan 1987 (Sichuan sheng wenwu guanli weiyuanhui et al): 'Chengdu Shi'erqiao Shangdai jianzhu yizhi diyiqi fajue jianbao,' Wenwu 1987(12): 1-23, 37.

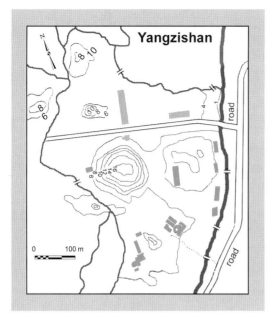

Figure 2 • *Topographical map of Yangzishan. After* Kaoguxuebao *1957(4): 18*

[8] Sichuan 1957 (Sichuan sheng wenwu guanli weiyuanhui): 'Chengdu Yangzishan tutai yizhi qingli baogao,' *Kaogu xuebao* 1957(4): 17-31; Lin Xiang 1988: 'Yangzishan jianzhu yizhi xin kao,' *Sichuan wenwu* 1988(5): 3-8.

early stratum, pottery spindle whorls with incised inscriptions have been found.

The Shierqiao site is the largest among a number of early remains in the area. Along the ancient Pijiang River stretching out to the north and to the southwest, there is a crescent-shaped region, about 10 square kilometres in area, where a group of early sites have been identified, similar in date and nature to the Shierqiao remains. None of these sites has a border: they are probably parts of a single large settlement. Pottery from these sites is extremely rich: to a depth of 20 centimetres, the number of pottery sherds from a single square metre can vary between 200 and 2,000.

To the north of the site, at Yangzishan (figure 2), archaeologists have also discovered a man-made earthen platform which has been dated to the late Shang period (figure 3).[8] The platform is square, and has three levels linked by steps. The upper level has an area of 36.1 square metres, the lowest level 103.6 square metres. The whole platform is built with clay bricks along the edges, and filled in with soil in the middle. It stands 10 metres high, with a total area of over 10,000 square metres: over 70,000 cubic metres of soil were used in its construction (figure 4, overleaf). The orientation of the platform is 55° north, the same as that of the sacrificial pits at the Sanxingdui site. It is probably no coincidence that the bronze statue from pit No 2 at Sanxingdui stands on a similar square base. The Yangzishan platform is probably a ceremonial centre overlooking the Chengdu plain.

To sum up, the Shierqiao and Yangzishan remains reflect an advanced level of construction techniques, with a concentration of natural resources and organisation of labour. Architects, labourers, professionals who had special knowledge of physics and mathematics, and people who managed the labourers, were all supported by the surplus produced by the agriculturists. The archaeological remains also indicate a complex social structure and relationship.

The Model of the Early Shu Cities

In the study of the origins and formation of early cities, we can apply a model which has an internal structure, functional system and spatial organisation, which determine the development of the city. To reconstruct the model of the early Shu cities, I shall employ both archaeological and textual evidence for my argument.

The model for the Sanxingdui city shows at the beginning a strong religious and political orientation. The social organisation and political structure surround the sacred and political body which also functions as a centripetal force in the process of urbanisation. Archaeologically, the Sanxingdui culture can be divided into four phases: Phase I is the neolithic period; from Phase II, the Sanxingdui culture entered a civilised stage. During the transition between Phases I and II, the culture had undergone a noticeable transformation. This change is quite sudden, reflecting changes in the social structure.

We shall first look at the religious nature and symbolism of the Sanxingdui city wall. The walls of Sanxingdui city were begun in the early Shang period, and lie directly over the cultural remains of the neolithic period. The city wall is the earliest evidence for the formation of this city. In other words, the urbanisation of Sanxingdui culture began at the same time as the construction of the wall: the wall is the landmark and most representative element of the Sanxingdui civilisation. We have described the wall of Sanxingdui city as thick and strong: what was the function of this huge and

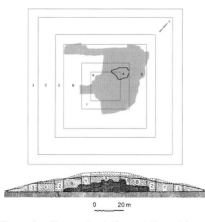

Figure 3 • *The earth platform at Yangzishan. After* Kaoguxuebao *1957(4): 20*

Figure 4 • Reconstruction of the Yangzishan platform. After Kaoguxuebao 1957(4): 20

permanent city wall? Scholars have generally agreed that its purpose was defensive; according to them, the wall at Sanxingdui undoubtedly served as protection for the early Shu city.

However, in terms of construction, the wall itself is quite different from the city walls of the Shang capital found at Zhengzhou. The Sanxingdui city wall is very large and thick, but its sides are not steep enough to provide good defence. Carbon dating of artefacts from different layers of the wall also show that it was constructed at different periods, so that it is unlikely to have been constructed at one time as a defence system. Other scholars think that the wall here was built as a protection from floods, like an embankment; but if we look at the topography and location of the city, the walls on the east and west run at right angles to the Yazi and the Mamu Rivers, so that they could not have offered protection from flooding by these two rivers. The southern wall, within which are the sacrificial pits discovered in 1986, runs parallel to the curve of the Mamu River, but the latter actually flows within the city wall and not outside. In my view, the explanation of the function of the city wall should be sought in the context of the cultural remains found in the city.

Until now, we have found very few weapons at the Sanxingdui site: those that have been found are of types such as jade and square-shaped bronze *ge* dagger axe, which were probably used in a ritual context rather than in warfare. Particularly, other objects made of gold, bronze, jade, pottery are strongly marked by their ritual use. Another very noticeable fact is that in the second period of the Sanxingdui culture, when the city wall began to be constructed, a special type of pottery occurred; this type is represented by the spoon-shaped object which has a handle in the form of a bird's head with a long beak (figure 5). This object reminds us of the images of the ruler known as Yuwu of the Shu kingdom described in ancient texts. It is obviously not an ordinary utensil, but is more likely to have been used in ritual ceremonies. It may not be a coincidence that this object and the city wall appeared at the same time, probably as the result of the sudden social changes.

We may be able to argue that a new incoming force conquered the local culture; the city wall and the spoon with a bird's head handle are the direct evidence of this cultural conquest. This seems to correspond to the ancient records such as the *Shuwang benji* (Biography of the King of Shu, attributed to Yang Xiong, 53 BC-AD 18) and *Huayang guozhi* (Records of the Huayang State, by Chang Qu, 4th century AD) where it is said that there were three early rulers of the Shu kingdom: Cancong, Bohuo and Yufu, and that Yufu had a birdlike head.[9] Thus, the bird-headed spoon is probably a representation of this new religious and political power. Put together with the evidence from the sacrificial pits, we can imagine that religious ceremonies were probably conducted on the top of the wall. In other words, military conquest might provide the foundation for the Shu kingdom, but in the building of this capital the fundamental force was religious power.

On the other hand, the formation of the early Chengdu city shows a different pattern from that of the Sanxingdui city. The only religious remnant

[9] For the textual references of the Shu, see Yuan Ke, Zhou Min 1985: *Zhongguo shehua ziliao cui bian*, Chengdu: Sichuan sheng shehui kexueyuan chubanshe, 384-391.

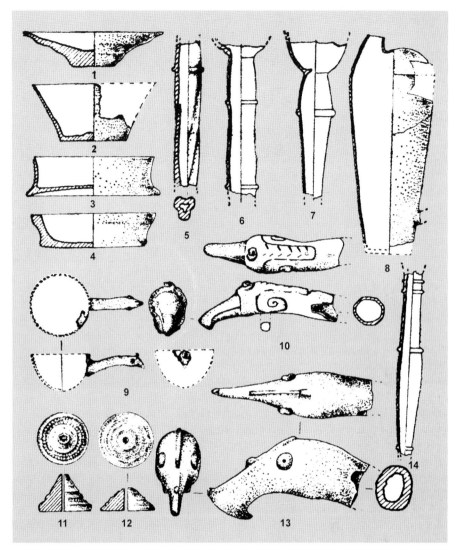

Figure 5 • Artefacts from the Sanxingdui site. After Kaoguxuebao 1987(2): 245

at Chengdu city is the platform at Yangzishan. The date of its construction is in the late Shang period, but the beginning of the city at this site goes back far earlier. The lower stratum of the Shierqiao site and several other sites, including Fuqinxiaoqu and Fangchijie have all been dated to c2000 BC. It is probably correct to say that the beginning of the early Chengdu city has little to do with religion, unlike the Sanxingdui city. Although some oracle bones dating to the Shang and Zhou periods have been found at the Chengdu city site, none of them are inscribed. The hollows cut into the bones are irregular and crude, and were probably made by folk priests, in contrast to the royal priests in the government. This evidence indicates that in the early Chengdu city there was probably no organised religious body at the highest level of society.

In the early Chengdu city, the earliest architectural remains are found at the Shierqiao site, from which the city spread out gradually. No defensive system or walls have been found at the early Chengdu city. This is not because, as some literary sources have suggested, there was any shortage of soil at Chengdu, but because, as Xu Zhongshu has argued, Chengdu in ancient times was a much more open city which had developed largely on the basis of economic activities.[10] This model differs greatly from the Sanxingdui model.

[10] Xu Zhongshu 1987: 'Chengdu shi gudai ziyou dushi shuo,' Xu Zhongshu ed. Ba Shu kaogu lunwenji, Beijing: Wenwu chubanshe, 151-152.

The Function and Networks of the Early Shu Cities

Both in Sanxingdui and in Chengdu cities, the population was large. If we take some specialist estimates of the ratio between the population and the land in the pre-Han times, every family used about 158.7 square metres.[11] As Sanxingdui city covered a total area of 2.6 square kilometres, this would have meant that about 16,383 households lived there. If a household comprised five persons, the population would be 81,915. So, is this figure correct?

By the Eastern Zhou period, the Chengdu city covered an area of 15 square kilometres, five kilometres east to west, and three kilometres north to south. Using the same ratio, there would have been 94,517 households and 472,585 persons at this time. This number, however, is much greater than the 35,000 population of Lingzi, the capital of Qi state in the Spring and Autumn period (770-745 BC), and seems too high. Ma Shichang, on the basis of the excavated area of Lingzi and the numbers found in historical records, has estimated that the ratio of land per household was about 268 square metres, instead of 158.7 square metres.[12] On this basis, the Chengdu city in the Eastern Zhou period would have had 55,970 households, or 279,850 head of population. This figure is bigger than that arrived at for the early Sanxingdui city, and smaller than the Han dynasty population of Chengdu city. This is probably closer to the actual fact.

The high population density in the city must have been organised in an orderly way through an urban mechanism. There were different professions and divisions of labour, all within a framework of class and rank. From textual and archaeological evidence, the urban population of Shu was divided into rulers and subjects: each of these was further divided into different ranks. There were courtiers, officials, warriors, merchants, priests, farmers and craftsmen or artisans. They were also divided into different ethnic groups, such as Shu, Ba, Pu, and Di, Qiang, etc. The complicated social structure indicates a complex urban system. In terms of the economy, the concentration of the population and the divisions of labour led to great advances in industry and trade, which enabled the city to function more efficiently.

The next question is how did these cities relate to each other? During the Shang period, there were two major cities in Sichuan: Sanxingdui city and Chengdu city, one in the south and the other in the north. Around these two large centres, there were a number of smaller settlements. There seem to have been links between the cities and the countryside, forming the early city networks of the Shu kingdom. In the early period, Sanxingdui city, probably as the political capital and religious centre, obviously occupied a more important position than Chengdu city, which mainly functioned as a trading centre. In that period, economics had to serve the needs of religion.

However, at the same period, the trade network expanded, providing the huge population living in the cities with the necessities and luxuries of life, and even with works of art. It is likely that markets had also appeared in Sanxingdui city. Luxury goods were consumed by the ruling house and the upper classes of officials. The lower and middle ranks of the ruling class mainly relied on the produce of their own lands, though they used trade to obtain goods that they could not produce themselves. Ordinary residents in the city, in particular craftsmen and traders, relied in the main on the market, obtaining the necessities for their daily life through exchange. This division also determined the social framework of each group. To manage and control such trade and markets, we can imagine that a well-organised bureaucracy would have been essential.

Trade was presumably also conducted between Sanxingdui and different regions through official or private organisations. Some of the goods were imported from other places: these included ivory, jade, cowrie shells, gold, copper and tin. Archaeologists have found many cowrie shells in the sacrificial pits at Sanxingdui, which have been identified as coming from the Indian Ocean. They are similar to those discovered in Han dynasty tombs in Yunnan, and were probably used as currency in trade. Thus the early Sanxingdui city

[11] Lin Yun 1986: 'Guanyu Zhongguo zaoqi guojia xingcheng de jige wenti,' *Jilin daxue shehui kexue xuebao* 1986(6): 1-12.

[12] Ma Shizhi 1988: 'Luelun Chu Yindu chengshi renkou wenti,' *Jiang Han kaogu* 1988(1): 56-61.

may have functioned as the political capital and religious centre of the Shu kingdom, but it was also involved in trade to certain degree.

From about the same time, Chengdu city began to develop more quickly as the centre of commercial and industrial activities. Archaeology has shown that there were workshops for bronzes, pottery, jade, stone and bone. Some carved lacquer objects found at Sanxingdui probably originally came from Chengdu city. The population of early Chengdu city must have been considerable, and the market also emerged and developed on a large scale. The turtle shells and cowrie shell from the early remains did not originate from the Chengdu plain itself, but came from the sea. At the Zhihuijie site, dated to the Zhou period, pollen analysis has revealed some species of plants which were not indigenous to the area.[13] For the production of bronze, copper and tin were not among local resources, so the supply of raw materials for the workshops must have come in as traded goods.

The development of the early Chengdu city entered a new phase in the Spring and Autumn period, when Chengdu actually functioned as the main trading centre for handicrafts and the exchange of different types of goods. Merchants from different regions gathered there, with special areas for merchants to live and to trade. In the tombs at Qingchuan and Yingyang, dated to the Spring and Autumn and Warring States periods, many lacquer wares were excavated with the mark *Cheng* or *Chengzao* or *Chengting*, all of which were obviously goods produced and traded at the Chengdu market. They did not use a local script, but used the standard Chinese writing in order to sell them to distant areas. As I have discussed elsewhere, there are many textual references to Chengdu's market and trade: there seem to have been two sections in the city, with the markets concentrated in the smaller southern section. This system was already in place before the Qin period, and was reorganised under the Qin dynasty (221-206 BC).[14]

There is another interesting question of when and how the southern silk road opened. From archaeological evidence, we can assume that the trade between the Shu cities (Sanxingdui and Chengdu) and South and West Asia had begun as early as the Shang and Zhou periods. The bronze human figurines, bronze trees, golden staff and face mask found at the sacrificial pits at Sanxingdui may be influenced by the civilisations of Western Asia.[15] By the Eastern Zhou period, we know that it was fashionable in the Shu area to wear glass pendants, which might be an influence from Iran.[16] By the Han dynasty Chengdu had become an international trading centre, along the eastern section of Sichuan many objects of Central Asian, Western Asiatic and South Asian style have been found. This aspect of east-west cultural relations certainly needs further investigation.[17]

Now let us investigate further the networks of the early Shu cities. By the Western Zhou and in the early Spring and Autumn period, as the central power of the Zhou royal house was in decline, different rulers began to assert themselves, and the function and position of cities also began to change dramatically. A new group of cities emerged, forming an urban network within which different types of production and trade could expand and flourish. The ruler of the Shu state during the early Western Zhou period was Duyu, also known as Wangdi. According to ancient texts, the city built by Wangdi was called Pi, situated at the foot of Mt Minshan. This area is today called Pi xian, to the west of Chengdu. Another record found in the *Huayang guozhi* says that Duyu built another city called Jushang to the southwest of Chengdu, in what is today Shuangliu xia.[18] These two cities built by Duyu in the late period are similar to the early Sanxingdui and Chengdu cities, respectively, in their spatial organisation. Pi in the north was the main capital, while Jushang in the south was the second capital. Pi functioned as the political and military centre of Duyu's realm. This two-capital system was different from the Shang and closer to that of the Western Zhou. In the early Western Zhou period, King Cheng established the second capital in Luoyang, stationing Zhou troops there in order to consolidate their power and prevent any resurgence of the Yin descendants in the central and

[13] Luo Erhu *et al* 1989: 'Chengdu Zhihuijie yizhi baofeng fenxi yanjiu,' *Nanfang minzu kaogu* 2: 299-309.

[14] Duan Yu 1991: 'XianQin Qin Han Chengdu de shi ji shifu zhineng de yanbian,' *Huaxi kaogu yanjiu* 1: 324-348.

[15] Duan Yu 1993: 'Lun Shangdai Changjiang shangyou Chuanxi pingyuan qingtong wenhua yu Huabei he shijie gu wenmin de guanxi,' *Dongnan wenhua* 1993(2): 1-21.

[16] Such pendants were called *sese* which is probably a transliteration of the word for gems in Arabic or a South Asian language. In the Tang dynasty such ornaments were commonly found in tombs.

[17] Liu Hong 1991: *Nanfang sichou zhi lu wenhua lun*, Kunming: Yunnan minzu chubanshe.

[18] Yuan Ke, Zhou Min 1985: 386-389.

eastern plains In his choice of sites for the capitals, Duyu was probably also attempting to prevent the previous defeated ruler from staging a comeback.

Later, during the Eastern Zhou period, there were three major cities in Sichuan: Chengdu, Guangdu and Xindu. All of them were centres of much larger urban networks. Chengdu, originally an industrial and trading centre, had by the middle and later Spring and Autumn period become a political centre as the new ruler Kaiming moved his capital there. Trade and industry also developed further, many lacquers and textiles which were made in Chengdu were sold to other provinces.

The history of Guangdu probably began in the Shang period, but only reached city status in the Zhou period. It was probably used as one of the Shu capitals. Guangdu is mentioned in the *Shanhaijing* (Classic of Mountains and Seas) and in the *Huainanzi* as the symbolic centre of the world where there is a *jianmu* or the cosmological tree and all the gods and spirits come and go from there.[19] The bronze trees discovered at the sacrificial pit No 2 at Sanxingdui probably relate to the mythology of the cosmological tree. According to Meng Wentong, the *Shanhaijing* was likely written by a Shu author, around the middle of the Warring States period.[20] The history of Xindu certainly goes back to the early Warring States period. Some Shu tombs of the Warring States period have been found there, and there are traces of megalithic worship.

Apart from these three major cities, there were also many other new cities during the Eastern Zhou period. They include Linqiong, the walls of which are described in the *Huayang guozhi* as being six *li* around and five *zhang* tall, with about 2,300 households and a population of about 11,500, making it a medium-sized city. Other records mention that King Kaiming had his capital in Lushan, in the west of Sichuan; but he also ruled Nan'an, which is today known as Leshan.[21]

In the northern part of Sichuan, the Guangyuan region was controlled by the Shu. Nanzhen, in southern Shaanxi, is a famous ancient city which was also under the rule of the Shu, in the period before the Eastern Zhou. Archaeologists have excavated a great number of tombs of the middle and late Spring and Autumn periods, along the Yandao circuit in southwestern Sichuan. All the evidence shows that the urban network of the Shu expanded greatly during the Eastern Zhou period over the whole of the Chengdu plain, reaching into the neighbouring mountainous regions. In the Eastern Zhou period, the urban network reached a balance and comparative stability. Chengdu was the primary city, controlling the whole of the Shu region, while Xindu in the north had links with southern Sichuan, and Nanzhen held the key military position between Sichuan and the central plains. Pi to the west of Chengdu was linked with the nomadic cultures of the high plateau of western Sichuan. Linchong bridged the area between the Chengdu and the western Sichuan plains. Nan'an to the south of Chengdu supplied the capital with salt and also linked the urban economy with the southern mixed agricultural and pastoral economy. Yandao in the mountainous region of southwestern Sichuan controlled the local rich mineral resources of copper as well as the international trade route to the south. Thus the urban network of the Shu kingdom was well organised and functioned efficiently. This model made an important landmark in the early history of Shu and continues to have an impact in the modern city network of Sichuan province.

In 1995, archaeologists in Chengdu discovered a new site near Xinjin Longma.[22] It has since been named the Baodun site. The site dates earlier than the Sanxingdui site. The discovery includes city walls, architectural remains and a large amount of pottery. It provides new information for the study of early Shu cities. The initial investigation, however, has shown that the Baodun site differs greatly from the Sanxingdui culture. Further research is expected in the near future.

[19] Yuan Ke, Zhou Min 1985: 20-21.

[20] Meng Wentong 1962: 'Luelun "Shanhaijing" de xiezuo shidai jiqi changsheng diyu,' *Zhonghua wenshi luncong* I: 43-70.

[21] *Huayang guozhi*, juan 3, see Liu Lin 1984: *Huayang guozhi jiao zhu*, Chengdu: Ba Shu shushe, 175-331.

[22] Personal communication from the Chengdu city Archaeological Team.

Conclusion

To conclude, we have to consider the question of the significance of early Shu cities in the general history of China. It has been generally accepted that the origin of cities in China mainly relates to the concentration of political power, and for purposes of defence. For example, K C Chang argued that the rise of urbanism in early China is not a result of economic development, but a political development.[23] In other words, the driving force of early cities ispolitical and military power, and only after that the economy becomes a part of the elements and functions. This interpretation may be right for the model of the early cities of the Central Plains.

However, the study of the early Shu cities has suggested another model which differs from the one of the central plains. The evidence of the Sanxingdui and Chengdu cities shows that different models could coexist. In the Eastern Zhou period, in the central plains, cities largely derived from the old fiefdoms and long established settlements. But in the Shu kingdom, the development of cities is largely based on local economics, in particular in relation to the commercial activities developed with the neighbouring regions and a long-distance international trade. The major force driving the development of a city had to be one of economy and trade. Thus the origins of cities could be, like those of civilisation itself, multifaceted.

[23] Chang, K C 1985: 'Guanyu Zhongguo cuqi "chengshi" zhege kainian,' *Wenwu* 1985(2): 61-67.

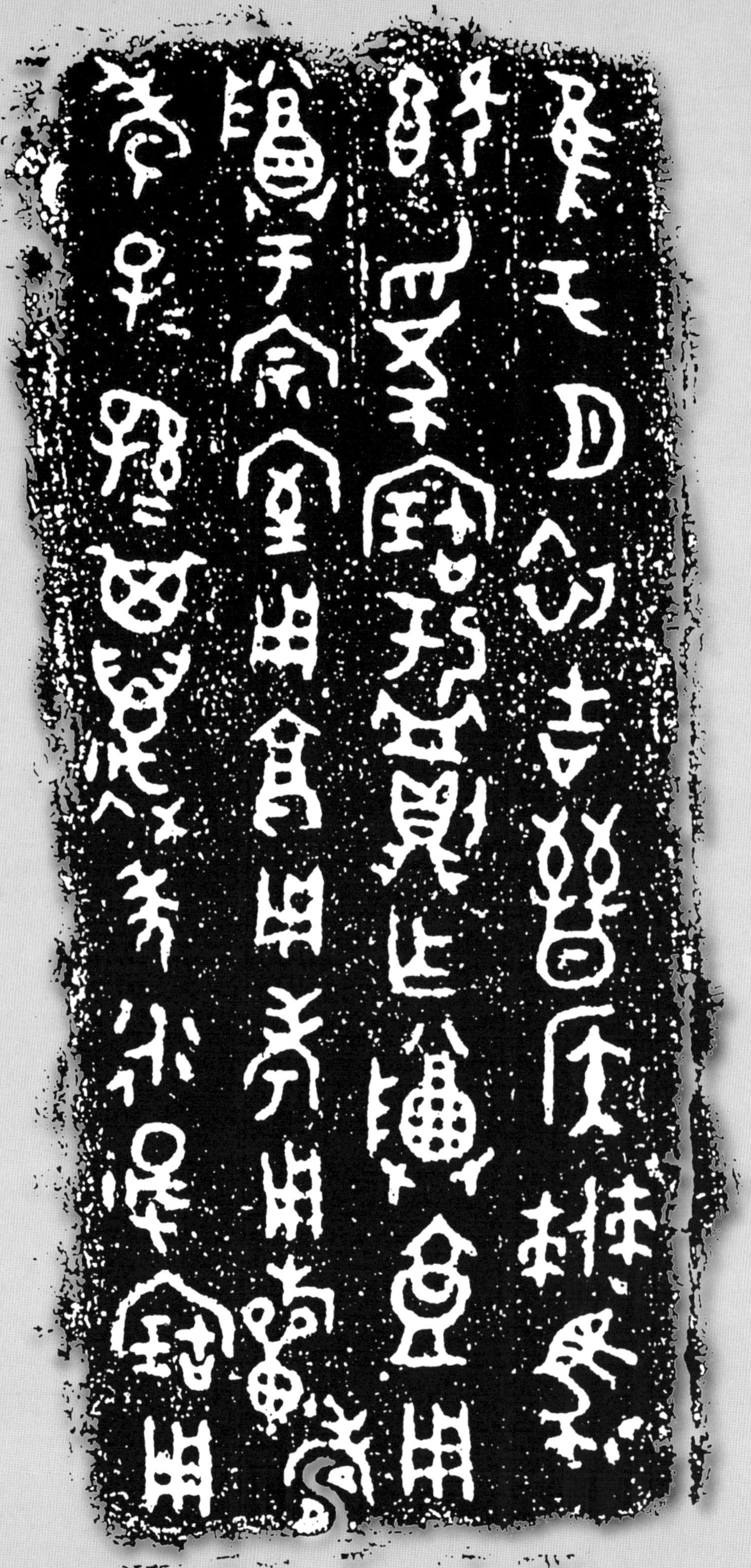

of the tombs with three *ding* should have been of lower status than marquis. Usually, we would expect that tombs of rank of marquis rank would contain five *ding*, but in the early Western Zhou period the regulation governing the number of *ding* to be buried was not strictly enforced. This tomb with four *ding* is earlier than the other royal tombs of Jin. It is possible that it belonged to a marquis, or even that the occupant of this tomb was Shu Yu himself. If this place has yielded so many tombs of Jin aristocrats of the Western Zhou period, then it cannot be other than the earliest capital of Jin, Tang.

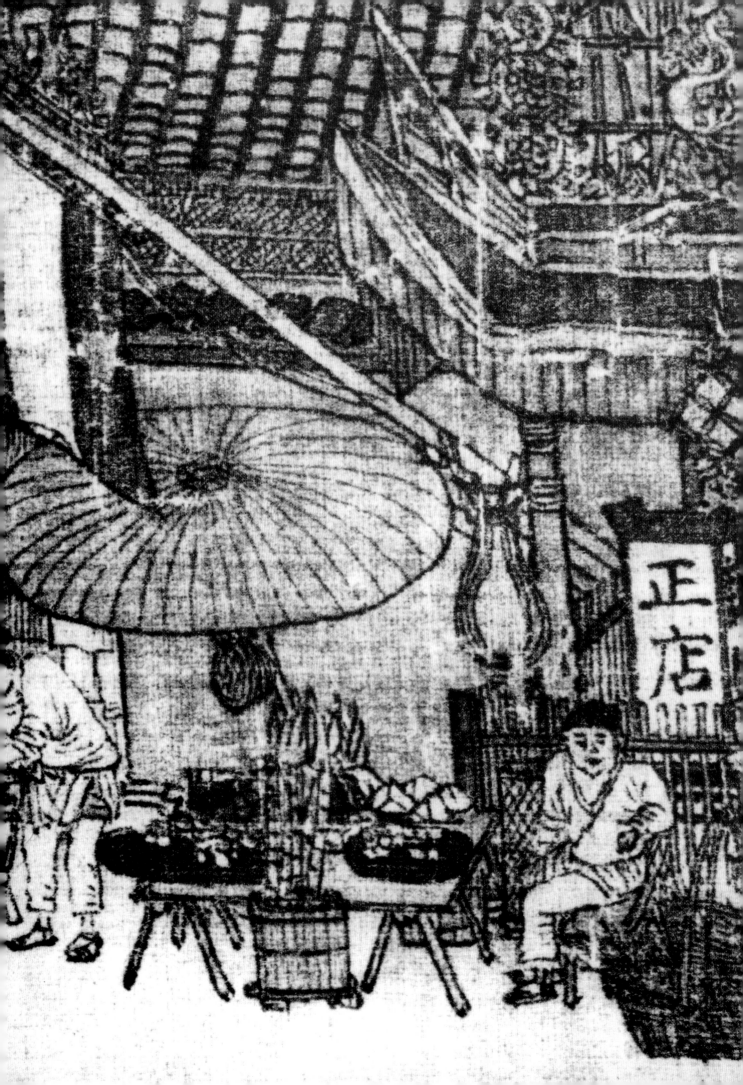

Wang Tao

A City with Many Faces: Urban Development in pre-Modern China

*U*rbanism is an important phenomenon in human history. Comparative studies have, however, shown that each city possesses its own characteristics within a particular historical context. The fundamental elements that determine the construction and functions of a city, such as economic, political, military and religious factors, play different roles in different cases. In other words, each city may potentially be unique.

Modern scholars have now realised that the most appropriate way to approach a city is to approach it in its own cultural tradition. To understand the cultures of different cities and the idea of urbanism and its manifestations in various contexts, we must consider the experiences and feelings of the people who lived in these cities rather than just the half-buried city walls and broken roof tiles. In this paper I will examine different models and the crucial stages of urbanisation in pre-modern China, mainly from an archaeological perspective, but also in conjunction with some contemporary historical sources. The aim is to reveal a general pattern, if there is one, and the key elements that underlay the development of Chinese cities from 3000 BC to AD 900.

The 'Ideal City' and Some Basic Terms

A good way to detect what people think of their cities is to find out what they call them. The most common word in the Chinese language for 'city' is *cheng*, meaning a walled settlement. The term y*i* is interchangeable with *cheng* and is older, first appearing in Shang oracle bone inscriptions (c12th century BC). The idea of the 'city-wall' is a significant one, providing a physical distinction between town and village. Though the 'wall' is not the only important element of a city, it has been widely employed by archaeologists in China as the working criterion by which to identify city remains.

Another important term is *du,* meaning imperial cities, *i e* capitals. The morphology and functions of imperial cities differ considerably from those of ordinary towns and cities. In terms of physical layout, a typical Chinese city was often divided into two parts: the *cheng* inner-city, and the *guo* outer city; the former was for the king and his officials, while the outer city was usually occupied by those providing a service, such as soldiers and craftsmen.

From a very early time, the residential area in a city was divided into living quarters, called *li* or *fang*. This tradition probably originated from the residential groupings in earlier neolithic villages, which later were replaced by the walled

Facing page • Detail from Qingming shanghe tu (Up the river on the Qingming festival), by Zhang Zeduan. After Wenwu jinghua 1 (1959), 27. See also figure 7

enclosures which came to dominate Chinese medieval city landscapes.

Religion also played an important role in Chinese cities. *Zong* and *she* were the major religious centres — the former refers to the Ancestral Temple and the latter to the Altar of Earth. The two are essential for any settlement, and are always found together within a city context, patronised directly by the royal courts. In addition, the commercial centre such as the *shi* market also played a crucial role in the development of cities, but its function may have varied according to different situations.

Outside the city, the *jiao* suburbs were again divided into many smaller settlements. The majority of agriculturalists who worked on the land lived further out in the *ye* fields. These features are important elements in the development of a city, for not only do they sustain the cities with basic supplies, they also mark the contrast, both mentally and physically, between city and rural ways of life.

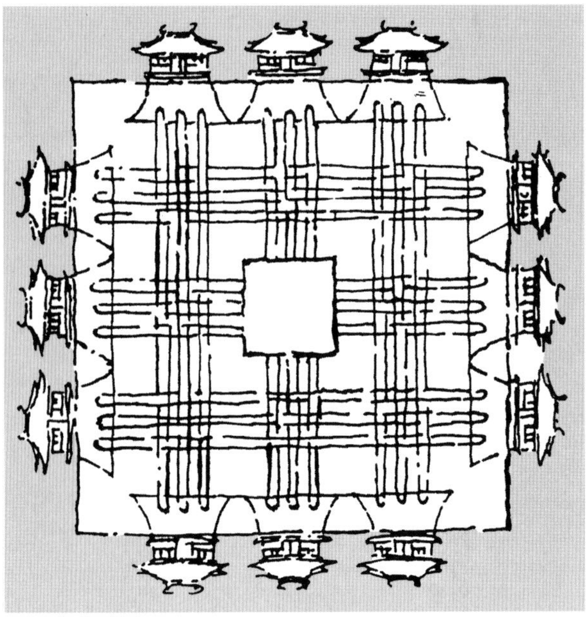

Deep down inside the core of Chinese idea of urbanism there lies the model of an 'ideal city.' In the *Zhouli*, an ancient document retrieved from the imperial library in the 1st century BC, we can read the earliest description of the 'ideal city' in which the kings lived: it was square-shaped, surrounded by suburbs which were further subdivided into several zones where people of different professions and status lived (figure 1). The city had 12 gates, three on each side. The palace was located in the middle, with the Ancestral Temple on the left, the Altar of Earth on the right and the Market at the back. Within the city there were nine streets aligned north to south, and another nine aligned east to west. This ideal model of the kings' city was not based on an actual city, but was probably derived from ancient cosmology. Nonetheless it contains key elements relating to Chinese urbanism, and its impact on later city planning is apparent.[1]

Figure 1 • The 'ideal city' described in the Zhouli. *After Nalan Chengde 1676, plate 1,* juan *4/2b*

Moats to Walls: Early Cities

Artificial ditches or moats appear to have been a prominent feature in a number of early neolithic settlements from 6000-3500 BC in northern China. The famous Banpo village of the Yangshao culture, excavated in the 1950s, represents the basic form of a neolithic village in the middle Yellow River valleys.[2] The residential houses, common halls, animal pens and storage pits are surrounded by a moat 6-8 metres wide and five-six metres deep. The cemetery and kilns are located outside the moat. Another village site of the Yangshao culture, Jiangzhai, excavated in the 1970s, is perhaps the best preserved site[3] (figure 2). It comprises more than 100 houses, divided into five groups, occupying nearly 20,000 square metres. Three ditches dug separately to the north, south and east protect the village, and to the southwest is a river that functioned as a natural defence. Both the Banpo and Jiangzhai sites are C14 dated to 4800-3600 BC. In recent years, settlements with artificial ditches have been found with an even earlier date; for instance, the Xinglongwa site in Inner Mongolia, dated to 6200-5400BC.[4] It has more than 160 house remains, arranged in rows, occupying about 24,000 square metres. The artificial ditch surrounding the village is 1.5-2 metres wide and 570 metres long; access was retained on the northwestern side. These large moated neolithic settlements, in particular Jiangzhai village, revealed an already sophisticated organisation of space, and the moats themselves, built primarily for defensive purposes, led to the construction of fortified walls.[5]

In about 3000 BC, a number of walled settlements, or 'cities,' began to appear on the Chinese landscape. Dozens of city sites have been identified in

[1] Wright, A 1977. 'The cosmology of the Chinese city.' William Skinner ed. *The city in late imperial China.* (California): Stanford University Press, 33-73; He Yeju 1982. 'Zhouguang' wangji guihua chutan. *Jianzhu lishi yanjiu* 1, 96-118.

[2] Zhongguo kexueyuan kaogu yanjiusuo 1963. *Xi'an Banpo.* Beijing: Wenwu chubanshe.

[3] Banpo Bowuguan (and Shaanxi Kaogu yanjiusuo xian bowuguan Lindong 1988). *Jiangzhai.* Beijing: Wenwu chubanshe.

[4] Zhongguo shehui kexueyuan Kaogu yanjiusuo 1984. *Xin Zhongguo de kaogu faxian he yanjiu.* Beijing: Wenwu chubanshe; Ren Shinan 1994: 'Xinglongwa wenhua de faxian jiqi yiyi.' *Kaogu* 1994(8), 710-18.

[5] Yan Wenming 1994. 'Zhongguo huaihao juluo de yanbian.' *Guoxue yanjiu* 2, 483-92; Cao Bingwu 1996. Zhongguo shiqian chengzhi luelun. *Zhongyuan wenwu* 1996(3), 37-46.

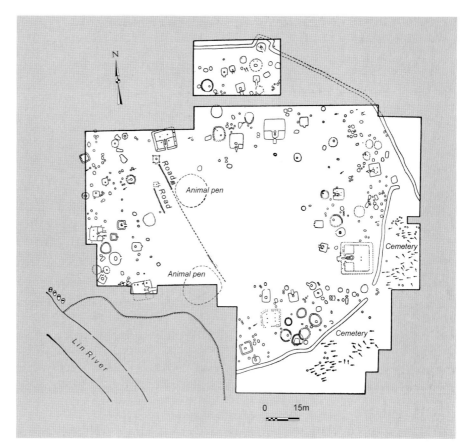

Figure 2 • Layout of Jingzhai Village. After the Institute of Archaeology, CASS 1984, 55

6 Zhang Yushi Yang Zhaoqing 1995. 'Xinshiqi shidai kaogu huo zhongda faxian - Zhengzhou Xishan Yangshao wanqi chengzhi mianshi.' *Zhongguo wenwubao* (10 September 1995).

7 Henan sheng wenwu yanjiusuo (and Zhoukou diqui wenwuju) 1983. 'Henan Huaiyang Pingliangtai Lngshan wenhua chengzhi shijue jianbao.' *Wenwu* 1983(3), 8-20.

8 Henan sheng wenwu yanjiusuo (and Zhongguo lishi bowuguan Kaogu bu) 1992. *Tengfeng Wangchenggang yu Yangcheng,* Beijing: Wenwu chubanshe.

9 An Jinhuai 1985. 'Shilun Tengfeng Wangchenggang Longshan wenhua chengshi yu Xiadai Yangcheng.' *Zhongguo kaogu xuehui disici nianhui lunwenji.* Beijing: Wenwu chubanshe.

10 Cao Bingwu 1996. 'Zhongguo shiqian chengzhi luelun.' *Zhongyuan wenwu* 1996(3), 37-46.

11 Xu Guanji 1986. 'Chifeng Yingjinhe Yinhe liuyu shicheng yizhi.' *Zhonguo kaoguxue yanjiu* bianweihui ed. *Zhonguo kaoguxue yanjiu.* Beijing: Wenwu chubanshe, 82-93.

the central plains, in the north and south, and along the east coast. The most recent discovery is the Xishan site near Zhengzhou[6], covering approximately 100,000 square metres. The remains of the city wall are about 300 metres long, with its base measuring 11 metres wide, narrowing to five to six metres at the top. The corners of the wall are thicker, about eight metres. The remaining wall stands three metres above ground level. The wall was constructed of rammed-earth (*hangtu*) and was built in sections. This construction technique is a distinctive trait for all later architecture in the central plains — the power base of Chinese civilisation. The city is round, and outside the wall is a moat 5-7.5 metres wide, and four metres deep. Archaeologists have ascertained that the city was built during the later Yangshao period (c3300-2800 BC).

Other important walled settlements of the central plains include the Pingliangtai[7] and Wangchenggang[8] sites, dated between 2500-2000 BC. Pingliangtai is a square-shaped enclosure measuring c185 metres along each side. The remains of the wall stand three metres high, with a base 13 metres wide, narrowing to eight-10 metres at the top. There are gates in both the southern and northern walls. Excavation has also uncovered the roads and drainage system of the city. The Wangchenggang site is somewhat different. It consists of two separate enclosures. Compared to Pingliangtai, Wangchenggang is smaller, but, significantly, both sites have yielded traces of using bronze, and the latter has been associated with the Xia, the first legendary dynasty, and linked archaeologically with the Erlitou culture.[9]

Along the east coast, the nuclear Longshan culture area, the remains of a number of cities have been reported. Further excavations have also been made at Chengziya, which was first excavated in the 1930s.[10] In northeast China, in western Liaoning and eastern Inner Mongolia, many stone-walled sites were built during the period 2300-1600 BC.[11] The evidence indicates that from 3000 BC onwards, in central and northern China, a revolutionary transformation was taking place from neolithic villages to prehistoric cities.[12]

What was the driving force behind such changes? And what were the social conditions like? As K C Chang observed, the 3rd/2nd millennium BC was a period of innovation within the Longshan cultural sphere, which quickly spread.[13] These developments, in addition to growing cities, included new technology in the ceramics industry and the emergence of a metal industry, public works and, importantly, the emergence in society of an élite, who controlled ritual practices and the right to interpret them. There was evidence of an institutionalised violence. The economic divisions, the concentration of manpower and the stratification of social classes also paved the way for the transition to an urbanised society.

The most astonishing new discoveries, however, have come from the south. In the middle ranges of the Yangzi River, archaeologists have uncovered several large walled settlements dated to c2800-2000 BC, including Pengtou-shan, Shijiahe, Jimingcheng and Yingxiangcheng.[14] Shijiahe is the largest site, covering about 1,200,000 square metres, and including a cluster of nearby settlements. Excavation of the site has revealed systematic spatial arrangement. Evidence of the manufacture of many ritual objects indicates that Shijiahe was probably a religious centre. Some evidence of bronze-casting has also been found within the city.

Building massive walled cities of the south required a technology quite different from the rammed-earth method commonly used in the north. Analysis of the early section of the remaining wall at Yinxiangcheng shows it is about 40 metres wide at the base narrowing to five metres at the top. The wall was constructed not by the rammed-earth method, but by layering different soils on top of one other. Outside the wall was a huge 45 metres wide moat, from which had been taken the soil used for building the wall. Remains of wooden boats have been retrieved from the moats, indicating that the moats were probably used for protecting against floods, or maybe even for fishing. The distinctive morphology and technology of the cities along the Yangzi River suggest that urban centres in this region might derive from an independent origin from those of the north, and that they may have performed different functions.

The City for Kings

In China, like many other places, the development of cities is closely associated with the formation of states. The 'Bronze Age' in China started in approximately 2000 BC, which corresponds to the rise of dynastic power in the Chinese historical tradition. At the Erlitou site (c1900 BC) in Henan, archaeologists have found the most convincing evidence of the use of bronze for making ritual vessels. In Erlitou, more than 10 architectural remains have been identified as palaces and temples. Although no city wall has been found so far, many archaeologists believe that Erlitou was probably the old capital of the Xia dynasty, or, as others have suggested, an early city of the Shang people.[15]

In 1983-84, archaeologists excavated a city site at Yanshi in Henan. The enclosure is rectangular; the southern wall is no longer extant and the northern wall is partly damaged, but the western and eastern walls remain, measuring 1,710 metres and 1,640 metres respectively. There were gates on each side and the main street of the city was about eight metres wide. Scholars believe that the Yanshi site is likely to be Xibo, the capital of the Shang king Tang.[16]

Another city site discovered in Zhengzhou, Henan, is undoubtedly a Shang capital (c1600 BC). It is larger than the Yanshi site, with a rammed-earth wall 6,960 metres long. Within the enclosure, architectural remains of palaces have been found; outside the city are cemeteries, workshops and a number of dwellings.[17] Recent excavations at the site have revealed the earliest use of a wheeled vehicle in China.[18] As K C Chang argues, the Shang city at Zhengzhou meets all the criteria for a mature city, clearly associated with the state machine.[19]

However, the city wall may not be indispensable for every royal city. The Xiaotun site at Anyang was the last capital of the Shang dynasty. Contrasting with

[12] Qu Yingjie 1989. 'Lun Longshan wenhua shiqi gu chengzhi.' Tian Changwu and Shi Xingbang eds. Zhongguo yuanshi wenhua lunji. Beijing: Wenwu chubanshe, 267-80.

[13] Chang, K C 1986. The Archaeology of Ancient China (Fourth Edition). New Haven and London: Yale University Press.

[14] Zhang Xuqiu. 1994. 'Qujialing wenhua gucheng de faxian he chubu yanjiu.' Kaogu 1994(7), 629-634; Ren Shinan 1996. 'Chang-jiang zhongyou wenming qiyuan tansuo — yi Qujialing, Shijiahe wenhua wei zhongxin.' Zhongguo shehui kexueyuan lishi yanjiusuo eds. Hua Xia wenming yu chuanshi cangshu — Essays of the International symposium on Sinology, Haikou, China, 1995. Beijing: Chinese Social Sciences Press, 252-284. See also Zhang Chi and Okamura's article in this volume.

[15] Yin Weizhang 1986. 'A re-examination of Erh-li-t'ou culture.' K C Chang, ed. Studies of Shang Archaeology. New Haven and London: Yale University Press, 1-13.

[16] Zhao Zhiquan Xu Diankui 1988. 'Yanshi Shixiangguo Shangdai zaoqi chengzhi.' Zhongguo kaogu xuehui eds. Zhongguo kaogu xuehui diwuci nianhui lunwenji. Beijing: Wenwu chubanshe.

[17] An Jinhuai 1986. 'The Shang city at Cheng-chou and related problems.' In K C Chang ed. Studies of Shang Archaeology. New Haven and London: Yale University Press, 15-48.

[18] People's Daily [Overseas Edition], (31-12-96).

[19] Chang, K C 1985. 'Guanyu Zhongguo chuqi 'chengshi' zhege gainian.' Wenwu 1985(2), 61-67.

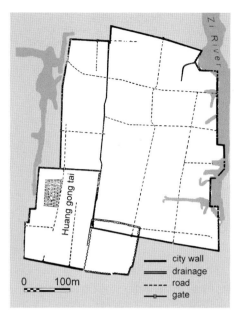

Figure 3 • Layout of Linzi city of the Qi state. After the Institute of Archaeology, CASS 1984, 272

the Zhengzhou site, no city walls have yet been found at Xiaotun. The current view is that the powerful Shang did not need a fortified wall as protection, and that natural barriers such as rivers and artificial ditches were sufficient defence. However, in the Shang divination records, we read that the Shang kings frequently went out to inspect the different settlements around the capital. This suggests that the Shang may have already established the *jiao* suburb and *ye* fields system, in areas that were outside the direct rule of the Shang kings.

During the Western Zhou period (c11th century-771 BC), after the Shang had been overthrown by the Zhou people from the northwest in about 1040 BC, the new rulers inherited the Shang writing system, metal industry and, to a degree, the Shang rituals. Politically, they established a system of enfeoffment, dividing their territory into petty 'states' ruled by the *zhuhou* or dukes, who were members of the royal family or old heads of various tribes. Only a limited number of Western Zhou cities have been excavated; contemporary literary sources, however, relate the close association of urbanisation with statecraft during this period.[20] The lands under heaven all belonged to the king. A hierarchical administrative zone system was established to control the fief/dukedoms. The symbolism of space order was apparent in both political and ritual thinking.

Inner City, Outer City

In the beginning of the Western Zhou dynasty, in addition to the capital Zongzhou, King Cheng ordered the construction of a second capital, Chengzhou, near modern-day Luoyang. The project was directed by the Duke of Zhou, and in terms of city planning Chengzhou city marks a significant development. It was, according to contemporary sources, built in two parts: the inner city, *wangcheng*, occupied by the king's palaces, and the outer city, *guo*, mostly for the military and the old Shang aristocrats who had now become citizens subject to the new regime.[21]

Recent archaeology has pushed for an even earlier origin for the inner and outer cities structure. In 1986-7, outside the enclosure of the Shang city at Zhengzhou, to the south and west, archaeologists uncovered the remains of the base of a rammed-earth wall, which could be a wall of the outer enclosure.[22] The function of the outer city was obviously to control and protect, but the increase of population and an intensification of commercial activities could also account for the appearance of the outer city. This is clearly demonstrated by the excavation of a number of city sites of the Eastern Zhou period (771-221 BC).

For instance, the excavation of Linzi in Shandong, the capital of the Qi State revealed a double city, where a small enclosure was located in the southwest corner of a much larger walled surround (figure 3).[23] The northern and southern sides of the city were protected by moats. The remaining eastern wall of the inner city is 2,195 metres long, the western wall 2,274 metres, the northern wall 1,404 metres, and the southern wall 1,402 metres. There were five gates altogether, with two leading to the outer city, which was rectangular with a 3,316 metres long northern wall and 5,209 metres long eastern wall. Archaeologists have also identified gates on all sides and roads within the outer city. Examination of the walls shows that the inner city was built later than the larger enclosure, probably during the Warring States period when trade intensified in the cities, and at a time when warfare between states was commonplace.

The majority of the Eastern Zhou cities, including Xinzheng of the Zheng and Han States, Xintian of the Jin State, Handan of the Zhao State, but excepting Jinancheng of the Chu State in the south, share a similar layout, with the inner city located in the western part of the outer city, and the main gate facing to the east. This custom lasted for several hundred years until the 1st century AD. When the Eastern Han dynasty constructed its capital in Luoyang, the orientation of the

[20] Lu Liancheng 1993. 'Zhongguo gudai ducheng fazhang dezaoqi jieduan - Shangdai Xi-Zhou ducheng xingtai de kaocha.' Zhongguo shehui kexueyuan kaogu yanjiusuo eds. *Zhongguo kaoguxue luncong*. Beijing: Kexue chubanshe.

[21] Hsu Cho-yun and Linduff, K M 1988. *Western Zhou Civilization*. New Haven and London: Yale University Press.

[22] Henan Sheng wenwu yanjiusuo 1991. 'Zhengzhou Shangcheng wai hangtu qiangji de tiaocha yu shijue.' *Zhongyuan wenwu* 1991(1), 87-95.

[23] Qun Li 1972. 'Linzi Qiguo gudu kantan jiyao.' *Wenwu* 1972(5), 45-54.

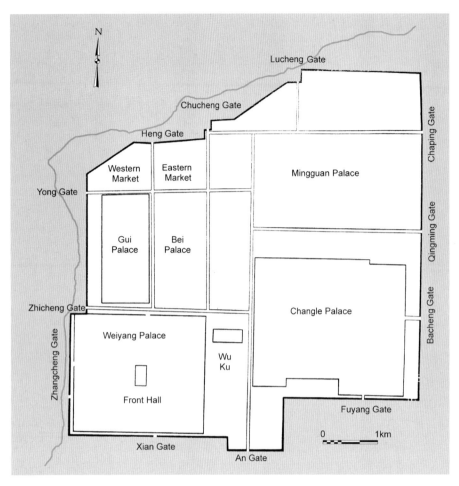

Figure 4 • Layout of the Han dynasty capital Chang'an. After the Institute of Archaeology, CASS 1984, 394

city was now set to face south.

The inner/outer city model represents the second transformation of Chinese urbanism.[24] From the 8th to the 3rd century BC, improvements in agricultural technology, *e g* the use of iron tools, resulted in surplus which allowed trade to develop in an urban context. Commercialism encouraged politicians, craftsmen, artists and philosophers to integrate further within society, and bronze and ceramic manufacturing centres, even academies for philosophers, mushroomed throughout the country. Cities and markets often served as places to exchange goods and ideas. At the same time, though, the decline of the central power of the Zhou kings also made the traditional city model untenable. The concept of the classical 'ideal city' had to be shelved to wait for its revival in a new context.

The Warring States were unified by the first emperor of Qin, Shihuangdi, in 221 BC. The old capital of the Qin dynasty has been badly eroded by the Wei River and archaeological work has proved extremely difficult there. However, on the southern banks of the Wei River stands the capital of the Western Han dynasty, Chang'an, one of the most important capital cities of the ancient world, and one which has been under archaeological investigation since the 1950s (figure 4).

As Wu Hung points out, Han Chang'an was not a single construction but consists of different strata.[25] When the Han dynasty was first established in 206 BC, it reused the old palaces left by the Qin Empire. Systematic construction of the city wall did not start until 194 BC. When the wall was finally completed and new palaces had been added, the Han rulers did indeed seem to have had some idea of city planning. Han dynasty Chang'an was an impressive city: the remaining eastern wall is 6,000 metres, the southern wall 7,600, the western wall

[24] Du Zhengsheng (Tu Cheng-sheng) 1992. *Gudai shehui yu guojia*. Taipei: Yunsheng Cultural Company, 609-727.

[25] Wu Hung 1995: *Monumentality in Early Chinese Art and Archaeology*, California: Stanford University Press, 148-149.

[26] Zhongguo shehui kexueyuan kaogu yanjiusuo 1984. *Xin Zhongguo de kaogu faxian he yanjiu.* Beijing: Wenwu chubanshe, 393-397.

[27] Yang Kuan 1993. *Zhongguo gudai ducheng zhidushi yanjiu.* Shanghai: Guji chubanshe, 114-133, 573-613.

[28] Liu Qingzhu 1996. 'Han Chang'an cheng de kaogu faxian ji xiangguan wenti yanjiu — jinian Han Chang'an cheng kaogu gongzuo sishi nian.' *Kaogu* 1996(10), 1-14.

[29] Yang Kuan 1993. *Zhongguo gudai ducheng zhidushi yanjiu.* Shanghai: Guji chubanshe, 186-187, 191-200.

4,900 metres and the northern wall 7,200 metres, with 2,570 metres of the perimeter remaining. The city had 12 gates, three on each side. The road network consisted of eight avenues running north to south and east to west, the longest of which is Anmen Avenue, 5,400 metres long and 45-56 metres wide. Within the enclosure were five royal palaces, one armoury in the middle and two markets behind the palaces. A ritual complex built by Wang Mang in AD 4 has also been uncovered in the suburbs south of the city.[26]

The size of Han dynasty Chang'an is large (36 square kilometres), but could even a city this size have been adequate for the population of a quarter of million recorded in contemporary documents, when we consider that the city was mostly occupied by royal residences? As a consequence, Yang Kuan has suggested that Chang'an was only the inner city of the Western Han capital, and that there was an even larger outer city.[27] However, several archaeologists disagree with him for no traces have been found to date of such an outer enclosure.[28]

In AD 25, the Eastern Han dynasty established its capital in Luoyang. This city has also been excavated. It is rectangular, and consists of two palaces, the Northern Palace and Southern Palace. Compared with Chang'an, the Luoyang city is much smaller (9.5 square kilometres), and is likely to have been the inner-city. We would expect there to be a much larger outer city surrounding it. The most significant difference between Chang'an and Luoyang is that the main gate of Luoyang was the southern gate, instead of the eastern gate of earlier times. This change of orientation probably reflects the ideological and ritual changes of the Eastern Han period.[29]

A Grid City

One of the most distinctive characteristics of Chinese medieval city planning is that the city landscape is divided into numerous regularly shaped wards, often described as similar to a chess board. From literary sources we read that as early as the Eastern Zhou period, the population of a city was divided into different groups, which lived in separate enclosed wards, called *li*. Each ward had its own administrators and guards. This system may have started with military units in mind, and its purpose was clearly for easier control of the movements of population.

Historical documents record that during the Western Han dynasty, Chang'an had about 160 *li* wards, and about 50-100 families lived in each ward. However, archaeological excavations of Han dynasty Chang'an do not show a regular layout of wards. The first clear evidence of the use of a grid plan in China is Luoyang during the Northern Wei period (No 386-535). Luoyang, as the capital of the Eastern Han dynasty, was burned down in AD 190, then rebuilt as the capitals of the Cao-Wei court and the Western Jin dynasty for another 100 years. In 312 it fell once again, this time to attack from Xiongnu horsemen. The Northern Wei dynasty moved its capital from Pingcheng in Shanxi to Luoyang in 494, and decided that the new city ought to be properly designed and constructed. Compared with older Chinese cities, the new Luoyang capital had certain distinguishing features: *a*) the royal palaces were located on the axis of the city; *b*) the city was based on a grid system, with 320 residential wards and the royal palace and park complexes. The wards were square. Each ward had four gates, one on each side, and was controlled by two officers, four administrators and eight gatekeepers.[30]

[30] Su Bai 1978a. 'Bei Wei Luoyang cheng he Beimang lingmu.' *Wenwu* 1978(7), 42-52.

[31] Meng Fanren, 1994. 'Shilun Bei Wei Luoyangcheng de xingzhi yu zhongya gucheng xingzhi de guanxi - jiantan silu yanxian chengshi de zhongyaoxing.' *Han Tang yu bianjiang kaogu yanjiu* 1, 97-110.

Was the idea of the grid plan indigenous to China or was it imported? Several Chinese archaeologists have argued that this model was probably diffused from a western tradition.[31] The invention of the grid plan has been attributed to the Greek town planner Hippodamus of the 5th century BC, whose model spread beyond the Greek world, reaching Central Asia with the conquest of Alexander the Great in the 4th century BC. Many Central Asian cities were based on the grid system. The Northern Wei dynasty was established in the 4th century AD by a non-Chinese ethnic group — the Tuoba or the Xianbei. Though there is a substantial time difference of several hundred years between the Hellenistic cities and Northern Wei Luoyang, the nomadic origins of the Xianbei

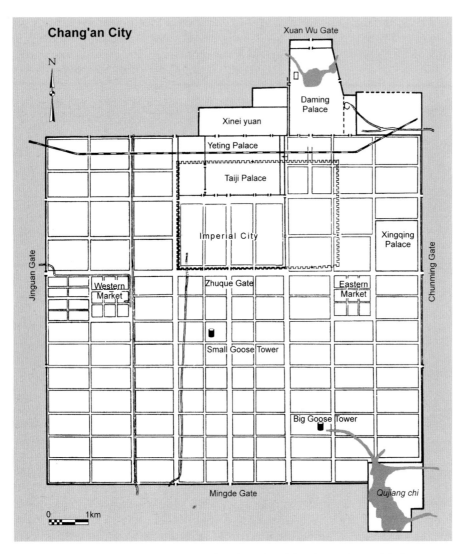

Figure 5 • Layout of the Tang dynasty capital Chang'an. After the Institute of Archaeology, CASS 1984, 573

may have brought them in contact with other peoples of Central Asia, from whom they learned such knowledge.

Between the 6th and 8th centuries, the royal capitals of the Tang dynasty (618-906) were designed along a grid. The Tang dynasty had two capitals: the western capital, Chang'an, was built to the southeast of the Han dynasty Chang'an (figure 5); and the eastern capital was built at Luoyang. Archaeological investigation of Tang dynasty Chang'an, has revealed both an inner and outer city.[32] The inner city is roughly square, located in the centre, and measuring 3,335 metres north to south and 2,820 metres east to west, with the palace complex at the back. The outer city is rectangular, 8,651 metres north to south, 9,721 metres east to west, covering a total area of 84 square kilometres. The outer city was divided into more than 100 wards, now known as *fang*, of three regular sizes. There were two markets, the Western Market and the Eastern Market.

The basic layout of Tang dynasty Chang'an clearly follows the Northern Wei model at Luoyang. It was symmetrical, with the position of palaces and the rectangular wards exactly as previously, but on a much larger and more sophisticated scale. The classical model of the 'ideal city,' as well as geomancy, also influenced city planning for Tang dynasty Chang'an.

Luoyang was much smaller than Chang'an, about 47 square kilometres. Whilst Luoyang was designed with an inner and outer city and a grid plan, it was

[32] Zhongguo shehui kexueyuan kaogu yanjiusuo 1984. *Xin Zhongguo de kaogu faxian he yanjiu*. Beijing: Wenwu chubanshe, 572-581.

[33] Su Bai 1978b. 'Sui Tang Chang'an cheng he Luoyang cheng. *Kaogu* 1978(6), 406-25.

less elaborate than Chang'an, where the layout was determined by ideological factors, such as the palace in the centre according to the classical model.[33] In Luoyang, the palaces and the imperial city were located in the northwest corner of the city. The outer city was divided by the Luo River into northern and southern sections, and many canals ran through the city. The advanced canal system provided good transportation, particularly for business. Luoyang had three markets, all close to the canals. In other words, commercial factors played an important role here.

City and Market

The market is a place for trade. It is a result of economic divisions and the expansion of craft production. Goods need to be distributed. By the time of the Eastern Zhou period, many markets appeared in an urban context. However, they were probably multifunctional and were firmly controlled by the state. At Yong, the old capital of Qin State, near modern-day Fengxiang in Shaanxi, archaeologists have identified structural remains, close to the northern city wall, as the marketplace. This was a rectangular enclosure (160 metres north to south and 180 metres west to east, a total area of almost 30,000 square metres) with one gate on each side.[34] The walled marketplaces could have made tax-collecting easy and, like the closed residential wards, appear to be designed to prevent the free movement of people. Newly excavated Qin-Han bamboo slips also show that the markets were strictly regulated by the government.

[34] Yang Yubin 1993. 'Zhengzhou Shang cheng de kaogu faxian he yanjiu.' *Zhongyuan wenwu* 1993(3), 81.

The markets in Han dynasty Chang'an were divided into eastern and western sections, and stood behind the palaces. They may have been further divided into subsections for different trades. This model was followed in Tang dynasty Chang'an, where archaeologists have excavated both the eastern and western markets. The western market measured 1,031 metres north to south, 927 metres west to east, and the eastern market was almost the same size, 1,000 metres north to south, 924 metres west to east. The markets were surrounded by walls and within each market there were two vertical and two horizontal streets crossing each other. Along the streets were shops and stalls, and at the end of one street stood two storage buildings. The government set up special offices in each market to conduct daily business and arbitrate among traders. There was a clear division between the eastern and western markets: the former was mostly for tailors and butchers, the latter for medicine stores, gold and silversmiths and jewellery shops. Foreign traders to Tang Chang'an all gathered in the western market where the wine bars served by foreign ladies and music were famously popular places for Chinese poets.

By the 10th century, however, the rigid market system was no longer appropriate. In Tang dynasty Luoyang, considerable changes were taking place. There were three markets, instead of two, in the outer city of Luoyang, all near canals for easy transport of goods. The growing importance of commercial concerns in city planning can be better seen in another Tang city — Yangzhou in Jiangsu (figure 6).

The city of Yangzhou was located by the Grand Canal, built by Emperor Yangdi of the Sui dynasty in AD 605-10. The original purpose of the canal was to transport supplies from the south to the north to support the war against Korea. In the 7th century, the traditional land trade route via the 'Silk Road,' between China and Europe was obstructed by the Tibetans, making sea trade more safe and economical. Foreign goods were loaded in the Persian Gulf, transported to coastal ports such as Guangzhou (Canton), Jiaozhou and Quanzhou, then shipped along the rivers to Yangzhou, whence they were distributed throughout the country. Goods exported from China also followed the same route. Yangzhou became a very important commercial centre for west-east trade.[35] It was also the national base for ship building.

[35] Yu Yongbing 1994. 'Shitang Sichouzhilu shang de Yangzhou Tangcheng,' *Han Tang yu bianjiang kaogu yanjiu* 1, 169-172.

Archaeological excavation in Yangzhou has shown that the old city consisted of two parts: the date of the old town, Zicheng, can be traced back to the Han period, but the new town, Luocheng, was entirely constructed in the Tang dynasty, around AD 783.[36] The new part was almost three times bigger than the old Zicheng. To the east of Luocheng ran the Grand Canal, and two rivers ran north to south through the city. The two rivers provided the city with its main transport, and markets were probably set up along the river banks. Contemporary writers described 24 bridges on the rivers, and this is largely confirmed by archaeological investigations.[37] It is difficult to think why there was a need for so many bridges along the rivers if they were not for flourishing commercial activities. Excavations have also yielded many foreign objects, such as glass, gold, Persian ceramics, and a flask with Arabic writing on it.

Commerce transformed the landscape of Chinese cities, and by the Song period (960-1279), the main feature of big cities was the predominance of crowded streets and shops. The most vivid picture of this comes not from archaeology but from a contemporary artist, Zhang Zeduan, whose painting, *Qingming shanghe tu* [Up the river on Qingming festival], painted in the 11th century, depicted the busy riverside street scenes of Kaifeng, the capital of the Northern Song dynasty (figure 7).[38] People were no longer confined to enclosed wards but moved out onto the streets, planting trees and digging wells. New features developed in the market, too, with inns, restaurants and theatres. This marks another important transformation in Chinese urbanism, from the traditional 'closed wards' to the 'open market.'

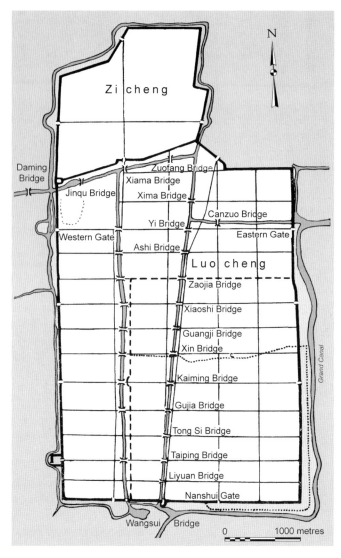

Figure 6 • Layout of the Tang dynasty city of Yangzhou. After Jiang Zhongyi 1994, 163

Conclusion

Urbanisation in China seems to coincide with global cycles. The first urbanisation took place around the 3rd and 2nd millennia BC, at the turning point of the transition from the neolithic to the Bronze Age. Archaeologists have offered different interpretations for the emergence of early cities in China.[39] What drove people to move from open fields into walled settlements? It should be noted that furious warfare was becoming commonplace during the later neolithic period in the central plains, probably due to an increase in population and, at the same time, the decrease of natural resources. We should also pay attention to the deep divisions within society and the emergence of institutionalised religion. Religious objects from many of the sites seem to show that the worshipping of earthly gods and making sacrifices to ancestors became the key factor in the establishment of a supreme power. Rulers always acclaimed their superior spiritual power, in addition to their military power over ordinary men. In this sense, urbanisation is closely associated with the formation of a state religion.

The second urban revolution in China is associated with the use of new technology and the decentralisation of political powers, together with intensified warfare among petty states, during the later half of the 1st millennium BC. Once China had become an empire, the city, or the imperial capital, always fulfilled its function as the centre of political, military and religious affairs.

[36] Yangzhou kaogu dui 1990. 'Yangzhoucheng kaogu gongzuo jianbao,' *Kaogu* 1990(1), 36-44.

[37] Jiang Zhongyi 1994. 'Tangdai Yangzhou hedao yuershici qiao kao.' *Han Tang yu bianjiang kaogu yanjiu* 1, 162-68.

[38] Whitfield, Roderick 1998. 'Material culture in the Northern Song dynasty: the world of Zhong Zeduan.' Lo, Kaiyin, ed. *Bright as Silver, White as Snow,* Hong Kong, Yunmintang.

[39] Yu Weichao 1985. 'Zhongguo gudai ducheng guihua de fazhan jieduanxing.' *Wenwu* 1985(2), 52-60.

Figure 7 • Section of Qingming shanghe tu *[Up the river on the Qingming festival], by Zhang Zeduan. After* Wenwu jinghua *1 (1959), 27*

These functions more or less determined the basic features of city planning in pre-modern China. Before the 10th century, a typical Chinese city was a closed, socially rigidly defined place, where different classes exercised their powers or struggled to survive.

Growing commercial activities and social mobility from the 10th century onwards shook the traditional 'closed' urban model. However, the inception of many capitalist elements did not bring China into a capitalist society, for after the Song dynasty, China came under the rule of the Ming dynasty and several non-Chinese governments (Tanguts, Mongol and Manchus). There had never developed fully an independent city economy in traditional China.[40] City planning returned time and again to the closed model. This classical model is the result of Chinese social development, reflecting the social relationships and ideology which mainly derived from Confucianism. Many neighbouring countries, such as Japan, took this model and developed it in their own cultural traditions.[41]

[40] Fu Zhufu 1980. *Zhongguo jingjishi luncong*. Beijing: Sanlian chubanshe, 321-386.

[41] Ueda Masaaki 1976. *Tojo*. Tokyo: Shakai shisosha; Steinhardt, N S 1990. *Chinese imperial city planning*. Honolulu: University of Hawaii Press, 108-118.

Tattoos found on bodies in the Pazyryk tombs

The Cultural Frontiers

CHEN FANG-MEI

Bronze Weapons from the South: the Xin'gan Case

*L*ate Shang (c1300-1045 BC) bronze weapons were distributed over a large part of southern China including the present provinces of Jiangxi, Jiangsu, Anhui, Hunan, and Guangxi. Most of these southern excavations, however, have been on a small scale. The Xin'gan Dayangzhou (Bronze Age) site in Jiangxi is an exception to this rule. It was excavated in 1989, as the result of a chance find beneath a sandy mound on the east side of the Gan River. Local archaeologists believe that it was a burial: traces of a lacquered tomb chamber and coffin could be detected, although the wood of both had decayed away. The tomb was a rectangular pit, oriented at 271°, with a chamber 3.6 metres wide and 8.22 metres long, and a coffin 0.85 metres wide and 2.34 metres long. One thousand and three hundred and seventy-four (1,374) burial objects were retrieved from the burial site (figure 1).[1]

Presently, the Xin'gan tomb is unique among southern burials, on account of its large size and great amount of bronze weapons and vessels, jades, and pottery. The discovery of the Xin'gan site has revealed the complexity of Late Shang bronze weapons in the south.

Scholars, however, have different opinions about the dating of the Xin'gan tomb. One group of scholars has dated it to the Late Shang,[2] but another group argues that it is as late as the Western Zhou or even the Eastern Zhou.[3] The disparity in the dating of the Xin'gan tomb reveals the difficulties encountered when dating archaeological sites outside the central plains, partly because the relationship and interaction between the centre and periphery has been less understood, but mainly on account of the lack of a chronological sequence for the outer regions. This may simply be because more archaeological excavation has been done in the central plains, or because large quantities of bronze artefacts were continuously produced and used there, whereas in the outer regions it may be that the casting and use of bronze artefacts was intermittent.

Therefore, at the moment, establishing a basic chronological sequence for the regions outside the central plains is made possible only by the fact that their artefacts often betray a typological relationship with those of the central plains. The Xin'gan tomb is one example of this. Based on a stylistic comparison between the Xin'gan and Anyang bronze weapons, many scholars believe that they were contemporary; others insist that the central plain had imposed its influence on the regions surrounding it, and that accordingly stylistic elements of the central plains were retained much later in the outer regions.

[1] Jiangxi 1997 (Jiangxi sheng wenwu kaogu yanjiusuo *et al*): *Xin'gan Shangdai damu*, Beijing, Wenwu chubanshe.

[2] Peng Shifan, Liu Lin, Zhan Kaixun 1991: 'Guanyu Xin'gan Dayangzhou Shangmu niandai wenti de taolun.' *Wenwu* 1991 (10): 27-32; Li Xueqin 1991:'Xin'gan Dayangzhou Shangmu ruogan wenti.' *Wenwu* 1991 (10): 33; Zou Heng 1990: 'Youguan Xin'gan chutu qingtongqi de jige wenti.' *Zhongguo wenwu bao* December 6,1990.

[3] Ma Chengyuan 1992: 'Wu Yue wenhua qingtongqi de yanjiu – jianlun Dayangzhou chutu de qingtongqi.' *Wu Yue qingtongqi yanjiu zuotanhui*, 19-21; Hayashi 1994: 'Kachu seidoki jiakanshu no ukamon no dento.' *Senoku Hakkokan Kiyo* 10: 3-56.

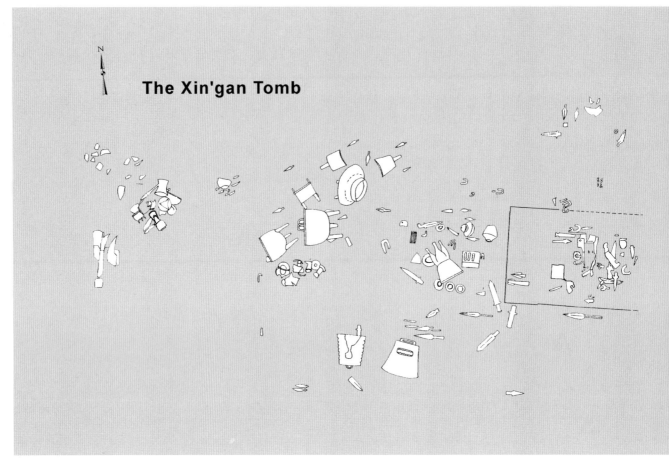

The Xin'gan Tomb

Figure 1 • Location of artefacts in the Xin'gan tomb

Scholars who have doubts about the possibility of indigenous development in the areas outside the central plains prefer to date the cultural remains from regional areas as being later than those with similar forms in the Central plains. They may do so either because of the lack of a chronological sequence for the outer regions, or because they are unconsciously influenced by the 'nuclear' theory which has dominated Chinese archaeology in the last 40 years. However, it is not possible to conduct a complete analysis of the styles of the Xin'gan bronze weapons solely on the basis of the chronological sequence of the central plains. By conducting a new stylistic analysis of the bronze weapons found there, I believe that the Xin'gan tomb can be dated to a period no later than the Late Shang period. This discussion will focus on two aspects: the indigenous style of the bronze weapons from the Xin'gan tomb and the stylistic parallels between the Xin'gan bronze weapons and those from areas such as Anyang and the northwest.

Bronze Weapons and Burial Systems

The wealth of bronze weapons at the Xin'gan tomb suggests a strong parallel with the tombs of the Anyang area, which can be classified into several categories according to the objects buried in them.[4] Among tombs containing bronzes, two main types can be distinguished: *Type I*, tombs in which the majority of the bronze objects are weapons; and *Type II*, tombs with bronze weapons but in which the majority of the bronze objects are vessels. Further subdivisions are possible, such as whether the bronze weapons are of one or more kinds, whether a human sacrifice is found in addition to bronze weapons. The tombs of Type II are normally thought to be those of Shang kings (with four ramps), or of members of a royal family, or of the nobility.

[4] Chen Fangmei 1997: 'Shang houqi qingtong fu yue zhi de fazhan ji qi wenhua yiyi.' *Zhongguo kaoguxue yu lishixue zhenghe guoji yantaohui lunwenji*. Taipei: Institute of History and Philology, 983-1052; The same author 1997: *The Bronze Weapons of the Late Shang Period* (PhD dissertation), London: University of London, School of Oriental and African Studies, 172-94.

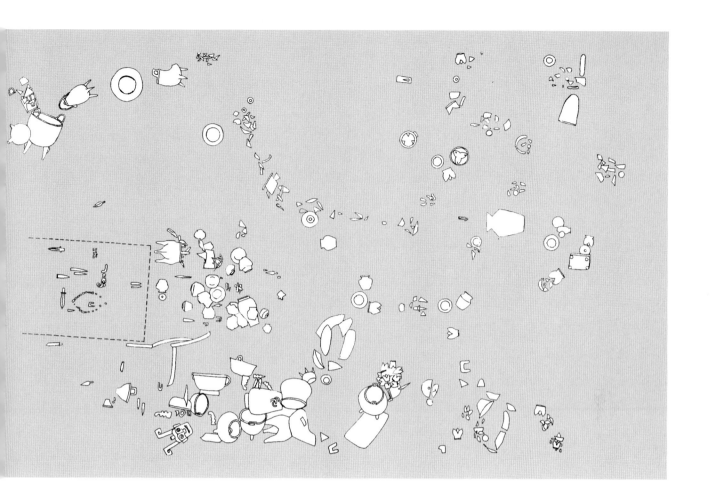

Following the Anyang classification, the Xin'gan tomb can be classified as being of Type I, in which bronze weapons were in the majority but in which bronze vessels still played an important role. The scale of both bronze weapons and bronze vessels at the Xin'gan tomb matches that found at Guojiazhuang M160 at Anyang, and tomb M1713 of the western sector of Yinxu, both of Type I.

The Xin'gan tomb contained 232 bronze weapons (including 123 arrowheads) together with 59 bronze vessels. This is comparable with Guojiazhuang tomb M160, which contained over 200 bronze weapons (and an additional 902 arrowheads) and 40 bronze vessels; and with tomb M1713 of the western sector of Yinxu, which had 65 bronze weapons (no arrowheads) and 17 bronze vessels.

In addition, the above three tombs share other common characteristics such as size of the tomb chamber and coffin, the presence of a tomb shelf (probably intended for sacrificial victims), and the main kinds of bronze weapons found in them, the most important of which are the *ge* dagger-axe and *mao* spearhead. The Xin'gan tomb contained 35 *mao* and 31 *ge*; Guojiazhuang tomb M160, 95 *mao* and 118 *ge*; tomb M1713, 30 *mao* and 30 *ge*. These figures show how the Xin'gan tomb can be seen in the context of Type I tombs at Anyang.

If one can judge the status of the occupant on the basis of the number of *ge* and *mao* as well as by the number of bronze vessels and the scale of their decoration, the occupant of the Xin'gan tomb could be a noble with considerable military and political powers. His status might be close to or slightly higher than that of the occupant of tomb M1713 at Yinxu if we consider the close similarities in the number of *ge* and *mao*. The total number of bronze weapons and bronze vessels in the Xin'gan tomb, however, is much greater than those in tomb M1713.

Typology, Assemblage, Forms and Decoration

The inventory of bronze weapons at Xin'gan is as listed below:

mao spearhead: 35

ge dagger-axe: 31

yue axe: 6

gouji hooked halberd: 1

dao knife: 15

bishou dagger : 2

jian sword: 2

zu arrowheads:123

zou helmet: 1

dun ferrule: 19

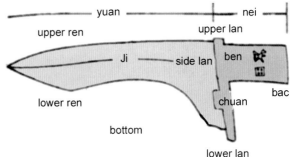

Figure 2 • Traditional terminology of ge *dagger axe*

Of all the different bronze weapons, the *ge* and *yue* have the most complex typology. The terminology used by modern scholars for the various parts of the *ge*, such as *yuan* (the full length of the blade), *nei* (tang inserted into and projecting beyond the wooden shaft), *lan* (small projections providing a more secure attachment for binding the weapon to the shaft) and *hu* (downward extension of the lower edge) is derived from ancient classics (figure 2). At Anyang, six sub-types of double-bladed *ge* can be distinguished on the basis of variations of form or method of attachment to the shaft (in some of these, the shaft is inserted in a socket, rather than the *nei* passing through the shaft). There are three main types of *yue* axe and further sub-types, fastened either by means of the *nei* or with a socket (*qiongku*).

Among the burials of a similar date, the inventory of the Xin'gan tomb is second only to that of the Fu Hao tomb at Anyang.[5] However, it is worth noting that at the Xin'gan tomb, the large number of bronze weapons, a total of 232 pieces, greatly surpassed that of the bronze vessels, only 59 pieces, which is very different case from the Fu Hao tomb. It is clear that the assemblage of bronze weapons in the Xin'gan tomb includes not only all the various types of bronze weapons found in the Anyang area, with the exception of the bow-shaped implement, but also some types which were rare at Anyang such as the hooked *ji* halberd, *jian* sword and socketed *yue* axe.

There are several reasons why the *ge* is a significant for dating. At Anyang, the *ge* is one of the principal bronze weapons: there is an ample number of examples, sufficient to provide a clear outline of its development. In the Xin'gan tomb also, the *ge* is a major weapon: the number of *ge* in the Xin'gan tomb is second only to the number of *mao* spearheads, with a total of 31 examples. There are 24 *ge* with rectangular *nei*, four *ge* with curved *nei*, and three *ge* with a descending blade, *hu*. The *ge* with rectangular *nei* counts for the majority of the *ge* types, while it is worth noting that there are no examples of socketed *ge*.

The three major utilitarian forms of the central plains *ge* are the *ge* with rectangular *nei*, the socketed *ge*, and the *ge* with *hu*. In nearly 300 years of the Anyang period, the comparatively few finds of the socketed *ge* with *hu* identify Late Shang Phases III and IV as the initial period for this type, while the *ge* with rectangular *nei* and the socketed *ge* are the most common types of utilitarian weapons. In the development of the *ge*, the *ge* with rectangular *nei* gradually gives way to the socketed *ge*. This shift occurs between Late Shang Phases II and III. As the socketed *ge* becomes more popular, the *ge* with rectangular *nei* passing through the shaft becomes less common. In Phases III and IV the utilitarian *ge* with *hu* appears in a small number of tombs. A more ritualised form of the *ge*, the *ge* with curved *nei*, is retained through Phases IV.

[5] Bagley 1992: 'Changjiang Bronzes and Shang Archaeology' *Zhonghua minguo jianguo bashinian Zhongguo yishu wenwu taolunhui lunwenji*, Taipei, 209-256.

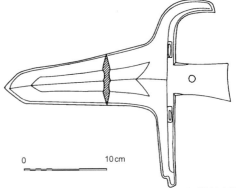

Figure 3 • A bronze gouji *hooked halberd, XDM 135*

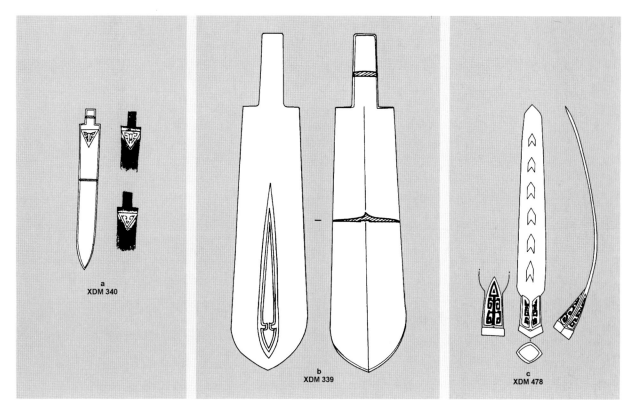

Figure 4 • *Three bronze* bishou *hand daggers:* **a** *XDM 340,* **b** *XDM 339,* **c** *XDM 478*

The decoration on this type of *ge,* first seen late in Phase I in the shape of a sculptured bird, is traditionally applied on the curved part of the *nei.*

The *ge* with rectangular *nei* accounts for the majority of *ge* in the Xin'gan tomb. Among them, those with a straight *nei* and a long blade are similar to Erligang examples. The remaining *ge* with rectangular *nei* assume a style similar to Anyang examples dating to Late Shang Phases I and II. The Xin'gan tomb also contains some *ge* of forms that have not appeared at Anyang: for example, the three examples of *ge* with curved *nei* from Xin'gan, when compared with those found at Anyang, approximate the forms of Yinxu Phase I, but replace the traditional form with a distinctly regional style and realistic décor such as tiger (figure 9) or *kui* dragon.

In comparison with the styles and forms of *ge* from Anyang, the *ge* from the Xin'gan tomb manifest a strong indigenous style, not typical of other regions. It should be noted that examples of *ge* with rectangular and curved *nei* of the Erligang tradition, the forerunners of the Anyang *ge,* are also seen in the south at Huangpi Panlongcheng, Hubei. Could it be that the south and Anyang were both developing from that tradition? While not denying the possibility of their mutual interaction, they appear to be independent developments from one original tradition.

The forms of *ge* from the Xin'gan tomb are not limited to those found at Anyang, but represent a parallel development and a high degree of independent initiative within this tomb. Not only was the *ge,* the principal weapon of the Anyang tombs, important in the Xin'gan tomb, but its function was embellished with the development of the *gouji* hooked halberd (figure 3), a weapon then unknown in the Anyang area. Balancing the extended *hu* found on one type of *ge,* a backwards-curving part was added to the top of the *hu* for hooking. The Xin'gan *gouji* with its cross-like form bears some resemblance to the *ji* of the Western Zhou period, all of which consisted of the *ge* with *hu* in combination with a *mao* spearhead. However, there are several differences between them. The upward extension of the Xin'gan *gouji*

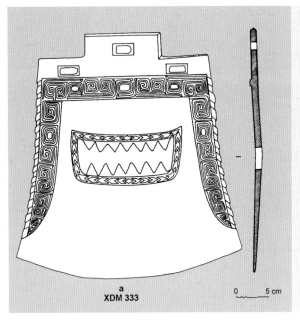

Figure 5 • *Type I bronze* yue *axes:* **a** *XDM 333,* **b** *XDM 335*

is hooked, hence its name. It may have evolved as an experiment to provide an additional function for the *ge* with *hu*. Only one *gouji* was excavated from the Xin'gan tomb. However, since it was put inside the coffin, it must have been considered important.

Another important bronze weapon in the Xin'gan tomb is the *bishou* or hand dagger, very few of which have been excavated at Anyang. In contrast, two *bishou* (figure 4), and a third blade with openwork decoration (figure 4c), were excavated at the Xin'gan tomb. Their forms, with a flat grip and no pommel, are unique, different from both the Anyang sword with a hollow cylindrical grip and from the sword with the flat grip and pommel of the north. It seems that the three different regions developed different sword forms. At the Xin'gan tomb, these reveal some experimentation with the length and profile of the sword. It appeared either as short as l4.3 centimetres or as long as 35.7 centimetres. The shorter sword (figure 4a) has a slender profile like a willow leaf. The longer one (figure 4b) has an arch profile. The sunken grooves on the body of the longer sword were specifically made to allow blood to flow along them, hence the name blood grooves.

In the case of the *yue* axe also, its importance within the Xin'gan tomb and its indigenous form are manifestions of regional character. Six *yue* were found at the Xin'gan tomb, thus revealing the importance of this weapon, in contrast to its role in the Anyang area where, except for royal tombs where the number of *yue* buried is not known, it is normal for only one or two *yue* to be found in a single tomb. Even the Fu Hao tomb, the tomb of a member of the royal family, contained only four *yue*. The six found in the Xin'gan tomb may indicate either or both of two possibilities: that the *yue* was of great importance in the south; or that, as a military officer, the occupant of the Xin'gan tomb was likely to have been of high rank.

The *yue* from the Xin'gan tomb are not only relatively numerous: their various forms indicate a new way of using this weapon. There are two types of *yue* at the Xin'gan tomb:

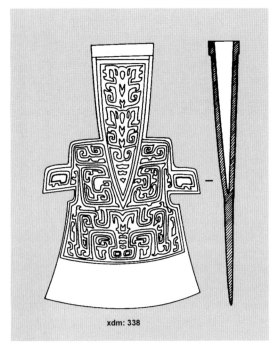

Figure 6 • *Type II bronze* yue *axe, XDM 338*

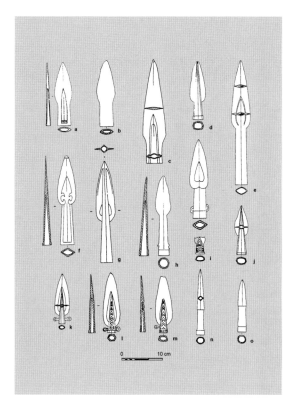

Figure 7 • Bronze mao *from the Xiangian tomb*

6 Personal communication

one, with a flat *nei* (figure 5ab), was common in the Anyang area; the other, with *qiongkou* socket (figure 6), is not seen in the Anyang area. In this type, instead of the usual flat *nei,* there is a cylindrical socket at right angles to the blade edge. While the shaft itself was possibly parallel to the blade, at the point where it was hafted the blade and shaft are perpendicular. This manner of hafting the *yue* is not found with *yue* with a flat *nei*.

The décor on the *yue* is composed of an intaglio design forming a very stylized zoomorphic mask. This form of embellishing the *yue* is not found in the Anyang area where zoomorphic masks are distinguished by protruding or distinct eyes, nose and horns. From the tomb sketch this piece was centrally placed within the tomb. According to the excavator Peng Shifan, "all weapons were placed outside the coffin, while this revolutionary Type II *yue* was placed inside the coffin...it displayed a brilliant black lustre."[6] It may have been a special weapon for the Xin'gan tomb.

This socketed form of *yue* is unique: it is not found either in the central plains or in the north. However, following the Spring and Autumn period the socketed *yue* became the standard form of *yue* in southwestern China. Perhaps this form was suitable for the particular environment of the south.

As for the *mao* spearhead, in the Xin'gan tomb this weapon is found in greater numbers than the *ge* (figure 7), whereas the opposite was usually the case in the Anyang area. Moreover, the hollow socket of several of the Xin'gan *mao* is hexagonal in cross-section. This feature is rare among the *mao* from Anyang. On some of the Xin'gan spearheads there are two small rings which are not directly attached to the socket. Such rings are again rare among the *mao* from Anyang.

Assessing the creativity seen in the bronze weapons from Xin'gan, the *ge* with lower extension *(hu)* and the *gouji* from the Xin'gan tomb represent new forms, but with a close affinity to the standard *ge* form. Can their origin be accounted for by an innate creativity and not as proceeding from developments made at Anyang? Taking development in the central plains as a standard, the *ge* with *hu* extension appears at Anyang only in Phase III or IV. The *gouji* (hooked halberd) does not appear until early in the Western Zhou as exemplified by those found at Xunxian Xincun, Shaanxi. In the case of the Xin'gan hooked *gouji*, the backward-arching hook is particularly long, parallel to the main blade of the halberd and perpendicular to the *hu*. The 90° angle of the hooked portion of the blade differs from the early Western Zhou *ji* halberd, and they are not necessarily close in date.

The Differences and Parallels between Xin'gan and Other Areas

The bronze weapons at the Xin'gan tomb reveal strong indigenous styles but also offer stylistic parallels to other areas including Anyang and Chenggu, Shaanxi. First, the Anyang style was transformed in the Xin'gan style as regards shape. For instance, the *ge* dagger-axe with an elongated straight-edged blade was common in the Anyang area but this was subtly transformed and given a concave profile on the Xin'gan *ge*.

The decoration on some of the weapons found at the Xin'gan tomb is quite alien to that found at Anyang. The design of two human heads on the *ge* just mentioned (figure 8), and of a tiger head with open mouth and teeth on a *ge* with curved *nei* (figure 9) contrast with the Anyang *ge* which were commonly decorated with a bird design. The tiger motif was a particularly common motif on bronze vessels from the Xin'gan tomb. Although only four *ge* decorated with

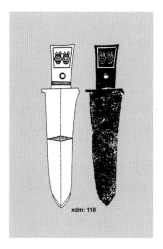

Figure 8 • Bronze ge
XDM 118 with concave profile

tiger heads and only one decorated with two human heads were found among the 31 *ge* at Xin'gan, these few examples clearly demonstrate the indigenous nature of their designs. Another example can be found among the *mao* spearheads; one type which was common in the Anyang area also appeared in the Xin'gan tomb but with a shortened socket decorated with a design of openwork chevrons (figure 7c). Both the design of the motif itself and the openwork technique are alien to the Anyang area.

The indigenous design of bronze weapons from the Xin'gan tomb can be related to the design of bronze vessels from the same tomb. The chevron design found on the spearhead frequently embellishes the bronze vessels from the same tomb. Moreover, the animal mask design on another *yue* from the Xin'gan tomb omits teeth and mouth of the animal mask, leaving only the horn, eyes and nose in low relief *leiwen* background pattern (figure 6). This form of animal mask in low relief is closer to the Erligang tradition than to the Anyang tradition.

However, certain of the bronze weapons from the Xin'gan tomb are close to those of the Anyang area. These include three types of *ge* dagger-axe, and one type of *yue* axe. In particular two of the *ge* types are almost identical in the two areas. In order to determine whether these two types of *ge* at the Xin'gan tomb had developed from the Erligang tradition at Panlongcheng which is close to Xin'gan, or from the contemporary tradition at Anyang, one may notice that these, which were the two most common forms of the *ge* found in the Xin'gan tomb, were also the core of the bronze weapons found in the Anyang area. In other words, the Anyang tradition plays an important part in the bronze *ge* from the Xin'gan tomb. These two *ge* types are the vehicle which connects the Xin'gan tomb with the Anyang tombs. Moreover, the big knife (figure 10) from the Xin'gan tomb resembles the knife from the Fu Hao tomb in shape, again revealing a close relationship between the Xin'gan tomb and the Anyang tombs.

The *yuan* main blade and *hu* lower extension of the special *ge* with *hu* from Xin'gan (figure 11) are almost perpendicular to each other, similar to the *ge* from Chenggu in Shaanxi (figure 12), but differing from the *ge* with *hu* from Anyang, raising the possibility of parallel developments in the south and west. The 90° angle of the Chenggu *ge* implies an awkward relationship between the *hu* and *yuan* and possibly represents an earlier form.

Although archaeological excavations in the south have been scattered, it is still possible to establish the indigenous elements of Xin'gan bronze weapons and trace the typological development of some examples such as *yue* axe and *mao* spearhead.

The importance of the *yue* axe in both quantity and quality is one of the indigenous characteristics of the bronze weapons at the Xin'gan tomb. This characteristic is difficult to explain in the context of the development of the *yue* in the Anyang area. For instance, Xiaotun M331, M232, M338, M333, M188, which are all undisturbed finds, have been dated to Phase I of the Late Shang period, yet no *yue* were excavated from the above tombs. Although one *yue* was excavated from M1 at Sanjiazhuang, it was plain without decoration.

It was only during the later phases of the Late Shang period that the *yue* became important in some particular tombs. This accords well with the fact that in the Erligang period at Zhengzhou, where only a single *yue* with a damaged plain *nei* has been found, the *yue* seems to have been of very minor significance.

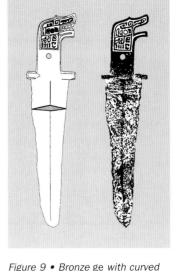

Figure 9 • Bronze ge *with curved nei XDM 127*

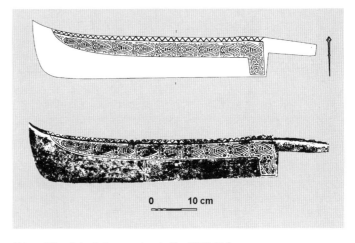

Figure 10 • A large bronze dao *knife, XDM 319*

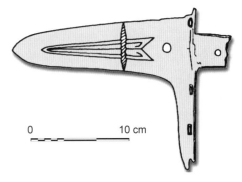

Figure 11 • Bronze ge *with* hu *extension XDM 132*

Figure 12 • A bronze ge from Chenggu, Shaanxi (after Kaogu 1980/3, 213, fig 3-2)

Figure 13 • A bronze yue axe, Panlongcheng, Hubei (after Wenwu 1976/2, p33, fig 34)

In contrast, the significance of bronze *yue* and the characteristics of its size, shape and decoration at the Xin'gan tomb can be traced earlier at other sites in the south. At Huangpi Panlongcheng, three *yue* were excavated from two out of 11 tombs. Two *yue* were excavated from M2 at Lijiaju. One of the two is quite large, extending to 41 centimetres in length (figure 13). This is similar to the examples from Xin'gan. Of the two large *yue* from the Xin'gan tomb, one is 35.2 centimetres in length and the other is 36.5 centimetres. The Panlongcheng *yue* and Xin'gan *yue* are related on account of their comparatively large size, indicating their importance. Furthermore, the design on a *yue* axe at the Xin'gan tomb reveals a close connection to the Panlongcheng tradition rather than to the contemporary Anyang design. Instead of a *taotie* mask with gaping mouth and teeth facing the blade like those of the Anyang area, the body of the Xin'gan *yue* is decorated with *leiwen* pattern along the three unsharpened edges. In the centre of the blade is a large horizontal perforation with a saw-tooth design (figure 5a). On the Anyang *yue*, it is obvious that the openwork teeth were designed to face the blade; on the Xin'gan *yue* axe, however, the connection between the surrounding *leiwen* pattern and the openwork teeth is ambiguous: since there is no *taotie* mask, it is not clear to whom the teeth belonged. The *leiwen* design rendered along the three non-bladed sides of the Xin'gan *yue* represents a scheme of arrangement that can be traced back to the Panlongcheng *yue* axes of the Erligang period, on one of which *kui* dragons appear along the three non-bladed edges. The large perforation in the centre can be traced back to neolithic jade or stone *yue* axes. We will return to this point below.

On the whole, it would appear that the Xin'gan *yue* axe was possibly more influenced by the Panlongcheng tradition than by any other. However, it tried to alter the neolithic perforation into the motif of a gaping mouth and teeth. This idea may in part have been adopted from the Anyang *taotie* tradition, in which case the design of the Xin'gan *yue* axe is unique as it combines the southern and Anyang traditions.

On the other *yue* from the Xin'gan tomb (figure 6), the teeth and mouth of the animal mask are omitted and the horn, eyes and nose are depicted in low-relief *leiwen* pattern. The primal mask represented by the eye motif in the *leiwen* more closely parallels the Erligang than the Anyang tradition.

The Indigenous Origins of the Xin'gan Bronze Weapons

The large perforation on the body of the Panlongcheng *yue* is particularly revealing of the relationship between bronze *yue* and jade and stone *yue* from the south in the neolithic period. In other words, the development from jade and stone to bronze *yue* in the south not only explains the importance of the bronze *yue* at the Xin'gan tomb but also explains the significance of the *yue* in the later stages of the Anyang period.

From the neolithic to the Erligang period, the stone *yue*, jade *yue* and bronze *yue* share one basic shape—a rectangular body with a single blade and a rectangular *nei* for hafting. During the neolithic period, the heavy stone axe was widespread throughout China in the Northeast (Liaoning and Jilin); the Northwest (Inner Mongolia, Gansu), the Southwest (Sichuan) and in the South (Fujian). For some of the stone axes without a perforation, the stone axe could be inserted into a slotted shaft and then bound. Some have small perforations which facilitated attaching the thongs. The earliest form of stone axe *(fu)* was thick and heavy and bears marks of use. As a tool for production, it was widely distributed throughout China during the neolithic period.

A special transformed type of stone axe is referred to as the 'stone *yue*.' Another even more unusual type is referred to as 'jade *qi*.'[7] The characteristic shapes and burial context of the stone *yue* and jade *qi* are related to those of

[7] Zhang Minghua 1989: 'Liangzhu yuqi yanjiu.' *Kaogu* 1989 (7).

the bronze *yue* of the Late Shang period. This particular type of stone *yue* is flat, has a slender body and no trace of having been used. It has been considered as a ritual object and named as 'stone *yue*' to distinguish it from the 'stone *fu*' which was considered to be a production tool. Stone *yue* and stone *fu* axes were all hafted with the shaft parallel to the edge of the blade. However, methods for binding the axe blade to the shaft vary. According to the depiction on the pottery urn at Linru Yanchun, Henan (figure 14), the stone *fu* axe was inserted into a slot on the shaft and then bound with thongs. In contrast, the stone *yue*, being perforated, was attached to the shaft by inserting the shaft through the perforation.

The stone *yue* was widely distributed, and according to Fu Xianguo's compilation they have been found in the south at Qujiang Shixia, Guangdong,[8] in the north in Hebei province, in the east including Shandong, and in the west including Gansu and Qinghai. This area includes the Yangshao culture and Longshan culture of the central plains, Dawenkou culture of Shandong, Majiayiao culture and Qijia culture of Gansu and Qinghai, Daxi culture and Qujialing culture of the middle region of the Yangzi. However, it was particularly densely spread over the south including Jiangsu, Zhejiang, and Anhui. It can be traced back from the Hemudu culture to the Majiabang, Songze, and Liangzhu cultures.[9] The transformation of the stone *fu* axe, a tool for production, to the *yue* axe, a ritual object, can be more clearly traced in the south.

The process of development of the ritual character of the *yue* was much more obviously revealed in the Liangzhu culture where the jade *yue* axe was distinguished from the *yue* made of stone. The jade *yue* is made of nephrite belonging to the tremolite-actimolite group of stones. The jade *yue* was distinguished from stone *yue* by its elaboration, demonstrating the status of the occupant of the tomb. The jade *yue* seems to have been buried with higher-ranking officials as exemplified by the tombs at Yuhang Fanshan in Zhejiang.

Jade *yue* were excavated from five of 11 tombs at Yuhang Fanshan. They are tombs M12, 14, 16, 17 and 20. In M20 and 24, stone *yue* and jade *bi* were placed near the legs of the occupant of the tomb, and one jade *yue* was placed near the left side of the occupant with a finial ornament belonging to it found above the jade *yue*. The shaft of the jade *yue* was possibly grasped in the hand by the tomb occupant. Among the tombs at Fanshan, M20 was lavishly furnished, and was one of the more complete tombs. In the tomb there were 170 jade sets (511 pieces), 24 stone objects, nine ivory objects, a shark's tooth and two pieces of pottery. One jade *yue* with animal mask and bird design and six jade *cong* were buried in M12 at Fanshan. Although the total number of the burial objects of M12 was unknown because of robbery, the abundance of burial objects can be guessed from the eight jade *cong* which still remained within the tomb.

The use of nephrite jade for the *yue* in the five tombs of the Fanshan tomb group reveals that the status of the occupant in each of the five tombs might have been higher than in the case of the other tombs at Fanshan. The shift from stone to jade *yue* is the culmination of a long process from the culture of Hemudu (c5005-3380 BC) through the Majiabang-Songze cultures (c4300-3200 BC) to the Liangzhu culture (c3300-2200 BC). The ritual meaning was emphasised in the development from the stone axe through stone *yue* to jade *yue*. The jade *yue* along with jade *cong* and jade *bi* are important elements from which to judge the status of the tomb occupant. The animal mask on the jade *yue* of tomb M12 at Fanshan resembles that on the jade *cong* of the same tomb. Jade *bi* and *yue* were placed at the bottom of tomb M3 at Sidun, Wujin, Jiangsu, where a jade *bi* and three jade *yue* with traces of being burned were surrounded with jade *cong*.

It is obvious that during the late stage of the Liangzhu culture the jade *yue* is distinguished from the stone *yue* within the tomb. The jade *yue* from tombs

Figure 14 • A painted pottery urn, c3900 BC Linru Yancun, Henan (after Zhongyuan kaogu 1981/1, 4, fig 1-1)

[8] Fu Xianguo 1985: 'Shilun Zhongguo xinshiqi shidai de shiyue.' *Kaogu* 1985(9), 820-832.

[9] Zhang Minghua 1989: 624-635.

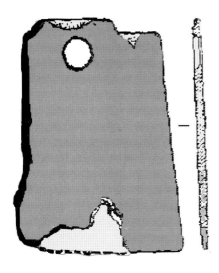

Figure 15 • A shouldered stone bronze axe, Heian, Jiangsu (after Kaogu xuebao 1983/2, 167, fig 22-7)

T27M2,T22M5, T15M3 and T4M6 at Fuquanshan have been dated to the late stage of the Liangzhu culture. A jade *yue* was excavated from tomb M3 at Sidun which was C14-dated and dendro-chronologically calibrated as 2790±230 BC. The importance of bronze *yue* during the Late Shang period can be traced back to the importance of the jade *yue* in the late Liangzhu culture.

From present archaeological evidence, the transformation of the *yue* from jade to bronze and its important role in the burial system of the south are most obvious in the upper Erligang period. The *yue* from M2 of Lijiazui, Huangpi, Hubei were cast in bronze. The majority of furnishings in this tomb consists of bronze objects (63 pieces) compared with only a few jade pieces. The number of bronze weapons was greater than the number of bronze vessels (40 bronze weapons and tools, 24 bronze vessels). Three human victims were buried along with the bronze vessels and bronze weapons. The significance of bronze *yue* within this burial system foreshadows its importance in the South during the Late Shang period.

Not only was the bronze *yue* important in the burial system, but also its shape can be traced back to the jade *yue* and stone *yue* of the neolithic period from the south. For instance, a stone axe from M28 at Heian Qingdong, Jiangsu (figure 15) carries shoulders on the upper portion distinguishing the body from the *nei*. This differs from the typical stone axe with a rectangular body without shoulders. The origin of the bronze *yue* form can be traced back to the shouldered stone axe.

The socketed *yue* axe is distinguished by the perpendicular positioning of the socket in relation to the blade edge. Similar forms of the *yue* hafted in the same manner are seen widely distributed over the south and southwest during the 5th to 3rd centuries BC. This indicates that the socketed *yue* and its method of use were possibly particularly evolved in those areas. However, the body of the Xin'gan socketed *yue* is square and the sides of the blade are concave. The decoration of the Xin'gan socketed *yue* (figure 6) consists of an animal mask in low relief. It resembles the *yue* of the Erligang period and differs from the much later socketed *yue* of the fifth to third centuries BC, in both profile and decoration.

The significance of bronze *mao* spearhead within the Xin'gan tomb (figure 7) is marked by the quantity and the various indigenous shapes found nearby in the Wucheng area, where Erligang-style bronze and pottery have been found. The pottery from the Xin'gan tomb is comparable to the pottery and proto-porcelains excavated from Period II of the Wucheng site.[10] This can also be seen on the *ge* dagger-axe. Both actual *ge* and pottery vessels marked with *ge* are also seen in the Period II stratum at Wucheng. Such a phenomenon can hardly be found at the Anyang area during the early part of the Late Shang period. For example, no spearhead was excavated from among the four Period I tombs at Xiaotun containing bronze weapons, such as tombs, M338, M333, M232, M188. A spearhead in the simplest shape was excavated at M3 of Sanjiazhuang. The spearhead was also rarely used for burial in central plains tombs of the Erligang period, but was more developed in the south during the Erligang period. Spearheads were excavated from M3 and M2 of Lijiazhuang, near Panlongcheng, Hubei. The socket of the Lijiazhuang spearhead is square with rings which were attached to the shaft by a short connection. This characteristic paved the way to the development of the spearhead as seen in the Xin'gan tomb.

To sum up, from the examples of *yue* axe and *mao* spearhead, the characteristics of the bronze weapons at the Xin'gan tomb can be traced back to those appearing in the south during the Erligang period. This phenomenon can be applied to the complete assemblage of bronze objects. including both bronze weapons and bronze vessels.[11] The same condition can also be applied to the five tombs of Anyang and the tombs of Chenggu, Shaanxi.[12] During the early phases of the Late Shang period many areas faced the same problem: how to create new elements based on the traditions of the Erligang period. Most of the bronze

[10] Li Boqian 1981: 'Shi lun weicheng wenhua,' *wenwujikan* 3.

[11] Peng Shifan *et al* 1991: 27.

[12] Chen Fangmei 1991: 'Xiaotun wuzuomu de qingtongqi – cong Erligang dao dianxing Yinxu fengge fazhan de zhuyao qushi,' *Kaogu lishi yu wenhua – Gao Xiaomei xiansheng bazhi daqinglunwenji.* Taipei: Zhengzhong shuju, 181-232.

weapons from the Xin'gan tomb reflect this trend. On the one hand, they continued some features of the Erligang tradition seen at both Panlongcheng and in the central plains, such as the *ge* with the elongated blade. On the other hand, they developed indigenous styles of the *yue* axe and the *mao* spearhead on the basis of local traditions. The creativity is also exemplified in the *ge* which are intimately related to those of the central plains.

Swords were well developed in the south during the fifth to third centuries BC indicating the use of the weapon in the region. However, the Xin'gan sword without a guard or pommel differs from these later southern swords. The Xin'gan sword is possibly related to the sword without a guard and pommel of the 11th to 10th century BC, but with some differences. With respect to the creativity displayed in the weapons of the Xin'gan tomb, the Xin'gan sword is possibly one of the earliest types in the south.

Conclusion

In conclusion, the bronze weapons from the Xin'gan tomb exemplified a common trend of Late Shang, absorbing and transforming the Erligang tradition to create a unique Late Shang style. As the Erligang tradition did not only simply originate from culture of the central plains but also had roots in the south, it can be linked to an indigenous southern tradition as far back as the neolithic period. These weapons are imbued with clearly recognisable regional characteristics. Both the *yue* and the *mao* serve as evidence of this phenomenon. Hence the Xin'gan bronze weapons and coeval bronze weapons from Anyang probably represent two parallel developments. On the other hand, the bronze weapons from the Xin'gan tomb do reveal interactions with the central plains. The *ge* serves as evidence of this phenomenon. In addition, such interactions were not restricted to the central plains but also extended to the Chenggu region in southern Shaanxi. The *ge* with a long *hu* provides evidence of this phenomenon. Moreover, knives similar to the long large knives of the Xin'gan tomb have been found in both the north and the central plains; their rectangular tangs, however, differ from those on the knives of the central plains and possibly represent a northern influence, either direct or mediated through the central plains. Present materials make it difficult to give conclusive answers to this question.[13]

[13] See Li Xueqin 1991: 33-38.

The indigenous style of the bronze weapons of the Xin'gan tomb is difficult to discuss with respect to the context and typology of the Anyang bronzes. However, from the intermittent chronological sequence of bronze weapons in the south it appears the style of the Xin'gan bronze weapons was developed during a particular stage, evolving from the strong Erligang tradition to the new phase of the Late Shang period. The styles of bronze vessels from the tombs at Xiaotun as well as those from the Chenggu finds evolved according to a similar development. Scholars have been debating the question of how long it took to transfer the Erligang tradition into the new phase of Late Shang. The style of the bronze weapons at the Xin'gan tomb is parallel with that at the Anyang area, and will provide more information for discussion.

The dynamic interaction of the Xin'gan bronze weapons with regional bronze weapons outside Anyang makes their indigenous style more obvious. It is also possible to suggest that the bronze weapons from Xin'gan initiated the Western Zhou development, as some of the elements within the development of the Western Zhou can not be explained as succeeding from the Late Shang central plains culture.

TU CHENG-SHENG

The 'Animal Style' Revisited

S cholars who have studied the material culture of the northern steppes have all been concerned with one essential question: what is the origin of the 'animal style'? Did it originate in southern Siberia, the Karasuk culture in the Yenisei River in the Minussinsk Basin, or with the Shang culture in the Yellow River valley? Most Western scholars tend to accept the former hypothesis; however, there are some dissenting views.[1]

In order to discuss the origins of the northern Chinese animal style, we have first to classify the artefacts into different groups, and then place these in their historical context.

The Origins of Animal Pommel Decoration on Weapons

Bernhard Karlgren[2] agreed with W P Yetts and W C White, considering the Yellow River region as the place where the animal style made its first appearance. Yetts and White included decorations on the Shang and Zhou ritual vessels within the categories of the animal style; Karlgren defined the animal style as the 'Scythian-Siberian style,' and traced its origins to China. The majority of western scholars, however, disagreed with Karlgren, and continued to trace the origins of the animal style to the Minussinsk basin. As artefacts from the Yellow River region consist mainly of Shang objects from Anyang, the crux of the debate lies in the question of which is earlier, the Shang culture or the Karasuk culture? The problem is how to establish the chronology of these two cultures from different regions. Karlgren dated the Yinxu culture to the period from 1300-1028 BC; in his view, the Scythian-Siberian animal style only became popular in the 7th century BC, and therefore could not have influenced the art of the much earlier Shang dynasty, nor could it be the origin of the Eurasian animal style: even following S A Teploukhov's dating of the Karasuk culture to c1000 BC, this would still be later than the Shang.[3] H Kühn pushed the date of the Karasuk culture to the 13th and 12th centuries BC, similar to the date of the Yinxu period.[4] Karlgren's objection to such a date was that objects of the Karasuk culture were in the main collected items rather than from controlled excavations, so that it was not possible to fix an absolute date based purely on shapes and styles.

[1] See for instance E H Minns, Karlgren, Loehr, Karl Jettmar and most recently Chinese scholars such as Wu En, Tian Guangjin and Guo Suxin. Some Russian scholars have also debated this question.

[2] Karlgren 1945: 'Some weapons and tools of the Yin dynasty,' *Bulletin of the Museum of Far Eastern Antiquities* 17: 101-144.

[3] Teploukhov, S 1929: 'Essai de classification des anciennes civilisations métalliques de la région de Minoussinsk,' *Materialy po etnografii*, IV, cited by Karlgren 1945.

[4] Kühn 1938: *Chronologie der Sino-Siberischen Bronzen*, IPEK 1938, cited by Karlgren 1945.

This is originally a part of the article, 'Ou Ya caoyuan dongwu wenshi yu Zhongguo gudai beifang minzu zhi kaocha,' first published in Chinese in the *Bulletin of The Institute of History and Philosophy Academia Sinica*, Vol 64, Part 2 (1993).

Other scholars disagreed with Karlgren. According to V A Gorodzov, the Karasuk culture should be dated to c1500 to 1000 BC; Tallgren dated a bronze knife from the Minussinsk basin, similar to a knife from Anyang, to 1500 BC.[5] According to Max Loehr,[6] the Afanasieva culture in the Minussinsk area should be dated to 2000 BC, followed by the Seima culture around 1700 BC, and the Seima-Andronovo culture around 1600 BC. The Karasuk culture would be around 1400 BC. The Shang culture at Anyang is later, around 1300 BC. In terms of typology of objects, chronology and the Stone Age substrata, everything indicates that Siberia is the origin of the animal style, and that the northern animal style played a part in Anyang.

Loehr's cultural chronology of southern Siberia seems to have pushed the date too early: according to M P Gryaznov the Andronovo culture began around the middle of the 2nd millennium BC, the Karasuk culture and the animal style around the 13th century BC.[7] But his argument, on the same line as Loehr's, that Minussinsk influenced Anyang is not convincing, because he only took the latest date of the Shang. The so-called Stone Age substrata refers to the decorative motifs on the bone, horn and wooden objects of the neolithic and mesolithic periods. Gregory Borovka found in northern Russia and Finland stone weapons and wooden finial ornaments decorated with naturalistic sculptures, which date to the Stone Age.[8] Some bone and stone sculptures from the Ulashan and Krasnoyarsk region feature motifs of deer and horses, and are also dated to the Stone Age. Through the remains of such artefacts are few, Borovka thought that they were related to the animal style on metal objects. E H Minns also held the same view, believing that the inventors of such animal style were the people who lived in the northern region of deer hunting, different from the sheep and oxen herded by the nomads. The raw materials used for such artefacts were also different, including wood, bone, bark and metal. Minns also believed that the northern deer-hunters passed through the regions inhabited by peoples who possessed metal crafts, such as Krasnoyarsk-Minussinsk and Altai. They transferred the original animal style from bone and wood to metal; the same applied to the Chinese, Iranians, Greeks and Western Asian peoples. Thus the origin of this animal style was neither in China, nor in Central Asia, nor in southern Russia colonised by the Greeks, nor yet in the Caucasus.[9]

We should, however, note that the sculpture of the animal style is a general phenomenon in the cultures of different regions. The animal-style sculptures in northern Asia in the neolithic era are no exception: on the evidence provided by Borovka, apart from the animal decoration on the wooden finial discovered in a Finnish peat-bog, the rest can be thought of as the generic animal art of the neolithic period, not closely related to the animal style we are discussing here. Also, the distance between the neolithic material and that from the Bronze Age is too great to establish a link between them in the case of the animal style on bronze weapons.[10]

Let us take a close look at the examples cited by Max Loehr from Tallgren's book (figure 1). There are four Seima short swords dated to c2000 BC or later. One of the swords (1a) is decorated with a deer's head (though to me it looks like a horse); the pommel has no ring, and there are five horizontal lines incised on the hilt. Two of them (1c, 1d) are decorated with two and three standing horses, respectively: the handles were incised

[5] Tallgren, A M 1937: 'Some north Eurasian sculptures,' *Eurasia Septentrionalis Antiqua* 12.

[6] Loehr, M 1949: 'Weapons and tools from Anyang and Siberian analogies,' *American Journal of Archaeology* 53: 126-144.

[7] Gryaznov, M P 1969: *South Siberia* (trans J Hogarth), London: The Cresset Press, 89-97.

[8] Borovka, G 1928: *Scythian art* (trans V G Childe), London: Bouverie House.

[9] Minns, E H 1942: 'The art of the northern nomads,' *Proceedings of the British Academy* 28: 47-99.

[10] Tallgren, A M 1937: 117, n2; Karlgren, B 1945: 140, n1.

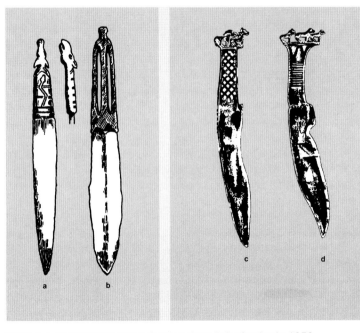

*Figure 1 • Short swords of the Seima culture (**a-b** after Loehr 1956, **c-d** after Gimbutas 1965)*

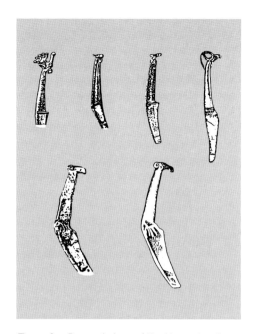

Figure 2 • *Bronze knives of the Karasuk culture (after Jettmar 1950)*

[11] Chernykh, E N 1992: *Ancient metallurgy in the USSR: the early metal age* (trans S Wright), Cambridge: CUP, 268-9, 194.

[12] Gimbutas, M 1965: *Bronze Age cultures in central and eastern Europe*, The Hague, 104-105.

[13] Suliminski, Tadeusz 1970: *Prehistoric Russia: an outline*. London: John Baker.

[14] Kiselev 1951: *Ancient History of Southern Siberia* (Chinese edition) 1981, Urumqi: Xinjiang shehui kexueyuan minzu yanjiusuo.

[15] Wu En 1986: 'Zhongguo beifang qingtong wenhua yu Kalasuke wenhua de guanxi, *Zhongguo kaoguxue yanjiu — Xia Nai xiansheng kaogu wushinian jinian wenji*, vol 2, Beijing: Kexue chubanshe, 135-150.

[16] Jettmar, K 1950: 'The Karasuk culture and the southeastern affinities,' *BMFEA* 22: 83-126.

with horizontal or cross-hatched patterns. Based on the shape of these bronze swords, N L Chlenova dated the Seima culture to the 9th to 8th century BC. Some scholars have disagreed with her, and date it to the 16th and 15th centuries BC.[11] Other scholars date it as contemporary with the Yinxu phases of Shang culture, between 1450-1400 BC and 1300-1250 BC.[12] Generally speaking, therefore, Max Loehr's chronology is too early, the distribution of the Seima-Turbino culture is rather broad, and cannot be discussed in detail here. Sulimirski argues that the ring on the hilt and the length of the handle indicate the Seima culture cannot be earlier than the Karasuk culture, and that it came from the south and central Ula mountains. These knives and swords cannot be taken as prototypes of the Karasuk culture, especially the handles with standing animals, which are obviously rather late in both China and Siberia.

However, these differing views cannot be reconciled because the archaeological chronology of southern Siberia is still unclear. Scholars' dating of the Karasuk and Andronovo cultures varies greatly and has been placed as early as 1500-1000 BC or 1000-700 BC. Current research indicates that the Karasuk culture is a migratory culture following the Andronovo culture which entered the Minussinsk basin around the 12th century BC.[13] S V Kiselev used the typical white jade ring from Gelazikewo and a bronze knife decorated with a donkey to argue that the Karasuk style of bronzes from Inner Mongolia appeared at the same time as the Anyang bronzes, around the 14th to 13th centuries BC.[14] This theory is, in my view, more acceptable.

Kiselev observed that the animals decorating bronze weapons of the Karasuk culture have no eyes or nostrils, and that their ears have no ear canal. Looking at the examples (figure 2), the style of these animal sculptures is quite different from the knives decorated with animal heads from China (Shanxi, Shaanxi and northern Hebei), and their casting is rather clumsy. Therefore it is unlikely that they represent the origins of the animal style.

The prolonged debate on the origins of the animal style has shifted between the Minussinsk basin and Anyang, and much effort has been spent on establishing the chronology of these two regions. Comparatively, Anyang is easier to date, but Minussinsk remains controversial. In fact, there is a gap between the traditional animal style and the knives and short swords of the Karasuk culture. The bronze weapons decorated with animal heads from Anyang are not typical even though the number of northern-style bronze weapons and tools from Anyang is huge. But if we view Shang bronzes as a whole, the animal style is not the mainstream: this is also the practical criteria for differentiating the Huaxia (Chinese) from the Rongdi (nomads). The knife decorated with an animal head from Anyang has a traditional central plains body, with no rings on the hilt; the ears of the horse and the horns of the sheep and oxen do not project, unlike those from the northern areas. Based on the most recent archaeological evidence, the animal style Shang and Zhou weapons from the region of the Great Wall are closer to those found in the area of Lake Baikal than to those from the Minussinsk basin. Wu En analysed some examples from Mongolia and Lake Baikal and confirmed that they are almost identical to pieces from northern China. He therefore argues that there was a close link between the bronze cultures of these two regions, and that they developed in parallel.[15]

Forty years ago, Karl Jettmar tried to sidestep the question of whether the Minussinsk culture or that of Anyang was earlier. He proposed that there was a cultural exchange between Trans-Baikalia and northern China, the Ordos region and the upper and middle range of the Yenisei River, each of which might have developed independently.[16] Jettmar also used the anthropologist Debets' study which showed that the people of the Karasuk culture were 'Sinid' rather than 'Europoid' to make a hypothesis of a migratory trend from the Ordos region to the Minussinsk basin in the early 2nd millennium BC, since the people who produced the Karasuk and Ordos bronzes are genetically related. The Ordos-style bronzes of the Shang period found in Anyang were made by the Sinides.[17] Kiselev, in his *Ancient History of Southern Siberia*, cited a theory that the Minussinsk basin during the Karasuk period suffered an invasion from the southeast or from Mongolia. The invaders integrated with the local population of Afanasieva-Andronova type. The appearance of the Europoid population did not take place in this region until the Tagarski period; this anthropological evidence may provide support for the origins of cultural diffusion.

On the basis of typological studies and craftsmanship, the Chinese scholars Wu En, Tian Guangjin and Guo Suxin have argued that the northern-style bronzes derived from the Ordos region. Tian and Guo have also discussed the connection between the ecology of inner Mongolia and the appearance of nomadism and the invention of such animal-style weapons.[18] These Chinese scholars were of the opinion that the opening of the route between the Yellow River, Mongolia to Trans-Baikalia, Tuva and the Yenisei region goes back as early as the Shang and Zhou periods. This view coincides with Jettmar's opinion of 40 years ago. As a matter of fact, the link, whether direct or indirect, between northern China and the West must have existed since early times. In a tomb discovered in Ujunjul in southern Siberia, dated between the 10th to 7th centuries BC, the occupant was buried with a bronze knife at his waist.[19] At his right side there was a crane-necked axe. In tomb No 12, discovered in Panomaravo in the Lake Baikal region, the occupant was buried with a dagger, four axes and some arrows. This phenomenon is similar to what has been found in Jixian Shangdongcun, Shanxi.[20] Although at the moment there is little material evidence, its historical significance cannot easily be ignored.

As more and more bronze weapons with pommels decorated with animal motifs are discovered, scholars have come to focus on Mt Yanshan and the region of the Great Wall as the origin of the animal style. It is certainly worthwhile to explore further the relationship between this region and Anyang, Mongolia, Trans-Baikalia and the Minussinsk region, in relation to the development of the Eurasian animal style. We have, however, to take two points into consideration: first, the large number of knives with animal decoration from the Minussinsk Karasuk culture which have bent backs; many bronze knives of this type do not have animal decoration.[21] This phenomenon does not occur in northern China. The second point to be borne in mind is whether the link between the Minussinsk basin and the region of the Great Wall is limited to Mongolia and its eastern part. The archaeology of Xinjiang and Outer Mongolia is limited at this period, so we are unable to make a precise judgement, but early cultural links on the Eurasian grasslands are multifaceted.

Foreign Elements and the Motifs of the Northern Animal Style

Discussion concerning the origins of the animal style has been largely based on the theory of cultural diffusion, which many scholars have strongly opposed. The recognition of similarities between the Ordos animal style and the motifs of Minussinsk ornament does not of itself prove that the one must be derived from the other: similar backgrounds of beliefs, custom and tradition may lead to similar results. There is a regional, geographical and temporal gap between the two cultures. The common characteristics of the Ordos style bronzes are the result of grassland economics and lifestyle.[22] However, we cannot easily dismiss the diffusionist view; the speed of cultural exchange on the grasslands, particularly after the appearance of the nomadic lifestyle, was much faster than that of agricultural societies. If there already existed a direct or indirect contact between the Mt Yanshan/Great Wall region and the Gobi desert/Trans-Baikalian region as early as the Shang period, this communication must have intensified in the Spring and Autumn period, when the northern region was gradually pastoralised.

[17] Jettmar, K 1950: the same author 1967: *Art of the Steppes: the Eurasian animal style*, London: Methuen.

[18] Tian Guangjin and Guo Suxin 1992: 'Zailun Ordos shi qingtongqi de yanyuan,' conference paper, *Zhongguo gudai beifang minzu kaogu wenhua guoji xueshu yantaohui*, Huhehaote, August 11-18, 1992.

[19] Watson, W 1971: *Cultural frontiers in ancient East Asia*, Edinburgh: EUP, 62.

[20] Jixian 1985 (Jixian wenwu gongzuozan): 'Shanxi Jixian chutu Shangdai qingtongqi,' *Kaogu* 1985(9): 848-849.

[21] Martin, F R 1893: *L'Age du bronze au musée de Minoussinsk*, Stockholm: Samson E Wallin.

[22] Carter, D 1957: *The Symbol of the Beast: the animal style art of Eurasia*, New York: The Ronald Press, 87-88.

Cultural integration may have taken place more speedily in such a context. Since there is a considerable variation in the dating of different Eurasian cultures, I shall discuss the foreign elements rather than concentrating solely on questions of origin and development.

Animal Motifs on Weapons and Tools

Let us first compare the animal decoration on the hilt and pommel, which is where such decoration is most commonly seen. A damaged bronze knife has been collected in Jianping (figure 3); its style is similar to what has been found in southern Siberia. A bronze knife found in Tuva has a bear- or boar-like animal on the pommel and four elks on the hilt; it can be dated quite early.[23] E H Minns also recorded a similar one found in southern Siberia.[24] The hollow or inlay technique used for the Tuva knife is very similar to that found in northern China. The arrangement of the animal patterns is also similar to the short sword found in the Upper Xiajiadian culture tomb in Pingquan Dongnangou, Hebei province.[25] In style, however, the specimen from Tuva is much finer and more realistic. It is quite common to find examples with an animal on the pommel; within China, there are places such as tomb M8 Sandaoling Luotuoliang, Longhua, Hebei and tombs at Ningcheng Nanshan'gen and M95 Jundushan Yuhuangmiao, Yanqin, Beijing. Two examples in the collection of the State Hermitage, St Petersburg, were collected in Koryakovo and Beiskoye, in Krasnoyarsk, western Siberia. These two examples were decorated with a goat and a boar on the pommels, and belonged to the Tajiaer culture.[26] Similar examples have been found in the Minussinsk area; they include an axe with a beak, animal motifs including wild animals and goats, and they too belong to the Tajiaer culture.[27] The objects discussed above are dated between the 7th and the 5th centuries BC. This is around the time of the Spring and Autumn period, when the northern-style swords were popular in China.

Figure 3 • A damaged bronze hilt, Jianping, Liaoning (after Kaogu 1983/8)

We now look at the antenna-hilt type of knife. Early examples in China came from the Maoqinggou tombs in Inner Mongolia, with typical examples in M59, M58 and M70, belonging to Maoqinggou Phase I, dated by archaeologists to the late Spring and Autumn period, or slightly earlier. Similar examples were also found nearby in tomb M1 at Gongsumao, dated to the late Spring and Autumn period.[28] Bronze or occasionally iron knives of this antenna-hilt type were also found in Batoy and Kordachin, near Krasnoyarsk, Siberia.[29] They are similar in shape and style to those from Maoqinggou, and may be dated to the 5th to 4th century BC, equivalent to the late Warring States period. A M Tallgren also recorded a different Siberian type, belonging to the second and third phases of the Tajiaer culture, about the fourth century BC.[30] Therefore, we can assume that this type of sword was popular from the late Spring and Autumn period to the early Warring States period, in both northern China and in Siberia (figure 4).

[23] Piotrovsky, Boris *et al* 1991: The Scythian Gold from the Hermitage, Seoul: No 185

[24] Minns, E H 1913: *Scythians and Greeks*, Cambridge: CUP, figure 165.

[25] Hebei 1977 'Hebei Pingquan Dongnangou Xiajiadian shang ceng wenhua mufen.' *Kaogu* 1977 (1): 51-53. Similar objects have also been found in Longhua Sandaoying Luotuoliang, Hebei province and in Ningcheng Nanshangen, Liaoning province; Beijing Yanqing Jundushan Yuhuangmiao.

[26] Piotrovsky 1991: *l'Or des Scythes*, Trésors de l'Hermitage, Leningrad, Paris, Nos 166, 168.

[27] Gryaznov, M P 1969: *South Siberia* (trans J Hogarth), London: The Cresset Press, 213.

[28] Tian Guangjin and Guo Suxin 1976: 'Taohongbala de Xiongnu mu,' *Kaoguxuebao* 1976 (1): 131-143.

[29] Piotrovsky 1991: Nos 177, 178.

[30] Tallgren 1937, No 52.

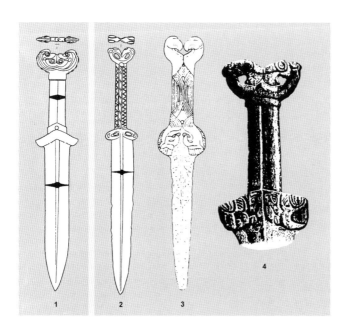

*Figure 4 • Antenna-style swords from Siberia and China: **1** M70 Maoqingguo (after Tian Guangjin and Guo Suxin 1986, 258); **2-4** Siberia (after Minns 1913)*

Two daggers (figure 5) found in Ningchengdianzi Xiaoheishigou, Inner Mongolia, have straight-edged blades decorated with animals covered with circular patterns.[31] This decoration is rather strange, and is unknown elsewhere; its origins are also obscure. However, it may be related to the West, since S J Rudenko has observed that the 'mythological eagle' on the horns of a gold foil deer-like beast from the Scythian tomb near Kiev, Zourovka, also has this pattern, as do similar gold sheet animals found at the Karagodeushkh tombs of the Taman group; the two examples are dated to the 6th to 5th and 4th to 3rd centuries BC, respectively. Gold sheet animal-shaped ornaments from Elizavetovski on the Don River, dated to the 5th century BC, also have a bird's head with geometrical patterns.[32] Similar patterns are also found on Scythian gold ornaments from southern Russia. Chinese archaeologists dated the daggers from Xiaoheishigou to the early Spring and Autumn period, around the 8th century BC, which is much earlier than the pieces from Siberia, but there are no other comparable examples of this animal style within the Chinese border.

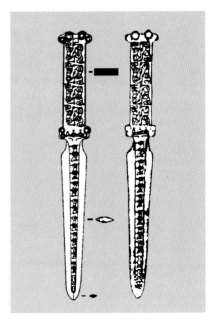

Figure 5 • Bronze hand dagger, Inner Mongolia (after Xiang Chunsong 1984)

Plaque Decorations

From the Warring States period onwards, the animal style became prominent on belt-hooks and plaques. The main motifs are of animals in combat or facing each other. Examples of such motifs can be found in both Siberia and China: for instance, the 'two oxen' plaque collected at Kanterevaya in Krasnoyarsk is similar to the one found in Xichagou (figure 6a); the 'two horses' plaque found in Oznachennaya is also found in Inner Mongolia (figure 6b).[33]

The recumbent 'B' shaped plaque is another example: the one with a tiger attacking a donkey in the Hermitage is very similar to those found in northwestern China, particularly the one from Guyuan Yanglang, Ningxia (figure 7).[34] The two of them are stylistically very similar: the design and decorations on the tiger are almost identical and typical of the Siberian style, but it is possible that the Hermitage piece may originally have come from China. The design on the plaques include eagle, wild and domestic animals, and strange beasts, either singly or in group combat. Chinese archaeological evidence includes tomb M25 in Tongchuanzaomiao, Shaanxi province,[35] which is similar to those found in the northwest, though less fine, vivid and complex. It is therefore not likely that they originated from China.

Both on the frame and on the animal motifs, there is often sunken decoration; the plaques may originally have been made to be inlaid, as for example the golden plaque inlaid with coral, garnets, and glass from tomb No 3, Khapry cemetery, Chaltyr, Rostov. Some pieces in museum collections were originally also inlaid, such as the oxen and horse plaques mentioned above. Another disturbed tomb from Rostov also yielded a golden plaque on which the animal's ear, eye and hoof were decorated with sunken patterns. A gold necklace from Khokhlatch, Novotcherkassk has an animal motif with turquoise, glass and coral inlay.[36]

The technique of inlay was widely used: the dagger discovered in Fengxiang, Nan'ganhe, Shaanxi had two animals resembling tigers back-to-back on its hilt, again with sunken areas originally made to hold inlays. A similar example from a Scythian tomb in Rostov has a camel motif with some of the inlay still intact.[37]

Some animal-shaped plaques from China have turquoise inlays: the tradition of turquoise inlay in China can be traced back to Yanshi Erlitou, but glass, garnets and coral were rarely used, and the sunken shapes are also different. In northern China, although there are some gem mines in Liaoning and Ningxia, these are not very common. The tradition of such inlaid animal plaques and other objects is unlikely to prove indigenous to China. Yetts long ago argued that the peoples of the Yellow River started to produce inlaid bronzes under the inspiration of Scythian and Sarmatian gold; his argument coincides with our new evidence.

[31] Cheng Dong and Zhong Shaoyi 1990: *Zhongguo gudai bingqi tuji.* Beijing: Jiefangjun chubanshe, 4-139; Xiang Chunsong 1984: 'Xiaoheishigou faxian de qingtongqi,' *Neimenggu wenwu kaogu* 1984 (3).

[32] Rudenko 1958: 'The mythological eagle, the gryphon, the winged lion and the wolf in the art of northern nomads,' *Artibus Asiae*, 21/2, plate III.3.

[33] Borovka 1928: *Scythian art* (trans V G Childe), London: Bouverie House, plate 53; Piotrovsky 1991: Nos 181, 182; Sun Shoudao 1957: 'Xiongnu Xichagou wenhua gumuqun de faxian,' *Wenwu* 1960 (8,9).

[34] *Wenwu*, 1978(12), 86.

[35] *Kaogu*, 1986(2).

[36] Piotrovsky, Boris et al 1991: *The Scythian Gold from the Hermitage*, Seoul: National Museum of Korea: 240-1, No 156; Roztovzeff, M I 1929: *Animal Style in South Russia and China*, Princeton: Princeton University Press, plate XIV:1.

[37] *Kaogu* 1989(11): 1046, figure 2, No 6.

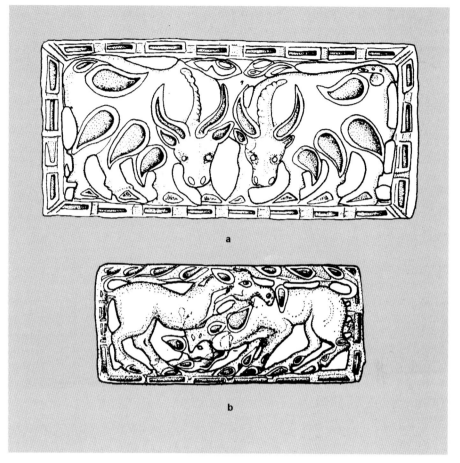

Figure 6 • *Bronze plaques: **a** Xichagou, Liaoning (after Sun Shoudao 1957); **b** Inner Mongolia (after Tian Guangjin and Guo Suxin 1986, 82, fig49-2)*

The Griffin Motif

Foreign elements in the design and decoration of animal plaques are mostly seen in the griffin motif and the animal with the lower limbs turned upside down. These two are related, and I will examine the griffin motif first.

Roztovzeff has distinguished the Scythian from the Sarmatian style: the former is represented in a realistic manner, and the latter includes imaginary or supernatural animals, which he termed the 'new animal style'. These supernatural or imaginary animals are also known as 'griffin'. They have a lion's body, two wings, occasionally a horse's body and the beak of an eagle. Alternatively they have elk's horns, or horns transformed into a bird's head. Rudenko has classified them as mythological eagle, griffin, winged lion, etc. This artistic motif is found throughout the Eurasian grasslands, from Hungary and Turkey to the Ukraine, Central Asia, southern Siberia, Trans-Baikalia and Mongolia. Although the actual representation of this motif varies according to region, the most popular one is the raptor-feline base. On the plaque, the griffin is often in combat with other beasts, and scholars have interpreted this motif as a shamanistic ritual in the context of the myths and legends of the grassland, saying that they symbolise the heavenly god, shamans and kings.[38] Others have interpreted the subject as the struggle for survival, typical of the grasslands. I will not pursue the social significance of this motif but shall instead take it as evidence for exploring the relationship between China and the northwest.

The appearance of this griffin motif in northern China is around the period of the late Warring States, and can be divided into three types according to the different forms it takes. The first type generally

[38] Horvath, I 1992: 'The roles of the Griffin in the art and society of the steppe-dwelling peoples of Eurasia.' The International Academic Conference of Archaeological Cultures of the Northern Chinese Ancient Nations, 1992/8/11-18 (conference paper).

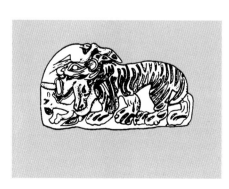

Figure 7 • *'B' shaped plaque, Guyuan Yanglang, Ningxia (after* Wenwu *1978/12)*

Figure 8 • The griffin motif (Type I): **a** Loo collection (after SSA, p124); **b** M30 Xingzhuangtou, Yi xian, Hebei (after Bunker 1992); **c** M2 Xigoupan, Inner Mongolia (after Tian Guangjin and Guo Suxin 1986); **d** M47 Shuihudi, Yunmeng, Hubei (after Kaogu xuebao 1986/4, 515, fig38-5)

has an animal body with an eagle's beak: a plaque from the Loo collection has a bird's head on the end of the long tail of a horse (figure 8a). Other examples have a lion biting a horse, with a goat between them.[39] A recent discovery from tomb M30 Yi xian Xinzhuangtou, Hebei includes a belt-hook also decorated with a goat's head in the middle with a two-headed beast biting a kneeling horse on each side (figure 8b).[40] A simpler version has been found in a fragment from tomb M5 Tongxing Daodunzi, Ningxia.[41] The beak of this beast is turned upwards, in a very similar fashion to the decoration on the gold sheet from tomb M2, Xigouban Zhunge'erqi, Inner Mongolia.[42] A simpler belt-hook, also found in this tomb, was decorated with two kneeling griffins with horse bodies and eagle's beaks (figure 8c). The examples from Xinzhuangtou and Xigouban are dated to the late Warring States, and the Daodunzi example is as late as the middle or late Western Han. The Qin tomb No 47 in Yunmeng Shuihudi, Hubei yielded a wooden comb carved with a griffin with horse's body and eagle's beak (figure 8d).[43] This indicates that the motif also travelled to the south.

In the Loo collections there was a plaque with a motif of a winged lion biting a horse, similar to the piece in the Hermitage Museum; among Chinese archaeological material, only a limited number of examples of a winged griffin have been found, at Shanxi,[44] but the motif was widespread in the Altai region. Examples include the embroidered textile from the Pazyryk tomb.[45]

The second type, or bird-headed beast, is more common in China than the winged griffin motif (figure 9): a bronze plaque discovered in a tomb at Xinjixiang Baiyanglincun, Pengyang, Ningxia, decorated with a tiger biting a goat, features an eagle's head on the back of the tiger (figure 9a).[46] Similar examples are also found on plaques from Chenyangchuan (a Warring States tomb), Xiji, Ningxia (figure 9b),[47] and the early Western Han tomb at Shuo

[39] Salmony, A 1933: Sino-Siberian Art in the Collection of C T Loo, Paris: C T Loo, plates XIII:4, XXIII:2, 3.

[40] Bunker, E 1992: 'Sino-nomadic art: Eastern Zhou, Qin and Han artifacts made for nomadic taste,' Zhongguo yishu wenwu taolunhui lunwenji (qiwu xia), Taipei: National Palace Museum: No 52.

[41] Kaogu xuebao 1988: No 3, 344, figure 9/7.

[42] Tian Guangjin and Guo Suxin 1986: 356-357, figures 4/4, 5/2.

[43] Kaogu xuebao, 1986(4): 515, figure 38/5.

[44] Shanxi 1996:16.

[45] Rudenko 1970: Frozen tombs of Siberia: the Pazyzyk burials of Iron Age horsemen (trans M W Thompson), California: UCP, 236, figure 115; Piotrovsky 1991, No 101, 185.

[46] Luo Feng and Han Kongyue 1990: 'Ningxia Guyuan jinnian faxian de beifang xi qingtongqi,' Kaogu 1990 (5): plate 12/1.

[47] Yan Shizhong and Li Huajiang 1992: 'Ningxia Xiji faxian yizuo qingtong shidai muzang,' Kaogu 1992 (6).

*Figure 9 • The griffin motif (Type II): **a** Pengyang Baiyanglin; **b** Xiji Chenyangchuan; **c** Xi'an Sandian; **d** Taohongbala, Inner Mongolia*

[48] *Wenwu*, 1987: 14.

[49] Borovka, G 1928: *Scythian art* (trans V G Childe), London: Bouverie House, 107, plate 66a.

[50] Zhu Jieyuan and Li Yuzheng 1983. 'Xi'an dongjiao Sandiancun Xi Han mu.' *Kaogu yu wenwu* 1983 (2): 22-25.

[51] Tian Guangjin and Guo Suxin 1986: *Ordos shi qingtongqi*, Beijing: Wenwu chubanshe, 343, figure 69/4.

[52] Borovka 1928: 103.

[53] Dai Yingxin and Sun Jiaxiang 1983: 'Shaanxi Shenmu xian chutu Xiongnu wenwu,' *Wenwu* 1983 (12), figure 4.

[54] Rudenko 1970: 297.

[55] M P Gryaznov 1969: figure 134.

[56] Rudenko 1958: 101-122.

xian, Shanxi province.[48] The tiger motifs all have birds' heads on their backs, sometimes more than one, at the end of the tail or on the ear of the tiger. Sometimes the motifs developed into more complicated forms, with multiple bird-like heads at the ends of wings or tails of the principal animals: an example is the plaque in the Hermitage Museum with two confronted tigers.[49]

A related motif is that of bird's heads incorporated in the frame of plaques in which the main motif is one of animal combat. Examples have been found in tombs of the early Western Han in Xi'an (figure 9c)[50] and at Yulongtai in Inner Mongolia (figure 9d). The latter is inlaid with gems and has eight birds' heads with S-curved bodies.[51] This motif is probably related to those where bird's heads are combined with beasts.

The third type is the deer body with an eagle's beak, or occasionally with a bird's head (figure 10). The gold ornament found in tomb M2 Xigouban has the motif of a standing deer with an eagle's beak and long antlers (figure 10a); a second example is similar except that the deer is kneeling (figure 10b). The antlers in these examples spread out like the branches of a tree. This motif can also be found on plaques from Verkhneudinsk[52] and Trans-Baikalia; others can be found in western museums, such as the Museum of Far Eastern Antiquities in Stockholm and the British Museum, London. The finest example is a gold deer sculpture found in Shenmu Nalinggaotu, with pointed ears, protruding eyes, bird's beak, and large curving antlers with birds' heads on the ends of the tines. Its tail is also in the form of a bird's head (figure 11).[53]

This griffin motif found in China can be compared to Central Asian materials such as textiles from Pazyryk and tattoos on the bodies of the tomb occupants, which all show similar motifs, close in style to those found in China. Sometimes in the case of the textiles and the tattoos, the pattern may be simplified. According to the excavator, Rudenko, the tombs at Pazyryk date before the 5th century BC.[54] This is equivalent to the late Spring and Autumn or the early Warring States period. Other scholars have dated them to the 5th to the 3rd century BC, but still no later than the Warring States period.[55]

The appearance of the griffin motif in the Eurasian animal style is later than the naturalistic style. Around the 6th century BC, on artefacts from Scythian tombs in Kuban and Dniepre, we can see motifs of kneeling animals and deer with birds' beaks, but not as prominent as those of the earlier period. Only after the 5th century BC does this particular motif acquire a flavour of the supernatural, with antlers of deer transformed into birds' heads. The material from Pazyryk may represent a transitional phase: its origins need to be further explored. Comparing the bird's head animal motif with the material from Pazyryk, Chinese examples seem to have been derived from the winged lion motif from north of the Black Sea. The wooden-winged lion found in the Scythian tomb at Tuektin developed further into the form represented on the 'golden man' plaque found at Issyk, Alma-Ata, Kazakhstan.[56] The Chinese griffin, with no wings but with a bird's head growing from its back, may be a result of this development. In general, we can trace the origins of the modern Chinese animal style to the region between the north of the Black Sea and the Altai Mountains. They are later than the examples from this region, and most of them are dated to the late Warring

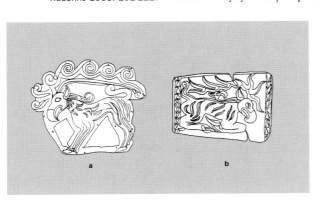

*Figure 10 • The griffin motif (Type III): **a-b** M2 Sigouban*

States period, when trade and exchange between inland China and the Altai region had begun. Chinese textiles were found in the Pazyryk tomb No 5. However, the exact relationship between the Chinese and the Scythians to the north of the Black Sea needs further investigation.

Animals with Inverted Hindquarters

This motif was found on the tattoo of the occupant in tomb No 2, Pazyryk (figure 12). The hindquarters of the animal are turned at 180 degrees to the forepart of the body in a rather unnatural fashion. This expression is used on many other objects found at Pazyryk, such as the saddles, one of which, from tomb No 1, is slightly unusual, having both tiger and deer with inverted hindquarters, although usually this treatment is reserved for small animals. A similar motif is also found on the coffin of tomb No 2 at Bash-Adar, 100 kilometres west of Pazyryk. The golden headdress of two gold figures from Scythian tomb at Alma-Ata features a standing leopard motif, whose hindquarters are turned. In the same tomb, horse and deer motifs on a scabbard similarly have their bodies turned through a 180 degrees. They are dated between the 5th and 4th centuries BC.[57]

Figure 11 • A gold deer sculpture (after Wenwu *1983/12)*

[57] Nara (Nara National Museum) 1988: *The Oasis and Steppe Routes*, Nos 134-2, 3, 4.

Within the Chinese border, a gold sheet with two facing tigers was found in tomb M30 at Alagou, south of Urumqi, Xinjiang. The tigers have curving bodies with inverted hindquarters. The Alagou site is dated to the Warring States period, and belongs to the same cultural sphere as the Pazyryk tombs. Some examples in Peter the Great's collection from Siberia in the Hermitage Museum also have similar motifs, indicating that they may have come from the same region. From Xigouban M2, two plaques also bear the horse motif with inverted hindquarters (figure 13). All these examples of inversion of the animals' hindquarters occasionally have additions of a bird's head, transforming them into griffins, so the form may be complex or simplified.

A triangular-shaped plaque from tomb No 1, Daodunzi, dated to the middle or late Western Han, in the 1st century BC, has a tree in the middle, flanked by

Figure 12 • Tattoos found on the bodies of the Pazyryk tombs, Altai (after Rudenko 1970)

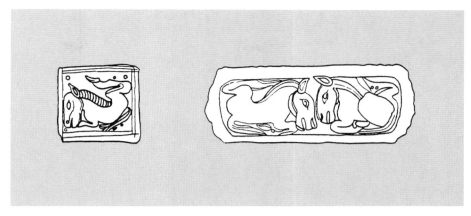

Figure 13 • Two plaques from M2 Xigouban (after Tian Guangjin and Guo Suxin 1986)

[58] Borovka 1928: plate 52b; Artamonov, M I 1973: *The art of ancient Central and South Siberia* (in Russian), Nos 208, 157.

[59] Kato Kyuso 1991: 'Sarumatan no kogei to sono shuhen' (Sarmatian Arts and their surroundings), *Nan Roshiya chiba minzoku no ihoten zuroku*, Tokyo: Asahi shimbunsha.

[60] Horvath 1992.

[61] Wu En 1984: 'Lun woguo beifang gudai dongwu wenshi de yanyuan,' *Kaogu yu wenwu* 1984(4): 46-59, 104.

[62] Rudenko 1958.

two equines. There are sunken patterns on the frame, the tree leaves, the ears, knees and hooves of the horses. Similar examples with finer decoration and dated to the 4th century BC have been collected by the Russians from southern Siberia in earlier years.[58]

The tree on the Daodunzi plaque is also known as the 'tree of life' in a long Scythian tradition, but the guardian animals in such cases are usually winged lions, which protect the tree and the souls of men from evil spirits (snakes). Rempel argues that in this 'tree and guardian lions' motif, the lions represent the hero or the ruler: the tree must be guarded, otherwise the people would disperse.[59] The kings possessed magical powers to protect life,[60] but on the plaques from Ningxia and southern Siberia the guardian animals are not lions but horses. We do not know how this change took place, but the foreign influence is obvious.

This influence was not limited to the region along the Great Wall, but extended to the south of the Yangzi River in the early years of the Han dynasty. On the middle coffin from Mawangdui Han tomb No 1, there are painted tigers and a horse, all of which have inverted hindquarters (figure 14a); the dragon also has an inverted body (figure 14b), but in the Chinese tradition the dragon is related to the snake, so that people may not have considered this unusual. In fact, this may have been an effect of northern influence, at any rate during the Western Han dynasty.

Exchanges between south and north became frequent after the occupation of the northern grasslands by nomads: this influence was reciprocal and long-term in character. For instance, on the gold plaque found at Xigouban, there is a Chinese inscription on the back, with characters whose calligraphic style is close to the Qin small seal script. Chinese archaeologists believe it to have been made in the Qin state. The evidence for northern animal style in China is accumulating, but scholars are still arguing over its origins. Chinese scholars tend to believe that Siberian plaques were made in imitation of Chinese examples, because the variety of animal style plaques found within China is much greater than those found in southern Siberia, as well as finer in casting quality.[61] Russian scholars, however, such as Rudenko, argue that Pazyryk motifs are far more complicated than those found in Mongolia and northern China; the latter were influenced by the Altai culture.[62] In view of the examples I have cited, the foreign elements of the griffin motif cannot easily be ignored. Chinese ideas, however, also made some impact on the cultures of the northern peoples of the Great Wall region. Some northern bronze plaques with the typical Chinese dragon-tiger motif, and the earrings from tomb M4, Xigouban represent a combination of Chinese and grassland elements. The bronze plaque with turtle-dragon motif from tomb M14 Daodunzi seems to be related to Xuanwu, the Dark Warrior. This phenomenon probably represents a sinicisation of the border area during the Han dynasty.

Figure 14 • Painted coffin from the Han tomb (M1) in Changsha, Hunan (after Changsha Mawangdui yihao Han mu, *fig22, 25)*

Conclusion

Based on archaeological materials and museum collections, I have discussed the northern animal style from late Shang, Western Zhou, Spring and Autumn period to the Warring States, Qin and Han dynasties, over a period of more than 1,000 years. These artefacts may be divided into groups reflecting three different stages of economic and social life. The first group consists of the swords and daggers with animal heads on the pommels, which represent the culture of a mixed agricultural and pastoral economy during the late Shang and Western Zhou period; they spread over the Great Wall region, eastwards towards Yanshan Mountain, south to the Shaanxi and Shanxi plains. The second group are the antenna-hilt style of swords, which began in the Spring and Autumn and early Warring States period, mainly to the south and north of the Yanshan region. Finally, the third group consists of plaques with relief and openwork designs, dated between the middle and late Warring States and the Qin-Han periods, and representing the pastoral culture of the northern grasslands.

The animal style itself, with a distribution over a limited range of territory, represents the change from a mixed agricultural tradition to nomadism. If we may borrow names from traditional literature, we can divide its progress into three stages, first of all the Guifang (Yanyun) culture (Shang period); secondly the Rongdi (Zhou period); and thirdly the Xiongnu (Qin-Han period). In the early stage, infantry was the main form of warfare, with the occasional use of chariots; mounted cavalry appeared in the second stage, while the third stage saw the formation of the Xiongnu federation in the north of China.

Along the Great Wall, the Mt Yanshan region and the Shaanxi-Shanxi plains, cultures developed independently, differing from the Huaxia culture of the middle and lower Yellow River, and also from the Minussinsk and Karasuk cultures of Siberia. The south and north may have met here, but this area did not merely serve as a mediator between the two: it is quite possible that it may have been the homeland of the first group. It has links with Anyang as well as with Mongolia and Trans-Baikalia, and is quite different from the Minussinsk area, but because the chronology of these related areas is not yet clear, our discussion has to be cautious. The third group contains strong foreign elements, indicating exchanges that were taking place in the grasslands, with the development of pastoralism. The second group represents the transitional period. We realise that the northern culture was a state of constant transformation throughout the Shang, Zhou and until the Warring States period, but that nomadism was the marker indicating the dividing line between the different stages.

Figure *a* • Bronze container, Jiangchuan Lijiashan M69:157

Li Kunsheng

The Bronze Age of Yunnan

The Chinese Bronze Age is identified with the so-called Three Dynasties of Xia, Shang and Zhou. However, Yunnan, formerly known as Dian, lies somewhat outside this definition. Yunnan province, in the south-west of China, borders on Sichuan, Tibet, Guangxi and Guizhou. The creators of the ancient Dian culture belonged to ethnic groups other than the Han Chinese. This combination of geographical and human factors led to different characteristics and time-scale for the Bronze Age in Yunnan, which corresponds roughly to the period from the late Shang dynasty to the end of Western Han dynasty, *i e* from the 11th century BC to the 1st century BC. Based on the archaeological materials that have accumulated over the last 50 years, we can divide the bronze culture of Dian into four major regions: the Dianchi region; the Erhai region; the northwest of Yunnan; and the Honghe region (figure 1).

1 The Dianchi Region

The distribution of the bronze culture of this region was centred on Lake Dianchi. In the northeast it reached as far as Qujing, in the west to Lufeng and in the south to Yuanjiang. More than 40 sites have been excavated, spread over 14 counties and cities, including Kunming, Jinning, Jiangchuan, Anning, Chenggong, Chengjiang, Qujing. The most important of them are the ancient tombs in Jinning Shizhaishan. Between 1955 and 1960, archaeologists conducted four seasons of excavation and excavated 50 tombs, recovering more than 4,000 artefacts, including the gold seal inscribed *Dianwang zhi yin* (Seal of the King of Dian) from tomb No 6, confirming that the cemetery belonged to the royal house of the Dian kingdom during the Western Han dynasty.[1]

The second most important discovery was the group of 20 ancient tombs in Jiangchuan Lijiashan, which were excavated in 1972 (figures a, b and c); between December 1991 and April 1992 more tombs were excavated, with a further discovery in 1994, making a total of 86 tombs in all.[2] In Chenggong Tianzimiao, 44 tombs were excavated in 1974,[3] in Anning Taijishan, 17 tombs were excavated in 1964;[4] in Qujing Zhujie Batatai, more than 250 tombs of Bronze Age date were excavated in seven seasons between 1977 and 1982.[5]

[1] Yunnan 1959 (Yunnansheng bowuguan): *Yunnan Jinning Shizhaishan gu muqun fajue baogao*, Beijing: Wenwu chubanshe

[2] Yunnan 1975 (Yunnansheng bowuguan): Yunnan Jiangchuan Lijiashan gu muqun fajue baogao,' *Kaogu xuebao* 1975(2); Zhang Xinning 1993: 'Jiangchuan Lijiashan gu muqun dierci fajue jiankuan,' *Yunnan wenwu* 1993(6). The reports of new discoveries are forthcoming.

[3] Kunming 1985 (Kunming shi wenguanhui): 'Chenggong Tianzimiao Dianmu,' *Kaogu xuebao* 1985(4): 507-545.

[4] Yunnan 1965 (Yunnansheng wenwu gongzuodui): 'Yunnan Anning Taijishan gu muqun qingli baogao,' *Kaogu* 1965 (9).

[5] The archaeological report has yet to be published. Information based on the author's own excavation notes.

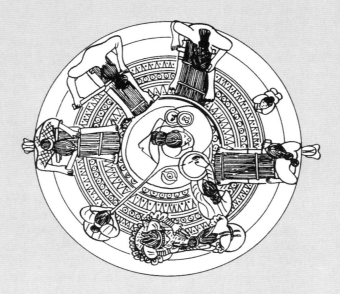

*Figure **b** (above) • Bronze container, unearthed at Jiangchuan Lijiashan 1992 and figure **c** (below) • Bird-view of the container*

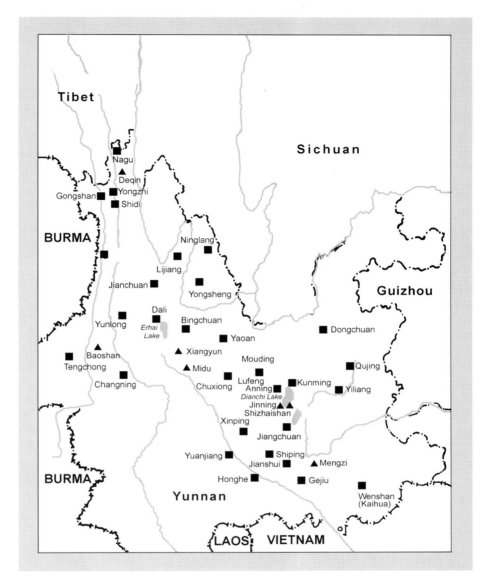

Figure 1 • Map of Yunnan

2 The Erhai Region

The bronze culture of the western region of Yunnan was centred on Lake Erhai. In the north, this region extends to Jianchuan, in the south to Changning, east to Chuxiong. The western border is still unclear. Ancient bronzes of this type have been found in Dali, Jianchuan, Yongsheng, Ninglang, Weishan, Changning, Midu, Xiangyun, Baoshan, Yaoan. The most important among these is the Haimenkou site in Jianchuan county, where 14 bronzes were excavated in 1957 and a further 12 pieces in 1978.[6] Among these 26 pieces, several can be identified as early Dian bronzes. Next in importance is the bronze coffin found in Xiangyun Dabona.[7] The tomb, excavated in 1964, had a wooden chamber. The coffin, weighing 257 kilogrammes, was decorated with geometrical and animal patterns (figure 2). In 1977 another wooden-chambered tomb was excavated nearby, but this did not contain a bronze coffin. Some early tombs were also found in Aofengshan, Jianchuan county, where 342 tombs containing more than 572 artefacts were found in 1980.[8]

The ancient tombs in Wanjiaba, Chuxiong, excavated between 1975 and 1976,[9] combined the characteristics of both the Dianchi and the Erhai regions. Seventy-nine tombs with a total of 1,243 artefacts have been found. Among

[6] Yunnan 1958 (Yunnansheng bowuguan choubeichu): 'Jianchuan Haimenkou guwenhua yizhi qingli jianbao,' *Kaogu tongxun* 1958 (6): 5-12.

[7] Yunnan 1964 (Yunnansheng wenwu gongzuodui): 'Yunnan Xiangyun Dabona muqu Tongguan mu qingli baogao,' *Kaogu* 1964 (12): 607-614.

[8] Yunnan 1986 (Yunnansheng bowuguan gongzuodui): 'Yunnan Jianchuan Aofengshan mudi fajue jianbao,' *Wenwu* 1986 (7): 1-20.

[9] Yunnan 1983 (Yunnansheng wenwu gongzuodui): 'Chuxiong Wanjiaba gu muqun fajue jianbao,' *Kaogu xuebao* 1983 (3): 347-382.

them were five bronze drums, dated to the Spring and Autumn period; they are the earliest bronze drums so far known.

3 The Northwest of Yunnan

The northwest of Yunnan is less well-known: only a small number of tombs have been excavated, in Deqin, Ninglang and Zhongdian. The bronzes found at these sites differ greatly in style from those of the bronze cultures of the Dianchi and Erhai regions. Instead, they are stylistically related to the ancient cultures of Sichuan, Gansu and Qinghai, and the nomadic cultures of the Scythians and Xiongnu.

4 The Honghe Region

We lack materials for the bronze culture of southern Yunnan. About 200 pieces have been found in Shiping, Hekou, Honghe, Mengzi, Tengchong, Wenshan and elsewhere. From their style and shapes, they represent a new type of bronze culture.

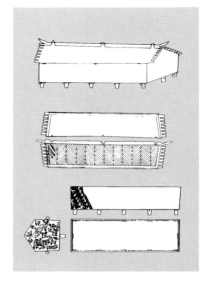

Figure 2 • Bronze coffin from Xiangyun Dabona

Classification

The main classifications of ancient Chinese bronzes are as follows: agricultural tools; weapons; cooking and wine vessels; water vessels; musical instruments; and miscellaneous objects. However, many of the bronze objects which were popular in the central plains seldom appeared in Yunnan, *e g li* tripod, *xian* steamer, *gui* food vessel, *xu* and *fu* containers, *dui* covered dish. The most common Shang-style wine vessels, such as *jia*, *jue*, *guang* and *fangyi*, are also absent in Yunnan. Thus, to deal with ancient bronzes in Yunnan we have to classify them into slightly modified categories.

a) There is a great variety of production tools, including axe, pickaxe, hoe, spade, sickle, knife, axe, adze, chisel, saw, awl, and needle; warping beam, weft beating knife and spinning whorl; and tools for fishing.

b) The weaponry is rich, including dagger-axe, spearhead, sword, pike, halberd, hook, crossbow, mace, arrow, scabbard and so on.

c) There are many food vessels: cooking pot, chopping-stand, wine vessels, covered box, wine jar, goblet and cup. Water vessels are mainly basins.

d) There are also many musical instruments: drum, gourd-shaped pipe, bell, cymbals and jingle.

e) There is a great variety of miscellaneous objects, such as belt hook, mirror, earrings, water-dropper, bed warmer, pillow, coins and seals.

f) Some types are unique to Yunnan bronzes, such as cowrie container, barrel, coffin and decorative buttons.

Technology

The piece-mould method was known to the ancient craftsmen of Yunnan; some bronzes from the Haimenkou site were cast by moulds,[10] but the main method in the Bronze Age of Yunnan was the lost-wax technique. The earliest use of the lost-wax method is the Chu culture, about 6th century BC, but it very quickly reached Yunnan and was widely used by the craftsmen of the Dian culture.

The bronze craftsmen of the Dian culture also used some special techniques such as incising, using sharp tools (probably made of iron) to incise patterns on bronzes. The best example of this technique was found at Jinning Shizhaishan (M13:67), on fragments of an incised bronze piece belonging to the Western Han period (figure 3). The fragment is 42 centimetres long, 12.5 centimetres wide and 0.1 centimetres in thickness. On it are incised human figures, phoenixes, ox and tiger and horse heads, shells, and complicated patterns with lines as fine as a human hair.

A second technique is that of gold and silver inlay, using a sharp iron tool to cut into the surface of the bronze, and then inlaying with gold, silver

[10] Xiao Minghua 1991: 'Jianchuan Haimenkou 1978 nian fajue suohuo tongqi jiqi youguan wenti,' Yunnansheng bowuguan ed. *Yunnan qingtong wenhua lunji*, Kunming: Yunnan renmin chubanshe, 174-179.

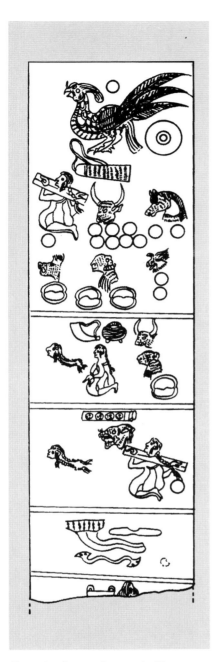

Figure 3 • Bronze fragment with incised decoration, Jinning Shizhaishan M13:67

or copper wire. Sometimes on silver objects, gold wire or gold foil was also inlaid. For example, a silver belt-plaque of triangular shape, found in Shizhaishan, has in the centre a winged tiger, grasping a tree branch with its claws and with its tail erect. Its body is inlaid with gold foil and the eyes with yellow agate (M7:72). Other materials such as agate, jade and turquoise were also inlaid.

The inlay technique had been widely used in the central plains during the Spring and Autumn and Warring States periods, and came to Yunnan slightly later, where it was most common during the Warring States and Western Han periods. Among 88 decorative pieces from 13 tombs at Shizhaishan, over 90 per cent were inlaid with agate, jade or turquoise. For example, the round-shaped bronze decorative piece (M10:17), whose diameter is 16.8 centimetres, has a red agate inlaid in the centre, surrounded by a ring of turquoise, another narrow white ring, and a further turquoise ring creating a pattern of red, green, white and green, and making this inlay technique especially effective.

Yet another bronze-working technique is gilding. This was probably a central plains invention whose use began in the Spring and Autumn period. The basic method was to mix gold and mercury, in a proportion of one to seven. The liquid amalgam was applied to the surface previously treated with salt and alum. By heating the bronze, the mercury was driven off, leaving the gold on the surface of the object as it cooled. This use of gold appeared in Yunnan during the Western Han period. The best example is the openwork gilt bronze plaque (M13: 109), 15 centimetres long and 9 centimetres wide, depicting a group of Dian warriors defeating the local tribesmen. An armoured warrior holds a head in his left hand and leads a woman carrying a baby as captive with his right hand. Behind her follow a cow and two sheep. Another armed Dian warrior follows behind and also carries a human head. Beneath them are headless bodies and a huge serpent. All of them are gilded. After 2,000 years of burial, the gilding is still complete and shining, reflecting the advanced gilding technique of the Dian people.

Animal Art

Animal sculpture is an important and unique part of the Yunnan bronze art. More than 40 species are depicted, including tiger, leopard, bear, wolf, fox, wild boar, monkey, deer, rabbit, oxen, sheep, horses, pigs, dogs, chickens, snakes, otter, lizard, crocodile, pigeon, cuckoo, cormorant, ducks, eagle, swallow, parrot, sparrow, crow, owl, pheasant, peacock, phoenix, kingfisher, harrier, fish, prawns, frogs and rats, bees and beetles.These bronze animal sculptures can be divided into four types:

1 **Sculptures in the Round:** These are usually domesticated animals or birds: the best example was found inside the bronze coffin at Xiangyun Dabona, depicting the six domesticated animals: ox, pig, horse, dog, sheep, chicken. Such subjects reflect a concern with animal husbandry.

2 **Animals in Groups:** Sometimes similar species are depicted together, such as oxen, peacocks and waterfowl. The best examples feature a motif known as 'animal combat.' They are similar to the Ordos animal art of Northern China, as well as to the animal combat motifs in Scythian art, but there are differences: the animal combat plaques from Yunnan do not have framing elements, and are freer and more imaginative. A representative example is the bronze plaque from Jinning Shizhaishan (M10:4) depicting a wild boar being attacked by two leopards, in openwork (figure 4).

3 **Men and Animals in Combination:** These are of two kinds: in the first, men and animals are seen in a harmonious relationship, such as a herdsman and his ox (figure 5); in the second, man is seen as a hunter, as in the bronze plaque showing two noblemen on horseback hunting deer (M13:7) (figure 6). Both examples come from Jiangchuan Lijiashan.

4 Three-dimensional Animal Sculpture as Ornament on Bronze Weapons: These include ox, leopard, wild boar, snake, monkey and tiger, sometimes as attachments to the weapon (figure 7), sometimes forming part of the weapon itself, such as a snake head forming the hilt of a sword (figure 8). Another example is the bronze axe from Jinning Shizhaishan in the form of a fish tail (figure 7a).

In general, the characteristic of Yunnan bronze animal sculpture is naturalism, the depiction of real animals, differing from the ritual bronzes of the Shang and Zhou, where the *taotie* mask and the *kui* dragon are not representations of real animals. The composition of animal sculpture is generally well-balanced, with considerable detail and occasional exaggeration of certain elements. Not only are the physical features of the animal described but its mood is vividly expressed, showing the craftsmen's understanding of the nature of these animals.

Architecture

The earliest architectural remains, dated to the 12th century BC, were found in Jianchuan Haimenkou in 1957 and 1978.[11] They are buildings of timber construction. At the site, hundreds of timber posts were found, and a bronze axe was originally attached to one of them. The buildings can be reconstructed as ganlan or pile-dwellings. Two bronze architectural models in the form of such timber structures were found inside the bronze coffin at Dabona. Each of them has two storeys, the lower one empty and the upper level projecting outwards, with windows. The roof is steeply sloped, with a long ridge beam and short rafters; the gable ends have swallow-tail timbers, while the roof has incised lines to indicate the roofing material. This is very similar to the architecture of the Jingpo minority people who still live in Yunnan province.[12] These models of pile-dwellings can be dated to the 5th century BC; a similar one retrieved from tomb No 21, Lijiashan, is 10.5 centimetres high, and 9.5 centimetres wide, has similar characteristics and dates from the same time.

A slightly later model, dated to the 2nd century BC, was discovered at Shizhaishan (M12:26). It was cast on the lid of a bronze container (figure 9). This model is 17.5 centimetres high, and is supported on two round pillars; the floor is raised above ground level and there are no surrounding walls. The roof is supported by a beam and rafter structure: apart from the two main pillars, there are smaller supplementary pillars at three of the four corners. Only five pillars are found, but it should have had six in all. The one missing was probably omitted during the casting process. The roof is steeply sloping and the ridge beam is longer than the building itself; the gable ends have swallow-tail timbers. Although there are no surrounding walls, it was placed together with a number of bronze drums, indicating that it was not a residential building but a religious structure. Interestingly, one can find engravings of similar architecture on the back of bronze mirrors of the Yayoi period in Japan. Three other pieces have been found at the Shizhaishan site (M3:64, M6:22, M13:259).

Apart from this, another cast bronze building in the form of a granary has been found, on a container from Shizhaishan (M12:1). The granary was supported on four sides with 13 timbers along each side. It has two storeys: the upper level has timber walls of log-cabin type, differing from the open

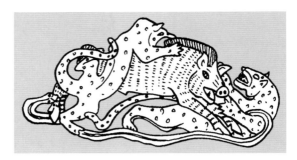

Figure 4 • *Bronze plaque, Jinning Shizhaishan M10:4*

Figure 5 • *Bronze plaque, Jiangchuan Lijiashan, unearthed 1992*

[11] Yunnan 1958 (Yunnansheng bowuguan choubeichu): 'Jianchuan Haimenkou guwenhua yizhi qingli jianbao,' *Kaogu tongxun* 1958 (6): 5-12.

[12] An Zhimin 1963: 'Ganlan' shi jianzhu de kaogu yanjiu,' *Kaogu xuebao* 1963 (2): 65-85.

Figure 6 • *Bronze plaque, Jiangchuan Lijiashan M13:7*

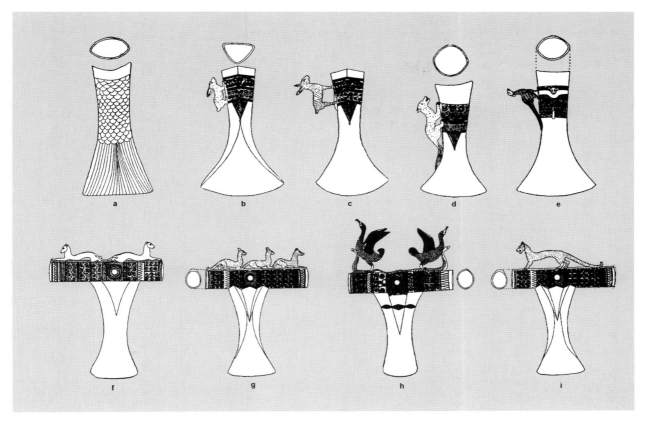

Figure 7 • *Bronze axes unearthed at Jinning Shizhaishan:* **a** *M6:98,* **b** *M12:6,* **c** *M13:105,* **d** *M13:253,* **e** *M12:6* **f** *MM6:93,* **g** *M13:210,* **h** *M13:235,* **i** *M3:85*

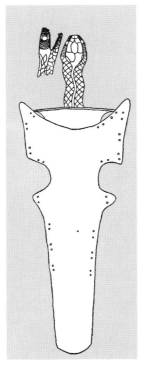

Figure 8 • *A bronze dagger from the Shizhaishan site (M6:48)*

architectural scheme in other examples. The roof is similar to the latter, and at its summit are some small birds. Outside the granary a hen and chickens are looking for food. It dates to the second stage, in the 2nd century BC.

Music

A number of musical instruments have been identified among the bronze pieces in Yunnan, including a gourd-shaped mouth-organ (*hulusheng*) and flute (*xiao*), *chunyu* drum, *zhong* bell, goathorn-shaped bell and *ling* bell, *luo* gong, *ba* cymbals and *gu* drum. The gourd-shaped *sheng* was invented by the people of the Bronze Age in Yunnan: tomb M24 at Lijiashan contained two examples (figure 10), and another four were found in tombs No 15, 16, and 17 at Shizhaishan. They are of two kinds, with either a straight or a curved tube. The shape imitates a gourd, but is wholly cast in bronze, with five or seven holes to serve as stops. When one blows in the tube and stops the holes with the fingers, it can make pleasing sounds. This type of musical instrument can be found between the 5th and 1st centuries BC. Many of the ethnic minorities still living in Yunnan continue to play this type of instrument, but their instruments are made of organic materials rather than bronze.

Only one example of the gourd-shaped bronze *xiao* has been archaeologically excavated in Yunnan, from the bronze coffin at Xiangyun Dabona. Its shape is similar to the gourd-shaped *sheng*, but there are three pipes, one longer one in the centre with two smaller pipes beside it. It was played in a similar way as the gourd-shaped *sheng*.

The *chunyu* drum derived from the central plains. It consists of an oval cylinder, with a handle cast in the form of a tiger. The shoulder is usually wide and the neck is constrained with a narrow waist. No actual examples have been excavated in Yunnan, but among the 127 bronze figurines on the lid of a bronze container (M12: 26), one is shown playing the *chunyu* (figure 11). Another example is the bronze plaque (M13: 65) on which are eight musicians playing musical instruments: one of them is a *chunyu*. Both pieces date to the 2nd century BC.

The *zhong* bell is another object from the central plains, which was slightly modified after its arrival in Yunnan. It has been found in many places in Yunnan, such as Xiangyun, Changning, Mouding, Jinning and Jiangchuan. sometimes in sets, between the 5th and 1st centuries BC. From Shizhaishan M6, a set of six bells was found (figure 12).

A bell with a goat-horn-shaped suspension loop (*yangjiao niuzhong*) is only found in Yunnan, Guangxi and Guangdong provinces and in Vietnam. Altogether several dozen have been found. The suspension loop is shaped like the horns of a goat. Eleven pieces are known from Yunnan, six of them in tomb No 1 at Chuxiong Wanjiaba. They are dated to the 6th century BC, corresponding to the late Spring and Autumn Period in central China. Their size ranges from large to small in regular stages, the biggest 21.6 centimetres high, the smallest 15 centimetres high, and they have no decoration. Apart from this set, some similar *yangjiaoniu* bells of later date, around the 2nd century BC, have been found in Jinning and Changning.

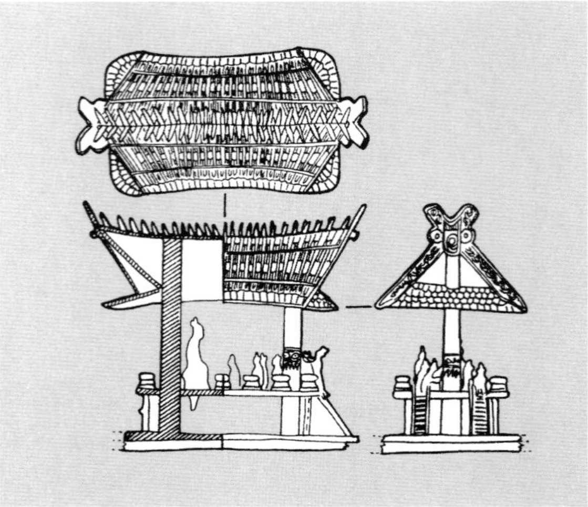

Ling jingles. These are of two main types. One is called *maling* or horse jingle: at Shizhaishan this type of *maling* was found together with horse harness in six tombs; another kind was used by priests during ritual ceremonies. Some small bells could also be attached to the ankles of dancers.

Luo gong. Only two examples have been found so far. One is from tomb No 1 at Guixian Luobowan, Guangxi province, dated to the 2nd century BC. Another *luo* of 50.5 centimetres diameter, decorated with beautiful patterns, was found in tomb No 12 at Shizhaishan, which was also dated to the 2nd century BC.

Ba cymbals. These originally came from India. A bronze plaque found in tomb No 13 at Shizhaishan depicts two men playing cymbals and dancing. The plaque was gilded, 13 centimetres high and 19 centimetres wide. Two men with large noses and deep-set eyes, wearing long trousers and tightly tied jackets, are dancing and singing and holding cymbals. The base line is formed by a snake. The shape of the cymbal is round, with a knob at the back to provide a hold. They were struck against each other to make a sound.

Games and Bull-fighting

Some bronze objects from Yunnan were used for playing or associated with performances. At Shizhaishan, tombs No 14 and 17 contained a special kind of bronze vase or *touhu*. This kind of vase was used during banquets and games, and was about 40 centimetres in height, with a round body and narrow cylindrical neck. When playing the game, the player stands at a distance from the vase, throwing an arrow into the mouth of the vase, some of which are decorated with incised motifs (figure 13).

Another kind of object, found in tombs No 3, 6 and 7 at Shijiashan, is a model audience platform, from which to watch contests between bulls, or men bull-fighting. This kind of platform dates to the 2nd century BC. In ancient China there were special warriors or fighters for taming wild animals. A bronze dagger from a tomb at Shizhaishan (M13:172) has a scene of a man in combat with a tiger incised on both sides of the blade (figure 14).

Figure 9 • *A bronze architectural model in the* ganlan *style, Jinning Shizhaishan M12:26*

Figure 10 • *A bronze* hulusheng *mouth-organ, Jiangchuan Lijiashan M24:a*

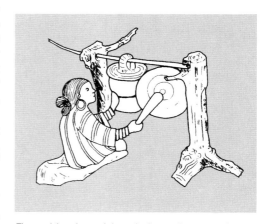

Figure 11 • *A musician playing a* chunyu *and a drum, Jinning Shizhaishan M12:26*

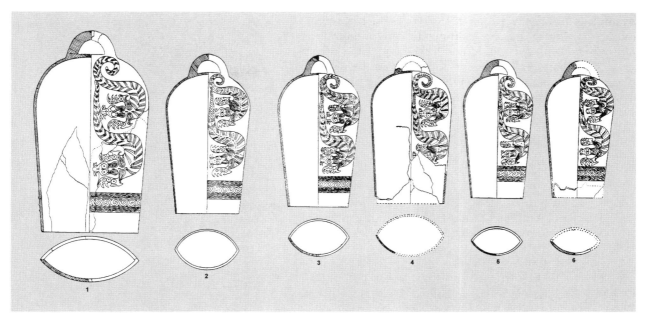

Figure 12 • A set of six bronze bells, Jinning Shizhaishan M6:114-119

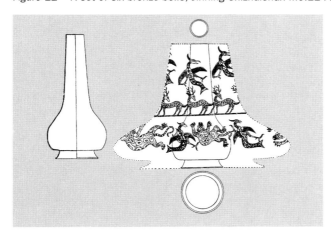

Figure 13 • Two bronze touhu vases, Jinning Shizhaishan: M17:24

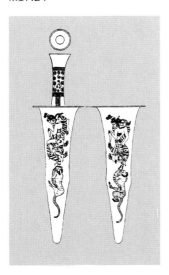

Figure 14 • A bronze dagger with incised motif, Jinning Shizhaishan: M13:172

Dance

There are different types of dance represented in the Yunnan bronzes. One of these is a religious dance, usually associated with the aristocracy and performed in temples, similar to dances in the central plains. Dance was one of the arts taught at the Zhou court; the dances represented on Yunnan bronzes, which include both civil and military dances, can all be identified with textual references of the late Zhou period.

The first type is known as the *yuwu* or feather dance. The dancers either hold feathers or wear feather headdresses. This kind of feather dance is depicted on the bronze *luo*-gong from tomb No 12 at Shizhaishan (M12:1). It depicts 23 dancers: the leader wears a long coat and a long sword; the remainder have naked upper bodies and go barefoot, with only a cloth belt at the waist. They wear feather headdresses and hold a long half-open bird's feather in their hands.

Another dance is known as *maowu*, in which the dancer holds a yak tail. On the famous Kaihua bronze drum dated to the Western Han period, 15 dancers are depicted wearing feather headdresses with cloth belts, and each holding a yak's tail (figure 15). In another dance, the dancers do not hold any objects in their hands but only perform a sleeve dance. An example can be seen on the bronze drum-shaped container found in Shizhaishan tomb No 12 (M12:2) on which a dancing scene is cast in the round on the lid: along the edge of the lid are a group of dancers holding their arms up with the palms facing outwards, performing a sleeve dance (figure 16).

Another dance is known as *ganwu* or shield dance. It is a military dance, in which the dancers hold a shield. This type of dance can be seen on the bronze drum found in Shizhaishan (M14:1), dated around the 2nd century BC.

There are also many representations of folk dances which were unique to the ancient Dian people: for example, the dance with a *hulusheng*. The sculpture on the bronze container from Shizhaishan (M17:23) includes four figurines, one of whom is playing a *hulusheng* while the other three are dancing. The Kaihua bronze drum of the Western Han period, already referred to, has a similar dancing scene: four men in a line and wearing feather

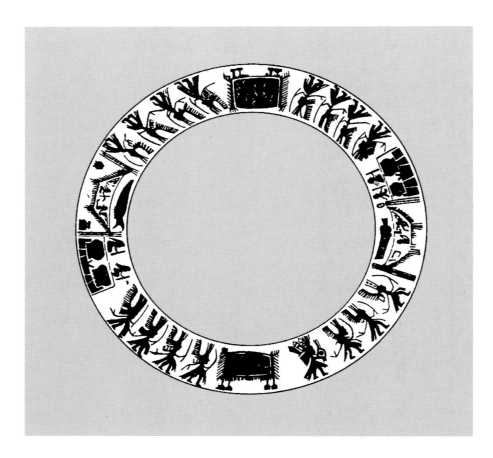

Figure 15 • Motif on the bronze drum unearthed in Kaihua

Figure 16 • Motif on the bronze drum unearthed in Jinning Shizhaishan M12:2

Figure 17 • Dancing shamans on a bronze plaque, Jinning Shizhaishan M13:64

Figure 18 • Ritual scene on the bronze drum unearthed in Guangnan

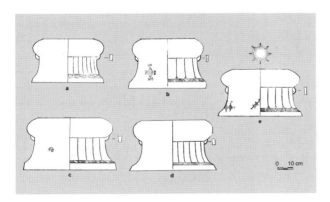

*Figure 19 • Bronze drums, Wanjiaba type: **a** M23:160, **b** MM23:161, **c** M23:159, **d** M23:158, **e** M1:12*

headdresses, naked to the waist, with a cloth belt; the three in front raise their arms and stamp their feet, while the fourth is blowing away on a *hulusheng*. A depiction of men imitating dancing cranes is found on the waist of a bronze drum from Lijiashan (M24:42B): the dancers are wearing feather headdresses, wings and tails, with their arms stretched out and fingers spread, vividly imitating the movements of cranes. There is another special kind of circle dance, in which the dancers' movements are circular. A circular plaque from Jiangchuan Lijiashan, inlaid with turquoise, has 18 figures in a circle, dancing hand in hand.

Some dancing scenes can be associated with ancient shamanistic dances. A bronze plaque from Shizhaishan (M13:64) and a bronze container from Lijiashan (M69:162) both have four shamans performing a ritual dance. They all wear a high cap with a pointed top, and hold bells (figure 17). Both pieces probably date from the Western Han period. On the waist of a bronze drum from Guangnan there is another ritual scene of slaughtering an ox: two groups each surrounding a tall pole with feather decoration (figure 18). An ox is tethered to the pole, and in front of the ox a man wearing a feathered headdress is standing with his hands raised. Behind the ox is another man wearing a feather headdress and holding an axe ready to slaughter the beast. There are 10 groups of figures dancing nearby, with about 20 people in each group.

Bronze Drums

In the Bronze Age of Yunnan, the most significant object is bronze drum. Bronze drums are seen in southern China and South East Asia. It first appeared as early as the 6th century BC and is still in use among smong some ethnic groups today. Being mainly for ceremonial use, it is a popular and treasured instrument, and therefore has a greater significance. In China, a total of over 1,500 examples are kept in museum and public collections in the 12 southern provinces. Private collections account for about a further 800 examples. They can be divided into eight types: Wanjiaba; Shizhaishan; Lengshuichong; Zunyi; Majiang; Beiliu; Lingshan; and Ximeng.

The Wanjiaba and Shizhaishan types can be safely dated to the Bronze Age. Although the Shizhaishan type was first classified by the Austrian archaeologist Franz Heger in 1902 as the earliest type in the total of 165 bronzes classified by him,[13] recent archaeology has proven that the Wanjiaba type, which Heger had no chance to see, is earlier than the Shizhaishan type.

The Wanjiaba type of bronze drum dates to between the 6th and the 3rd centuries BC (figure 19).[14] Its shape is simple and the casting is crude. The body of the drum is divided into three sections; the top is smaller and the neck is wider, with a narrowed waist and projecting foot. In the centre of the top of the drum there is a sun motif in relief (figure 20), some with rays but most without. The shoulder is usually plain, but the waist is often decorated with straight vertical lines dividing it into different zones. The majority of drums of this type have no further decoration within these zones, but a few have geometric or animal patterns. The foot is usually decorated with spirals or curved lines. The peculiar feature of this kind of bronze drum is that it has decoration on the inside wall, often of crocodile skin pattern. The shape of this early type of bronze drum is

[13] Heger, Franz 1902: *Alte Metalltrommeln aus Sudostasien*, Leipzig.

[14] Li Kunsheng and Hung Derong 1990: 'Lun Wanjiaba xing tonggu,' *Kaogu* 1990(5): 456-566.

Figure 20 • Incised decoration found on Wanjiaba bronze drums

derived from that of a bronze cooking pot. To my knowledge, 37 pieces are in existence, 28 in Yunnan, three in Guangxi and six from Vietnam and Thailand.

The Shizhaishan type of bronze drums date from the 3rd century BC to the 1st century AD (figure 21). They have a well-developed type of decoration and the casting is improved. They are circular and pillow-shaped, divided into shoulder, waist and foot. The shoulder is broader than the top, the narrow waist and projecting foot make it look like a trumpet. A sun motif is usually found on the top, with radiating rays, from four to 32 in number. It may reflect ancient sun-worship. Around the edge of the top, there is often a decoration of flying cranes, depicted in a realistic manner. They usually number four, six, 14 or 16. Apart from these, geometric patterns such as saw-tooth and checkerboard patterns are also found on the top. Sometimes the body is decorated with oxen, deer, boats and figures wearing long feather headdresses. Some of the drums are covered with triangular patterns and small circles, the most typical decoration of the Shizhaishan type. There are more than 156 bronzes of this type in existence, over 56 of which are in China, 39 of them in Yunnan.

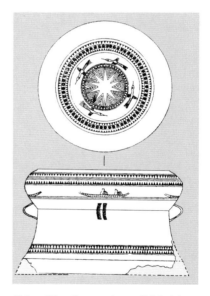

Figure 21 • Bronze drum, Shizhaishan type, Jinning Shizhaishan M3:3

Conclusion

To sum up, the Bronze age of Yunnan began in the 11th century BC, originating in the Erhai region, and reached its peak in the Dianchi region around the 3rd century BC to the 1st century BC, declining after the 1st century AD.

Archaeology of the Bronze Age in Yunnan is a very significant branch of the study of ancient bronze culture in China. There are over 100 sites in all, and more than 1,000 pieces have been discovered. They have their own characteristics and time frame, differing from those of the central plains. The people who created this unique bronze culture were not Han Chinese: they had a different economic and social culture which is so vividly reflected in their choice of subject-matter and bronze-casting techniques. Their material culture also provides an opportunity for exploring the art and spiritual world of the Dian culture.

Sacrifice, Rituals and the Afterlife

CHEN XIANDAN

The Sacrificial Pits at Sanxingdui: Their Nature and Date

S ince the controlled archaeological excavation began in 1980 at the Guanghan Sanxingdui site, Sichuan province, there have been many seasons of excavations.[1] In 1986, two pits (Nos 1 and 2) were discovered, and striking artefacts were found which have attracted great attention.[2] Many experts have tried to discuss their significance, and have offered many interpretations of the objects found in the pits. Now we can see that common ground has been reached on many questions, but there is still considerable debate on certain important questions, such as the nature of these pits and their date.

The Problem of Dating

In the preliminary excavation report, we dated these two pits to the Shang period, contemporary to the first and second phases of the Yinxu period (c14th-13th century BC). There are however, some different views on dating them, as follows:

a) First phase of the Yinxu period (c14th century BC);[3]

b) Late Shang or early Western Zhou period (c12th-11th century BC);[4] and

c) Middle or late Western Zhou period (10th century BC).[5]

The first view is close to the date proposed in the preliminary archaeological report; the second and particularly the third theories, however, differ substantially from that proposal. For instance, the last view asserts that the Shu culture did not have an advanced bronze technology and that no bronze objects dating earlier than Western Zhou have ever been discovered in Sichuan. According to this theory, the Shu culture only developed bronze technology after the conquest of Shang by the Zhou; therefore one may say that the objects from the pits were probably made in the Western Zhou and were used for two or three hundred years, until the time when they were invaded by outsiders, when the objects were buried.

In the preliminary report, we briefly discussed the material from the excavation of pits No 1 and 2, but faced with these different opinions, this paper will offer a way of re-examining the evidence and offer a further discussion. First let us look at the carbon-14 dating evidence. More than 20 sacrificial specimens collected from various strata at the site were submitted for carbon

[1] Sichuan 1987a (Sichuan wenwu guanli weiyuanhui *et al*): 'Guanghan Sanxingdui yizhi,' *Kaogu xuebao* 1987(2): 227-254; Chen Xiandan 1989a: 'Sanxingdui yi er hao keng liangge wenti de tantao,' *Wenwu* 1989(5): 36-38.

[2] For excavation reports, see Sichuan 1987a, ibid; Sichuan 1987 (Sichuan sheng wenwu kaogu yanjiusuo *et al*): 'Guanghan Sanxingdui yizhi yihao jisi keng fajue jianbao,' *Wenwu* 1987(10): 1-15; Sichuan 1988 (Sichuan sheng wenwu kaogu yanjiusuo *et al*): 'Guanghan Sanxingdui yizhi erhao jisi keng fajue jianbao,' *Wenwu* 1989(5): 1-20. For an English study, see Ge Yan and C Linduff 1990.

[3] Sun Hua 1993: Guanyu Sanxingdui qiwu keng ruogan wenti de bianzheng,' *Sichuan wenwu* 1993(4): 3-11; 1993(5): 3-7; Sheng Zhongchang 1987: 'Sanxingdui erhao jisi keng qingtong li renxiang chuji,' *Wenwu* 1987(10): 16-17.

[4] Hu Changyu, Cai Ge 1992: 'Yufu kao-ye tan Sanxingdui,' *Sichuan wenwu*: Special issue on the studies of the Sanxingdui culture, 26-33.

[5] Song Yemin 1990: 'Guanghan Sanxingdui yihao, erhao jisi keng jige wenti de tantao,' *Nanfang minzu kaogu* 3: 69-84.

tests at the Institute of Archaeology, Chinese Academy of Social Sciences and Peking University archaeological laboratories. The earliest dates obtained are 4900 ±130 bp. and 4760 ± 130 bp; the latest dates are 2875 ± 80 bp. These figures have been calibrated as 2950 BC, 2810 BC and 840 BC. Based on this scientific dating, we see that the latest cultural deposit at the Sanxingdui site is around 840 BC, still within the Western Zhou period. These dates refer to the time during which the site was occupied: if we look at the two sacrificial pits, No 1 is under the sixth stratum in section B, and pit No 2 is beneath the fifth stratum. Thus the stratigraphical evidence supports an earlier date for these pits.

Secondly, we can select a group of objects to compare with the evidence from stratification and typology together with the carbon-14 dating. Many important artefacts such as bronze sculptures, bronze trees and gold objects have been discovered for the first time and offer no comparisons with objects already known elsewhere in China. We can only compare artefacts such as jade *ge* dagger axe, *zhang* sceptre, and bronze *zun*, *lei* wine vessels, and pottery with similar objects from other places of similar date.

If we look at the jade *ge* and *zhang* from the two pits, the *ge* are of two types (figure 1), while the *zhang* are of four types (figure 2): they are very close to those that have been found at Yanshi Erlitou, Zhengzhou Erligang and Anyang Yinxu. Among several hundred jade and stone implements, we have found no single object that can be dated later than the Yinxu style. The bronze *zun* and *lei* containers (figure 3) from pit No 2 are close in both shape and decoration to vessels found in the second and third phases at Anyang Yinxu. In terms of decoration, the bird motifs on these objects have similar features, such as crest and curved beak, with raised or sometimes depressed tail feathers. For example, the bronze *zun* from pit No 1 is decorated with dragon and tiger motifs (figure 4); its shape and decoration are similar to the bronze *zun* decorated with dragon and tiger found in the Yuer River at Funan, Anhui province, which has been dated to the period later than the Erligang phase and close to the first Yinxu phase. Another similar piece has been found in Shaanxi. In southern China, in sites such as Yueyang in Hunan and Zaoyang and Shashi in Hubei, similar bronze vessels have been discovered, dated to the late Shang period.

Now we should examine the pottery from Sanxingdui. From pit No 1, many pottery containers have been found (figure 5): all of them

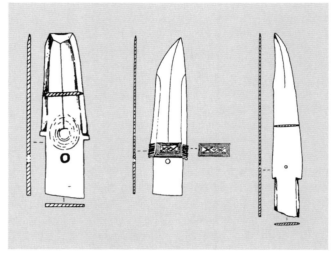

Figure 1 • *Jade* ge *dagger axes found at the Sanxingdui site (K1:126, 142, 158)*

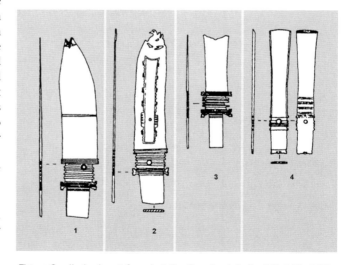

Figure 2 • *Jade* zhang *found at the Sanxingdui site (K1:146, 235, 01, 78)*

have a deeply curved belly, sloping sides, round rim and pointed bases. They were used together with a separate stand, which has a narrow waist, straight mouth and barrel or cylinder-shaped body. They are made of a tempered dark brown clay. Several archaeologists have debated whether this type of pottery should belong to the Western Zhou period. They say that "this kind of vessel with pointed base represents a set of objects that became popular in a wide area centred around Chengdu around the Duyu period of the Shu kingdom, in the late Western Zhou and early Spring and Autumn period."[6] This view would date pit No 2 to the late Western Zhou and early Spring and Autumn

[6] Xu Chaolong 1992: 'Sanxingdui jisi keng shuo chang yi-jiantan Yufu he Duyu zhi guangxi,' *Sichuan wenwu* 1992(5): 32-38; (6): 40-47.

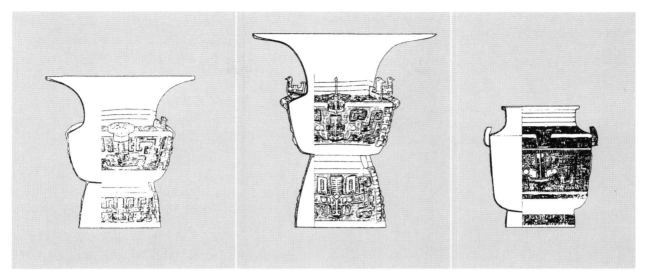

Figure 3 • Bronze zun and lei vessels found at the Sanxingdui site (K2:127,146,70)

period, mainly on the evidence of these vessels with pointed base.

However, this kind of pottery lamp is only one of the many kinds of pottery objects: it first appeared during the third phase of the Sanxingdui site, in the ninth stratum of section B, about 1400-1200 BC, and increased in numbers during the fourth phase, that is during the period 1000-840 BC. Apart from the contextual seriation, it appeared in differing quantities in the different periods. In terms of typology, the early pointed-base lamp has a wide mouth, rounded rim, and deep belly, with a sharply-pointed base. Later it became smaller in size, with a shallower body, and the base becomes round and flattened. Comparing their form with that of similar pottery lamps found at Chengdu Shi'erqiao and Chengdu Zhihuijie sites, dated to the Shang and Western Zhou period, respectively, those from Sanxingdui pit No 1 are clearly earlier than the examples dated to the Western Zhou but closer to those from the early and middle Shang period, such as type A from the Shi'erqiao site. Therefore, we date those pointed-base lamps before the middle and late Western Zhou.

Figure 4 • Tiger motif on a bronze zun found at the Sanxingdui site (K1:258)

Another important fact is that pits No 1 and No 2 are of different dates. We can compare the stratigraphical evidence and typology of the objects from pit No 1 and pit No 2. They show some clear differences, as follows:

a) The two pits lie beneath different strata of the Sanxingdui site. The cultural deposit at the Sanxingdui site can be divided into eight layers; pit No 1 is beneath the sixth stratum and No 2 is in the fifth stratum.

b) The two pits are of different shapes and layout (figure 6). Pit No 1 is between 450 and 464 centimetres in length and 330-380 centimetres in width. It has three passages leading to it, one at each end and one in the centre of one long side; the width of these passages is between 80 and 200 centimetres, and they are between 26 and 34 centimetres deep. Pit No 2 is triangular in shape, 530 centimetres long and 220 to 230 centimetres in width, and 140 to 168 centimetres deep. The base of the pit is somewhat smaller, 500 centimetres long and 210 centimetres in width.

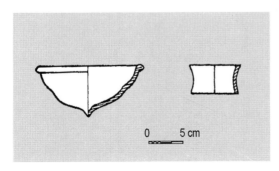

Figure 5 • Pottery objects found at the Sanxingdui site (K1:24, 27)

c) Objects from pit No 1 are usually smaller, such as bronze masks and bronze figurines in a kneeling position (figure 7). They total 439, far fewer than the 1,164 objects

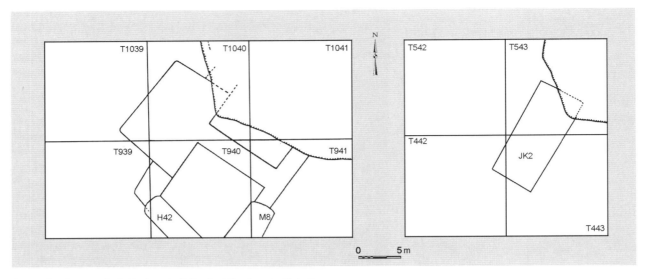

Figure 6 • Layout of pit No 1 and pit No 2 at the Sanxingdui site

in pit No 2. Objects such as bronze masks, the standing figure and bronze trees from pit No 2 are also much bigger in size, with heights ranging from 138 to 395 centimetres. The bronze heads and masks from pit No 1 are usually shaped in the round, and are fewer in number, while those from pit No 2 are square and long, with more variations.

d) In pit No 1, there was found only one bronze *zun* decorated with dragon and tiger motif, together with a *zun* with goat decoration and a *pou* vessel. In pit No 2 there were found more than a dozen bronze *zun*, *lei* and square *hu*.

e) Among all the objects from pit No 1, the largest single group are jade and stone implements, 195 out of the total of 439; in pit No 2, bronze objects number 732 out of the total of 1,164, or more than half of the total number.

f) From pit No 1 there was found a gold scabbard, which had probably belonged to the king or a royal figure, while in pit No 2 there were several bronze trees, one of which has been restored to a height of almost 395 centimetres. Examples of jade *zhang* from pit No 1 are of a greater variety but smaller in size than those found in pit No 2.

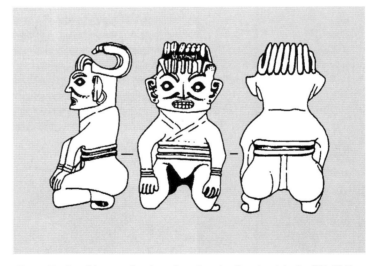

Figure 7• Small bronze figurines found at the Sanxingdui site (K1:293)

g) From pit No 1 there are the remains of elephants, such as teeth, skull and broken pieces, as if a whole elephant was sacrificed; in pit No 2 only elephant tusks were found, over 60 in all, representing 30 individuals (figure 8).

Taking all the above differences into account, it would seem that there is a time gap between the two pits. The jade *ge* and *zhang* from pit No 1 are close to those of Yinxu Phase I. The jade *ge* from pit No 2 are similar to those of types A and B from the tomb of Fu Hao at Xiaotun, of Phase II. However, despite the difference of time, the orientation of the pits, the artefacts within them and the evidence of burning are the same in both cases, indicating that they are probably related to each other in a sequence.

In general, all the artefacts from both pits, no matter whether considered individually or in groups, carry the period characteristics of the Shang. Scholars who have regarded this phenomenon as the result of cultural diffusion have

Figure 8 • *Location of artefacts in pit No 2, top level*

overlooked the reciprocal influences between different regions. This mutual influence could be the result of official rewards, tributes, ordinary commerce or war. It is too simplistic to state that, when a particular type of object first appeared in one cultural area, it automatically had originated in that culture, so that when one sees similar types of object appearing in another area, one assumes that it derived from the other area and must be later than it. Based on this kind of logic, some scholars have argued that it would have been impossible for the Shu people to make such superb bronze objects, because none of the bronze objects previously found in Shu could be dated before Western Zhou; they even think that the bronze containers and other bronze objects from Sanxingdui were made in Shang and imported directly from there to Sichuan. However, the enormous bronze figurines, masks and bronze trees have never been found before the excavation of the Sanxingdui site: could we say that they were from somewhere else?

These bronze figurines bear no similarity to the Shang style of the central plains, and they are cast in a more sophisticated manner than the wine containers such as *zun* and *lei*. From the Sanxingdui site we have discovered a large number of clay sculptures, such as pig, tiger, owl, rat, sheep, horse and cormorant, dated to the early and middle Shang period. They represent an advanced skill in sculpture of the Shu culture. From the jades discovered from the site we can also see a developed technology and the use of metal tools. In the western part of Sichuan there are rich copper mines, and from the site itself we have retrieved fragments of crucibles for molten bronze. This evidence shows that the Shu people had mastered bronze technology as early as the middle and late Shang period. Even though we have not found any bronze vessels earlier than this date, we cannot rule out the possibility of their existence. As archaeologists, we know that it is difficult to say that something never existed simply because it has never been found. The most recent finds of Chinese archaeology have brought up many hitherto unknown types of objects.

The Nature of the Pits

I have previously argued that pits No 1 and 2 at Sanxingdui were ritual pits.[7] There are, however, several other different theories: one group regards the pits as some kind of burial; the other considers that the objects were buried because they had lost their magical power or might bring misfortune. The scholars who espouse the latter view seem to be in the majority. The debate concerning the nature of these two pits will undoubtedly continue, but here I would like to offer some of my own observations.

First, let us consider the theory that the two pits were burials or cremated remains. In the preliminary archaeological report we have argued that within the excavated area of the Sanxingdui site, no cemetery has yet been found. A local brick factory was digging clay in the area surrounding these two pits for over 10 years without ever coming across any burials. The pits that were discovered in this area were mostly hoards. One instance is the hoard discovered in 1929 at Yueliangwan, containing many jade and stone ritual objects, such as *zhang, zong, gui, fu, yuan* and *bi*. These objects were placed one on top of the other, and no bodies or skeletons were ever found with them. Most scholars agree that this was a ritual pit. In 1964, 50 to 60 metres away from this pit, another hoard containing polished and half-finished stone implements was discovered. In May 1986, another pit of triangular form was discovered close to pits No 1 and 2; it contained some bronze fragments. Another pit was found in 1988, containing jade ritual objects. In all these pits, no bodies or skeletal remains have ever been found. In 1987, when we discovered pit No 1 at Sanxingdui, it contained some fragments of bone, which we sent for analysis to the scientific department: the preliminary results indicate that they were not human bones. Therefore, it is unlikely that pit No 1 was a human burial.

The second theory, that both pits were hoards for objects that had lost their magic or which would bring bad luck, can be divided into two camps:

a) The objects were buried by the new ruler Duyu after he subdued the Yuwu reign, regarding these objects as bringing bad luck;

b) The hoards were made as the result of a foreign invasion of the Shu kingdom, when the temple was destroyed and the objects in it were broken and buried.

I however disagree with both of these interpretations. I have mentioned earlier in this paper that pits No 1 and 2 are not from the same period: pit No 2, which is later, can be dated to the early Western Zhou period, while even the latest cultural deposits are not as late as late Western Zhou or the Spring and

Figure 9 • Jade zhang *with carved motifs found at the Sanxingdui site (K2:201)*

[7] Chen Xiandan 1989b: 'Guanghan Sanxingdui yizhi fajue gaikuan, chubu fenqi,' *Nanfang minzu kaogu* 2: 213-231.

Autumn period, although the argument that these two pits were the result of Duyu's succession would place them in the late Western Zhou or early Spring and Autumn period. The second theory also contradicts the dating evidence: because the two pits belong to different periods, they cannot have been destroyed in the course of a single invasion. Furthermore, there is the question of why the objects should have been buried in two separate pits, and why they should differ substantially between them. By focusing only on the fact that these objects were broken and buried, these two arguments have both overlooked the difference of dating and the different contents of the two pits. The objects were arranged in a purposeful and orderly fashion, not thrown in at random, so they do not appear to be the result of sudden destruction. The evidence of burning, the breaking up of animal remains and the passageway specially made at pit No 1, indicate that there was an organised ritual accompanying the burying of objects.

Near pits No 1 and 2, three earthen mounds are arranged along the same axis, 35 degrees east of north. We have conducted a trial excavation of these mounds and confirmed that they are man-made; the objects found within them can be dated to the Shang period. It is possible that these man-made mounds were actually some kind of altar. The southwest section of the Sanxingdui walled enclosure seems to have been related to ritual sacrifice. The hoards and pits discovered here may have been related to these activities. Significantly, a jade *zhang* found in pit No 2 was incised with a scene with people performing sacrifice to the mountains (figure 9), and two small bronze temples were also found. Around the four sides of the temples were small figures in kneeling position, probably also in relation to a ritual performance.

Conclusion

To sum up, we still insist that pits No 1 and 2 at Sanxingdui are sacrificial pits, not a special kind of burial, but definitely intended for a religious ceremony, which might relate to war, the climate, harvesting or ancestral worship. Such rituals played an important role in ancient China. The study of these two pits and the objects found within them can provide vivid evidence for our understanding of Shu religious beliefs.

TANG JIGEN

The Burial Ritual of the Shang Dynasty: a Reconstruction

*I*n archaeological research we often face the difficulty of dealing with incomplete remains of the human past, yet it is sometimes possible to reconstruct the context of the archaeological evidence, and from this to understand aspects of human behaviour in the past. This paper considers material from scientific excavations at Yinxu during the last 70 years and aims to reconstruct the funeral rite performed by the Shang people and to explore its cultural significance. In order to achieve this, I have used the method of reduction, an analytical tool commonly employed by processual archaeologists.

Reconstruction of the funeral rite is object-specific; it has to be based on the analysis of material remains from burials. In looking at the actions involved in a ritual and the ensuing results of that ritual, we can see the objects in specific context and thereby try to establish their function and cultural meaning. In this respect, the study of the funeral rite offers us a unique opportunity to study Shang culture to a higher level.

The Placing of Grave Goods within the Tomb

Since the beginning of scientific excavation of Yinxu in 1928, over 6,000 tombs have been excavated.[1] The archaeological evidence shows clearly that, with very few exceptions, all burials there followed a certain pattern. The burial itself was complex, involving the preparation of a shaft pit and secondary ledge (the latter not present in all tombs), and a wooden chamber for the larger tombs. The coffin and burial goods were then placed in the coffin and the pit was refilled with earth and stamped firm. This was the basic procedure followed for most tombs, regardless of whether they belonged to nobles or commoners. The exceptions are tombs which manifest human sacrifice, and the simpler graves of slaves.

The placing and arrangement of burial goods was part of the rite. Burial goods from late Shang dynasty tombs can be classified into two categories:

a) objects used by the person when he or she was alive; and

b) objects made specially for the funeral rite.

To know whether a object was a part of ritual remains, we need to prove that it was in fact used during the rite. The majority of burial goods were placed in the tomb after the coffin was laid down, usually on the secondary ledge near the head of the occupant. Sometimes goods were also placed to both sides of the coffin or on top of it. This was particularly so when a large number of burial goods had been placed in a tomb. Many large tombs had a wooden chamber,

[1] Zhongguo 1994 (Zhongguo shehui kexueyuan kaogu yanjiusuo): *Yinxu de faxian yu yanjiu,* Beijing: Kexue chubanshe.

Facing page • Two of the inscriptions found on the bronze vessels of the Fu Hao tomb. See also figure 1

Figure 1 • Inscriptions found on the bronze vessels of the Fu Hao tomb

and ritual objects were also placed in the gap between the coffin and the chamber wall. In the tombs of aristocrats, the arrangement of bronze ritual vessels was significant.

A superb example of this is Fu Hao's tomb (M5),[2] where several large vessels were placed between the coffin and the chamber wall on the northern side. Three of these bear the name Fu Hao or Hao (Lady Hao) (figure 1a). Important vessels bearing the same name(s) were also found on the eastern and western sides. Square *ding*-vessels bearing the name Hou Mu Xin (figure 1b) were placed in the northeastern and northwestern corners. The round *ding*-vessel bearing the name Yan Bi (figure 1c) was also found in the northwestern corner. Two vessels bearing the name Si Tu Mu (figure 1d) were found on the eastern, northern and southern sides, and at the southern end of the western wall. Three objects bearing the name Zi Su Quan (figure 1e) were found on top of the chamber; these were obviously less important than the other objects bearing Fu Hao's own name, and their importance may depend in part on the status of the participant who supplied these objects.

In general, larger tombs tend to contain larger numbers of objects. These cannot have been placed in the tombs simultaneously, but must have been placed in groups in some sort of order. Again, Fu Hao's tomb serves as an excellent example: those burial objects which were placed outside the coffin were probably placed in the tomb in nine different groups, and were placed in the tomb from the bottom upwards. The large vessels are found in the gap between the coffin and chamber walls, and are concentrated on the eastern, western and northern sides (figure 2). On top of the chamber two jade *gui* food containers—one white (321), one green (322)—were found 6.2 metres below the surface (figure 3). The white *gui* contained two bone knives and one bronze knife. Also above the chamber (5.7 metres below the surface), on the secondary ledge, a bronze *zun* vessel had been placed in the northeastern corner, a bronze *jia* vessel and a bronze *zun* vessel in the southeastern corner (the *jia*, whose three legs were missing, had been placed on the top of the *zun*); and on the northern side of the *zun* was a stoneware jar. In the middle of the chamber there had been placed a stone musical instrument known as a *qing*, and a stone ox incised with the name Si Xin (figure 4). To the south of the ox lay a jade bracelet, a pottery *xun* mouth organ, three bronze arrowheads and a large piece of turquoise. On the same level, on the northeastern side of the chamber, against the eastern wall, two dogs were buried. Two more dogs,

[2] Zhongguo 1980 (Zhongguo shehui kexueyuan kaogu yanjiusuo): *Yinxu Fu Hao mu*, Beijing: Wenwu chubanshe.

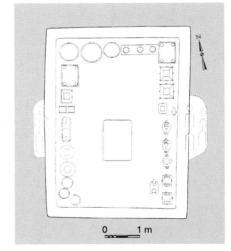

Figure 2 • Location of the large vessels inside the Fu Hao tomb

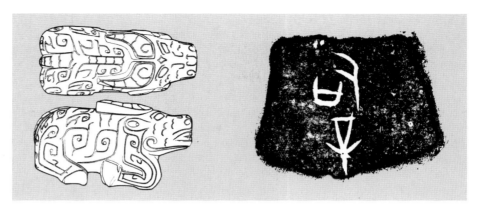

Figure 4 • Stone ox with an inscription (M5: 315)

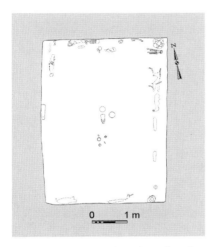

Figure 3 • Location of artefacts found on the top of the Fu Hao tomb

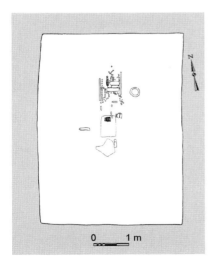

Figure 6 • Location of artefacts found in the upper layers (1-5) of the Fu Hao tomb

facing one another, had been placed at the southern side. Another dog was placed at the centre of the northern section of the chamber. Two bones were also found in the eastern section, but these have not yet been identified.

In the sixth layer (5.6 metres below the surface, figure 5), a wooden box was found which contained tightly packed bone hairpins and a number of ivory objects. Unfortunately, the box has not survived. To the south of the box were a further 80 artefacts, including a jade plate, jade *ge* dagger-axe with bronze fitting, stone *dou* container, stone bird, bone carving knife, cowrie-shells, pottery *xun* mouth organs, bronze mirrors, bronze arrowheads, bow-shaped object, small stone ox, stone jar, bone knife, agate beads and pieces of bone painted with red pigment.

In the fifth layer (4.6 metres below the surface), a jade *ge* dagger axe was found in the central part of the western side, and a jade *gui* vessel in the central part of the southern side. In the fourth layer (4.3 metres below the surface) a group of objects had been laid in an orderly manner in the central part of the northern side; these included bronze ornament, bronze *ge*, bronze bow-shaped object, bone arrowheads and jade items.

In the third layer (3.5 metres below the surface) a stone spade and a stone *qing* chime, both damaged, were found in the centre of the northern side. In the second layer (3 metres below the surface) a jade mortar was found, placed upside down, in the northeastern section. In the first layer (1 metre below the surface) a pottery *jue* vessel, slightly damaged, had been placed in the centre (figure 6).

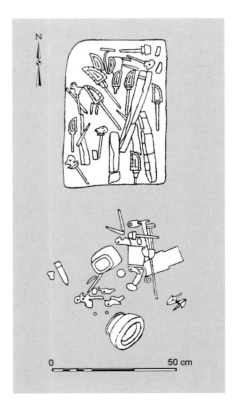

Figure 5 • Location of artefacts found in the sixth layer of the Fu Hao tomb

Grave Goods in the Royal Tombs

Burials for kings were much grander and more complicated. A good example of a king's tomb is Tomb M1004 at Xibeigang,[3] on the northern bank of the Huan River. Although the tomb had previously been disturbed, the southern section near the entrance of the tomb was intact at the time of excavation. The tomb had four layers. The lowest layer contained chariot fittings, armour and a leather shield. The third layer contained 100 helmets and 370 bronze *ge* dagger-axes. The second layer contained 360 bronze *mao* spearheads, tied into batches of 10, and placed head down. The top layer contained a stone *qing* chime, a jade rod and two bronze square *ding* vessels decorated with oxen and deer motifs. Clearly, the different layers contained different types of objects.

In 1991 a set of stone objects was found in Tomb 91HGM3. It bears the posthumous names of ancestors. These names are the direct results of actions which took place during the Shang funeral rite.

Intentional Damage to Grave Goods

There is evidence in the Yinxu tombs that some grave goods may have been intentionally damaged during the burial ritual. This appears to be particularly true for pottery vessels. The archaeologists who worked at the site believe the pottery objects were broken before burial. This practice is seen in Tomb M656 in the Yinxi xidi (the western sector of Yinxu), where a pottery *dou* vessel had been placed on the western side of the secondary ledge and a bronze *ge* on the eastern side of the ledge. Fragments of pottery had been scattered on the secondary ledge and on top of the coffin.[4] In other tombs it is clear that many jade and bronze weapons were also broken or bent as part of the funeral rite.

The tombs at Yinxu also shed light on the offerings made during the burial rite. Small fragments of animal bones are often found lying beside vessels, usually pottery vessels, probably the remains of meat offerings originally placed in the vessels. A particularly interesting example is Tomb CM233 at Yinxu xidi, where over 20 burial objects were unearthed, including a lacquer plate placed by the head of the tomb occupant. On the plate were the leg bones of cattle and sheep, and beneath the plate were a *ding* tripod, a *zun* vessel and a *you* vessel, all made of pottery.[5]

Human and Animal Sacrifice

Both humans and animals were sacrificed in the Shang funeral rite. In the large royal tombs remains of human sacrifice were commonly found on the secondary ledge, or in the 'waist pit' (*yaokeng*) specially made in the centre of the chamber. Human sacrifice played an important role in the funeral rite and the procedure may have been very complicated. Fu Hao's tomb, for example, contained the remains of 16 humans: one was found in the *yaokeng*, eight were found inside the chamber but outside the coffin; three were in the niches made on the walls of the shaft pit. The human remains found on the top of the chamber include a child, in the northwestern corner, and the upper body of another victim on the northern side; the third body lay face down in the northeastern corner, and a skull was found in the middle of the northern section. The evidence shows that these human sacrifices were not carried out simultaneously.[6]

Another important example of sacrifice can be seen in Tomb M1001 in the royal cemetery at Xibeigang.[7] M1001 is a large tomb with four sloping entrances, which had nine small pits in the floor of the chamber: one in the centre and eight placed at the corners. With one exception each pit contained the remains of a man and a dog, the exception containing no dog. Each man had a *ge* dagger axe; apart from the man in the centre pit who had a stone *ge*, those on the sides had bronze *ge*; they were apparently the guards of the tomb master. Outside the chamber, the remains of one man were found in the southwestern section, 11 on top of the chamber, six of them on the northwestern side (five had coffins) and five on the eastern side (only one had a coffin). At the southern entrance were

[3] Liang Siyong, Gao Quxun 1970: *Houjiazhuang, 1004 hao damu,* Taipei: Zhongyang yanjiuyuan.

[4] Zhongguo 1979 (Zhongguo shehui kexueyuan kaogu yanjiusuo Anyang gongzuodui): '1969-1977 nian Yinxu xiqu muzang fajue baogao,' *Kaogu xuebao* 1979(4): 99-117.

[5] Zhongguo 1987a (Zhongguo shehui kexueyuan kaogu yanjiusuo): *Yinxu faxian baogao 1958-1961,* Beijing: Wenwu chubanshe.

[6] Zhongguo 1980 (Zhongguo shehui kexueyuan kaogu yanjiusuo): *Yinxu Fu Hao mu,* Beijing: Wenwu chubanshe: 8-9.

[7] Liang Siyong, Gao Quxun 1962: Houjiazhuang, *1001 hao damu,* Taipei: Zhongyang yanjiuyuan.

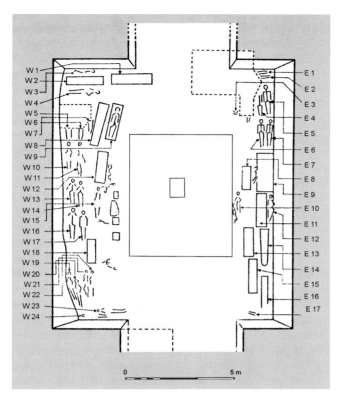

Figure 7 • Layout of the Wuguan M50 and the burials of human sacrifice

[8] Liang Siyong, Gao Quxun 1970: *Houjiazhuang, 1004 hao damu,* Taipei: Zhongyang yanjiuyuan: 26-29.

[9] Guo Baojun 1951: '1950 nian chuan Yinxu fajue baogao,' *Zhongguo kaogu xuebao* 5: 1-61.

[10] Zhongguo 1987b (Zhongguo shehui kexueyuan kaogu yanjiusuo Anyang gongzuodui): 'Yinxu 259, 260 hao mu fajue baogao,' *Kaogu xuebao* 1987(1): 99-117.

[11] Zhongguo 1979 (Zhongguo shehui kexueyuan kaogu yanjiusuo Anyang gongzuodui): '1969-1977 nian Yinxu xiqu muzang fajue baogao,' *Kaogu xuebao* 1979(4): 99-117.

found 59 headless bodies, split into eight groups and buried at different depths. One headless body was found at the eastern entrance and another in the eastern side room. Human skulls were found at all the entrances, about three metres below the surface, facing up towards the chamber. At the eastern entrance there were six skulls in three groups; at the southern entrance 11 skulls in four groups; at the southern entrance 42 skulls in 14 groups; and at the northern entrance 14 skulls in six groups.

M1004 is another large tomb which also had four sloping entrances. On the eastern side of the chamber, near the southern wall of this tomb, there was a small pit with the remains of a man face down. Beneath him was another small pit, which contained the remains of a dog. Although the tomb had been disturbed, five skulls were found in the chamber; seven skulls in two groups (one group of four, and one group of three) were found at the northern entrance.[8]

The famous tomb at Wuguan (50WGKM1), excavated in 1950,[9] also showed evidence of human sacrifice (figure 7). The remains of a man with a *ge* dagger-axe were found in the small pit in the centre of the tomb. On the secondary ledge, there were the remains of 17 human bodies in the eastern section and 24 in the western section. Some of these human sacrifices had their own coffins and burial goods such as bronze *ding, gui, gu, jue, ge* and jades. A further 29 skulls were found in the soil used to refill the pit, but at different depths, corresponding to three layers, and all the skulls were facing the chamber. There were two entrances to the tomb. At the northern entrance, four triangular pits had been laid out in the form of a cross; six horses were found in the eastern and northern pits; four horses were found in the western pit; two kneeling men were found in the southern pit, one holding a *ge,* the other holding a bell. At the southern entrance, there were three triangular pits, each containing four horses. Near the chamber the remains were found of another man in kneeling position, and beside him the remains of a dog.

Another large tomb, though with only one entrance, is M260 (84AWBM260),[10] where the famous Si Mu Wu *ding* was unearthed. Again, the remains of a man and a dog were found in a pit in the centre of the chamber. A total of 22 skulls were found at the entrance, with the remains of a further six bodies found in the chamber and another five bodies found between the coffin and the chamber walls.

Dogs were the most popular animals used in the Shang burial rite. They are often found in the small pit in the centre of a tomb, and sometimes in the layers of soil, or buried on the secondary ledge. Of the 939 tombs excavated in Yinxu xidi, 339 contained dogs: of these 197 were found in the *yaokeng* and 105 were found in soil used to refill the pits; another 91 tombs had dogs in both the *yaokeng* and refill soil.[11] In most cases the dogs were placed with the heads in the same direction as the occupants, indicating that they were killed before burial. A few examples are known where the dogs were buried alive, usually indicated by the unusual position of the dogs.

The Funeral Rites

Before the excavation of the tombs at Yinxu, there was no primary evidence from which to consider the question of ancient funeral rites. Scholars interested in this matter were therefore restricted to early texts, such as the *Liji* (A record of rituals). Whilst it is legitimate to use literary records as secondary sources, these are usually records compiled during later periods, and should not be considered as direct witness to the Shang ritual. In the case of the funeral rite at Yinxu, the archaeological evidence speaks for itself. It is possible from this important primary evidence to identify some of the key features of the Shang funeral rite:

Preparation of the Burial Pit: The Shang people buried their dead underground, and preparation of the burial pit was the first step (we are not concerned here with the preparation of the body). The choice of location was straightforward: most people were buried in the family or clan cemetery. The orientation of the tombs is usually facing northeast, though there are occasional exceptions laid out east-west or without obvious orientation. In some cemeteries all the early tombs were uniformly oriented east-west, and all the later tombs were uniformly oriented north-south. The reason for the change in orientation is unclear.

The size and shape of the tomb depended on the status of the deceased. Royal tombs had four entrances, and the ground plan resembled a *ya*-shape, with the entrances up to 10-20 metres in length. Large tombs belonging to the nobility had only one or two entrances, and occasionally no entrance at all, just a large shaft pit. Medium-sized or small tombs had no entrance, just a shaft pit. The *yaokeng* or central pit in the base of the floor of the chamber was a special feature of Shang tombs. These central pits were triangular or oval, usually 70 centimetres long by 30-40 centimetres wide. They were used for burying humans or dogs used in sacrifices. Most tombs had a single *yaokeng*, though some small tombs had none, and more elaborate tombs had more than one. For example, Tomb M1001 had nine pits in the floor.

Performance of Sacrifice: Once the pit had been dug, a sacrifice was performed, such as the burial of a human or dog in the central pit. The sacrifice depended on the status of the deceased. Victims were usually killed before burial, but occasionally the victims were buried alive. The significance of the sacrifice is unclear. During later periods of Chinese history, sculpted models of animals were placed in tombs to eliminate future negative disturbance. It is feasible that the Shang people buried dogs with a similar intention. Certainly the number of dogs buried and the age and sex of the occupants suggests that the dogs did not necessarily belong to the deceased.

Construction of the Wooden Chamber: Wooden chambers were built only in tombs of the nobility, and their size reflected the status of the deceased. The floor and walls were constructed of timber, piled closely to form a rectangular chamber. Sometimes, though not frequently, a small gap was left between the timber and earth wall. Forty-seven tombs excavated between 1969 and 1977 had a tomb chamber, with the chamber usually 2.2-2.5 metres long and 1-1.2 metres wide. In early texts such as the *Liji* it is said that the species and quality of timber used for coffin and chamber also depended on the status of the deceased.[12] However, we have not been able to verify this with the Shang evidence.

Placing of the Coffin in the Tomb Chamber: Early texts also describe the different equipment used for lowering coffins into the chamber; however, no tools and/or functional objects associated with the procedure, such as stone stelae or elaborate robes, have been found in Shang tombs. Sometimes a gap was left between the four sides of the coffin and the chamber walls; sometimes the coffin was against the walls.

The Yinxu tombs indicate that during the Shang dynasty, coffins were usually 180-210 centimetres long by 60-80 centimetres wide, and the wood planks were about seven centimetres thick. Some tombs had no chamber, and in these the coffin was placed directly on to the earth, though in some cases a timber support was built to raise the coffin off the ground.

Placing of the Burial Goods between the Coffin and the Walls of the Chamber: Burial goods from the Yinzu tombs can be divided into two categories: *a* small objects from inside the coffin, such as cowrie-shells placed in the mouth of the deceased and pendants worn by the deceased. Sometimes, objects which had been used by the person were also placed inside the coffin,

[12] Sun Xidan 1989: Liji jijie, Beijing: Zhonghua shuju: 1179-1180.

for example the coffin in Tomb M733 in Yinxu xidi yielded bronze adzes, chisels, stone *gui* and *zhang*, and shells. In category *b* are objects placed in the tomb during the funeral and burial. These objects were placed in the gap between the coffin and the chamber walls, or on the secondary ledge, or together with the refill soil. The objects were arranged in a certain order. The objects placed between the coffin and chamber were very important and played a role in the performance of the ritual, and therefore should be regarded as significant ritual objects.

Sealing off the Top of the Chamber: After the objects had been placed between the coffin and chamber walls, the top of the chamber needed sealing and the pit filling up with soil. Some important tombs had a mat or painted cloth on top of the chamber; for example tomb M219 in Yinxu xidi showed remains of matting and traces of painted cloth.[13]

Placing More Grave Goods and Performance of Human Sacrifice: Only when the matting and painted cloth was in position, and the secondary ledge had been prepared, could the most important part of the funeral rite take place. Vessels were presented in sets and often contained food. A number of tombs had small niches hollowed out of the pit walls in which to place such vessels. For example, in Tomb M733 in Yinxu xidi, there was a niche on the secondary ledge hollowed out directly above the head of the deceased. It contained burial goods: bronze *gu, jue*, and pottery *gu, jue* and *li*, jar and plate. Human and animal sacrificial victims were placed in the tombs at this stage, whether dead or alive. In Tomb M166 in Yinxu xidi, a human victim was found, face down in a foetal position, one foot on top of the other, apparently bound with ropes. In Tomb M358 in the same area, a human sacrificial victim's head was found to have been sliced in two.

Filling the Pit with Soil: Finally, the pit would be refilled with soil and stamped down. There may also be a ritual significance here, too, as human remains, dogs and objects are frequently found in different layers of the infill soil. For example, in the large tomb at Wuguancun mentioned earlier, 29 skulls were placed in three different layers, all facing the chamber.

Tombs in the Shang period did not have a mound constructed above ground, and the funeral rite might seem to end here. Early texts mention a special rite called *yuji* that was performed after the completion of the burial, and that the purpose of this rite was to comfort the soul of the deceased. However, this is difficult to detect from the archaeological evidence, and such activities are open to future discovery and discussion. The chariot pits that are sometimes unearthed near large tombs may also have played a part in the funeral rite; however, the details of how and when the chariots were buried are not yet clear and need further attention.

Some Observations

Ritual is a complicated concept, yet it also reflects social behaviour. It is usually accepted by the majority of the community in which the concept is formed and enacted. It is an ideology shared by a particular social group and is considered as being at the core of tradition. To a degree, ritual controls action. However, it survives only partially in the archaeological record, and any interpretations will have limitations to a greater or lesser degree. This is true for a study of the funeral rites of the Shang dynasty, yet a study of the archaeological remains of Shang tombs throws light on Shang society and culture. Several points stand out as being relevant to the Shang funeral rite:

Social Division

The funeral rite reflected the social divisions and ranking system in Shang society. From analysis of thousands of Shang tombs, it is possible to detect a pattern in the performance of the funeral rite, which was broadly followed by all ranks of Shang society, from king to commoner. However, two facts stand out: *a)* there is a small number of graves which show no trace of any funeral rite having been performed; *b)* there was huge disparity in the level of the funeral rite that was

[13] Zhongguo 1979 (Zhongguo shehui kexueyuan kaogu yanjiusuo Anyang gongzuodui): '1969-1977 nian Yinxu xiqu muzang fajue baogao,' *Kaogu xuebao* 1979(4): 99-117.

performed at different tombs.

Those graves which show no traces of the funeral rite fall into two groups:

a) The majority were sacrificial pits of human victims;

b) The tombs were found in habitation areas, and were simple burials. Human sacrificial victims were not buried in coffins or in specially prepared pits, and were seldom buried with burial goods. Some were even beheaded or piled up in heaps. As the victims themselves played a role in the funeral rite, there was apparently no need to perform a funeral rite for them. The general consensus is that sacrificial victims were prisoners of war. The graves found in habitation areas, with few or no burial goods, probably belonged to slaves. In these graves, the bodies were simply wrapped in mats and buried in simple pits.

The rank of a tomb occupant is reflected in the size and shape of the tomb, the chamber and coffin, the number of burial objects and the presence and quantity of human sacrifice. In terms of burial objects alone, tombs can be ranked in ascending order as follows:

a) No burial goods;

b) No wine vessels among the burial goods;

c) Wine vessels made of pottery;

d) A set of bronze *gu* and *jue*;

e) Two sets of bronze *gu* and *jue*;

f) More than two sets of bronze *gu* and *jue*; and

g) More than two sets of bronze *gu*, *jue* and *ding*, *zun*, *pou* and *gui*.

For a true representation of rank, the burial objects need to be considered alongside the scale of human sacrifice.

The level of the funeral rite was probably determined by the social status and wealth of the deceased. Rich and prominent members of society no doubt had greater material resources with which to demonstrate their importance and adherence to the accepted ideology through funeral rite. Those who could not afford the fullest funeral rite would have had one commensurate with their budget. In this way, slaves were unable to afford any rite at all..

Changes in Belief

The funeral rite reflected changes in the Shang belief of the spiritual world. Archaeological remains and oracle bone inscriptions attest to the strong Shang belief in the spirit world. Yet in the Shang period, the traditional concepts of the spirit world changed, and this is reflected in the funeral rite. As Yang Xizhang and Yang Baocheng point out, the use of *mingqi*, or objects made specially for burials, appeared in the latter half of the second phase of the Yinxu period.[14] These objects coexisted with other ritual objects and show different ideas about how the spirits could be served. Traditionally, scholars believed this change took place in the Zhou period. However, archaeology demonstrates clearly that the change was already under way in the late Shang period.

In terms of the funeral rite, the gradual increase in the use of *mingqi* in burials coincides with a reduction in the food offerings prepared for the funeral rite, as the smaller *mingqi* could not be used for containing food. This simplification of the rite shows that Shang belief in the spirit world was, as Yang argues, being challenged. There is another, more important implication, that the use of *mingqi* reflected a different approach to death, that the distinction between life and death was being reassessed, and that greater emphasis was being placed on the present life rather than on the other world. This is a very significant change.

[14] Yang Xizhang, Yang Baocheng 1985: 'Yindai qingtong liqi de fenqi yu zuhe,' Zhonggguo shehui kexueyuan kaogu yanjiusuo ed. *Yinxu qingtongqi*, Beijing: Wenwu chubanshe, 79-102.

Adults and Children

In the burials, there was a distinction between adults and children. Children were usually buried in the habitation area, near the houses, whereas adults were buried in family or clan cemeteries. Children's graves had few burial objects, often none at all, and children's graves seldom contained coffins. Instead, the children were placed in pottery vessels. Burial pits and sacrifice are not associated with graves of children under 12 years of age, and suggests that the funeral rite was not applicable to children under 12.

The Concept of Family

[15] Tang Jigen 1995: 'Yinxu jiazu mudi chutan,' Zhonggguo shehui kexueyuan kaogu yanjiusuo ed. *Zhongguo Shang wenhua guoji xueshu taolunhui lunwenji.*

The burials reveal that a general pattern of funeral rite was adhered to by the majority of people, although details varied according to different circumstances, particularly in burials associated with individual families or clans.[15] For example, in the east section III of Yinxu xidi, there were two cemeteries belonging to different clans. In one, the bodies were oriented north-south, and pottery *li* were the main burial goods. The other reveals an earlier and later phase: in the earlier phase the tombs are oriented east-west, and the main burial objects were *gu* and *jue*, with hardly any *li*. Among clans then, the funeral rite varied.

To conclude, the funeral rite is an important part of the Shang ritual system, and is comparatively well-preserved in the archaeological record. Over the last few decades archaeologists have been trying to find a way to deal with different cultural remains, in particular the question of racial identity. Numerous methods have been tried, such as typology, which has been used most commonly for discussion of a particular culture or a particular group of people. Typology is effective, yet its users take the risk that different peoples have similar material culture, but differ in terms of language, custom and ideology. The study of ritual should be able to help with this shortcoming.

LI BOQIAN

Jades from Tomb 63 at the Jin Cemetery at Tianma-Qucun

*T*he Jin vassal state was established in the early Western Zhou period (mid-11th century-771 BC) to serve as the northern frontier of the Zhou kingdom. Its founder was Tang Shu Yu, son of King Wu (r 1027-1025 BC) and brother of King Cheng (r 1024-1005 BC). In recent years, fieldwork at the Tianma-Qucun site, in the region straddling the modern counties of Quwo and Yucheng (Shanxi province), and in particular the excavation (1992-95) of the cemetery in the central part of this area (figure 1), have confirmed that this site probably marks the earliest capital of the Jin state.[1]

The Tianma-Qucun Cemetery of Jin

Excavations of the Jin cemetery at Tianma-Qucun unearthed tombs belonging to eight of the 11 marquises of the Jin state. One tomb, No 63, which I believe to belong to the consort of Marquis Mu, yielded an impressive number of jade items with distinctive characteristics. In this paper I will discuss these jades, which reflect significant changes in social structure and ideology towards the end of the Western Zhou period. In his historical work *Shiji* (Records of the Historian), Sima Qian presents a chronology of 11 *hou* (marquises) of Jin, starting with Tang Shu Yu:[2]

1 Tang Shu Yu
2 Jinhou (Xie Fu)
3 Wuhou (Ning Zu)
4 Chenghou (Fu Ren)
5 Lihou (Fu)
6 Jinghou (Yi Jiu)
7 Xihou (Si Tu)
8 Xianhou (Ji or Su)
9 Muhou (Fei Wang)
10 Shang Shu (brother of Muhou)
11 Wenhou (Chou)

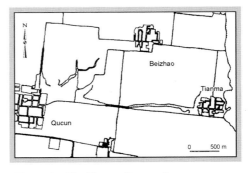

Figure 1 • The Tianma-Qucun site

The excavations at Tianma-Qucun seem to attest to the reliability of Sima Qian's chronology. The excavation of the Jin cemetery is now largely complete. The site itself measures 150 metres east-west and 130 metres north-south. A total

[1] Li Boqian 1993: 'Jin guo shi fengdi kaolue,' *Zhongguo wenwu bao* 12-12-93; see also Zou Heng: 'Lun zaoqi Jin du,' *Wenwu* 1994(1): 29-32., and his article 'The early Jin capital discovered: a personal account' in this volume. For archaeological reports, see Beijing 1993 (Beijing daxue kaoguxi): '1992 nian chun Tianma-Qucun yizhi muzang fajue baogao,' *Wenwu* 1993 (3), 1994 (Beijing daxue kaoguxi, Shanxi sheng kaogusuo): 'Tianma-Qucun yizhi Beizhao Jin hou mudi dier ci fajue,' *Wenwu* 1994(1), 1995 (Beijing daxue kaoguxi, Shanxi sheng kaogusuo): 'Tianma-Qucun yizhi Beizhao Jin hou mudi diwu ci fajue,' *Wenwu* 1995(7).

[2] *Shiji* (by Sima Qian, b 145 BC), Beijing: Zhonghua shuju, 1969, *juan* 39.

Facing page • Jade figure found in a bronze box in tomb M63 of Muhou's consort. See figure 7

of 17 large tombs have been found (figure 2): there are seven groups of paired tombs (one tomb of each pair for the husband and one for his wife) and one group of three tombs. The paired tombs are arranged in two parallel rows: the northern row has four groups of paired tombs and the southern row has three groups of paired tombs. The single group of three tombs lies to the west of the southern row, and appears to have belonged to one of the marquises and his two consorts. The typology of the artefacts, mainly pottery and bronzes, recovered from each of the 17 tombs allows us to reconstruct the chronological sequence of the tombs as follows:

> Group A: M9 and M13 — located at the eastern end of the northern row
> Group B: M6 and M7
> Group C: M33 and M32
> Group D: M91 and M92 — located between the two rows
> Group E: M1 and M2
> Group F: M8 and M31
> Group G: M64, M62 and M63 — at the western end of the southern row
> Group H: M93 and M102 — located at western end of northern row

The earliest tombs (M9 and M13) appear to date to the reign of King Mu (r 947-928 BC). The latest tombs (M93 and M102) date to the beginning of the Spring and Autumn period (770-480 BC). There is reason to believe that the tombs belong to only eight of the 11 Jin marquises, and that the first, second and tenth marquises were not buried here.

Although precise dates are not known for the marquises of Jin, early historical records state that the second marquis, Xie Fu, served during the reigns of King Cheng (r 1024-1005 BC) and King Kang (r 1004-967 BC). Xie Fu's dates should therefore be placed in the middle of the Western Zhou period. As the earliest tomb at Tianma-Qucun dates to the reign of King Mu, it is unlikely that the first and second marquises, Tang Shu Yi and Xie Fu, were buried here. The tenth marquis, Shang Shu, came to power following the death of his brother, Muhou. This was a breach of convention, and Shang Shu was killed by his nephew Chou (Muhou's son), who became the eleventh marquis with the title Wenhou. Ancient custom dictated that no persons who had been killed could be buried in the royal cemetery, and it is unlikely that Shang Shu was buried there.

Thus there is no difficulty in identifying the remaining eight marquises with the eight pairs of large tombs. Bronze vessels found in the tombs bear inscriptions which can be identified with six of the marquises: Jin hou Bo Ma (M33, M91 and M92), Jinhou Xi Fu (M91 and M92), Jinhou Dui (M92, M1 and M2), Jinhou Su (M8), Jinhou Pi (or Si) (M8) and Jinhou Bang Fu (M64).

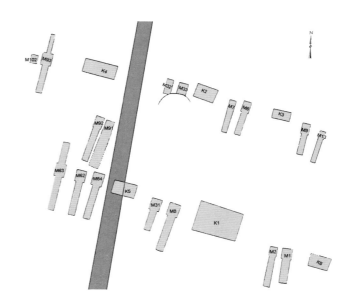

Fig 2 • Plan of the Jin Cemetery at the Tianma-Qucun site

The name Jinhou Bo Ma is identified with the fifth marquis, Lihou. Bronzes bearing this name were found in tombs M33 and M32, which are slightly earlier than tombs M91 and M92, and are likely to be the tombs of Lihou and his wife.

The name Jinhou Xi Fu can be identified with the sixth marquis, Jinghou (Yi Jiu) and his wife. Bronzes bearing this name were found in tombs M91 and M92, which may belong to this couple. A damaged bronze vessel found in tomb M91 bears the inscription: 'Jinhou Xi Fu made this valuable [vessel] for his late father Li.' This vessel can only have been cast by Jinghou (Yi Jiu) for his father the fifth marquis, Lihou. In the cemetery, a son's tomb is usually beside that of his father.

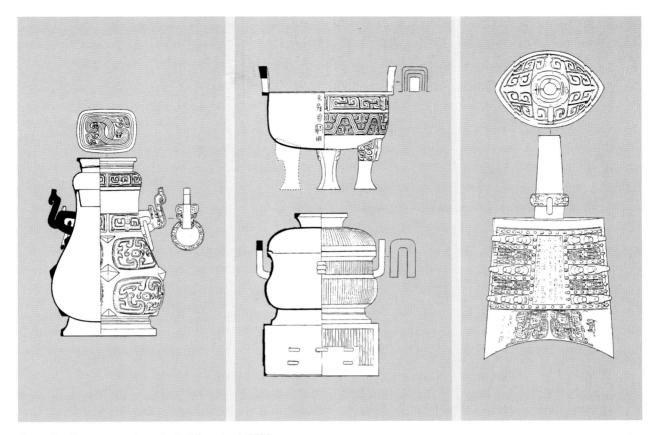

Figure 3 • Bronze vessels and a bell from tomb M64

[3] For a different view, see Xu Jay 1996: 'The cemetery of the Western Zhou lords of Jin,' *Artibus Asiae*, LVI, 3/4: 193-231.

[4] Qiu Xigui 1994: 'Guanyu Jin hou tongqi mingwen de jige wenti.' *Chuantong wenhua yu xiandaihua* 1994(2).

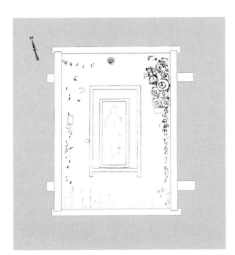

Figure 4 • Location of the artefacts from tomb M62

The name Jinhou Dui is identified with the seventh marquis, Xihou. Bronzes bearing this name were found in tombs M1 and M2, which are slightly later than M91 and M92. Xihou can be identified as the occupant of M1.

The name Jinhou Su matches a record in the *Shiji*, and can be identified as the eighth marquis, Xianhou. Eleven bronze objects (five *ding* vessels and 16 bells, both of which are indicators of rank and social status) bearing the name Jinhou Su were found in tomb M8, which suggests this was Xianhou's tomb. Bronzes bearing the name Jinhou Pi (or Si) were also found in this tomb: the name may be a variation of Jinhou Su.[3]

The name Jinhou Bang Fu can be identified as the ninth marquis, Muhou (Fei Wang, son of Xianhou). Bronze vessels bearing this name were found in tomb M64, which is later than tomb M8; the typology of the artefacts from M64 (figure 3) suggest a date corresponding to the late Western Zhou period (9th-early 8th centuries BC).[4] The *Shiji* ('Jin Shijia') states that Muhou lived during the reign of King Xuan (r 827-782 BC).

Based on the location of the tombs and on the typology of the artefacts, tomb M6 probably belonged to the fourth marquis, Chenghou (Fu Ren), tomb M9 to the third marquis, Wuhou (Ning Zu), and tomb M93, to the eleventh marquis, Wenhou (Chou).

The Jades Found in Tomb M63

As we have seen, both from the archaeological evidence and from the inscriptions, the occupant of M64 was undoubtedly the ninth marquis Muhou, with his two consorts buried in tombs M62 (figure 4) and M63 which lie one after the other to the west of his tomb. The position of their tombs suggests that his first wife was buried in tomb M62, which is closer, and his second wife in tomb M63, which is the tomb farthest west in the southern row. However, the construction of the two tombs suggests that although she was his second consort, she was also his favourite: M63 has two entrances and a large number of jade items. Of all the 17 tombs in the cemetery, tomb M63 contained the largest number of jade items in the cemetery, and those with the most interesting characteristics.

Jades from M63 can be described as belonging to two categories. The first category, burial or ritual jades, includes jade face-covers,[5] necklace, pendants, *gui* sceptre, *bi* rings and *ge* dagger axe. These items were placed both inside and outside the coffin.

The face-cover, known in Chinese as *mingmu*, consisted of many pieces of new and recycled pieces of jade sewn on to a textile veil to form a facial representation, and was placed over the face of the deceased. The necklace was made up of numerous jade tubes and beads made of agate and turquoise, strung together. The pendant found on the chest of the deceased consisted of over 50 pieces (*cong* tubes, *huang* pendants and beads). This decorative adornment was probably made specially for the burial, as a symbol of the status of the deceased. Jade *gui*, *bi* and *ge* were certainly symbolic of status, and were used for ritual purpose: larger ones were found inside the coffin and smaller ones were used in the decoration of the coffin. All these types of jade items were also found in other tombs in the Tianma-Qucun cemetery, for example in tombs M8 and M31, associated with Marquis Xian and his wife (figures 5 and 6).

The second category of jades is more unusual. During the excavation of tomb M63, a bronze box was found inside the burial chamber, but outside of the coffin, in the northwest section of the tomb. It contained a large number of jades. Although the box almost entirely disintegrated after excavation, traces of the remains showed that the original had been square in shape. The box had contained over 30 pieces of jade, stuck together in three layers, though some had fallen out of the box. Eleven of these pieces were illustrated in the preliminary report (figure 7). This is the only known example of jades being placed in a box for burial before the end of the Zhou dynasty. The jades found in the box have distinctive features and can be broadly described as follows:

a) Varied types. Many carved animals: ox, deer, sheep, tiger, bear, turtle, bird, owl and woodpecker. Also some small imitations of bronze vessels (*e g ding*) and of musical instruments (*e g* drum). There are very few burial jades or symbolic ritual jades.

b) Jades of exceptionally good quality, and far superior to those of the first group.

c) Jades showing masterful carving. Many pieces are well-designed and executed, *e g* a resting sheep looking back over its shoulder, a kneeling bear with a terrifying expression on its face, and a horse standing still. All are carved with the utmost care and are exceptional pieces.

d) Jades made over a long period. From the characteristics of the carving technique and the style, these pieces are mostly of Shang date (c16th-11th centuries BC), except for the jade figurines and deer which were probably made in the Western Zhou period (1027-771 BC). The kneeling bear is very similar to the one found in the Fu Hao's tomb at Yinxu (M5: 430); the dragon-owl with a crown of feathers is also similar to one found in Fu Hao's tomb (M5: 993). The representations of oxen (M63: 162, 90-35, 90-14) and turtles (M63: 156, 90-10) are all of typical Shang style.

It is clear that the two categories of jade objects had different functions, and it may be that their cultural significance is also varied. Jade items in the first

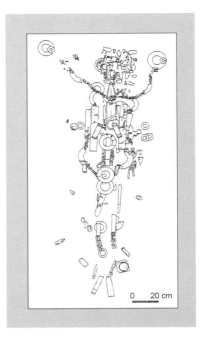

Figure 5 • Jade remains in Tomb M8.

[5] For a discussion on jade face-covers, see Wang Tao and Liu Yu 1997: 'The face of the other world: jade face-covers from ancient tombs,' R Scott, ed. *Chinese Jades*, Colloquies on Art and Archaeology in Asia No 18, London: Percival David Foundation of Chinese Art, 133-46

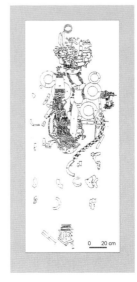

Figure 6 • Jade remains in Tomb M31

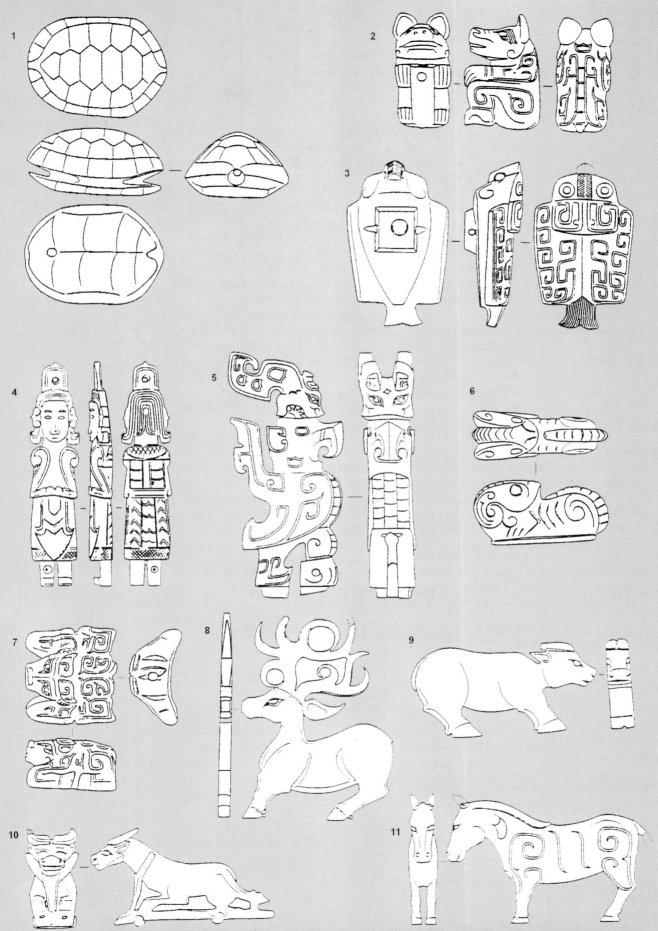

*Figure 7 • Jades found in a bronze box in tomb M63 of Muhou's consort: **1** tortoise; **2** bear; **3** ray; **4** figure; **5** eagle; **6** sheep; **7** crouched cow; **8** deer; **9** standing cow; **10** prostrate cow on a wheeled platform and **11** horse*

category are fairly familiar as burial jades or ritual jades. The second category appears to be a private collection of jades, contained in a bronze box, for the personal enjoyment of the owner. Although the original box is no longer intact, its remains indicate its similarity with another box from the same tomb (M63: 123), which also contained objects apparently for the personal enjoyment of the owner.

The jade items found in the box once held important and potent meanings. The dragon-owl with its crown of feathers is a combination of dragon and phoenix, mythic creatures of earlier times. One piece represents a turtle with its head withdrawn (M63: 90-10). In ancient Chinese belief, the turtle was a spiritual animal: the earliest representation of a jade turtle was found at the Hanshan Lingjiatang site, Anhui province, of a neolithic date (c3000 BC).[6] The Shang people also used turtles in divination and incised divinatory inscriptions on to turtle plastrons. Another piece represents an ox prostrate on a wheeled flatbed. Clearly in earlier times these jade objects were associated with a ritual context. Yet in tomb M63 this diverse collection of jade items appears to be solely for the personal enjoyment of the owner, where, removed from their original ritual context, these beautiful pieces are regarded as ornaments or works of art

Over 700 jade items were found in Fu Hao's tomb at Yinxu, and many of these are representations of animals.[7] Unfortunately, archaeological details of the excavation are lacking, rendering it even more difficult to ascertain the functions of these objects. The context for the jades in the tomb of Muhou's consort is easier to reconstruct: they were separated from the burial jades and were specially put into a bronze box, divested of whatever religious significance they may once have held. Even the imitation *ding* tripod and drum, once potent symbols in ritual, had lost their sacred meaning.

To sum up, if we consider this burial in its historical perspective, we see that by the late Western Zhou period, the central power of the royal Zhou court was waning and changes in society directly influenced intellectual thought. The sacred power of gods was rigorously questioned and the ritual required for gaining the spirits' consent also underwent some reform. This gave a rise to peoples' desire to make, seek out and collect beautiful things. The rising trends towards humanism were challenging the old ritual codes, and loosening the clear-cut distinction between cult objects and works of art. If my observation of the jades in the box found in the Muhou's consort's tomb is valid, this private collection of beautiful jades of earlier times reflects transformations in both social structure and ideology, which led to a conscious appreciation of viewing and collecting these objects.

[6] Zhongguo 1980 (Zhongguo shehui kexueyuan kaogu yanjiusuo): *Yinxu Fu Hao mu*, Beijing: Wenwu chubanshe: 164, 166, figure 86:10; plate 141:2

[7] Zhongguo 1980: 157-171.

ALAIN THOTE

Continuities and Discontinuities: Chu Burials during the Eastern Zhou Period

Among the major discoveries made in the past 20 years, Chu graves occupy a prominent place. The most recent synthesis of studies on Chu tombs was published by Guo Dewei.[1] A wealth of archaeological material providing new perspectives on Chu burial practices has been excavated from Dangyang Zhaojiahu in Hubei,[2] Xichuan Xiasi in Henan,[3] and from more than 2,400 of the 4,700 or so tombs in the vicinity of Jiangling in Hubei, the site of one of the Chu capitals.[4] With all these recent excavations, we now have at our disposal a fairly complete series of Chu tombs from the 8th to the 3rd century BC (figure 1 and table 1). Archaeologists are now able to date Chu tombs much more precisely than ever before. For instance, at Jiangling Yutaishan, six periods were distinguished on the basis of the succession of ceramic assemblages: Mid-Chunqiu period (c680-580 BC); Late Spring and Autumn period (c580-480 BC); Early Warring States period (c480-400 BC); Mid-Warring States period (c400-320 BC) and first half of the Late Warring States period (c320-278 BC).

At Jiangling, the dating of the Jiudian tombs is even more precise than that of the Yutaishan tombs. The chronology used for the Jiudian tombs is also divided into six periods, but it is much shorter: Late Spring and Autumn period, last phase (c510-480 BC); Early Warring States period, initial phase (c480-440 BC); Early Warring States period, second phase (c440-400 BC); Mid-Warring States period, initial phase (c400-360 BC); Mid-Warring States period, last phase (c360-320 BC); Late Warring States period, initial phase (c320-278 BC); Late Warring States period, last phase (c278-223 BC). Yindu, the capital of the Chu kingdom, was invaded and destroyed by the state of Qin in 278 BC, and consequently new burial practices were introduced in the Jiangling area, showing a marked contrast with earlier funerary traditions.

This article aims at a reconsideration of Chu burial practices and their evolution as seen in tombs of medium size, whose study is too often neglected by comparison with much wealthier tombs. It goes without saying that large tombs are also important for the study of burial customs, and we shall take them into account in this study. However, the large tombs excavated until now are still few, especially those of early periods (seventh-5th century BC). Moreover, the

[1] Guo Dewei 1995: *Chu xi muzang yanjiu*, Wuhan: Hubei Jiaoyu chubanshe.

[2] Hubei 1992 (Hubei sheng Yichang diqu bowuguan, Beijing daxue kaoguxi): *Dangyang Zhaojiahu Chu mu*, Beijing: Wenwu chubanshe.

[3] Henan 1991 (Henan sheng wenwu yanjiusuo, Henan sheng Danjiang muqu kaogu fajuedui, Xichuan Xian Bowuguan): *Xichuan Xiasi Chunqiu Chu mu*, Beijing: Wenwu chubanshe.

[4] Guo Dewei 1995: *Chu xi muzang yanjiu*, Wuhan: Hubei Jiaoyu chubanshe, 122. The main reports on Chu tombs excavated in the area of Jiangling are the following: Hubei 1984 (Hubei sheng Jingzhou diqu bowuguan): *Jiangling Yutaishan Chu mu* Beijing: Wenwu chubanshe; Hubei 1985 (Hubei sheng Jingzhou diqu bowuguan): *Jiangling Mashan yi hao Chu mu*, Beijing, Wenwu chubanshe; Hubei 1991 (Hubei sheng Jing Sha tielu kaogudui):, *Baoshan Chu mu*, Beijing: Wenwu chubanshe; Hubei 1995 (Hubei sheng wenwu kaogu yanjiusuo):*Jiangling Jiudian Dong Zhou mu*, Beijing: Kexue chubanshe; Hubei 1996 (Hubei sheng wenwu kaogu yanjiusuo): *Jiangling Wangshan Shazhong Chu mu*, Beijing: Wenwu chubanshe. In addition, numerous preliminary reports on Chu tombs unearthed in the Jiangling area appeared in various archaeological journals such as *Jiang Han kaogu*, *Wenwu*, *Kaogu* and others.

This article is based on a paper read at the conference 'Mysteries of Ancient China' (British Museum, 6-8 December 1996). I wish to thank Dr Jessica Rawson for her invitation to participate in the conference.

sites are spread out across four provinces (Hubei, Hunan, Henan, Anhui). Therefore they defy attempts at classification and typology. Medium-sized tombs can be defined as composed of one (in rare cases, two) inner coffins (*guan*) and one outer coffin (*guo*) whose area does not exceed six to seven square metres. By comparison, the outer coffins at Jiangling Wangshan tombs Nos 1 and 2 and Jiangling Shazhong tomb No 1 measure respectively 6.14 metres by 4.08 metres (25 square metres), 5.08 metres by 2.96 metres (15 square metres) and 4.2 metres by 2.34 metres (nearly 10 square metres).[5] We may assume that the form and furnishing of the burials were guided by the Chu people's beliefs about death. Their evolution should therefore reflect changes in their conception of the afterlife. By focusing on medium-sized tombs, we should also have a much larger range of examples pertaining to a wider range of social classes.[6]

Table 1 | Chronology of Tombs at Dangyang Zhaojiahu, Jiangling Jiudian and Jiangling Yutaishan

	Dangyang Zhaojiahu Period No	Jiangling Jiudian Period No	Jiangling Yutaishan
Late Western Zhou	I.1		
ca 770-730	II.2		
ca 730-680	II.3		
ca 680-630	III.4		{ I ca 680-580
ca 630-580	III.5		{
ca 580-530	IV.6		{ II ca 580-480
ca 530-480	IV.7	I	{
ca 480-440	V.8	II.2	{ III ca 480-400
ca 440-400	V.9	II.3	{
ca 400-360	VI.10	III.4	{ IV ca 400-360
ca 360-320	VI.11	III.5	{ V ca 360-320
ca 320-278	VII.12	IV.6	{ VI ca 320-278
ca 278-223		IV.7	

New Evidence from Dangyang Zhaojiahu

The cemetery at Dangyang Zhaojiahu is a key site for understanding the earliest Chu burial customs. Based on the study of ceramic and bronze typologies, the chronology of this cemetery has been divided into seven periods and 12 phases. The first period is said to belong to Late Western Zhou and the last to the first stage of Late Warring States period, which gives a span of about five centuries, between the late 9th century BC and the end of the 4th century BC.[7] The tombs from the early phases, between the late 9th and the 6th centuries BC, show that the Chu people had already perfected techniques, and used specific methods, to protect the underground structure and its precious contents efficiently. The early tombs at Dangyang consisted of a vertical pit with a wooden structure built at the bottom. Made of heavy wooden beams 16-20 centimetres thick, the entire outer coffin was protected by layers of pounded white clay (*bai gaoni*) or grey-green clay (*qing gaoni, qinghui ni*). Such a construction called for a considerable supply of raw materials, but the Hubei-Hunan area seemingly benefited from much larger wood resources than other parts of China, and had excellent kaolin-type clay.[8] Chu carpenters also had no shortage of material, judging from the huge timbers they felled to build the tombs. Such massive wooden outer coffins, a prerequisite for protecting the contents of the tomb, would remain almost unchanged for centuries throughout the Hubei-Hunan area,[9] as later exemplified by the three tombs at Changsha Mawangdui, Hunan. Though these tombs date to the early 2nd century BC, to a great extent their mode of construction follows that of the Chu burial traditions.[10]

By comparison with the wooden structures used for tombs elsewhere in China, the joint-making techniques revealed by Chu wooden outer and inner coffins were complex and in many respects much more advanced (figure 2). Compare the mode of construction of tombs from metropolitan China, for instance at Houma Shangmacun, Shanxi, in the Jin area, with carpenters' work

[5] Hubei 1996 (Hubei sheng wenwu kaogu yanjiusuo): *Jiangling Wangshan Shazhong Chu mu*, Beijing: Wenwu chubanshe, 10, 113, 166.

[6] On ranking expressed in the burial and the grave-goods, see Renfrew, Colin 1994: *Archaeology, Theories, Methods and Practice*, London, Thames and Hudson Ltd, 174-179.

[7] Hubei 1992 (Hubei sheng Yichang diqu bowuguan, Beijing daxue kaoguxi): *Dangyang Zhaojiahu Chu mu*, Beijing: Wenwu chubanshe, 160-215.

[8] The properties of the so-called 'white clay' or 'grey-green clay' are described and analysed in Wen Daoyi 1959: 'Changsha Chu mu,' *Kaogu xuebao* 1959(1): 41-58.

[9] Wen Daoyi 1959: 43.

[10] Hunan 1973 (Hunan sheng bowuguan, Zhongguo kexueyuan kaogu yanjiusuo): *Changsha Mawangdui yi hao Han mu*, Beijing: Wenwu chubanshe; Pirazzoli-t'Serstevens 1992: 'Mawangdui, les tombes d'une maison royale, 186-165 av J-C,' 110-144, in *Chine Antique — Voyage de l'âme*, Daoulas: Centre culturel Abbaye de Daoulas, 83-97.

Figure 1 • *The evolution of Chu medium-sized tombs from the 8th to 3rd century BC.*
1 *Dangyang Zhaojiapang tomb No ZH M2 (8th to 7th century BC);* **2** *Dangyang Zhaojiapang tomb No ZH M3 (7th century BC);* **3** *Dangyang Jinjiashan tomb No J M2 (7th to 6th century BC);* **4** *Dangyang Jinjiashan tomb No JM 229 (5th century BC);* **5** *Jiangling Yutaishan tomb No 159 (4th century BC);* **6** *Jiangling Mashan tomb No 1 (circa Late 4th-Early 3rd century BC); After* Dangyang Zhaojiapang Chu mu, *figures 11 p28 [1], 13 p30 [2], 28 p47 [3], 24 p41,* Jiangling Yutaishan Chu mu, *figure 23 p33 [5],* Jiangling Mashan yi hao Chu mu, *figure 12 p10 [6]*

[11] Shanxi 1994 (Shanxi sheng kaogu yanjiusuo): *Shangma mudi,* Beijing: Wenwu chubanshe, 199-202, figure130 (A-E); 230-234, figure 152 (A-G); Hubei 1992: 22, figure 9; 29, figure 12; 33, figure 15; 35, figure 19; 48, figure 29; 50 figure 31; 56, figure 37; 58, figure 39.

[12] Hubei 1992: 51-52.

at Dangyang Zhaojiahu.[11] Close examination of Chu tombs, whatever their size, always reveals careful woodworking. Most of the Dangyang Zhaojiahu tombs were medium-sized or small tombs, but nearly half of them (142 of a total of 297) possessed an outer coffin 3.15 to 2.00 metres long and 1.80 metres wide. The walls of the wooden structure and those of the coffin inside were each made with thick wood panels that involved the use of expert joint-making techniques.

To secure the coffin firmly, hemp ropes tied in both directions were already used at Dangyang Zhaojiahu in the 8th or early in the 7th century BC, as shown by tombs M2 and M6 at Zhaojiapang.[12] In the Chu kingdom this mode of fastening lasted for centuries and disappeared only at the end of the 4th century BC. The process was gradually improved upon during the Eastern Zhou period, first with the addition of sticks to tighten the ropes, and later with their eventual replacement by lacquered textile bands (figure 3). At Jiangling Wangshan, two large tombs (Nos 1 and 2) from the second half of the 4th century BC illustrate the transition during which ropes were replaced by textile bands. The inner coffin from tomb No 1 was closed with the help of ropes and silk bands while silk bands only were used for the inner coffin from tomb

No 2.[13] To sum up, the specific character of Chu burial traditions appeared quite early. In the Chu conception of the afterlife, an efficient protection for the dead was of primary importance, whereas magical practices were secondary. Differing from the burial customs of other states, the Chu people rarely put cinnabar into the coffins, a magic process to prevent the corpse from decaying.[14] To preserve the corpse they relied on other techniques which were continually perfected until the end of the 3rd century BC.

Surprisingly, in spite of its massive aspect, the outer coffin from the 8th to 6th centuries BC rarely contained more than thirty pieces of tomb furniture. Twenty-two medium-sized tombs from Dangyang Zhaojiahu are reviewed here. They belong to the phases I-1 (late Western Zhou) to IV-7 (late Spring and Autumn). Six of them which had been plundered in earlier times may have lost a part of their furnishings. With the exception of tomb JI M9, which contained 32 pieces (six bronze containers, 21 pottery vessels and five wooden small tables), the remaining tombs did not have more than 30 pieces.[15] These were almost exclusively bronze ritual vessels, pottery imitations of bronze vessels and more common ceramics (figure 4). At Dangyang Zhaoxiang tomb No 4, vessels modelled on ritual bronzes had even been carved in wood and lacquered.[16] Until the 3rd century BC, pottery imitations of bronze vessels would always occupy a prominent place, if not the first rank, among the categories of furniture deposited in Chu medium-sized tombs. These ceramic imitations of bronzes are so numerous that the chronology of the Chu tombs is in most cases solely based on pottery typologies. However, as observed by many scholars, it happened that pottery assemblages of different types overlap chronologically.[17] The exact role of those vessels is still not clear to us. Were they put into tombs as offerings to the deceased, or to contain offerings for him, like those made in temples above ground during ceremonies for the ancestors? Were they, on the contrary, provided to the dead person so that he or she could use them and perform sacrifices during his or her afterworldly existence? If we consider the way all the

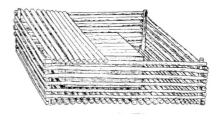

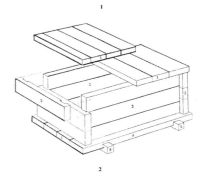

Figure 2 • Comparison between Jin and Chu guo outer coffins. **1** the wooden structure of a large tomb at Houma Shangmacun, Shanxi (Tomb 1283, ca750-700 BC), **2** the wooden structure of a medium-sized tomb at Dangyang Zhaojiahu, Hubei. After Shangma mudi, figure 130 E p202, and Dangyang Zhaojiahu Chu mu, figure 9 p22

[13] Hubei 1996 13-19, 117-121.

[14] Some of the early tombs from Dangyang-Zhaojiahu contained cinnabar (Hubei 1992: op cit 21), as well as tombs No 7 and 10 at Xichuan Xiasi (Henan 1991: 28, 249). However, the use of cinnabar is not mentioned in any other report on Chu tombs. By contrast, in tomb No 251 at Taiyuan Jinshengcun (Shanxi), which dates to the second half of the 5th century BC, a layer of cinnabar had been put under (or into) the coffin of the owner. See Tao Zhenggang, Hou Yi 1994: Chunqiu Jin guo qingtongqi baozang — Shanxi Taiyuan Zhao qing mu, Taipei/Beijing: Kwang Fu shuju wenwu chubanshe, 111.

[15] Hubei 1992: 224-5, 227-228.

[16] Yichang 1990 (Yichang diqu bowuguan): 'Hubei Dangyang Zhaoxiang 4 hao Chunqiu mu fajue jianbao,' Wenwu 1990(10): 25-32.

[17] Li Ling 1991: 'On the Typology of Chu Bronzes' [Translated and edited by L von Falkenhausen], Beiträge zur Allgemeinen und vergleichenden Archäologie, Band 11, Mainz am Rhein, Verlag Philipp von Zabern, 1991, 57-113, 70-71.

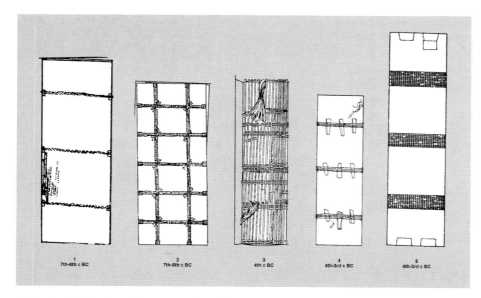

Figure 3 • Coffins from Chu graves closed by ropes and silk bands. **1** Dangyang Zhaojiahu Jinjiashan tomb No 1; **2** Dangyang Zhaojiahu Caojiagang tomb No. 3. **3** Jiangling Jiudian tomb No 295; **4** Jiangling Jiudian tomb No 712; **5** Jiangling Jiudian tomb No 744. After Dangyang Zhaojiahu, figures 30 p49 and 20 p35, Jiangling Jiudian Dong Zhou mu, figures 56 p90, 54 p88, and 65 p100

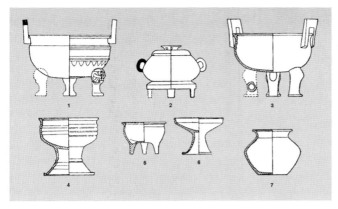

Figure 4 • Bronze and earthenware ritual vessels from Dangyang Zhaojiapang tomb No ZH M3. From left to right: **1** bronze ding tripod, **2** gui tureen, **3** earthenware ding, **4** cup, **5** li tripod, **6** dou cup, and **5** jar. After Dangyang Zhaojiahu Chu mu, figure 119 p176

vessels were deposited inside the tombs at Dangyang, two points should be noted:

1) In the tombs of the 6th century BC, offerings of meat, rice and jujube were put on small wooden tables or into bamboo baskets; in one tomb a pair of chopsticks accompanied the food containers.[18] Remains of food offerings were recovered from tomb M9 (animal bones, seeds, jujube) and tomb M1 (rice, jujube).[19] Bronze *zhou* or *he* oval small cups also appeared for a short time in the tombs before being finally replaced by lacquered eared-cups some time after the end of the 6th century BC[20] Since the vessels were piled up one on top of the other inside the tombs, some of them, like *dou* stem-cups, could not be used for presenting or containing food offerings, as for example, in tomb M3 at Dangyang Zhaojiahu.[21] Hence some of the ritual vessels could only have had a symbolic function.

2) All these vessels were tightly stacked into the outer coffin at the head section of the coffin only (figure 1:1-6). Such a position must have been of primary importance for the Chu people until the 4th century BC. By contrast, not a single vessel was placed alongside the coffin, where there was just enough room for storage. Judging from the plans of the tombs published in the Dangyang Zhaojiahu, Yutaishan and Jiangling Jiudian reports, not a single exception is to be mentioned here. By the end of the 4th century BC a dramatic change occurred, on which tentative explanations will be provided in this article. This change is illustrated for example by 4th to 3rd century BC Tombs 25, 26 and 47 at Changde Deshan in Hunan.[22] In Tombs 25 and 26 a sword protected by a wooden box was deposited at the head of the coffin instead. In smaller tombs the ritual vessels were sometimes deposited in niches dug out of the pit wall at the head of the outer coffin.[23] In a few tombs without an outer coffin (and therefore excluded from the group of medium-sized tombs reviewed in this article), niches for the storage of ritual vessels were excavated in one of the long sides of the pit.[24] Furthermore, the location of these items reveals that during the final stages of a funeral the inner coffin was lowered first into the tomb. Next, the various burial furnishings were stored at the head of the coffin, and finally, flat timbers were deposited to cover the outer coffin.

Grave Goods: Weapons, Food, Vessels and Figurines

At Dangyang Zhaojiahu no weapon was brought into tombs dating to before the 6th century BC. The chronology at Yutaishan should probably be amended on the basis of the results obtained from more recent excavations. Also, periods of a century are not of great help for characterizing the evolution of burial goods over three to four centuries. Since there is no reason to assume that all the early tombs in this cemetery were those of women, we must suppose that storing weapons in medium-sized graves came into practice at Chu only around the 5th century BC

Apparently, only Chu aristocrats of higher ranks were allowed (or were wealthy enough) to be interred with a large amount of weapons, as shown by tomb No 8 and tomb No 2 at Xichuan Xiasi in Henan.[25] These two large tombs date respectively to the beginning of the 6th century BC (tomb No 8) and the middle of the 6th century BC (tomb No 2). Though it had been plundered on repeated occasions many centuries ago, tomb No 8 still contained two *ji*-halberds, 14 *ge* dagger axes and 23 *mao* spearheads while four *ji*, four *ge* and 17 *mao* were deposited in tomb No 2. Of great interest is the fact that the only

[18] At Dangyang Zhaojiahu a bamboo basket filled with jujube and a pair of chopsticks were deposited in tomb J M2.

[19] Hubei 1992: 47, 155, 225 (Table 2), 227 (Table 3).

[20] Thote, Alain 1997: 'Intercultural Contacts and Exchanges illustrated by the burial goods from Xichuan Xiasi cemetery (6th century BC),' *Hanxue yanjiu* 15.1: 263-89: p277-228, note 37.

[21] Hubei 1992: 30, figure 13.

[22] Hunan 1963 (Hunan sheng bowuguan): 'Hunan Changde Deshan Chu mu fajue baogao,' *Kaogu* 1963(9): 461-473, 479.

[23] Hubei 1995: 71-72, figures 42-43.

[24] Hubei 1992: 67, figure 47; 69, figure 49.

two swords found in this cemetery came from tomb No 11, which is probably the latest in the site (c late 6th century to early fiftth century BC).[26] In contrast, from the middle of the 5th century BC, even tombs with very few pieces of furniture contained swords. At Jiudian and Yutaishan the high proportion of swords found — in approximately one third of the tombs (see Table 2) — did not decrease significantly throughout the Warring States period. Medium-sized tombs as well as small tombs are taken into account here. At Jiudian, 41 per cent of the tombs from the *yi* category contained weapons. This sudden development of the sword at the turn of the 5th century BC was a direct consequence of wars with the state of Wu. In 506-505 BC, Wu armies invaded Chu and besieged the capital, forcing the king of Chu to flee to the north.[27] From that time on, swords cast in the Wu-Yue area were buried in Chu tombs, within a few years or even several decades after they had been seized from the enemy. For instance, a sword that had belonged to the King of Yue was found in tomb No 1 at Jiangling Wangshan, dating to c350-300 BC. In other words, it was buried far from the place where it was made, and more than a century

Table 2 | Swords at Jiangling Yutaishan and Jiangling Jiudian cemeteries

(Number of tombs with swords/total of tombs, for each period)

t = tombs   tsw = tombs with swords

YUTAISHAN Chronology [423 t]		JIUDIAN Chronology [464 t]		YUTAISHAN & JIUDIAN [887 t]
I (680-580) [9 t]	[1 sw]			
II (580-480) [65 t]	[10 sw] 15%	I (530-480) [3 t]		[2 sw] 18%
III (480-400) [115 t]	[31 sw] 27%	II.2 (480-440) & II.3 (440-400) [19 t]	[9 sw] 47%	30%
IV (400-360) [139 t]	[44 sw] 32%	III.4 (400-360) [54 t]	[28 sw] 52%	37%
V (360-320) [56 t]	[16 sw] 29%	III.5 (360-320) [196 t]	[69 sw] 35%	34%
VI (320-278) [39 t]	[9 sw] 23%	IV.6 (320-278) [54 t]	[51 sw] 31%	[158 t] 32%
		IV.7 (278-223) [34 t]	[13 sw] 38%	
	[111 sw] 26%		[172 sw] 37%	[283 sw] 32%

after it was cast. Moreover, the Chu even started to produce swords on the model of those from the Wu-Yue area, which were superior in quality. The typical swords made in the Wu-Yue area were derived from daggers cast in the area surrounding Lake Tai since the Late Western Zhou period. Moreover on the best examples and their prototypes the pommel guards are decorated with a face motif imitating the famous Liangzhu mask of the neolithic period.[28] These swords have V-shaped guards with two rounded shoulders. Two rings encircle the cylindrical handles (figure 5).

Chu tombs also contained *ge* dagger-axes, bows and arrows, helmets, spearheads, etc. Providing the deceased with weapons (swords, bows and arrows, halberds, etc) marked a decisive turn in the evolution of Chu medium-sized and small tombs. Gradually new categories of objects, especially personal belongings and household articles, came to be associated with the traditional sets of ritual vessels and were accompanied by auspicious sculptures placed at the head section of the coffins, or less frequently in a side compartment. These categories comprised utensils for dressing (combs, mirrors and belt-hooks), musical instruments for personal use (*se* zithers), utensils for eating and drinking (eared-cups, boxes, etc), bamboo cases, mats, pillows and fans (figure 6).

Frequency analysis of the number of different artefact types in each grave shows that these new burial furnishings did not find their way into the tombs at once, but gradually over a period of time (table 3). For instance, the two kinds of combs with thin or thick teeth (*shu* and *bi*), that were among the most common burial items, appeared a century or so earlier and in much greater proportion than did the mirrors with which they began to be associated at the end of the 4th century BC. At Yutaishan, the proportion of combs rises to 10 per cent during period III (c480-400), 41 per cent during period IV (c400-360)

[25] Henan 1991: 186-193.

[26] For the dating of Xiasi cemetery (c600-500 BC), see Li Ling 1996: 'Zai lun Xichuan Xiasi Chu mu — du "Xichuan Xiasi Chu mu,"' *Wenwu* 1996(1), 47-60.

[27] Sima Qian, *Shiji* (Beijing: Zhonghuashuju, 1959), 1715-6.

[28] Thote, Alain 1996: 'Note sur la postérité du masque de Liangzhu à l'époque des Zhou orientaux,' *Arts Asiatiques* 51: 60-72 and Thote 1997: 263-89; also Yu Xiucui 1991: 'Dangyang Zhijiang Chu mu chutu de qingtong jian jieshao,' *Jiang Han Kaogu* 1991(1): 44-46.

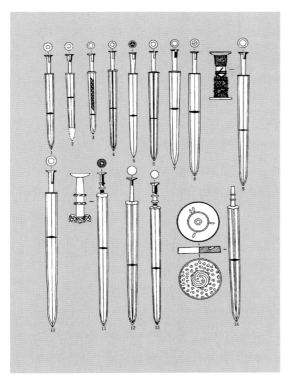

Figure 5 • The two main types of swords from Jiudian: the current type from Chu (Nos 1 to 10), a sword from Wu-Yue with the Liangzhu mask (No 11) and the type derived from the Wu-Yue sword (Nos 12-14). After Jiangling Jiudian Dong Zhou mu, *figure 145 p215*

and 38 per cent during period V (c360-320), while the proportions of tombs containing mirrors are respectively 0.7 per cent (period IV), four per cent (period V) and 10 per cent (period VI, c320-278). At Jiudian, the first mirrors appear in three per cent of the tombs during phase III.5 (c360-320) and in 16.5 per cent of the tombs during phase IV.6 (c320-278). No mirror is associated with earlier tombs. The association of mirrors with combs can only be evidenced in tombs whose furnishings of perishable material did not decay: at Mashan tomb No 1,[29] at Jiudian (11 tombs with combs and mirror, five with mirror and no comb, 22 without any furnishings of perishable material), at Yutaishan (three tombs with combs and mirror, four with mirror and no comb, two without any furnishings of perishable material). The frequent association of mirrors with combs should rule out the hypothesis that Chu mirrors were buried for prophylactic purposes at that early time. The Chu mirrors of the Mid- and Late Warring States periods were decorated with various different motifs, such as 'T' shaped patterns. Without question these motifs have an iconographic significance. Whether zoomorphic or geometric, they were also probably associated with magic and considered by the Chu people as auspicious. However, this does not mean that the Chu people believed that the mirrors themselves possessed magic properties (as people would do two or three centuries later during the Han dynasty). Nor does it mean that mirrors were deposited into tombs for a supposed prophylactic function. On the contrary, the archaeological evidence shows that mirrors began to be deposited into Chu tombs at the same time as other personal belongings, and that they were put close to such objects inside the tombs. Diane O'Donoghue in her detailed examination of the Chu mirrors remains cautious concerning the

[29] Hubei 1985: 87.

[30] O'Donoghue, Diane M 1990: 'Reflexion and Reception: The Origin of the Mirror in Bronze Age China,' *Bulletin of the Museum of Far Eastern Antiquities* 62: 5-183.

[31] Kong Xiangxing, Liu Yiman 1984: *Zhongguo gudai tongjing*, Beijing: Wenwu chubanshe, 53.

[32] Hubei 1985: 92 (Table 13).

functional and iconographic issues of these objects.[30] It seems that the Changsha area was an important manufacturing centre for mirrors. According to Kong Yangxing and Liu Yiman, nearly one quarter of the Chu tombs in that area contained mirrors.[31]

Many of these items, and even food, were carefully packed inside bamboo cases.[32] Only in very few medium-sized tombs did the Chu people put all of these new items together. Instead, they selected some objects from these categories. Jiangling Mashan tomb No 1 is exceptional in this respect. It contained pottery ritual vessels, one set for eating and drinking, one set for washing and clothing (one mirror, two combs, etc), eight wooden figurines, an auspicious sculpture, bamboo mats, a fan, a pillow, 19 bamboo caskets (including 18 with lids), and personal adornments. In many cases tombs with outer coffins of similar size have compara-

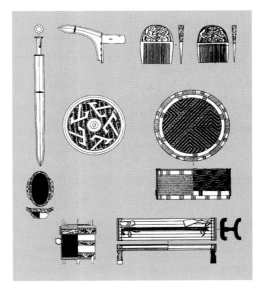

Figure 6 • Standard pieces of furniture from Chu graves (here, from the cemetery at Jiangling Jiudian). After Jiangling Jiudian Dong Zhou mu, *figure 145.10 p215 (sword), figure 148 p226 (ge), figure 164 p251 (mirror), figures 190.2 and 192.1 pp290 and 294 (combs), figure 185 p283 (eared-cup), figure 177 p271 (lacquer container zhi), figure 214 p317 (bamboo casket), figure 219 p324 (pillow)*

tively different structures. Compare for example Jiangling Mashan tomb No 1 (circa late 4th century-early 3rd century BC) with Cili Shibancun tomb No 36 in Hunan (4th century BC): their outer coffins are respectively 2.89 metres long, 1.49 metres wide and 1.06 metres high and 3.3 metres long, 1.4 metres wide and 1.3 metres high. However the vertical pit at Jiangling Mashan had no step while the pit at Cili Shibancun was much larger and had three steps. The gender and status of the deceased (a woman at Mashan, a male officer at Shibancun) may have determined the structures of their tombs both below and above ground as well as the equipment of the burials.[33] Wooden figurines were added to the furnishings some time around the middle of the 4th century BC, slightly earlier than mats, fans and pillows. At Jiudian, figurines began to be deposited into tombs during Period III.5 (c360-320). The proportion of tombs containing figurines at that early stage is quite small (2.5 per cent). During Periods IV.6 and IV.7 the proportion rises to 7 per cent and 9 per cent respectively. At Yutaishan, the proportions are 4 per cent (Period IV, c400-360), 12.5 per cent (Period V, c360-320) and 5 per cent (Period VI, 320-278).

Of all these items, the role of figurines remains fairly puzzling. The common explanation of figurines as substitutes for human sacrifices does not provide a reason for them to be deposited into tombs. In a few tombs (outside the Chu area), human sacrificial victims and wooden or pottery figurines were found buried together.[34] It is worth noting that *yong* figurines are mentioned in the bamboo slips from Sui Xian Leigudun tomb No 1 (433 BC), which contained 21 human victims.[35] This phenomenon appeared in the Chu area in the 4th century BC, when human sacrifices had become extremely rare. The question of human sacrifices associated with tombs, which is rather complex, should be studied case by case, since the interplay between various contrasted factors such as local traditions, status of the deceased, and influence of new religious or philosophical ideas as well, resulted in the maintenance or extinction of those practices. In the area of Jiangling there is no archaeological evidence of human sacrifices associated with burials to date. With the exception of the cemetery at Xichuan Xiasi in Henan (6th century BC) and of tombs No 5 at Dangyang Caojiagang in Hubei (6th to early 5th century BC), Nos 3, 4 and 5 at Echeng Baizifan in Hubei (4th century BC) and No 1 at Changsha Liuchengqiao in Hunan (early 4th century BC), the few remaining tombs with human sacrifices excavated in the Chu area were culturally associated with other traditions, those of Zeng (Sui Xian Leigudun tomb No 1 and tomb No 2 in Hubei, late 5th century BC), of Cai (Shou Xian Ximennei tomb No 1 in Anhui, early 5th century BC), and of Wu (Gushi Hougudui tomb No 1 in Henan, late 6th century-early 5th century BC).[36]

The gender of a sacrificed victim is often difficult to determine, due to poor conditions of preservation. On the other hand, many figurines were adorned with attributes which leave no doubt as to their status. Judging from their attributes, some were soldiers, whereas others would be considered as high officers. Ornaments such as *huang* arc-shaped pendants and rings strung with beads were depicted with ink and colours in the dress of some wooden figurines. Pendants are shown hanging from the shoulders or the waist of the figures like jade pendants, which were insignia or symbols of power and wealth in antiquity.[37] A wooden figure representing a warrior was found in tomb No 1 at Taoyuan Sanyuancun (Hunan). Though the figurine is described in the report as a woman, a model of a shield was discovered close to it, which indicates that it represented a man, more precisely a soldier.[38]

On the contrary, in large tombs from the 5th to 4th century BC, the sacrificial victims were mainly young women, probably concubines, musicians and dancers, as in the case of Sui Xian Leigudun tomb No 1, in which 21 young women were buried in coffins.[39] The human victims at Gushi Hougudui were five men, nine women (the gender of three other victims could not be determined). At Gushi Baizifan, they were 13 males. At Dangyang Caojiagang, two women were sacrificed. In other cases, information about the gender of the victims is lacking.[40] Consequently, it seems that the figurines had a symbolic

[33] Hubei 1985: 3-4, 71-93; Hunan 1990 (Hunan sheng wenwu kaogu yanjiusuo, Cili Xian Wenwu Baohu Guanli Yanjiusuo): 'Hunan Cili Shibancun 36 hao Zhanguo mu fajue jianbao,' *Wenwu* 1990(10): 37-47.

[34] Shanxi 1984: (Shanxi sheng kaogu yanjiusuo): 'Shanxi Changzi Xian Dong Zhou mu,' *Kaogu xuebao* 1984(4): 503-529; Shandong 1977 (Shandong sheng bowuguan): 'Linzi Langjiazhuang yi hao Dong Zhou xunren mu,' *Kaogu xuebao* 1977(1): 73-104.

[35] Hubei 1989 (Hubei sheng bowuguan): *Zeng Hou Yi mu*, Beijing: Wenwu chubanshe: 500; 530, note 276.

[36] Huang Zhanyue 1990: *Zhongguo gudai de rensheng renxun*, Beijing: Wenwu chubanshe: 184-196.

[37] Jiangling 1989 (Jiangling xian wenwuju): 'Hubei Jiangling Wuchang Yidi Chu mu,' *Wenwu* 1989 (3): 35-50, 48 (figure 35), 62; and Henan 1986 (Henan sheng wenwu yanjiusuo), *Xinyang Chu mu*, Beijing: Wenwu chubanshe: 115 (figure 79); colour plate, 14; plates 106.1, 106.3, 107.4.

[38] Changde 1987 (Changde diqu wenwu gongzuodui, Taoyuan xian wenhuaju): 'Taoyuan Sanyuancun yi hao Chu mu,' *Hunan kaogu jikan* 4: 22-32; figure 18.2 and figure 19.

[39] Hubei 1989.

[40] Huang Zhanyue 1990: 184-196.

Table 3 | Furniture Deposited in Chu Tombs

◆◆◆◆◆◆ Large tombs (Xichuan Xiasi, Suixian Leigudun Tomb No 1, etc)

▼▼▼▼▼▼ Tombs of medium size (cemeteries at Dangyang Zhaojiahu, Jiangling Yutaishan, Jiangling Jiudian, and a few other tombs)

	8th Century	7th Century	6th Century	5th Century	4th Century	3rd Century
Ritual vessels (bronze and earthenwares)	◆◆◆◆◆◆◆ ▼▼▼▼▼▼	◆◆◆◆◆◆ ▼▼▼▼▼▼	◆◆◆◆◆◆ ▼▼▼▼▼	◆◆◆◆◆ ▼▼▼▼▼	◆◆◆◆◆◆ ▼▼▼▼▼	◆◆◆◆◆◆ ▼▼▼▼▼
zu offering tables		? ? ? ▼▼▼▼▼▼	◆◆◆◆◆◆ ▼▼▼▼▼	? ? ? ▼▼▼▼	◆◆◆◆◆◆ ▼▼▼▼	
wooden *ji*		◆◆	◆◆◆◆◆◆	◆◆◆◆◆◆	◆◆◆◆◆◆ ▼▼▼▼▼	▼▼▼▼▼
ge dagger-axes	◆◆◆◆◆◆◆	◆◆◆◆◆◆	◆◆◆◆◆◆	◆◆◆◆◆◆ ▼▼▼▼▼	◆◆◆◆◆◆ ▼▼▼▼▼	▼▼▼▼▼
daggers/swords			◆◆◆◆	◆◆◆◆◆◆ ▼▼▼▼▼	◆◆◆◆◆◆ ▼▼▼▼▼	▼▼▼▼▼
zhou oval containers		▼▼▼▼▼▼	? ? ? ▼▼▼▼▼▼	◆◆◆◆◆◆		
eared-cups			◆◆◆	◆◆◆◆◆◆	◆◆◆◆◆◆ ▼▼▼▼▼	◆◆◆◆◆◆ ▼▼▼▼▼
zhenmushou			◆◆◆◆◆◆	◆◆◆◆◆◆ ▼▼▼▼▼▼	◆◆◆◆◆◆ ▼▼▼▼▼	◆◆◆◆◆◆ ▼▼▼
figurines				◆◆◆◆◆◆	◆◆◆◆◆◆ ▼▼▼▼▼	◆◆◆◆◆◆ ▼▼▼▼▼
se zithers				◆◆◆◆◆◆	◆◆◆◆◆◆ ▼▼▼▼▼	◆◆◆◆◆◆ ▼▼▼▼▼
combs				◆◆◆◆◆◆	◆◆◆◆◆◆ ▼▼▼▼▼	▼▼▼▼▼
mirrors					▼▼▼▼▼▼	▼▼▼▼▼▼
wooden caskets			◆◆◆◆			
bamboo caskets					▼▼▼▼▼▼	▼▼▼▼▼▼
pillows					▼▼▼▼▼▼	
fans					▼▼▼▼▼▼	
guo with compartments	◆◆◆◆◆◆	◆◆◆◆◆◆	◆◆◆◆◆◆ ▼▼▼▼▼	◆◆◆◆◆◆ ▼▼▼▼▼	◆◆◆◆◆◆ ▼▼▼▼▼	◆◆◆◆◆◆ ▼▼▼▼▼

presence, of exactly the same kind as the household items. They might express the desire of the deceased to have followers or servants of comparable status and quality.

The assemblages of ritual vessels contrast strongly with these new categories of burial furnishings. They remained fairly static all along the period considered (Table 4): standard sets comprised *fou* or *hu* containers for beverages, *ding* tripods, *fu* or *dui* containers for food, and *dou* high cups for presenting food offerings (figure 7). The extinction of one type of vessel, such as the *gui* tureen disappearing after the period IV.6 at Dangyang Zhaojiahu, and the emergence of new types, for instance the appearance of the *dui* vessels in early 5th century BC, are useful chronological indicators. However, the types did not change significantly during the period considered — nearly five centuries — while shape and decoration followed the current fashion of the time. The examination of Table 4 reveals that the combination of *ding* tripods with *fu* or *dui* containers and *hu* or *fou* vessels for liquids was the most common assemblage. The chronology is therefore mainly based on the evolution of shapes for each vessel type. Other types of vessels were frequently added to the standard assemblages, but with less regularity. It is worth noting that the typologies made at Yutaishan were considered obsolete by archaeologists soon after the publication of the report on Jiudian cemetery (especially the dating of the tombs containing pottery vessels of 'daily use,' a category that would need further research). Earthenware imitations of bronzes and more common ceramics were low-fired wares. Therefore all of the vessels in these two categories should be considered as ritual containers intended for tombs.[41] At Yutaishan, *fu* and *dui* that have perfectly symmetrical shapes were interchangeable. In wealthy medium-sized tombs these vessels were grouped in pairs. Containers for holding and pouring water were the rather common *yi* and *pan*, *lei* and a small *ding* tripod with a small opening, a typical Chu shape. Their shape and decoration gradually changed. Since they were low-fired earthenware intended for burial, they were made shortly before being put into the graves. What did not really change throughout the Warring States period is, on the one hand the care taken to make close imitations of bronzes (even if their quality is uneven), and on the other, the composition of sets and fixed numbers of items within each assemblage.

The use of auspicious sculptures with antlers such as *zhenmushou*, deer, long-necked birds standing on tigers and drum-stands, etc, lasted, on a large scale, only around one and a half centuries, from about 450 BC to 300 BC. At Jiangling Jiudian, the average proportion of small tombs containing *zhenmushou* is 11 per cent, with the following frequency seriation : 83 per cent (Period II.2, c480-440), 25 per cent (Period II.3), 61 per cent (Period III.4), 20 per cent (Period III.5), 10 per cent (Period IV.6), six per cent (Period IV.7, c278-223). The bronze sculpture from Leigudun, which is a drum-stand imitating a wooden model, testifies to an early dating for such objects in the Chu area.[42] Cultural contacts with the states from central and eastern China renewed and strengthened by Chu during her northern and eastern expansion might explain the diminishing use of these very specific cult objects.

Construction of the Tombs

By the 5th century BC, the structure of the medium-sized tombs underwent a major change: the *guo* outer coffin became compartmentalised, allowing a clear

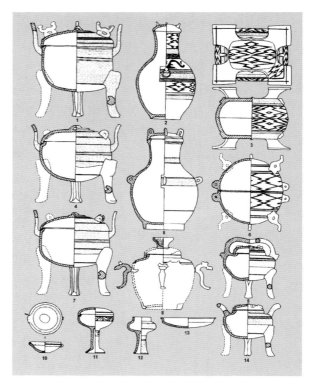

Figure 7 • *Ritual vessels from Tomb No 231 at Jiangling Jiudian (4th century BC): the tomb contained vessels for cooking ding (1), for containing food offerings* fu *(2),* dou *(3) and* dui *(4), for holding beverages* hu *(5, 6) or containing liquids* lei *(7), for the ritual ablutions* yi *and* pan *(8), and of unknown use* ding *with small opening (9) and high cups (10). Most of the vessels were grouped in pairs. After* Jiangling Jiudian Dong Zhou mu, *figure 235, p362*

[41] On the usual chronology of the Chu graves and problems concerning their dating, see the remarkable survey by Donald B Wagner (Wagner 1987: 'The Dating of the Chu Graves of Changsha: the Earliest Iron Artifacts in China?' *Acta Orientalia* [Copenhagen], Vol XLVIII: 111-156).

[42] Thote 1987: 'Une sculpture chinoise en bronze du Ve siècle avant notre ère : essai d'interprétation,' *Arts Asiatiques* 42: 45-58.

Table 4 | Sets of Earthenware and Bronze Ritual Vessels in Three Chu Cemeteries

[*ding, dou, dui, fang, fou , fu, gui*, box *he, hu, lei, li, zhan*, oval container *zhou* or *he, yu*]
[*ding* with small opening *jiao-ding, hu* with long neck *changling-hu*]

After *Dangyang Zhaojiahu Chu mudi*, 224-234; *Jiangling Yutaishan Chu mu*, 129; *Jiangling Jiudian Dong Zhou mu*, 357, 369.

Dangyang Zhaojiahu Medium sized and small tombs *jia* and *yi* types	**Jiangling Yutaishan** Medium-sized and small tombs	**Jiangling Jiudian** 22 medium-sized tombs group *yi*, type *jia*	**Jiangling Jiudian** 299 small/medium-sized tombs group *yi* type, type *yi*
II.3 = (four tombs) *ding + gui + li + dou* + small jar or *li + dou + yu* + (small jar)			
III.4 = (four tombs) *ding + gui + dou* + small jar + *(li)* or *li + dou + yu* + (small jar)	**I** = *li + yu + (dou)* + jar		
III.5 = *ding + gui + dou* + small jar + *(li)* + *zhou + zhan* or *ding* or *li* + small jar + *yu + (dou)* + *(zhou + zhan)*			
IV.6 and **IV.7** = (five tombs) *ding + dui* + various containers	**II** = *li + yu* + jar or *li + yu + hu* with long neck	**I.1**	**I.1** = *ding + fu + fou* (large *hu*) + *dou*
V.8 = *ding + hu + dui* and/or *dou* + *(pan)*	**III** = *li + yu + hu* with long neck or *ding + fu + hu + (dou)*	**II.2** = *ding + fu + fou* (large *hu*) + *dui + hu + dou* + *ding* with small opening	**II.2** = *ding + fu + fou* (large *hu*) + *dui + li + hu + dou* + (*hu* with long neck)
V.9 = *ding + hu + dui* and/or *dou* + *(fu)* or *ding* + *(hu) + (fu)* + *(ding* with small opening or *jiao-hu)* + *(pan) + (yi)*	or *ding + dui + hu + lei* (+ *ding* with small opening)	**II.3** = *ding + fu + fou* (large *hu*) + *dui + hu + lei + dou* + *ding* with small opening	**II.3** = *ding + fu + fou* (large *hu*) + *dui + hu + lei + dou* + *ding* with small opening + (*hu* with long neck)
VI.10 = *ding + hu + dui + (fu) + (dou)* + *ding* with small opening or *jiao-hu*	**IV** = *li + yu + hu* with long neck or *ding + fu + hu* or *ding + dui + hu* + *(dui) + (dou)* + (*ding* with small opening)	**III.4** = *ding + fu + fou* (large *hu*) + *dui + hu + lei + dou* + *ding* with small opening	**III.4** = *ding + fu + fou* (large *hu*) + *li + lei* + (*hu* with long neck) + *ding* with small opening
VI.11 = *ding + hu + dui + (fu) + (dou)* or *ding + hu + fu + (dou)* + *ding* with small opening	**V** = *ding + fu + hu + (dui) + (dou)* or *ding + dui + hu + (dui) + (dou)* + (*ding* with small opening)	**III.5** = *ding + fu + fou* (large *hu*) + *dui + hu + lei + dou* + *ding* with small opening	**III.5** = *ding + fu + fou* (large *hu*) + *fang + dui + (li)+ lei* + (*hu* with long neck) + *ding* with small opening
VII.12 = (four tombs) *ding + hu + dui + (fu) + lei + (fang)* + *ding* with small opening	**VI** = *ding + dui + hu* or *ding + fang* + box *he* + (*ding* with small opening)	**IV.6** = *ding + fu + fou* (large *hu*) + *dui + hu + lei + fang* + box *he* + *ding* with small opening	**IV.6** = *ding + fu + fou* (large *hu*) + *fang + dui + (li)+ lei* + (*hu* with long neck) + box *he + ding* with small opening
			IV.7 = *ding + dui + hu*

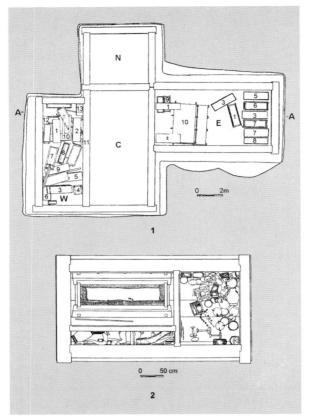

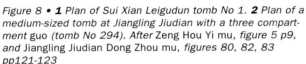

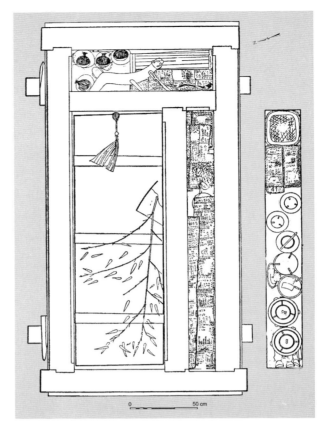

Figure 8 • **1** Plan of Sui Xian Leigudun tomb No 1. **2** Plan of a medium-sized tomb at Jiangling Jiudian with a three compartment guo (tomb No 294). After Zeng Hou Yi mu, figure 5 p9, and Jiangling Jiudian Dong Zhou mu, figures 80, 82, 83 pp121-123

Figure 9 • Plan of Jiangling Mashan tomb No 1 (late 4th century BC-early 3rd century BC). After Jiangling Mashan yi hao Chu mu, figure 12 p10

distribution of the burial furnishings by categories. It seems that this shift occurred a century or so earlier in larger tombs, as exemplified by tomb No 7 at Xichuan Xiasi which dates from the beginning of the 6th century BC.[43] In turn, a century later, medium-sized tombs began to follow the models provided by larger tombs, echoing their structure and content on a much smaller scale (see also Table 3).

> The coffin was put inside a narrow compartment and separated from burial furnishings by a wooden panel. In broader outer coffin structures a side compartment could be added alongside the coffin, and further compartments added at its foot and along the opposite side wall. Compartmentalising the outer coffin remained specific to Chu tombs until the end of the Warring States period, even though it was not applied to all of them. This has led some archaeologists to suggest that through the use of compartments and new categories of burial furnishings, Chu tombs had some sort of relationship with buildings of the living.

> The first example to date of a compartmentalised outer coffin found in Hubei is provided by a medium-sized tomb excavated at Yingshan Wudian dating to Late Western Zhou-Early Eastern Zhou (circa 8th century BC). In this tomb the guo, which was three metres long and 1.5 metres wide, had a foot compartment and a side compartment. Bronze ritual vessels were deposited in both compartments. It seems that the area where the tomb is located (close to Suizhou in Hubei and Xinyang in south Henan) did not yet belong to the Chu kingdom at that early time.[44] In fact, such an interpretation does not take into account that household items and personal belongings never replaced the ritual vessels, but were merely added to them. Moreover, the borrowing of architectural elements from actual buildings remained a rare phenomenon. At

[43] Henan 1991: 27, figure 20.

[44] Yingshan 1989 (Yingshan xian wenhuaguan wenwuzu): 'Hubei Yingshan Wudian gu muzang qingli jianbao,' Wenwu 1989(3): 51-56.

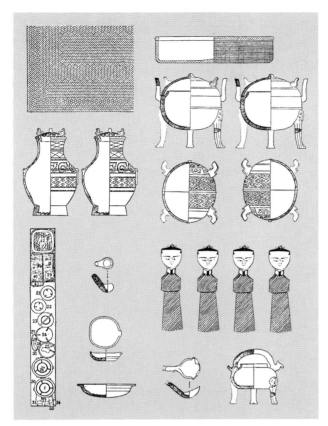

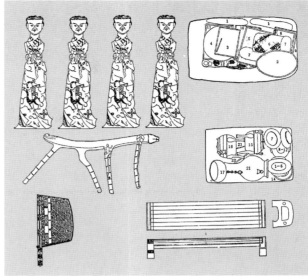

Figure 11 • Furniture from the head compartment of Jiangling Mashan tomb No 1 (late 4th century BC-early 3rd century BC): wooden puppets, bamboo casket with a set for drinking and eating, bamboo casket with a set for washing and clothing, auspicious sculpture, fan and pillow. After Jiangling Mashan yi hao Chu mu, figures 66 p81, 68 p83, 69 p84, 70 p85, 73 and 74 p87

Figure 10 • Furniture from the side compartment of Jiangling Mashan tomb No 1 (late 4th century BC-early 3rd century BC): mats, bamboo caskets with food, earthenware ritual vessels (hu, dui, ding, yi and pan, ding with small opening), wooden puppets. After Jiangling Mashan yi hao Chu mu, figures 63 p76, 67 p82, 71 and 72 p86

[45] Yu Weichao 1980: 'Han dai zhuhou wang yu liehou muzang de xingzhi fenxi — jian lun "Zhou zhi," "Han zhi" yu "Jin zhi" de san jieduanxing,' Zhongguo kaoguxuehui di yi ci nianhui lunwenji 1979, Beijing: Wenwu chubanshe, 334.

[46] Hubei 1995 31. For other sites, see Thote, Alain 1991: 'The Double Coffin of Leigudun Tomb No 1: Iconographic Sources and Related Problems,' in Thomas Lawton (ed), New Perspectives on Chu Culture during the Eastern Zhou Period, Arthur M Sackler Gallery, Smithsonian Institution, Washington, DC, 45, note 17.

[47] Hubei 1995 122, figure 81; 114, figure 74.

[48] Hubei 1982 (Hubei sheng Jingzhou diqu bowuguan): 'Jiangling Tianxingguan yihao Chu mu,' Kaogu xuebao 1982(1): 77; Hubei 1991: 50, figure 33.

[49] Hubei 1995: 28.

Jiangling Jiudian only four compartmentalised tombs from a total of 154 had an outer coffin with doors and windows. Such architectural elements were as rare at other Chu sites.[45] Similarities between the tomb and the house of the living may equally be the result of the use of techniques or aesthetic features shared by both.[46] The doors were closed, but could swing towards the head or side compartments (Jiangling Jiudian tombs No 294 and No 526), so that the coffin was probably put outside and in front of the compartments equipped for the furniture.[47] At Jiangling Tianxingguan tomb No 1, murals representing double doors were painted on the walls of three side compartments. Their location leaves no doubt that they were meant as symbolic openings from the side compartments towards the adjoining compartments. At Jiangling Tianxingguan tomb No 1 and Baoshan tomb No 2, and in many smaller tombs, a double roof was added to all compartments, except for the central one.[48]

The new ideas on afterlife that undoubtedly inspired the introduction of household and personal articles into tombs seem to have equally inspired the addition of architectural elements in the guo. Intermediary solutions between wooden structures with compartments and those without could also explain that real or symbolic openings through the walls were needed.

The types and sub-types defined by Chinese archaeologists for the tombs at Jiudian (group yi) amount to seven types and no less than 36 sub-types.[49] It must be borne in mind that the cemetery was in use for about 300 years. These high numbers indicate that new ideas on death and the afterlife, when they became widespread by the end of the 5th century BC, generated many variations in the preparation of a tomb and its contents. Innovative features were mixed with traditional elements. Consequently, the notion of an 'underground home' prepared for the deceased, as later exemplified at Changsha Mawangdui,[50] developed gradually at Chu without following a direct line towards its full achievement. Prototypes appeared for the first time in the second half of the 5th century BC in large tombs such as Sui Xian Leigudun tomb No 1,[51] before being progressively adopted in medium-sized tombs (figure 8). Hence a great deal of variation existed in the concrete expression of new ideas about the otherworldly existence of the dead.

At the very end of the 4th century BC, the organisation of tombs underwent a further evolution. As a case in point, the burial furnishings at Mashan tomb No 1 in the vicinity of Jiangling were exchanged between the head and side compartments (figure 9). Instead of being deposited at the head of the coffin, the pottery ritual vessels were grouped together on the floor of the side compartment. The assemblage comprised, as usual, pairs of *hu, ding* and *dui,* as well as the standard *ding* with small opening and a set of *yi* and *pan* for ablutions, as well as ladles (figure 10). Bamboo cases for food were stored beside this typical Chu assemblage of ritual vessels. Obviously food brought into the tomb was not a part of traditional offerings, but was intended as provisions. These caskets contained remains of animals (sheep, chicken, sparrow bones, etc).[52]

The head compartment contained the artefacts of the best quality (figure 11). With the exception of the bamboo mats, which could not be put into this compartment because of their length, all the burial furnishings at the head of the coffin were household utensils (figure 12): a complete set for eating and drinking carefully wrapped within a bamboo casket, a pillow and a fan. Put over the previous case, a set for washing and clothing comprised a *pan* basin for water, two pairs of shoes, two combs, a bronze mirror, cloth, a belthook and personal adornments.

The organisation of both compartments was almost symmetrical, with four figurines in each of them. A sacrificed dog watched over the long side compartment whereas an auspicious sculpture was deposited over the furnishings in the head compartment.

It appears that all of the necessities for daily life were not only of the highest quality, but were also more valued than the traditional ritual vessels, as indicated by their position at the head of the tomb. For instance, the tomb's owner was provided with two *pan* basins, one for personal use and the other to fulfil ritual requirements.[53] The refined craftsmanship of the first strongly contrasted with the conspicuous lack of quality of the second. It seems to me that the lacquered *pan* had probably been used for washing the corpse while the pottery basin which belongs to the set of ritual vessels was used for ablutions during the sacrifices.

This shift from previous burial customs can equally be observed in late Chu tombs of medium size in Hunan and Hubei, though these are less well documented than at Mashan due to poor conditions of preservation. When all the pieces of furniture were stored inside the head compartment of these tombs, they were deposited one over the other by categories. In tomb No 617 at Jiudian, household and washing furniture were stored on the ground. They were then covered by a drum, on top of which was a *zhenmushou*. The ritual vessels were stacked together beside the drum, with the *yi* and *pan* containers leaning against the household furniture. This was also the case in tombs Nos 51 and 451. The compartments in these tombs were so tightly packed that the items they contained did not move with the course of time, enabling us to reconstruct in which order they were put into the tombs during the funerals.[54] Tomb No 1 at Changsha Shi Hehuachi (Hunan) is characterized by the same features as observed in Jiangling Mashan tomb No 1.[55]

Conclusion

To summarize, the spatial organisation and content of Chu medium-sized tombs gradually evolved in such a way as to follow, one or two generations later, the same evolution as larger tombs. In the meantime, the increasing quality and number of furnishings in medium-sized tombs probably reflected important

[50] Pirazzoli-t'Serstevens, Michèle 1992.

[51] Thote, Alain 1986: 'Une tombe princière chinoise du Ve siècle avant notre ère,' in *Comptes rendus de l'Académie des Inscriptions & Belles-Lettres*, avril-juin: 407; von Falkenhausen, Lothar 1993: *Suspended Music. Chime-Bells in the Culture of Bronze Age China*, Berkeley/Los Angeles/Oxford: University of California Press, 7.

[52] Hubei 1985: 87.

[53] Hubei 1985: plate XXXV and colour plate XXIX.

[54] Hubei 1995: figure 51, 83, figure 67, 105, figures 59 and 60, 94-5.

[55] Changsha 1989 (Changsha shi wenwu gongzuodui): 'Changsha shi Hehuachi yi hao Zhanguo muguo mu fajue baogao,' *Hunan kaogu jikan* 5 : 52-60, 6.

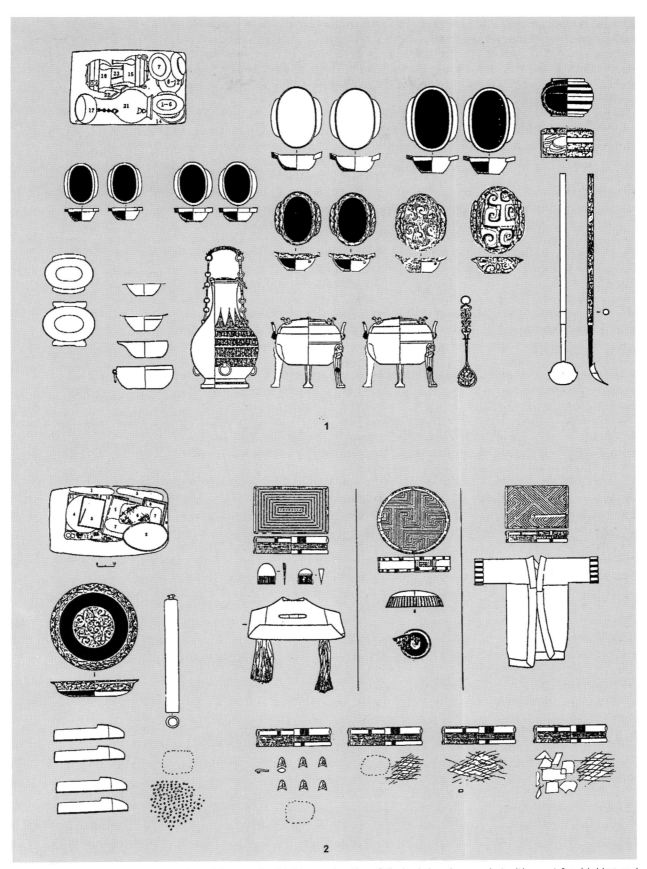

Figure 12 • **1** (above): bamboo casket with a set for drinking and eating. **2** (below): bamboo casket with a set for drinking and clothing. Jiangling Mashan tomb No 1 (late 4th century BC-early 3rd century BC). After Jiangling Mashan yi hao Chu mu, figures 61.1-5 and 61.9-10 p72, 62 p73, 64.1-4 p78, 65.1-5 p79, and figures 25 and 26 p24, 28.1 and 28.6 p27, 61.6 p72, 64.5 p78, 65.6-7 p79, 75 p88, 77 p90, 78 p91

changes in Chu society. Unfortunately, information on the deceased is cruelly lacking: such important information as age at death, sex, family, social status or class, wealth, and relation to persons buried nearby are not supplied to us. However, it seems to me that changes in the general pattern of medium-sized tombs should mirror a parallel evolution in the concept of the afterlife. At the outset, burial furnishings were primarily ritual vessels and food offerings probably of the same kind as those used in temples dedicated to the ancestors. To these ritual vessels new categories of objects were added in stages, beginning with weapons. The tombs gradually departed from the initial temple model or symbolism to become more like an underground home divided into compartments, equipped with personal belongings of the deceased, household items and food provisions. The role of the ritual vessels deposited into the tombs seemingly changed at the same time. I would suggest that they might have been provided to the dead so that he or she could use them and perform sacrifices during his or her afterworldly existence, as also suggested by Hayashi Minao.[56] Ritual texts from antiquity such as the *Liji* (Record of rituals) and the *Yili* (Book of rites) abound in information on ceremonies held when a high-ranking officer died. They did not describe actual tombs in detail, but stipulated above all the process of rituals, with the interdicts and recommendations. Even though they provided some interesting details on graves, they mentioned almost nothing, with the exception of Lu, about the states and areas in China which commonly shared such practices. However, some indications may be useful to interpret the general evolution during the Eastern Zhou period. In particular it is said in the *Liji* (Tangong) that the deceased should not be treated as if he or she were dead. This may be why the new types of burial furnishings and offerings were adopted to express comparable feelings towards the deceased.[57] Many scholars whose studies have inspired mine, Yu Weichao and Wu Hung for instance,[58] have highlighted significant changes during the Eastern Zhou period in the organisation of tombs for the élite. In the case of medium-sized tombs at Chu, the evolution was slower, and much more complex. This should help us to understand how the new ideas that inspired this evolution spread into wider classes in Chu society.

[56] Hayashi, Minao 1993: 'Concerning the Inscription "May Sons and Grandsons Eternally Use this [Vessel],"' *Artibus Asiae* 53 (1/2): 51-58.

[57] Couvreur, Séraphin 1950: *Mémoires sur les bienséances et les cérémonies*, Paris: Cathasia/ Les Belles Lettres, tome 1, première partie: 169-70.

[58] Yu Weichao 1980: 332-37; Wu Hung 1988: 'From Temple to Tomb. Ancient Chinese art and Religion in Transition,' *Early China* 13: 78-115.

Art and Technology

Figure 1 • *The eight-pointed motif found on artefacts of the neolithic period and Bronze Age:*
a *White pottery plate (M1:1), Daxi culture, Anxiang Tangjiagang, Hunan*
b *Pottery spindle whorl, Majiabang culture, Wujin Panjiatang*
c *Pottery jar (M33:4), Songze culture, Qingfu Songze, Shanghai*
d *Painted pottery basin (M44:4) and spindle whorl (T3:1), Dawenkou culture, Pi xian Dadunzi, Jiangsu*
e *Pottery dou, Dawenkou culture, Taian, Shangdong*
f *Painted pottery basin (M35:2), Dawenkou culture, Zou xian Yedian, Shandong*
g *Pottery spindle whorl (M17:3), Liangzhu culture, Haian Qingdun, Jiangsu*
h *Painted pottery pot (P1130), Yangshao culture, Xi'an Banpo, Shaanxi*
i *Pottery spindle whorl (T2M8:1), Yangshao culture, Jing'an, Jiangxi*
j *Bronze mirror, Qijia culture*
k *Stone object (T4:13), Qijia culture, Wuwei Huangniangniangtai, Gansu*
l *Painted pottery base, Xiaoheyan culture, Aohanqi Xiaoheyan, Inner Mongolia*
m *Bronze chariot part, Shang dynasty, Anyang Xiaotun (M20), Henan*
n *Pottery spindle whorl, Upper Xiajiadian culture (Western Zhou period), Ningcheng Nanshangen, Inner Mongolia*
o *Bronze chariot part, Eastern Zhou period, Zhenjiang Jianbiwangjia, Jiangsu*
p *Pottery architectural part, Warring States period, Luoyang, Henan*

WANG XU

The Eight-pointed Star Pattern
and the Prehistoric Loom

A number of pieces of pottery excavated from the neolithic era in China are decorated with a symmetrical eight-pointed cross, usually with a square or a round hole at the centre. This design is generally called 'the eight-pointed star pattern.' Although we immediately recognise its form, its significance is mystifying. We read in excavation reports since 1964 that the eight-pointed star pattern has been discovered in different locations and from different periods, however no reasonable or sound explanation has yet been found for it and it has become rather a puzzle.

Rough statistics show that there are over 10 types of pottery or stone artefacts decorated with the eight-pointed star (figure 1). These fall into several archaeological culture types and last for a very long period:

- Daxi culture (c4200-3200 BC)
- Songze culture (c4000-3300 BC)
- Dawenkou culture (c4200-2500 BC)
- Xiaoheyan culture (c2000 BC)
- Qijia culture (c2000 BC)
- Shang and Zhou dynasties (16th-3rd centuries BC)

The distribution of the pattern is concentrated in the area between the lower reaches of the Yangzi and the lower reaches of the Yellow River, stretching as far west as the middle of the Hexi corridor and as far north as the eastern edge of the loess plateau. In time the pattern is found over a period of more than two millennia. Yet despite the differences in location, time and archaeological culture of these discoveries, the eight-pointed star patterns reveal a startling similarity. They are obviously a standardised symbol for a certain object.

The eight-pointed star appears again and again on spindle whorls (*fanglun*), and apart from its decorative purpose or religious meaning it may also convey to us information about prehistoric tools and production facilities. Certainly the eight-pointed star in frontal view and in side view found on pottery spindle whorls among the neolithic remains at Wujin, Panjiatang,

---

This paper was first published in *Zhongguo wenhua* No 2 (1990) and has been revised for this volume.

Jiangsu province seem to be representations of mechanical parts made 6,000 years ago. From this starting point we can begin to examine the evidence for textile equipment of historical times — from Han down to the Qing dynasty, and also from modern folk textile equipment (figure 2), and to unravel the mystery of this persistent eight-pointed star motif. Originally it was the most recognizable component of the standing frame loom (*taijia zhiji*) — an exact image of the eight-pointed star ratchets at either end of the warping beam (*juanjingzhou*). The stone artefact from the Qijia culture in the form of an eight-pointed star (figure 1k) is a three-dimensional model of an object actually used at that time. If we compare it with the corresponding component of the modern Dingqiao loom (figure 3), we find an astonishing similarity between the two. Thus the eight-pointed star, persisting in a standard form for over six millennia, indicates that a loom with a standard warping beam was already in existence and had reached an advanced stage during neolithic times.

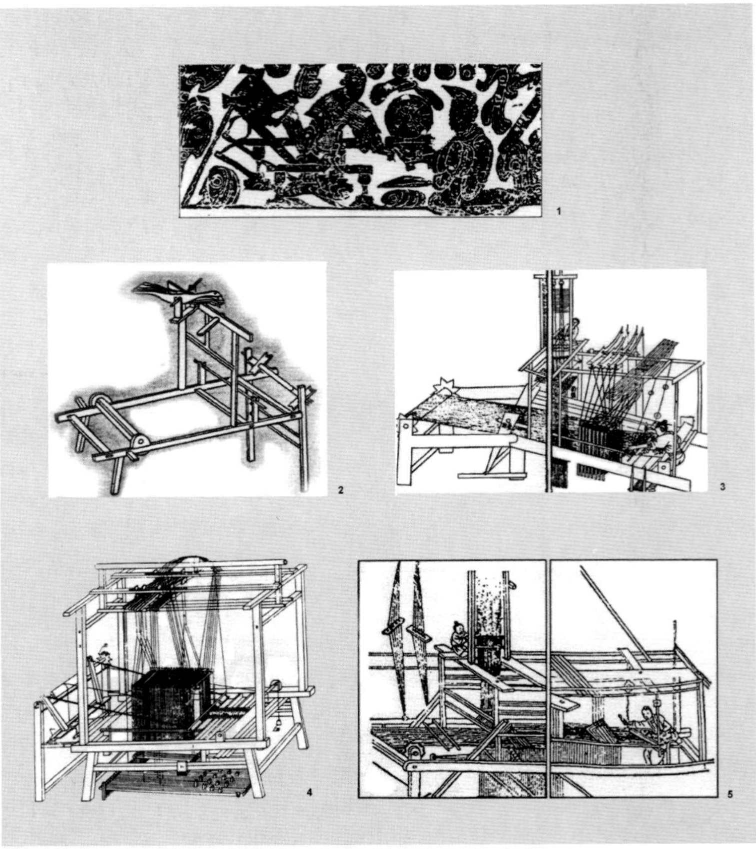

The warping beam of both ancient looms and modern folk looms is generally called the *sheng*. The eight-pointed star depicts the ratchet at either end of the warping beam, being known as the *shenghua* in Henan and as the *yangjiao* (sheep's horns) in Sichuan. By

Figure 2 • Pictorial evidence for early looms:
a *Han dynasty brick relief carving, Caizhuang, Jiangsu*
b *Illustration in Xie Jingshi's* Ziren yizhi *(Yuan dynasty)*
c *Illustration in Song Yingxing's* Tiangong kaiwu *(Ming dynasty)*
d *Diangqiao loom (after* Zhongguo fangzhi kexue jishu shi*)*
e *Illustration in Wei Jie's* Cansang suibian *(Qing dynasty)*

their means, the weaver can control the unwinding of warp threads from the warping beam as weaving progresses. The eight-pointed *shenghua* carved and painted on pottery dishes and spindle whorls is not an accidental form of decoration, but is a symbol related to the textile craft. The appearance of the warping beam marks an important technological achievement 6,000 years ago in the course of the transformation from the primitive frameless waist loom to work at which the weaver had to sit on the ground (see figure 7) into the frame loom. As the prototype of later frame looms, the *sheng* became the symbol both of the loom itself and of the textile craft.

From literary texts we find that the *sheng* later developed into a woman's head ornament, such as the jade *sheng* and the wooden *sheng'a*, which became a sign of the division of work in Chinese society between the women who wove and the men who worked in the fields.[1] In the *Shanhaijing* (Classic of Mountains and Seas) there is a reference to the Queen Mother of the West and to the *sheng* that she wears. The commentary states that the *sheng* is made of jade. Although the story is a myth it shows the earliest reference to this tradition. In the *Hou Hanshu* (History of the Later Han) (*'Yufuzhi'*) we read that when attending ritual ceremonies, emperors, queens and the ladies of the court would adorn their hair with a hairpin a foot long which bore a *sheng* on each end.[2] The ornament showed the respect commanded by these court women. In the *Huainanzi*, the character for *sheng* is written with a variant, explained in the *Shuowen* as the warping beam of the loom.[3] From the Han tomb at Yinan there were found two engraved stone depictions of the Queen Mother of the West wearing a *sheng* (figure 4). And in the story of filial son Dong Yong, engraved on a stone

[1] *Jing Chu suishiji* (by Zong Ling, 6th century AD) informs us of its development into an ornament for women's hair, and that people would make *sheng* from flowers or gold (Tang Ling 1985, *Jing Chu suishiji yizhu* Wuhan, Hubei renmin chubanshe: 25). Cao Zijian (192-232) in *Qi qi* writes that before entering the temple, the Empress would put on her *sheng*.

[2] *Hou Hanshu* (by Fang Hua 398-446), Beijing: Zhongguo shuju ed. 1965.

[3] In the *Shuowen jiezi*, Xu Shen (1st century AD) says that *sheng* is "that which holds the warp threads of the loom" (Duan Yucai (1735-1815), *Shuowen jiezi zhu*, Shanghai: Guji chubanshe, 1991, 262); in Anyang village people today still call the warping beam the *sheng*.

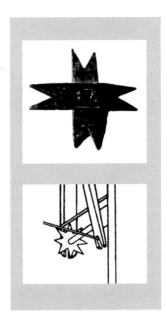

Figure 3 • Warping beam of the Dingqiao loom

[4] Chen Weiji 1984: *Zhongguo fangzhi kexue jishushi*, Beijing, Kexue chubanshe: 24-29.

Figure 4 • Xiwangmu (Queen Mother of the West) in Han dynasty art, Yinan, Shandong

sarcophagus of the Northern Qi dynasty, we see the Heavenly Daughter Weaving Girl descending to the mortal world with a *sheng* in her hand, indicating her profession (figure 5). All these examples show the symbolic meaning of the *sheng* and the importance of its role in the history of Chinese textile equipment.

Sheng made of gold or jade have been found in many Han and Jin tombs, but the shape of these *sheng* is much smaller and more intricate than the *sheng* in the portraits of the Queen Mother of the West in Han tomb art. We also find the eight-pointed star still extant in the textiles and embroideries of some minority peoples living in remote areas of China today (figure 6). However, these people can no longer identify the original function or meaning of the design.

If we take the *sheng* to be a standard component of the warping beam, we must also ask ourselves whether among the neolithic cultures of Daxi, Majiabang, Songze and Dawenkou, there was already in use a loom more advanced than the primitive waist loom. In other words, if there was a standard warping beam then there must first have been a frame loom on which to use it. According to specialist research, the primitive waist looms existing today among minority peoples have either no warping beam or only the crudest of warping beams, little more than wooden sticks. It was only after the frame loom had been developed that the warping beam became necessary and was then standardised.[4] It seems likely that 6,000 years ago the people of China who used stone tools went a stage beyond the waist loom and invented the frame loom.

On the Dawenkou culture painted pottery basins and *dou* found at Pi Xian Dadunzi, Zou xian Yedian and Taian, there are pairs of vertical lines between the eight-pointed star motifs (figures 1d-e). These probably represent the parting sticks (*fenjingban*), used to separate the upper and lower warp threads. Another motif is a narrow board with rounded ends and four holes, which may have had the same function, though we cannot be certain of this. However, on the rim of the two pottery basins there is a motif shaped like a shuttle. In weddings today in Shandong, the bride sends a gift to the bridegroom, including a pair of such objects about a foot long and made of flour: these are the symbol of women's work. So the motifs painted on neolithic

Figure 5 • Carving on the stone coffin, Northern Qi dynasty

Figure 6 • The eight-pointed motif found on textiles of the minorities living in China today

pottery are representations of important loom parts. In the neolithic period women were responsible for both pottery making and weaving, so it is not difficult to understand why such patterns appeared on these objects. The shuttle motif also appeared on the foot of a pot from the Songze site (figures 1c). Another pattern found on Majiabin pottery spindle whorl may also be related to the weaving process (figure 1b). From this evidence, we propose that the frame loom with a warping beam had appeared, and with a ratchet at either end could control the tension on the warp. The shuttle was also depicted.

Figure 7 • *Weaving scene on a Dian bronze container, Han period, Jinning Shizhaishan, Yunnan*

But what were the other components of this frame loom? And what was the frame like? In the neolithic cultures mentioned earlier we find no materials concerning such objects. Yet if we look at the site of Yuyao Hemudu, Zhejiang province, in the lower reaches of the Yangzi River, we find that some wooden weaving tools have been unearthed.[5] These have been dated to 7,000 years ago, and were part of a primitive waist or backstrap loom, similar in form to the waist looms depicted on the bronze cowrie shell holders discovered at Jinning, Shizhaishan, Yunnan province (figure 7), contemporary with the Han period.[6] However, it is my opinion that some objects from the same stratum at Hemudu show us that the construction of looms at that time was more advanced than experts have supposed.

The first report of the excavation mentions seven wooden tubes,[7] somewhat like hollow bamboo, each made of one piece of wood polished very smooth inside and out. Their function was not known. One tube (T17 4: 23) is 32.6 centimetres long, 9.4 centimetres in diameter and 0.7 centimetres in thickness of the wall. This thickness varies a little, and around the two ends were rings of rattan or bamboo (figure 8). By its length and shape I think it may be the tubular rear heddle *(tongshi houzong)* or the warp-dividing heddle *(fenjing tong)* of a loom. Also found were 18 wooden sticks, the longest of which measured 40 centimetres; further research will be necessary before we can know whether these were pattern sticks *(zonggan jiaobang)*.

More important than these were a number of pottery spindle whorls unearthed during the second excavation, on which was carved in intaglio the cross figure pattern where there is a hole in the central circle (figure 9). This I believe to be another standardised symbol of the ratchet of a warping beam, with its own tradition. If we compare it with the Han dynasty loom and the engraved stone sarcophagus of the Six Dynasties with the Weaving Girl holding her *sheng*, we can see the line of development connecting them. We can also draw the

[5] Zhejiang 1978 (Zhejiang sheng wenwu guanli weiyuanhui, Zhejiang sheng bowuguan): 'Hemudu yizhi diyi qi fajue baogao,' *Kaogu xuebao* 1978 (1): 39-94; Hemudu 1980.

[6] Chen Weiji 1984: 25-26.

[7] Zhejiang 1978: 62; Liu Jun and Yao Zhongyuan 1993, *Zhongguo Hemudu wenhua*. Hangzhou: Zhejiang renmin chubanshe: 116

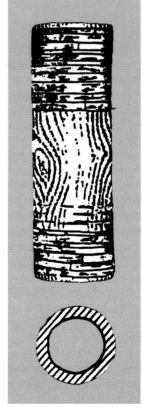

Figure 8 • *Wooden tube (possible warp-dividing heddle) found at the Hemudu site*

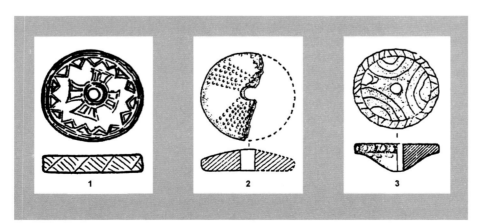

Figure 9 • *Pottery spindle whorls found at the Hemudu site*

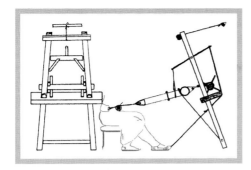

Figures 10-11 • Reconstruction of the loom of the Hemudu culture

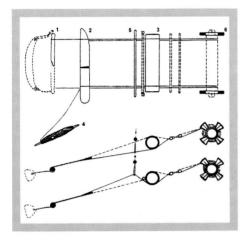

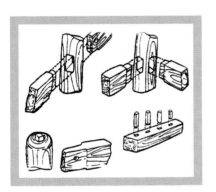

Figure 12 • Architectural timber joints of the Hemudu culture architecture

[8] Hemudu 1980 (Hemudu yichi kaogu dui), 'Hemudu yizhi di'er ci fajue de zhuyao shouhuo,' Wenwu 1980 (5): 1-15.

conclusion that a framed loom with its standardised warping beam already existed in the Hemudu culture.

Using existing materials and specialist research, I will try now to reconstruct the central part of the loom and the method of feeding the weft (*kaikou fangshi*). But the structure of the frame can only be conjectured with reference to the following known types of looms: *1)* the framed loom (*taijia zhiji*) of the Han dynasty (figure 2-1); and *2)* the vertical frame loom (*tijiashi zhiji*) in use today by the Miao people of Wenshan, Yunnan.

The second of these is the primary form of frame loom, using only a warping beam and a single direction heddle rod, controlling the lifting of the heddles: the frame stands vertically and does not extend horizontally. This type of loom is in the transitional stage from the seated waist loom to the frame loom. From my investigations, I would say that the central part of the looms from Hemudu and the Miao people of Wenshan are very similar.

If we look at the two archaeological cultures of Hemudu and Majiabang Songze we find the eight-pointed star patterns on the spindle whorl are again similar, with only a few disparities. Both patterns are in the shape of a cross, and their function is the same.

To sum up, we can now reconstruct the vertical frame loom of the Hemudu culture 7,000 years ago, which may have been much more developed than we suppose at present (figures 10,11). Certainly the level of technology at that time was high enough to produce such a loom. We can judge this from the construction of woodwork joints and from the timber architecture of the time (figure 12).

We can now draw the following conclusions:

1) That the frame loom existed along the lower reaches of the Yangzi and the southeast coast 7,000 years ago.

2) That the invention of the frame loom enabled the use of a warping beam to maintain tension on the warp threads, thus making possible the production of fine silks.

3) That the use of the frame allowed the weaver's feet to play a part in the weaving. This helped to develop the skill of weaving, and to lay the foundation for the later development of the loom and the production of high quality textiles.

4) That the appearance of the frame loom increased production capacity, which in turn may have influenced the way of collecting raw materials for textiles, *i e* gathering the fibres and their cultivation.

5) That the frame loom was probably the first machine made by prehistoric peoples. Its fundamental structure is the primary model of the modern loom.

The latter half of this century is generally agreed to be the golden age of Chinese archaeology. Field excavation during the last 30 years has brought forward a vast amount of new material from neolithic times, allowing us a deeper understanding of neolithic cultures throughout China. During that time, the wide areas along the Yangzi and Yellow rivers had already become regions of a predominantly agricultural economy, where settled life was stable with livestock farming and crafts (textiles and pottery) well developed even in remote areas.[8] Against this background there appeared the revolutionary breakthrough in textile technology from the primitive waist loom to the vertical frame loom.

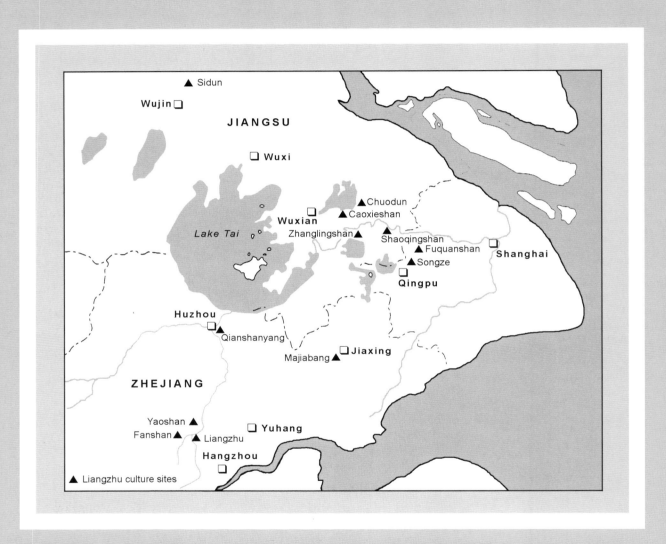

Map showing the distribution of Liangzhu culture sites in the Lake Tai area (after Yang Boda 1994)

FILIPPO SALVIATI
Decorated Pottery and Jade Carving of the Liangzhu Culture

T he discovery of the Liangzhu culture (c3300-2200 BC) is regarded as one of the most important achievements of Chinese archaeology. It has contributed to our knowledge of neolithic developments in South China and has offered new evidence for the study of the origins of Chinese civilisation.[1]

Initially known through finds at a limited number of sites in the 1930s,[2] the Liangzhu culture is now known to have occurred over quite a large area: hundreds of sites, many of which are located in the region of Taihu, have been identified and excavated in the Shanghai municipality, northern Zhejiang and southern Jiangsu provinces.

Liangzhu-type artefacts, especially jade objects, have been found in neolithic sites located in Jiangxi, Anhui, Hubei and Guangdong provinces, indicating a wide diffusion of this culture. One of the most characteristic marks of the Liangzhu culture is its highly developed jade industry, which has been the subject of the majority of Liangzhu studies. Liangzhu jades have not only offered abundant and fresh material for the study of the origin of the Chinese jade-carving tradition, but have also attracted interest by virtue of the images carved on them. These images provide some of the earliest evidence of the emergence of 'ritual art' in ancient China.[3] Jades, however, represent only one aspect of the artistic tradition of Liangzhu, the other being decorated pottery vessels.

This paper investigates the close relationships between the decorative motifs found on pottery and jade in the available archaeological material of the Liangzhu culture.

Environment and Technology

Lake Tai is located in southern Jiangsu province, in an area between 30° to 32°30' north latitude (which includes the Hangzhou bay in the south and the Yangzi River delta further north) and 119° to 122° east longitude. The area is principally delimited by rivers, the Yangzi to the north and the Qiantang in the south, and by the East China sea to the east. The reliefs bordering the Lake Tai area are Mt Maoshan (a possible source of raw jade in prehistoric times) to the west and the Tianmushan range to the southwest, both guaranteeing inland access through valleys and passes.

The Taihu region is a large span of water in a huge flatland dotted with numerous other smaller lakes and crisscrossed by streams and canals, creating a communication network of waterways. The high rainfall, the risk of floods, the

[1] Mou Yongkang and Wu Ruzuo 1993: 'Shuidao, cansi he yuqi. Zhonghua wenming qiyuan de ruogan wenti,' *Kaogu* 1993(6): 543-453.

[2] Sun Zhixin 1993: 'The Liangzhu Culture: Its Discovery and Its Jades,' in *Early China* 18: 1-40, for a detailed account of the discovery of the Liangzhu culture.

[3] Wu Hung 1990: 'A Great Beginning. Ancient Chinese Jades and the Origin of Ritual Art,' introduction to the catalogue *Chinese Jades from the Mu-Fei Collection*, London, Bluett & Sons Ltd. —1995: *Monumentality in Early Chinese Art and Archaeology*, California: Stanford University Press: 24-44.

humid and often marshy environment imposed on the local neolithic communities the necessity of either of settling on slightly elevated sites or of providing above-ground foundations for their dwellings. Ample evidence in this sense is provided by the copious remains of long wooden houses excavated at the Hemudu site (Yuyao, Zhejiang), the most ancient neolithic culture discovered in the southern portion of the Taihu area, dated to c5000-3600 BC.[4]

The neolithic cultures which flourished in the Taihu area may be regarded as forming a 'cultural complex' with characteristics and peculiarities differentiating it from those in other parts of neolithic China. In the Taihu area specific features have been elaborated and transmitted from one culture to the other — from Hemudu to Liangzhu — over a time span of about two and a half millennia.

Besides the earliest attested evidence of rice cultivation in the whole of East Asia, the importance of the Hemudu site is attested also by a wooden lacquered cup and by wooden elements thought to have been parts of a loom.[5] The latter point to an advanced level in textile manufacturing, and some argue that silk was known to Hemudu, as indirectly attested by the motif of two 'silkworms' incised on a bone bowl.[6] So far, however, these findings, which represent the advanced technological level reached by the Hemudu culture, are primarily confined to the type-site: thus the knowledge we have of this important neolithic culture is still rather hazy.

Finds of simple ornaments in the shape of bold 'earrings,' plain rings and rudimentary *huang* pendants, usually referred to as 'jade' but actually made of other, similar-looking stones,[7] testify to the beginnings of a hardstone-working tradition in this area of neolithic China. The Hemudu pseudo-jades are, moreover, roughly contemporary with the most ancient artefacts in nephrite discovered to date anywhere in the world, those found in the Chahai site (Fuxin, Liaoning) in northeast China. However, at the moment, there is no direct evidence of any influence in either direction between the Taihu area and northeast China.[8] It is thus plausible to assert, considering the available archaeological evidence, that Chahai and Hemudu represent two of the oldest areas in China where independent jade-working traditions were initiated and developed in the following centuries.

Roughly contemporary to Hemudu is the Majiabang culture (c5000-4000 BC), whose type site is located south of Lake Tai and north of Hangzhou Bay. Majiabang shares some characteristics with Hemudu, such as certain pottery types, rice cultivation, techniques of wood construction and pseudo-jade working tradition, with a slight increase in the repertory of shapes now including, in addition to *jue* earrings and *huang* pendants, also *guan* beads and *zhuo* bracelets, found in the Majiabang graves of the eighth and ninth strata of the Caoxieshan site in Wu xian, Jiangsu province.[9]

The cultural sequence in the Taihu area continues with the Songze culture (c4000-3000 BC), cultural deposits of which have been found in the layers of the Caoxieshan site just above Majiabang ones, the same cultural succession having already been attested at the Songze site itself (Qingpu, Shanghai), where a large cemetery was excavated during two seasons in 1960-1961 and 1974-1976.[10] Despite differences, such as ceramic types or the orientation of the bodies in the graves — head towards the north in the Majiabang burials and towards the south in Songze ones — archaeologists are inclined to regard the Majiabang culture as an initial stage from which Songze developed.[11]

A remarkable increase in sophistication, however, is clearly attested amongst artefacts of the Songze culture: pottery shapes are extremely varied and present also a surprising range of decorative motifs, from cutout geometric patterns on the bases of *dou* stands and shallow basins, to painted and engraved decoration including complex, interlaced designs. The jade-working tradition increases as well: Songze jades have been proved to be tremolite nephrite[12] and the simple objects yielded by Songze sites — *jue* slit rings, earrings, *huang* pendants — show an unprecedented degree of refinement, often having been polished to a high sheen. However, the climax in the jade-carving tradition was reached with the Liangzhu culture which, following Songze, concludes the neolithic sequence in the Taihu area.

[4] Zhejiang 1976 (Zhejiang sheng wenwu guanli weiyuanhui): 'Hemudu faxian yuanshi shehui zhongyao yizhi,' *Wenwu* 1976(8): 6-12. Zhejiang 1978 (Zhejiang sheng wenwu guanli weiyuanhui): 'Hemudu yizhi diyiqi fajue jianbao,' *Kaogu xuebao* 1978(1): 39-94.

[5] See Wang Xu's paper in this volume.

[6] Zhou Kuangming 1982: 'Yangcan qiyuan wenti de yanjiu,' *Nongye kaogu* 1982 (1): 133-138.

[7] Wen Guang and Jing Zhichun 1992: 'Chinese neolithic jade: a preliminary geo-archaeological study,' *Geoarchaeology, An International Journal* 7/3: 251-275.

[8] Although Jessica Rawson advances the hypothesis that "...perhaps under influence from the northeast, jade working began on a small scale in the southeast, or, more specifically, *jue* (slit rings) probably spread from the north to the southeast of Zhejiang province, where they are found at Hemudu." (Rawson, Jessica 1995: *Chinese Jade: From the Neolithic to the Qing*, London: British Museum Press: 28 and 119). In another context, Rawson speaks of the Liangzhu people as having "inherited skills and traditions from the Dawenkou and Hongshan peoples" (Rawson, Jessica 1992 ed: *The British Museum Book of Chinese art*, London: British Museum Press: 51), a theory which remains, at the moment, pure speculation. Still Rawson finds "rather surprisingly [that] jade working arose not in the centre of China in the Yellow River area, but in the far northeast, in areas we know today as Inner Mongolia and Liaoning province." (Rawson, Jessica 1995: *Chinese Jade: From the Neolithic to the Qing*, London: British Museum Press: 111), which demonstrates how hard to die is the old assumption that "North comes first."

[9] Nanjing 1980 (Nanjing Bowuyuanl): 'Jiangsu Wuxian Caoxieshan yizhi,' *Wenwu ziliao congkan* 1980(3): 1-24.

[10] Huang Xuanpei et al 1987: *Songze: xinshiqi shidai yizhi fajue baogao*, Beijing: Wenwu chubanshe, 1987.

[11] Chang, K C 1986: *The archaeology of ancient China* (4th ed), New Haven and London: Yale University Press, 203-204.

[12] Wen Guang and Jing Zhichun 1992: 260-261.

[13] Discussed in Huang Xuanpei, Song Jian and Sun Weichang 1992: *Shanghai bowuguan cang Liangzhu wenhua zhenpin zhan*, Hong Kong, 80-81. See also Jiangsu 1963: 'Jiangsu Wujing Meiyan xinshiqi shidai yizhi,' *Kaogu* 1963(6): 308-310; Nanjing 1984: 'Jiangsu Kunshan Chuodun yizhi de diaocha yu fajue,' *Wenwu* 1984(2): 8-9.

[14] Huang Xuanpei, Song Jian and Sun Weichang 1992: 78-79.

[15] Changshu 1984: 'Jiangsu Changshu Liangzhu wenhua yizhi,' *Wenwu* 1984(2): 14.

[16] Nanjing 1982: 'Jiangsu Yuecheng yizhi de fajue,' *Kaogu* 1982(5): 467.

[17] Longnan 1988: 'Jiangsu Wujian Meiyan Longnan yizhi 1987 nian fajue jiyao,' *Dongnan Wenhua*. 1988(5): 49-53; Suzhou 1990: 'Jiangsu Wujian Longnan xinshiqi shidai cunluo yizhi diyi, erci fajue jianbao,' *Wenwu* 1986(10): 1-27.

[18] Qian Gonglin 1990: 'Wujian Longnan yizhi fangzhi chutan,' *Wenwu* 1990(7): 28-31.

[19] Chang, K C 1986: *The archaeology of ancient China* (4th ed), New Haven and London: Yale University Press, 254.

[20] Nanjing 1982: 471-472.

[21] Jiangsu 1963: 'Jiangsu Wujing Meiyan xinshiqi shidai yizhi,' *Kaogu* 1963(6): 311.

[22] Zhejiang 1988: 'Zhejiang Yuhang Fanshan Liangzhu mudi faxian jianbao,' *Wenwu* 1988(1): 30

[23] Huang Xuanpei, Song Jian and Sun Weichang 1992: 68-69.

[24] Changshu 1984: 'Jangsu Changshu Liangzhu wenhua yizhi,' *Wenwu* 1984(2): 14; Nanjing 1982: 467.

[25] In the Taihu area, wooden wells are firstly attested amongst the finds of the Hemudu culture (Zhejiang *et al* 1978), and they remained in use during the following Majiabang and Songze cultures. For faunae or botanical species see Zhejiang 1992: 218-219; for a survey of well structures in neolithic China, see Zhang Minghua 1990: 'Zhongguo xinshiqi shidai shuijing de kaogu faxian,' *Shanghai bowuguan jikan* 5.

[26] Huang Xuanpei, Song Jian and Sun Weichang 1992: 29-30; 38.

[27] Zhejiang 1988b: 'Yuhang Yaoshan Liangzhu wenhua jitan yizhi faxian jianbao,' *Wenwu* 1988(1): 38.

[28] Zhejiang 1988a: 'Zhejiang Yuhang Fanshan Liangzhu mudi faxian jianbao,' *Wenwu* 1988(1): 30; Wang Mingda 1997: 'A Study of the Jades of the Liangzhu Culture: the Functions of Liangzhu Jades, based on Evidence from Tomb No 20 at Fanshan' in R Scott ed. *Chinese Jade*, London 1997, 39.

In Liangzhu sites, rice remains have been found at Qianshanyang and stone weeding tools related to rice cultivation have been unearthed at Tinglin, Jinshan county, Shanghai.[13] Amongst other agricultural tools excavated so far, the stone ploughshares used to till the fields are of great interest, since Liangzhu was one of the first cultures to make use of such tools. Often provided with holes to secure them onto a wooden ploughboard, they have a triangular shape, with two bevelled blade edges, to help break the soil for cultivation.[14] Stone sickles like those found at Changshu[15] and Yuecheng[16] were used in harvesting.

The luxuriant forests that once covered the area around Lake Tai provided the main source for building material, a source exploited since the Hemudu culture as documented by finds of numerous dwellings at the site itself. Very few habitation sites of the Liangzhu culture have been investigated, a limitation probably due to the fact that many modern villages or small towns, including Liangzhu, are built over prehistoric sites, thus making them almost inaccessible to modern archaeologists. An early Liangzhu site which has yielded a fair amount of house remains is Longnan.[17] Here the houses are mostly large shelters, with a lowered floor and simple roofs touching the ground.[18]

The abundance of water in the Taihu area favoured navigation through the many rivers and canals. Rafts and simple boats, remains of which are attested in sites of the Liangzhu culture,[19] were used for such a purpose. Communication by sea and navigation along the coast were probably quite common as well, as indirectly attested by objects of Liangzhu type found far away from the Taihu area and in sites along the coast. Ample archaeological evidence testifies to fish in the diet of the Liangzhu people, as attested by net weights — such as those unearthed at Yuecheng[20] — and fishing hooks or small harpoons.[21] The shark's tooth found in one of the graves of the Fanshan cemetery (Yuhang, Hangzhou)[22] is another clue pointing to connections with the sea, further strengthened by the Liangzhu remains found on Zhoushan Island just off Hangzhou Bay.

Wood was cut and worked by means of quite sophisticated tools which have been found in a number of Liangzhu sites. Stepped stone adzes have been excavated at Fuquanshan, although since these do not bear signs of use, archaeologists think they must have been ritual objects.[23] Similar tools from other sites were hafted onto a wooden handle and used for woodworking, including different kinds of stepped stone adzes, chisels and knives with holes.[24]

Other important remains testify to other uses for wood, such as that of using it to line wells, as in the case of the well unearthed at Xiyangdian (Qingpu, Shanghai)[25] or at Taishidian (Kunshan, Jiangsu).[26] Wood was also used to make coffins for the most important burials. The coffins were made out of a large trunk, cut into two halves which were then hollowed out to provide space for the corpse. Evidence of such coffins has come to light in quite a number of sites, as in Fanshan, Yaoshan (Yuhang, Zhejiang) and Fuquanshan. For the most elaborate burials there is evidence of the use of two coffins, which were probably also lacquered. The use of lacquer is already attested among neolithic cultures of the Taihu area, in the Hemudu culture. Liangzhu continued this craft, as documented by remains of lacquered objects found in some of the most richly furnished graves, such as at Yaoshan M9, which has yielded a lacquered cup with parts inlaid with tiny pieces of jade.[27] However, lacquer was predominantly used to protect the wooden coffins used in the most important burials, and was hence probably linked to other materials intended as symbols of social status.

In the Taihu area, ivory obtained from mammals was already worked in the Hemudu culture. This tradition continued with the Liangzhu culture as testified by a limited number of artefacts, such as small objects in ivory found in tombs of the Fanshan cemetery.[28] By far the most important object in ivory so far discovered is a plaque broken in two pieces found in tomb No 6 of the Fuquanshan site (T4 M6:36a and 36b), probably used to cover or protect the wooden handle of an axe. One of the two fragments is partly engraved with a complex *shoumian* animal mask design.

The earliest remains to date of silk fabrics discovered in China have been found in sites of the Liangzhu culture, namely Qianshanyang and Caoxieshan.

The first site yielded, during the 1958 excavation, some silk threads, a small fragment of woven silk and what has been described as a "round silk belt, spun together with 10 strands of silk, each containing three threads,"[29] all found inside what remained of a basket. Though the evidence is still scanty, it seems likely that the Liangzhu people knew how to produce silk.[30]

Pottery vessels of the Liangzhu culture are usually very refined in terms of shapes and manufacture, and within them it is also possible to distinguish between vessels of more daily use (generally red and grey wares) and ceramic types destined for the élite, if not specifically made for burial or ritual requirements.[31] Some of the finest black wares were constructed on the wheel and polished to a high lustre, and may antedate by a millennium the so-called 'eggshell' wares typical of the Shandong area.[32] In shape, some of the Liangzhu vessels share some characteristics with the pottery of the previous Songze culture, as well as with that of contemporaneous neolithic cultures of East China, particularly Dawenkou and Longshan.

For the most part, pottery vessels of the Liangzhu culture are undecorated. An exception to this rule is represented by a limited number of specimens ornamented with whirling geometric motifs or with bird patterns. Although a few sherds with incised patterns of stylised birds have been recovered from sites located to the south and southwest of Lake Tai, the majority of intact vessels with complex and refined decoration come from sites east of Lake Tai, namely Caoxieshan, Zhanglingshan and Fuquanshan. The concentration of pottery vessels exhibiting incised motifs at this cluster of sites indicates a possible local practice of making use of decorated vessels, a custom already attested in the Songze culture remains found in the same area, hinting at a long tradition of decorated pottery vessels established before the Liangzhu culture.

Typological Analysis of the Motifs on Jade and Pottery

All major decorative motifs of the Liangzhu culture — 'mask' motifs, images of birds, geometric and abstract patterns — occur both on pottery and jade, with obvious differences and peculiarities but pointing to a strong uniformity in the Liangzhu artistic tradition. Liangzhu iconography is characterised by a limited number of standardised images which can occur singly or combined together according to fixed schemes. The following typological analysis attempts to provide a classification of the motifs.

The *sanjiao* 'Three-pointed' Motif

To illustrate the homogeneity of decoration in both Liangzhu pottery and jade, I will at first take into consideration the motif conventionally called by Chinese scholars *sanjiao* or 'triangular,' which I will refer to as the 'three-pointed' motif. Since a number of the pottery vessels presenting this motif antedate the full development of the Liangzhu jade-carving tradition, it is possible to assume that the decoration of pottery was to a certain extent influential in the latter. This is evident in the way the three-pointed motif has been rendered on the two different media, pottery and jade. Furthermore, this comparison seems to raise the possibility that certain features of the *shoumian* carved on the jades may have evolved from originally abstract motifs used to decorate the pottery vessels.

The three-pointed motif basically consists of a triangular shape whose three extremities can be elongated, while the central hole from which they radiate can be either narrowed or enlarged. The three-pointed motif can appear alone or serially repeated on the surface to be decorated, but it is also frequently found in association with a circle or dot, usually placed between a pair of three-pointed motifs.

In pottery, the motif is almost exclusively found on the feet or pedestals of *dou* stands, *gui* vessels, *guan* jars and *pan* basins. Though it can be incised on the surface, it is usually rendered through cutout perforations, a decorative technique extensively used in many neolithic cultures of East China (Longshan, Dawenkou) and the southeast.[33]

[29] Huang Xuanpei, Song Jian and Sun Weichang 1992: 30.

[30] Zhou Kuangming 1982 'Yangcan qiyuan wenti de yanjiu,' *Nongye kaogu* 1982 (1); Mou Yongkang and Wu Ruzuo 1993: 'Shuidao, cansi he yuqi. Zhonghua wenming qiyuan de ruogan wenti,' *Kaogu* 1993(6): 545-548.

[31] Jiang Yueping 1993: 'Liqi 'ding' de yuanyuan tansuo,' *Nanfang wenwu* 1993(2): 102-105.

[32] Barnes, Gina 1993: *China, Korea and Japan: The Rise of Civilisation in East Asia*, London: Thames and Hudson, 112.

[33] The area of distribution of such a motif is actually quite large and includes also neolithic cultures located further inland, along the middle reaches of the Yangzi River and along the east coast. Two examples are represented by a pottery stand with cutout perforations of triangles and circles found at Zouxian Yedian (M7:45), Shandong, and by a tall, cylindrical support found in T109:2(1) at the Jingshan Qujialing site, Hubei province. These finds are congruous with the hypothesis of contacts between Liangzhu and other cultures located along the East Coast or further inland, along the middle reaches of the Yangzi River: examples from neolithic sites of this latter region are reproduced and discussed by Gao Menghe 1992: 'Changjiang zhongyou de shiqian qizuo jiqi xiangguan wenti,' *Jianghan kaogu* 1992(3).

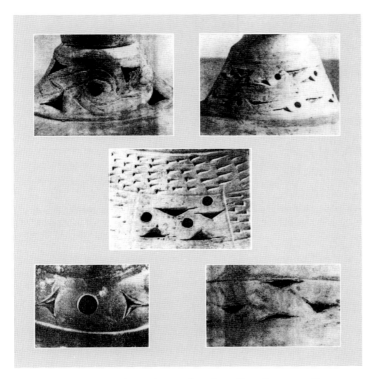

Figure 1 • Examples of the 'three-pointed' motif on Songze pottery vessels. (After Huang Xuanpei et al 1987, plates LXVIII, top and centre, and LXVII, bottom)

The area of distribution of such a motif is actually quite large and includes also neolithic cultures located further inland, along the middle reaches of the Yangzi river and along the East Coast. Two examples are represented by a pottery stand with cutout perforations of triangles and circles found at Zouxian Yedian (M7:45), Shandong, and by a tall, cylindrical support found in T109:2(1) at the Jingshan Qujialing site, Hubei province.[34] These finds are congruous with the hypothesis of contacts between Liangzhu and other cultures located along the East Coast or further inland, along the middle reaches of the Yangzi River.[35]

In the Taihu area the three-pointed motif makes its first significant appearance on pottery vessels of the Songze culture (figure 1), such as on the foot of some *dou*-stands excavated from the middle layer of the Songze site dated to about 3800 BC.[36] A number of *dou* vessels from the lowest, Songze culture layer of the Zhanglingshan site have their feet decorated with the 'three-pointed' motif.[37]

Slightly later than Songze is the Longnan site (Wujiang, Jiangsu). The motif, in a stylised version and repeated several times alternated with dots, appears on a vessel belonging to the first period (5360±92 BP),[38] while a low *dou* of the second period (5135±92 BP) has the motif of triangles and dots cut out all around its foot[39].

Some more and interesting examples are provided by objects excavated in the Caoxieshan site. A curious, oblong vessel resting on four feet has its upper border hollowed out, with triangular perforations arranged on either side of circular perforations (figure 2). It was found in tomb M8:3 in the sixth stratum which has yielded 89 tombs attributed to the Songze culture. Other objects with the three-pointed motif come from the same layer. Noteworthy amongst them is a flattened *dou*, which shows a variation in the treatment of the motif cut out in the foot of the vessel: the slanting triangular forms are separated by a row of three parallel, vertical lines.[40]

A vessel found in the richly-furnished Liangzhu tomb located in the second layer of the Caoxieshan site provides another instance of the parallels occurring in the decoration of pottery and jade artefacts. The vessel is a lidded *ding* (figure 3, left) resting on three flattened legs decorated with perforations in the shape of dots alternated with comma-like motifs:[41] the same pattern occurs on a jade finial found in a tomb in the third layer of the eastern mound at the Zhanglingshan site and used to decorate the top part of the wooden handle of an axe (figure 3, right).[42]

The jade objects found in the two Liangzhu tombs of the Caoxieshan and Zhanglingshan sites show that the working of jade had already attained a degree of sophistication — in terms of technique as well as in terms of

[34] The examples cited are reproduced in Gao Menghe 1993: 'Shiqian qizuo chutan,' *Kaogu* 1993(1): 42-51.

[35] For examples from neolithic sites of this latter region, see Gao Menghe 1992: Changjiang zhongyou de shiqian qizuo jiqi xiangguan wenti,' *Jianghan kaogu* 1992(3).

[36] Huang Xuanpei and Zhang Minghua 1980: 'Qingpuxian Songze yizhi dierci fajue,' *Kaogu xuebao* 1980(1): figures 9:5 (from M85:8), 10 (from M69:7), 14 (from M59:8).

[37] Huang Xuanpei et al 1987: plates LXVII and LXVIII.

[38] Qian Gonglin 1990: 'Wujian Longnan yizhi fangzhi chutan,' *Wenwu* 1990(7): figure 8:2.

[39] See Qian Gonglin 1990: figures 21/6 and 18/1, 2. Also the *gui* in figure 16:4 *(ibid)* has its foot decorated with the same motif. Further examples of the motif on vessels from the same site are illustrated in Longnan 1988: 'Jiangsu Wujian Meiyan Longnan yizhi 1987 nian fajue jiyao,' *Dongnan wenhua.* 1988(5): figures 5:4 and 5:6.

[40] Nanjing 1980 plate 1/3 (M87:9). See also *ibid*: Figure 72/1-6.

[41] Nanjing 1980 figure 69/1.

[42] Nanjing 1986(10): 'Jiangsu Wuxian Zhanglingshan dong shan yizhi,' *Wenwu* 1986(10): figure 9/7 (M1:15).

Figure 2 • Pottery vessel with cutout decoration from tomb M8:3 of the Caoxieshan site. Length, 21 cm; height, 10.5 cm (after Nanjing bowuyuan 1980, plate 2, No 1)

forms — unknown in the preceding cultural phases of the Songze and Longnan sites. The latter have yielded jade objects, but they are small, undecorated ornaments — semilunar pendants, rings, beads — which anticipate some of the later Liangzhu shapes but cannot compete with them on the technical level. The only perforations they have are small holes of varying size which played a utilitarian function, for suspension of the objects themselves. On the other hand, the perforations on the top part of the jade finial (itself a completely new form in the jade repertory) from the tomb at Zhangling-shan are more elaborate and essentially decorative: they show, in my opinion, that at a certain stage in the evolution of carving techniques, Liangzhu jade craftsmen had started to carve openwork, and the cutout perforations on pottery vessels were transferred to jade objects.

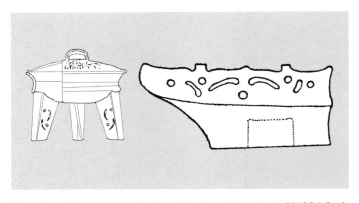

Figure 3 • **Left** drawing of pottery ding tripod from tomb M198.I.2 of the Caoxiehan site. Height, c42 cm; diameter, c43 cm. **Right** drawing of jade axe finial from tomb M1:15 of the Zhanglingshan site. Height, 4.4 cm; upper length, 9.1 cm (after Nanjing bowuyuan 1980, figure 9:1 and Nanjing bowuyuan 1986, figure 9:7)

On jade objects, the first occurrence of the three-pointed motif can be seen in a jade *xi* pendant found in a tomb from the upper layer of the western mound of the Zhanglingshan site (figure 4).[43] The three-pointed motif is visible on the right and left sides of the object, when seen frontally and in a horizontal position. Three oblong deep cuts radiate from the two holes, and the motif is completed by the addition of a central dot in the form of an incomplete perforation, carved from both sides of the object, so that the decoration matches that already seen on pottery vessels.

Further examples of the application of the three-pointed motif on jades can be seen on objects excavated in the two Liangzhu cemeteries of Fanshan and Yaoshan. Three objects in particular are pivotal in our discussion: they are two jade *huang*-pendants from Fanshan (M16:3) and Yaoshan (M11:84), and a badge from Yaoshan.

All three objects show a treatment of the motif extremely close to that seen on the jade *xi* from Zhanglingshan, from stylistic as well as technical points of view. In the Yaoshan pendant (M11:84; figure 5, top), the motif appears at the top and on the left and right sides, with a small hole in between, exactly in the same way as it had been used in the previous centuries to decorate the feet of the pottery vessels. In the *huang*-pendant from Fanshan (M16:3; figure 5, bottom left), seven 'three-pointed motifs' have been used to frame three large, round openings.

Both pendants from Fanshan and Yaoshan show the first significant departure from the purely geometric nature of the motif. In fact, in both jades the perforations, in conjunction with lightly incised lines around some of the holes, conjure up what seems to be the eyes of an enigmatic face: the impression is further enhanced by the symmetrical placement of all the elements. The badge from Yaoshan (M7:55; figure 5, bottom right) exemplifies the process: by eliminating all 'redundant' elements, only a pair of three-pointed motifs with a

[43] M5:16. Though of difficult interpretation given its highly abstract outline, the pendant — on the basis of its possible resemblance with a find from the Zhanglingshan site — has been interpreted as representing "a human figure wearing a high headdress" (Rawson, Jessica 1995: *Chinese Jade: From the Neolithic to the Qing*, London: British Museum Press, 219, figure 3).

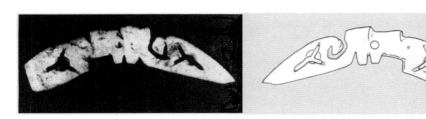

Figure 4 • Photograph and drawing of a jade xi from tomb M15:16 of the Zhanglingshan site. Length, 6 cm; height, 1.2 cm (after Zhejiang sheng et al 1989 plate 203 (left) and Rawson 1995, 219 figure 3 (right)

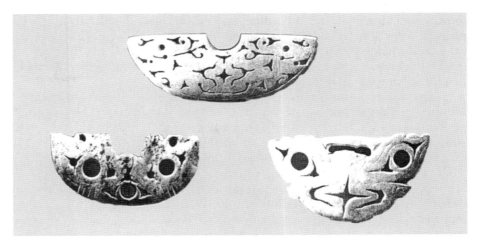

Figure 5 • Three jades with cutout decoration. **Top** pendant from tomb M11:84 of the Yaoshan site. Height 4.8 cm, length 12.7 cm. **Bottom left** pendant from tomb M16:3 of the Fanshan site. Height 3.7 cm, length 7.5 cm. **Bottom right** pendant from tomb M7:55 of the Yaoshan site. Height: 3.9 cm, length 7.1 cm (after Zhejiang sheng et al 1989, plates 159, 160 and 220 respectively)

hole in between have been left and placed symmetrically at both extremities of the jade. The final effect is that of a pair of eyes which, together with a few other perforations, give the impression one is looking at a face seen frontally. These jades may thus represent a point of confluence between two decorative traditions of pottery and jades.

On the basis of the available evidence, it seems that the three-pointed motif, apparently purely ornamental when used to decorate pottery vessels, became representational when transferred to jades. It is difficult to say if this result was accidental, but it could be that at a certain stage some motifs of the pottery tradition were transferred to jade objects and used there to stress some specific features and details — the eyes — of the *shoumian* which had entered the artistic vocabulary as a new motif since the Zhanglingshan period.

It is also relevant to observe that the three-pointed motif continues to be used in the background decoration of many of the most elaborate jades found in the Fanshan and Yaoshan sites, a fact which shows how conservative was the tradition but also how flexible it was in changing the medium on which the motifs were expressed.

The *shoumian* and its Variations

The principal motif used to decorate jade artefacts of the Liangzhu culture is certainly represented by the 'animal mask,' which occurs in a limited number of variations also on pottery and, in one instance, as we shall see, on ivory.

In the literature in the Chinese language, the term most frequently used to describe this particular motif and its variants is *shoumian*. As pointed out by Li Xueqin,[44] this term (which had already been used by Chen Mengjia in the 1950s as a substitute for *taotie*), although roughly equivalent to the English 'animal mask,' has a more specific meaning, *shou* signifying 'wild animal or beast.'

Since nowadays scholars agree that the two principal variations of the 'mask' motif carved on the Liangzhu jades are recognizable as possessing, respectively, animal and human characteristics, the indiscriminate use of the term *shoumian* could give rise to some confusion unless these variations are distinguished.

In the following discussion I will retain the term *shoumian* when referring, in general, to the 'animal mask' motif, but I will adopt also the specifications 'theriomorphic' and 'anthropomorphic' when using the term with specific reference to one or another kind of mask.

[44] Li Xueqin 1992: 'Liangzhu jades and the Shang dynasty *taotie* motif' in Whitfield ed, *The Problem of Meaning in Early Chinese Ritual Bronzes* 1993, 56.

The presence of different types of masks on jade *cong* had already been recognised by some scholars in the past, at a time when the present archaeological data were not available and the Liangzhu jades — without being known or labelled as such — were known only from specimens housed in public and private collections.

C T Loo, for example, in describing a *cong* reproduced in the publication accompanying an exhibition of jades held in 1950 at the Norton Gallery of Art, noticed that the ornamentation was the same "in each field: two bands, two engraved eye-circles and a shorter band below."[45] Another *cong* reproduced in the same book is distinctively described as having its "corner panels containing two styles of mask."[46]

In 1952 Alfred Salmony went even further, by detecting that one of the "two styles of mask" possessed anthropomorphic features and that the same masks helped in establishing the correct orientation of the *cong*, which, as we now know, have quite often been photographed — or positioned in museum cases — upside down. This is the description offered by Salmony of a *cong* in the Edward and Louise B Sonnenschein collection:

> Beginning from above, the sequence of (decoration) is: two full-length crossing bands in relief, two incised circles, one short crossing bar in relief. When one compares the earth symbols of the collection with more clearly delineated examples (Salmony, *Carved Jade*, plate XXVIII.1), it becomes quite obvious that these three patterns together constitute an anthropomorphic face with forehead, eyes and mouth. This reading may also be confirmed by comparison with similarly decorated objects of the same period, such as plaques, rings, and three-lobed hangings? The identification of the anthropomorphic faces has some bearing on the ritual position of the earth symbol. Since the decor motif must be recognisable, *the object cannot be shown or reproduced as a truncated but as an inverted pyramid.*[47]

Jades found in controlled excavations have confirmed Salmony's interpretations while providing modern scholars with a large body of material, on which stylistic analysis and classifications of the various types of *shoumian* have been based. Some recent but pioneering studies have been made by Wang Wei, Che Guangjin and Liu Bin, who have classified the different types of *cong*.

Wang Wei has proposed to divide the *cong* into two types, A and B, according to their proportions.[48] Those whose width exceeds their height belong to Type A, those whose height exceeds their width to Type B. Variations in the ways of rendering the *shoumian* carved on the objects lead to five subgroups in Type A and three in Type B.

Che Guangjin instead focused primarily on the types of *shoumian* carved on jades of the Liangzhu culture. He points to three main motifs:

   a) the *shoumian* or theriomorphic mask;
   b) the compound man-and-animal image;
   c) the anthropomorphic motif. Each of the these comprises two subgroups.[49]

A similar classification has been proposed by Liu Bin, whose analysis is however somewhat less sophisticated than those of the other two scholars. He detects three main categories of *shoumian* motif:

   a) the complex image formed by the combination of human and animal elements;
   b) the *shoumian* motif carved in its complex form — the theriomorphic variant — and
   c) the simplified or anthropomorphic version of the *shoumian*, serially repeated along the corners of the tallest types of *cong*.[50]

The three authors agree in recognizing the presence of different types of *shoumian*, which can be basically reduced to the two main types mentioned above, the theriomorphic mask or mask with animal characteristics and the other with anthropomorphic features.

[45] Loo, C T 1950: *An exhibition of Chinese Archaic Jades. Arranged for the Norton Gallery of Art, West Palm Beach, Florida*, Norton Gallery of Art, plate XXXIV.4.

[46] *Ibid*. Plate XXXV.2.

[47] Salmony, Alfred 1952: *Archaic Chinese Jades from the Edward and Louise B. Sonnenschein Collection*, Chicago: The Art Institute of Chicago, plates XXVIII, 1; XXVIII, 2-6; LIX. For further notes on Salmony's perceptions, see Pearlstein, Elinor 1993: 'Salmony's Catalogue of the Sonnenschein Jades in the Light of Recent Finds,' *Orientations*, 24-6 (June 1993): 48-58.

[48] Wang Wei 1986: 'Liangzhu wenhua yucong chuyi,' *Kaogu* 1986(11): 1009.

[49] Che Guangjin 1987: 'Liangzhu wenhua yucong wenshi tanxi,' *Dongnan Wenhua* 1987(3): 19-21

[50] Liu Bin 1990: 'Liangzhu wenhua yucong chutan,' *Wenwu* 1990 (2): 30-33.

In the light of archaeological discoveries, the earliest examples to date of the *shoumian* of the theriomorphic type are to be found on two objects recovered from sites located in Wu xian, Jiangsu. The first object is a jade *zhuo* bracelet excavated in 1977 from tomb M4:02 of the Zhanglingshan site and the second is a pottery jar recovered from a well located in the proximity of Lake Denghu.[51]

The bracelet (figure 6) has four theriomorphic masks carved within well-defined square registers on its exterior surface and equally spaced between them. The face is characterised by round eyes made up of two concentric circles, large 'eyebrows' and a mouth with four pointed teeth, all elements recurring in later, more refined examples of the *shoumian* motif.

Figure 6 • *Jade bracelet from Zhanglingshan tomb M4:02. Height, 3.5 cm; diameter 10 cm (after Zhejiang sheng et al 1989, plate 12)*

The jar (figure 7), found together with other pottery vessels dated by archaeologists to the early phase (Zhanglingshan type) of the Liangzhu culture, is 9.8 centimetres high and the diameter of its mouth is 8.5 centimetres. The belly of the jar is richly decorated with a variety of engraved motifs, including birds, butterflies, snakes, chickens and others, according to the description given by excavators of the well.[52] The motif indicated in the report as representing a 'cat' — a sort of feline face seen frontally, provided with slanting eyes and fang-like appendages — is the *shoumian* referred to above, and it is believed by some scholars[53] to be the antecedent of the *shoumian* motif seen on later Liangzhu jades.

Another remark can be made on the three-pointed motif analysed before. Amongst the Liangzhu pottery vessels found in the Lake Denghu well together with the pottery jar decorated with the *shoumian*, a *pan*-basin covered with black slip has its rim decorated with elongated forms of the three-pointed motif, in two instances encircling two concentric, bold rings taking the aspect of eye-like patterns.[54] The treatment of the motif and the particular visual effect it provokes accord well with the archaeological material from the Zhanglingshan site, a fact which seems to corroborate the dating of the material found in the well.

The Anthropomorphic Mask: This highly stylised mask is generally found carved on the tiers marking the outer perimeter of many *cong* (figure 8, left). The mask is characterised by round eyes which, particularly on the more elaborate objects belonging to the Late Liangzhu phase, are inscribed in an elliptical form provided with two opposite, pointed edges. A central, horizontal bar in relief set below and between the eyes suggests the nose, and it can be

[51] Nanjing 1985 (Nanjing bowuyuan et al): 'Jiangsu Wuxian Denghujing cun de fajue,' *Wenwu ziliao congkan* 9: 1-22.

[52] Nanjing 1985: 6.

[53] An Zhimin 1988: 'Guanyu Liangzhu wenhua de ruogan wenti-wei jinian Liangzhu wenhua faxian wushi zhounian erzuo,' *Kaogu* 1988(3): 241; Teng Shu-p'ing 1988: 'Kaogu chutu xinshiqi shidai yushicong yanjiu,' *Gugong Xueshu Jikan* 6/1: 8 and figures 7a, 7b.

[54] Nanjing 1985: 7, figures 26:1, 10:9.

Figure 7 • *Drawing of the decorative motifs incised on a pottery jar from Denghu (after Nanjing bowuyuan et al 1985, figure 10:1)*

either plain or carved with a simple design which gives a more 'naturalistic' aspect to the nose. Above the eyes, two narrow, parallel bars in relief, separated by a central strip which is usually undecorated, are generally incised with series of parallel lines, standing as an abbreviated version of the feathered headdress. This is the commonest anthropomorphic mask familiar for decades, because of its almost ubiquitous appearance on many *cong* kept in collections around the world.

The Theriomorphic Mask: This is a more elaborate mask. Although some of its essential features, the eyes and the nose, are practically the same as those of the anthropomorphic one, their treatment differs from the latter. In the basic form of the *shoumian* motif, the eyes are round and made up of two concentric circles enclosed by slanting, oval shapes joined in the middle by a wide bar, often arched at a sharp angle (figure 8, right). Another feature is the mouth, carved in relief or engraved below the nose, provided with four pointed teeth, two emerging from the lower jaw and two from the upper one, stressing the sense of awe inspired by the mask. Additional details can eventually include sophisticated geometric patterns filling the oval spaces around the eyes or the bar joining them: the same can be used to cover the background, the surface of the jade objects, from which the mask emerges.

The use of these 'filling patterns' in the decoration of a complex *shoumian* motif carved on an object not of jade is visible on a unique ivory fragment found in tomb M6 of the Fuquanshan site (figure 9). Probably used to protect the wooden handle of an axe, the ivory – found beside the skeleton and paired by another, undecorated ivory fragment – has one side highly decayed and corroded, while the other is partly covered with a complicated *shoumian* motif, carved in extremely minute and distinct lines,[55] described also as "geometric design of cloud pattern" and "dense network of fine decorative lines."[56] Zhang Minghua, in an article devoted to the study of jade axes of the Liangzhu culture describes the ivory fragment as follows:

> At the moment of the discovery, it appeared broken in pieces of a brownish-yellowish colour; the border being totally irregular and incomplete: moreover, the object was broken in two parts. The larger one (T4 M6:36a) is 25.4 centimetres long and 7 centimetres wide and is somewhat shaped like a knife. One of its sides was severely damaged, the concave and convex parts not even, one of them carved with a *shoumian*. The small section of the ivory object (T4 M6:36b) measures 16.8 centimetres and has the lower portions of its extremities incomplete and damaged.[57]

The variant of the *shoumian* just described can occur alone — on objects ranging from *cong* to small 'boxes,' tubular objects, rod-shaped ornaments, *huang*-pendants — but is more frequently associated, especially on *cong*, with the anthropomorphic mask, which appears always on top, though the two masks are kept separate by the frameworks within which they are carved (figure 10).

A more integrated version of the two motifs is far more evident in the complex, compound image which presents the anthropomorphic image, complete with a torso and limbs, imposed over the *shoumian* (figure 11). Contrary to the previous types of mask motifs, which occur on jades from a number of Liangzhu sites, the complex version of the combined motifs is, at the moment,

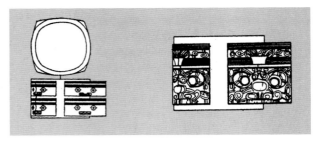

Figure 8 • Cong *decorated with the anthropomorphic (left) and theriomorphic mask motifs (right).* **Left** *from tomb T22M5:49 of the Fuquanshan site. Height, 4.7 cm; width, 6.7 cm.* **Right** *from tomb M12:1 of the Yaoshan site. Height, 5.8 cm; width, 7 cm (after Shanghai shi 1986, figure 59:2, and Zhejiang sheng 1988b, figure 5:1 respectively)*

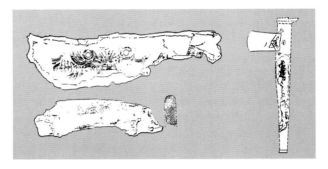

Figure 9 • *Drawing of the elaborate 'mask' motif on two ivory fragments from tomb T4M6:36 of the Fuquanshan site (left) and hypothetical reconstruction of the axe to which they belonged (after Zhang Minghua 1989, figures 8 and 11:4)*

[55] Shanghai 1984 (Shanghai shi wenwu baoguan weiyuanhui): 'Shanghai Fuquanshan Liangzhu wenhua muzang,' *Wenwu* 1984(2): 3.

[56] Huang Xuanpei, Song Jian and Sun Weichang 1992: 230.

[57] Zhang Minghua 1989: 'Liangzhu yuqi yanjiu,' *Kaogu* 1989(7): 629-630.

Figure 10 • Cong *decorated with the anthropomorphic and theriomorphic masks, From tomb M4:1 of the Wujin Sidun site. Height 7.2 cm; width 8.6 cm; diameter of hole, 6.8 cm (after Zhejiang sheng* et al *1989, plate 24)*

[58] Rui Guoyao and Shen Yueming 1992: 'Liangzhu wenhua yu Shang wenhua guanxi sanli,' *Kaogu* 1992(11): 1042-1043.

[59] On this 'diamond' pattern, see Allan 1993: 170 and 176 note 17.

[60] The repertory of animal forms in Liangzhu art includes a very few jade carvings in the shape of a frog (Zhanglingshan M4:1), a fish, a turtle and a cicada (Fanshan M22:23, M17:39 and M14:187 respectively).

[61] Childs-Johnson, Elizabeth 1989: 'The Shang Bird: Intermediary to the Supernatural,' *Orientations* 20-11 (November 1989): 61.

Figure 11 • *The man-and-animal motif carved on jades from Fanshan and Yaoshan (after Zhejiang sheng 1988a, figure 20)*

found carved only on jades excavated from the two cemeteries of Fanshan and Yaoshan, such as *cong*, tubular objects, *guan* headdress shaped ornaments, *yue* axes, ritual badges and *huang* pendants.

The head of the anthropomorphic figure is always characterised by what seems to be a large feathered hat, almost rectangular in shape, with a pointed top. The face has a large, open mouth showing two rows of teeth, a flat nose and round, open eyes, invariably marked by the two opposite, pointed indentations which characterise the motif in its simplified form when it occurs carved on the tiers of the *cong*. The anthropomorphic figure and the *shoumian* below it are characterised by a more defined body, engraved in minute lines on the jade surface. Although the sketched torso and two long arms, stretching outside and then turning, at a sharp angle, towards the eyes of the *shoumian* below, are clearly meant to belong to the human-like figure, the interpretation of the lower limbs, which are provided with claws, is more controversial.

The last mask motif to be discussed represents an interesting version of the *shoumian*, and is generally described by Chinese scholars[58] as a sort of 'dragon' mask because of its supposed resemblance with later representations of dragons in Chinese art. What cannot be doubted is that the 'dragon' mask shows distinctive features which differentiate it from the former ones described above.

This *shoumian* (figure 12) is characterised by two round eyes sometimes in relief, accentuated 'eyebrows' (in some cases resembling 'horns') and a flat nose below which is carved a mouth with the teeth clearly in evidence. One of the most distinctive features is a kind of diamond pattern, set between the eyes and the nose, a geometrical motif similar to that which later on will occasionally characterise examples of *taotie* masks and *long*-dragon motifs of the Shang period.[59] Seemingly associated only with the Yaoshan site, the 'dragon' mask is to be found on the edges of round or semicircular objects such as bracelets, badges, *huang*-pendants, or tubular objects.

The Bird Motif

Closely connected to the *shoumian* motif is the bird motif, which because of its frequency, can be regarded as the second most important decorative motif in the art of the Liangzhu culture.[60] The *shoumian* and the bird motif are closely connected not only because the two quite often occur together, but also because the most complex version of the *shoumian* seems to be in some way related to the bird motif, particularly with reference to the feathered headdress customarily seen on the head of the human-like figure (figure 11).

The two motifs are associated together on jade objects such as *cong*, *guan*-headdress-shaped ornaments, *huang*-pendants and three-pronged ornaments, while on pottery artefacts the *shoumian* and bird motifs occur in only one case. The ceramic bowl described above and coming from the well near Lake Deng includes amongst its decorative motifs a *shoumian* on whose sides are stylised figures of birds seen in profile,[61] all executed in intaglio on the body of the bowl (figure 7).

When they occur on the jades, the two motifs are always arranged in the same way: the centrally-positioned mask of the *shoumian* is flanked by images of birds in profile and turned outwards. Examples of this iconographic scheme can be found on three *cong* from Fanshan (M12:98, 93 and M20:124); on another *cong* excavated at Fuquanshan (M6:21); on headdress-shaped ornaments such as those from Fanshan (M22:11) and Yaoshan (M2:1; figure 13); on the three-pronged ornament excavated at Fanshan (M14:135); on a *huang*-pendant from Fanshan (M23:67); and on a *yue*-axe from Fanshan (M12:100).

It is worth noticing that, with the exception of the *cong* found at Fuquanshan (M6:21), the other jades which present the bird motif associated with the *shoumian* all have been excavated from the graves of the Yaoshan and Fanshan cemeteries, with the highest percentage in the latter. Moreover, some Fanshan graves have also yielded small jades carved in the shape of birds (M14:259, M15:5, M16:2 and M17:20), while one has been found at Yaoshan (M2:50).

Three of the birds from Fanshan have been found placed at the foot of their respective graves, the fourth in the head area of M15. Their function, as stated in the archaeological report,[62] is not clear, although they may have been pendants, as the one or two pairs of holes on the back would indicate. All birds are represented seen from above, with their wings outstretched, as if flying.

The bird motif is primarily found on jades excavated from Fanshan and less often on those from the Yaoshan sites. It occurs also on objects from the Fuquanshan site, where the bird motif occurs twice on the jades — on the *cong* mentioned above and on a small jade carved in the shape of a bird (M126:3) — and on some pottery vessels excavated from the tombs of this cemetery and related sites of the same geographical area. By virtue of their decoration, these vessels constitute an important group in the pottery production of the Liangzhu culture, which is predominantly undecorated.

The first relevant group of vessels has come to light in the Liangzhu layer of the Caoxieshan site, where three burials have been found. Tomb M198 contained two graves, the first of which contained a three-legged, lidded *ding* (M198.I:2; figure 14, left). The lid is incised with motifs described as "spiralling, winding and hooked patterns joined together and turning round": on the handle of the lid there are, not visible in the drawing accompanying the report but mentioned in the description, "motifs of fishes."[63] Furthermore, the legs of the *ding* are pierced with geometric motifs, circle and comma-shaped patterns.

The second grave of the same burial contained two lidded *hu*, both in fragmentary condition and reconstructed by restorers. The first (M198.II:7, 8; figure 14, right) has the central, upright portion of the body decorated with thin, zigzagging vertical lines: the globular, bottom part of the body bears incised motifs of birds, represented in profile and as if flying. The second *hu* (M198.II:6, 13; figure 14, centre) has the central, upright portion of the body decorated with complex, apparently geometric motifs, amongst which there is a stylised representation of a bird in profile, similar to that of the other *hu*.

Similar patterns occur on the second group of vessels (including a ewer, a *ding* and three *hu*) brought to light in the Fuquanshan site. The *ding* (T22M5:90) is similar to the one from Caoxieshan, with the difference that the spiralling patterns are present not only on the lid of the vessel but also partly on the body, which quite likely was originally covered all over with such patterns (figure 15, left).[64] Similar motifs occur also on the central portion of the body of the first *hu* (T27M2:166; figure 15, right) whose lid, lower portion of the body and footrim all carry patterns interpreted as birds in profile and flying; on the footring, they are alternated with motifs of flying birds seen frontally.

The same pattern of a flying bird in profile can be discerned on the lower portion of the body and the footring of a second *hu* found at the Fuquanshan site (T27M2:66; figure 16, left);[65] the central portion of the body of this latter *hu* is again decorated with spiralling, hooked geometric motifs executed in bold lines.

A third *hu* found at the Fuquanshan site (T22M5:2; figure 16, right) differs in shape and decoration from others excavated in the same site and at Caoxieshan. It has a round body and a short ring foot, a tilted and wide-open spout and a handle decorated with striated, parallel lines. The body presents a background decoration formed by vertical, parallel zigzagging lines against which are set motifs of flying birds in profile, spaced and distributed all over the body of the vessel. Another bird, but seen frontally with its wings outstretched as if flying, is incised just below the spout.

Figure 12 • Jade bracelet decorated with the 'dragon' mask motif from tomb M1:30 of the Yaoshan site. Diameter, 7.4 cm; height, 2.6 cm (after Zhejiang sheng et al 1989, plates 102, 157 and 219)

[62] Zhejiang 1988a (Zhejiang sheng wenwu kaogu yanjiusuo Fanshan kaogudui): 'Zhejiang Yuhang Fanshan Liangzhu mudi faxian jianbao,' *Wenwu* 1988(1): 29.

[63] Nanjing 1980 11.

[64] Reproduced and discussed in Huang Xuanpei, Song Jian and Sun Weichang 1992: 90-91.

[65] Ibid 104-105.

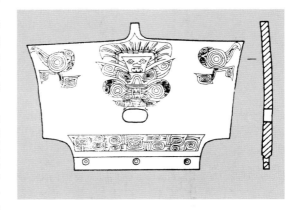

Figure 13 • Jade *guan*-headdress-shaped ornament decorated with mask motif flanked by images of birds, from Yaoshan M2:1. Height 5.8 cm; upper length, 7.7 cm (after Zhejiang sheng 1988b, figure 24)

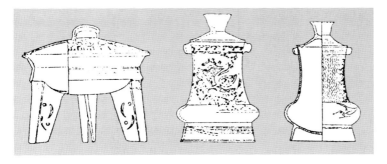

Figure 14 • *Decorated pottery vessels from the Caoxieshan site.* **Left** *ding tripod from tomb M198.II.2, height c42 cm.* **Centre** *hu from tomb M198.II.6, height c30 cm.* **Right** *hu from tomb M198.II.7, height c28 cm (after Nanjing bowuyuan 1980, figure 69:1-3)*

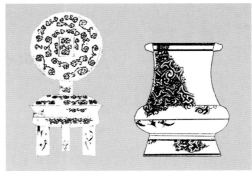

Figure 15 • *Decorated pottery vessels from Fuquanshan.* **Left** *ding tripod from tomb T22M5:90, height 26 cm.* **Right** *hu from tomb T27M2:166, height c20 cm (after Huang Xuanpei et al 1992, entry No 22, and Shanghai shi 1986, figure 24:2)*

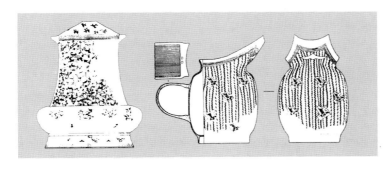

Figure 16 • *Decorated pottery* hu *vessels from Fuquanshan.* **Left** *from tomb T27M2:66, height 19 cm.* **Right** *from T22M5:2, height 5 cm (after Huang Xuanpei et al 1992, Nos 29 and 33)*

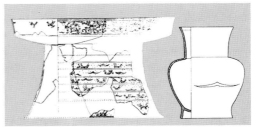

Figure 17 • *Decorated pottery vessels.* **Left** *dou-stand from Fuquanshan M101:90, height 18.8 cm.* **Right** *zun from Xiyangdian, height 16.9 cm (after Huang Xuanpei et al 1992, Nos 25 and 37)*

This latter variation of the bird motif, already encountered on the footring of the second *hu* from Fuquanshan, occurs on some other pottery vessels excavated from several Liangzhu sites. The first is a tall *dou* found at Fuquanshan (M101:90; figure 17, left), whose surviving decoration suggests that the vessel was originally completely covered with incised motifs. These are: *1*) spiralling patterns alternated with groups of birds — two in profile with their heads turned towards a central flying bird seen frontally — incised on the interior and exterior surfaces of the top basin; and *2*) alternated bird motifs in profile and frontal views, incised within the seven registers which form the bamboo-shaped ring foot.

A flying bird, represented frontally, is also incised on the body of a *zun* found at Xiyangdian, Qingpu county (figure 17, right), this time alternated with the motif of a running bird with long neck, interpreted as an 'ostrich.'[66]

Finally, a fragmented *hu* discovered in 1972 at Jiaxing Quemuqiao, has its body decorated with the regularly repeated pattern of a flying bird seen frontally,[67] a motif seen also, repeated twice, inside the top basin of a *dou* found at Nanhu, Yuhang xian.[68]

Considering the archaeological material as a whole, the bird motif on pottery vessels of the Liangzhu culture basically occurs in two versions: the bird seen in profile and the bird seen frontally. Both these versions of the bird motif on pottery vessels have their counterparts in jade material: representations of birds in profile appear on *cong*, on three-pronged and headdress-shaped ornaments, flanking the central *shoumian* mask with their heads turned outwards. Finally, on jade objects of the Liangzhu culture, the frontal bird occurs only once: on a tall *cong* in the Shanghai Museum, which has the motif of "a bird

[66] *Ibid* 120-121.

[67] Zhejiang 1974 (Zhejiang sheng Jiaxingxian bowu zhanlanguan): 'Zhejiang Jiaxing Quemuqiao faxian yipi heitao,' *Kaogu* 1974(4): 249-250.

[68] Yuhang 1991 (Yuhang xian wenguanhui): 'Yuhangxian chutu de Liangzhu wenhua he Maqiao wenhua de taoqi kehua fuhao,' *Dongnan Wenhua* 1991(3): figure 1.

with outstretched wings incised on one side of the protruding rounded inner edge at the upper end."[69]

The 'Writing' on the Pottery and Jade

Occasionally, certain 'signs' are found incised on pottery, which have been interpreted as 'proto-characters,' although at the moment there is no proper evidence of a developed writing system, and nothing has yet been found which would be comparable to the proto-characters on a pottery sherd from the Longshan culture site of Dinggong (Zouping, Shandong).[70]

A pottery basin with a number of these 'signs' incised on its rim was first published by He Tianxing in 1937.[71] By that time some other pottery wares bearing similar 'signs' had occasionally been found by Chinese archaeologists. The 'signs' occur either isolated or grouped together, such as those inscribed on a pottery *guan* jar found at Nanhu, Yuhang xian, which include a sort of 'branch' repeated several times,[72] or those incised on the side of another *guan* recovered from a well near Lake Denghu.[73] Some scholars have also linked these engraved 'signs' on pottery with others incised on the surface of a number of Liangzhu jades (including three large *bi* disks in the Freer Gallery of Art, Washington), relating them in turn to other symbols found on Dawenkou culture pottery receptacles.[74]

Conclusion

The typological analysis of recurrent motifs in the iconography of the Liangzhu culture shows that the artistic vocabulary of this late-neolithic culture was primarily limited to images of birds and mask motifs. These motifs are represented alone or together, in a highly standardised manner and according to fixed schemes.

Most of Liangzhu iconography is to be found on the jades produced by this culture and on a group of pottery vessels decorated with incised motifs of birds. With the exception of the jar from Denghu, the mask motif, the most recurrent icon adopted in the decoration of jades, does not occur on ceramic vessels. A link between the two media, pottery and jade, is however provided — besides the case of the three-pointed motif illustrated above — by bird motifs, which occur, in various forms, in both media. In both cases, pottery and jade, the objects bearing decorations were quite likely intended for ritual and not for daily use.[75] Decorative motifs therefore seem to have been used to highlight artefacts which had a special significance for the Liangzhu people and which probably played a important role in their rituals.

[69] Huang Xuanpei, Song Jian and Sun Weichang 1992: 158.

[70] Fang Hui 1994: 'Shandong sheng Zouping xian Dinggong yizhi fanxian de Longshan wenhua dui zi taowen,' *Gugong wenwu yuekan* 133 (April 1994): 98-103.

[71] Reproduced in Chang, K C 1986: *The archaeology of ancient China* (4th ed), New Haven and London: Yale University Press, 258.

[72] Yuhang 1991 (Yuhang xian wenguanhui): 'Yuhangxian chutu de Liangzhu wenhua he Maqiao wenhua de taoqi fuhao,' *Dongnan wenhua* 1991(3): 182, 184

[73] Nanjing 1985; Zhang Minghua, Wang Huiju 1990: 'Taihu diqu xinshiqi shidai de taowen,' *Kaogu* 1990(10): 904; Huang Xuanpei et al 1992: 31.

[74] Li Xueqin 1987: 'Lun xin chu Dawenkou wenhua taoqi fuhao,' *Wenwu* 1987(12): 75-80; Zhang Minghua and Wang Huiju 1990: 905-907.

[75] On the decorated *ding* tripod of the Liangzhu culture, see the discussion by Jiang Yueping 1993: 'Liqi 'ding' de yuanyuan tansuo,' *Nanfang wenwu* 1993(2).

New Discoveries

Table 1 | The 50 Most Important Discoveries Listed by Locations

Province/Region	City/County	Site	Date
Anhui	Tianchang	Western Han cemetery	206 BC-AD 23
Anhui	Mengcheng	Weichisi Dawenkou culture site	c4300-2500 BC
Gansu	Dunhuang/Anxi	Western Han Xuanquanzhi postal remains	206 BC-AD 23
Guangdong	Guangzhou	Nanyue Kingdom palace remains	206 BC-AD 23
Guizhou	Pan xian	Dadong palaeolithic site	c300,000 bp
Hebei	Dingzhou	Beizhuangzi Late Shang/Early Western Zhou cemetery	c13th-11th century BC
Hebei	Zhangjiakou	Xuanhua Xiabali Liao cemetery	AD 907-1211
Heilongjiang	Ning'an	Bohai state cemetery	AD 618-906
Heilongjiang	Ning'an	Hongzun Fish Farm Mohe-Bohai cemetery	5th-10th century AD
Henan	Anyang	Huayuanzhuang Shang oracle bone hoard	c13th century BC
Henan	Sanmenxia	Shangcunling Western Zhou tomb (No 2009)	c11th-8th century BC
Henan	Yongcheng	Mangshan Western Han Liang state cemetery	206 BC-AD 23
Henan	Xichuan	Danjiangkou Reservoir Chu state cemetery	8th-5th century BC
Henan	Luoyang	Zhongzhoulu Northern Song garden remains	AD 960-1127
Henan	Dengzhou	Baligang Yangshao culture site	c5000-3000 BC
Henan	Yongcheng	Western Han Liang state royal cemetery	206 BC-AD 23
Henan	Zhengzhou	Xishan Yangshao culture walled site	c3350-2950 BC
Henan	Zhengzhou	Xiaoshuangqiao Shang dynasty site	c15th century BC
Henan	Huixian	Mengzhuang Longshan culture walled site	c2500-2000 BC
Hubei	Jiangling	Jigongshan palaeolithic site	c50,000-10,000 bp
Hubei (Sichuan)	Sanxia	Three Gorges archaeological survey	various
Hunan	Fengxian	Chengtoushan Qujialing culture site	c3000-2600 BC
Hunan	Changsha	Western Han Changsha state cemetery	206 BC-AD 23
Hunan	Daoxian	Yuchanyan neolithic site	c10,000 bp
Inner Mongolia	Aohanqi	Xinglongwa neolithic site	c6000-5000 BC
Inner Mongolia	Aluke'erxinqi	Liao dynasty tomb of Yelü Yuzhi	AD 941
Inner Mongolia	Aluke'erxinqi	Baoshan Liao cemetery	AD 907-1211
Jiangsu	Kunshan	Zhaolingshan Liangzhu culture site	c3300-2200 BC
Jiangsu	Gaoyou	Longqiuzhuang neolithic site	c7000-5000 BC
Jiangsu	Yangzhou	Tang city remains	AD 618-907
Jiangsu	Nanjing	Tangshan palaeolithic site	c300,000 bp
Jiangsu	Xuzhou	Western Han Shizishan Chu state cemetery	206 BC-AD 23
Jiangxi	Ruichang	Tongling Shang/Zhou mining site	c15th-7th century BC
Jiangxi	Fengcheng	Hongzhou kiln remains	AD 23-960
Jiangxi	Wannian	Xianrendong and Diaotonghuan palaeolithic/neolithic sites	c20,000-9,000 bp
Liaoning	Suizhong	Yuan shipwreck	AD 1271-1368
Shaanxi	Xi'an	Sui Baqiao bridge	AD 581-618
Shaanxi	Linyou	Sui Renshou and Tang Jiucheng palace remains	AD 518-907
Shandong	Zouping	Dinggong Longshan culture walled site	c2500-2000 BC
Shandong	Tengzhou	Qianzhangda Shang/Zhou cemetery	c12th-11th century BC
Shandong	Changqing	Xianrentai Si state cemetery	c8th-5th century BC
Shanxi	Quwo	Qucun Beizhao Jin state cemetery	c11th-8th century BC
Shanxi	Quwo	Qucun Beizhao Jin state cemetery	c11th-8th century BC
Shanxi	Datong	Yungang cave No 3	AD 386-534
Tibet	Lhasa	Qugong Bronze Age culture site	c1750 BC
Xinjiang	Minfeng	Niya site	2nd century BC-5th century AD
Yunnan	Jiangchuan	Lijiashan cemetery	206 BC-AD 220
Zhejiang	Yuhang	Huiguanshan Liangzhu culture altar and tombs	c3300-2200 BC
Zhejiang	Yuhang	Mojiaoshan Liangzhu culture architectural remains	c3300-2200 BC
Zhejiang	Hangzhou	Lin'ancheng Southern Song grand temple remains	AD 1127-1279

Wang Tao with the assistance of Li Xinwei
The Important Archaeological Discoveries: 1991-1995

*B*etween 1991 and 1995, *Zhongguo wenwu bao* (China Cultural Relics Newspaper) invited leading Chinese archaeologists from different institutions to identify the 10 most important archaeological discoveries of each year, so that it could make annual awards. At first, this annual event was solely the initiative of the n ewspaper, but it soon became clear that the event was not only making national headlines—a clear illustration of the boom in archaeology in China today—but was also acknowledging gradual progress in the field over the years. The selection here is very broad, ranging from the palaeolithic to the Yuan dynasty (300,000 bp-AD 14th century). The discoveries have either yielded significant new archaeological material or have thrown light on important historic issues. To a degree, the selection process was also an indication of the politics of the state-run archaeological network. It is important to note that these discoveries have not been judged in terms of perfect excavation planning and scientific technique. This paper is a summary of the 50 sites selected over the five-year period (Table 1).

In order to understand the significance of the archaeological discoveries of the 1990s, a brief look at the history of modern archaeology in China is necessary. In the first decades of this century, Chinese archaeology had a mixed fortune of traditional antiquarianism and western influence. In the 1920s, the Swedish scholar J G Andersson (1874-1960) excavated at Zhoukoudian, a palaeolithic site near Peking (Beijing), where 'Peking Man' was later found. Andersson also discovered a neolithic site with distinctive painted pottery at Yangshao village in western Henan, and named the assemblage 'Yangshao culture.' This marks the beginning of studying prehistory in China. At the same time, the discovery of oracle bone inscriptions at the end of the 19th century led to the scientific excavation of Yinxu (Ruins of Yin), today's Anyang, by the Institute of History and Philology (IHP), Academia Sinica from 1928 to 1936, which marked the real birth of field archaeology in China. Through archaeology, the existence of the Shang dynasty, previously considered to be legendary, was confirmed. Later, in the 1930s, the Longshan culture, distinguished by its black pottery, was identified. The Yangshao and Longshan cultures were then regarded as the two successive neolithic cultures which laid down the foundation for Chinese civilisation.

For about 10 years, until the interruption of the Sino-Japanese War, the archaeological work of the IHP concentrated mainly on Yinxu. The civil war that followed brought field archaeology in the country to a standstill. After 1949, when the Nationalist government withdrew from the mainland, the Academia Sinica moved to Taiwan, where its work was mostly limited to local digging and to research and publication of the old materials they had taken with them. On the mainland, archaeology was enthusiastically promoted by the Communist government in the hope that it would lend support to their new ideology and raise the international status of the nation. The Institute of Archaeology, initially under the Chinese Academy of Sciences (CAS), was set up in 1950. In 1952, Peking University inaugurated the first archaeological course in China to train its own archaeologists.

Chinese archaeology today operates on different levels. From the capital Beijing, the State Bureau of Cultural Relics (SBCR) controls the administration of excavations and the conservation of cultural relics nationwide. The Institute of Archaeology, now attached to the Chinese Academy of Social Sciences (CASS), is the highest academic organisation conducting planned excavations, and has its own permanent archaeological stations and mobile teams working around the country. A number of universities where archaeological training is offered also conduct excavations, and some of the more established departments such as the Department of Archaeology at Peking University also play an important role at the national level. At the local level, each province or autonomous region has its own Institute of Archaeology and Cultural Relics (IACR); many cities and counties or even townships may also have a Cultural Relics Office (CRO). Museums, though their main task is to house and display artefacts, are also sometimes involved in field work. It is fair to say that nowhere else in the world can one find so many people practising archaeology!

The scale and progress of archaeology in China during the last three decades has been phenomenal. The number of archaeological sites that have been excavated and surveyed runs to over 10,000. The picture of Chinese archaeology looks very different from that of 40 years ago. Palaeolithic remains have been found all over China, and these discoveries contribute to the international study of human evolution. For the neolithic period, a new framework has been established and the problems of the origins of agriculture and the formation of Chinese civilisation have been the focus of intensive archaeological research. For a long time, the central plains (*zhongyuan*) had been thought of as the 'cradle' of Chinese civilisation from where culture diffused. However, during the 1970s and 1980s, with the help of C14 dating, archaeology witnessed a number of breakthroughs. In the central plains, several pre-Yangshao cultures (c6000-5500 BC) have been identified. The Yangshao culture itself is now known to include different branches such as the Banpo and Miaodigou types. In the northeast, the complex religious sites of the Hongshan culture (c3500 BC) were found, indicating a high level of cultural development. Along the east coast, the chronology of the Beixin (c5400-4400 BC), Dawenkou (c4300-2500 BC) and Longshan (c2500-2000 BC) cultures has been established. In the lower Yangzi River, the Hemudu culture (c5000-3300 BC) revealed abundant evidence of rice farming and animal domestication. The Liangzhu culture (c3000-2200 BC) in the Hangzhou Bay region also yielded a large number of sophisticated religious artefacts. In the middle reaches of the Yangzi River, the evidence begins to show a different cultural pattern from that of the Yellow River valley.

Until recently, Chinese archaeologists seldom ventured later than the Han dynasty (206 BC-AD 220). The situation has now changed and excavation of historic sites such as mediaeval cities and tombs has become more important. Archaeology plays a key role in confirming, and questioning, the validity of historic records. Scientific analysis and modern technology also constitute an essential part of archaeological practice; and new branches such as underwater archaeology are being developed. A younger generation of archaeologists is now establishing itself and applying new methods. Foreign archaeologists, banned for many years from working in China, are now welcomed to participate in joint excavation projects. Chinese archaeology is gradually integrating itself into the mainstream of world archaeology.

Palaeolithic

Between 1991-1995, three new discoveries stand out among the numerous palaeolithic sites already known. Important for palaeo-anthropological studies is the discovery of two hominoid skulls and an early *homo erectus* fossil tooth found in a lava cave at Tangshan near Nanjing (Jiangsu).[1] The area is known for its hot springs, which have been developed as a tourist attraction. On 13 March 1993, during the clearing of a newly discovered cave, a team of construction workers accidentally dug out an intact hominoid skull. Archaeologists from the Nanjing City Museum were called in and found a second skull in the cave. Between December 1993 and January 1994, a joint team from Peking University and Nanjing City Museum carried out further excavations at the site and found the fossil tooth. A systematic record of the stratigraphy was made. There are four strata of deposits: at the top is a calcified layer; the second layer is brownish clay; the third layer contains fossils; the fourth is again brownish clay. Preliminary uranium-series and ESR tests indicate the date of the site is around 300,000 bp, *i e* Middle Pleistocene. Analysis shows that one of the skulls is female and the other male, and that the morphological features of the male bears resemblance to that of Peking Man, found in 1926 at Zhoukoudian near Beijing. The fauna remains at Tangshan are also similar to those found at Zhoukoudian. Despite Tangshan's southern locality, it shares similarities with palaeo-anthropological development in the north. The Tangshan site has provided new evidence for studying early climatic and environment changes as well as early human origins in Asia.

The second important discovery is the Pan xian Dadong cave site near Liupanshui (Guizhou).[2] The site was first noticed in the late 1970s when hydrologists were surveying the area and found mammal fossils in the cave. Between April and May 1993, a joint team from the Institute of Vertebrate Palaeontology and Palaeo-anthropology (CAS), Guizhou Teachers' University, Liupanshui City CRO and the Pan xian CRO excavated at the cave and confirmed it to be an upper palaeolithic dwelling site. It is a karst-type limestone cave, about 1,660 metres long, and divided into five different levels. The cultural deposit in the cave is rich: from the entrance inwards about 200 metres long and 30 metres wide, reaching a maximum depth of 19.5 metres. The total area covers nearly 8,000 square metres; the actual excavated area covers 92 square metres. Finds included four hominoid teeth and over 2,000 stone implements, mostly choppers, anvils and balls. Uranium-series tests show the upper layer of the cultural deposit to be c300,000 bp. The site was occupied by early humans over a long period, probably throughout the Middle and Late Pleistocene. The fauna fossils are also typical of this period. Compared with other palaeolithic cultures in China, the lithic tradition at the Dadong site is unique, comprising mostly scrapers and chopping tools, with a small percentage of hammer and hand-axes, made of flint, basalt or limestone. In terms of technology, there are similarities with those of the Guanyingtong site in western Guizhou, but at Guanyingtong there are fewer limestone tools. Furthermore, about 10 per cent of the Tangshan stone tools have a prepared striking platform, a feature often associated with the palaeolithic tradition in Europe. This well-preserved site offers excellent data for establishing the chronology of palaeolithic development in southwest China and for reconstructing the evolution of *homo erectus*. It may also offer some new clues for the study of early human migration and contacts between continental Europe and East Asia. The work at Pan xian Dadong still continues, and in 1995 the joint team included a number of American participants.

The third discovery concerns the Jigongshan upper palaeolithic remains in Jiangling (Hubei).[3] The site is located on a small hill, five kilometres northwest of Jingzhou Town, and its northern and western sides overlook a lake. The site was excavated by archaeologists from the Jingzhou Museum and the Archaeology Department of Peking University in October 1992. The site is divided

[1] Tangshan kaogu fajuedui: 'Nanjing Tangshan fajue chu gurenlei huashi,' *Zhongguo wenwu bao* 18-12-94; Wei Zhengjin: 'Nanjing Tangshan Huludong zhiliren huashi didian kaogu fajue de zhongyao shouhuo,' *Wenwu* 1996(10): 58-63.

[2] Zhang Hangang: 'Dadong yizhi fajue you huo zhongyao chengguo,' *Zhongguo wenwu bao* 29-8-93; — 'Pan xian Dadong jiushiqi yizhi de jiazhi he yiyi,' *Zhongguo wenwu bao* 14-11-93; Si Xinqiang *et al*: 'Pan xian Dadong fajue jianbao,' *Renleixue xuebao* 1993(5): 113-121; Huang Weiwen, Si Xinqiang *et al*: 'Excavations at Pan xian Dadong, Guizhou Province, Southern China,' *Current Anthropology* 36-5 (1995): 844-846.

[3] Liu Deyin: 'Woguo jiushiqi shidai kaogu de zhongda tupo,' *Zhongguo wenwu bao* 2-5-93; Zhongguo shehui kexue yuan kaogu yanjiusuo: 'Xinglongwa juluo yizhi fajue huo shuoguo,' *Zhongguo wenwu bao* 13-12-92.

Table 2 | The 50 Most Important Discoveries by Year of Award

Year	Province/Region	City/County	Site	Date
1991	Heilongjiang	Ning'an	Bohai state cemetery	AD 618-906
1991	Hebei	Dingzhou	Beizhuangzi Late Shang/Early Western Zhou cemetery	c13th-11th century BC
1991	Henan	Sanmenxia	Shangcunling Western Zhou tomb (No 2009)	c11th-8th century BC
1991	Jiangxi	Ruichang	Tongling Shang/Zhou mining site	c15th-7th century BC
1991	Henan	Anyang	Huayuanzhuang Shang oracle bone hoard	c13th century BC
1991	Gansu	Dunhuang/Anxi	Western Han Xuanquanzhi postal remains	206 BC-AD 23
1991	Henan	Yongcheng	Mangshan Western Han Liang state cemetery	206 BC-AD 23
1991	Shandong	Zouping	Dinggong walled Longshan culture site	c2500-2000 BC
1991	Zhejiang	Yuhang	Huiguanshan Liangzhu culture altar and tombs	c3300-2200 BC
1991	Tibet	Lhasa	Qugong Bronze Age culture site	c1750 BC
1992	Hubei	Jiangling	Jigongshan palaeolithic site	c50,000-10,000 bp
1992	Hunan	Feng xian	Chengtoushan Qujialing culture site	c3000-2600 BC
1992	Henan	Luoyang	Zhongzhoulu Northern Song garden remains	AD 960-1127
1992	Henan	Xichuan	Danjiangkou Reservoir Chu state cemetery	8th-5th century BC
1994	Henan	Huixian	Mengzhuang Longshan culture walled site	c2500-2000BC
1992	Shanxi	Quwo	Qucun Beizhao Jin state cemetery	c11th-8th century BC
1992	Anhui	Tianchang	Western Han cemetery	206 BC-AD 23
1992	Yunnan	Jiangchuan	Lijiashan cemetery	206 BC-AD 220
1992	Inner Mongolia	Aluke'erxinqi	Liao dynasty tomb of Yelü Yuzhi	AD 941
1992	Jiangsu	Kunshan	Zhaolingshan Liangzhu culture site	c3300-2200 BC
1992	Inner Mongolia	Aohanqi	Xinglongwa neolithic site	c6000-5000 BC
1993	Jiangsu	Gaoyou	Longqiuzhuang neolithic site	c5500-3300 BC
1993	Zhejiang	Yuhang	Mojiaoshan Liangzhu culture architectural remains	c3300-2200 BC
1993	Liaoning	Suizhong	Yuan shipwreck	AD 1271-1368
1993	Hebei	Zhangjiakou	Xuanhua Xiabali Liao cemetery	AD 907-1211
1993	Jiangxi	Fengcheng	Hongzhou kiln remains	AD 23-960
1993	Jiangsu	Yangzhou	Tang city remains	AD 618-907
1993	Shanxi	Datong	Yungang cave No 3	AD 386-534
1993	Guizhou	Pan xian	Dadong palaeolithic site	c300,000 bp
1993	Shanxi	Quwo	Qucun Beizhao Jin State cemetery	c11th-8th century BC
1993	Hunan	Changsha	Western Han Changsha state cemetery	206 BC-AD 23
1994	Shandong	Tengzhou	Qianzhangda Shang/Zhou cemetery	c12th-11th century BC
1994	Hubei, Sichuan	Sanxia	Three Gorges archaeological survey	Various
1994	Shaanxi	Linyou	Sui Renshou and Tang Jiucheng palace remains	AD 581-907
1994	Inner Mongolia	Aluke'erxinqi	Baoshan Liao cemetery	AD 907-1211
1994	Shaanxi	Xi'an	Sui Baqiao bridge	AD 581-618
1994	Henan	Yongcheng	Western Han Liang state royal cemetery	206 BC-AD 23
1994	Anhui	Mengcheng	Weichisi Dawenkou culture site	c4300-2500 BC
1994	Henan	Dengzhou	Baligang Yangshao culture site	c5000-3000 BC
1994	Jiangsu	Nanjing	Tangshan palaeolithic site	c300,000 bp
1995	Henan	Zhengzhou	Xishan Yangshao culture walled site	c3350-2950 BC
1995	Zhejiang	Hangzhou	Lin'ancheng Southern Song Grand Temple remains	AD 1127-1279
1995	Heilongjiang	Ning'an	Hongzun Fish Farm Mohe-Bohai cemetery	5th-10th century AD
1995	Xinjiang	Minfeng	Niya site	2nd century BC-5th century AD
1995	Henan	Zhengzhou	Xiaoshuangqiao Shang dyansty site	c15th century BC
1995	Shandong	Changqing	Xianrentai Si state cemetery	c8th-5th century BC
1995	Guangdong	Guangzhou	Nanyue Kingdom palace remains	206 BC-AD 23
1995	Jiangsu	Xuzhou	Western Han Shizishan Chu state cemetery	206 BC-AD 23
1995	Hunan	Dao xian	Yuchanyan neolithic site	c10,000 bp
1995	Jiangxi	Wannian	Xianrendong and Diaotonghuan (palaeolithic/neolithic)	c20,000-9,000 bp

stratigraphically into two cultural levels: the upper stratum is about 10-25 centimetres deep, of a yellowish manganic sub-clay deposit, and dates to 20,000-10,000 bp. About 500 stone implements, mostly small scrapers, have been found from this level. The lower stratum is deeper, about 50 centimetres, of a brownish sub-clay deposit, and dates between 50,000-40,000 bp. From the lower level archaeologists have identified a residential and production area of the upper palaeolithic. In the centre-north section of the site there are five circles of gravel and stone implements, which were probably .the living quarters. Many used stone tools have been found within the circles. In the southern section there was a lithic workshop, where stone hammers and hammering blocks have been found, and even traces of the stoneworkers' footprints. A sharp cleaver was found in the open ground to the south of the workshop, suggesting that the area may originally have been used as a slaughtering ground. The lithic technology here is relatively sophisticated. The main types of tools are cleavers, scrapers, hammers, hammering blocks, and a number of sharp-pointed implements, made of pebbles. Many tools have sharp prismatic blades. They were made by anvil percussion, direct percussion and bipolar percussion, sometimes hit from opposite directions, sometimes struck only from one side, and retouched. The Jigongshan palaeolithic site is the first of its kind to have been found in southern China. It is fortunate that it was discovered in a very good state of preservation.

Neolithic

In East Asia, evidence for studying the early neolithic period, in particular the question of the origins of agriculture, is largely defined in the context of mainland Southeast Asia and southern China. Two recent archaeological discoveries in Hunan and Jiangxi provinces have reinforced the theory that rice cultivation and pottery making in China began earlier in the south than in the north.

Between September and November 1994, a joint team from the Jiangxi provincial ICRA and the Andover Foundation for Archaeological Research (USA) carried out excavations at the Xianrendong and Diaotonghuan sites in Wannian (Jiangxi).[4] Xianrendong had been discovered in the 1960s; Diaotonghuan was a new site, only 800 metres from Xianrendong. At the time of excavation in the 1960s, the Xianrendong site was identified as an early neolithic site, but many questions remained unanswered. The new project was designed to investigate the stratification and to try to confirm the exact date of the site. The cultural deposits are divided into four strata: the lower two layers represent a much earlier period from which only chipped quartz or quartzite implements were found. Later polished stone implements and sand-tempered pottery sherds were found in the upper layers. The stratification of the Diaotonghuan site is almost identical. Carbon 14 dating for the upper layers suggests c14,000-9,000 bp and for the lower layers c20,000-15,000 bp. The two sites were contemporary and it is likely that they were related in some way, with Diaotonghuan probably used as a temporary camp and slaughtering place. Some modern technology such as phytolithic and isotopic analysis was used to study materials collected from the site. The results offer new evidence for studying early agriculture and for the transition from palaeolithic to neolithic in China.

Recent excavations by the Hunan provincial ICRA at the Daoxian Yuzhangyan cave site[5] also provide important evidence for studying the neolithic transformation and plant cultivation in China. The cave was first discovered in the early 1980s and further excavations took place in 1993 and 1995. Finds consisted mainly of stone choppers and spades and a small quantity of primitive pottery with cord-impressed pattern. The cultural deposit is 1.2 - 1.8 metres deep. There are rich animal remains at the site, with a high percentage of fowl remains. Pollen analysis shows there was a great variety of plant-life. The most important discovery, however, is the earliest evidence in the world of cultivated rice (Oryza sativa japonica). The silicate rice represents a transitional stage between wild rice and fully cultivated rice. Although no C14 dating is available yet, comparative analysis indicates the early stratum of the site is about 10,000 years old.

[4] Liu Shizhong: 'Jiangxi Xianrendong de Diaotonghuan yizhi fajue huo zhongyao jinzhan,' Zhongguo wenwu bao 28-1-96; Liu Shizhong, Xu Zhifan: 'Jiangxi shiqian kaogu huo zhongyao shouhuo,' Nanfang wenwu 1995(4): 125.

[5] Yuan Jirong: 'Yuzhangyan huo shuidao qiyuan zhongyao xin wuzheng,' Zhongguo wenwu bao 3-3-96.

For the later neolithic, an important breakthrough was the discovery of the Xinglongwa neolithic site in Aohanqi (Inner Mongolia).[6] It is located in the small hills in the upper reaches of the Muniu River, a branch of the Daling River. The site had been excavated previously, and the fifth season was conducted by the Institute of Archaeology, CASS, between July and October 1992. The excavation covered an area of over 10,000 square metres and revealed house foundations, storage pits, graves and a surrounding ditch. The site can be divided into early and late phases. The houses belonging to the early phase were originally half-underground, triangular or square in plan, and arranged in rows. The average size of these houses was between 50-80 square metres, with the largest covering 140 square metres. There are two of these large houses in the centre of the settlement, which may have been used as public meeting places. The houses of the later phase were smaller, not necessarily in rows, and were built beyond the surrounding ditch. The pottery from the Xinglongwa site was made of dark grey or yellow-sanded clay, with a limited variety of shapes. The most common types are jars, bowls and cups, usually decorated with irregular impressed patterns. Artefacts made of other materials, such as stone and bone, have also been found. The two nephrite jade earrings found in one of the graves are the earliest jade ornaments known to date. In another grave, two pigs were buried on the right of the deceased. The Xinglongwa site represents a unique well-developed neolithic culture in the north, which, in terms of settlement patterns, differs greatly from the neolithic cultures in the Yellow River region. Preliminary C14 dating (uncalibrated) indicates its age: 6000-5000 BC.

In the central plains, archaeology has revealed new aspects of the Yangshao culture. In 1992 and 1994, a joint team from the Archaeology Department of Peking University and the Nanyang Regional ICRA (Henan) excavated the Baligang site[7] of the later phase of the Yangshao culture. The site is located three kilometres north of Baizhuangcun village, near Dengzhou, Henan province, just south of the Duan River. The site covers some 50,000 square metres and the cultural deposit is 3.5 - 5 metres thick. The most significant discovery comprises the architectural remains in the lower stratum, dating to the later Yangshao and Miaodigou periods. The architectural remains are primarily two long rows of houses parallel to each other, and are further divided into suites and smaller rooms. Hearths, stone tools and pottery vessels were found in the houses. The construction of the houses appears to belong to different periods, suggesting some multiple occupation. The two rows of houses have opposite orientations, and this may indicate some sort of social division. The evidence from the Baligang site is important for studying the settlement pattern of the later Yangshao culture.

The Weichisi site[8] in Mengcheng (Anhui) is another important settlement site which relates to the Dawenkou culture in the East Coast region. The Institute of Archaeology, CASS, has been conducting excavations here for the last 10 years and finds have included a large quantity of pottery, stone tools, over 200 tombs, many storage and sacrificial pits and, most importantly, architectural remains. The small groups of houses were built in the east, west and south sections of the site. Large houses were built in rows in the centre-north of the site, and the centre-south is a large public square. Surrounding the settlement was a moat, some 30 metres wide and 1.2 - 3.5 m deep. The settlement shows links with the Dawenkou culture in the Shandong peninsula: several burial urns are incised with a symbol identical to that found on Dawenkou urns. However, the pottery vessels used as funerary objects at Weichisi differ substantially from the typical Dawenkou burials in Shandong. The custom of tooth extraction common in Dawenkou is not seen here. The Weichisi settlement represents a new development of the late Dawenkou type. Further research is needed on its relationship to the Dawenkou culture in Shandong and the neolithic cultures in Jiangsu.

Neolithic development in the region between the Yangzi and Huai rivers has its own distinctive characteristics. Between April and June 1993 a joint team of archaeologists from the Nanjing Museum and the Yangzhou and Yancheng Museums excavated the Longqiuzhuang site[9] near Gaoyou city (Jiangsu), which

[6] Zhongguo shehui kexue yuan kaogu yanjiusuo: Nei Menggu Aohanqi 'Xinglongwa juluo yizhi fajue baogao,' *Kaogu* 1997(1): 1-26; Ren Shinan: 'Xinglongwa wenhua de faxian jiqi yiyi - jian yu Huabei tong shiqi de kaoguxue wenhua xiang bijiao,' *Kaogu* 1994(8): 710-718.

[7] Zhang Shuai: 'Bali yizhi fajue huo zhongyao shouhuo,' *Zhongguo wenwu bao* 28-3-93; Zhang Chi: 'Baligang shiqian juluo fajue huo zhongyao chengguo,' *Zhongguo wenwu bao* 25-12-94.

[8] *Zhongguo wenwu bao* 1993a: 'Weichisi yizhi chutu daxing paifang shi jianzhu,' *Zhongguo wenwu bao* 3-1-93; —1993b: 'Weichisi yizhi zai huo zhongyao faxian,' *Zhongguo wenwu bao* 13-6-93; Liang Zhonghe: 'Weichisi xinshiqi shidai juluo yizhi chujian guimo,' *Zhongguo wenwu bao* 12-2-95; Liang Zhonghe: 'Weichisi yizhi juluo fajue shuoguo leilei,' *Zhongguo wenwu bao* 21-8-94; Zhongguo shehui kexue yuan kaogu yanjiusuo Anhui dui: 'Anhui Mengcheng Weichisi yizhi fajue jianbao,' *Kaogu* 1994(1): 1-13; Kaogu 1995: 'Zhuanjia zuotan Anhui Mengcheng Weichisi yizhi fajue de shouhuo,' *Kaogu* 1995(4): 338-345.

[9] Zhang Min *et al*: 'Gaoyou Longqiuzhuang yizhi fajue huo zhongda chengguo,' *Zhongguo wenwu bao* 5-9-93; Zhang Min *et al*: 'Longqiuzhuang yizhi fajue zai huo zhongda chengguo,' *Zhongguo wenwu bao* 27-2-94; Zhang Min: 'Gaoyou Longqiuzhuang yizhi de fajue jiqi yiyi,' *Dongnan wenhua* 1995(4): 95-98.

has been identified as a new type of later neolithic culture. Longqiuzhuang is a large habitation site, rectangular in shape, covering some 40,000 square metres and surrounded by water, which joins large rivers to its south and west. The cultural deposit is about two metres deep and can be divided into eight strata: the top three layers are of modern or later times, but from the fourth to eighth strata, the cultural remains are clearly of the neolithic culture particular to this region. Finds include stone and bone implements, pottery and a small number of jade objects. There are the foundations of a house between the fifth and sixth layers. There is a great variety of bone or horn implements at Longqiuzhuang, and many of these are finely carved and have incised patterns. The pottery is mostly made of grey clay tempered with powdered shell, with a small quantity of dark-red clay vessels. Pottery typology indicates that a change took place between the early and later periods: the early phase is represented by bowls, jars and basins, and the later phase by the addition of tripods and high-footed cups. Painted pottery also appears in the later phase; it is decorated with geometric designs and animal or plant motifs in red and black pigments. In the sixth stratum, archaeologists found remains of cultivated rice, indicating a mixed economy based on rice cultivation, fishing and hunting. The date of the Longqiuzhuang culture is c7000-5000 bp. It represents a new cultural type differing from the Dawenkou culture in Shandong and the Majiaban-Songze cultures in southern Jiangsu. It disappeared after 5000 bp.

The discovery of sophisticated jade objects of the Liangzhu culture in 1980s attracted much attention both in China and abroad. The early 1990s saw a marked advancement in the study of the Liangzhu culture. In 1990 and 1991, a joint team from the Nanjing Museum, Suzhou Museum and Kunshan City CRO excavated the Zhaolingshan site[10] near Kunshan (Jiangsu). The site is a raised earth mound surrounded by ancient river courses and an area of 1,000 square metres was excavated, including the clearing of 83 tombs. In the centre of the site is an artificial platform made of fine soil, measuring 60 metres east to west, 50 metres south to north and four metres deep. The cultural deposit is about nine metres deep, and consists of Songze culture and Liangzhu culture sections, and an upper layer of the Eastern Zhou period. To the south of the platform are two very thick layers of burned earth, underneath which were a number of burials. The wooden coffins were originally painted with pigments. Artefacts such as jades, pottery, ivories and gems have been found in the tombs and much of the pottery was painted or had incised patterns. The jades are mainly tools and ornaments, with a high degree of polish and carved motifs. They are typical of Liangzhu jades belonging to the early, middle and later periods. A group of burials in the northwestern section of the site shows that the bodies were mainly those of young people, and that they had been dismembered before burial. They may have been sacrificed.

More Liangzhu culture remains were found in Zhejiang province. A team from the Zhejiang provincial ICRA excavated a Liangzhu culture altar and several graves at Huiguanshan[11] in 1991. They also excavated Liangzhu culture architectural remains at the Mojiaoshan site[12] in 1992. Both sites are in Yuhang county, where there is a concentration of important Liangzhu culture remains.

The Huiguanshan site is near Pinyao town, located on top of a natural hill. It was discovered during a rescue operation. The altar is rectangular in shape, with a north-south orientation, and covers a total area of 1,600 square metres. Its two-metre wide foundation was cut out of the rock and filled with soil, thereby forming the inner and outer sections. The inner section measures eight by 10 metres. There are two narrow water ditches on the east and west sides of the outer section. About two metres below the altar is another area of level ground, which may have served as the lower lever of the altar. Four large graves were also excavated on the southwestern side of the altar, where they had been cut into the ground. These graves contain a large number of jade objects, such as *cong*, *bi, yue* and ornamental head pieces. Tomb 4 is the largest Liangzhu culture grave known to date: it measures 4.75 by 2.6 metres, comprises a wooden chamber and coffin, and is rich in burial goods.

[10] Qian Feng: 'Zhaolingshan yizhi fajue huo zhongda chengguo,' *Zhongguo wenwu bao* 2-8-92; Jiangsu sheng Zhaolingshan kaogudui: Jiangsu sheng Kunshan Zhaolingshan yizhi diyi, dier ci fajue jianbao, *Dongfang wenming zhi guang*, Hainan: Guoji xinwen chuban zhongxin 1986, 18-31.

[11] Liu Wu, Wang Yunlu: 'Huiguanshan yizhi faxian jitan he damu,' *Zhongguo wenwu bao* 11-8-91; Zhejiangsheng wenwu kaogu yanjiusuo, Yuhangshi wenwu guanli weiyuanhui: 'Zhejiang Yuhang Huiguanshan Liangzhu wenhua jitan yu mudi fajue jianbao,' *Wenwu* 1997(7): 4-33.

[12] Yang Nan, Zhao Hua: 'Yuhang Mojiaoshan qingli daxing jianzhu jizhi,' *Zhongguo wenwu bao* 10-10-93; Yan Wenming: 'Liangzhu suibi,' *Wenwu* 1996(3): 28-35.

The Mojiaoshan site is located 25 kilometres northwest of Hangzhou, in the Greater and Smaller Mojiao Mountains, the Wugui Mountain and the hilly area around them. The site stretches 670 metres east to west and 450 metres north to south, over a total area of 300,000 square metres. It is triangular in shape and surrounded by water, with the two large rivers to its north and south linked by means of a tunnel. The site was first discovered during a construction project and was excavated between September 1992 and July 1993. The imposing stamped earth platform and the stratification of the site shows that the architectural remains lie between the early and later phases of the Liangzhu culture, belonging to the middle transitional period. It was during this period that the Liangzhu culture reached its peak. The spatial distribution of Liangzhu culture sites in this area suggests that Mojiaoshan may have had a political or religious importance. Important Liangzhu culture sites have been identified in the vicinity: Yaoshan, Fangshan and Huiguanshan.

In recent years, the study of early cities has become a key area in Chinese archaeology, and a number of remarkable discoveries have contributed to our understanding of early urban development in China. Between 1993-1995, the archaeological training programme organised by the SBCR carried out field work at sites near Zhengzhou (Henan). The Xishan site,[13] located 23 kilometres north of Zhengzhou, has been identified as a late Yangshao culture settlement. Finds here included house foundations, storage pits, ditches, graves, and many animal and pollen remains. There is also a stamped earth structure, which may have been an original wall built to protect the settlement. The remains of the wall in the west, north, northeast and southeast of the site form a circle: they stand about three metres tall with a width of five to six metres, and eight metres at the corners. Beyond the wall is a ditch, about five to 7.5 metres wide and four metres deep; it is likely that the earth used to build the wall came from the ditch. Examination of the wall shows that the stamped earth technique was used in its construction. A typological analysis of the pottery found at the Xishan site indicates the site was used for a long period and that the wall was probably built c5300-4800 bp, i e the late Yangshao culture period (Qinwangzhai type).

In Henan province, a joint team from the Henan provincial ICRA, the Xinxiang Regional CRO and the Huixian CRO discovered a new walled settlement at Mengzhuang, in Huixian city.[14] Excavations were carried out between July and November 1994. The remains of the stamped earth wall extend for 400 metres on each side and cover a total area of about 16,000 square metres. There was originally a moat (5.7 metres deep) surrounding the wall. Pottery sherds from the stamped earth wall and beneath the wall are rich and of great variety; many with impressed basket, cord and square patterns. Examination of the stratigraphy and pottery typology shows that the wall was probably constructed in the middle Longshan culture period, but was continuously used until the Erlitou, Shang and Zhou periods. It is the largest walled neolithic site that has ever been found in Henan. The remains are complex, and further research is needed.

In the east coast region — the core area of the Longshan culture—several walled settlements have been discovered, including the Dinggong site in Zouping county (Shandong).[15] It was discovered in 1990 by the Archaeology Section of the History Department, Shandong University, which had been excavating there since the mid-1980s. The site is square, with stamped earth walls on each side: 350 metres north to south, 310 metres east to west, and covering a total area of over 10,000 square metres. The early part of the wall was built in the middle phase of the Longshan culture. It was later rebuilt in the late Longshan period. A moat 20 metres wide and three metres deep, surrounds the wall. The cultural deposit in the site is about 1.5 to two metres deep, and finds are very rich, including houses, storage pits, kilns and graves. Burials were found beneath the house foundations. Three kilns stand close to one another and their construction is very advanced. Pottery includes some white clay vessels and a number of very finely made eggshell cups. Analysis of these artefacts shows that the site was used throughout the entire Longshan period, c4600-4000 bp. Near

[13] Zhang Yushi, Yang Zaoqing: 'Xinshiqi shidai kaogu huo zhongda faxian,' *Zhongguo wenwu bao* 10-10-95; Xu Shunzhan: 'Zhengzhou Xishan faxian Huangdi shidai gucheng,' *Zhongyuan wenwu* 1996(1): 1-5.

[14] Yuan Guangkuo: 'Huixian Mengzhuang faxian Longshan wenhua chengzhi,' *Zhongguo wenwu bao* 16-12-92.

[15] Shandong daxue lishixi kaogu jiaoyanshi: 'Zouping Dinggong faxian Longshan wenhua chengzhi,' *Zhongguo wenwu bao* 12-1-92; Shandong daxue lishixi kaogu jiaoyanshi: 'Shandong Zouping Dinggong yizhi dier, san ci fajue jianbao,' *Kaogu* 1992(6): 496-504; Shandong daxue lishixi kaogu jiaoyanshi: 'Shandong Zouping Dinggong yizhi disi, wu ci fajue jianbao,' *Kaogu* 1993(4): 295-299; Kaogu 1993: 'Zhuanjia tan Dinggong yizhi chutu taowen,' *Kaogu* 1993(4): 344-354; Feng Shi: 'Shandong Dinggong Longshan shidai wenzi jiedu,' *Kaogu* 1994(1): 37-54; Bian Ren: 'Guanyu Dinggong taowen de taolun,' *Kaogu* 1994(9): 825-831; Cao Dingyun: 'Shandong Zouping Dinggong "Longshan taowen" bianwei,' *Zhongyuan wenwu* 1996(2): 32-38.

the site, artefacts of the earlier Beixin, Dawenkou and Yueshi cultures, and later periods such as Shang and Zhou, were also found. They provide evidence for reconstructing the chronology of the regional cultural development.

Many walled settlements have also been identified in south China, particularly in the middle reaches of the Yangzi River. These are almost as early as the ones in the north and East Coast region, but are often bigger. The most important discovery is the Chengtoushan walled site[16] in Feng xian (Hunan), located on the raised terrace of the Danshui River, a branch of the Fengshui River, about 20 kilometres northwest of Feng xian town. First discovered in 1979, the site was excavated in December 1992 by a joint team from the Hunan provincial ICRA and the Feng xian CRO. A circular wall, about 310 metres in diameter, surrounds the site, and northwest of the site is a water course 35-50 metres wide and four metres deep, part natural part man-made. The walled city has four gates. These are located in the four directions, and the eastern gate is the best preserved, with a paved passage about five metres wide. Within the wall there are traces of streets and in the southwest section are the remains of a group of rectangular-shaped stamped earth platforms. Trial excavation of the wall revealed 13 cultural layers from different periods and showed that the wall was built during the middle and late phases of the Qujialing culture, c4700-4000 bp. Pottery found at the site is also typical of the Qujialing culture. The Chengtoushan site provides important evidence for a comparative study of the development of cities in northern and central China.

Bronze Age (c1900-300 BC)

Although, strictly speaking, neither Shang nor Zhou, the Qugong site[17] near Lhasa (Tibet) has yielded new and extremely important evidence for studying the beginning of the Bronze Age in China. At 3680-3690 metres above sea level, it is the highest site in China. It was excavated by a joint team from the Institute of Archaeology, CASS, and the Tibet CRO in 1990 and 1991, and yielded evidence for a new advanced Chalcolithic culture which was supported by a mixed economy. The excavated area was over 1,000 square metres and many storage pits and stone slab tombs were found, along with rich remains of polished stone implements and animal bones—horses, oxen, sheep, deer and fish—and artefacts made of bone. The ceramic production here is also well developed. Pottery was mostly made on a slow turntable, burnished, and decorated with a geometric patterning. The most significant discovery, however, is the bronze arrowhead found in the lower stratum dated to 3700 bp, making it the earliest bronze object ever found in this region. The arrowhead was examined at the University of Science and Technology, Beijing, and the result shows a metal composition of 83.67 per cent copper and 12.51 per cent tin. Jade arrowheads in the same form were also found at the site, suggesting that the bronze arrowhead is probably also of local manufacture. The cultural remains of the Qugong site differ substantially from the Karuo culture (c3300-2100 BC) excavated in eastern Tibet in the 1970s, hence the new term 'Qugong culture.'

There have been some unexpected surprises during the excavation of Shang and Zhou dynasty sites in recent years. Between March and May 1995, a joint team from the Henan provincial ICRA and the Faculty of Culture and Museum Studies, Zhengzhou University, excavated the Xiaoshuangqiao site,[18] 20 kilometres to the northwest of Zhengzhou. The excavation revealed storage pits, sacrificial burials, stamped earth foundations and ditches. The sacrificial pits contain human victims, oxen and dogs. Artefacts include stone tools and musical instruments, bronze architectural components and pottery. There is a high percentage of high-fired glazed ceramic vessels, which were probably used for a ritual purpose. Several pottery fragments have been found, as well as a jar bearing brush-writing in red. This is the earliest known Shang writing. Whilst there is evidence of bronze-casting, few bronze vessels have been found. The date of the Xiaoshuangqiao site is close to the second phase of the upper Erligang period, just after the end of the Zhengzhou Shang occupation,

[16] Shan Xianjin, Cao Chuansong: 'Fengxian Chengtoushan Qujialing wenhua chengzhi bei queren,' *Zhongguo wenwu bao* 15-3-92; Zhang Xuqiu: 'Qujialing wenhua gucheng de faxian he chubu yanjiu,' *Kaogu* 1994(7): 629-634.

[17] Zhongguo shehui kexueyuan kaogu yanjiusuo: 'Lasa Qugong yizhi chutu zaoqi qingtongqi,' *Zhongguo wenwu bao* 26-1-91.

[18] Song Guoding *et al*: 'Zhengzhou Xiaoshuangqiao yizhi fajue huo zhongda chengguo,' *Zhongguo wenwu bao* 13-8-95; Chen Xu: 'Zhengzhou Xiaoshuangqiao Shang dai yizhi de niandai he xingzhi,' *Zhongyuan wenwu* 1995(1): 1-8; Chen Xu: 'Zhengzhou Xiaoshuangqiao Shangdai yizhi ji Aodu shuo,' *Zhongyuan wenwu* 1997(2):45-50; Henan sheng wenwu kaogu yanjiusuo, Zhengzhou daxue wenboxueyuan kaoguxi. Nankai daxue lishixi bowuguanxue zhuanye: '1995 nian Zhengzhou Xiaoshuangqiao yizhi de fajue,' *Huaxia kaogu* 1996(3): 1-56; Pei Mingxiang: 'Lun Zhengzhou Xiaoshuangqiao Shangdai qianqi jisi yizhi,' *Zhongyuan wenwu* 1996(2): 4-8.

but before the beginning of the Yinxu period. Scholars are currently debating whether Xiaoshuangqiao may have been the site of one of the Shang capitals.

The biggest surprise came in September 1991 in Anyang (also known as Yinxu, capital of the late Shang dynasty), with the discovery of a hoard of 1,583 pieces of turtle-plastrons and a small number of ox scapulae, of which 579 bore inscriptions. The hoard was discovered by the Anyang Archaeology Team of the Institute of Archaeology, CASS, in the east section of Huayuanzhuang, just 400 metres south of the central area of Yinxu, i e Yinxu Museum.[19] From the stratification and pottery typology, this hoard is of an early date, probably of the first phase of the Yinxu period. The content covers subjects such as ritual, hunting, weather and the well-being of the royal family. The archaeological context and the style of the inscriptions indicates that it is most likely that they belong to the non-kings' diviners' school of the Wu Ding period. This is the most important discovery of oracle bone inscriptions (OBI) at Anyang since the finds of OBI hoard YH127 in 1936, when 17,096 pieces of inscribed bones were unearthed, and of 1973, when over 5,000 pieces were found during the excavation at Xiaotun nandi.

In the north, in Dingzhou (Hebei), a team from the Hebei provincial ICRA discovered, during a rescue operation, over 100 ancient tombs, of which 42 were of the Shang period.[20] The Shang tombs are in different sizes and are vertical pits, with a wide base and a narrow opening, and with a special ledge made on which to place burial goods. There are traces of timber chambers and painted wooden coffins in some of the tombs. It seems to have been common practice to bury dogs in tombs, and a few of the large tombs showed evidence of human sacrifice. Artefacts found in the tombs include pottery, jade and stone objects, cowrie shells, lacquerware and bronze vessels. The bronze vessels are mostly in the Shang metropolitan style but with local characteristics. Several of the bronze vessels bear inscriptions, and archaeologists have deciphered one of the inscriptions as You, probably the name of a *fangguo* (or regional state) of the Shang dynasty. The date of the tombs is probably from the late Shang period to the beginning of the Western Zhou dynasty. It is the largest Shang find in northern China, and the material from this site is crucial in determining the relationship between the Shang court and the north during this period.

In Shandong, archaeologists from the Institute of Archaeology, CASS, excavated a large cemetery of the late Shang and early Western Zhou period at Tengzhou Qianzhangda between October and December 1993.[21] Eleven tombs, two horse pits and a well were unearthed. Finds included over 200 bronze objects, many jades, much lacquerware, and a large amount of pottery. Turtles were used in the burials. About 20 of the bronze vessels bear inscriptions, and quite remarkably, five sealed bronze jars and vases were found full of liquid, probably Shang dynasty wine. The artefacts from the site are of a very high quality and in Tomb 18 a chariot was found, all reflecting great wealth. Although the inscriptions on the bronze vessels have yet to be fully deciphered, it is believed that the cemetery may have belonged to the Xie people, who formed a sub-state of the Shang dynasty, and survived into the Western Zhou dynasty. The Shang tombs were concentrated mainly in the north section of the village. Many tombs of Western Zhou date have been identified in the south of the village, but await further excavation.

Good news also came from the south. Much has been learnt of early mining technology following the excavation of the Ruichang Tongling mining site (Jiangxi) over the last seven to eight years.[22] The site was first discovered in 1988, not far from the Daye Tonglushan mining site, and over a period of four years, the Jiangxi provincial ICRA conducted a series of excavations there. The total excavated area measured over 1,800 square metres, about 600 square metres of which have now been identified as belonging to an ancient mining area. Finds include 102 mine pits, 18 passages, two furnaces, several wells, and a large number of mining tools and utensils. The furnaces are well preserved and it is likely that further research on them will be of great importance for the study of China's early metallurgy. The site was used over a long period, probably until the early Warring States period. Carbon

[19] Zhongguo shehui kexueyuan kaogu yanjiusuo: 'Yinxu Huayuanzhuang faxian zaoqi jiagu keng,' *Zhongguo wenwu bao* 22-12-91; Zhongguo shehui kexueyuan kaogu yanjiusuo: '1986-1987 nian Anyang Huayuanzhuang nandi fajue baogao,' *Kaogu xuebao* 1992(1): 97-128.

[20] Hebei sheng wenwu yanjiusuo, Baoding diqu wenwu guanlisuo, Dingzhou wenwu guanlisuo: 'Dingzhou faxian Shangdai daxing fangguo guizu mudi,' *Zhongguo wenwu bao* 15-12-91; Hebei sheng wenwu yanjiusuo: 'Dingzhou Beizhuangzi Shang mu fajue jianbao,' *Wenwu chunqiu* 1992 (special issue): 231-241.

[21] *Zhongguo wenwu bao* 1995a: 'Tengzhou Qianzhangda yizhi you zhongyao faxian,' *Zhongguo wenwu bao* 8-1-95.

[22] Jiangxi sheng wenwu kaogu yanjiusuo Tongling yizhi fajuedui: 'Jiangxi Ruichang Tongling Shang/Zhou kuangye yizhi diyici fajue jianbao,' *Jiangxi wenwu* 1990 (3): 1-12; Zhou Weijian, Lu Benshan, Hua Jueming: 'Ruichang Tongling gu kuangye yizhi de duandai jiqi kexue jiazhi,' *Jiangxi wenwu* 1990(3):13-24; Peng Shifan, Liu Shizhong: 'Guanyu Ruichang Sang/Zhou tongkuang yicun yu gu Yang Yueren,' *Jiangxi wenwu* 1990(3): 25-31; Jiangxi sheng wenwuju: 'Ruichang Tongling kuangye yizhi fajue huo zhongda chengguo,' *Zhongguo wenwu bao* 19-1-92.

[23]*Zhongguo wenwu bao* 1992: 'Guoguo mudi fajue you huo zhongda faxian,' *Zhongguo wenwu bao* 2-2-92; Xu Yongsheng: 'Cong Guoguo mudi kaogu faxian tan Guoguo lishi kaikuan,' *Huaxia kaogu* 1993(4): 92-95; Hu Xiaolong: 'Qian tan Shangcunling Guoguo mudi chema keng,' *Huaxia kaogu* 1993(4): 96-97; Tian Shuangyin: 'Cong Guoguo mudi chutu de zuiyi mianzhao kan gu zhi lianyu,' *Huaxia kaogu* 1993(4): 98-100; Henan sheng wenwu kaogu yanjiusuo, Sanmenxia shi wenwu gongzuodui: 'Shangcunling Guoguo mudi M2006 de qingli,' *Wenwu* 1995(1): 4-31; Ma Chengyuan: 'Guoguo damu canguanji,' *Zhongguo wenwu bao* 3-3-91; Zhang Changshou: 'Guoguo mudi de xin faxian,' *Zhongguo wenwu bao* 17-3-91; Zou Heng: Xin faxian Guoguo damu guan hou gan,' *Zhongguo wenwu bao* 17-3-91; Yu Weichao: 'Shangcunling Guoguo mudi xin faxian suo jieshi de jige wenti,' *Zhongguo wenwu bao* 3-2-91; Li Xueqin: 'Sanmenxia Guo mu xin faxian yu Guoguo shi,' *Zhongguo wenwu bao* 3-2-91; Jiang Tao: 'Guoguo de zao fajue yu renshi,' *Zhongguo wenwu bao* 8-12-91.

[24]*Zhongguo wenwu bao* 1993: 'Quwo Qucun fajue Jin hou mudi,' *Zhongguo wenwu bao* 10-1-93; Beijing daxue kaoguxi, Shanxi sheng kaogusuo: 'Tianma-Qucun yizhi Beizhao Jin hou mudi dier ci fajue,' *Wenwu* 1994(1): 4-28; Shanxi sheng kaogusuo, Beijing daxue kaoguxi: 'Tianma-Qucun yizhi Beizhao jin hou mudi disan ci fajue,' *Wenwu* 1994(8): 22-33; Beijing daxue kaoguxi, Shanxi sheng kaogusuo: 'Tianma-Qucun yizhi Beizhao jin hou mudi diwu ci fajue,' *Wenwu* 1995(7): 4-39; Zou Heng: 'Lun zaoqi Jin du,' *Wenwu* 1994(1): 29-32; Zhang Han: 'Jin hou xi gui mingwen chushi,' *Wenwu* 1994(1): 33-34; Sun Hua: 'Guanyu Jin hou Dui zu mu de jige wenti,' *Wenwu* 1995(9): 50-57; Sun Huan: 'Jinhou Yu/Si zu mu de jige wenti,' *Wenwu* 1997(8): 27-36; Li Xueqin: 'Jin hou Su bianzhong de shi, di, ren,' *Zhongguo wenwu bao* 1-12-96; Qiu Xigui: 'Guanyu Jinhou tongqi mingwen de jige wenti.' *Chuantong wenhua yu xiandaihua* 1994(2); Zou Heng: 'The early Jin capital discovered: a personal account' in this volume; *Zhongguo wenwu bao* 1994: 'Quwo fajue Jin hou bangfu ji furen mudi,' *Zhongguo wenwu bao* 30-1-94; Shanxi sheng kaogusuo, Beijing daxue kaoguxi: 'Tianma-Qucun yizhi Beizhao jin hou mudi disi ci fajue,' *Wenwu* 1994(8): 1-21; Li Boqian: 'Jades from tomb 63 at the Jin cemetery at Tianma-Qucun' in this volume.

[25] Ren Xianghong *et al*: 'Shandong Changqing Xianrentai yizhi faxian Siguo guizu mudi' *Zhongguo wenwu bao* 17-12-95; Cui Dayong *et al*: 'Shandong Changqing xian Xianrentai faxian Zhou dai juluo yu Siguo guizu mudi,' *Zhongguo wenwu bao* 1996(5). (Mainly photographs).

14 dating indicates that the site may be as early as the middle Shang period, making it the earliest mining site known in China.

In Western Zhou archaeology the discovery and excavation of the royal cemeteries of the Guo state in Sanmenxia Shangcunling (Henan),[23] and the one of the Jin state in Tianma-Qucun (Shanxi) are unsurpassed. Earlier excavations at Sanmenxia Shangcunling had brought to light Tomb 2001 of the Guo state during the Western Zhou period. In 1990 the Henan provincial ICRA discovered two new tombs in the northern section of the cemetery. These two tombs were vertical shaft tombs, about 20 metres deep, and the coffin had originally been placed in the centre. The occupant of Tomb 2009 had been buried with a jade face-cover and the tomb yielded a large number of artefacts, including bronze vessels, musical instruments, textiles and leather, and jade slips with brush writing. Also notable are an iron weapon and three iron tools. The tomb is believed to belong to one of the rulers of the Guo state. His burial probably took place in the late Western Zhou period.

The Department of Archaeology, Peking University, has been conducting fieldwork in Tianma-Qucun since 1980. A number of settlement sites had been discovered, but it was only in 1991 that the important royal tombs were found near Beizhao village. By then, nine large tombs had unfortunately been disturbed by tomb robbers. In 1992, a joint team from Peking University and the Shanxi Provincial Institute of Archaeology carried out rescue excavation at Qucun Beizhao to prevent further tomb plundering. The nine tombs were investigated and a further five large tombs were excavated, as well as several sacrificial pits. The tombs were mostly in pairs, all with a long sloping entrance. Finds from the tombs included many fine bronze vessels and jade objects. Inscriptions on the bronze vessels confirm that the cemetery belonged to the Jin royal house and that it was used from the Western Zhou to early Eastern Zhou periods.

Further excavation at the Jin royal cemetery in Qucun Beizhao took place in 1993, when three more tombs located in the southwestern corner of the cemetery were excavated.[24] These tombs had the same orientation as the earlier tombs and were intact. A large number of bronze and jade objects were retrieved from the tombs. The three occupants each had a jade face-cover and elaborate jade pendants. A number of bronze vessels from Tomb 64 carry the inscription "Jin Hou Banfu" (Banfu, Duke of Jin), suggesting that this tomb may have belonged to Duke Mu of Jin and that the other two tombs, Tombs 62 and 63, may have belonged to his consorts. The tombs are of the late Western Zhou period, probably of the reign of King Xuan of Zhou. The discovery is significant for these are the only Jin royal tombs which allow a clear identification of the occupants. The discovery of the Jin royal cemetery confirms that Quwo was indeed the Jin capital at that time.

For the Eastern Zhou period, there was also an important rediscovery, this time of the long-lost Si state of the Spring and Autumn period. Previously the locality of the Si state had been sought in southern Shandong. In 1995, archaeologists from Shandong University made an important discovery of the Xianrentai site[25] in Changqing, near Jinan in central Shandong. The site is located on a terrace on the northern bank of the Nandashahe River. Excavation there revealed habitation remains, storage pits, kilns and tombs. The site was occupied over a long period, from the late neolithic to the Han period. The most important finds were the six tombs of the Si state. They are all vertical shaft tombs but of different sizes, with the largest, Tomb 6, measuring over 20 square metres. The tombs all have the same orientation—45 degrees northwest—and share similar burial customs, such as the burial of a dog, the use of cinnabar and the wrapping of coffins in mats. Burial goods are rich, and include bronze vessels, musical instruments, weapons, chariot parts, and many jade items. Many of the bronzes bear inscriptions which indicate that the tombs belong to the royal house of the Si state, and that they date from the late Western Zhou to the early Spring and Autumn period. The Si state is mentioned in the *Zuozhuan* where it is said that the Si state was destroyed by Duke Xiang of the Lu state in 560 BC. This important excavation has determined the true location of the Si state and and the bronzes and jades from the tombs provide rich material for studying the Si culture.

In Henan province, the discovery of aristocratic tombs of the Chu state at the Dajiangkou reservoir has also added significantly to the study of Chu culture in the Eastern Zhou period. Between 1991 to 1992, the Henan provincial ICRA excavated some 50 tombs which were under threat of tomb robbery. These tombs, all in the Dangjiangkou reservoir area, lie close to the Chu cemetery at Xichuan Xiasi, of the Spring and Autumn and Warring States periods.[26] A bronze *ding* tripod with the inscription *Kehuang zhi sheng* was found in Tomb 1 at the Heshangling site. Kehuang is mentioned in the *Zuozhuan* as being the grandson of the Chu minister, Ziwen. The bronze *ding* was cast c605 BC. The occupant of Tomb 2 is a young female, buried with three human sacrificial victims and numerous burial goods including jades, wooden objects, bronze vessels and musical instruments. The inscriptions on a set of bells record that they were made in 600 BC. At the Xujianling site, the tombs are large and there is a large number of burial goods. For example, Tomb 10 was 13.8 metres long, and 13 metres wide, had a sloping entrance at its eastern side, and contained almost 200 burial items. A number of chariots and horses were found close to the tombs. The discovery of this cemetery has provided new clues for locating the capital of the Chu state during the Spring and Autumn period.

[26] Cao Guichen: 'Danjiangkou shuiku faxian Chuguo guizu mu,' *Zhongguo wenwu bao* 30-8-92.

Han (206 BC-AD 220)

Remarkable progress has been made in the archaeology of the Han dynasty, in particular the important excavations of a number of tombs belonging to Han noblemen. At Yongcheng Mangshan (Henan), a jade suit and many bronze objects had been found from a Han dynasty tomb in 1985. Between 1987 and 1993, the Shangqiu Regional Archaeological Team and the Henan provincial IACR carried out a series of excavations at the cemetery of the Han dynasty Liang state.[27] It is located in the Mt Mangdang, 30 metres north of Yongcheng, and most of the tombs are cut into the rocks. The tomb of King Xiao of the Liang is located on the slope of Mt Baoan, facing the east, with an entrance, corridors, tomb chamber and side chambers; it is 60 metres long and had a maximum width of 30 metres. Another large tomb (Tomb 2) was found 200 metres away, and probably belonged to King Xiao's consort. The tomb is divided into the eastern and western sections, with two entrances, three corridors, and 81 side-chambers and halls. It is 180 metres long, with a maximum width of over 70 metres, covering a total of 1,550 square metres. A number of pottery figurines and over 10,000 components of chariot fittings or horse harnesses were found in the tomb, many of which were made of gilt bronze. Some 10,000 kg of coins were found in the tomb; these have been identified as *banliang* and *yujia banliang* types. The evidence confirms that the construction of the cemetery probably began in the Jindi and Wudi reigns (156-105 BC) and that the cemetery was abandoned at the end of the Western Han dynasty. Tomb 2 also revealed the earliest and best preserved wall paintings of this period. On the surface, the cemetery was originally surrounded by walls and a drainage system has been discovered. The architecture follows the style of the Warring States period and the Qin dynasty, and many of the building materials are marked with inscriptions such as *Donggong* (Eastern Palace), *Xigong* (Western Palace) and *Xiaoyuan* (Filial Garden).

[27] Yan Daoheng: 'Yongcheng Mangshan Han Liangwang ling chutu dapi zhengui wenwu,' *Zhongguo wenwu bao* 25-8-91; Henan sheng wenwu kaogu yanjiusuo: *Yongcheng Xi Han Liangguo wangling yu qingyuan*, Zhengzhou: Zhengzhou guji chubanshe, 1996; Zheng Qingshen: 'Yongcheng qingli Liang Xiaowang ling qin jianzhu jizhi,' *Zhongguo wenwu bao* 22-5-94.

In Jiangsu province, between December 1994 and March 1995, archaeologists from the Nanjing Museum and Xuzhou Terracotta Museum successfully excavated the mausoleum of the King of the Han dynasty Chu state at Mt Shizi in Xuzhou.[28] The tomb was also cut deep into the rock, about 117 metres long (including the passage), and 13.2 metres wide, covering total of 851 square metres. The passage is in three sections, and there is a courtyard near the burial chamber. Over 15,000 objects were found: these include a jade suit, five silver and over 150 bronze seals, a large number of gold and jade objects and iron weapons. The most interesting finds are the terracotta soldiers buried around the

[28] *Zhongguo wenwu bao* 1995b: 'Xuzhou Shizishan Han Chu wang ling fajue huo zhongda chengguo,' *Zhongguo wenwu bao* 25-11-95.

[29] Cao Yannong, Song Shaohua: 'Changsha fajue Xi Han Changsha Wang shimu,' *Zhongguo wenwu bao* 22-8-93.

tomb, similar to the ones found at Qin Shihuangdi's tomb complex, but of a smaller size. Scholars now believe that the tomb probably belonged to Liu Wu, one of the third generation of Chu kings enfeoffed by the Han emperors. The excavation of the mausoleum provides the best information for studying Western Han history, in particular its enfeoffment system.

A number of important Western Han tombs have also been unearthed in Hunan, Anhui and Yunnan provinces. In 1993, the Archaeological Team of Changsha city excavated a large Han tomb which probably belonged to one of the queens of the Changsha state. It is located on the west bank of the Xiang River in Wangchengpo Gufengyuan, Changsha (Hunan).[29] The tomb is vertical, carved into the rock, with a sloping entrance and a wooden chamber. The tomb measures 37 x 15.98 metres at a depth of 13.1 metres from the surface, and with an orientation of 287 degrees. The wooden chamber is constructed in the form of the *tizhou* (timbers piled up so that the ends present a net-like appearance, *reticulatum*) and is divided into inner and outer compartments: the outer compartment measuring 7.48 metres long, 5.8 metres wide and 2.25 metres high; and the inner 3.50 metres long, 2.70 metres wide, and of the same height as the outer compartment. Both compartments are covered with timbers of a triangular section. There is a passage between the inner and outer compartments. There are two coffins, one placed inside the other, both painted in red and black. Two clay figurines were found at the entrance. A large number of artefacts have been found in the burial chamber: these include gold and silver objects, jades, glass, bronzes, iron, lacquerware, bamboo, wooden objects, bone, pottery and musical string instruments. The seal marks from the tomb read *Changsha houfu* (Queen's Residence of the Changsha state), indicating that the occupant could be female. Three other burial pits were found near the tomb: Pit 1 is a kitchen, Pit 2 contains a chariot, and Pit 3 contains many clay animal figurines.

[30] Deng Chaoyuan: 'Tianchang Han muqun chutu dapi zhengui wenwu,' *Zhongguo wenwu bao* 5-7-92; Huang Shengzhang: 'Tianchang yihao Han mu niandai wenti,' *Zhongguo wenwu bao* 21-11-93.

In Anhui province, several tombs were discovered during the construction of a reservoir in Tianchang, towards the end of 1991. A joint team from the Anhui provincial ICRA and the Tianchang county CRO undertook rescue archaeology there in spring 1992.[30] They excavated 25 tombs and found 750 objects. The tombs are dated to the Western Han period, with one exception dated to the later Warring States period. Tomb 1 is the largest and measures 4.8 by 3.5 metres. It was a joint burial of husband and wife. Five seals from the tomb show that the main occupant was Heng Ping, a courtier who worked for the wife of the King of Guangling, probably during the reign of Xuandi (73-49 BC). Finds from the Tianchang cemetery include coins, bronzes, iron, pottery, jades, wooden objects and lacquerware. In terms of quality, this is one of the best burial groups ever found of a Western Han date, in particular the lacquerware. The complete set of 28 pieces of carpenters' tools from Tomb 1 is unique.

[31] He Jinlong, Zhang Xinning: 'Lijiashan mudi fajue huo shuoguo,' *Zhongguo wenwu bao* 10-1-93; Zhang Xinning *et al*: 'Jiangchuan Lijiashan gu muqun di'er ci fajue jianbao,' *Yunnan wenwu* 1993(6): 123.

In southwest China, to the north of the Xingyun Lake in Jiangchuan (Yunnan), a cemetery of the Dian Kingdom of the 1st and 2nd centuries AD was found at Lijiashan.[31] The Lijiashan site was previously excavated in 1966 and 1972, when over 1,300 objects were retrieved. The new discovery came about during the 1992-3 session conducted by the Yunnan provincial ICRA, when a total of 58 tombs were excavated and 2,066 artefacts were found. The tombs are oriented east to west, with the large tombs buried much deeper into the ground than the smaller ones. The majority are single burials, with a smaller number of double burials, either single sex or of both sexes. A huge stone — not found locally — had been placed on each of the large tombs: these weighed from several hundred to several thousand kilogrammes each. The stones appear to have been burned. The finds include bronze, jade, gold and iron objects and various gems. Most finds came from the large tombs on the hilltop, and were found in the coffins or placed between the inner and outer coffins. The outstanding quality of the objects raises once again the question of the relationship between Lijiashan and Shizhaishan, another major site of the Dian Kingdom of the same period.

The archaeology of the Qin and Han periods is of course not restricted to tombs. In northwest China, important discoveries have been made in Gansu and Xinjiang, along the ancient 'Silk Road,' which are very significant for understanding the history and culture of the 'Silk Road.' Between 1990 and 1991, in the area between Dunhuang and Anxi, the Gansu provincial ICRA excavated the Xuanquanzhi site of the Han dynasty.[32] The site was an important postal station set up in the middle of Western Han dynasty and used until the Eastern Han period. From the architectural remains, archaeologists unearthed about 150,000 wood-slips and over 2,650 other artefacts, including writing on paper. The paper has been dated to the reigns of Xuandi and Yuandi (73-33 BC), much earlier than the traditional date for the invention of paper. The content of the wood-slips is rich and covers subjects such as economics, law, ethnic relations and social production; and most importantly, it records official communications between the Han court and the western regions.

In Xinjiang, in 1994, a joint team of Chinese and Japanese archaeologists conducted an archaeological survey of the Minfeng Niya site (Xinjiang), followed by a small scale excavation.[33] Niya is believed to be the capital of the Jingjue Kingdom, which lasted from the 1st to 3rd century AD. The excavation first revealed a habitation site where three wooden slips written in the Kharosthi script and a number of Chinese documents were found. Remains of a small Buddhist temple were also found; a stupa surrounded by an earth wall, only five metres long. A cemetery was found in the northwest of the site and eight tombs were excavated. They are double burials, each containing one man and one woman. The coffins and bodies were all well preserved, and there were rich finds, particularly textiles, some of which bear Chinese inscriptions. A pottery jar also bears the Chinese character *wang* (king).

In the south, the Guangzhou City IACR carried out a trial dig within the city at the fourth road of the Zhongshan Main Street in 1994.[34] Huge structural remains of stone were found 4.5 to seven metres below ground level. These remains included wells, ponds, tiles, bricks, pillars and, most importantly, stone paved floors with a wooden drainage system underneath. Many tiles and bricks were inscribed with tribal names such as *Fan*. Coins of the Qin and Western Han *banliang* were found. The site has been identified as the royal residence of the Nanyue Kingdom of the early Western Han period. Its architectural style and particularly its stone slab paved floors are rare in China, unlike in Europe.

Northern Wei to Tang (AD 386-907)

A noticeable change in archaeology in the 1990s is the increasing number of excavations of known historic sites. In 1993, a joint team from the Shanxi provincial Institute of Archaeology, the Datong Museum and the Yungang Institute of Cultural Relics investigated Cave 3 at Yungang (Shanxi).[35] The cave is divided into two chambers, one at the front and one at the back, with a courtyard at the front, measuring about 50 by 15 metres. Construction of the original cave had begun in the Northern Wei period but it had not been completed. Excavation of the front courtyard revealed two stone walls of the Northern Wei period, and many carved stone architectural parts and sculptures in animal forms. The unfinished floor shows the techniques used for cutting into rock and cave construction. Remains include a stamped earth ground and a low water barrier of the later Jin and Liao periods, and small finds such as coins and tiles.

In order to study the ceramic technology of the famous Hongzhou kiln (Jiangxi), in 1992, a joint team from the Jiangxi provincial ICRA and the Department of Archaeology of Peking University carried out a series of excavations at several sites where evidence had indicated an association with ceramic production at the Hongzhou kiln during the Tang period.[36] The excavation yielded a number of artefacts and, more importantly, the 'dragon kilns' built in the Sui period (AD 589-618), and saggers that date as early as the Southern Dynasties (AD 420-589).

In terms of architecture and city planning, there have been some remarkable discoveries of the Sui and Tang periods. Since 1989, the Institute of Archaeology, CASS, has been excavating the Renshougong and Jiuchenggong palaces recorded in written sources as being located in Linyou county (Shaanxi).[37] According to the records, the Renshougong palace was designed as the imperial

[32] *Zhongguo wenwu bao* 1991: 'Han Xuanquanzhi yizhi fajue huo zhongda chengguo,' *Zhongguo wenwu bao* 25-8-91.

[33] *Zhongguo wenwu bao* 1996: 'Xinjiang Niya yizhi kaogu huo fengshuo,' *Zhongguo wenwu bao* 4-1-96.

[34] Chen Weihan: 'Guangzhou faxian Xi Han Nanyueguo guanshu yizhi,' *Zhongguo wenwu bao* 11-2-96.

[35] 'Yungang ku qian yizhi fajue huo zhongda chengguo,' *Zhongguo wenwu bao* 16-1-94.

[36] 'Hongzhou yaozhi daiocha ji fajue huo zhongda chengguo,' *Zhongguo wenwu bao* 2-5-93; Jiangxi sheng wenwu kaogu yanjiusuo, Beijing daxue kaoguxi, Jiang sheng Fengcheng shi bowuguan: 'Jiangxi Fengcheng yao yizhi tiaocha baogao,' *Nanfang wenwu* 1995(2): 1-29.

[37] 'Sui Renshougong Tang jiuchenggong 37 hao dianzhi fajue huo zhongda chengguo,' *Zhongguo wenwu bao* 30-10-94.

summer palace by Yu Wenliao, the royal architect of the Sui court, and was constructed in AD 593. It continued to be used by the Tang emperors and was renamed the Jiuchenggong in AD 631. In 1994, a new architectural foundation (No 37) was accidentally revealed during construction work at the old royal palace area. Archaeologists were called in to excavate. The foundation measures 42.62 metres east to west, 31.72 metres north to south, is raised 1.09 metres above the ground, and faces south. It is well preserved in its original layout: with paved stone floor, entrance steps and 46 stone pillar bases forming the inner and outer sections. The architectural details of the building are well preserved, providing rich information of the architecture of this period.

In 1993, after six years of hard work, a joint team from the Institute of Archaeology, CASS, the Nanjing Museum and the Yangzhou City Cultural Bureau announced their new discoveries at Yangzhou (Jiangsu).[38] Yangzhou is known to have been an important trading city from before the Tang dynasty, serving as a link between the interior of China and the growing trade centres along the coast. The new excavations revealed the basic layout of the city, some 6,030 metres north to south and 3,120 metres east to west, comprising the old Zicheng and the new Luocheng sections built in the Tang dynasty. City walls, gates, streets and drainage systems were also unearthed. The evidence shows that by the middle of the Tang dynasty, Yangzhou was a rising metropolitan city, densely populated, and geared towards trade.

Another highlight was the discovery of the old Baqiao bridge in 1994 in Xi'an (Shaanxi),[39] excavated by archaeologists from the Shaanxi provincial Institute of Archaeology. According to written records, the Baqiao bridge was constructed in AD 583 to link the new Sui capital at Daxingcheng with Tongguan, Pujingguan and Lantianguang. The bridge remained in use until the Song dynasty. The remains show the bridge was several hundred metres in length, and that it was supported by four arched piers and decorated with beautiful stone carvings. It is the largest bridge ever excavated in China.

Archaeology of the Tang period also provides new evidence for studying the relationship between China and neighbouring regions. In 1990, the Heilongjiang IACR found a number of burials associated with the Bohai (Parhae) kingdom at Sanlingxiang in Ning'an (Heilongjiang).[40] The Bohai kingdom was founded in AD 699 with the name Chin'guk by T'ae Cho-yong, a refugee general from Koguryo, supported by other Koguryo refugees and descendants of the Suksin and Yemack peoples, with the intention of reviving the Koguryo kingdom. The name of the kingdom was changed to Parhae (Chinese: Bohai) in AD 713, when the third king received the title of Parhaegunwang from Emperor Xuanzong. Parhae is recorded in the *Tangshu* (Tang History) as the flourishing country of Haedong (Korea). It maintained close relations, from its foundation until AD 926, with Japan, while importing Tang culture, the Tang administrative system and planning of the five capital cities, the chief of which (Sangyong), called Yongchengbu, was in present-day Jilin.

In autumn 1990, archaeologists first excavated a large tomb built with stone slabs. It has an entrance, a corridor and a burial chamber. The chamber is 3.90 x 3.30 metres with a height of 2.45 metres. The corridor is 2.70 by 1.40 metres wide with a height of 1.70 metres. Over 10 bodies were found in the tomb, including those of infants. Artefacts included ceramic vessels, tiles and animal sculptures. The tomb is decorated with plant motifs and figurative painting.

Following the success of the 1990 excavation, the Heilongjiang ICRA embarked on another large project. Between 1992 and 1995, archaeologists excavated a large cemetery of the Bohai Kingdom at the Hongzun Fish Farm at Bohaizheng in Ning'an.[41] A total of 323 tombs and seven altars were cleared, yielding over 2,000 artefacts. The tombs are in a variety of different forms and sizes, and can be classified into three types according to their construction material: *a)* stone slabs, *b)* bricks, and *c)* mixed use of stone slabs and bricks. The bricks are red and/or green in colour and come in various shapes. There are both single and group burials, and some are secondary burials or cremations. There are rich burial goods, including pottery vessels, bronze and iron weapons,

[38] Wang Qinjin: 'Yangzhou Tang cheng kaogu huo zhongda jinzhan,' *Zhongguo wenwu bao* 21-11-93.

[39] 'Xi'an faxian Sui dai Banhe guqiao yizhi,' *Zhongguo wenwu bao* 10-7-94.

[40] Jin Taishun: 'Ning'an Hongzun yuchang Mohe Bohai muqun fajue you zhongda shouhuo,' *Zhongguo wenwu bao* 4-2-96.

[41] Heilongjiang sheng wenwu kaogu yanjiusuo: 'Heilongjiang fajue Bohai daxing shishi bihua mu,' *Zhongguo wenwu bao* 19-1-92.

tools, horse harnesses and ornamental objects made of gold, silver, jade and agate. The altar is the earliest known example of its kind. Generally, these altars range from 5.4 x 7 metres to 3 x 4.8 metres, they are surrounded by stone walls, and artefacts found by them include pottery, jewellery made of gilt bronze, silver or agate, and, interestingly, horse teeth. It is unusual to find such a large concentration of tombs associated with the Bohai Kingdom.

Song-Liao-Yuan (AD 960-1368)

Architectural remains and tombs still feature strongly in the archaeology of this period. In 1991, during a rescue operation, the Luoyang Archaeological Team of the Institute of Archaeology, CASS, excavated a Northern Song (AD 960-1127) garden opposite the old magistrate's building.[42] The garden is located at the southern end of Zhongzhou Road, corresponding to the southeastern part of the city during the Tang dynasty. The excavated area covers 1,500 square metres, and the remains include two paved corridors to the east and west, about 50 metres long and 4.5 metres wide. A flower bed meets the corridor on the western side, and a patterned brick path links the two corridors. Halfway down the path lie the foundations of a gatetower and a stamped earth wall running north to south, which divides the garden into eastern and western sections. A narrow path runs beside the eastern wall. Beside the eastern wall runs another narrow path and a parallel drainage channel which connects with a water-pool to the south of the brick path, where pavilions once stood. Above the Song architectural remains there are Jin, Yuan, Ming and Qing cultural deposits, but the ceramics and coins found in the early deposits confirm that the garden is of Northern Song date.

In 1995, the Imperial Temple of the Southern Song (AD 1127-1279) was excavated in Hangzhou (Zhejiang).[43] According to historical records, the temple was built in AD 1134. The archaeological evidence confirms this and shows that it was probably rebuilt several times. The excavation area measures about 1,000 square metres and the remains include the eastern wall, the gate and an earth platform. This is the largest temple ever discovered of such an early date.

Remarkable discoveries relating to the Liao kingdom have been made in Inner Mongolia, although it is unfortunate that the discoveries were made after the tombs had been robbed. From September to October 1992, a joint team from the Inner Mongolia IACR, the Chifeng City Museum and the Aluke'erxin Banner CRO excavated the tomb of a Khitan nobleman.[44] The tomb is located on Mt Aketu, also known as Lefengshan, located about 30 kilometres southeast of Hansumusumu, Aluke'erxin Banner. Rescue excavation was carried out following two incidents of tomb robbery. The tomb lies 10.2 metres below the surface and is over 30 metres long. A tomb gate and passageway lead to the chamber, so that the tomb consists of the main chamber, the passageway and two side chambers on both sides. There are two coffin beds in the main chamber. The tomb was constructed in stone and green-glazed bricks were used for the inner walls and ceiling. The interior was originally painted and the stone doors were polished and painted with plant and bird motifs. Many burial goods have been retrieved, including ceramics, and gold and silverware, with design and craftsmanship of superb quality. The epitaph found in the tomb identifies the occupant as the 52-year-old Yelü Yuzhi (AD 890-941), a prominent member of the Khitan royal clan, who merited a biography in the *Liaoshi*. During his lifetime, Yelü Yuzhi attained many important official positions, such as Right Supervisor of the Central Pavilion of the Dongdan Kingdom (*Dongdanguo zhongtai youping zhangshi*) and Grand Master of the Eastern Capital (*Dongjing taifu*). The discovery of his tomb provides important material for the study of Khitan culture and history.

In Aluke'erxin Banner (Inner Mongolia), the same team excavated two more tombs which had been plundered. The two Liao tombs are located on the southern side of Mt Baoshan, together with many other tombs surrounded by a wall.[45] The tombs were constructed using stone slabs and comprise an entrance, door, corridor, burial chamber and side chamber. Inside the tombs, the structure

[42] Luo Tang: 'Luoyang zaixian Bei Song yashu tingyuan yizhi,' *Zhongguo wenwu bao* 14-6-92; Zhongguo shehui kexue yuan kaogu yanjiusuo Luoyang Tang cheng gongzuodui: 'Luoyang Song dai yashu tingyuan yizhi fajue baogao,' *Kaogu* 1996(6): 1-5.

[43] Hangzhou shi wenwu kaogusuo: 'Hangzhou faxian Nan Song Lin'an cheng taimiao yizhi,' *Zhongguo wenwu bao* 31-12-95.

[44] Qi Xiaoguang: 'Nei Menggu faxian Qidan huangzu Yelü Yuzhi mu,' *Zhongguo wenwu bao* 31-1-93; Nei Menggu wenwu kaogu yanjiusuo, Chifeng shi bowuguan, Aluke'erxinqi wenwu guanlisuo: 'Liao Yelü Yuzhi mu fajue jianbao,' *Wenwu* 1996(1): 4-32; Zhao Feng, Qi Xiaoguang: 'Yelü Yuzhi mu sichou zhong de tuancai he tuan huawen,' *Wenwu* 1996(1): 33-35; Qi Xiaoguang: 'Yelü Yuzhi muzhi dui wenxian jizai de qibu,' *Wenwu* 1996(2): 41-44.

[45] Qi Xiaoguang: 'Nei Menggu fajue Baoshan Liao chu bihua mu,' *Zhongguo wenwu bao* 1-1-95.

imitates contemporary living quarters and the walls are decorated with figurative and flower paintings and calligraphy. Tomb 1 is 22.5 metres long and an inscription found on the wall of the side chamber says that the occupant was the 14-year old son of a Khitan noble family, buried in AD 923. Although Tomb 2 is smaller and has no inscription, it is likely to belong to another member of the same family.

Five Liao tombs of a later date, c11th-12th century AD, were excavated by Hebei provincial Institute of Cultural Relics at Xuanhua Xiabali (Hebei) in 1993.[46] The construction of the tombs again resembles contemporary living quarters, with a wooden door and wooden furniture, and with ceramic vessels, food and fruit on the tables. The walls are painted with scenes depicting processions, musicians, chess-players and the tea ceremony. An interesting burial custom was noted here: the bodies were cremated, and the ashes were placed inside anthropomorphic models made of wood or straw, dressed in clothes, and the models were then placed inside the coffins. On the coffins are inscriptions from Buddhist sutras. The epitaphs found in the tombs show that the dead were members of the Zhang family, a Chinese clan which served at the Khitan court.

Another important project of a very different nature has also been noted. In 1991-1992, archaeologists from the National Museum of Chinese History, with the assistance of scientists from the No 1 Team of Oceanic Survey of the Ministry of Mining, made successful underwater investigations of the Yuan dynasty shipwreck at Suizhong Sandaogan (Liaoning).[47] A third session took place between May and July 1993. The wreck was a commercial vessel of the Yuan dynasty (AD 1206-1368), filled with goods of trade, mostly glazed ceramics, some of which were Cizhou ware. The part of the wreck jutting out from the sea bed measures 16 x 7 metres. The wreck has provided primary evidence of early shipbuilding technology, as well as evidence for oceanic trade between China and the outside world. This is the first major Chinese project concerning underwater archaeology.

Archaeological Survey of the Three Gorges Area

With the state project to construct the Three Gorges Dam well under way, the archaeological survey of the area which will be affected by subsequent flooding has gained momentum. About 18 institutions have participated in the survey and a total area of over 200,000 square metres has been excavated.[48] About 800 sites have been registered and some 10,000 objects found. A broad range of sites from different periods have been unearthed, the most significant being the palaeolithic and neolithic sites. The survey confirms that the middle reaches of the Yangzi River have very rich remains of early human activity, and a new type of neolithic culture has been identified, which differs from the Daxi culture. The survey has also provided material for the study of local traditions and for cultural contact between the local culture and the Shang and Zhou culture in the central plains. The survey employed many new scientific methods and has raised the standard of general archaeological practice in the region significantly.

[46] Zheng Shaozong: 'Zhangjiakou qingli Liao bihua muqun, *Zhongguo wenwu bao* 8-8-93; Hebei sheng wenwu yanjiusuo, Zhangjiakou wenwu guanlichu, Xuanhua qu wenwu guanlisuo: 'Xuanhua Liao dai bihua muqun,' *Wenwu Chunqiu* 1995(2)-1-23; Hebei sheng wenwu yanjiusuo, Zhangjiakou wenwu guanlichu, Xuanhua qu wenwu guanlisuo: 'Hebei Xuanhua Liao Zhang Wencao bihua mu fajue jianbao,' *Wenwu* 1996(9): 14-46.

[47] *Zhongguo wenwu bao* 1994: 'Suizhong Yuan dai chenchuan yizhi disan ci diaocha chengguo xi ren,' *Zhongguo wenwu bao* 6-2-94.

[48] *Zhongguo wenwu bao* 1994: 'Sanxia kaogu huo da mianji fengshou,' *Zhongguo wenwu bao* 24-7-94; *Zhongguo wenwu bao* reporter: 'Sanxia baqu kaogu qude fengshuo chengguo,' *Zhongguo wenwu bao* 20-2-94.

Chinese Historical Chronology

Shang dynasty	c1600 - 1145 BC
Western Zhou dynasty	c1145 - 771 BC
Eastern Zhou dynasty	771 - 221 BC
Qin dynasty	221 - 206 BC
Western Han dynasty	206 BC – 9 AD
Wang Mang interregnum	9 - 23 AD
Eastern Han dynasty	25 - 220 AD
The Three Kingdoms	220 - 265 AD
Western Jin dynasty	265 - 313 AD
Eastern Jin dynasty	317 - 419 AD
Wei dynasty	385 - 557 AD
Northern Qi dynasty	550 - 577 AD
Northern Zhou dynasty	557 - 580 AD
Sui dynasty	581 - 618 AD
Tang dynasty	618 - 906 AD
Five Dynasties	907 - 960 AD
Northern Song dynasty	960 - 1127 AD
Southern Song dynasty	1127 - 1279 AD
Yuan dynasty	1279 - 1368 AD
Ming dynasty	1368 - 1644 AD
Qing dynasty	1644 - 1912 AD

Glossary

Aluke'erxinqi 阿鲁科尔沁旗
An Zhimin 安志敏 (1924-)
Anhui 安徽
Anning 安宁
Anxi 安西
Anyang 安阳
Aofengshan 鳌凤山
Aohanqi 敖汉旗
Aoxiangshan 翱翔山

Ba 巴
Bahe 灞河
baigaoni 白膏泥
Baiyanglincun 白杨林村
Baizifan 百子畈
Baligang 八里岗
Banpo 半坡
Bangfu 邦父
Baodun 宝墩
Baoshan 包山 (Hubei)
Baoshan 保山 (Yunnan)
Baoshan 宝山 (Liaoning)
Baotou 包头
Batatai 八塔台
Beiliu 北流
Beixin 北辛
Beizhao 北赵
Beizhuangzi 北庄子
bi 箄
bi 璧
bishou 匕首
Bian Ren 卞仁
bianxiang 边箱
bo 钹
Bohai 渤海

Bohuo 柏馘

Cancong 蚕丛
Cao Chuansong 曹传颂
Cao Guiqin 曹桂芩
Cao Yannong 曹砚农
Cao Zijian 曹子建 (192-232)
Caojiagang 曹家岗
Caoxieshan 草鞋山
Chahai 查海
Changdao 长岛
Changning 昌宁
Changqing 长清
Changsha 长沙
Changshu 常熟
Changzi xian 长子县
Che Guangjin 车广金
Chen Chen 臣辰
Chen Fang 陈放
Chen Shengyong 陈剩勇
Chen Weihan 陈伟汉
Chen Xu 陈旭
Cheng'guan xiang 城关乡
Cheng hou 成侯 (Marquis Cheng,
    Furen 服人)
Cheng wang 成王(King Cheng,
    *r*1402-1006)
cheng 城
Chengbeixi 城背溪
Chengdu 成都
Chenggong 成公 (Duke of Cheng)
Chenggong 呈贡
Chenggu 城固
Chengjiang 澄江
Chengting 成亭

Chengtoushan 城头山
chengzao 成造
Chenyangchuan 陈阳川
Chiyou 蚩尤
Chongli 重黎
Chongshan 崇山
Chu 楚
Chuxiong 楚雄
Cili 慈利
Cishan 磁山
cong 琮
Cui Dayong 崔大庸

Dabona 大波那
Dadiwan 大地湾
Dadong 大洞
Dadunzi 大墩子
Dai Yingxin 戴应新
Dali 大理
Dangyang 当阳
Danjiangkou 丹江口
Daodunzi 倒墩子
Dao xian 道县
Datong 大同
Dawenkou 大汶口
Daxi 大溪
Daxia 大夏
Deng Chaoyuan 邓朝源
Denghu 澄湖
Dengjiawan 邓家湾
Dengzhou 邓州
Deqin 德钦
Deshan 德山
Dian 滇
Dianchi 滇池
Dianwang zhi yin 滇王之印
Diaotonghuan 吊桶环
Dilizhi 地理志 (*Hanshu*)
ding 鼎
Dinggong 丁公
Dingqiao 丁桥
Dingzhou 定州
Dingzhuang 丁庄
Di 氏
Dong Yong 董永
Donghuishan 东灰山
Dongnangou 东南沟
Dongshanzui 东山嘴
Dongting 洞庭
dou 豆
du 都
Duyu 杜宇
dui 敦
Dunhuang 敦煌
Dushi fangyu jiyao 读史方舆纪要 (by
Gu Zuyu 顾祖禹, 1631-1692)

Echeng 鄂城

Erhai 洱海
Erligang 二里岗
Erlitou 二里头

Fan 番
Fangchijie 方池街
fangguo 方国
fanglun 纺轮
fangyi 方彝
Fanshan 反山
Fen 汾
Feng Shi 冯时
Fengcheng 丰城
Feng xian 沣县
Fengxiang 凤翔
fenjingbang 分经棒
fenjingtong 分经筒
fou 缶
fu 釜
Fu Langyun 付朗云
Fufeng 扶风
Fuhe 滏河
Fujian 福建
Funan 阜南
Fuqinxiaoqu 抚琴小区
Fuquanshan 福泉山
Fuxin 阜新

Gan Zhigeng 干志耿
Ganjiang 赣江
ganlan 干栏
Gansu 甘肃
Gao Quxun 高去寻
Gao Wei 高玮
Gaoyou 高邮
ge 戈
gong 觥
Gongsuhao 公苏耗
Goujian 勾践
gu 鼓
Gu Yanwu 顾炎武 (1613-1682)
Guan 管
guan 罐
Guangdong 广东
Guangdu 广都
Guanghan 广汉
Guangnan 广南
Guangxi 广西
Guangxu Yuchengxianzhi
光绪羽城县志
Guangyuan 广元
Guangyun 广韵
Guanpingyan 贯平堰
Guanzhou 广州
Gucheng 故城
Guifang 鬼方
gui 簋
Guihuashu 桂花树

Guilin 桂林
Gui xian 贵县
Guizhou 贵州
Gu Jiang 故绛
Guo Baojun 郭宝钧 (1893-1971)
Guojiacun 郭家村
guo 椁
Guo moruo 郭沫若 (1892-1978)
Guo Suxin 郭素新
Gushi 固始
Guyuan 固原

Haimenkou 海门口
Han 韩
Han 汉
Han Kongle 韩孔乐
Handan 邯郸
Hangjiahu 杭嘉湖
Hangzhou 杭州
Hanshan 含山
Hanshu 汉书 (by Ban Gu 班固, 32-92)
He Jinlong 何金龙
He Tianxing 何天行
Hebei 河北
Hehuachi 荷花池
Heilongjiang 黑龙江
Heishantou 黑山头
Hejiawan 何家湾
Hekou 河口
Hemudu 河姆渡
Henan 河南
Hetao 河套
Hohhot 呼和浩特
Honghe 红河
Hongzhou 洪州
Hongzun 虹鳟
Hou Ji 后稷
Hou Mu Xin 后母辛
Hougudui 侯古堆
Houhan shu 后汉书 (by Fan Ye 范晔, 398-445)
Houma 侯马
hu 壶
Hu 胡
Hu Sheng 胡绳
Hu Xiaolong 胡小龙
Hua'nan 华南
Huaihe 淮河
Huainanzi 淮南子(by Liu An 刘安, 179-122 BC)
Huaiyi 淮夷
huang 璜
Huang Shengzhang 黄盛璋
Huangdi 黄帝
Huangdi 皇帝
Huangpi 黄陂
Huangquan 黄泉

Huaxia 华夏
Hua xian 华县
Huayangguozhi 华阳国志 (by Chang Qu 常璩, 291?-361?)
Huayuanzhuang 花园庄
Hubei 湖北
Huiguanshan 汇观山
Hui xian 辉县
Huliuhe 壶流河
hulu 葫芦
Hunan 湖南

ji 戟
Ji xian 吉县
jia 家
Jiahu 贾湖
Jiameng 葭萌
Jianchuan 剑川
Jiangchuan 江川
Jiangling 江陵
Jiangshan 绛山
Jiangsu 江苏
Jiangting 降亭
Jiangxi 江西
jianmu 建木
Jianping 建平
Jiaodong 胶东
Jiaqingyitongzhi 嘉庆一统志
Jiaxing 嘉兴
Jieshi 碣石
Jigongshan 鸡公山
Jijiahu 季家湖
Jijiaocheng 鸡叫城
Jilin 吉林
Jimingcheng 鸡鸣城
Jin 晋
Jin hou 晋侯 (Marquis Ji, Xiefu 燮父)
Jin hou 靖侯 (Marquis Jin, Yijiu 宜臼)
Jin Jinggong 晋景公 (Duke Jing of Jin)
Jin Taishun 金太顺
Jin Wengong 晋文公 (Duke Wen of Jin)
jing 粳
Jing Chu suishiji 荆楚岁时记
Jingpo 景颇
Jingshan 京山
Jinning 晋宁
Jinshan 金山
Jinshengcun 金胜村
jinshixue 金石学
Jinxi 锦西
Jinzhong 晋中
Jiucheng 九成
Jiudian 九店
Jizhou 冀州

juanjingzhou 卷经轴
jue 爵
Jundushan 军都山
Juzhanghe 沮家河

Karuo 卡若
Kaihua 开化
kaikoufangshi 开口方式
Kaiming 开明
Kang wang 康王 (King Kang ,
    r1005-978BC)
Kazuo 喀左
Ke Jun 柯俊
Kunming 昆明
Kunshan 昆山
Kuodizhi 括地志

Langjiazhuang 郎家庄
Lanzhou 兰州
Laohahe 老哈河
Laoguantai 老官台
Leigudun 擂鼓墩
Lengshuichong 冷水冲
Leshan 乐山
li 里
li 鬲
Li hou 厉侯 (Marquis Li, Fu 福)
Li Huairen 李淮仁
Lushun 旅顺
Li Xueqin 李学勤
Li Yuzheng 李域铮
Liang 梁
Liang Siyong 梁思永 (1904-1954)
Liang Zhonghe 梁中合
Liangzhu 良渚
Liao 辽
Liaoshi 辽史
Liaodong 辽东
Liaohe 辽河
Liaoning 辽宁
Li Chi (Li Ji) 李济 (1896-1979)
Liji 礼记
Lijiacun 李家村
Lijiashan 李家山
Lin'ancheng 临安城
Linjia Dongxiang 林家东乡
Lin Xiang 林向
Lin Yun 林云
ling 铃
Lingjiatan 凌家滩
Lingnan 岭南
Lingshan 灵山
Lingyuan 凌源
Linqiong 临邛
Lintong 临潼
Linyou 麟游
Linzi 临淄

liqi 礼器
Liu Bin 刘斌
Liu Deyin 刘德银
Liu Dunzhen 刘敦桢
Liu Hong 刘弘
Liu Shizhong 刘诗中
Liu Zhihui 刘智慧
Liuchengqiao 浏城桥
Li xian 礼县
Lizhaixiang 里砦乡
long 龙
Longgangsi 龙岗寺
Longhua 隆化
Longnan 龙南
Longqiuzhuang 龙虬庄
Longshan 龙山
Loo, CT 庐芹斋
Lu Sixian 陆思贤
Lufeng 禄丰
luo 锣
Luo Erhu 罗二虎
Luo Feng 罗丰
Luo Kaiyu 罗开玉
Luo Tang 洛唐
Luobowan 罗泊湾
Luohe 洛河
Luojiaboling 罗家柏岭
Luojiajiao 罗家角
Luotuoliang 骆驼梁
Luoyang 洛阳
Lushan xian 芦山县

Ma Shizhi 马世之
Majiabang 马家浜
Majiang 麻江
Majiayan 马家院
Majiayao 马家窑
Mamuhe 马牧河
Mangshan 芒山
mao 矛
Maoqinggou 毛庆沟
Maoshan 茅山
Maoshi Tangpu 毛诗唐谱
maowu 旄舞
Machang 马厂
Mashan 马山
Mawangdui 马王堆
Meinian 梅埝
meishu kaogu 美术考古
Meixian 梅县
Mencheng 蒙城
Meng Wentong 蒙文通
Mengzhuang 孟庄
Mengzi 蒙自
Mianchi 渑池
Mianshan 绵山
Miao 苗
Miaodigou 庙底沟

Midu 弥渡
Minhe 民和
Minfeng 民丰
Minle 民乐
mingqi 明器
Minshan 岷山
Mojiaoshan 莫角山
Mouding 牟定
Mozi 墨子
Mu hou 穆侯 (Marquis Mu, Feiwang 费王)
Mu wang 穆王 (King Mu, *r* 956-918 BC)

Nan'an 南安
Nan'ganhecun 南干河村
Nanhu 南湖
Nanjing 南京
Nanliang xiang 南梁乡
Nanshan'gen 南山根
Nanyang 南阳
Nanyue 南越
Nanzheng 南郑
Nanzhuangtou 南庄头
nei 内
Ning'an 宁安
Ningcheng Dianzi 宁城甸子
Ninglang 宁蒗
Ningshao 宁绍
Ningxia 宁夏
Ningzhen 宁镇
Niuheliang 牛河梁
Niya 尼雅
Nuwa 女娲

pan 盘
Panjiatang 潘家塘
Panlongcheng 盘龙城
Pan xian 盘县
Peiligang 裴李岗
Peng Shifan 彭适凡
Pengtoushan 彭头山
Pengyang 彭阳
Pi 郫
Pijiang 郫江
Pingquan 平泉
Pi xian 邳县
Poyang 鄱阳
Pu 濮

Qi 齐
Qixiong 七雄
Qi Xiaoguang 齐小光
Qi Yuzhen 戚玉箴
Qian Feng 钱峰
Qiang 羌
Qianshanyang 钱山漾
Qiantang 钱塘

Qianzhangda 前掌大
Qijia 齐家
Qin 秦
Qin Shihuangdi 秦始皇帝
qing 磬
qinggaoni 青膏泥
Qinghai 青海
qinghuini 青灰泥
Qinglian'gang 青莲岗
Qinglongquan 青龙泉
Qingpu 青浦
Qingtaocun 青台村
Qinling 秦岭
Qinwangzhai 秦王寨
Qinzhou 青州
qiongkou 銎口
Qionglai 邛崃
Qixia 栖霞
Quanhucun 泉护村
Qucun 曲村
Quemuqiao 雀幕桥
Qugong 曲贡
Qujialing 屈家岭
Qujiang 曲江
Qujing 曲靖
Qushang 瞿上
Quwo 曲沃

Ren Xianghong 任相宏
Rong 戎
Rong-Di 戎狄
Ruichang 瑞昌
Ruicheng 芮城

Sandaoying 三道营
Sanfangwan 三房湾
Sangganhe 桑干河
sanjiao 三角
Sanjiazhuang 三家庄
Sanmenxia 三门峡
Sanxia 三峡
Sanxingdui 三星堆
Sanyuancun 三元村
Sanzhang 三张
se 瑟
sese 瑟瑟
Shaanxi 陕西
Shaguotun 沙锅屯
Shan Xianjin 单先进
Shandong 山东
Shang 商
Shangcunling 上村岭
Shangdongcun 上东村
Shanghai 上海
Shangmacun 上马村
Shangshu 殇叔 (Marquis Mu's brother)
Shanhaijing 山海经

Shantou 汕头
Shanxi 山西
Shao Wangping 邵望平
Shazhong 沙冢
she 社
Shennong 神农
Shen Zhongchang 沈仲常
sheng 塍 (胜)
sheng 笙 (a musical instrument)
Shenyang 沈阳
shi 士
Shi Xingbang 石兴邦 (1923-)
Shibanchong 石板冲
Shibancun 石板村
Shi'erqiao 十二桥
Shiji 史记 (by Sima Qian 司马迁, *b* 145 BC?)
Shijiahe 石家河
Shimen 石门
Shiping 石屏
Shishou 石首
Shixia 石峡
Shizhaishan 石寨山
Shizishan 狮子山
Shou xian 寿县
shoumian 兽面
Shu 蜀
Shuangliu xian 双流县
Shuitianfan 水田畈
Shun 舜
Shuowen jiezi 说文解字 (by Xu Shen 许慎, 1st century AD)
Shuwang benji 蜀王本纪 (by Yang Xiong 扬雄, 53BC‐18 AD)
Shuzhi 蜀志
Si Kong 司空
Si Tu 司土
Si Tu Mu 司菟母
Si Xin 司辛
Si Yue 四岳
Sichuan 四川
Song 宋
Song Guoding 宋国定
Song Shaohua 宋少华
Song Zhaolin 宋兆麟
Songze 崧泽
Sui Xian 随县
Suizhong 绥中
Suizhou 随州
Sun Hua 孙华
Sun Jiaxiang 孙嘉祥
Sun Shoudao 孙守道
Susong 苏淞

Ta'ershan 塔儿山
Taian 泰安
Taigubaiyan 太谷白燕
Taihu 太湖

Taihuang Taihou 太皇太后
taijia zhiji 台架织机
Taishidian 太史淀
Taiyuan 太原
Tang 唐
Tangshan 汤山
Tangshu 唐叔
Tangshu Yu 唐叔虞
Tangtao 唐陶
Tanjialing 谭家岭
Taosi 陶寺
taotie 饕餮
Taoyuan 桃源
Tengchong 腾冲
Tengzhou 滕州
Tian Changwu 田昌五
Tian Guanjin 田广金
Tian Shuangyin 田双印
Tianchang 天长
Tianma-Qucun 天马‐曲村
Tianmushan 天目山
Tianxingguan 天星观
Tianzimiao 天子庙
ticou 题凑
Tinglin 亭林
Tongling 铜岭
tongshihouzong 筒式后综
Tongxiang 桐乡
Tongxin 同心
Tucheng 土城

Wang Feng 王逢
Wang Jihuai 王吉怀
Wang Qinjin 王勤金
Wang Wei 王巍
Wang Yi 王毅
Wang Yunlu 王云路
Wangdi 望帝
Wangshan 望山
Wanjiaba 万家坝
Wannian 万年
Wei 魏
Weiyanggong 未央宫
Wei Zhengjin 魏正瑾
Weichisi 尉迟寺
Weishan 巍山
Wen hou 文侯 (Marquis Wen, Chou 仇)
Wenshan 文山
Wuba 五霸
Wu En 乌恩
Wu Hong 巫鸿
Wu hou 武侯 (Marquis Wu, Ningzu 宁族)
wu 巫
Wu 吴
Wu-Yue 吴越
Wuan 武安

Wuchang 武昌
Wucheng 吴城
Wudi benji 五帝本记 (*Shiji*)
Wudi 五帝
Wugong 武功
Wujiang 吴江
Wujin 武进
Wuliangci 武梁祠
Wuxian 吴县
Wuyang 舞阳

Xi'an 西安
Xi hou 僖侯 (Marquis Xi, Situ 司徒)
Xia 夏
Xia Nai 夏鼐 (1910-1985)
Xiabali 下八里
Xiajiadian 夏家店
Xian hou 献侯 (Marquis Xian, Ji or Su 籍/苏)
Xiangfen 襄汾
Xiangjiang 湘江
Xiangshan 翔山
Xiangyun 祥云
xian 籼
Xianrendong 仙人洞
xiao 萧
Xiaoheishigou 小黑石沟
Xiaoheyan 小河沿
Xiaojiawuji 肖家屋脊
Xiaoshuangqiao 小双桥
Xia xian 夏县
Xichagou 西岔沟
Xichuan 淅川
Xichuang Xiasi 淅川下寺
Xifu 喜父
Xigoupan 西沟畔
Xiheying 西河营
Xiji 西吉
Xijiang 西江
Xilamulunhe 西拉木伦河
Ximeng 西盟
Xin'gan Dayangzhou 新干大洋洲
Xindu 新都
Xingcheng 兴城
xinggong 行宫
Xinglongwa 兴隆洼
Xingyang 荥阳
Xinjiang 新疆
Xin Jiang 新绛
Xinjin Longma 新津龙马
Xinjixiang 新集乡
Xinle 新乐
Xinyang 信阳
Xinzheng 新郑
Xinzhuangtou 辛庄头
Xiongnu 匈奴
Xishan 西山

Xiwangcun 西王村
Xiwangmu 西王母
Xiwusi 西吴寺
Xixiang 西乡
Xiyangdian 西漾淀
Xiyincun 西阴村
Xu Chaolong 徐朝龙
xu 簋
Xu Yongsheng 许永生
Xu Zhifan 许智范
Xu Zhongshu 徐中舒
Xuandi 宣帝 (*r* 73－49 BC)
Xuanwu 玄武
Xuang wang 宣王 (King Xuan, *r* 817-782 BC)
Xuanhua 宣化
Xuanquanzhi 悬泉置
Xuchang 许昌
Xuejiagang 薛家岗
Xushui 徐水
Xushuling 蓄树岭
Xuyi 徐夷
Xuzhou 徐州

ya 亚
Ya Bi 亚弼
Yan Daoheng 阎道衡
Yan Shizhong 延世忠
Yan Wenming 严文明
Yandao 严道
Yandi 炎帝
Yang Nan 杨楠
Yang Xizhang 杨锡璋
Yang Zhaoqing 杨肇清
Yangcheng 阳城
yangjiaoniu 羊角钮
Yangjiaquan 杨家圈
Yangjiawan 杨家湾
Yanglang 杨郎
Yangshao 仰韶
Yangzhou 扬州
Yangzishan 羊子山
Yanqing 延庆
Yanshan 燕山
Yanshi 偃师
Yantai 烟台
Yanzhou 兖州
Yao 尧
Yaoan 姚安
Yaodian 尧典
Yaodu 尧都
yaokeng 腰坑
Yaoshan 瑶山
Yazihe 鸭子河
Yedian 野店
Yelu Yu 耶律羽
Yi 翼

yi 邑
Yichang 宜昌
Yicheng 翼城
Yidi 义地
Yihe 伊河
Yili 仪礼
Yin Da 尹达
Yin 殷
Yingshan Wudian 应山吴店
Yinxiangcheng 阴湘城
Yinxu xidi 殷墟西地
Yiwulushan 医巫闾山
Yi xian 易县
Yongcheng 永城
Yongsheng 永胜
Yuan Guangkuo 袁广阔
Yuan Jiarong 袁家荣
Yuan 元
Yuanhejunxiantuzhi 元和郡县图志
Yuanjiang 元江
Yu Wenkai 宇文恺 (555-612)
Yuchanyan 玉蟾岩
Yudi jisheng 舆地纪胜
Yue 越
Yueshi 岳石
Yue wang 越王 (King of Yue)
Yucheng 羽城
Yue'erhe 月儿河
yue 钺
Yueliangwan 月亮湾
Yufu 鱼凫
Yufuzhi 舆服志
Yugong 禹贡
Yuhang 余杭
Yuhuangmiao 玉皇庙
yuji 虞祭
Yujiahu 余家湖
Yuyao 余姚
Yungang 云冈
Yunmeng Shuihudi 云梦睡虎地
Yunnan 云南
Yutaishan 雨台山

Zaoshi 皂市
Ze Lu 泽潞
Zeng 曾
Zengpiyan 甑皮岩
Zhang Chi 张弛
Zhang Guangzhi 张光直
Zhang Han 张颔
Zhang Hangang 张汉刚
Zhang Min 张敏
Zhang Minghua 张明华
Zhang Shuai 张帅
Zhang Xinning 张新宁
Zhang Xuqiu 张绪球
Zhang Yushi 张玉石
Zhang Zhengming 张正明

Zhang Zhongpei 张忠培
Zhangjiabanhe 张家板河
Zhangjiakou 张家口
Zhanglingshan 张陵山
zhang 丈
Zhao 赵
Zhao Feng 赵丰
Zhao Ye 赵晔
Zhaobaogou 赵宝沟
Zhaohua 昭化
Zhaojiahu 赵家湖
Zhaojialai 赵家来
Zhaokang 赵康
Zhaolingshan 赵陵山
Zhaoxiang 赵巷
Zhejiang 浙江
Zheng Qingsen 郑清森
Zheng Shaozong 郑绍宗
Zhengding 正定
Zheng Xuan 郑玄 (127-200)
Zhengzhou 郑州
zhenmushou 镇墓兽
Zhi Nu 织女
Zhihuijie 指挥街
Zhijiang 枝江
Zhongdian 中甸
Zhongguo kaogu xuehui
中国考古学会
Zhongwei xiang 中卫乡
Zhongzhoulu 中州路
zhou 舟
Zhou 周
Zhoukoudian 周口店
Zhoushan 舟山
Zou xian 邹县
zhu 祝
Zhu Jieyuan 朱捷元
Zhuanxu 颛顼
Zhujie 珠街
Zhunge'erqi 准格尔旗
zhuo 镯
Zhuolu 涿鹿
Zi Shu Quan 子束泉
zongfa 宗法
Zoumaling 走马岭
Zou xian 邹县
zun 尊
Zunyi 遵义
Zuozhuan 左传

Bibliography

Abe, Stanley K 1993: 'Wonder House: Buddhist Art and the West,' Unpublished MS.

Ackerman, P 1945: *Ritual Bronzes of Ancient China*, New York.

Adams, R M 1956: 'Some hypotheses on the development of early civilisation,' American Antiquity 21: 227-32.

Allan, Sarah 1991: The *Shape of the Turtle: Myth, Art and Cosmos in Early China*, Albany, New York.

— 1993: 'Art and Meaning' and 'Epilogue,' in Whitfield 1993: 9-33, 161-76.

Alsop, Joseph 1982: *The Rare Art Traditions*. New York: Harper and Row.

American Antiquity 21: 227-232.

An Jinhuai 1985: Shilun Tengfeng Wangchenggang Longshan wenhua chengshi yu Xiadai Yangcheng. *Zhongguo kaogu xuehui disicinianhui lunwenji.* Beijing: Wenwu chubanshe.

— 1986: The Shang city at Cheng-chou and related problems. In K C Chang (ed). *Studies of Shang Archaeology*. New Haven and London: Yale University Press, 15-48.

An Zhimin 1963: 'Ganlan' shi jianzhu de kaogu yanjiu,' *Kaogu xuebao* 1963 (2): 65-85.

— 1988: 'Guanyu Liangzhu wenhua de ruogan wenti-wei jinian Liangzhu wenhua faxian wushi zhounian erzuo,' *Kaogu* 1988(3): 236-45.

Antal, F 1949: 'Remarks on the Method of Art History.' *Burlington Magazine* 91: 49-52, 73-75.

Artamonov, M I 1973: *The art of ancient Central and South Siberia* (in Russian).

Bachhofer, Ludwig 1944: 'The Evolution of Shang and Early Chou Bronzes,' *Art Bulletin* 26: 107-16.

— 1945: 'Reply to Maenchen-Helfen,' *Art Bulletin* 27: 243-246.

— 1946: *A Short History of Chinese Art*. New York: Pantheon.

Bagley, Robert W 1987: *Shang Ritual Bronzes in the Arthur Sackler Collection*, Cambridge, Mass: Arthur M Sackler Foundation.

— 1992: 'Changjiang Bronzes and Shang Archaeology' *Zhonghua minguo jianguo bashinian Zhongguo yishu wenwu taolunhui lunwenji*, Taipei, 209-256.

Ban Gu: *Hanshu*, Beijing: Zhonghua shuju, 1962.

Banpo Museum (and Shaanxi Provincial Institute of Archaeology, Lintong County Museum) 1988: *Jiangzhai*. Beijing: Wenwu chubanshe.

Baoding 1992 (Baoding diqu wenguansuo, Beida kaoguxi, Hebei daxue lishixi): 'Hebei Xushui xian Nanzhuangtou yizhi shi jue jianbao,' *Kaogu* 1992(11): 961-970.

Barnes, Gina 1993: *China, Korea and Japan: The Rise of Civilisation in East Asia*, London: Thames and Hudson.

Beasley, W G and E G Pulleyblank 1961: *Historians of China and Japan*. London: Oxford University Press.

Beijing 1992 (Beijing daxue kaoguxi): 'Shijiahe yizhi diaocha baogao,' *Nanfang minzu kaogu* 5: 213-294.

— 1993. '1992 nian chun Tianma-Qucun yizhi muzang fajue baogao,' *Wenwu* 1993 (3): 11-30.

— 1994 (Beijing daxue kaoguxi, Shanxi sheng kaogusuo): 'Tianma-Qucun yizhi Beizhao Jin hou mudi dier ci fajue,' *Wenwu* 1994(1): 4-28.

— 1995 (Beijing daxue kaoguxi, Shanxi sheng kaogusuo): 'Tianma-Qucun yizhi Beizhao Jin hou mudi diwu ci fajue,' *Wenwu* 1995(7): 4-39.

Bian Ren 1994: 'Guanyu Dinggong taowen de taolun,' *Kaogu* 1994(9):825-831.

Binford, Lewis 1962: 'Archaeology as Anthropology,' *American Antiquity* 28-2: 217-225.

Borovka, G 1928: *Scythian art* (trans V G Childe), London: Bouverie House.

Bunker, E 1992: 'Sino-nomadic art: Eastern Zhou, Qin and Han artifacts made for nomadic taste,' *Zhongguo yishu wenwu taolunhui lunwenji*, Taipei: National Palace Museum.

Burke, Peter 1992: *New Perspectives on Historical Writing*. Philadelphia: Pennsylvania State University Press.

Cao Bingwu 1996: Zhongguo shiqian chengzhi luelun. *Zhongyuan wenwu* 1996(3), 37-46.

Cao Dingyun 1996: 'Shandong Zouping Dinggong "Longshan taowen" bianwei,' *ZYWW* 1996(2): 32-38.

Cao Guichen: 'Danjiangkou shuiku faxian Chuguo guizu mu,' *Zhongguo wenwu bao* 30-8-92.

Cao Yannong, Song Shaohua: 'Changsha fajue Xi Han Changsha Wang shimu,' *Zhongguo wenwu bao* 22-8-93.

Carpenter, Rhys and Ackerman, James 1963: *Art History and Archaeology*. Englewood Cliffs: Prentice Hall.

Carter, D 1957: *The Symbol of the Beast: the animal style art of Eurasia*, New York: The Ronald Press.

Chang, K C 1981: 'The Animal in Shang and Chou Bronze Art,' *Harvard Journal of Asiatic Studies* 41: 527-554.

— 1983: *Art, Myth and Ritual: The Path to Political Authority*, Cambridge, Mass: Yale University Press.

— 1985: 'Guanyu Zhongguo chuqi "chengshi" zhege kainian,' *Wenwu* 1985(2): 61-67.

— 1986a: "Tan 'cong' jiqi zai Zhongguo gushishang de yiyi," *Wenwu yu kaogu lunji*, Wenwu chubanshe biejibu ed. Beijing: Wenwu chubanshe, 252-260.

— 1986b: *Kaogu xue zhuanti liu jiang*, Beijing, Wenwu chubanshe.

— 1986: *The Archaeology of Ancient China* (fourth edition), New Haven: Yale University Press.

— 1989: 'Zhongguo xiangfu zuoyong quan yu wenming de xingcheng,' *Qinzhu Su Bingqi kaogu wushiwu nian lunwen ji*. Beijing, Wenwu chubanshe, 1-26.

— 1990: 'The Meaning of Shang Bronze Art,' *Asian Art* 3.2 (Spring 1990): 9-17.

— 1993: *Meishu, shenhua yu jisi*, Taipei: Daoxiang chubanshe.

— *forthcoming*: 'Wang de xingqi yu chengbang de xingcheng,' *Zhongguo wenming de xingcheng*, K C Chang and Xu Pingfang, eds. New Haven/Beijing: Yale University Press/China New World Press.

Changde 1987 (Changde diqu wenwu gongzuodui, Taoyuan xian wenhuaju): 'Taoyuan Sanyuancun yi hao Chu mu,' *Hunan kaogu jikan* 4: 22-32.

Changsha 1989 (Changsha shi wenwu gongzuodui): 'Changsha shi Hehuachi yi hao Zhanguo muguo mu fajue baogao,' *Hunan kaogu jikan* 5 : 52-60, 6.

Changshu 1984 (Changshu shi wenwu guanli weiyuanhui): 'Jiangsu Changshu Liangzhu wenhua yizhi,' *Wenwu* 1984(2): 12-16.

Chavannes, Édouard 1913: *Mission archéologique dans la Chine septentrionale.* Paris: E Leroux.

Che Guangjin 1987: 'Liangzhu wenhua yucong wenshi tanxi,' *Dongnan wenhua* 1987(3): 18-24.

Chen De'an, Luo Yaping 1989: 'Zaoqi Shuguo ducheng cu lu duanni,' *Zhongguo wenwu bao* 15-9-89.

Chen Fangmei 1991: 'Xiaotun wuzuomu de qingtongqi – cong Erligang dao dianxing Yinxu fengge fazhan de zhuyao qushi,' *Kaogu lishi yu wenhua – Gao Xiaomei xiansheng bazhi daqinglunwenji.* Taipei: Zhengzhong shuju, 81-232.

— 1997a: 'Shang houqi qingtong fu yue zhi de fazhan ji qi wenhua yiyi.' *Zhongguo kaoguxue yu lishixue zhenghe guoji yantaohui lunwenji.* Taipei: Institute of History and Philology, 983-1052.

— 1997b: *The Bronze Weapons of the Late Shang Period.* (PhD dissertation. London: University of London, School of Oriental and African Studies).

Chen Shenyong 1995: 'Xia wenhua dongnan shuo,' *Xungeng*, 1995(1): 10-13.

Chen Weihan 1996: 'Guangzhou faxian Xi Han Nanyueguo guanshu yizhi,' *Zhongguo wenwu bao* 11-2-96.

Chen Weiji 1984: *Zhongguo fangzhi kexue jishushi*, Beijing, Kexue chubanshe.

Chen Xiandan 1989a: 'Guanghan Sanxingdui yizhi fajue gaikuan, chubu fenqi,' *Nanfang minzu kaogu* 2: 213-231.

— 1989b: 'Sanxingdui yi er hao keng liangge wenti de tantao,' *Wenwu* 1989(5): 36-38.

Chen Xu 1995: 'Zhengzhou Xiaoshuangqiao Shang dai yizhi de niandai he xingzhi,' *Zhongyuan wenwu* 1995(1).

Chen Xu 1997: 'Zhengzhou Xiaoshuangqiao Shangdai yizhi ji Aodu shuo,' *Zhongyuan wenwu* 1997(2):45-50.

Cheng Dong, Zhong Shaoyi 1990: *Zhongguo gudai bingqi tuji*. Beijing: Jiefangjun chubanshe.

Chernykh, E N 1992: *Ancient metallurgy in the USSR: the early metal age* (trans S Wright), Cambridge: Cambridge University Press.

Childe, Gordon 1950: 'The Urban Revolution,' *Town Planning Review* 21: 3-17.

Childs-Johnson, Elizabeth 1987: 'The Ancestor Spirit and Animal Mask in Shang Ritual Art' (conference paper), The International Symposium on the Yin-Shang Culture of China, 10-16 September, 1987, Anyang.

— 1989: 'The Shang Bird: Intermediary to the Supernatural,' *Orientations* 20-11 (November 1989): 53-61.

Clifford, James 1988: 'On Collecting Art and Culture.' *The Predicament of Culture*, 215-251. Cambridge, Mass: Harvard University Press.

Clunas, Craig 1993: 'East Asian Art and Oriental Antiquities: British and American Views,' unpublished MS.

Cohen, Warren I 1992: *East Asian Art and American Culture*. New York: Columbia University Press.

Couvreur, Séraphin 1950: *Mémoires sur les bienséances et les cérémonies*, Paris: Cathasia/Les Belles Lettres.

Creel, Herlee G 1936: 'Notes on Professor Karlgren's System for Dating Chinese Bronzes,' *Journal of the Royal Asiatic Society,* 1936.3: 463-473.

Crump, James and Irving 1963: *Dragon Bones in the Yellow Earth*. New York: Dodd, Mead and Company.

Cui Dayong *et al* 1996: 'Shandong Changqing xian Xianrentai faxian Zhou dai juluo yu Siguo guizu mudi,' *Zhongguo wenhua huabao* 1996(5).

Dai Yingxin, Sun Jiaxiang 1983: 'Shaanxi Shenmu xian chutu Xiongnu wenwu,' *Wenwu* 1983 (12), 23-30.

Daniel, Glyn 1968: *The Origins and Growth of Archaeology*. New York: Crowell.

— 1975:*150 Years of Archaeology*, second edition, London: Duckworth.

Davidson, J Leroy 1937: 'Toward a Grouping of Early Chinese Bronzes,' *Parnassus* 9.4 (April 1937): 29-34, 51.

Davis, Whitney 1990: 'Style and History in Art History' in *The Uses of Style in Archaeology* (M Conkey and C Hastorf, eds). New Directions in Archaeology. Cambridge: Cambridge University Press.

Deng Chaoyuan 1992: 'Tianchang Han muqun chutu dapi zhengui wenwu,' *Zhongguo wenwu bao* 5-7-92.

Ding Ying 1959: 'Jiang Han pingyuan xinshiqi shidai hongshaotu de daoguke kaocha,' *Kaogu xuebao* 1959(4): 31-34.

Duan Yu 1991a : 'Ba Shu guwenzi de lianxi jiqi qiyuan,' *Chengdu wenwu* 1991(3): 20-33.

— 1991b: 'Xian Qin Qin Han Chengdu de shi ji shifu zhineng de yanbian,' *Huaxi kaogu yanjiu* 1: 324-348.

— 1993: 'Lun Shangdai Changjiang shangyou Chuanxi pingyuan qingtong wenhua yu Huabei he shijie gu wenmin de guanxi,' *Dongnan wenhua* 1993(2): 1-21.

Duan Yucai:*Shuowen jiezi zhu*, Shanghai: Guji chubanshe, 1991.

Du Zhengsheng 1992: *Gudai shehui yu guojia*. Taipei: Yunsheng Cultural Company.

Elkins, James 1987: 'Remarks on the Western Art Historical Study of Chinese Bronzes, 1930-1980.' *Oriental Art* 33.3: 250-260.

Fairbank, Wilma C 1984: 'Liang Ssu-ch'eng: A Profile,' *A Pictorial History of Chinese Architecture* (Liang Ssu-ch'eng), xiii-xix. Cambridge: MIT Press.

Fang Hua: *Hou Hanshu*, Beijing: Zhongguo shuju 1965.

Fang Hui 1994: 'Shandong sheng Zouping xian Dinggong yizhi faxian de Longshan wenhua dui zi taowen,' *Gugong wenwu yuekan* 133 (April 1994): 98-103.

Feng Shi 1994: 'Shandong Dinggong Longshan shidai wenzi jiedu,' *Kaogu* 1994(1): 37-54.

Ferguson, John C 1919: *Outlines of Chinese Art*. Chicago: University of Chicago Press.

Fong, Wen C 1980, ed: *The Great Bronze Age of China*, London: Thames and Hudson.

Fontein, Jan and Wu Tung 1973: *Unearthing China's Past*. Boston: Museum of Fine Arts.

Fu Langyun 1993: 'Niuheliang, Nüshenmiao, zushu kao,' *Beifang wenwu* 1993(1): 46-50.

Fu Xianguo 1985: 'Shilun Zhongguo xinshiqi shidai de shiyue.' *Kaogu* 1985 (9), 820-832.

Fu Zhufu 1980: *Zhongguo jingjishi luncong*. Beijing: Sanlian chubanshe.

Gan Zhigeng, Sun Shoudao 1992: 'Guanyu Niuheliang zhi xing de tongxin,' *Beifang wenwu* 1992(3): 3-7.

Gansu 1982 (Gansu sheng bowuguan, Qinan xian wenhuaguan): 'Yijiu baling nian qinan Dadiwan yiqi wenhua yicun,' *Kaogu yu wenwu* 1982(2): 1-4.

— 1984 (Gansu sheng wenwudui *et al*): 'Gansu Dongxiang Linjia yizhi fajue baogao,' *Kaoguxue jikan* 4: 111-161.

— 1989 'Minle xian Huishan xinshiqi yizhi gu mu nongye yicun xin faxian,' *Nongye kaogu* 1989(1), 56-69, 73.

Gao Hanyu 1981: 'Cong chutu wenwu zhuishuo cansiye de qiyuan,' *Cansang tongbao* 12 (1): 17-24.

Gao Menghe 1992: Changjiang zhongyou de shiqian qizuo jiqi xiangguan wenti,' *Jiang Han kaogu* 1992(3): 42-46.

— 1993: 'Shiqian qizuo chutan,' *Kaogu* 1993(1): 42-51.

Gao Wei 1989: 'Longshan shidai de lizhi,' *Qinzhu Su Bingqi kaogu wushiwu nian lunwen ji*, Beijing, Wenwu chubanshe, 235-44.

Gardner, Charles S 1938: *A Union List of Selected Western Books on China in American Libraries.* second edition. American Council of Learned Societies.

Ge Yan and K Linduff 1990: 'Sanxingdui, a new Bronze Age site in southwest China,' *Antiquity* 64/244: 501-513.

Gimbutas, M 1965: *Bronze Age cultures in central and eastern Europe.* The Hague.

Gombrich, E H 1966a: 'Norm and form: the stylistic categories of art history and their origins in Renaissance ideals,' *Norm and Form*, 81-98. London: Phaidon.

—1966b: 'The Renaissance Conception of Artistic Progress.' *ibid*, 1-10.

Goodrich, L Carrington 1957: 'Archaeology in China: The first decades.' *Journal of Asian Studies* 17: 5-15.

Goody, Jack 1968 ed: *Literacy in Traditional Societies*, Cambridge: Cambridge University Press.

Gryaznov, M. P. 1969: *South Siberia* (trans. J. Hogarth), London: The Cresset Press

Gu Fei 1993: 'Ping Zhongguo yuqi shidai,' *Kaogu* 1993(6): 554-555.

Gu Haibing 1996: 'Hunan Lixian Chengtoushan yizhi chutu de xinshiqi shidai shuidao jiqi leixing,' *Kaogu* 1996 (8), 81-89.

Gu Yanwu: *Rizhilu*, 'Guoxue jiben congshu,' Shanghai: Shangwu yinshuguan, 1935.

Gu Zuyi: *Dushi fanyu jiyao* (1631-1692), Shanghai: Zhonghua shuju, 1955.

Guangdong 1978 (Guangdong sheng bowuguan): 'Guangdong Qujiang Shixia muzang fajiu jianbao,' *Wenwu* 1978(7): 1-15.

Guangming ribao, May 14, 1995.

Guo Baojun 1951: '1950 nian chuan Yinxu fajue baogao,' *Zhongguo kaogu xuebao* 5: 1-61.

Guo Dewei 1995: *Chu xi muzang yanjiu,* Wuhan: Hubei Jiaoyu chubanshe.

Guo Moruo 1954: *Zhongguo gudai shehui yanjiu.* Beijing: Renmin chubanshe.

Guo Ru 1987: 'Cong Hebeisheng Zhengding Nanyangzhuang chutu de taochangyong shilun woguo jiachang de qiyuan wenti,' *Nongye kaogu* 1987(1): 302-309.

Guojia 1990 (Guojia wenwuju kaogu lingdui peixunban): *Baozhou Xiwusi,* Beijing: Wenwu chubanshe.

Hangzhou shi wenwu kaogusuo: 'Hangzhou faxian Nan Song Lin'an cheng taimiao yizhi,' *Zhongguo wenwu bao* 31-12-95.

Haskell, Francis and Nicholas Penny 1981: *Taste and the Antique: The Lure of Classical Sculpture. 1500-1900.* New Haven: Yale University Press.

Hayashi, Minao 1993: 'Concerning the Inscription "May sons and grandsons eternally use this [vessel],"' *Artibus Asiae* 53 (1/2): 51-58.

— 1994: 'Kachu seidôki jakanshû no ukamon no dentô,' *Senoku Hakkokan Kiyo,* 10: 3-56.

He Jinlong, Zhang Xinning 1993: 'Lijiashan mudi fajue huo shuoguo,' *Zhongguo wenwu bao* 10-1-93.

Hebei 1977 (Hebei sheng bowuguan and wenwu guanlichu): 'Hebei Pingquan Dongnangou Xiajiadian shang ceng wenhua mufen.'*Kaogu* 1977 (1): 51.

— 1981 (Hebei sheng wenguanchu and Handanshi wenguansuo): Hebei Cishan yizhi, *Kaogu xuebao* 1981(3): 303-338.

— 1991 (Hebei sheng wenwu yanjiusuo, Baoding diqu wenwu guanlisuo, Dingzhou wenwu guanlisuo): 'Dingzhou faxian Shangdai daxing fangguo guizu mudi,' *Zhongguo wenwu bao* 15-12-91.

— 1992 (Hebei sheng wenwu yanjiusuo): 'Dingzhou Beizhuangzi Shang mu fajue jianbao,' *Wenwu Chunqiu* 1992 (Special Issue).

— 1995 (Hebei sheng wenwu yanjiusuo, Zhangjiakou wenwu guanlichu, Xuanhua qu wenwu guanlisuo): 'Xuanhua Liao dai bihua muqun,' *Wenwu Chunqiu* 1995(2).

— 1996 (Hebei sheng wenwu yanjiusuo, Zhangjiakou wenwu guanlichu, Xuanhua qu wenwu guanlisuo): 'Hebei Xuanhua Liao Zhang Wencao bihua mu fajue jianbao,' *Wenwu chunqiu* 1996(9).

Heger, Franz 1902: *Alte Metalltrommeln aus Sudostasien*, Leipzig.

Heilongjiang 1992 (Heilongjiangsheng wenwu kaogu yanjiusuo): 'Heilongjiang fajue Bohai daxing shishi bihua mu,' *Zhongguo wenwu bao* 19-1-92.

Hemudu 1980 (Hemudu yichi kaogu dui), 'Hemudu yizhi di'er ci fajue de zhuyao shouhuo,' *Wenwu* 1980 (5): 1-15.

— 1983 Henan Provincial Institute of Cultural Relics (and the Cultural Bureau of Zhoukou District): Henan Huaiyang Pingliangtai Langshan wenhua chengzhi shijue jianbao. *Wenwu* 1983(3), 8-20.

Henan 1986 (Henan sheng wenwu yanjiusuo), *Xinyang Chu mu*, Beijing: Wenwu chubanshe.

— 1991 (Henan sheng wenwu yanjiusuo, Henan sheng Danjiang muqu kaogu fajuedui, Xichuan Xian Bowuguan): *Xichuan Xiasi Chunqiu Chu mu*, Beijing: Wenwu chubanshe.

— 1991 Henan Provincial Institute of Cultural Relics (Zhengzhou shangcheng wai hantu qiangji de tiaocha yu shijue): *Zhongyuan wenwu* 1991(1), 87-95.

— 1992 Henan Provincial Institute of Cultural Relics (and the Department of Archaeology of The National Museum of Chinese History): Tengfeng Wangchenggang yu Yangcheng, Beijing: Wenwu chubanshe.

— 1995 (Henan sheng wenwu kaogu yanjiusuo, Sanmenxia shi wenwu gongzuodui): 'Shangcunling Guoguo mudi M2006 de qingli,' *Wenwu* 1995(1):4-31.

— 1995 (Henan sheng wenwu kaogu yanjiusuo, Zhengzhou daxue wenboxueyuan kaoguxi and Nankai daxue lishixi bowuguanxue zhuanye): '1995 nian Zhengzhou Xiaoshuangqiao yizhi de fajue,' *Huaxia kaogu* 1996(3) .

— 1996 (Henan sheng wenwu kaogu yanjiusuo: *Yongcheng Xi Han Liangguo wangling yu qingyuan*, Zhengzhou): Zhongzhou guji chubanshe, 1996.

Hentze, Karl 1932: *Mythes et symboles lunaires*, Anvers.

— 1937: *Frühchinesische Bronzen und Kultdarstellungen*, Antwerp.

— 1941: Die *Sakralbronzen und ihre Bedeutung in den Frühchinesischen Kulturen*, 2 volumes, Antwerp.

He Yeju 1982: 'Zhouguang' wangji guihua cutan. *Jianzhu lishi yanjiu* 1, 96-118.

Hodder, Iain 1986: *Reading the Past: Current Approaches to Interpretation in Archaeology*, Cambridge: Cambridge University Press.

Hopkirk, Peter 1980: *Foreign Devils on the Silk Road*. London: John Murray

Horvath, Isabella, 'The roles of the Griffin in the art and society of the steppe-dwelling peoples of Eurasia.' (Conference paper). The International Academic Conference of Archaeoloigical Cultures of the Northern Chinese Ancient Nations, 1992/8/11-18.

Hsu Cho-yun and Linduff, K M 1988: *Western Zhou Civilization*. New Haven and London: Yale University Press.

Hu Changyu, Cai Ge 1992: 'Yufu kao-ye tan Sanxingdui,' *Sichuan wenwu* 26-33.

Hu Xiaolong 1993: 'Qian tan Shangcunling Guoguo mudi chema keng,' *Huaxia kaogu* 1993(3).

Huang Shengzhang 1993: Tianchang yihao Han mu niandai wenti,' *Zhongguo wenwu bao* 21-11-93.

Huang Shengzhang 1992, ed : *Yazhou wenming*, volume II. Hefei: Anhui jiaoyu chubanshe.

Huang Weiwen, Si Xinqiang *et al* 1995: 'Excavations at Panxian Dadong, Guizhou Province, Southern China,' *Current Anthropology* 36-35 (1995): 844-846.

Huang Xuanpei, Zhang Minghua 1980: 'Qingpuxian Songze yizhi dierci fajue,' *Kaogu xuebao* 1980(1): 29-58.

— *et al* 1987: *Songze: xinshiqi shidai yizhi fajue baogao*, Beijing: Wenwu chubanshe, 1987.

— Song Jian, Sun Weichang 1992: *Shanghai bowuguan cang Liangzhu wenhua zhenpin zhan (Gems of Liangzhu culture from the Shanghai Museum)*, exhibition catalogue in Chinese and English, Hong Kong, Hong Kong Museum of History.

Huang Zhanyue 1990: *Zhongguo gudai de rensheng renxun*, Beijing: Wenwu chubanshe.

Hubei 1982 (Hubei sheng Jingzhou diqu bowuguan): 'Jiangling Tianxingguan yihao Chu mu,' *Kaogu xuebao* 1982(1): 71-116.

— 1984 (Hubei sheng Jingzhou diqu bowuguan): *Jiangling Yutaishan Chu mu* Beijing: Wenwu chubanshe.

— 1985 (Hubei sheng Jingzhou diqu bowuguan): *Jiangling Mashan yi hao Chu mu*, Beijing, Wenwu chubanshe.

— 1989 (Hubei sheng bowuguan): *Zeng Hou Yi mu*, Beijing: Wenwu chubanshe.

— 1991 (Hubei sheng Jing Sha tielu kaogudui): *Baoshan Chu mu*, Beijing: Wenwu chubanshe.

— 1992 (Hubei sheng Yichang diqu bowuguan, Beijing daxue kaoguxi): *Dangyang Zhaojiahu Chu mu*, Beijing: Wenwu chubanshe.

— 1994 (Hubei sheng wenwu kaogu yanjiusuo, Zhongguo shehui kexueyuan kaogu yanjiusuo): 'Hubei Shijiahe Luojiaboling xin shiqi shidai yizhi,' *Kaogu xuebao* 1994(2): 191-229.

— 1995 (Hubei sheng wenwu kaogu yanjiusuo): *Jiangling Jiudian Dong Zhou mu*, Beijing: Kexue chubanshe.

— 1996 (Hubei sheng wenwu kaogu yanjiusuo): *Jiangling Wangshan Shazhong Chu mu*, Beijing: Wenwu chubanshe.

Hunan 1963 (Hunan sheng bowuguan): 'Hunan Changde Deshan Chu mu fajue baogao,' *Kaogu* 1963(9): 461-473, 479.

— 1973 (Hunan sheng bowuguan, Zhongguo kexueyuan kaogu yanjiusuo): *Changsha Mawangdui yi hao Han mu*, Beijing: Wenwu chubanshe.

— 1990 (Hunan sheng wenwu kaogu yanjiusuo, Cili Xian Wenwu Baohu Guanli Yanjiusuo): 'Hunan Cili Shibancun 36 hao Zhanguo mu fajue jianbao,' *Wenwu* 1990(10): 37-47.

Institute of Archaeology, CA (Chinese Academy) 1963: *Xi'an Banpo*. Beijing: Wenwu chubanshe.

Institute of Archaeology, CASS (Chinese Academy of Social Sciences) 1984: *Xin Zhongguo de kaogu faxian he yanjiu*. Beijing: Wenwu chubanshe.

Jettmar, K 1950: 'The Karasuk culture and the south-eastern affinities,' *Bulletin of the Museum of Far Eastern Antiquities* 22: 83-126.

— 1967: *Art of the Steppes: the Eurasian animal style*, London: Methuen.

Jiang Tao 1991: 'Guoguo de zao fajue yu renshi,' *Zhongguo wenwu bao* 8-12-91.

Jiang Yueping 1993: 'Liqi 'ding' de yuanyuan tansuo,' *Nanfang Wenwu* 1993(2): 102-105.

Jiang Zhongyi 1994: Tangdai Yangzhou hedao yuershici qiao kao. *Han Tang yu bianjiang kaogu yanjiu* 1, 162-168.

Jiangling 1989 (Jiangling xian wenwuju): 'Hubei Jiangling Wuchang Yidi Chu mu,' *Wenwu* 1989 (3): 35-50, 62.

Jiangsu 1963 (Jiangsu sheng wenwu gongzuodui): 'Jiangsu Wujing Meiyan xinshiqi shidai yizhi,' *Kaogu* 1963(6): 308-318.

— 1983 (Jiangsu sheng Zhaolingshan kaogudui): Jiangsu sheng Kunshan Zhaolingshan yizhi diyi, dier ci fajue jianbao, *Dongfang wenming zhi guang*, Hainan: Guoji chuban zhongxin.

Jiangxi 1990 (Jiangsu sheng wenwu kaogu yanjiusuo Tongling yizhi fajuedui): 'Jiangxi Ruichang Tongling Shang/Zhou kuangye yizhi diyiqi fajue jianbao,' Jianxi wenwu 1990 (3): 1-12.

— 1992 (Jiangxi sheng wenwuju): 'Ruichang Tongling kuangye yizhi fajue huo zhongda chengguo,' *Zhongguo wenwu bao* 19-1-92.

— 1995 (Jiangxi sheng wenwu kaogu yanjiusuo, Beijing daxue kaoguxi, Jiang sheng Fengcheng shi bowuguan): 'Jiangxi Fengcheng yao yizhi tiaocha baogao,' *Nanfang wenwu* 1995(2): 1-29.

— 1997 (Jiangxi sheng wenwu kaogu yanjiusuo *et al*): *Xin'gan Shangdai damu*, Beijing, Wenwu chubanshe 1997.

Jin Taishun 1996: 'Ning'an Hongzun yuchang Mohe Bohai muqun fajue you zhongda shouhuo,' *Zhongguo wenwu bao* 4-2-96.

Jixian 1985 (Jixian wenwu gongzuozhan): 'Shanxi Ji xian chutu Shangdai qingtongqi,'*Kaogu* 1985 (9), 848-849.

Kane, Virginia 1973: 'The Chronological Significance of the Inscribed Ancestor Dedication in the Periodisation of Shang Dynasty Bronze Vessels,' *Artibus Asiae* 35: 335-370.

— 1975: 'A Re-examination of Anyang Archaeology,' *Ars Orientalis* 10: 93-110.

Kaogu 1989: 'Zhongguo wenming qiyuan zuotan jiyao: (9 September 1989),' *Kaogu* 1989(12): 1110-1120.

— 1992: 'Zhongguo wenming qiyuan zuotan jiyao: (November 27-30 1991),' *Kaogu* 1992(6): 526-549.

— 1993: 'Zhuanjia tan Dinggong yizhi chutu taowen,' *Kaogu* 1993(4): 344-354.

— 1995: 'Zhuanjia zuotan Anhui Mengcheng Weichisi yizhi fajue de shouhuo,' *Kaogu* 1995(4): 338-345.

Karlgren, Bernhard 1930: 'Some Fecundity Symbols in Ancient China,' *Bulletin of the Museum of Far Eastern Antiquities* 2.

— 1936: 'Yin and Chou in Chinese bronzes,' *Bulletin of the Museum of Far Eastern Antiquities*. 8: 9-156.

— 1937: 'New Studies on Chinese Bronzes,' *Bulletin of the Museum of Far Eastern Antiquities* 9:1-117.

— 1945: 'Some weapons and tools of the Yin dynasty,' *Bulletin of the Museum of Far Eastern Antiquities* 17:101-144.

Kato Kyusô 1991: 'Sarumatan no kôgei to sono shûhen' (Sarmatian Arts and their surroundings), *Nan Roshiya chiba minzoku no ihôten zuroku*, Tokyo: Asahi shimbunsha.

Kesner, Ladislav 1991: 'Taotie Reconsidered: Meanings and Functions of Shang Theriomorphic Imagery,' *Artibus Asiae* 41 (1/2): 29-53.

Kiselev 1951: *Ancient History of Southern Siberia* (Chinese edition 1981, Urumqi: Xinjiang shehui kexueyuan minzu yanjiusuo).

Kong Xiangxing, Liu Yiman 1984: *Zhongguo gudai tongjing*, Beijing: Wenwu chubanshe.

Kong Yingda: *Maoshi zhengyi*, Shisanjing zhushu edn, Beijing: Zhonghua shuju 1980.

Kristeller, Paul O 1965: 'The Modern System of the Arts,' *Renaissance Thought II: Papers on Humanities and the Arts*, New York: Harper, 163-227.

Kristiansen, K 1981: 'A social history of Danish archaeology (1805-1975), *Towards a History of Archaeology* (Glyn Daniel, ed), London: Thames and Hudson, 20-44.

Kubler, George 1991: *Esthetic Recognition of Ancient Amerindian Art*. New Haven: Yale University Press.

Kunming 1985 (Kunming shi wenguanhui): 'Chenggong Tianzimiao Dianmu,' *Kaogu xuebao* 1985(4).

Lach, Donald F 1965-77: *Asia in the Making of Europe*. 2 vols. Chicago: University of Chicago Press.

Langer, Susanne K 1953: *Feeling and Form*, New York.

Laufer, Berthold 1912: *Jade: a Study in Chinese Archaeology and Precision*. Chicago: Field Museum of Natural History.

Li Boqian 1981: 'Shilun Wucheng wenhua,' *Wenwu jikan 3*.

— 1993: 'Jin guo shi fengdi kaolue,' *Zhongguo wenwu bao* 12-12-93.

Li Chi 1927: *Xiyingcun shiqian de yicun*. Peking, Qinghua xuexiao yanjiuyuan congshu, no.3.

Li Fan *et al* 1989: 'Gansu Minle xian Huishan xin shiqi yizhi nongye yicun xin faxian,' *Nongye kaogu*, 1989(1): 56-69, 73.

Li Kunsheng, Hung Derong 1990: 'Lun Wanjiaba xing tonggu,' *Kaogu* 1990 (5): 459-466.

Li Ling 1991: 'On the Typology of Chu Bronzes' [Translated and edited by Lothar von Falkenhausen], *Beiträge zur Allgemeinen und vergleichenden Archäologie*, Band 11, Mainz am Rhein, Verlag Philipp von Zabern, 57-113.

Li Ling 1996: 'Zai lun Xichuan Xiasi Chu mu — du "Xichuan Xiasi Chu mu,"' *Wenwu* 1996(1), 47-60.

Li Tai *et al* 1980: *Kuodizhi jijiao* Beijing: Zhonghua shuju.

Li Xueqin 1987: 'Lun xin chu Dawenkou wenhua taoqi fuhao,' *Wenwu* 1987(12): 75-80.

— 1991a: 'Xin'gan Dayangzhou Shangmu ruogan wenti.' *Wenwu* 1991 (10): 33-38.

— 1991b: 'Jin hou Su bianzhong de shi, di, ren,' *Zhongguo wenwu bao* 1-12-96.

— 1991c: 'Sanmenxia Guo mu xin faxian yu Guoguo shi,' *Zhongguo wenwu bao* 3-2-91.

— 1993: 'A Neolithic jade plaque and ancient Chinese cosmology,' *National Palace Museum Bulletin* 27 (5-6): 1-26.

— 1993: 'Liangzhu Culture and the Shang Dynasty *taotie* motif,' in Whitfield 1993: 56-66.

Li Youheng, Han Defeng 1978: 'Guangxi Guilin Zengpiyan yizhi dongwuqun,' *Gujizui dongwu yu gu renlei* 16-4: 244-254.

Liang Siyong, Gao Quxun 1962: *Houjiazhuang, 1001 hao damu*, Taipei: Zhongyang yanjiuyuan.

— 1970: *Houjiazhuang, 1004 hao damu*, Taipei: Zhongyang yanjiuyuan.

Liang Zhonghe 1994: 'Weichisi yizhi juluo fajue shuoguo leilei,' *Zhongguo wenwu bao* 21-8-94.

— 1995: 'Weichisi xinshiqi shidai juluo yizhi chujian guimo,' *Zhongguo wenwu bao* 12-2-95.

Lin Xiang 1988: 'Yangzishan jianzhu yizhi xin kao,' *Sichuan wenwu* 1988(5): 3-8.

Lin Yun 1986: 'Guanyu Zhongguo zaoqi guojia xingcheng de jige wenti,' *Jilin daxue shehui kexue xuebao* 1986(6): 1-12.

Liu Bin 1990: 'Liangzhu wenhua yucong chutan,' *Wenwu* 1990 (2): 30-37.

Liu Deyin 1993: 'Woguo jiushiqi shidai kaogu de zhongda tupo,' *Zhongguo wenwu bao* 2-5-93.

Liu Hong ed 1991: *Nanfang sichou zhi lu wenhua lun*, Kunming: Yunnan minzu chubanshe.

Liu Jun, Yao Zhongyuan 1993: *Zhongguo Hemudu wenhua*. Hangzhou: Zhenjiang renmin chubanshe.

Liu Lin 1984: *Huayangguozhi jiao zhu*, Chengdu: Ba Shu shushe.

Liu Qingzhu 1996: Han Chang'an cheng de kaogu faxian ji xiangguan wenti yanjiu — jinian Han Chang'an cheng kaogu gongzuo sishi nian. *Kaogu* 1996(10), 1-14.

Liu Shizhong, Xu Zhifan 1995: 'Jiangxi shiqian kaogu huo zhongyao shouhuo,' *Nanfang wenwu* 1995(4).

Liu Shizhong 1996: 'Jiangxi Xianrendong he Diaotonghuan fajue huo zhongyao jinzhang,' *Zhongguo wenwu bao*, 28-1-96.

Liu Wu, Wang Yunlu 1991: 'Huiguanshan yizhi faxian jitan he damu,' *Zhongguo wenwu bao* 11-8-91.

Loehr, Max 1936: 'Beiträge zu Chronologie der ältern Chinesischen Bronzen,' *Ostasiatische Zeitgeist* 22 (N F12): 3-41.

—1949: 'Weapons and tools from Anyang and Siberian analogies,' *American*

Journal of Archaeology, 53: 126-144.

— 1953: 'The Bronze Styles of the Anyang Period (1300-1028 BC).' *Archives of the Chinese Art Society of America* 7: 42-53.

— 1968: *Ritual Vessels of Bronze Age China*, New York.

Longnan 1988 (Longnan yizhi kaogu gongzuodui): 'Jiangsu Wujiang Meiyan Longnan yizhi 1987 nian fajue jiyao,' *Dongnan wenhua*. 1988(5): 49-53.

Loo, C T 1950: *An exhibition of Chinese Archaic Jades. Arranged for the Norton Gallery of Art, West Palm Beach, Florida*, Norton Gallery of Art.

Lu Liancheng 1993: Zhongguo gudai ducheng fazhang dezaiqi jieduan - Shangdai Xi-Zhou ducheng xingtai de kaocha. Institute of Archaeology, CASS eds. *Zhongguo kaoguxue luncong*. Beijing: Kexue chubanshe.

Lu Sixian 1993: 'Hongshan luoti nüshen wei Nüwa kao,' *Beifang wenwu* 1993(3):33-6.

Luo Erhu *et al* 1989: Chengdu Zhihuijie yizhi baofeng fenxi yanjiu,' *Nanfang minzu kaogu* 2: 299-309.

Luo Feng, Han Kongyue 1990: 'Ningxia Guyuan jinnian faxian de beifang xi qingtongqi,' *Kaogu* 1990 (5), 403-418.

Luo Kaiyu 1989: 'Chengdu cheng de xingcheng he Qin de gaijian,' *Chengdu wenwu* 1989(1): 56-61.

Luo Tang 1992: 'Luoyang zaixian Bei Song yashu tingyuan yizhi,' *Zhongguo wenwu bao* 14-6-92.

Ma Chengyuan 1991: 'Guoguo damu canguanji,' *Zhongguo wenwu bao* 3-3-91.

— 1992: 'Wu Yue wenhua qingtongqi de yanjiu – jianlun Dayangzhou chutu de qingtongqi.' *Wu Yue qingtongqi yanjiu zuotanhui*, Shanghai Museum 19-21.

Ma Shizhi 1988: 'Luelun Chu Yindu chengshi renkou wenti,' *Jiang Han kaogu* 1988(1): 56-61.

Ma Xuzhen *et al*, 1929: *Yicheng xian zhi,* Taipei: Chengwen shuju.

Maenchen-Helfen, Otto 1945: 'Some Remarks on Ancient Chinese Bronzes,' *Art Bulletin* 27: 238-243.

March, Benjamin 1929: *China and Japan in Our Museums*. New York: Institute of Pacific Relations.

Martin, F R 1893: *L'Age du bronze au musée de Minoussinsk*, Stockholm: Samson E Wallin.

Meng Fanren 1994: Shilun Bei Wei Luoyangcheng de xingzhi yu Zhongya gucheng xingzhi de guanxi - jiantang silu yanxian chengshi de zhongyaoxing. *Han Tang yu bianjiang kaogu yanjiu* 1, 97-110.

Meng Wentong 1962: 'Luelun "Shanghaijing" de xiezuo shidai jiqi changsheng diyu,' *Zhonghua wenshi luncong* I: 43-70.

Minns, E H 1913: *Scythians and Greeks*, Cambridge: Cambridge University Press 1913.

— 1942: 'The art of the northern nomads,' *Proceedings of the British Academy* 28: 47-99.

Mirsky, Jeannette 1977: *Sir Aurel Stein: Archaeological Explorer*. Chicago: University of Chicago Press.

Mitter, Partha 1977: *Much Maligned Monsters: History of European Reactions to Indian Art*. Oxford: Clarendon Press.

Mou Yongkang, Wu Ruzuo 1990: 'Shi tan yuqi shidai-zhonghua wenming qiyuan de tansuo,' *Zhongguo wenwubao* 1-11- 90.

— 1993: 'Shuidao, cansi he yuqi - Zhonghua wenming qiyuan de ruogan wenti,' *Kaogu* 1993(6): 543-553.

— 1997: ' Shi lun yuqi shidai-Zhongguo wenming shidai chansheng de yige zhongyao biaozhi,' Su Bingqi ed. *Kaoguxue wenhua lunji* 4: 164-87, Beijing: Wenwu chubanshe.

Mungello, David 1985: *Curious Land: Jesuit Accommodation and the Origins of Sinology*. Stuttgart: Steiner.

Nalan chengde 1676: *Sanli tu.*

Nanjing 1980 (Nanjing bowuyuan): 'Jiangsu Wuxian Caoxieshan yizhi,' *Wenwu ziliao congkan* 1980(3): 1-24.

— 1981 (Nanjing bowuyuan): 'Jiangsu Pi xian Dadunzi yizhi dierci fajue,' *Kaoguxue jikan* 1: 27-81.

— 1982 (Nanjing bowuyuan): 'Jiangsu Yuecheng yizhi de fajue,' *Kaogu* 1982(5): 463-473.

— 1984 (Nanjing bowuyuan *et al*): 'Jiangsu Kunshan Chuodun yizhi de diaocha yu fajue,' *Wenwu* 1984(2): 6-11.

— 1986 (Nanjing bowuyuan *et al*): 'Jiangsu Wuxian Zhanglingshan dong shan yizhi,' *Wenwu* 1986(10)26-35.

Nara 1988 (Nara National Museum): *The Oasis and Steppe Routes.* Exhibition catalogue.

Neimeng 1996: Nei Menggu wenwu kaogu yanjiusuo, Chifeng shi bowuguan, Aluke'erxinqi wenwu guanlisuo: 'Liao Yelü Yuzhi mu fajue jianbao,' *Wenwu* 1996(1): 4-32.

Ningcheng 1985: 'Ningcheng xian xin faxian de Xiajiadian shangceng wenhua muzang jiqi xiangguan yiwu de yanjiu,' *Wenwu ziliao congkan,* 1985(9), 23-58.

O'Donoghue, Diane M 1990: 'Reflexion and Reception: The Origin of the Mirror in Bronze Age China,' *Bulletin of the Museum of Far Eastern Antiquities* 62: 5-183.

Okamura, Hidenori 1996: Exacavations at Yingxiangcheng in Hubei province. Conference paper read at the conference 'Mysteries of ancient China,' held at the British Museum, 6-8 December 1996.

— , Zhang Xuqiu 1997: 'Kôhoku Inshôjô ishi kenkyû (I),' *Tôhô Gakuhô,* Vol 69: 459-510.

Panofsky, Erwin 1955: 'The History of Art as a Humanistic Discipline,' *Meaning in the Visual Arts: Papers in and on Art History,* 1-25. New York: Doubleday.

Paper, Jordan 1978: 'The Meaning of the T'ao-t'ieh,' *History of Religions* 18.1: 18-41.

Pearlstein, Elinor 1993: 'Salmony's Catalogue of the Sonnenschein Jades in the Light of Recent Finds,' *Orientations* 24-6 (June 1993): 48-58.

Pei Anping 1989: 'Pengtoushan wenhua de daozuo yicun yu Zhongguo shiqian daozuo nongye,' *Nongye kaogu* 1989(2): 102-8.

Pei Mingxiang 1996: 'Lun Zhengzhou Xiaoshuangqiao Shangdai qianqi jisi yizhi,' *Zhongyuan kaogu*1996(2): 4-8.

Peng Shifan, Liu Lin, Zhan Kaixun 1991: 'Guanyu Xin'gan Dayangzhou Shangmu niandai wenti de taolun.' *Wenwu* 1991 (10): 27-32.

Peng Shifan, Liu Shizhong 1990: 'Guanyu Ruichang Shang/Zhou tongkuang yicun yu gu Yang Yueren,' *Jiangxi wenwu* 1990(3): 25-31.

People's Daily [Overseas Edition], 31 December 1996.

Piotrovsky, Boris *et al* 1991: *L'Or des Scythes, Trésors de l'Hermitage,* Leningrad, Paris 1991.

Pirazzoli-t'Serstevens, Michèle 1992: 'Mawangdui, les tombes d'une maison royale, 186-165 av J-C,' in *Chine Antique— Voyage de l'âme,* Daoulas: Centre culturel Abbaye de Daoulas, 83-97.

Podro, Michael 1982: *The Critical Historians of Art.* New Haven: Yale University Press.

Pope, John A 1947: 'Sinology or Art History: Notes on Method in the Study of Chinese Art.' *Harvard Journal of Asiatic Studies* 10: 388-417.

Powers, Martin J 1991: *Art and Political Expression in Early China.* New Haven: Yale University Press.

Preziosi, Donald 1989: *Rethinking Art History: Meditations on a Coy Science.* New Haven: Yale University Press.

—1992: 'The Question of Art History.' *Critical Inquiry* 18: 363-386.

Qi Xiaoguang 1993: 'Nei Menggu faxian Qidan huangzu Yelü Yuzhi mu,' *Zhongguo wenwu bao* 31-1-93.
— 1995: 'Nei Menggu fajue Baoshan Liao chu bihua mu,' *Zhongguo wenwu bao* 1-1-95.
— 1996: 'Yelü Yuzhi muzhi dui wenxian jizai de qibu,' *Wenwu* 1996(2).
Qi Yuchen 1993: 'Zhonghua diyi cun lanshen,' *Beifang wenwu* 1993(1): 3-8.
Qian Feng 1992: 'Zhaolingshan yizhi fajue huo zhongda chengguo,' *Zhongguo wenwu bao* 2-8-92.
Qian Gonglin 1990: 'Wujiang Longnan yizhi fangzhi chutan,' *Wenwu* 1990(7): 28-31.
Qinghai 1990 (Qinghai sheng wenwu kaogu yanjiu suo): *Minhe Yangshan*, Beijing: Wenwu chubanshe.
Qiu Xigui 1994: 'Guanyu Jin hou tongqi mingwen de jige wenti.' *Chuantong wenhua yu xiandaihua* 1994(2).
Qun Li 1972: Linzi Qiguo gudu kantan jiyao. *Wenwu* 1972(5), 45-54.
Qu Yingjie 1989: Lun Longshan wenhua shiqi gu chengzhi. Tian Changwu and Shi Xingbang eds. *Zhonguo yuanshi wenhua lunji*. Beijing: Wenwu chubanshe, 267-80.

Rawson, Jessica 1990: *Western Zhou Ritual Bronzes from the Arthur M. Sackler Collections*, Cambridge, Mass: Arthur M Sackler Foundation.
— 1992 ed: *The British Museum Book of Chinese art*, London: British Museum Press.
— 1993: 'Late Shang Bronze Design: Meaning and Purpose,' in Whitfield 1993: 67-95.
— 1995: *Chinese Jade: From the Neolithic to the Qing*, London: British Museum Press.
Ren Shinan 1993: 'Zhongguo shiqian yuqi leixing chuxi,' *Zhongguo kaoguxue luncong* (Zhongguo shehui kexueyuan kaogu yanjiusuo ed), Beijing: Kexue chubanshe, 106-130.
— 'Xinglongwa wenhua de faxian jiqi yiyi - jian yu Huabei tong shiqi de kaoguxue wenhua xiang bijiao,' *Kaogu* 1994(8): 710-718.
— 1996: Changjiang zhongyou wenming qiyuan tansuo — yi Qujialing, Shijiahe wenhua wei zhongxin. Institute of History, CASS eds. *Hua Xia wenming yu chuanshi cangshu — Essays of the International symposium on Sinology, Haikou, China, 1995*. Beijing: Chinese Social Sciences Press, 252-284.
Ren Xianghong *et al*: 'Shandong Changqing Xianrentai yizhi faxian Siguo guizu mudi' *Zhongguo wenwu bao* 17-12-95.
Renfrew, Colin 1982: 'Explanation revisited,' *Theory and explanation in archaeology* (A C Renfrew, M J Rowlands and B A Segraves, eds). New York: Academic Press, 5-23.
— 1994: *Archaeology, Theories, Methods and Practice*, London, Thames and Hudson Ltd.
Ridgway, Brunhilde Sismondo 1986: 'The State of Research on Ancient Art.' *The Art Bulletin* 68.1:7-23.
Roztovzeff, M I 1929: Animal Style in South Russia and China, Princeton: Princeton University Press.
Rudenko 1958: 'The mythological eagle, the gryphon, the winged lion and the wolf in the art of northern nomads,' *Artibus Asiae*, 21: 101-122.
Rudenko 1970: *Frozen tombs of Siberia: the Pazyzyk burials of Iron Age horsemen* (trans M W Thompson), California: UCP
Rudolph, Richard C 1963: 'Notes on Sung Archaeology.' *Journal of Asian Studies* 22: 169-177.
Rui Guoyao and Shen Yueming 1992: 'Liangzhu wenhua yu Shang wenhua guanxi sanli,' *Kaogu* 1992(11): 1039-1044.

Said, Edward 1978: *Orientalism*. New York: Knopf.

Salmony, Alfred 1933: *Sino-Siberian Art in the Collection of C T Loo*, Paris: C T Loo.

— 1952: *Archaic Chinese Jades from the Edward and Louise B. Sonnenschein Collection*, Chicago: The Art Institute of Chicago.

Ségalen, Victor *et al* 1923-24: *Mission archéologique en Chine. 1914 et 1917*. Paris: P Geuthner.

—1977: *The Great Statuary of China*. trans E Levieux, Chicago: University of Chicago Press.

Shaanxi 1990 (Shaanxi sheng kaogu yanjiusuo): *Longgangsi Xinshiqi shidai yizhi fajue baogao*, Beijing: Wenwu chubanshe.

Shan Xianjin, Cao Chuansong 1992: 'Fengxian Chengtoushan Qujialing wenhua chengzhi bei queren,' *Zhongguo wenwu bao* 15-3-92.

Shandong 1977 (Shandong sheng bowuguan): 'Linzi Langjiazhuang yi hao Dong Zhou xunren mu,' *Kaogu xuebao* 1977(1): 73-104.

— 1992 (Shandong daxue lishixi kaogu jiaoyanshi): 'Shandong Zouping Ding-gong yizhi dier, san ci fajue jianbao,' *Kaogu* 1992(6): 496-504.

— 'Shandong Zouping Dinggong yizhi disi, wu ci fajue jianbao,' *Kaogu* 1993(4): 295-299.

— 'Zouping Dinggong faxian Longshan wenhua chengzhi,' *Zhongguo wenwu bao* 12-1-92.

Shanghai 1984 (Shanghai shi wenwu baoguan weiyuanhui): 'Shanghai Fuquanshan Liangzhu wenhua muzang,' *Wenwu* 1984(2): 1-5.

— 1986 (Shanghai shi wenwu baoguan weiyuanhui): 'Shanghai Qingpu Fuquanshan Liangzhu wenhua mudi,' *Wenwu* 1986(10): 1-25.

Shanxi 1984: (Shanxi sheng kaogu yanjiusuo): 'Shanxi Changzi xian Dong Zhou mu,' *Kaogu xuebao* 1984(4): 503-529.

— 1994 (Shanxi sheng kaogu yanjiusuo): *Shangma mudi*, Beijing: Wenwu chubanshe.

—1994a (Shanxi sheng kaogusuo, Beijing daxue kaoguxi): 'Tianma-Qucun yizhi Beizhao Jin hou mudi disan ci fajue,' *Wenwu* 1994(8): 22-33.

— 1994b 'Tianma-Qucun yizhi Beizhao Jin hou mudi disi ci fajue,' *Wenwu* 1994(8): 4-21.

Shao Wangping *forthcoming*: 'Wenming de xingcheng - Longshan shidai yu Longshan jiaofu zuoyong quan,' *Zhongguo wenming de xingcheng* (K C Chang and Xu Pingfang, eds), New Haven/Beijing: Yale University Press/China New World Press.

Sheng Zhongchang 1987: 'Sanxingdui erhao jisi keng qingtong lirenxiang chuji,' *Wenwu* 1987(10): 16-17.

Shi Xingbang 1983: 'Cong kaoguxue wenhua tantao woguo siyouzhi he guojia de qiyuan wenti,' *Shiqian yanjiu* 1983(1): 27-45.

— 1997, 'Zhongguo wenhua yu wenming fazhan he xingcheng de kaoguxue tantao,' *Zhongguo kaoguxue yu lishixue zhi zhenghe yanjiu* (Tsang Cheng-hwa ed), Taipei: Zhongyang yanjiuyuan, 85-130.

Shihe 1990 (Shihe kaogudui): 'Hubei sheng Shihe yizhiqun 1987 nian fajue jianbao,' *Wenwu* 1990(8): 1-16.

— 1994 (Shihe kaogudui): 'Hubei Tianmen Dengjiawan yizhi 1992 nian fajue jianbao,' *Wenwu* 1994(4): 32-41.

Shiji (by Sima Qian), Beijing: Zhonghua shuju, 1969.

Shilong 1956 (Shilong guojiang shuiku zhihuibu wenwu gongzuodui): 'Hubei Jingshan Tianmen kaogu fajue baogao,' *Kaogu tongxun* 1956(3): 11-21.

Si Xinqiang *et al* 1993: 'Panxian Dadong fajue jianbao,' *Renleixue xuebao* 1993(5): 113-21.

Sichuan 1957 (Sichuan sheng wenwu guanli weiyuanhui): 'Chengdu Yangzishan tutai yizhi qingli baogao,' *Kaogu xuebao* 1957(4): 17-31.

— 1987a (Sichuan wenwu guanli weiyuanhui *et al*): 'Guanghan Sanxingdui yizhi,' *Kaogu xuebao* 1987(2): 227-254.

— 1987b (Sichuan sheng wenwu kaogu yanjiusuo *et al*): 'Guanghan Sanxingdui yizhi yihao jisi keng fajue jianbao,' *Wenwu* 1987(10): 1-15.

— 1988 (Sichuan sheng wenwu kaogu yanjiusuo *et al*): 'Guanghan Sanxingdui yizhi erhao jisi keng fajue jianbao,' *Wenwu* 1989(5): 1-20.

— 1987c (Sichuan sheng wenwu guanli weiyuanhui *et al*): 'Chengdu Shi'erqiao Shangdai jianzhu yizhi diyiqi fajue jianbao,' *Wenwu* 1987(12): 1-23, 37.

Sickman, L and A Soper 1956: *The Art and Architecture of China.* Harmondsworth: Pelican.

Sima Qian: *Shiji*, Beijing: Zhonghua shuju, 1969.

Siren, Osvald 1930: *A History of Early Chinese Art*, Vol I, *The Han Period.* London: E Benn.

Snodgrass, Anthony M 1987: *An Archaeology of Greece: The present state and future scope of a discipline.* Berkeley: University of California Press.

Song Guoding *et al* 1995: 'Zhengzhou Xiaoshuangqiao yizhi fajue huo zhongda chengguo,' *Zhongguo wenwu bao* 13-8-95.

Song Yemin 1990: 'Guanghan Sanxingdui yihao, erhao jisi keng jige wenti de tantao,' *Nanfang minzu kaogu* 3: 69-84.

Soper, Alexander C 1966: 'Early, Middle and Late Shang: A Note.' *Artibus Asiae* 28: 5-38.

—1976: 'The Relationship of Early Chinese Painting to Its Own Past,' *Chinese Culture,* 21-47 Princeton.

Spiro, Audrey 1981: 'Max Loehr's Periodisation of Bronze Vessels.' *Journal of Asian Culture* 5: 107-133.

Steinhardt, N S 1990: *Chinese imperial city planning.* Honolulu: University of Hawaii Press.

Su Bai 1978a: Bei Wei Luoyang cheng he Beimang lingmu. *Wenwu* 1978(7), 42-52.

— 1978b: Sui Tang Chang'an cheng he Luoyang cheng. *Kaogu* 1978(6), 406-425.

Su Bingqi 1984: *Kaoguxue lunshu xuanji.* Beijing: Wenwu chubanshe, 157-189.

— 1986: 'Liaoxi gu wenhua gucheng guguo,' *Wenwu* 1986(8): 41-44.

— 1994a, ed, *Zhongguo tongshi*, vol2. Shanghai: Renmin chubanshe.

— 1994b, *Zhongguo kaogu wenwu zhi mei*, 10 vols, Beijing/Taipei: Wenwu chubanshe and Guangfu shuju.*Zhongguoren - kaogu xungenji*, Shenyang: Liaoning University Press.

— 1994c, *Huaren - longde chuanren.*

Suliminski, Tadeusz 1970: *Prehistoric Russia: an outline.* London: John Baker.

Sun Hua 1993: Guanyu Sanxingdui qiwu keng ruogan wenti de bianzheng,' *Sichuan wenwu* 1993(4): 3-11; 1993(5): 3-7.

— 1995: 'Guangyu Jinhou xi zu mu de jige wenti,' *Wenwu* 1995(9).

— 1997 'Jinhou Yu/Xi mu de jige wenti,' *Wenwu* 1997(8): 27-36.

Sun Shoudao 1957: 'Xiongnu Xichagou wenhua gumuqun de faxian,' *Wenwu* 1960 (8,9).

Sun Xidan: *Liji jijie*, Beijing: Zhonghua shuju 1989.

Sun Zhixin 1993: 'The Liangzhu Culture: Its Discovery and Its Jades,' *Early China* 18: 1-40.

Sutton, Denys 1973: 'The Lure of Ancient China.' *Apollo* 97 (March 1973): 2-11.

Suzhou 1986 (Suzhou bowuguan *et al*): 'Jiangsu Wujiang Longnan xinshiqi shidai cunluo yizhi diyi, erci fajue jianbao,' *Wenwu* 1986(10): 1-27.

Tallgren 1937: 'Some north Eurasian sculptures,' *Eurasia Septentrionalis Antiqua* 12.

Tang Jigen 1995: 'Yinxu jiazu mudi chutan,'*Zhongguo Shang wenhua guoji xueshu taolunhui lunwenji,* Zhongguo shehui kexueyuan kaogu yanjiusuo ed. Beijing: Kexue chubanshe.

Tang Ling 1985, *Jing Chu suishiji yizhu* Wuhan, Hubei renmin chubanshe.

Tang Shengxiang, Wen Shaokai and Y I Sato 1994: 'Zhongguo jingdao qiyuan de tantao,' *Nongye kaogu* 1994(1): 59-67.

Tang Yunming 1985: 'Woguo yuchang zhichou qiyuan shidai cutan,' *Nongye kaogu* 1985(2): 320-323.

Tangshan 1994 (Tangshan kaogu fajuedui): 'Nanjing Tangshan fajue chu gurenlei huashi,' *Zhongguo wenwu bao* 18-12-94.

— 1996 (Tangshan kaogu dui): 'Nanjing Tangshan Huludong zhiliren huashi didian kaogu fajue de zhongyao shouhuo,' *Wenwu* 1996(10): 58-63.

Tao Zhenggang, Hou Yi 1994: *Chunqiu Jin guo qingtongqi baozang — Shanxi Taiyuan Zhao qing mu*, Taipei/Beijing: Kwang Fu Book Enterprises Co. Ltd/ Cultural Relics Publishing House.

Taylor, W 1948: *A Study of Archaeology,* American Anthropologist Memoir 69, Washington DC.

Teng Shu-p'ing 1988: 'Kaogu chutu Xinshiqi shidai yushicong yanjiu,' *Gugong xueshu jikan* 6.1: 1-65.

Thorp, Robert L 1985: 'The growth of early Shang civilisation: New data from ritual vessels.' *Harvard Journal of Asiatic Studies* 45.1: 5-75.

—1988: 'Archaeology of Style at Anyang: Tomb 5 in Context,' *Archives of Asian Art* 41: 47-69.

—1991: 'Bronze Catalogues as Cultural Artifacts.' *Archives of Asian Art* 44: 84-94.

—1993: '*Hao dongxi*: Reflections on the Curious Status of Objects,' paper presented at the CAA Annual Meeting, Seattle, 4 February, 1993.

Thote, Alain 1986: 'Une tombe princière chinoise du Ve siècle avant notre ère,' *Comptes rendus de l'Académie des Inscriptions & Belles-Lettres,* avril-juin, 393-413.

— 1987: 'Une sculpture chinoise en bronze du Ve siècle avant notre ère: essai d'interprétation,' *Arts Asiatiques* 42: 45-58.

— 1991: 'The Double Coffin of Leigudun Tomb No 1: Iconographic Sources and Related Problems,' *New Perspectives on Chu Culture during the Eastern Zhou Period* (Thomas Lawton ed), Arthur M Sackler Gallery, Smithsonian Institution, Washington, DC, 23-46.

— 1996: 'Note sur la postérité du masque de Liangzhu à l'époque des Zhou orientaux,' *Arts Asiatiques* 51: 60-72.

— 1997: 'Intercultural Contacts and Exchanges illustrated by the burial goods from Xichuan Xiasi cemetery (6th century BC),' *Hanxue yanjiu* 15.1: 263-89.

Tian Cangwu 1986: 'Xian Xia wenhua tansuo,' *Wenwu yu kaogu lunji,* Beijing: Wenwu chubanshe, 93-109.

Tian Guangjin and Guo Suxin 1976: 'Taohongbala de xiongnu mu,' *Kaogu xuebao* 1976 (1): 131-144.

— 1986: *Ordos shi qingtongqi,* Beijing: Wenwu chubanshe.

— 1992: 'Zailun Ordos shi qingtongqi de yanyuan,' conference paper, Zhongguo gudai beifang minzu kaogu wenhua guoji xueshu yantaohui, Huhehaote, August 11-18, 1992.

Tian Shuangyin: 'Cong Guoguo mudi chutu de zuiyu mianzhao kan gu zhi lianyu,' *Huaxia kaogu* 1993(3):.

Tong Enzheng 1989: 'Youguan wenming qiyuan de jige wenti,' *Kaogu* 1989(1): 51-59.

Trigger, Bruce 1989: *A History of Archaeological Thought.* Cambridge: Cambridge University Press.

Ueda Masaaki 1976: *Tojo.* Tokyo: Shakai shisosha.

Vanderstappen, Harrie 1977-78: 'Ludwig Bachhofer (1894-1976).' *Archives of Asian Art* 31: 110-112.

Vasilev, L S 1976: *The questions of the origins of Chinese civilisation* (in Russian; Chinese translation, *Zhongguo wenming qiyuan wenti,* Beijing: Wenwu chubanshe, 1989).

von Falkenhausen, Lothar 1993: *Suspended Music - Chime-Bells in the Culture of Bronze Age China,* Berkeley/Los Angeles/Oxford: University of California Press.

Wagner, Donald B. 1987: 'The Dating of the Chu Graves of Changsha: the Earliest Iron Artifacts in China?' *Acta Orientalia*, Vol XLVIII: 111-156.

Waley, Arthur 1923: *An Introduction to the Study of Chinese Painting*. London.

Wang Mingda 1997: 'A Study of the Jades of the Liangzhu Culture: the Functions of Liangzhu Jades, based on Evidence from Tomb No 20 at Fanshan,'*Chinese Jades* (R Scott ed). London 1997, 37-47.

Wang Qinjin 1993: 'Yangzhou Tang cheng kaogu huo zhongda jinzhan,' *Zhongguo wenwu bao* 21-11-93.

Wang Tao and Liu Yu 1997: 'The face of the other world: jade face-covers from ancient tombs,'*Chinese Jades* (R Scott, ed), Colloquies on Art and Archaeology in Asia No 18, London: Percival David foundation of Chinese Art, 133-146.

Wang Wei 1986: 'Liangzhu wenhua yucong chuyi,' *Kaogu* 1986(11): 1009-1016.

Wang Yi 1988: 'Chengdu shi Shu wenhua yizhi de faxian ji yiyi,' *Chengdu wenwu* 1988(1): 10-16.

Waterbury, Florance 1942: *Early Chinese symbols and literature: vestiges and speculations*, New York.

Watson, William 1968: 'The Five Stages of Shang,' (Review of Max Loehr, *Ritual Vessels of Bronze Age China*), *Art News* 67.7 (November 1968): 42-47, 62-64.

— 1971: *Cultural frontiers in ancient East Asia*, Edinburgh: Edinburgh University Press.

Wen Daoyi 1959: 'Changsha Chu mu,' *Kaogu xuebao* 1959(1): 41-58.

Wen Guang and Jing Zhichun 1992: 'Chinese neolithic jade: a preliminary geo-archaeological study,' *Geoarchaeology, An International Journal* 7/3: 251-275.

Wenley, A G 1946: *Descriptive and Illustrative Catalogue of Chinese Bronzes Acquired during the Administration of John Ellerton Lodge*, Washington: Smithsonian Institution.

Whitfield, Roderick 1965: *Chang Tse-tuan's 'Ch'ing-ming shang-ho t'u.'* PhD dissertation, Princeton University.

— 1993, ed: *The Problem of Meaning in Early Chinese Ritual Bronzes*, Colloquies on art and Archaeology in Asia, No 15, London: Percival David Foundation of Chinese Art, School of Oriental and African Studies.

Wenwu jinghua 1 (1959) Beijing: Wenwu chubanshe.

Willey, Gordon R and Jeremy A Sabloff 1974 (second ed 1980): *A History of American Archaeology*. San Francisco: Freeman.

Wilson, Marc F 1989: 'Laurence Chalfant Stevens Sickman (1906-1988),' *Archives of Asian Art* 42: 82-84.

Wiseman, James 1984: 'Scholarship and Provenience in the Study of Artifacts.' *Journal of Field Archaeology* 11: 67-77.

Wright, A 1977: 'The cosmology of the Chinese city,' William Skinner ed. *The City in Late Imperial China*. California: Stanford University Press, 33-73.

Wu En 1984: 'Lun woguo beifang gudai dongwu wenshi de yanyuan,' *Kaogu yu wenwu*, 1984 (4), 46-59, 104.

— 1986: 'Zhongguo beifang qingtong wenhua yu Kalasuke wenhua de guanxi, *Zhongguo kaoguxue yanjiu — Xia Nai xiansheng kaogu wushinian jinian wenji*, Beijing: Kexue chubanshe.

Wu Hung 1988: 'From Temple to Tomb. Ancient Chinese art and Religion in Transition,' *Early China* 13: 78-115.

— 1989: *Chinese Pictorial Art*, Stanford: Stanford University Press.

— 1990: 'A Great Beginning. Ancient Chinese Jades and the Origin of Ritual Art,' introduction to the catalogue *Chinese Jades from the Mu-Fei Collection*, London, Bluett & Sons Ltd.

— 1992: 'Art in a ritual context: rethinking Mawangdui,' *Early China* 17: 110-44.

— 1995: *Monumentality in Early Chinese Art and Archaeology*, California: Stanford University Press.

Wu Ruzuo 1987: 'Taihu wenhuaqu de shiqian nongye,' *Nongye Kaogu* 1987(2): 103-11.

Wu Yaoli 1994: 'Huanghe liuyu Xinshiqi shidai de daozuo nongye,' *Nongye kaogu* 1994(1): 78-84.

Xi'an 1988 (Xi'an Banpo bowuguan): *Jianzhai - Xinshiqi shidai yizhi fajue baogao*, Beijing: Wenwu chubanshe.

Xia Nai 1985: *Zhongguo wenming de qiyuan*. Beijing: Wenwu chubanshe.

—, Wang Zhongshu eds 1986: *Zhongguo dabaike quanshu: Kaoguxue,* Beijing and Shanghai: Zhongguo dabaike quanshu chubanshe.

Xiang Chunsong 1984: 'Xiaoheishigou faxian de qingtongqi,' *Neimenggu wenwu kaogu* 1984 (3).

Xiao Minghua 1991: 'Jianchuan Haimenkou 1978 nian fajue suohuo tongqi jiqi youguan wenti,' *Yunnan qingtong wenhua lunji* (Yunnansheng bowuguan ed), Kunming: Yunnan renmin chubanshe.

Xibei 1984 (Xibei shiyuan zhiwu yanjiusuo and Gansu sheng bowuguan): 'Gansu Dongxiang Linjia Majiayao wenhua yizhi chutu de ji yu dama,' *Kaogu* 1984(7): 654-655.

Xie Wei 1988: 'Anban yizhi huitu zhong suojian dao de nongzuowu,' *Kaogu yu wenwu*, 1988(5/6): 209-213.

Xie Zhongli 1994: 'Yuqi shidai —yige xin kainian de fenxi,' *Kaogu* 1994(9): 832-836.

Xu Chaolong 1992: 'Sanxingdui jisi keng shuo chang yi-jiantan Yufu he Duyu zhi guangxi,' *Sichuan wenwu* 1992(5): 32-38; (6): 40-47.

Xu Guanji 1986: Chifeng Yingjinhe Yinhe liuyu shicheng yizhi. Zhongguo kaoguxue yanjiu bianweihui ed. *Zhonguo kaoguxue yanjiu*. Beijing: Wenwu chubanshe, 82-93.

Xu Hui, Ou Qiuming 1981: Dui Qiansanyang chutu sizhipin de yanzheng, *Sichou* 1981(2): 43-45.

Xu Jay 1996: 'The Cemetery of the Western Zhou Lords of Jin,' *Artibus Asiae* LVI, 3/4: 193-231.

Xu Shunzhan: 'Zhengzhou Xishan faxian Huangdi shidai gucheng,' *Zhongyuan wenwu* 1996(1): 1-5.

Xu Yongsheng: 'Cong Guoguo mudi kaogu faxian tan Guoguo lishi kaikuan,' *Huaxia kaogu* 1993(3):.

Xu Zhongshu 1987: 'Chengdu shi gudai ziyou dushi shuo,' *Ba Shu kaogu lunwenji* (Xu Zhongshu ed). Beijing: Wenwu chubanshe, 151-2.

Yan Daoheng 1991: 'Yongcheng Mangshan Han Liangwang ling chutu dapi zhengui wenwu,' *Zhongguo wenwu bao* 25-8-91.

Yan Shizhong, Li Huajiang 1992: 'Ningxia Xiji faxian yizuo qingtong shidai muzang,' *Kaogu* 1992 (6): 573.

Yan Wenming 1992: 'Luelun Zhongguo wenming de qiyuan,' *Wenwu* 1992(1): 40-49.

— 1994: Zhongguo huaihao juluo de yanbian. *Guoxue yanjiu* 2, 483-492.

— 1997: 'Longshan shidai chengshi de chubu yanjiu,' *Zhongguo kaoguxue yu lishixue zhi zhenghe yanjiu*, (Tsang Cheng-hwa, ed), Taipei: Zhongyang yanjiuyuan, 235-256.

— 'Liangzhu suibi,' *Wenwu* 1996(3).

Yang Kuan 1993: *Zhongguo gudai ducheng zhidushi yanjiu*. Shanghai: Guji chubanshe.

Yang Nan, Zhao Hua 1993: 'Yuhang Mojiaoshan qingli daxing jianzhu jizhi,' *Zhongguo wenwu bao* 10-10-93.

Yang Shiting 1978: 'Qiantan Shixia faxian de Zaipeidao yiji,' *Wenwu* 1978(7): 23-28.

Yang Shuda 1980: *Chunqiu Zuozhuan zhu*, Beijing: Zhonghua shuju.

Yang Xizhang, Yang Baocheng 1985: 'Yindai qingtong liqi de fenqi yu zuhe,' *Yinxu qingtongqi* (Zhonggguo shehui kexueyuan kaogu yanjiusuo ed), Beijing: Wenwu chubanshe, 79-102.

Yang Yubin 1993: Zhengzhou Shang cheng de kaogu faxian he yanjiu. *Zhongyuan wenwu* 1993(3), 1-10, 22.

Yangzhou Archaeological Team 1990: Yangzhoucheng kaogu gongzuo jianbao, *Kaogu* 1990(1), 36-44.

Yichang 1990 (Yichang diqu bowuguan): 'Hubei Dangyang Zhaoxiang 4 hao Chunqiu mu fajue jianbao,' *Wenwu* 1990(10): 25-32.

Yingshan 1989 (Yingshan xian wenhuaguan wenwuzu): 'Hubei Yingshan Wudian gu muzang qingli jianbao,' *Wenwu* 1989(3): 51-56.

Yin Weizhang 1986: A reexamination of Erh-li-t'ou culture. K C Chang ed. *Studies of Shang Archaeology.* New Haven and London: Yale University Pree, 1-13.

You Xiuling, Zheng Yunfei 1995: 'Hemudu daogu yanjiu jinzhan ji zhanwan,' *Nongye kaogu* 1995(1): 66-70.

Yu Ke, Zhou Min 1985: *Zhongguo shehui ziliao cui bian*, Chengdu: Sichuan sheng shehui kexueyuan chubanshe.

Yu Weichao 1980: 'Han dai zhuhou wang yu liehou muzang de xingzhi fenxi — jian lun "Zhou zhi," "Han zhi" yu "Jin zhi" de san jieduanxing,' *Zhongguo kaoguxuehui di yi ci nianhui lunwenji 1979*, Beijing: Wenwu chubanshe, 332-37.

— Zhongguo gudai ducheng guihua de fazhang jieduanxing.*Wenwu* 1985/2, 52-60.

— 1991a: 'Kaogusuo sishinian chengguo zhan bitan,' *Kaogu* 1991(1): 75-76.

— 1991b: 'Shangcunling Guoguo mudi xin faxian suo jieshi de jige wenti,' *Zhongguo wenwu bao* 3-2-91.

Yu Xiucui 1991: 'Dangyang Zhijiang Chu mu chutu de qingtong jian jieshao,' *Jiang Han Kaogu* 1991(1): 44-46.

Yu Yongbing 1994: Shitan Sichouzhilu shang de Yangzhou Tangcheng, *Han Tang yu bianjiang kaogu yanjiu* 1, 169-72.

Yuan Jiarong 1996: 'Yuzhanyan huo shuidao qiyuan xin wuzheng,' *Zhongguo wenwubao* 3-3-1996.

Yuan Guangkuo 1992: 'Huixian Mengzhuang faxian Longshan wenhua chengzhi,' *Zhongguo wenwu bao* 16-12-92.

Yuhang 1991 (Yuhang xian wenguanhui): 'Yuhangxian chutu de Liangzhu wenhua he Maqiao wenhua de taoqi kehua fuhao,' *Dongnan wenhua* 1991(3): 182-184.

Yunnan 1958 (Yunnansheng bowuguan choubeichu): 'Jianchuan Haimenkou guwenhua yizhi qingli jianbao,' *Kaogu tongxun* 1958 (6): 5-12.

— 1964 (Yunnansheng wenwu gongzuodui): 'Yunnan Xiangyun Dabona muqu Tongguan mu qingli baogao,' *Kaogu* 1964 (12): 607-614.

— 1965 (Yunnansheng wenwu gongzuodui): 'Yunnan Anning Taijishan gu muqun qingli baogao,' *Kaogu* 1965 (9): 459-461.

— 1975 (Yunnansheng bowuguan): *Yunnan Jinning Shizhaishan gu muqun fajue baogao*, Beijing: Wenwu chubanshe.

— 1983 (Yunnansheng wenwu gongzuodui): 'Chuxiong Wanjiaba gu muqun fajue jianbao,' *Kaogu xuebao* 1983 (3): 347-382.

— 1986 (Yunnansheng bowuguan gongzuodui): 'Yunnan Jiangchuan Aofengshan mudi fajue jianbao,' *Wenwu* 1986 (7): 1-20.

Zhang Changshou 1991: 'Guoguo mudi de xin faxian,' *Zhongguo wenwu bao* 17-3-91.

Zhang Chi 1990: 'Shijiahe yizhi diwuci fajue huo xin chengguo,' *Zhongguo wenwu bao* 5-4-90.

— 1994: 'Baligang shiqian juluo fajue huo zhongyao chengguo,' *Zhongguo wenwu bao* 25-12-94.

Zhang Fupeng 1986: 'Guzi de qiyun yu fenleishi yanjiu,' *Zhongguo nongshi* 1986(1): 110-115.

Zhang Han'gang 1993a: 'Dadong yizhi fajue you huo zhongyao chengguo,' *Zhongguo wenwu bao* 29-8-93.

— 1993b: 'Panxian Dadong jiushiqi yizhi de jiazhi he yiyi,' *Zhongguo wenwu bao* 14-11-93.

Zhang Han 1994: 'Jin hou Xi gui mingwen chushi,' *Wenwu* 1994(1): 33-4.

Zhang Juzhong, Kong Shaochen, Liu Changjiang 1994: 'Wuyang shiqian daozuo yicun yu huang Huai tiqu shiqian nongye,' *Nongye kaogu* 1994(1): 68-77.

Zhang Min *et al* 1993: 'Gaoyou Longqiuzhuang yizhi fajue huo zhongda chengguo,' *Zhongguo wenwu bao* 5-9-93.

— 1994: 'Longqiuzhuang yizhi fajue zai huo zhongda chengguo,' *Zhongguo wenwu bao* 27-2-94.

Zhang Min 1993: 'Gaoyou Longqiuzhuang yizhi de fajue jiqi yiyi,' *Dongnan Wenhua* 1993(4).

Zhang Minghua 1989: 'Liangzhu yuqi yanjiu,' *Kaogu* 1989(7): 624-635.

— 1990: 'Zhongguo Xinshiqi shidai shuijing de kaogu faxian,' *Shanghai bowuguan jikan* 5: 67-76.

—, Wang Huiju 1990: 'Taihu diqu Xinshiqi shidai de taowen,' *Kaogu* 1990(10): 903-907.

Zhang Shuai 1993: 'Bali yizhi fajue huo zhongyao shouhuo,' *Zhongguo wenwu bao* 28-3-93.

Zhang Xinning *et al* 1993: 'Jiangchuan Lijiashan gu muqun dierci fajue jiankuan,' *Yunnan wenwu* 1993(6).

Zhang, Longxi 1988: 'The Myth of the other China in the eyes of the West.' *Critical Inquiry* 15 (Autumn): 108-131.

Zhang Xuqiu 1992: *Changjiang zhongyou Xin shiqi shidai wenhua kailun*, Wuhan: Hubei kexue jishu chubanshe.

— 1994: 'Qujialing wenhua gucheng de faxian he chubu yanjiu,' *Kaogu* 1994(7): 629-634.

— 'Qujialing wenhua gucheng de faxian he chubu yanjiu,' *Kaogu* 1994(7).

Zhang Yushi, Yang Zaoqing 1995: 'Xinshiqi shidai kaogu huo zhongda faxian,' *Zhongguo wenwu bao* 10-10-95.

Zhang Zhongpei 1994: *Zhongguo kaoguxue lilun shijian fangfa*, Zhengzhou: Zhongzhou guji chubanshe.

— *forthcoming*: 'Yangshao shidai - shiqian shehui de fanrong yu zhuanbian,' *Zhongguo wenming de xingcheng* (K C Chang and Xu Pingfang eds), New Haven/Beijing: Yale University Press and China New World Press.

Zhao Feng, Qi Xiaoguan 1996: 'Yelü Yuzhi mu sichou zhong de tuancai he tuan huawen,' *Wenwu* 1996(1): 33-35.

Zhao Zhiquan and Xu Diankui 1988. Yanshi Shixiangguo Shangdai zaiqi chengzhi. Zhongguo kaogu xuehui eds. *Zhongguo kaogu xuehui diwuci nianhui lunwenji*. Beijing: Wenwu chubanshe.

Zhejiang 1974 (Zhejiang sheng Jiaxingxian bowu zhanlanguan): 'Zhejiang Jiaxing Quemuqiao faxian yipi heitao,' *Kaogu* 1974(4): 249-250.

— 1976 (Zhejiang sheng wenwu guanli weiyuanhui): 'Hemudu faxian yuanshi shehui zhongyao yizhi,' *Wenwu* 1976(8): 6-12.

— 1978a (Zhejiang sheng wenwu guanli weiyuanhui, Zhejiang sheng bowuguan): 'Hemudu yizhi diyi qi fajue baogao,' *Kaogu xuebao* 1978 (1): 39-94.

— 1978b (Zhejiang sheng wenwu guanli weiyuanhui): 'Hemudu yizhi diyi qi fajue jianbao,' *Kaogu Xuebao* 1978(1): 95-107.

— 1988a (Zhejiang sheng wenwu kaogu yanjiusuo Fanshan kaogudui): 'Zhejiang Yuhang Fanshan Liangzhu mudi faxian jianbao,' *Wenwu* 1988(1): 1-31.

— 1988b (Zhejiang sheng wenwu kaogu yanjiusuo): 'Yuhang Yaoshan Liangzhu wenhua jitan yizhi faxian jianbao,' *Wenwu* 1988(1): 32-51.

— 1989 (Zhejiang sheng wenwu kaogu yanjiusuo, Shanghai shi wenwu guanli weiyuanhui and Nanjing bowuyuan) *Liangzhu wenhua yuqi*, Bejing/Hong Kong 1989.

— 1997 (Zhejiangsheng wenwu kaogu yanjiusuo, Yuhangshi wenwu guanli weiyuanhui): 'Zhejiang Yuhang Huiguanshan Liangzhu wenhua jitan yu mudi fajue jianbao,' *Wenwu* 1997(7): 4-33.

Zheng Qingshen 1994: 'Yongcheng qingli Liang Xiaowang ling qin jianzhu jizhi,' *Zhongguo wenwu bao* 22-5-94.

Zheng Shaozong 1993: 'Zhangjiakou qingli Liao bihua muqun, *Zhongguo wenwu bao* 8-8-93.

Zhongguo 1979 (Zhongguo shehui kexueyuan kaogu yanjiusuo Anyang gongzuodui): '1969-1977 nian Yinxu xiqu muzang fajue baogao,' *Kaogu xuebao* 1979(4): 99-117.

— 1980 (Zhongguo shehui kexueyuan kaogu yanjiusuo): *Yinxu Fu Hao mu*, Beijing: Wenwu chubanshe.

— 1987a (Zhongguo shehui kexueyuan kaogu yanjiusuo): *Yinxu faxian baogao 1958-1961*, Beijing: Wenwu chubanshe.

— 1987b (Zhongguo shehui kexueyuan kaogu yanjiusuo Anyang gongzuodui): 'Yinxu 259, 260 hao mu fajue baogao,' *Kaogu xuebao* 1987(1): 99-117.

— 1988 (Zhongguo shehui kexue yanjiuyuan kaogu yanjiusuo): *Wugong fajue baogao - Huxizhuan yu Zhaojialai yizhi*, Beijing: Wenwu chubanshe.

— 1991a: 'Lasa Qugong yizhi chutu zaoqi qingtongqi,' *Zhongguo wenwu bao* 26-1-91.

— 1991b: 'Yinxu Huayuanzhuang faxian zaoqi jiagu keng,' *Zhongguo wenwu bao* 22-12-91.

— 1992a (Zhongguo shehui kexue yuan kaogu yanjiusuo): 'Xinglongwa juluo yizhi fajue huo shuoguo,' *Zhongguo wenwu bao* 13-12-92.

— 1992b-c: '1986-1987 nian Anyang Huayuanzhuang nandi fajue baogao,' *Kaogu xuebao* 1992(1).

— 1994 (Zhongguo shehui kexueyuan kaogu yanjiusuo): *Yinxu de faxian yu yanjiu*, Beijing: Kexue chubanshe.

— (*Zhongguo kaoguxue nianjian* 1990. Beijing, Wenwu chubanshe, 1991.

— 1994 (Zhongguo shehui kexue yuan kaogu yanjiusuo Anhui dui): 'Anhui Mengcheng Weichisi yizhi fajue jianbao,' *Kaogu* 1994(1): 1-13.

— 1996 (Zhongguo shehui kexue yuan kaogu yanjiusuo Luoyang Tang cheng gongzuodui): 'Luoyang Song dai yashu tingyuan yizhi fajue baogao,' *Kaogu* 1996(6).

— 1997 'Xinglongwa juluo yizhi fajue baogao,' *Kaogu* 1997(1): .

Zhongguo wenwu bao reporter 1992: 'Guoguo mudi fajue you huo zhongda faxian,' *Zhongguo wenwu bao* 2-2-92.

— 1991: 'Han Xuanquanzhi yizhi fajue huo zhongda chengguo,' *Zhongguo wenwu bao* 25-8-91.

— 1993a: 'Weichisi yizhi chutu daxing paifang shi jianzhu,' *Zhongguo wenwu bao* 3-1-93.

— 1993b: 'Quwo Qucun fajue Jin hou mudi,' *Zhongguo wenwu bao* 10-1-93.

— 1993c: 'Hongzhou yaozhi daiocha ji fajue huo zhongda chengguo,' *Zhongguo wenwu bao* 2-5-93.

— 1993d: 'Weichisi yizhi zai huo zhongyao faxian,' *Zhongguo wenwu bao* 13-6-93.

— 1994a: 'Yungang ku qian yizhi fajue huo zhongda chengguo,' *Zhongguo wenwu bao* 16-1-94.

— 1994b: 'Quwo fajue Jin hou bangfu ji furen mudi,' *Zhongguo wenwu bao* 30-1-94.

— 1994c: 'Suizhong Yuan dai chenchuan yizhi disan ci diaocha chengguo xi ren,' *Zhongguo wenwu bao* 6-2-94.

— 1994d: 'Sanxia baqu kaogu qude fengshuo chengguo,' *Zhongguo wenwu bao* 20-2-94.

— 1994e: 'Xi'an faxian Sui dai Banhe guqiao yizhi,' *Zhongguo wenwu bao* 10-7-94.

— 1994f: 'Sanxia kaogu huo da mianji fengshou,' *Zhongguo wenwu bao* 24-7-94.

— 1994g: 'Sui Renshougong Tang Jiuchenggong 37 hao dianzhi fajue huo zhongda chengguo,' *Zhongguo wenwu bao* 30-10-94.

— 1995a: 'Tengzhou Qianzhangda yizhi you zhongyao faxian,' *Zhongguo wenwu bao* 8-1-95.

— 1995b: 'Xuzhou Shizishan Han Chu wang ling fajue huo zhongda chengguo,' *Zhongguo wenwu bao* 25-11-95.

— 1996: 'Xinjiang Niya yizhi kaogu huo fengshuo,' *Zhongguo wenwu bao* 4-1-96.

Zhou Kuangming 1982 'Yangcan qiyuan wenti de yanjiu,' *Nongye Kaogu* 1982 (1): 133-138.

Zhou Weijian, Lu Benshan, Hua Jueming: 'Ruichang Tongling gu kuangye yizhi de duandai jiqi kexue jiazhi,' *Jiangxi wenwu* 1990(3):13-24.

Zhu Jieyuan, Li Yuzheng 1983. 'Xi'an dongjiao Sandiancun Xi Han mu.' *Kaogu yu wenwu* 1983 (2), 22-25.

Zou Heng 1987: 'Zhongguo wenming de dansheng,' *Wenwu* 1987(12): 69-74.

—1990: 'Youguan Xin'gan chutu qingtongqi de jige wenti.' *Zhongguo wenwu bao* 6/12/1990.

— 1991: Xin faxian Guoguo damu guan hou gan,' *Zhongguo wenwu bao* 17-3-91.

— 1994: 'Lun zaoqi Jin du,' *Wenwu* 1994(1): 29-32.

Index

Site names appear in bold

abstract patterns 18, 52, 65, 66, 69, 72, 75, 216, 218

Academia Sinica, Taipei 8, 137, 229, 230

Ackerman, Phyllis 69

Adams, R M 95

Afanasieva culture 138, 140

Afang palace, Xianyang, Shaanxi 57

afterlife 163, 190, 192, 201, 204

agate 155, 175, 244

agriculture 6, 12, 18, 29, 33, 36, 41, 46, 79, 81, 84, 85, 93, 97, 107, 112, 230, 233;
   and nomadism 148; earliest centres of 85;
   and economy 84, 102, 148, 211;
   and society 84, 140; technology and tools 93, 96, 116, 154, 215

Alagou, Xinjiang 146

Altai 138, 144, 145, 146
   culture 147

altars 20, 46, 47, 171, 228, 235, 243, 244
   at Dongshanzui 20

Altar of the Earth 112

American archaeology 27, 30, 32

An Zhimin (1924-) 41, 156, 221

Anban, Fufeng, Shaanxi 82

ancestral worship 33, 36, 38, 171

Andersson, J G (1874-1960) 33, 229

Andronovo culture 138

Animal Art 155
   of the neolithic period 138
   animal and geometrical motifs 33, 153

and human characteristics 219
and human features 72
bone artefacts 237
clay figures 241 *see also* sculpture
husbandry 83, 84, 155
mask 134, 135, 215, 219
motifs 18, 65, 66, 68, 69, 71, 132, 158, 161, 235 *see also* motifs
motifs in Liangzhu jades 75
motifs on weapons 137, 138
pens and storage pits 112
sacrifice 73, 176, 179 *see also* sacrifice
sculpture 96, 155, 156, 243
sculpture on bronze weapons 156
style 13, 137, 138, 139, 140, 142;
style (Eurasian) 145

animals 72, 79, 80, 236
   domestication of 12, 29, 79, 82, 83, 84, 155, 230
   in burials 36, 176, 177
   in mythology 71

'animal combat' motif 155 *see also* motifs

anthropology 27, 28, 30, 35, 53, 231
   archaeology as 30

anthropomorphic mask 220, 222 *see also* motifs

antiquarianism 229

Anxi, Gansu 242

Anyang, Henan 34, 61, 114, 125, 127, 129, 130, 132-133, 229, 238, 238–240

Aohanqi, Inner Mongolia 20, 206, 234

Bronze container (detail), unearthed at Jiangchuan Lijiashan. See page 150

Arabic 101, 120
Archaeological Institute of America 53
archaic bronzes 12, 58 *see also* bronzes
architecture 21, 24, 29, 36, 37, 52, 57, 75, 84, 87, 89, 90, 96, 156, 201, 211, 234, 234–237, 235–237, 236, 237, 240, 242, 243, 243–244, 244
  in Haimenkou 156
  of Jingpo 156
  of the central plains 113
  stamped-earth 33 see also rammed-earth
art history, 52
  and archaeology 51
artists 52, 73, 95, 96, 116, 120
Asiatic 34
  Western 101
assemblage 14, 30, 128, 135, 189, 192, 198, 202, 229
Association for Chinese Archaeology 35
Assyriology 53
authenticity 58, 59

Ba culture (Zhou period) 95, 100
ba cymbals 157, 158
Bachhofer, Ludwig (1896-1976) 58, 59, 66
Bagley, Robert 67, 75, 128
Baizifan, Hubei 196
Baligang, Dengshan, Henan 228, 232, 234
bamboo slips 119
Ban Gu (AD 32-92), 105
Banpo, Shaanxi 18, 46, 82, 112, 206, 230
  and Yangshao culture 18, 42, 112
Banshan, Gansu 42
Banshan-Machang culture (c2300-1800 BC) 36
Baodun, Chengdu, Sichuan 102
Baqiao Bridge, Shaanxi 243
barley 82
baroque 59, 66
bas-reliefs 54 *see also* reliefs
Beishouling, Baoji, Shaanxi 18
Beixin, Shandong 83
Beixin culture (c5400-4400 BC) 83, 230, 237
bianxiang side compartment 200
bird motif 146, 223, 224 *see also* motifs
bishou hand dagger 128, 129, 130
boats 114, 162, 215
Bohai (Parhae) kingdom 243, 244
Bohai Gulf 19, 21
Bohaizheng, Ning'an 243

Borovka, Gregory 138
British archaeology 27
bronze 13, 21, 22, 24, 27, 29, 33, 36, 37, 38, 41, 54, 55, 57, 59, 63, 64, 66, 67, 96, 97, 98, 101, 106, 113, 114, 116, 126, 133, 138, 158 *see also* bronzes
  animal sculptures 155 *see also* sculpture
  art 66, 68, 69, 72, 76, 125, 155
  culture 13, 21, 32, 139, 151, 153, 154, 162
  drums 154, 156, 159, 161, 162 *see also* drums
  motifs 69, 71, 74, 75, 76
  plaques 75, 144, 147, 155, 158, 161
  sculpture 166, 198
  styles 59, 64, 75
  typologies 190
  vessels 21, 42, 54, 75, 108, 127, 128, 132, 135, 166, 169, 174, 184, 185, 186, 192, 200, 237, 238, 239, 240
  weapons 107, 125, 126, 127, 128, 130, 131, 132, 133, 135, 136, 138, 139, 140, 156, 176 *see also* weaponry
Bronze Age, the 38, 41, 43, 44, 82, 84, 114, 120, 125, 138, 151, 154, 157, 161, 162, 206, 237
bronze-casting 34, 35, 47, 162, 237
bronzes 54, 63, 174
  ceramic imitations of 192
  Dian 13
  Shang 59, 61, 67, 69, 71, 73, 75, 76, 139
  Zhou 55, 64, 65, 75
Buddhism 55, 59, 242, 245
Buddhist images 57
  pagodas 57
bull-fighting 158
bureaucracy 100
burial ritual 13, 173, 176
  system 126, 135

cabbage seed 82
Cahill, James 67
calendar 95
calligraphic inscriptions 54
canals 119, 120, 213, 215
Cancong, legendary ancestor of the Shu people 98
Caoxieshan, Wu xian, Jiangsu 93, 214, 215, 216, 217, 224, 225
carbon-dating 79, 80, 98, 112, 135, 165, 166, 230, 233, 234, 238
carpenters' tools 241 *see also* tools
CASS *see* Chinese Academy of Social Sciences

Caucasus 138
Cave of the Spirits, Wannian, Jiangxi 22
Central Asia 33, 55, 58, 101, 117, 118, 138, 143, 145
ceramics 57, 91–92, 116, 189, 190, 192, 198, 226, 244
  high-fired glazed 237
  Persian 120
  technology 242 *see also* technology
Chahai, Fuxing, Inner Mongolia 20, 214
Chang, K C (Zhang Guangzhi 1931-) 36, 38, 39, 43, 65, 71, 73, 103, 114
Chavannes, Édouard (1865-1918) 54, 55, 57
Che Guangjin 220
cheng city 38
Chengbeixi, Hubei 83
Chenggong Tianzimiao, Yunnan 151
Chengtoushan, Feng xian, Hunan 80, 82, 93, 145, 237
Chenyangchuan, Xiji, Ningxia 144
Chiang Ching-Kuo Foundation (Taiwan) 9
chiefdoms 35
Childe, Gordon (1892-1957) 28, 29, 35, 95
Childs-Johnson, Elizabeth 69, 71
Chinese Academy of Sciences (CAS), Beijing 230
Chinese Academy of Social Sciences (CASS), Beijing 230
Chiyou, legendary figure 45
Chlenova, N L 139
Christian art 52
Christianity 29, 54
chronology 29, 32, 43
Chu capitals 189
  culture 23, 154
    burial traditions 192
cinnabar 192, 239
Cishan, Hebei 81, 83
city 33, 95
  planning 242
civilisation vis à vis culture 33
Cizhou ware 245
classical archaeology 53
classification 43
clay 80, 81, 83, 84, 89, 96, 166, 169, 170, 190, 231, 233, 234, 235, 236, 241
coins 154, 240, 241, 242, 244
College Art Association 53
comma-shaped patterns *see also* motifs 224
compound man-and-animal motif *see also* motifs 220

Confucianism 54, 121
copper 41, 100, 101, 102, 155, 169, 237
cord-cutting 42
cord-impressed 233
cosmology 32
cowrie shells 100, 101, 154, 175, 178, 210, 238
craftsmen 36, 111
Creel, H G (1905-) 65
Cultural Revolution, the 27, 32

Dabona, Xiangyun, Yunnan 153, 155, 156, 157
Dadianzi, Aohanqi, Inner Mongolia 20
Dadiwan, Qin'an, Gansu 21, 46, 81, 82, 83
Dadong cave, Pan xian, Guizhou 231
Dadunzi, Pi xian, Jiangsu 83, 206, 209
Daheishan dao Beizhuang, Heilongjiang 19
dance 159, 161
Dangyang Caojiagang, Hubei 196
Dangyang Zhaojiahu, Hubei 189, 190, 191, 192, 193
Daniel, Glyn (1914-1986) 43
Danjiangkou reservoir, Xichuan, Henan 240
Daodunzi, Tongxing, Ningxia 144, 146, 147
Daoist images 54
Darwin, Charles (1809-1882) 28
Datong Museum, Shanxi 242
Davidson, J Leroy 65
Dawenkou, Zhejiang 36, 83, 207, 209, 230, 237
  second phase (c4300-2500 BC) 46
Daxi culture (c4400-3800 BC) 43, 80, 88, 92, 207
Dayangzhou, Xin'gan, Jiangxi 22, 125
de Perthes, Jacques Boucher 29
Deshan, Changde, Hunan 193
Dian culture 151, 154, 241
Dianchi 151
Diaotonghuan, Wannian, Jiangxi 80, 84, 233
diffusion of cultures 29, 33, 168, 213
ding vessel 22, 71, 90, 108, 174, 176, 177, 185, 193, 198, 202, 217, 224, 240
Dinggong, Zouping, Shandong 226, 236
dingqiao loom 208
Dingzhuang, Henan 82
division of labour 35
dogs 12, 33, 82, 83, 84, 89, 155, 174,

175, 1 76, 177, 178, 179, 202, 237, 238, 239 *see also* animals, sacrifice *and* domestication of animals
domestication of animals 33, 79, 82 *see also* animals
Donghuishan Minle, Gansu 82
Dongnangou, Pingquan, Hebei 141
Dongshanzui, Liaoning 20
'dragon kilns' 242
dragon mask 223
drums 42, 47, 154, 156, 157, 159, 161, 186, 188, 198, 202 *see also* bronze drums
du capitals 38, 111
dui vessel 43, 154, 198, 202
Duke Wu 108
Dunhuang, Gansu 57–58, 228, 232, 242
manuscripts 55
Dushi fangyu jiyao, by Gu Zuyi (1631-1692) 107
Duyu, legendary ancestor of the Shu people 101

early Jin capital, Tang 105
economic archaeology 31
Edwards, Richard (1916-) 61
Egyptology 53
eight-pointed star pattern 14, 207, 211
élite 36, 96, 114, 204, 216
enfeoffment 115, 241
Engels, Friedrich (1820-1895) 17, 34, 35
engraved decoration 214
environment 14, 28, 30, 31, 39, 79, 85, 91, 131, 213, 214, 231
environmental archaeology 30
Erhai region 153
Erligang, Zhengzhou, Henan 75
Erligang culture (c1600 BC) 34, 67
Erlitou, Yanshi, Henan 13, 34, 36, 37, 46, 75, 91, 113, 114, 142, 166, 236
Erlitou culture (c1900-1600 BC) 37
ethno-archaeology. 31
eurocentric 12, 33, 52, 53, 54, 55, 57, 59, 60, 62
'Europoid' 139
evolutionism 30
experimental archaeology 30

face-cover 186, 239
Fairbank, Wilma (1931-) 61
family 181
Fangchijie, Chengdu, Sichuan 99
fangguo regional state 20, 22, 238
Fanshan, Hangzhou, Zhejiang 43, 215, 218, 223, 224

Fengxiang, Nan'ganhe, Shaanxi 142
Ferguson, John C 54
Field Museum, Chicago 61
Fine Arts 52
floral motifs *see also* motifs 18
flute 157
food offerings 73, 180, 193, 198, 204
vessels 154
Forbidden City 61
Fu Hao 71, 174
funeral rite 173, 176, 177, 179, 180, 189
Fuqinxiaoqu, Chengdu, Sichuan 99
Fuquanshan, Shanghai 215, 222, 223, 224

games 158
ganlan architectural form 156
Gao Wei 36, 37
ge dagger axe 127, 128, 129, 130, 131, 132, 135, 136, 166, 194
gems 142, 235, 241
geometric patterns 22, 47, 65, 68, 69, 72, 75, 142, 153, 161, 162, 195, 214, 235, 237 *see also* motifs
gilding 155
global cycles 120
Gobi desert 18, 140
Goddess temple, Niuheliang, Liaoning 35
gold 100
and silver inlay 154
scabbard 168
seals 151
Gorodzov, V A 138
Gramineae 82
Grand Canal, the 119
Great Northwest region 21
Great Wall, the 20, 21, 139
Greeks 138
grid 117
griffin motif 72, 143, 144, 145, 146 *see also* motifs
Gryaznov, M P 138
Gu Yanwu (1613-1682) 106
Gu Zuyi (1631-1692) 107
Guangdu, Sichuan 102
Guifang (also Yanyun) ethnic group, Shang period 149
Guihuashu culture (c2500 BC) 87
Guo Dewei 189
Guo Moruo (1892-1978) 17, 34
Guo state (Western Zhou) 239
Guo Suxin 140
Guojiacun, Lishun, Liaoning 42

Haimenkou, Jianchuan, Yunnan 153, 154, 156
Han engraved stones 57

Han slips 55

Hanshu (History of the Former Han Dynasty), by Ban Gu 208

He Tianxing 226

Hedin, Sven (1865-1952) 55

Heger, Franz 161

hemp 82, 191

Hempel, C G 30

Hemudu, Yuyao, Zhejiang 81, 214, 230

Henan Longshan culture (c2600-2000 BC) 34

Hentze, Carl 69

Hermitage Museum, St Petersburg 146

Hetao Man 32

high-fired glazed ceramics 237

historical materialism 29

historiographic approach 31

hoards 63, 170, 228, 238

Hodder, Ian 31

homo erectus 231

Hongshan culture (c3500 BC) 20, 25, 35, 45, 47, 230

Hongzhou kiln, Jiangxi 242

horse 12, 82, 83, 84, 138, 139, 142, 143, 1 44, 146, 147, 154, 155, 158, 169, 177, 186, 237, 238, 240, 244

Hou Ji, legendary ancestor of the Zhou people 46

Hu Shun 24

Huainanzi, by Liu An (Han dynasty) 102, 208

Hua'nan region 21

Huang Shenzhang 43

Huangdi, Yellow Emperor, legendary ancestor of the Chinese 45

Huangquan (Yellow Springs) 73

Huaxia 21, 139

Huayang guo zhi (Records of The Huayang States) 98, 101, 102

Huayuanzhuang, Anyang, Henan 238

Hubei Longshan culture (c2500-2000 BC) 23, 87

Huiguanshan, Yuhang, Zhejiang 235

human and animal sacrifice 176, 177, 196

human behaviour 30

hunting 41

hypothetical-deductive approach 31

iconography 52

iconology 53

ideo-technic 30

ideographic 33

ideology 180

imperialism 53

India 54, 55, 58, 158

indigenous style of bronze weapons 132, 136 *see also* bronze, bronzes

Indus civilisation 45

Institute of History and Philology (IHP) 229

Iran 72, 101, 138

iron 239

Iron Age, the 41

Islam 54

ivory 100, 215

jade 20, 24, 100, 133, 134, 186, 213, 216, 235

suit 240

working 214

Jade Age, The 41

Janse, Olov 58

Japan 8, 14, 62, 121, 156, 229, 243

Japanese archaeology 242

Jettmar, Karl 139

jewellery 119, 244

Jiahu, Wuyang, Henan 83

Jiangling, Hubei 189

Jiangzai, Lintong, Shaanxi 19

jianmu cosmos tree 102

Jieshi palace, Liaoning 21

Jigongshan, Jiangling, Hubei 231, 233

Jijiahu culture (c2500 BC) 87

Jin royal cemetery 239

state 105, 183

jinshixue studies of bronzes and stones 27

Jiuchenggong, Shaanxi 243

Jiudian, Hubei 198

Kane, Virginia 67

Karasuk culture 137, 139

Karlgren, Bernhard (1889-1978) 54, 64, 137

Karuo culture (c3300-2100 bp) 237

Khitan 244

King Cheng (Western Zhou) 101, 108

King Kang (Western Zhou) 184

King Mu (Western Zhou) 75

King of Guangling (Western Han) 241

King Xiao of the Liang (Western Han) 240

Kiselev, S V 139

Korea 119, 243

Kühn, H 137

Kümmel, Otto 58

Kunstgeschichte 52

Kuodizhi (A Comprehensive Account of Geography) 106

labour force 31, 41
lacquer wares 57, 101, 191, 214, 241
Langer, Susanne K 68
Laoguantai culture (c6000 BC) 18
Laufer, Berthold 54
Leigudun, Sui xian, Hubei 196
Li Chi (Li Ji, 1896-1979) 71
Li Xueqin 219
Liang Siyong (1904-1954) 57
Liang state (Western Han) 240
Liangzhu culture (c3000-2200 BC)
    23, 34, 45, 47, 213, 216, 230, 235
    jades 43
Liao kingdom 244
Liaoshi (History of Liao) 244
Liji (Record of Rituals) 178, 204
Lijiacun, Shaanxi 81
Lijiashan, Jiangchuan, Yunnan 151,
    161, 241
Lingjiatang, Hanshan, Anhui 188
Linjia, Dongxiang, Gansu 82
liqi ceremonial objects 38
Liu Bin 220
Liu Dunzhen 57
Loehr, Max (1903-1988) 58, 66, 138
Longgangsi, Nanzhen, Shaanxi 42,
    82, 83
Longmen, Luoyang, Henan 61
Longnan, Wujian, Jiangsu 82, 217
Longqiuzhuang culture (c7000-5000
    bp), Gaoyou, Jiangsu 230, 234, 235
Longshan culture (c2600-2000 BC)
    18, 38, 229, 236
Loo, C T 220
loom 207, 208, 214
lost-wax casting 154
Lower Xiajiadian culture (c2000-1500
    BC) 20
lunar deity 69
Luobowan, Guixian, Guangxi 158
Luojiajiao, Tongxiang, Zhejiang 81,
    82
Luoyang Archaeological Team 244
Lyell, Sir Charles (1797-1875) 29

MacEnery, J 29
Machang, Gansu 42
Maenchen-Helfen, Otto 66
Majiabang culture (c5000-4000 BC)
    42, 81, 93, 214
Majiayao, Gansu 21
Majiayao culture (c3300-2050 BC) 36,
    82
Manchuria 62
Mangshan, Yongcheng, Henan 240
mao spearhead 127, 131
Maoqinggou, Inner Mongolia 141
Maoshi tangpu, by Zhang Xuan, Han
    Dynasty 105

marketplace 119
Marquis Mu *et al*, see King Mu *et al*
Marxism 17, 31
Mashan, Jiangling, Hubei 195, 196
matriarchal society 36
Mawangdui, Changsha, Hunan 190,
    202
Maya civilisation 39
Mediterranean region 53
Meinian, Wujiang, Jiangsu 84
Meng Wentong 102
Mengzhuang, Hui xian, Shandong
    236
mercury 155
metal industry 114
Miaodigou, Henan 18
microlithic 20
migration 29
migratory clan 48
millet 81, 82
    culture 33
mingqi funerary objects 180
Minhe, Qinghai 42
Minns, E H 138
Minussinsk basin 139
Miran, Xinjiang 55
mirrors 194
moats 96, 112
Mojiaoshan, Zhejiang 235
Montelius, Oscar (1843-1921) 28
mortuary figurines 57
motifs 14, 18, 64, 65, 66, 67, 68, 69,
    71, 72, 73, 74, 75, 131, 132, 133,
    138, 140, 142, 143, 145, 147, 155,
    176, 194, 195, 208, 209, 210, 214,
    216, 217, 218, 219, 220, 221, 223,
    235, 243
    animal and geometrical motifs 33,
    153
    'animal combat' motif 155
    bird motif 146, 223, 224
    three-pointed 216
    tiger 73
mouth-organ 157
Museum of Far Eastern Antiquities,
    Stockholm 61
musical instruments 154, 157, 158,
    194
myth and legend 66
'mythological eagle' 142-143
Naisitai, Barin youqi, Inner Mongo-
    lia 84
Nanhu, Yuhang, Zhejiang 225, 226
Nanyangzhuang, Zhending, Hebei
    84
Nanyue Kingdom (Western Han) 242
Nanzhuangtou, Xushui, Hebei 82,
    83
naturalism 145, 156

navigation 215
Near East, the 33, 39, 69
neolithic transformation 233
nephrite 134, 214, 234 *see also* jade
New Archaeology 27, 30
Ning'an, Heilongjiang 243
Niuheliang, Jianping, Liaoning 35, 47
Niya Minfeng, Xinjiang 242
nomadic cultures 13, 21, 102, 118, 140, 154
northern steppes 137
Nüwa 45

Oppenheim, Norbert 30
oracle bone inscriptions 36, 238
Ordos culture 20, 139
orientalism 54
ornaments 29

painted decoration 214
painting 52
palaeo-anthropological studies 231
palaeolithic remains in Abbeville and the Somme V 29
Panjiatang, Wujin, Jiangsu 207
Panlongcheng, Huangpi, Hubei 129, 132, 133
Paper, Jordan 69
park complexes 117
patriarchal society 36
Pazyryk, Altai Mt 145, 146, 147
Peiligang culture (c6000-5000 BC) 81
Peking Man 32, 231
Peng Shifan 131
Pengtoushan, Hunan 23, 80, 83
Persian Gulf 119
Petrie, Flinders (1853-1942) 29
piece-mould casting 154
Pingliangtai, Henan 113
Pitt-Rivers, Augustus (1827-1900) 29
Pokelofski 29
Pompeii 52
Pope, John 60
population 100
post-processual archaeology 31
postal station 242
pottery 7, 14, 18, 19, 20, 21, 22, 23, 24, 29, 32, 33, 37, 38, 42, 46, 47, 54, 59, 61, 68, 79, 80, 82, 84, 87, 89, 90, 91, 92, 96, 97, 98, 101, 102, 106, 107, 108, 125, 134, 135, 166, 167, 174, 175, 176, 179, 180, 181, 184, 192, 195, 196, 198, 202, 206, 208, 209, 210, 211, 213, 214, 216, 219, 221, 223, 224, 225, 229, 233, 234, 235, 236, 237, 238, 240, 241, 242, 244
pre-Yangshao culture 18

private ownership 36
processual archaeologists 173
protagonists 31
'proto-characters' 226
pseudo-jades 214
public works 114

Qi state (Eastern Zhou) 23, 100, 115
Qianhucun, Henan 46
Qianshanyang, Hangzhou, Zhejiang 84
Qianzhangda, Tengzhou, Shandong 238
Qijia culture (c2000 BC) 36, 207, 208
Qin Shihuangdi 241
Qin state 20, 119, 147
Qinglian'gang, Jiangsu 22
Qinglongquan culture III (c2500 BC) 23, 87
Qingtaicun, Xingyang, Henan 84
'Qingzhou archaeology' 23
Qixiong, Seven Powers 105
Qucun Beizhao, Shanxi 239
Quemuqiao, Jiaxing, Jiangsu 225
Qugong, Lhasa, Tibet 237
Qujialing, Jingshan, Hubei 23, 80, 88, 92, 217, 237

rammed-earth architecture 12, 113, 114, 115
ranking system 179
rape seed 82
reliefs 53, 57, 61, 66, 67, 132, 133, 135, 148, 161, 208, 213, 220, 221, 222, 223
religion 89, 95, 97, 98, 99, 100, 111, 112, 114, 120
Renfrew, C 28
representation 143
rice 12, 79, 80, 81, 92, 193, 214, 215, 233
    culture 33
ritual system 42, 163
    vessels 198 *see also* bronzes
Rizhilu, by Gu Yanwu (1613-1680) 106
Romans 28, 53
Rong-Di ethnic group (Zhou period) 149
Rostovtzeff, Michael 58, 143
Rowley, George (1893-1962) 58
Royal Ontario Museum, Toronto 61
Rudenko, S J 142, 143, 145
Rudolph, Richard 61
Russian archaeology 18

Sabloff, J 27
sacrifice 13, 20, 24, 73, 74, 75, 83, 97, 98, 100, 101, 102, 120, 126,

127, 163, 166, 168, 171, 173, 176, 177, 178, 179, 180, 181, 192, 196, 202, 204, 234, 235, 237, 238, 239, 240

Salmony, Alfred (1890-1958) 58, 220

Sandaogan, Suizhong, Liaoning 245

Sandaoling Luotuoliang, Longhua, Hebei 141

Sanxingdui, Chengdu, Sichuan 24, 95, 96, 97, 100, 101, 165

Sarmatian 142

Schliemann, Heinrich (1820-1890) 29

sculpture 10, 28, 52, 55, 57, 58, 61, 89, 96, 129, 138, 139, 145, 155, 156, 159, 166, 169, 194, 195, 198, 202, 242, 243

Scythian 137, 142, 143, 145, 146, 147, 155

Ségalen, Victor (1878-1919) 55

Seima-Turbino culture 139

semiotics 31

seriations and types 20

sericulture 33

Shaguotun, Jingxi, Liaoning 84

shaman 39, 42, 71, 73, 143, 161
    dance 161

Shang 21
    bronzes 59, 139
    capitals 238
    oracle bone inscriptions 55
    religion 73

Shangcunling, Sanmenxia, Henan 239

Shangdongcun, Ji xian, Shanxi 140

Shangmacun, Houma, Shanxi 190

Shanhaijing (Classic of Mountains and Seas) 71, 102, 208

Shao Wangping 36, 38

Shennong, legendary ancestor 47

Shibancun, Cili, Hunan 196

Shierqiao, Chengdu, Sichuan 24, 96, 97, 99

Shiji, by Sima Qian (c1st century BC) 45, 185

Shijiahe, Tianmen, Hubei 23, 87, 88

shipwreck 245

Shixia, Qujiang, Guangdong 22

Shizhaishan, Jinning, Yunnan 151, 154, 155, 156, 158, 159, 161, 162, 241

shoumian animal mask 219, 221, 222, 223

Shu kingdom 95, 96

Shuihudi, Yunmeng, Hubei 144

Shuitianfan, Hangzhou, Zhejiang 82

Shun, legendary ancestor 21, 46

Shuowen jiezi, by Xu Shen (1st century AD) 208

Shuwang benji (Biography of the Kings of Shu) 98

Si state (Shang/Zhou) 239

Siberia 137, 146

Sickman, Laurence 58, 61

Sidun, Wujin, Jiangsu 134

silk 84, 215
    weaving 84

silkworm 214

Silk Road, the 55, 101, 119, 242

silver 119, 154, 155, 240, 241

Sima Qian (b 145 BC?) 45

sinid 139, 140

Sino-Japanese War 32, 229

sinologists 58

Sirén, Osvald 58

slave and feudal societies 34

social archaeology 31

social history of art 53

social status 180

Songze, Qingpu, Shanghai 82

Songze culture (c4000-3000 BC) 207, 211, 214

Soper, Alexander 67

sorghum 82

Soviet archaeology 18, 31

stamped-earth architecture 33, 46

State Bureau of Cultural Relics (SBCR) 230

Stein, Sir Marc Aurel (1862-1943) 55

stelae 27, 54, 57

Steward, Julian H (1902-1972) 30

Stone Age, the 41

stratigraphy 27, 29, 166, 167, 231, 233, 236

structuralist approach 31

Su Bingqi (1909-1997) 34, 45, 47

Sulimirski, T 139

Sullivan, Michael 61

Sumerian civilisation 39

swords 128, 130, 136, 138, 139, 141, 148, 156, 159, 193, 194

symbolism 69

Tagarski period 140

Taigubaiyan, Jinzhong, Shanxi 20

Taimiao, Imperial Temple 244

Taishidian, Kunshan, Jiangsu 215

Tallgren, A M 138

Tangshan, Nanjing, Jiangsu 231

Tangshu (History of the Tang dynasty) 21

Taosi culture (c2500-1900 BC) 21, 45, 47

taotie 65, 66, 71, 75, 133, 156, 219, 223

technology 13, 14, 29, 32, 34, 35, 36, 39, 41, 42, 57, 93, 114, 116, 120, 154, 165, 169, 211, 213, 230, 231, 233, 238, 242, 245 temples 20, 35, 46, 47, 76, 95, 112, 114, 159, 170, 171, 192, 204, 242, 244

Teploukhov, S A 137

textiles 82, 84, 102, 144, 145, 186, 191, 208, 209, 214

theriomorphic 219, 222

Thomsen, C J 43

Three Age system 43

Three Dynasties 151

Three Gorges Dam 245

Tian Guangjin 140

Tianchang cemetery, Anhui 241

Tianma-Qucun, Shanxi 107, 108, 183, 239

Tianxingguan, Jiangling, Hubei 201

timber-structured buildings 156

tombs 13, 14, 20, 22, 23, 35, 42, 43, 46, 57, 63, 73, 81, 83, 89, 90, 95, 101, 106, 108, 125, 126, 127, 128, 129, 130, 131, 132, 135, 136, 140, 142, 144, 145, 146, 147, 151, 153, 155, 157, 158, 168, 173, 174, 176, 177, 178, 179, 180, 183, 184, 185, 186, 188, 189, 190, 191, 192, 193, 194, 195, 196, 198, 201, 202, 208, 215, 217, 221, 224, 230, 234, 235, 237, 238, 239, 240, 241, 243, 244, 245

Tongchuanzaomiao, Shaanxi 142

Tongling, Ruichang, Jiangxi 238

Tonglushan, Daye, Hubei 238

tools 21, 22, 29, 41, 42, 43, 79, 80, 96, 116, 139, 141, 154, 169, 178, 207, 209, 210, 215, 231, 233, 234, 235, 237, 239, 241, 244

trade 36, 39, 54, 55, 61, 95, 96, 100, 101, 102, 103, 115, 116, 119, 146, 243, 245

Trans-Baikalia 139

tree of life 147

tribal society 18

tumuli 54

Tuoba ethnic group 117

turquoise 75, 142, 155

turtle 71, 89, 101, 186, 188, 223, 238

turtle-dragon motif 147 *see also* motifs

two-capital system 101

typology 14, 27, 28, 29, 30, 47, 128, 136, 138, 166, 167, 181, 184, 185, 190, 2 35, 236, 238

Upper Cave Man 32

Upper Xiajiadian culture (c1000-300 BC) 141

urban revolution 95, 120

urbanisation 12, 34, 95, 96, 97, 111, 115, 120, 236, 296

urbanism 103, 111, 112, 116, 120

Vasilev, L S 33

walled settlement 87, 236, 243

Wang Wei 220

Wang Xu (1930-1997) 14, 207

Wangchenggang, Henan 113

Wangchengpo Gufengyuan, Changsha, Hunan 241

Wangshan, Jiangling, Hubei 191

Wanjiaba, Chuxiong, Yunnan 153, 158, 161

wards 117

warfare 47, 48, 115

Waterbury, Florance 69

weapons 13, 29, 37, 43, 73, 74, 98, 107, 12 5, 126, 127, 128, 129, 130, 131, 132, 135, 136, 137, 138, 139, 140, 141, 154, 156, 176, 193, 194, 204, 239, 240, 244

weaving 14, 42, 84, 208, 210, 211

Weichisi, Mengcheng, Anhui 234

Weiyang palace, Xian, Shaanxi 57

wells 120, 215, 238, 242

wheat 82, 85

White, L A 30

White, W C 137

Willey, Gordon R 27

winged lion motif 145 *see also* motifs

Wölfflin, Heinrich (1864-1945) 66

writing 17, 34, 35, 38, 72, 95, 101, 120, 226, 237, 239, 242

Wu En 140

Wu Liang shrines, Shandong 61

Wuba, Five Hegemons 105

Wucheng, Jiangxi 22

Wudi, Five Emperors 45-48

Xia Nai (1910-1985) 34

Xiabali, Xuanhua, Hebei 245

Xianbei ethnic group 117

Xianrendong, Wannian, Jiangxi 233

Xianrentai, Changqing, Shandong 239

Xiaoheishigou, Inner Mongolia 142

Xiaoheyan culture (c2000 BC) 207

Xiaoshuangqiao, Zhengzhou, Hennan 237

Xiasi, Xichuan, Henan 189, 193, 240

Xibeigang, Anyang, Henan 176

Xiejiagang, Anhui 37, 43

Xigouban, Zhunge'erqi, Inner Mongolia 144

Xincun, Xun xian, Shaanxi 131

Xindian culture (c1600) 36

Xinglongwa, Aohanqi, Inner Mongolia 20, 25, 42, 112, 234

Xinjixiang Baiyanglincun,

Pengyang, Ningxia 144
Xinle culture (c5300-4800 BC) 82
Xinzhuangtou, Yi xian, Hebei 144
Xiongnu ethnic group 149
Xiwangmu, Queen Mother of the
  West 208
Xiwu, Yanzhou, Jiangsu 82
Xixiang, Lijiacun, Shaanxi 81
Xiyangdian, Qingpu, Shanghai 215,
  225
Xiyincun, Xia xian, Shaanxi 84
Xu Wei 108
Xuanquanzhi, Gansu 242
Xuanwu, Dark Warrior 147

ya shaped 64
Yale University Art Gallery 61
Yan Wenming 36, 37
Yandi, legendary ancestor 45
Yang Baocheng 180
Yang Xiong (53 BC-AD 18) 98
Yang Xizhang 180
Yangshao culture (c5000-3000 BC)
  18, 34, 229, 234
Yangzishan, Chengdu, Sichuan 97
Yao, legendary ancestor 21, 46
Yaodian (Documents of Yao) 46
yaokeng waist pit 176
Yaoshan, Yuhang, Zhejiang 43, 215,
  218, 223, 224
Yedian, Zou xian, Shandong 209
Yetts, Walter Perceval (1878-1957)
  58, 137
Yili (Book of Rites) 204
Yin Da 17
Yindu, capital of the Chu kingdom
  189
Yinxiangcheng, Jiangling, Hubei 92
Yinxu, Anyang, Henan 34, 173, 229
yong figurines 196
you vessel 71, 176
Yu Wenkai (555-612) 243
Yuchanyan, Dao xian, Hunan 79,
  83, 84, 233
yue axe 43, 46, 130, 133, 134
Yueshi culture (c1900-1600 BC) 237
Yufu, legendary ancestor of the Shu
  people 98
Yulongtai, Inner Mongolia 145
Yungang cave, Shanxi 242
Yungang Institute of Cultural Relics
  242
Yutaishan, Jiangling, Hubei 189

Zengpiyan, Guilin, Guangxi 83
Zhang Minghua 222
Zhang Xuqiu 43
Zhang Zhongpei 36, 37
Zhanglingshan, Zhejiang 217, 221

Zhaobaogou, Aohanqi, Inner
  Mongolia 20
Zhaobaogou culture (c5200-4200 BC)
  48
Zhaojialai, Wugong, Shaanxi 46, 82
Zhaolingshan, Kunshan, Jiangsu
  235
Zheng Xuan (127-200) 105
zhenmushou, tomb guardian beast
  198
Zhihuijie, Chengdu, Sichuan 101
Zhinü Weaving Girl 209-210
zhongguo Central Kingdom 47
Zhou bronze inscriptions 55 *see also*
  bronze
Zhoukoudian, Beijing 62, 231
Zhuanxu, legendary ancestor 45
zongfa clan system 36, 38
zoomorphic masks *see also* motifs
  131
Zou Heng 36, 37
Zuozhuan (Zou commentaries) 106,
  239

An important title in EAR's Great Museums of the World Series

Eastern Art in the Ashmolean Museum Oxford

Contents

JAMES W ALLAN • The Ashmolean Museum's Oriental Collections: Past, Present and Future

OLIVER IMPEY • Arita Blue and White—Evolution and Development in the 17th Century

JAMES W ALLAN • Isfahan, Canton, Etruria—Persia and the China Trade in the 18th and 19th Centuries

SHELAGH VAINKER • Centuries of Seals—The Eric North Bequest to the Ashmolean Museum

CHUIMEI HO • Opulence, Luxury and Style—Life of the Aristocrat in Qing Dynasty China

HELEN BROWN AND LUKE TREADWELL • Oriental Acquisitions of the Heberden Coin Room

DAVID ARMITAGE • Restoration and Repair of Oriental Ceramics through the Millennia

CRISPIN BRANFOOT • Burmese Nats—Wooden Sculpture from the Richard C Temple Collection

TERESA FITZHERBERT • Preserving the Legacy of Islamic Art and Architecture Photographic Collections

RUTH BARNES • From Riches to Rags: Indian Printed Cotton Textiles in the Ashmolean

ANDREW TOPSFIELD • Indian Paintings in the Ashmolean and Bodleian Library Collections

MARIANNE ELLIS • Threads of History—Embroideries from Egypt in the Newberry Collection

Plus

The Khalili Collecton: Marvels of Meiji Japan—from a Consummate Collector of Islamic Art

Monograph edited by Sajid Rizvi • ISBN 1-872843-06-9 • Price £10.95/US$16.50

Order Form

Use any of the following options to order single or multiple copies of **Eastern Art in the Ashmolean Museum Oxford**

Single/ Multiple Copy Orders

❏ Please send _____ copy/copies of **Eastern Art in the Ashmolean Museum Oxford** at the price per copy of
❏ £10.95 (to a United Kingdom address) ❏ $22.50 outside the UK (inclusive of air mail delivery)

Please deliver ❏ to myself at: ❏ as a gift to:

Name ... ...
Professor/Dr/Mr/Mrs/Miss/Ms

　　　Address .. ..

City/Country .... Zip/Postcode ....

❏ I enclose cheque/bank draft payable to Eastern Art Publishing for £/US$_____
❏ Please debit my ❏ American Express ❏ Eurocard ❏ Mastercard ❏ Visa credit/chargecard
N° _____ Exp. ____ /20 ____

❏ Please invoice to the address above, quoting our VAT No. _____ (for orders from EU institutions)

Post or fax to Back Issues, Eastern Art Report, Eastern Art Publishing, P O Box 13666, London SW14 8WF, UK

T +44-[0]-20-8392 1122 • **F** +44-[0]-20-8392 1422 • **E** ear@eapgroup.com • **W** www.eapgroup.com | www.eapgroup.co.uk

Forthcoming in Saffron Books
International Series in Chinese Art and Archaeology • No 2

Art and Religion in pre-Modern China

Edited by Roderick Whitfield and Wang Tao

Contents

Representing the Unrepresentable: Words, Images and Representation
Wang Tao, School of Oriental and African Studies, London, UK

Homage to Heaven: The Concept of *Tian* and its Representation in Early Chinese Art
Liu Yang, New Southwest Museum, Sydney, Australia

The Art of Shang Ritual Bronzes: Evolution and Context
Chen Fangmei, National Palace Museum, Taipei, Taiwan

Wit in Shang Art
Paul Taylor, Warburg Institute, London, UK

Figurative Art at Sanxingdui
Chen Xiandan, Sichuan Provincial Museum, Chengdu, PR China

Jade Dragons: Image and Ideas
Jessica Rawson, Merton College, Oxford, UK

Fu Xi and Nu Wa in Han Mythology and Art
Mark Lewis, Cambridge University, Cambridge, UK

Religious Geography of the Qin/Han periods
Li Ling, Peking University, Beijing, PR China

Brick-built Paradise: A New Architectural Expression in Han China
Lukas Nickel, University of Heidelberg, Germany

Planet Gods in Dunhuang and Beyond
Lilla Russell-Smith, School of Oriental and African Studies, London, UK

Chinese Calligraphy and Religion
Zhao Chao, Institute of Archaeology, Chinese Academy of Social Sciences, Beijing, PR China

Saffron

Saffron Books, Eastern Art Publishing, P O Box 13666, London SW14 8WF, United Kingdom

T +44-[0]-20-8392 1122 • **F** +44-[0]-20-8392 1422 • **E** saffron@eapgroup.com
W www.eapgroup.com | www.eapgroup.co.uk